Principles of Group Accounting under IFRS

Principles of Group Accounting under IFRS

by Andreas Krimpmann

WILEY

This edition first published 2015
© 2015 John Wiley & Sons, Ltd

Registered office
John Wiley & Sons Ltd, The Atrium, Southern Gate, Chichester, West Sussex, PO19 8SQ, United Kingdom

For details of our global editorial offices, for customer services and for information about how to apply for permission to reuse the copyright material in this book please visit our website at www.wiley.com.

Wiley publishes in a variety of print and electronic formats and by print-on-demand. Some material included with standard print versions of this book may not be included in e-books or in print-on-demand. If this book refers to media such as a CD or DVD that is not included in the version you purchased, you may download this material at http://booksupport.wiley.com. For more information about Wiley products, visit www.wiley.com.

Designations used by companies to distinguish their products are often claimed as trademarks. All brand names and product names used in this book are trade names, service marks, trademarks or registered trademarks of their respective owners. The publisher is not associated with any product or vendor mentioned in this book.

Library of Congress Cataloging-in-Publication Data

Krimpmann, Andreas, 1963-
  Principles of group accounting under IFRS / by Andreas Krimpmann.
    pages cm
Includes bibliographical references and index.
ISBN 978-1-118-75141-1 (pbk.)
1. Accounting--Standards. 2. Financial statements, Consolidated. I. Title.
HF5626.K75 2015
657--dc23
                                2014046087

Cover Design & Image: Wiley

Set in 11/12.3pt, Times New Roman MT Std by Laserwords Private Ltd, Chennai, India

Printed in Great Britain by TJ International Ltd, Padstow, Cornwall, UK

To my family

CONTENTS

Contents

LIST OF FIGURES

LIST OF TABLES

PREFACE

Group accounting is often named as the flagship discipline of accounting. This is because group accounting is more than just financial accounting. It combines several disciplines under one umbrella: Financial accounting, management and cost accounting, taxation, law, organization and similar disciplines. Group accounting will even be complicated as there is often not only one jurisdiction to be considered. As a consequence, it may become a complex and challenging task to apply group accounting and to prepare consolidated financial statements. The challenge that needs to be mastered is not limited to large groups. Even small and medium-sized groups face the same or similar issues large groups have. To cope with these challenges, group accountants have to have not only an in-depth accounting knowledge but also knowledge on adjacent disciplines that are required for group accounting.

Literature that deals with group accounting can be found everywhere. The typical literature often focuses on general and theoretical aspects of groups. Literature that deals with practical problems is rarer to find. But group accounting literature that deals with practical problems in an international environment is virtually not present. This is where this book starts. Inspired by the daily problems of clients in preparing consolidated financial statements – both, in a local and an international environment – and the feedback gained in group accounting trainings, this book was written not only to systematically introduce to group accounting but also to present solutions on dedicated group issues. Therefore, this book provides a mixture of theoretical aspects and practical solutions on group accounting and adjacent areas. It not only explains theoretical aspects of dedicated accounting tasks in preparing consolidated financial statements, it also provides answers on typical recurring problems group accountants are confronted with. Solutions presented are comprehensive down to journal entry level. As these problems do not exclusively apply to accounting topics, the book does not stick to pure accounting issues. It tries to present an integrated view on group accounting and to catch group issues by its entirety. The various accounting topics and the solutions provided may predestine this book as a compendium for practitioners who seek answers for their accounting issues.

Due to the international focus of group accounting, group accounting subjects presented in this book are based on International Financial Reporting Standards. Even if several consolidation tasks and techniques are independent from any accounting standards, they are embedded in the examples to visualize their application under IFRS. A special emphasis is given to the new consolidation suite, IFRS 10 to IFRS 12. While this suite impacts the composition of the group, the companies to be consolidated and the way selected companies are consolidated are discussed in detail.

I would appreciate if this book appeals to readers and group accounting practitioners. The book in its current form is the result of long discussions on group accounting presentations, of discussions with clients and auditors regarding their most concerns on group accounting and the practical challenges groups face. In this context I would like to say thank you to my colleagues who are auditors, consultants and professors for their critical review of this book.

Berlin, August 2014
Andreas Krimpmann

INTRODUCTION TO THE BOOK

This book is designed as a handbook for practitioners, written by a practitioner. It does not only introduce in group accounting and the tasks that are necessary to prepare consolidated financial statements, it also provides answers and solutions to selected group accounting issues. Due to the intention of this book, it has to be assumed that the reader of this book has appropriate knowledge on accounting as the book does not introduce in general accounting topics.

Even if this book will give an overview of group accounting and discusses various aspects in preparing consolidated financial statements, the book should not be seen as the ultimate reference for all accounting details in applying IFRS on groups. Therefore, it is strongly recommended to apply the latest IFRS and refer to them when preparing consolidated financial statements. Only this official source offers the full set of accounting and disclosure requirements.

The structure of the book is based on the lifecycle of a company (regardless if it is a subsidiary, a joint venture or an associate) that is part of the group. General topics like accounting and legal requirements, definitions and organizational issues of groups are discussed upfront followed by the lifecycle of a company. The lifecycle itself is divided into the main stages of a company in the group: the initial and subsequent accounting, changes in the status of the company and finally the disposal from the group. General and special issues that impact the company and its accounting along the whole lifecycle complement the previous chapters. The preparation of consolidated financial statements, management consolidations, foreign currency translations, taxation and similar issues can be found in this area.

As a practitioner's handbook, examples are presented for selected topics to visualize the accounting treatment. These examples are taken from the consolidation of a midsize group. They represent one possible option to deal with accounting issues. Nevertheless, other options are available to cope with accounting issues. Therefore, the examples presented should not be understood as the one and only or ultimate solution. Which solution is feasible depends on the group, its accounting structure and the accounting problem to be solved.

To simplify the reading of this book, a set of conventions is used throughout the book. The following conventions are used in the book:

- Journal entries are presented using the Anglo-Saxon format.
- The structure of the balance sheet is based on the nature and liquidity of assets.
- All amounts presented in examples are in '000s of EUR unless otherwise mentioned.
- The presentation of figures in trial balances and calculations is following the accounting sign convention: Debits are presented as positive numbers and credits are presented as negative numbers.

A THE CASE STUDY

Based on the structure of a group, group accounting can become very challenging and complex. This applies particularly to large groups. Therefore, a certain knowledge of group accounting is required. While some accounting concepts as implemented in current IFRS might not be easy to understand, examples are used to illustrate the rationale, the accounting and their effects. Often, accounting standards interact with or complement each other. To illustrate this behaviour, either other examples are provided or interactions of examples are explained. While an example is better to understand if it is embedded in an environment, all examples provided are based on one accounting environment. Therefore, a case study accompanies this book. This case study consists of a smaller group with around 20 subsidiaries, associates and joint operations.[1] The group has to prepare consolidated financial statements as of 31.12.2013 based upon audited separate financial statements of the companies of the group. The group's transactions during the period and their accounting practices are used to provide examples of group accounting topics discussed throughout all chapters of the book. The examples will highlight selected issues discussed in each chapter. Each example covers an accounting issue without any reference to other chapters.

---

[1] The group used in this book is based on a real group in which financials are alienated and enhanced by additional companies to present all concepts of group accounting.

1. ABOUT THE GROUP

Flexing Cables is an international group which does business around the globe. Its ultimate parent is a European company, publicly listed on a European stock exchange. The core business of the group is the manufacturing of cables and cabling systems for specific purposes and applications, often based on customer specifications. This is a niche market and the group generates solid profits. Nevertheless, the invention in the overall market of new cables has affected the business of the group. Therefore, management has disposed of two manufacturing sites that produced copper-based cables and cabling systems, products which will not be demanded by clients in the near future. These products had faced a steady decline over recent years due to shifts in the market. Management has also acquired a new company specialized in individual cable solutions based on customer specifications. To strengthen the sales activities and control sales channels, the parent was able to increase its stakes in some of the investments in sales companies by taking over shares held by the former owners.

All activities of the group are arranged in five business units of which one business unit was jettisoned during the period. The group's management philosophy is to grant business units maximum freedom in making strategic decisions about the product portfolio, product invention, market presence and position in their special markets as long as the strategies fit into the group's overall strategy. Administrative functions (accounting, legal, HR and IT) are centralized at group level. For group purposes, the accounting function is implemented in a corporate centre that includes compliance, consolidation, financing and reporting tasks.

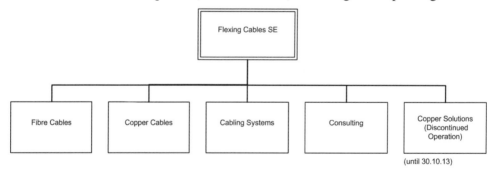

Fig. A-1   Business unit structure Flexing Cables

Production facilities of the group are allocated directly to that business unit for which they manufacture products. To minimize the legal structure of the group, sales companies serve all business units. An allocation of revenues and expenses to business units is ensured as the accounting departments in each sales company record all business unit specific transactions.

The legal structure of the group has grown by a mixture of organic growth and acquisitions. An optimization of the group due to legal and taxation did not take place. The group's legal structure during the 2013 period is presented below.

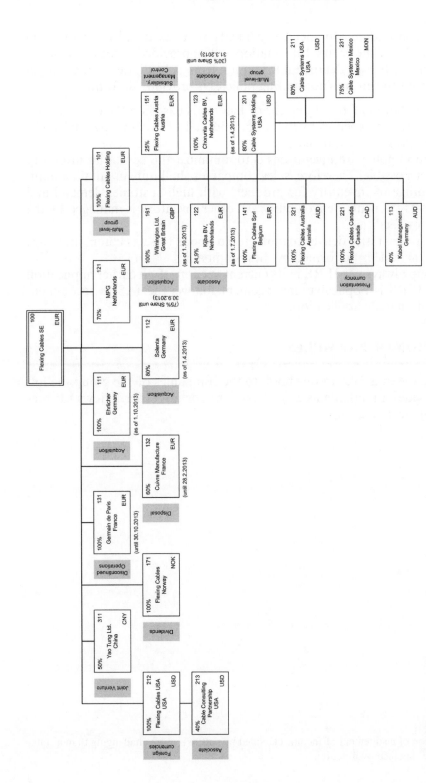

Fig. A-2 Group legal structure Flexing Cables

Preparing consolidated financial statements requires detailed information from all companies of the group. Information will be provided in the examples as appropriate. In addition to detailed information from subsidiaries, some general information about the group's accounting policies is provided upfront:

- The presentation of the statement of income is based on the classification of revenues and expenses by function. Internally, the company applies the profit & loss statement by nature.[2]
- The group's policy on inventories is to minimize and centralize inventory whenever possible. Therefore, sales companies shall only maintain a minimum storage of inventory for products with high customer demand and spare parts to ensure deliverability. All other inventory is managed by the production facilities.
- Production facilities deliver manufactured goods to sales companies only. No external sale is performed by these companies.
- The group always use IFRS in its current version. If an earlier application of new IFRS is applicable, management follows the IASB's recommendation of an early application.

2. ALLOCATION OF EXAMPLES

To allocate the examples in this book to the companies of the group the following list provides a mapping as a courtesy. The sorting order follows the lifecycle of a company in a group.

---

[2] The consolidation of a statement of income classified by nature is more challenging than a statement of income classified by function.

Example no.	Chapter	Case	Company involved	Page
42	F -5.2.1	Consolidation for own consumption	Flexing Cables SE, Flexing Cables Austria	165
43	F -5.2.2	Consolidation for immediate sale	MPG, Flexing Cables Belgium	167
44	F -5.2.2	Consolidation for later sale	MPG, Chorunta Cables	168
45	F -5.2.2	Consolidation for own use	Solenta, Flexing Cables Austria	169
46	F -5.2.2	Consolidation for own consumption	Flexing Cables SE, Flexing Cables Austria	170
47	F -5.2.3	Consolidation differences due to foreign exchange rates	Flexing Cables Norway, Flexing Cables SE	172
48	F -6.2	Transfer pricing system of a group	Flexing Cables SE	186
49	F -6.3	Unrealized profit elimination	MPG, Chorunta Cables	189
50	F -7.2	Profit allocation of non-controlling interests	Solenta	191
51	F -8.3	Netting of deferred taxes	Flexing Cables Norway	209
52	F -8.4	Reclassifications	Solenta	210
53	F -9.1.2	Ordinary profit distributions	Flexing Cables Belgium	212
54	F -9.2	Intercompany sales of fixed assets	Ehrlicher, Solenta	216
55	F -9.3.2	Multi-level groups, chain consolidation	Cable Systems USA, Cable Systems Holding, Flexing Cables Holding, Flexing Cables SE	223
56	F -9.3.2	Multi-level groups, simultaneous consolidation	Cable Systems USA, Cable Systems Holding, Flexing Cables Holding, Flexing Cables SE	231
57	G -2.1.1	Purchase price allocation associate	Kijba	247
58	G -2.1.2	Initial consolidation associate	Kijba	249

(continued)

Tab. A-1 List of examples

B LEGAL REQUIREMENTS FOR CONSOLIDATED FINANCIAL STATEMENTS

About this chapter:

The need to prepare consolidated financial statements is not only a requirement of IFRS to provide meaningful information to investors. It also interacts with the accounting standards of each country in which a group has some kind of presence. It even has to consider the taxation rules of those countries. Therefore, it is vital to understand the legal environment of a group. While local accounting standards and taxation rules have a direct impact on the preparation of consolidated financial statements under IFRS, adjustments, reconciliations and similar tasks are necessary to capture any divergent treatment of business transactions and align them towards the IFRS.

Therefore, this chapter will give an overview of the legal requirements that need to be kept in mind before preparing consolidated financial statements. These requirements not only relate to IFRS but also to the provision of information on how to deal with local accounting standards and taxation.

1. IFRS STANDARDS

The overall purpose of providing financial statements according to IFRS "...
is to provide financial information about the reporting entity that is useful to
existing and potential investors, lenders and other creditors in making decisions
about providing resources to the entity".[1] The standard focuses on the provision
of financial statements and does not differentiate between separate and consolidated financial statements. Accordingly, the information needed has to be borne
in mind while preparing the statements. Two dimensions will influence the information that will be disclosed:

- the accounting standards to be applied, including their mandatory disclosure requirements;
- the level of detail and voluntary information in the discretion of the
  preparers.

The preparation of financial statements is based on two accounting standards, *IAS 27 – Separate Financial Statements* and *IFRS 10 – Consolidated
Financial Statements*. Both standards define basic requirements, such as the
control concept, accounting requirements and the application of other IFRS as
appropriate. These standards are combined with *IAS 1 – Presentation of Financial Statements* that defines the format and basic disclosures of each statement
belonging to the full set of financial statements.

The basic standards are accompanied by more specific standards that focus
on selected types of company in a group:

- *IAS 28 – Investments in Associates and Joint Ventures* that deals with the
  accounting of associates and joint ventures.
- *IFRS 3 – Business Combinations* that covers the accounting of acquisition
  and other combinations of companies.
- *IFRS 9 – Financial Instruments* that cover the handling of investment in
  companies that qualify as financial assets.
- *IFRS 11 – Joint Arrangements* that includes the general principles of joint
  arrangements. This standard directly interacts with IAS28.
- *IFRS 12 – Disclosure of Interests in Other Entities* that includes the disclosure requirements of all kinds of company in the group.

Furthermore, a set of standards is required for group accounting:

- *IAS 21 – The Effects of Changes in Foreign Exchange Rates* that deal with
  the currency conversion of investments in foreign operations.
- *IAS 36 – Impairment of Assets* that ensures the recoverability of financial
  assets at parent level (in particular, investments in associates, joint ventures
  and subsidiaries) and assets at group level (e.g. goodwill and selected intangible assets).

---

[1] IFRS F.OB2

- *IAS 39 – Financial Instruments* that cover the handling of investment in companies that qualify as financial assets. This is an old standard but still applicable when a conversion of IFRS 9 has not yet been made.
- *IFRS 13 – Fair Value Measurement* that provides a basis for determining fair values.

All the above-mentioned standards build – from a group accounting perspective – the core standards that are mandatory in preparing consolidated financial statements. These standards include all rules and regulations that are necessary to account for the group. They are supported by additional IFRS that complement group accounting or are otherwise important for the preparation of and disclosures in the notes to consolidated financial statements.

- *IAS 7 – Statement of Cash Flow*
- *IAS 8 – Accounting Policies, Changes in Accounting Estimates and Errors*
- *IAS 10 – Events after the Reporting Period*
- *IAS 12 – Income Taxes*
- *IAS 24 – Related Party Disclosures*
- *IAS 32 – Financial Instruments: Presentation*
- *IAS 33 – Earnings per Share*
- *IAS 34 – Interim Financial Reporting*
- *IFRS 1 – First-time Adoption of International Financial Reporting Standards*
- *IFRS 5 – Non-current Assets Held for Sale and Discontinued Operations*

All other standards not explicitly mentioned are minor to the application for the preparation of consolidated financial statements. They are usually applied for the preparation of separate financial statements or for the adjustment of local accounting standards to arrive at IFRS. If such IFRS are applicable, they have the same importance as those standards that deal with pure group issues.

A fundamental concept that can be found across all IFRS is the accounting of transactions based on their fair value. The fair value is usually "the price that would be received to sell an asset or paid to transfer a liability in an orderly transaction between market participants at the measurement date".[2] While the determination of fair value is often an issue due to missing data or information in determining the fair value of an asset or transaction, the IASB have issued *IFRS 13 – Fair Value Measurement* as a guiding standard on all valuation issues dealing with fair value. As extensive fair value transactions are common in group accounting, this standard is also treated as one of the core standards that requires attention.[3]

> IFRS 13 has to be applied to periods beginning on or after 1 January 2013. It replaces various definitions of fair value in various standards.

---

[2] IFRS 13.A

[3] The items of IFRS 13 that are important for group accounting purposes are discussed in Appendix I: Fair value measurement on page 751.

In addition to the IFRS themselves, there is a set of **interpretations** regarding their application that need special attention. These interpretations as developed by the interpretation committee (the interpretation committee was formerly named the International Financial Reporting Interpretations Committee, IFRIC, and therefore the Standards Interpretation Committee) provide guidance regarding the accounting treatment and the interpretation of IFRS in selected cases. Interpretations are incorporated into IFRS as appropriate.

As far as group accounting is concerned, a small set of interpretations is important.[4] These interpretations focus on selected group accounting aspects only:

> *IFRIC 2 – Member's Shares in Cooperative Entities and Similar Instruments*
> *IFRIC 10 – Interim Financial Reporting and Impairment*
> *IFRIC 16 – Hedges of a Net Investment in a Foreign Operation*
> *IFRIC 17 – Distributions on Non-cash Assets to Owners*

In addition to the IFRS, the IASB has published IFRS for small and medium-sized entities (**IFRS for SMEs**). The intention of IFRS for SMEs is to have a "light version" that is easy to implement for smaller companies avoiding the complexity of full IFRS. Furthermore, IFRS for SMEs provide a simple and applicable accounting standard. IFRS for SMEs stand in parallel to full IFRS and are not designed to replace them. They are considered to be controversial as they are seen by some states as a competitor to local accounting standards; consequently, acceptance to apply IFRS for SMEs in these countries is low. The AICPA in the USA for example has issued a financial reporting framework (FRF) that can be applied by non-stock listed companies, private-held companies and any other preparers of financial statements instead of recommending IFRS for SMEs.[5]

IFRS are not necessarily IFRS. The authorized standards as published by the IASB are often adopted by nations as their **local accounting standards** in full or in part, for all accounting topics or for selected items only. Adoptions may be based on the standards as defined by the IASB or on modifications of the original standards. Furthermore, any improvements of IFRS made by the IASB may be adopted unchanged, modified or will not be adopted.[6] To fully frustrate preparers, the transfer into local law may either be taken over automatically or require an approval of the local government or even the parliament. Due to this conglomerate of options, adjustments and adoptions, two totally different approaches to application of IFRS can be observed:

1) Adoption as local accounting standard

    IFRS are used as the accounting standards of a nation without exception. IFRS are either adopted as they are or slightly modified. The same applies to improvements to IFRS. This practice can often be observed for nations that do not have a long history of accounting as it is practised

---

[4] The full list of all interpretations can be found in Appendix III: IFRS on page 766.
[5] The scope of this book is on full IFRS. IFRS for SMEs are not discussed any further.
[6] This book will stick to the IFRS as published by the IASB.

nowadays or for nations that have decided to abandon their accounting standards and shift towards IFRS.

2) Deviating local accounting standards

Nations that have a long track record in accounting stick to their accounting tradition and their accounting standards. A shift towards IFRS cannot be expected. Instead, those nations often adopt selected elements of IFRS as part of their local standards.

Even if an application of local accounting standards is given, some states allow a dual application of accounting standards for publicly listed companies. As far as taxation and the distribution of profits are concerned, these companies have to prepare separate financial statements by applying local accounting standards. By contrast, to satisfy information need of investors and requirements of stock exchanges, consolidated financial statement have to be prepared by applying IFRS. All other companies – and particularly privately held companies – are required to apply local accounting standards.

1.1. Transition to the new consolidation suite (IFRS 10 to IFRS 12, IAS 27 and IAS 28) from IAS 27 rev. 2008

To improve group accounting and to integrate all companies of a group subject to consolidation into consolidated financial statements, the IASB has issued **IFRS 10 to IFRS 12**, IAS 27 (rev. 2011) and 28 (rev. 2011) that belong to a suite of standards around group accounting for subsidiaries, joint ventures and associates. These standards are mandatory and applicable to periods that begin on or after 1 January 2013. These standards supersede the old group accounting standards IAS 27, 28 and 31. There is a clear division of work for these standards:

Issue	Standard(s)	Explanation
Scope of Standards		
• Separate financial statements	IAS 27	
• Consolidated financial statements	IFRS 10	
Definition and application of control		
• Control	IFRS 10	
• Joint control	IFRS 11	
Accounting for		
• Subsidiaries	IFRS 10	Application of the purchase method
• Joint ventures	IAS 28	Application of the equity method
• Associates	IAS 28	Application of the equity method
Disclosures for subsidiaries, joint ventures and associates	IFRS 12	

Tab. B-1   The group accounting suite: Division of work

Companies that have applied IAS 27 rev. 2008 so far are now required to apply the new standards. Therefore, a **transition** towards the new standards is necessary. The transition to IFRS 10 requires the application of IFRS 11, IFRS 12 and IAS 28 at the same time. Due to the effective date and application guidance, the initial application of and the transition to IFRS 10 is at the beginning of the period. To ensure a smooth transition, the transition should be executed in five steps:

1) Assessment and identification of the companies subject to transition
2) Adjustment of the carrying amounts in the statement of financial position to their appropriate levels[7]
3) Restatement of the prior period
4) Initial consolidation
5) Disclosure

From a technical point of view, the transition is similar to an initial application of IFRS. While IFRS 10.C2 and 10.C2B require a retrospective application at the beginning of the period, a level III restatement of selected balance sheet items of the affected companies combined with a consolidation at the date of transition is necessary. Differences that may result from the different accounting treatments are recorded in accordance with IAS 8. Due to the requirement to disclose comparative information, the prior period has to be restated by considering the transition and its subsequent effects.

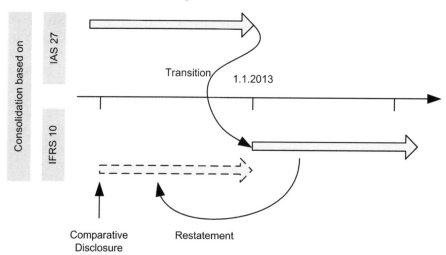

Fig. B-1   Overall transition procedure to apply IFRS 10

Step 1 – Assessment and identification of the companies subject to transition

Transition means that all companies of the group have to be checked whether or not a different treatment is demanded due to the changed definition of control, joint control and the application of the equity method for joint ventures.

---

[7] See chapter E -1.1 on page 116 regarding a detailed explanation of valuation levels.

Depending on the size of the group, this assessment may become a small project if subsidiaries and associates are considered as part of the consolidated companies whose consideration criteria are not based on voting rights. In such cases, the process in determining control and the outcome of that process should be covered by separate documentation. This documentation is required in preparing consolidated financial statements and its subsequent auditing.

Comparing the status of the companies by applying IFRS 10 and related standards (so the outcome of the assessment) with the current status of the companies prior to the application of IFRS 10, one of the following situations may occur for each company of the group:

- No change in the status of a subsidiary, associate or joint venture
- No change in the status of a company but application of different or modified valuation and measurement rules
- Not previously consolidated companies have to be consolidated
- Previously consolidated companies should not any longer be consolidated
- Companies consolidated on a proportionate basis have to be consolidated using the equity method
- Subsidiaries may become associates
- Associates may become subsidiaries

As a general rule, if control is established through voting rights without any side effects, such as contractual agreements between other investors, no changes should be expected. Also, a strict application of the new rules in determining control using the same assumption and estimation than before should not lead to tremendous changes in the group composition in all other cases (so, in those situations where control is not established through voting rights). In particular, any non-consolidations should not be expected until a consistent application of the underlying assumptions and estimations is ensured. Nevertheless, the range of, and options in, determining control that IFRS 10 offers, can be used by management to reconsider the composition of the group.

> Due to the new control concept several options and interpretations can be used for changes in the group composition. Final application depends on management discretion.

Step 2 – Adjustment of the carrying amounts in the statement of financial position

Depending on the assessment and its outcome, adjustments may be necessary. The execution of adjustments is a technical task that includes valuations, reclassifications and similar activities on the carrying amounts of balance sheet items. Due to the retrospective application, historical information is needed related to the life of a company within the group. Therefore, organizational aspects have to be considered: Is historical information available? Does it cover all the years up to the foundation or acquisition of the company? Where is the paperwork? Are electronic data available in the current IT accounting systems? Is data stored on legacy systems and is access to these systems available? Are staff available that have some knowledge of old transactions?

> Historical information is needed if a full application is demanded by management. Ensure that the archives are accessible; in particular, the data stored on legacy IT systems! Involve other departments, and particularly the IT department if necessary.

Due to the life of the company, historical information might no longer be available because documents have been removed, destroyed or are otherwise unavailable. Therefore, it might be **impracticable** to remeasure the company's assets, liabilities and non-controlling interests at the original acquisition date. A deemed acquisition date has to be assumed in such a situation. This date can be any date between the original acquisition date and the date of initial application of IFRS 10. It should be the first date of that period, where an application of the transition requirements is practicable. In the worst case, the deemed acquisition date is equal to the initial application date of IFRS 10. For auditing purposes, a document that includes a summary of all facts and circumstances regarding the selection of a deemed acquisition date is recommended.

Depending on the new status of the assessed company in the group, some of the following **tasks** have to be executed. While these tasks in most cases refer to valuation adjustments, these adjustments are recorded at level I to level III according to their classifications.

- Consolidation of a subsidiary that was not consolidated before
  If the assessment unveils that a company will be subject to consolidation because it now classifies as a subsidiary, a set of tasks is required depending on the type of company. The first task is the determination of which accounting standards have to be applied. IFRS 10.C4B and 10.C4C provide a combination of standards to be applied depending on the date control hypothetically was obtained.

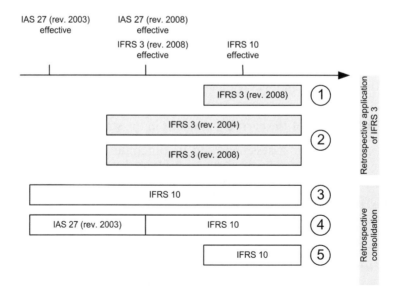

Fig. B-2 Application options of IFRS 3 and IFRS 10

> Even if several combinations of accounting standards are available, try to apply the latest version of the appropriate standards. This ensures integrity with the current period and prevents executing additional transitions.

Once the decision has been made which standards to apply, an investigation of the status and type of the company is required. Two alternatives are possible: the company is a business or the company is not a business. If the company has to be treated as a business, the application of the acquisition method (so a full purchase price allocation) as defined by IFRS 3 is necessary according to IFRS 10.C4a. By contrast, if the company is not a business, an application of a modified purchase price allocation is demanded by IFRS 10.C4b.

If the company is a **business**, a historical purchase price allocation is demanded. Due to the retrospective application, a virtual off-site calculation is needed. Based on the date the company hypothetically would become a subsidiary by applying IFRS 10, an application of the acquisition method according to IFRS 3 has to be performed.[8] The acquisition method has to use those facts and figures as of the historical date. The issue in this case is – again – the availability of details and conditions that existed at that date. Assuming a purchase price allocation is reasonable, any differences between the outcome and the carrying amount as of the historical acquisition date have to be virtually recorded at their appropriate valuation levels. The outcome of the purchase price allocation on each valuation level has to be carried forward to the date of initial application of IFRS 10. The carrying forward is done off-site. At the date of the initial application of IFRS 10, the differences between the carrying amounts and the calculated balances of all balance sheet items have to be accounted for.

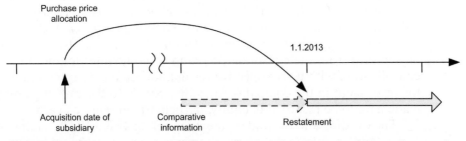

Fig. B-3 Retrospective handling as a subsidiary based on a purchase price allocation and its subsequent accounting

---

[8] See chapter E -3 on page 136 for the application of the purchase price allocation method.

The adjustments of all affected balance sheet items can be put into one journal entry.

Journal entry		Comment
dr.	Assets	Various assets
cr.	Liabilities	Various liabilities and provisions
cr.	Retained earnings	Separate account in retained earnings (contra-account for all adjustments)

The journal entry only adjusts the carrying amount of all balance sheet items of the subsidiary. It does not deal with any transactions at group level. Group transactions like the related goodwill are subject to consolidation that has to be executed in step 4.

If the company is **not a business**, a modified purchase price allocation has to be executed. The modification consists of an omitted accounting for goodwill only. Even if the journal entries and the valuation levels used are the same as within a business, they have no impact on the allocation of adjustments to the appropriate levels. No further changes apply. The wording of IFRS 10.C4b that deals with companies that are not businesses is identical to the wording of IFRS 10.C4a, with the exception of the goodwill application.

> You need to apply the following standards for all level I to level III adjustments:
>
> - IFRS 10 for the determination of the virtual acquisition date
> - IFRS 3 for the execution of the purchase price allocation
> - IFRS 10 for the initial consolidation
> - Other IFRS as appropriate for subsequent measurements and consolidations

- Deconsolidation

    If the assessment reveals that a company was consolidated before, but is no longer part of the consolidated companies due to new control criteria, a deconsolidation is necessary. Deconsolidation is a purely technical task that is similar to any other deconsolidation.[9] This deconsolidation consists of: removal from the consolidated group of companies followed by non-consolidation with a retrospective revaluation of the carrying amount of the investment in the company. Any adjustments to the carrying amounts made have to be recorded in equity, particularly in retained earnings.

    The wording and the underlying intention of IFRS 10.C5 is not easy to understand. It rules only the requirements regarding the deconsolidation and is silent about the status of the company afterwards. What is meant by the standard is clarified in IFRS 10.BC198: If control is determined by IFRS 10 for a subsidiary and control is not given, the "former subsidiary"

---

[9] See chapter J -Disposals and deconsolidation on page 569 regarding deconsolidation techniques.

has to be accounted for as a financial investment or an associate. The accounting has to start at the historical date where the interests in the company were acquired. The treatment is the same as for initial consolidation of a subsidiary.

If the former subsidiary is to be treated as an **associate**, an initial accounting as an associate is required (so, a purchase price allocation as part of a one-line consolidation). The purchase price allocation, the advance of all carrying amounts towards the initial application date of IFRS 10, and the calculation of the difference between the carrying amount and the calculated balances have to occur again off-site.

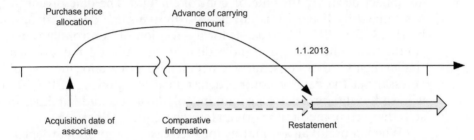

Fig. B-4 Retrospective handling as an associate based on a purchase price allocation and its subsequent accounting

The adjustment of the carrying amount of the investment in associates can be realized by one journal entry only:

Journal entry		Comment
dr.	Investment in associates	
cr.	Retained earnings	Separate account in retained earnings (contra-account for all adjustments)

Much simpler is the handling of the former subsidiary if it is to be treated as a **financial investment**. In such a case, the fair value of the financial investment has to be determined at the initial application date of IFRS 10 (and, if necessary, the historical acquisition date). Any differences between the determined fair value and the carrying amount of the financial investment have to be adjusted through equity.

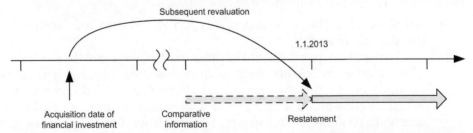

Fig. B-5 Retrospective handling as a financial investment based on fair value and its subsequent accounting

The accounting of any fair value adjustments can be realized again by one journal entry:

Journal entry		Comment
dr.	Investment in financial assets	
cr.	Retained earnings	Separate account in retained earnings (contra-account for all adjustments)

- Valuation issues

    Even if the assessment of step 1 comes to the conclusion that change in control is not given, an impact on valuation issues might be given. Such an impact occurs if the date of control changes. The date of control, as determined by IFRS 10, is not necessarily the same date as determined by IFRS 27 or SIC 12. Reasons for a deviation of control dates may be: contractual conditions, use and valuation of call and put options and similar items. As a consequence, a purchase price allocation would be necessary at the date of control determined by applying IFRS 10. This will lead to different carrying amounts of the assets and liabilities of the subsidiary compared to the original purchase price allocation.

    Whether or not an accounting for such cases is appropriate depends on the individual facts and circumstances and on the composition and size of the group. There may be reasons for an accounting of valuation changes; there may also be reasons not to consider such changes. Both ways – the accounting, as well as the non-accounting of valuation differences – is acceptable as IFRS 10.C3a offers an accounting of both alternatives. It is up to management to decide if a revaluation complies with cost-benefit aspects and adds additional value to consolidated financial statements.

Step 3 – Restatement of previous period

Whether the transition and its related accounting to the new consolidation suite are executed at the beginning of the reporting period, previous periods are involved as well. This is because IAS 1.38 requires comparative information for all amounts reported at the end of the period. Therefore, a restatement of the previous period is mandatory and demanded by IFRS 10.C (e.g. IFRS 10.C3B or 10.C4A). Because any revaluation is based on historical data, the restatement of the previous period can be achieved in two ways:

- Roll forward to the restated previous period and then roll forward to the initial application date

    The method makes use of the off-site calculation and the advancement of all changes in balance sheet items. In the first step, the new carrying amounts of the previous period are determined and differences to the actual carrying amount determined. Differences are incorporated into the consolidated financial statements. The restatement of the previous period is based on presentation tasks only; an accounting does not take place. The second step rolls all carrying amounts forward to the initial application date. At that date the regular transition tasks will continue.

- Roll forward to the initial application date of IFRS 10 and then one period back

    This method assumes that all accounting tasks are executed first before restating the previous period. Due to the recording of any adjustments, the carrying amounts of all items of the reporting period are properly stated. Based on these items and the results of the valuation at the historical acquisition date, the balances of the previous period and the deviations to the accounted carrying amounts for all items can be calculated.

Both methods provide the same results. Which method to prefer depends on the processes in preparing consolidated financial statements and the complexity of transitional adjustments.

Changes in the composition of the group can occur even before the transition to IFRS 10. A typical change would be the disposal of a subsidiary, joint venture or associate. In such cases, a restatement of the prior period by adjusting the carrying amount of the disposed company before the disposal does not really make sense nor does it provide additional information to investors. Therefore, any adjustments to the carrying amounts relating to the disposed company are not necessary.

Step 4 – Initial consolidation

Subsequent to the adjustment of all assets and liabilities and their related accounting, an initial consolidation has to be performed. This consolidation has to be performed at the beginning of the period at the initial application date of IFRS 10. This is because the figures of the consolidated statement of financial position have to be used in other statements and the notes. This applies particularly to the statement of changes in equity as the adjustments are recorded in equity, which requires a separate disclosure.

The initial consolidation is similar to any other regular consolidation. Specialities do not exist. The primary focus of the initial consolidation is on equity as this is the area where the most differences arise due to the revaluation of selected assets and liabilities and changes in goodwill. Changes in the carrying amount of assets and liabilities that arrive at group level via the aggregated trial balance do not require a debt consolidation unless intercompany items are involved. The debt consolidation therefore will focus on the carrying amounts of intercompany balance sheet items that already exist and that were already subject to a debt consolidation.

Step 5 – Disclosure

As with disclosures for all other issues, disclosure for the transition to IFRS 10 is required. These disclosures include comparative information of the previous period, which is mandatory. Due to the reference to IAS 8.28 and 8.28f in IFRS 10.C2A, the comparative disclosure is limited to line items affected in the financial statements. There is no requirement for additional explanation – a reporting of quantitative information is sufficient.

> For practical reasons, if changes in the list of companies subject to consolidation occur, all line items are usually involved. Therefore, the disclosures required should be incorporated into the comparative information provided for each statement of the consolidated financial statements of the period that begins on or after 1 January 2013. This applies particularly to the consolidated statement of financial position.

Nevertheless, options are available in deciding on the extent of disclosures. Due to the wording in IFRS 10.C6A and 10.C6B, management has the following options if the disclosure does not only cover the current and the previous period but also other prior periods:

- Full restatement

   All prior periods presented are adjusted and comply with IFRS 10.

- Limited restatement

   Only the immediately previous period is restated. All other prior periods are unchanged, which will result in unadjusted comparative information. If this disclosure option is used, additional disclosures are mandatory. Those items that are unadjusted have to be identified and supported by disclosures. The disclosures have to include a note that the unadjusted periods are prepared on a different basis. This basis has to been explained.

> The disclosure of a typical note could include phrases like:
> "The presentation of comparative numbers of the periods ended xxx, xxx and xxx for the consolidated statement of financial position, the consolidated statement of income, the consolidated statement of cash flows and the consolidated statement of changes in shareholder equity are prepared on a different accounting basis than the figures provided for the periods ended xxx and xxx. This accounting basis is subject to the application of IFRS as of xxx. IFRS as of xxx require the preparation of consolidated financial statements in accordance with IAS 27 – Separate and Consolidated Financial Statements. [...]"[10]

- Mandatory restatement

   Only the immediately previous period is adjusted and reported. There are no further comparative periods added.

1.2 Dependencies between IFRS 3 and IFRS 10

Due to the division of work, there is a dependency between IFRS 3 and IFRS 10. While IFRS 3 focuses on business combinations, the outcome of a business combination and, in particular, the accounting for the business combination is subject to consolidation according to IFRS 10. Therefore, both standards overlap regarding the handling of selected accounting issues. These accounting issues focus on the treatment of equity, particularly its allocation to the group and non-controlling interests.

---

[10] A reference to IFRS 10 is not necessary as a compliance statement required by IAS 1.16 is an integral part of the notes that refers to the application of and the compliance with the current IFRS.

The following table provides an overview of the dependencies between IFRS 3 and IFRS 10:

Subject	IFRS 3	IFRS 10
Group of consolidated companies	X	X
Balance sheet date		X
Group accounting policies		X
Equity consolidation	X	X
Debt consolidation		X
Consolidation of earnings & expenses		X
Unrealized profits		X
Non-controlling interests	X	X
Goodwill allocation	X	

Tab. B-2   Dependency between IFRS 3 and IFRS 10

1.3 Accounting transition of joint ventures

One part of the new consolidation suite is the new accounting of joint ventures in consolidated financial statements. While IAS 28.1 requires the application of the equity method as the default method for the consolidation of any investments in joint ventures, an accounting transition is mandatory. An application of the proportionate method is not acceptable any longer. This accounting transition differs from the transition due to changes in control that requires a separate handling.[11] Even if the status of the joint venture does not change, the accounting for the joint venture will change, depending on the accounting options provided by IAS 31. Therefore, three transitions may occur:

- From proportionate to equity
    The transition of joint ventures that were consolidated by applying a proportionate consolidation towards the application of the equity method is defined in IFRS 11.C2 to 11.C6. By applying the accounting rules of the transition, the initial carrying amount of the investment in the joint venture at group level is measured by the carrying amount of the net assets including goodwill that belongs to the joint venture. Goodwill effects that relate to cash generating units have to be considered. Therefore, the initial carrying amount of the investment in joint ventures at group level can be calculated:

	Pro-rata assets
+	Pro-rata goodwill as of the acquisition
-	Pro-rata liabilities
+/-	Goodwill adjustments due to cash-generating units
+/-	Deferred taxes
=	Initial carrying amount of investment in joint venture

Tab. B-3   Calculation of investment in joint ventures

---

[11] We will focus on the technical aspects of the transition only. An economic view of the transition to equity accounting can be found in chapter H -1 on page 479.

The transition itself has to consider the preparation process and its consolidation techniques. From a conceptual view on the transition, the integration of the joint venture in consolidated financial statements line by line is adjusted either at group level or at level II by using adjustment and reversal transactions. A technical realization of the transition can be applied in six steps:[12]

Step 1 – Derecognition

The first step will focus on a derecognition of the line items of the joint venture that are included in consolidated financial statements. Each asset and liability that belongs to the joint venture has to be eliminated. There are two ways available to derecognize assets and liabilities. The first is an elimination that can be realized by a simple reclassification towards investment in joint ventures. This account (which is also presented separately as an item in the consolidated statement of financial position) is equal to the account in the separate statement of financial position of the parent company.

The elimination can be realized by one journal entry only.

Journal entry			Company	Comment
dr.		Investment in joint ventures	Group	
dr.		Liabilities	Joint Venture	Various liabilities
	cr.	Assets	Joint Venture	Various assets
	cr.	Goodwill	Group	Goodwill as of the acquisition

The second way of derecognition is simply not to include the trial balance of the joint venture in the aggregated trial balance. Journal entries need not be performed. Going this way will not establish investment in joint ventures. This balance sheet position will be filled by the parent's account through the aggregated trial balance at a later step.

Step 2 – Remeasurement of carrying amount

The carrying amount of the investment in joint ventures has to be adjusted in the next step. Adjustments have to consider effects at group level that directly change the carrying amount of the investment in joint ventures. Typical items are goodwill adjustments, impairments and deferred taxes.

Goodwill that arises from the acquisition of the investment in joint ventures and that is allocated to the carrying amount of investment in joint ventures has to be adjusted by the portion of goodwill that belongs to cash-generating units. Depending on the composition of the cash-generating unit, goodwill may be allocated to or from the investment in joint ventures from or to the cash-generating unit. The determination of the cash-generating unit's goodwill that has to be allocated to the investment in joint ventures is based on the relative carrying amounts of the joint venture and the cash-generating unit. The determination can be executed in an off-site calculation.[13]

---

[12] The steps presented are based on a transition that is applied at group level.

[13] See chapter J -3.2.3 on page 585 for details regarding the determination of allocable goodwill.

While the carrying amount of investment in joint ventures at group level deviates from the carrying amount of investment in joint ventures at local level of the parent and also its tax base, deferred tax assets or liabilities have to be considered. Differences between the carrying amount at group level and the tax base of the parent belong to outside bases differences. The deferred tax calculation is based on the tax rate of the parent.[14]

The remeasurement of the carrying amount of investment in joint ventures can be recorded by using an additional journal entry.

Journal entry		Company	Comment
dr.	Investment in joint ventures		
cr.	Goodwill	Group	Goodwill-adjustments due to cash-generating units.
cr.	Deferred tax liabilities		Can also be a deferred tax asset.

Step 3 – Impairment test

The reclassification of assets, liabilities and goodwill to the investment in joint ventures does not guarantee that the resulting carrying amount is properly stated. Therefore, the execution of an impairment test is mandatory according to IFRS 11.C3. IFRS 11.C3 refers to IAS 28.40 to 28.43, which again refers to *IAS 39 – Financial Instruments: Recognition and Measurement* regarding the execution of an impairment test on financial assets.

The impairment test as defined in IAS 39.58 to 39.65 is similar to the impairment test in accordance with IAS 36. The first step – a check on objective evidences – is required. This check should determine if any signs exist that the investment in joint ventures is impaired. IFRS 39.59 provides a list of items that are indicators for potential impairments.

Once the check has unveiled the need for an impairment test, the test will compare the carrying amount of the investment in joint ventures with the present value of estimated future cash flows of the joint venture. The present value is derived from future cash flows and discounted using an appropriate interest rate. The estimation of future cash flows can be taken from the mid-term profit & loss planning of the joint venture.[15]

If an adjustment of the carrying amount is necessary, this adjustment has to be accounted through other comprehensive income in retained earnings. Therefore, the corresponding journal entry will reduce the carrying amount.

Journal entry	
dr.	Retained earnings
cr.	Investment in joint ventures

---

[14] See chapter K -2 on page 656 regarding the accounting of deferred tax assets and liabilities.

[15] See chapter F -8.2 on page 348 regarding the execution and requirements of impairment tests.

In addition to the adjustment of the carrying amount of investment in joint ventures, deferred taxes have to be considered as well.

Step 4 – Treatment of negative amounts

There are situations where the carrying amount of the investment in joint ventures will result in a negative amount. As a default treatment, the negative amount has to be compensated through retained earnings. The opening carrying amount therefore is zero.

Journal entry
dr.	Investment in joint ventures	
	cr.	Retained earnings

Exceptions to the default treatment are obligations the parent has to fulfil as an owner of the joint venture. If these obligations are either legal or constructive obligations the parent has to record a liability that reflects these obligations. Typical examples are guarantees the parent has given to third parties that enable the joint venture to run its business.

Journal entry
dr.	Investment in joint ventures	
	cr.	Liabilities

Step 5 – Consolidation

All transition tasks have so far focused on equity only. In addition to equity, debt may require attention. If any intercompany relationships exist and their corresponding carrying amounts are not consolidated, a debt consolidation is required.[16] Such tasks are not an integral part of the transition but they have an impact on the carrying amount of the investment in joint ventures.

Step 6 – Clean-up

Once the transition from a proportionate consolidation to the application of the equity method is finished, clean-up activities remain that have to be executed at the beginning of the following period. This is because the joint venture will not any longer be part of the aggregated trial balance which was required for a proportionate consolidation.

The clean-up activities consider all carrying amounts of balance sheet items involved that are recorded on the valuation levels. Furthermore, the initial equity consolidation has to be reversed at group level. Another

---

[16] See chapter G-2.2.3 on page 450 regarding the debt consolidation when the equity method is applied.

task is the reversal of any reclassification from assets and liabilities to the carrying amount of investment in joint ventures. The rationale for these clean-up activities is based on a shift in arriving at the carrying amount. While the opening carrying amount is based on a reclassification, the subsequent carrying amount is derived from the investment in joint ventures in the separate financial statement of the parent by considering valuation adjustments.

The extent of clean-up activities therefore depends on the recorded items at all levels. At a minimum, three journal entries have to be executed.

Journal entries			Company	Comment
dr.	Liabilities		Joint venture	Any adjustment of the underlying liabilities at level I to III.
	cr.	Assets	Joint venture	Any adjustment of the underlying assets at level I to III.
	cr.	Retained earnings	Joint venture	
dr.	Investment in joint ventures		Group	Reversal of the initial equity consolidation.
	cr.	Goodwill	Group	
	cr.	Equity	Group	
dr.	Assets		Group	Reversal of the reclassification.
dr.	Goodwill		Group	
	cr.	Liabilities	Group	
	cr.	Investment in joint ventures	Group	
	cr.	Retained earnings	Group	

By executing the above-mentioned journal entries, carrying amounts for selected balance sheet items remain at group level:

- Adjustments of the carrying amount of investment in joint ventures at parent level to arrive at group level. This adjustment includes any impairment issues.
- Goodwill allocation due to the influence of cash-generating units.
- Profits of the joint venture of previous periods that were contributed to the group's retained earnings until the transition to the equity method.
- Deferred taxes assets or liabilities.

The carrying amounts will remain at group level until the group is liquidated. As an alternate treatment, the remaining carrying amounts can be pushed-down on any valuation level.

Example[17]

Due to the new accounting rules, the accounting of the 50% investment in Yao Tung, the joint venture with Shenzhen Enterprises, has to be changed from a proportionate consolidation to an equity consolidation. The investment in Yao Tung was made five years ago for a purchase price of 5,100k EUR. The company has been profitable since then, impairment tests always passed. The parent (Flexing Cables SE) carries the investment in Yao Tung unchanged at a carrying amount of 5,100k EUR. Even if the company belongs to the Copper Cables business unit, it forms a separate cash-generating unit.

The balance sheet of Yao Tung (which is already converted to IFRS and EUR) at the beginning of the period is used to convert the investment in Yao Tung at group level from a proportionate consolidation into an equity accounting. We will call this balance sheet date the conversion date.

Statement of financial position Yao Tung as of 31.12.2012 (in k EUR)

Assets		Liabilities & Equity	
Cash at hand & bank	1,562	Trade payables	7,926
Trade receivables	10,968	Tax liabilities	40
Inventory	2,776	Accruals	4,676
Financial assets, short term	18	Other payables	5,096
Other assets	4,690	**Current liabilities**	**17,738**
Current assets	**20,014**		
		Loans	1,770
Property, plant & equipment	7,562	Deferred tax liabilities	156
Intangible assets	328	**Non-current liabilities**	**1,926**
Non-current assets	**7,890**		
		Share capital	250
		Retained earnings	7,990
		Equity	**8,240**
Total assets	**27,904**	**Total liabilities & equity**	**27,904**

To realize the conversion, additional information of the initial consolidation is required. This information is needed to verify that the investment in associates at group level reconciles with the carrying amount recorded by Flexing Cables.

- Net assets at the date of the initial consolidation were 4,400k EUR.
- There is a customer base of 2,400k EUR.
- Hidden reserves in property were detected with a value of 960k EUR.
- Deferred tax liabilities relating to the identified assets amounting to 840k EUR.

All identified items are recorded pro-rata (so 50% only) at level III. Net assets were also considered pro-rata only. At the date of the financial statement, their carrying amounts are:

---

[17] This example does not include the restatement of the previous period for comparative disclosures.

- Customer base: carrying amount 600k EUR, remaining useful live five years.
- Fair value adjustments of property, plant & equipment: carrying amount 180k EUR, remaining useful live three years.
- Deferred tax liabilities: carrying amount 195k EUR.

Furthermore, an amount of 1,640k EUR is allocated to goodwill. This goodwill represents the goodwill allocable to Flexing Cables. Its allocation is based on the following calculation:

	Consideration transferred		5,100
	IFRS net assets of the company	4,400	
+	Hidden reserves property	960	
+	Customer base	2,400	
−	Deferred tax liabilities	(840)	
=	Total assets Yao Tung	6,920	
−	Assets allocable to the Flexing Cables	50% of 6,920	3,460
=	Goodwill attributable to Flexing Cables		1,640

Based on this historical information and on the carrying amounts of level III assets, the equity contribution of Yao Tung at the conversion date can be estimated:

		Total	Pro-rata
	Equity Yao Tung @ conversion date	8,240	4,120
+	Initial amount level III items	2,520	1,260
−	Amortization & depreciation		(675)
−	Equity Yao Tung @ initial consolidation		3,460
=	Group equity contribution		1,245

In determining the initial carrying amount of the investment in Yao Tung, the carrying amounts of the following items need to be considered pro-rata (50%):

	Pro-rata assets	13,952
+	Pro-rata goodwill as of the acquisition	1,640
−	Pro-rata current liabilities	8,869
−	Pro-rata non-current liabilities	963
+	Level III assets of the purchase price allocation	780
−	Level III deferred tax liabilities	195
=	Initial carrying amount of investments in joint ventures	6,345

As the initial carrying amount of investments in associates at group level differs from the carrying amount recorded by Flexing Cables, a reconciliation will explain the difference:

	Initial carrying amount of investments in joint ventures at group level	6,345
−	Carrying amount of investment in joint ventures recorded by Flexing Cables	5,100
=	Difference (equals the group equity contribution of Yao Tung)	1,245

To safely convert Yao Tung to an associate, the outlined steps will be applied for the conversion at the conversion date, so at the **beginning of the period**. It will be assumed that the financial statement of Yao Tung is part of the consolidated financial statement of Flexing Cables.

Caution: Journal entries presented in the following steps are used for presentation purposes only. They do not roll forward and have to be reversed at the end of the period if recorded!

- Step 1 – Derecognition of assets and liabilities

  The following journal entries require a recording at the beginning of the period. Assets and liabilities will be derecognized pro-rata. The journal entries are executed at group level.

Journal entries				Comment
dr.		Investment in joint ventures	13,952		Assets as recorded
	cr.	Cash at hand & bank		781	in Yao Tung's
					financial statement.
	cr.	Trade receivables		5,484	
	cr.	Inventory		1,388	
	cr.	Financial assets, short-term		9	
	cr.	Other assets		2,345	
	cr.	Property, plant & equipment		3,781	
	cr.	Intangible assets		164	
dr.		Trade payables	3,963		Liabilities as
dr.		Tax liabilities	20		recorded in Yao
					Tung's financial
					statement.
dr.		Accruals	2,338		
dr.		Other payables	2,548		
dr.		Loans	885		
dr.		Debit	78		
	cr.	Investment in joint ventures		9,832	
dr.		Investment in joint ventures	585		Level III items.
dr.		Deferred tax liabilities	195		
	cr.	Property, plant & equipment		180	
	cr.	Intangible assets		600	
dr.		Investment in joint ventures	1,640		Group level.
	cr.	Intangible assets		1,640	

- Step 2 – Remeasurement of carrying amount

  As Yao Tung is treated as an own cash-generating unit, an allocation of further goodwill to the investment in joint ventures is not necessary. Also, due to the history of Yao Tung, any impairment losses are not recorded that need to be considered.

  As the carrying amount at group level differs from the carrying amount recorded by Flexing Cables, a deferred tax liability has to be recorded (carrying amount group level > carrying amount Flexing Cables). As stated before, Flexing Cables has never adjusted its carrying amount in Yao Tung. Therefore, it could be assumed that this amount reflects also the tax base. Accordingly, an amount of 374k EUR (1,245k EUR *30%, Flexing Cables tax rate) has to be recorded:

Journal entry

dr.   Investment in joint ventures   374

    cr.   Deferred tax liability   374

- Step 3 – Impairment test

  The equity value of Yao Tung successfully passed the impairment test. A recognition of an impairment loss is not necessary.

- Step 4 – Negative amounts

  Does not apply, step can be skipped.

- Step 5 – Consolidation

  A review of other matters that demand the execution of additional consolidation tasks unveiled nothing. Neither a debt, an expense–earnings consolidation, nor an elimination of unrealized profits is necessary.

Having successfully executed all conversion steps, a preparation of an auxiliary calculation is the only task that is pending at the conversion date. Using the above calculated items, the auxiliary calculation carries the following items:

Item	Goodwill	Hidden reserves	Non-accounted assets	Deferred taxation	Book value investment	Equity value
Balance @ initial recognition	1,640	180	600	(195)	4,120	6,345
Outside basis differences				374		
Depreciation & amortization						
Unrealized profits						
Profits						
• Cumulative						
• Current period						
Dividends						
Balance @ end of period	1,640	180	600	179	4,120	6,719

To complete the transition from a proportionate consolidation to the application of the equity method, a set of tasks is necessary at the **end of the period**.[18] It is recommended to execute these tasks when preparing consolidated financial statements. These tasks are purely technical tasks to ensure that appropriate balances are carried at all levels. The basis for these tasks is the omission of Yao Tung's trial balance in the aggregated trial balance due to the application of the equity method. The following tasks are executed:

- Reversal of conversion date journal entries

  Due to the omission of Yao Tung's trial balance as one part of the aggregated trial balance, journal entries executed at the beginning of the period will lose their underlying references. Accordingly, all these journal entries have to be reversed. An exception to this rule is the recording of the deferred tax

---

[18] We will only focus on the completion of the transition and therefore do not consider the performance of Yao Tung during the period.

liability that relates to outside basis differences. A reversal of this journal entry is not appropriate, it has to stay.

- Level III clean-up

     All balances at level III have to be removed. It is sufficient to record the elimination against retained earnings.

     Journal entry

dr.	Retained earnings	585	
dr.	Deferred tax liabilities	195	
	cr.	Property, plant & equipment	180
	cr.	Intangible assets	600

- Reversal of initial consolidation

     Similar to the situation of the journal entries of the conversion date is the situation of the journal entry of the initial consolidation. It will also lose its underlying reference and has to be reversed. By reversing the journal entry of the initial consolidation, the investment in joint ventures account of Flexing Cables will be re-established and passed through at group level. This balance will be used in forming part of the equity value.

     Journal entry

dr.	Investment in joint ventures	5,100	
	cr.	Goodwill	1,640
	cr.	Share capital	125
	cr.	Retained earnings	3,335

- Group equity adjustment

     During the period, Yao Tung was included in consolidated financial statements using the proportionate consolidation, the company contributed to performance of the group. Accordingly, a portion of the group's retained earnings are allocable to Yao Tung. That amount has to stay in retained earnings after the transition is completed in all subsequent periods. The amount also has to be considered in the equity value of Yao Tung. It will be realized by the following journal entry:

Journal entry			Comment
dr.	Investment in joint ventures	1,245	To be recorded at group level
	cr.	Retained earnings	1,245

     This journal entry has to be carried forward for each subsequent period to properly reflect the equity of the group. There are no future changes or adjustments to this journal entry necessary as long as Yao Tung is part of the group.

Having executed the clean-up task at the end of the period, the carrying amount is still the same as at the beginning of the period. The auxiliary calculation will also not change. Any changes from now on relate to the performance of Yao Tung and the adjustments necessary due to the one-line consolidation as required for associates and joint ventures.

- From equity to pro-rata

    The transition of joint ventures that are recognized by applying the equity method to an accounting for individual assets and liabilities is required when the status of the joint ventures changes to a joint operation.

    A technical realization of the transition can be applied in four steps:

Step 1 – Derecognition

The first step will focus on a derecognition of the net investment in joint ventures that is included in consolidated financial statements. The carrying amount of the investment in joint ventures and any other assets that belong to the net investment have to be eliminated in full. A typical example of another asset is a loan granted to the joint venture.

Step 2 – Estimation of assets and liabilities

Subsequent to the derecognition of the net investment in joint ventures, the assets and liabilities that belong to the joint operation have to be recognized. This assumes that the assets and liabilities that belong to the joint operation have to be known and identified. The recognition is based on the share in the joint operation, which includes a determination on the basis of contractual rights and obligations. The carrying amount of assets and liabilities is derived from the information used by applying the equity method.

The carrying amount of the investment in joint ventures may include goodwill that was established upon the initial application of the equity method. This goodwill has to be accounted for as a separate item. The carrying amount of goodwill can be taken from the calculation of the equity method.

As the carrying amounts of all assets and liabilities do not necessarily equal the net investment, the residual amount has to be recorded separately. The residual amount can be calculated as follows:

	Carrying amount of investments in joint ventures
−	Assets recognized
+	Liabilities recognized
−	Goodwill as applied by the equity method
=	Residual amount to be recorded in retained earnings

Tab. B-4 Calculation of retained earnings

The whole transaction can be executed by a few journal entries:

Journal entry		Company	Comment
dr.	Assets	Joint venture	
dr.	Goodwill	Joint venture	
cr.	Liabilities	Joint venture	
cr.	Investment in joint ventures	Joint venture	Derecognition

Step 3 – Adjustments

The cumulative assets and liabilities, including goodwill, are not necessarily identical to the net investment: there is a residual amount which needs to be off-set for full elimination. Depending on the residual amount, the following accounting requirements apply:

- Residual value is positive

    A positive residual value is an indication that the cumulative carrying amounts of all assets and liabilities are less than the net investment. Therefore, the residual value has to be charged to retained earnings.

Journal entry		Company	Comment
dr.	Retained earnings	Group	
cr.	Investment in subsidiaries	Group	

- Residual value is negative

    A negative residual value is an indication that all the cumulative carrying amounts of all assets and liabilities are higher than the net investment. Therefore, the residual value has to be charged against goodwill. If the goodwill has become zero due to this transaction, any remaining residual value is charged to retained earnings.

Journal entry		Company	Comment
dr.	Investment is joint ventures	Group	
cr.	Goodwill	Group	Until goodwill balance is zero.
cr.	Retained earnings	Group	

- From proportionate to pro-rata

    In rare cases, the status of a joint venture will change in a way that a transition from a proportionate consolidation to an accounting of assets and liabilities is required. IFRS 11 does not provide explicit accounting guidance for this case. Therefore, it is recommended to review the carrying amounts of all assets and liabilities according to the basis of the contractual rights and obligations. As far as deviations are detected, the asset or liability involved has to be adjusted to reflect contractual conditions. Similar to the other transitions, these differences should be recorded through retained earnings.

The accounting transition of a joint venture is accompanied by extended **disclosure requirements**. Regardless of which transition type is applied, an analysis of the differences between the carrying amount of the investment in joint ventures and the corresponding assets and liabilities is always required. The analysis varies depending on the type of transition. In case of a transition from a proportionate consolidation to the application of the equity method, a breakdown analysis is required. The breakdown has to explain the aggregation of assets and liabilities into a single line item. If more than one joint venture requires a transition, the breakdown required for all transitions can be accumulated into one analysis. If a transition from the equity method to the accounting of assets and liabilities is required, a reconciliation between the carrying amount of the investment in joint ventures and the assets, liabilities and retained earnings has to be disclosed.

2. EXEMPTIONS

If a company is the parent company of a group, it has to prepare consolidated financial statements. The standard does not differentiate between any types or size of groups or any industries groups operate in: equal application is mandatory. There is a requirement to prepare consolidated financial statements as long as there is a subsidiary that is subject to consolidation. Even if this requirement is not directly mentioned in the IFRS it can be derived from IFRS 10.20, which requires consolidation until control ceases. As a general rule, all subsidiaries have to be consolidated. This applies even if control is temporary, subsidiaries are held for sale (in accordance with IFRS 5) only, restrictions exist to transfer funds to the parent, the subsidiary's activities are substantially different from the group's activities, or the investor is a venture capital organization.

Exemptions from preparing consolidated financial statements are only available in limited cases. IFRS 10.4 lists six cases that are exempt from consolidated financial statements. In addition, exemption may arise due to the application of IFRS 8.8:

- The parent is a subsidiary of another parent (either wholly-owned or partially-owned). All owners of the parent are informed about the fact that the parent does not prepare and present consolidated financial statements and they do not object to this decision.
- The parent is the subsidiary of another parent that prepares consolidated financial statements that are publicly available in accordance with these IFRS.
- The parent has issued debt or equity instruments and these instruments are not publicly traded.

    Not publicly traded means that these instruments are not traded in a domestic or foreign stock exchange and in local or regional over-the-counter markets.

- The parent does and did not file its financial statements with a security commission or any other regulatory institution. It is also not in the process of filing financial statements for the intention of a public offering of these instruments.
- The parent maintains post-employment benefit plans or other long-term employee benefit plans.

- The parent is an investment entity that measures all of its subsidiaries through profit & loss.

  If the parent is a subsidiary and has a parent that is also an investment company that fulfils the same requirements, this (ultimate) parent is also exempt from preparing consolidated financial statements. By contrast, if that (ultimate) parent is not an investment company, it has to consolidate the parent and all of its investments.

- A parent may be exempt indirectly from preparing consolidated financial statements due to materiality considerations. If the parent has only one subsidiary that is treated as not material, a decision not to consider that subsidiary as part of the group might be appropriate. As a consequence, in the absence of another subsidiary, a preparation of consolidated financial statements is not necessary.

> This is rare. Therefore, inform your auditor upfront to avoid any unseemly effects during the auditing of financial statements.

Investment entities have to fulfil a set of requirements before they qualify as an investment entity as specified in IFRS 10.27. These requirements have to be fulfilled cumulatively. Considering these requirements, a parent is treated as an investment entity, if:

- it obtains funds from one or more investors for providing management services to them;
- the business purpose is to invest funds solely for returns from capital appreciation, investment income or both; and
- measures and evaluates the performance of substantially all its investments on a fair value basis.

To obtain evidence about meeting the requirements that define investment entities, IFRS 10.B85A to 10.B85W provide clarifying explanations.

Obtaining funds from investors and providing management services to them is a typical characteristic of an investment entity. The investment entity usually has more than one investor and more than one investment. Investors can be any unrelated party to the investment entity and other party of the group. An investment entity can also have a single investor if this investor represents a wider set of investors. IFRS 10.B85R mentions pension funds or family trusts as typical examples of such single investors. The investment entity uses the funds provided by investors to gain access to investment opportunities. Depending on the type, size and business of an investment opportunity, funds can be pooled or separately invested. Having only one investor temporarily does not disturb the status of an investment entity. Such cases arise on the formation and liquidation of an investment entity or in situations where investors are likely to change. Similar to investors, an investment entity usually has more than one investment to diversify, minimize risks and maximize returns. These investments can be held directly or indirectly through other investment entities. Again, with only one investment temporarily does not disturb the status of an investment entity. Having only one investment can arise upon the formation or liquidation of an investment entity, which temporarily suspends investment decisions and the funds pooling process for investing in a dedicated object.

The legal form of an investment entity is not important. Any legal form is sufficient, provided that ownership interests – or in special cases debt interests – are satisfied. This can be realized through equity, partnership interests or similar interests. Investors have to benefit from the net assets in the investments of the investment entity on a proportionate basis. Therefore, it is not important if they benefit through equity, debt or other forms of interest as long as the benefits are based on variable returns. It is also not important how the investor funds are managed: pooling of several funds in one investment, allocation of dedicated funds to specific investments, or allocation of an investor's fund in several investments all have the same effect as long as there is a variable return.

The second requirement, the **business purpose** focuses on the return of the investment. The investment can be any type of involvement. It can be an investee that is a separate legal entity; it can also be any other form of interest that is established through equity or similar interests. Returns can be based on capital appreciation or investment income or both. Investment income is defined as earnings or benefits from dividends, interests or rental income. Revenues from investment related activities and services, directly or indirectly provided, may of course be from an investment company. Contractual agreements between the investment entity and its investments, that define the extent, scope and involvement of the investment entity in the investment's business, can be used for evidence. It is not sufficient for one investment to meet the requirements; all investments have to fulfil them. Therefore, it might be useful to determine other sources of evidence – such as, the presentation of the investment entity or its overall activities – when considering whether other business areas apply or not. This is because any other benefit earned that arises from commercial transactions will disqualify a company from being an investment entity. Typical examples are companies that support their investees in developing their businesses: such companies have additional income to dividends received.

Any subsidiaries of the investment company that deliver services to the investment company and its investments have to be consolidated. As a consequence, consolidated financial statements of the investment parent company include all subsidiaries that do not classify as an investment.

The business purpose can be supported by other characteristics: the extent and duration of an investment, for example. As investment entities realize larger returns upon the disposal of an investment, exit strategies provide good evidence of business purpose. This applies to all types of investment, through equity and debt. As there are many exit strategies which apply to investment entities, it is wise to document such strategies. Activities that indicate exit strategies are: initial public offerings, private placements, sales of the investment to unrelated third parties or distributions to investors. Another characteristic of a business purpose is the type of return. All types of return that are not based on capital appreciation or investment income may disturb the status of an investment entity. Such returns are benefits of an investment that are not available to other parties, particularly to unrelated parties of the investment. IFRS 10.B85I lists a set of typical benefits:

- Acquisition, use, exchange or exploitation of the processes, assets or technology of an investee (the investment) including disproportionate or exclusive rights regarding the acquisition;
- Joint arrangements or other arrangements between the investment entity and the investee (the investment) to develop, produce, market or provide products or services;
- Financial guarantees or assets provided that serve as collateral;
- Options held by a related party to purchase ownership interests in the investment;
- Unusual transactions between the investment entity and the investment, such as terms and conditions not available to third parties, or not available at fair or equal value to a substantial portion of the business.

The third requirement, the **performance measurement** on a fair value basis, has to be applied consistently across the whole business. This assumes that the performance measurement, the internal reporting and management systems, the accounting of the investment and the external reporting to investors is executed on a fair value basis. Whenever possible, the fair value measurement has to be applied to all investments. Therefore, if IFRS permit a fair value measurement, such an application should be interpreted as required. The scope covers fair value measurement of investments, so all other assets and liabilities of the investment entity are exempt from a fair value measurement.

The **scope** and reach of exemptions finally consider all combination of groups that are not ultimate groups, publicly listed and managed funds. In other words, the focus is on groups of publicly listed companies.

3. LOCAL ACCOUNTING STANDARDS

Groups that operate in an international environment not only focus on the group's accounting rules and policies; they also have to follow compliance requirements of the legislation region they are located in. This applies to all companies of a group by considering their individual residences. One of these compliance requirements is the application of local accounting standards. These include dedicated accounting rules which companies have to follow, detailed allocation and presentation of selected transactions, and sometimes even the type of accounts charts they have to use. If a country or legislation has not adopted IFRS, either in their original version or as a modified version, application of these local accounting standards is mandatory. This mandatory application is often a legal requirement for various purposes. These purposes usually cover:

- Distribution of profits;
- Taxation;
- Filing at commercial registers.

Some legislations have adopted dual accounting requirements. Companies are required to prepare separate and consolidated financial statements based on local accounting standards by default. If companies are listed in stock exchanges, they are required to prepare consolidated financial statements based on IFRS. Other legislations additionally accept consolidated financial statements based on IFRS as an adequate replacement for consolidated financial statements that are prepared to local accounting standards. Nevertheless, the preparation of separate financial statements for all companies of the group is still subject to local accounting standards. For example, such practice is common in the European Union.

While local accounting standards cannot be overwritten by the group's accounting standards, policies and rules, an application of local accounting standards and IFRS in groups is common practice. In groups – and particularly in large groups – local accounting standards are often mixed with IFRS. Therefore, a system is needed in which local accounting standards interact with IFRS in a way that consolidated financial statements can be prepared by applying IFRS. This requires knowledge of the local accounting standards and IFRS of every country or legislation in which a group's company is located. While local accounting standards also interact with taxation, triangulation between local accounting standards, taxation standards and IFRS is desirable. One typical application of such knowledge is the conversion of financial statements based on local accounting standards into financial statements based on IFRS. Other applications are possible.

4. TAXATION

Similar to the preparation of separate financial statements, a consideration of taxation in consolidated financial statements is mandatory. This is because the IFRS do not differentiate between separate and consolidated financial statements and demand consistent application of standards, even for taxation. As a consequence, all tax effects of each company of the group, subject to consolidation and included in the consolidated financial statement, have to be considered. Such a requirement is easy to satisfy if all companies of the group are within one tax jurisdiction. But this is not usually the case. While international companies have global presences in almost all important nations, they face enormous taxation challenges:

- Taxation knowledge has to be available within the subsidiary. This is usually not an issue while the subsidiary resides in the tax jurisdiction: local tax know-how can be expected, either by the subsidiary or by its tax advisor.
- Taxation knowledge of each tax jurisdiction has to be available at the corporate centre. This knowledge is required to estimate and deal with tax effects that may arise at group level from the business transactions of subsidiaries.
- Transactions between companies of the group, allocation of profits in the group and transfer pricing issues require knowledge of international and foreign taxation for each legislation.

Depending on the size of the group, taxation knowledge varies. Large groups usually have separate tax departments within the corporate centre. Smaller (midsize) groups often have only limited knowledge, of select jurisdictions or types of tax. The remaining knowledge is covered by external tax advisors. Small groups lack dedicated tax knowledge: the full support of external tax advisors is required.

In addition to required knowledge of the group's tax structure, there is a further dimension – the local presence of the group. For each company within the group that operates in dedicated tax jurisdictions, tax knowledge is required at both local and group level. Such knowledge is not an issue at local level; however, it will be an issue at group level. This is because the tax department will need knowledge of each tax jurisdiction: not easy when several tax jurisdictions are involved. Therefore, even large groups may need tax advisors from time to time.

Taxation from the group's point of view is always an issue if the group's total tax burden needs to be minimized. Minimizing the tax burden and therefore tax payments to various tax jurisdictions often results in restructuring activities that cover the group's composition, by adding holding companies in tax havens, moving businesses or selected business tasks from one tax jurisdiction to another, or allocating/pooling profit or revenue streams to low-tax jurisdictions. Such tasks are common in large groups. Dedicated tax knowledge is required for such activities, often combined with legal and accounting knowledge.

The taxation of companies is not limited to one tax type only; it will cover several areas and business activities of the company subject to taxation. Taxation issues usually focus on the following tax types:

- Income tax

    The standard case is always the taxation of profits or losses generated in the ordinary course of the business. This will include the application and calculation of various types of tax charged on profits, the handling of losses subject to tax credits or reliefs, the offsetting of profit and losses with the profit and losses of previous or future periods or tax unities. Many other topics on the taxation of income have to be considered; those mentioned here are just some examples.

- Withholding taxes

    Withholding taxes are made on behalf of a third party for defined transactions such as dividend payments. The third party then can reclaim the taxes paid through their tax returns. The purpose of withholding taxes for tax jurisdictions is to ensure consistent taxation without any defaults, particularly on cross-border activities.

- International or foreign taxation

    Cross-border activities like the transfer of goods and services in a group are often subject to international or foreign taxations. Special tax rules exist that rule the place and type of taxation, typically defined in double tax treaties between autonomous states and often combined with additional local tax laws and regulations.

A totally separate area is the handling of transaction taxes. These do not focus on the performance of a company but on transactions instead. Examples of transaction taxes are sales taxes, value added taxes (VAT) or similar tax types. Such taxes have to be calculated based on the sale of goods and services, collected by a company and forwarded to the tax office. Transaction taxes therefore are accounted for as transit items and often included in other assets or liabilities. Due to the nature of these taxes, transaction taxes do not require special attention compared to other taxation issues.

Taxation issues are covered in the first instance in separate financial statements of each company of the group. The standard activity is the accounting and recording for current and deferred taxes, in the statement of income and the statement of financial position, either as assets or liabilities. This is because taxes are calculated and paid based on the performance and business activities of a company. They represent either obligations or receivables of the company against tax offices.

Taxation issues are also subject to consolidated financial statements. There are two dimensions that have to be considered: Local accounting of taxes and the IFRS' view of taxation. Local accounting means that current and deferred tax expenses, tax liabilities and tax assets are considered in consolidated financial statements as they are accounted for without any adjustments or modifications. The IFRS' view of taxation is slightly different. *IAS 12 – Incomes Taxes* demands a consideration of deferred tax items based on local tax rules and IFRS accounting rules. Therefore, an accounting of additional tax items may arise at group level.

The consideration of taxes both in separate and consolidated financial statements demand an integrated view of the taxation of companies. Local and group requirements have to be satisfied that demand a well-balanced system in groups.

5. DEFINITIONS

Some definitions need to be mentioned as they are vital in with a common understanding. These definitions are taken from IFRS 10.A:

Subject	Definition
Parent	An entity that controls on or more entities
Subsidiary	An entity that is controlled by another entity[19]
Group	A group consists of a parent and its subsidiaries
Control	See chapter C -1 for definition

Tab. B-5   General definitions

---

[19] The definition of an entity has been omitted from the current IFRS. IAS 27.4 (rev. 2008) has defined a subsidiary as "an entity, including an unincorporated entity such as a partnership [...] that is controlled by another entity (known as the parent)". It can be assumed that this definition is still valid and that a subsidiary can have various legal forms like partnerships or trusts and is not necessarily an incorporated entity.

C DEFINITION OF GROUPS

About this chapter:

A group is – at the end of the day – a set of companies that need to be considered in preparing consolidated financial statements. Depending on various criteria, companies have to be considered in specific ways – or even will not be considered. The key in defining a group is the control concept discussed in this chapter. The chapter will provide information on how and when a company has to be considered in preparing consolidated financial statements.

1. THE CONTROL CONCEPT

The control concept is the underlying principle in determining the composition of a group. The concept is tightly linked to the one entity theory. Entities have to be considered in preparing consolidated financial statements that are controlled by a parent according to IFRS 10.2. Therefore, control has to be checked for each company of the group. Control may be assumed directly by the parent or indirectly through other companies of the group. Other companies may be controlled directly through the parent or – again – through another company of the group that is controlled in any way.

The control concept was initially introduced with IAS 27 in 1989 as a part of accounting requirements in preparing separate and consolidated financial statements. Since that time, IAS 27 has been revised, expanded and renamed several times. A second element of control was introduced in 1998 by SIC 12. That interpretation defines the treatment of special purpose entities and incorporates an own control concept. The combination of IAS 27 and SIC 12 was finally superseded by IFRS 10 that defines **what control is**.

Date	Standard	Explanation
1987	Exposure Draft E 30 – Consolidated Financial Statements and Accounting for Investments in Subsidiaries	
1989	IAS 27 – Consolidated Financial Statements and Accounting for Investments in Subsidiaries	Initial definition, standard effective as of 1.1.1990
1998	Amendment of IAS 27 by IAS 39	
1998	SIC 12 – Consolidation – Special Purpose Entities	Expansion of the control concept by defined rules for SPE's
2001	SIC 33 – Consolidation and Equity Method	
2003	Revised version of IAS 27, SIC 33 incorporated	
2008	Amendment of IAS 27 by first time adoptions	
2011	IAS 27 and SIC 12 replaced by IFRS 10 – Consolidated Financial Statements	Revised definition of control, standard effective as of 1.1.2013

Tab. C-1   History of the control concept

The initial definitions of control as defined in IAS 27 (rev. 2008) and SIC 12 have been adjusted and refined by IFRS 10. The intention of this adjustment is the divergence in practice between both the old standard and the interpretation that led to an inconsistent application of the control concept. The new standard now provides a consistent control concept that should cover all types of group structure including those entities that are kept "outside" and not subject to consolidation. The adjusted definition of control is defined in IFRS 10.6 and 10.7

and refined in IFRS 10.B2 to 10.B85. According to the standard, control is given, if the following criteria are cumulatively fulfilled:

- Power over the investee[1] is given.
- The investor has the right to variable returns.
- The investor can use its power to affect the returns of the investee.

The cumulative fulfilment of the criteria establishes control and the investor who then has control is treated as a parent.

In addition to these criteria, the **purpose and design** of the subsidiary needs to be evaluated to understand the underlying rationales of decisions. This is vital for the determination of the above-mentioned criteria. The evaluation should cover two important aspects: relevant activities and decisions. All relevant activities of a subsidiary will ultimately lead to a return: such as, a distributable profit that has to be forwarded to a beneficiary. These activities significantly affect investors' returns. Typical activities as listed in IFRS 10.B11 are:

- Selling and purchasing of goods and services;
- Managing financial assets during their life;
- Selecting, acquiring or disposing of assets;
- Research and development of new products and processes; and
- Determining a funding structure or obtaining funding.

Other activities might be appropriate as well if they lead to a return. As administrative and similar activities usually have no or little impact on returns, these activities are not relevant and can be excluded from the determination of relevant activities. Therefore, it is important to know how activities are directed and how decisions about activities and their direction are made. A typical task in directing activities is to plan and budget activities that will lead to operating and capital decisions on the execution or realization of planned activities. Decisions are not limited to the activities themselves. As activities require a structure or some form of organization that needs to be managed, decisions about appointments, remuneration and termination of contracts with key management personnel and service providers may have the same importance as decisions about activities. As decisions are either made by a decision maker or derived from rules and agreements, such set-ups are reflected by the rights of the investor (through equity instruments) or by contractual agreements. While contractual agreements usually discard the investor's interest in the subsidiary, the inherent risk of the subsidiary and its business has to be considered as well.

There may be situations where a subsidiary is controlled by more than one investor. Depending on the current ability to direct relevant activities, the investor should be determined to be the one whose returns are most significantly affected.

---

[1] IFRS 10.5 defines an investee just as an entity. Such an entity can be a subsidiary, fund or any other type of entity. The legal form of an entity is irrelevant. To be consistent throughout the book, we will not use the term "investee" but use the terms "company", "entity" or "subsidiary" instead.

The timing of the direction of relevant activities has to be considered. Regular assessments of whether these conditions are still valid have to be made over time. Appropriate judgement is required taking all relevant facts and circumstances into account.

The first criterion to be determined is whether or not **power** is given. Power is more or less the ability to make decisions about the subsidiary and to direct its activities. Such a power is exercised through rights the investor has. In determining power, rights to be considered are either substantive rights or other rights. Power can also be supported by other interests of the investor. These interests have to be treated separately as they do not have the same meaning as rights. Protective rights are not subject to the determination of power even if the investor holds such rights.

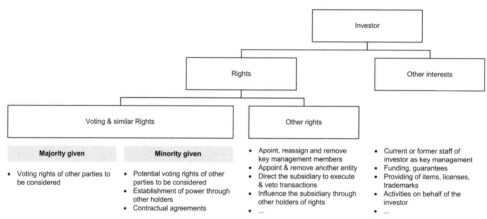

Fig. C-1   Structure of rights and interests

- Rights in general

    Rights as defined in IAS 27 (revised 2003) are carried forward and enhanced slightly. Under the new IFRS, the following rights should be considered in determining power:

    - Voting rights and potential voting rights

        The majority of voting rights will establish power. This can occur directly by the investor or via the governing body of the subsidiary if the majority of the members are appointed by the investor. Nevertheless, if other investors have rights that direct the activities of the subsidiary, there is no power, even with a majority of voting rights. The same applies to situations where relevant activities of the subsidiary are subject to direction by a government, court, administrator, liquidator or regulator. The majority of voting rights exist but power might not be given. An individual assessment of power is required in such cases.

> Scanning the contractual situation at investor level as a part of the determination of the purpose and design of the subsidiary will prevent unexpected surprises.

A minority of voting rights may establish de facto power. This can be realized either standalone or in a combination of contractual agreements between investors and other holders of rights, rights arising from contractual agreements, the types of voting rights and potential voting rights. Contractual agreements can transfer voting rights to an investor or direct other vote holders to act in the interest of the investor. Contractual agreements may also focus on decision-making rights instead of voting rights. They may also complement voting rights. Such decision-making rights require further investigation to ensure power. A two-step approach has to be followed in assessing *de facto* power.

The first step focuses on the relationship of voting rights over the subsidiary by considering rights arising from contractual arrangements, potential voting rights held by the investor and all other parties and the extent of the investor's voting rights relative to the extent of voting rights of other parties. Power due to relationships of voting rights can be based on several combinations: the absolute volume of voting rights of the investor, the proportion of his voting rights relative to other voting rights or the number of parties needed that act together to outvote the investor. A pure arithmetical calculation may not be helpful as other facts might be considered as well: nature of decisions to be made, other investors might be related parties, arrangements made between investors or the legal framework.

The second step is required only if a clear determination of power failed in the first step. An additional investigation is required considering additional facts and circumstances that may exist for the ability to direct relevant activities. IFRS 10.B42d mentions voting patterns of shareholders at previous shareholder meetings as a potential issue.

Potential voting rights have to be considered if these rights are substantive. They can be based on contractual agreements with other investors and include call or put options derived from convertible instruments. To decide whether or not these voting rights have to be considered in determining power, the nature, purpose and design have to be evaluated. This includes the terms and conditions on the exercising of the underlying instruments and agreements. The exercising is also influenced by the status of the potential voting right. If the underlying instrument is in the money[2], it can be presumed that the potential

---

[2] "In the money" means that the price where an option can be executed is favourable compared to the market price. For a call option, the execution price is below the market price, for a put option the execution price is above the market price.

voting right is substantive and has to be considered in determining power. If potential voting rights depend on the approval of third parties like antitrust agencies, these potential voting rights are exempt from consideration as long as the approval is not given or present at the decision date. The intention of the investor to make use of these rights is not important in determining the effects of potential voting rights.

Even if voting rights ensure power in most cases, there might be cases where voting rights are limited to selected activities only and not to the relevant activities. Power over relevant activities is then subject to separate agreements which need to be assessed to finally decide on the investor's power.

- Rights to appoint, reassign and remove key management members of the subsidiary.
  This may include members of the board, management or other governing bodies.
- Rights to appoint and remove another entity that directs relevant activities of the subsidiary.
- Rights to direct the subsidiary to execute or veto transactions for the benefit of the investor.
- Rights that give the holder the ability to direct relevant activities of the subsidiary.

  Holders can be any party that acts on behalf of the investor and his intention. Typical examples are managers that have defined authorizations in their employment contracts.

Even if the rights cover a large area, there might be circumstances and situations where it is difficult to decide if the rights are sufficient to establish power. In such cases, IFRS 10.B18 provides additional support in determining whether or not power can be established. Therefore, power is present if the investor is able to

- appoint or remove the key management personnel of the subsidiary without any contractual right,
- direct the subsidiary to enter into and veto changes to significant transactions for the benefit of the investor,
- dominate the election process of members of the governing body of the subsidiary,
- obtain proxies from other holders of voting rights and
- direct the subsidiary through related parties.

In the absence of any simple determination of power through voting rights, it is recommended to determine power by considering the whole situation of the investor and its involvement in the subsidiary.

> **Example**
>
> Flexing Cables Austria is a sales and service organization that serves the Austrian and East European market. The company is owner-driven; Flexing Cables SE owns only a 25% stake in the company. This investment was made several years ago to secure the former independent dealer from insolvency and to retain this important sales channel. The investment was accompanied by a set of conditions and activities:
>
> - Granting name rights for sales and service use combined with renaming the company into Flexing Cables Austria
> - Exclusive sale of Flexing Cables products and services only
> - Integration into the sales and service organization of Flexing Cables
> - Granting of an additional loan to expand the business activities
> - Veto-rights to significant changes in the business environment, unusual transactions and composition of Flexing Cables Austria
>
> Due to the involvement of Flexing Cables, Flexing Cables Austria was able to return to profitability and generate solid profits in all subsequent periods.
>
> The close integration of Flexing Cables Austria into the operations of Flexing Cables, the inability to cooperate with competitors of Flexing Cables and the veto rights of Flexing Cables led to the assumption that Flexing Cables Austria could not act independently. Thus, Flexing Cables was able to control Flexing Cables Austria by directing the distribution of products and the support of services. Consequently, control had been established even though the interest in Flexing Cables Austria was only 25%. The company had to be treated as a subsidiary and was subject to consolidation.

- Substantive rights

    Rights have to be exercisable anytime upon the discretion of the investor. This is, in particular, important if decisions have to be made about the subsidiary or its activities. Therefore, no reasons, facts or circumstances should exist that prevent the investor from exercising his rights. Only in such a case is a right a substantive right.

    An indicator of substantive rights is when the investor benefits from the execution of those rights. The type of benefits (monetary / non-monetary) is not important. The investor can also benefit in the case of potential voting rights if these rights are favourable to the investor. Potential voting rights that are out of the money are usually not favourable and therefore not substantive unless an implied control premium is favourable compared to the exercising price of the potential voting right.[3] If potential voting

---

[3] "Out of the money" means that the price where an option can be executed is unfavourable compared to the market price. For a call option, the execution price is above the market price, for a put option the execution price is below the market price.

rights are based on contracts, the timing and the execution of the underlying contracts have to be considered.

By contrast, reasons to prevent an investor in exercising his rights may have several reasons:

- Financial penalties or incentives
- Financial barriers due to exercising or conversion prices
- Terms and conditions of the exercising of rights: Time frames, conditions to be fulfilled, events to occur and other limitations
- Voting regulations or missing regulations in the corporate laws and regulations (also in the founding documents and bylaws)
- Inability of obtaining necessary information
- Operational barriers or incentives
- Legal or regulatory requirements
- Any other economic or otherwise barriers

The execution of rights by the investor may also be impaired if other parties are involved that have to agree on the execution of rights. To achieve a common opinion of the execution of rights, some kind of mechanism has to be in place that coordinates investors. This can be an agreement process at investor level, it can also be a governing body of the subsidiary like the board of directors. If a governing body of the subsidiary is involved, the type of right the investor has in appointing or removing their members is vital in determining if rights are substantive. The determination if rights are substantive depends also on the relationship between the investors and the mechanism investors will use. A missing mechanism is always an indicator that rights are not substantive.

- Protective rights

    Protective rights are excluded in determining whether or not power is present. The rationale behind this exclusion is that protective rights are designed to protect the interests of investors only, without giving them power over the subsidiary. Therefore, these rights stand in parallel to substantive rights. Protecting the investor's interests relates to fundamental changes of the activities of the subsidiary. In other words, if the business purpose changes, if the scope of the business changes, or if the nature of relevant activities changes, such transactions require the agreement of the investor. Protective rights can also be applied to exceptional circumstances.

    The assessment of protective rights is a standard task in determining voting rights and their impact on power. This assessment should consider not only the protective rights of the investor but also such rights of other investors.

- Other interests

    Rights can be combined with **other interests** of the investor. These interests may establish other rights that need to be considered in deciding whether or not power can be established:

- Key management of the subsidiary consists of current or previous employees of the investor.
- The subsidiary's operations depends on the investor's activities: funding the subsidiary's operation, guarantees issued to cover obligations, providing critical business items (services, technology, supplies, materials), providing use of licenses and trademarks or special knowledge.
- Activities of the subsidiary are conducted on behalf of the investor.
- The investor's exposure on returns is disproportionately greater than its voting or other rights.

The more an investor is actively involved in a subsidiary, the more it can be assumed that the investor has the ability to direct relevant activities and therefore has power.

A special evaluation regarding power is required for franchise agreements. Under a franchise agreement, the franchisee is entitled to use the franchisor's brand aligning the business to the operational requirements of the franchisor. This will give the franchisor some rights:

- Protective rights regarding the use of the brand.
- Decision-making rights in respect to the operations of the franchisee. These rights usually do not give the franchisor the right to direct the activities that significantly affect the franchisee's returns.

The second criterion required is the exposure to **variable returns**. The investor has to benefit from the returns of the subsidiary. Variable returns are subject to risk that will change depending on business activities, markets and performance. Therefore, returns can be positive or negative. Due to the risk exposure even fixed returns can be treated as variable returns if they are subject to risks. A broad interpretation of returns should be assumed. Typical examples of variable returns are:

- dividends, interest and other distributions of a subsidiary due to the performance achieved,
- changes in the value of the investor's investment in the subsidiary,
- fees, service charges, remuneration and similar charges provided for services,
- loss exposures for loans, guarantees, liquidity support and similar items,
- residual interest,
- tax benefits, and
- returns that are not available to others.

It is important to distinguish between control and returns. Even if only one investor has control, several investors are beneficiaries for returns.

The third criterion to be determined is a **link between power and variable returns**. Control is given only if power and variable returns are present and there is a link between both elements. This is because the investor can control variable returns only if he has power.

An investor is not necessarily the ultimate investor. The investor could be acting on behalf of another party, in which case his power is only a delegated power, which includes delegated decision-making rights. In such situations, there is no control as the investor acts as an agent and does not benefit from variable returns. A **principal–agent relationship** exists. Determination of the status of an investor – principal or agent – is standard procedure in determining control.

The determination of whether to treat an investor as an agent is based on the relationship between the investor, the subsidiary and the other investors. IFRS 10.B60 mentions four factors. Depending on the investor structure, some factors may be more important than others. All facts and circumstances that relate to the investor structure have to be considered in deciding on the importance of the factors and their weightings. Even if one factor indicates that the investor acts as an agent, an isolated view of this factor is not sufficient in determining whether or not an investor is an agent. Rather, all factors have to be considered.

- Scope of decision-making authority

    The scope of authority in decision making depends on the investor's discretion in deciding about activities and on the purpose and design of the subsidiary, the risks associated with the subsidiary and the involvement of the investor in the subsidiary's design. Activities refer to tasks that are permitted according to the underlying decision-making agreement and that are in line with laws and regulations.

- Rights held by other parties

    An investor does not operate in an isolated environment unless he wholly owns the subsidiary. Therefore, other investors exist that hold rights in the subsidiary. Rights may consist of substantive rights, protective rights or other rights, such as removal rights. In determining the role of an investor, these rights have to be considered. As rights of other parties may be exercised by management of the subsidiary, e.g. through the board of directors, an assessment of the management's authorities and the impact on the decision-making of the investor is necessary.

    Substantive rights limit and restrict the discretion of an investor in making decisions about the subsidiary. These rights are a strong indicator that the investor is an agent if substantive rights demand approval by others.

    Removal rights play an important role in determining if an investor acts as an agent. If at least one party has the ability to remove the investor without cause, this is a strong indication that the investor is an agent. In this case, it is not necessary to check other factors, such as remuneration, because the removal right will override such factors. If more than one other party is required to remove an investor, this cannot be relied on as an indication that the investor is acting as an agent. A typical scenario for such a case is the management of funds by a manager – funds usually have more than one investor. Rights that are similar to removal rights have to be considered as well. The most important rights are liquidation and withdrawal rights.

    Liquidation rights allow an investor to liquidate a subsidiary, even establish a new entity with the existing assets but under new management.

Specific attributes of assets or non-complete agreements may lead to the conclusion that a liquidation right is not equal to a removal right.

Withdrawal and redemption rights that have the ability to remove a decision-maker's authority have the same power as removal rights. To be effective, these rights should lead to the same result as liquidation rights.

- Remuneration

    Remuneration of an investor that does not depend on the magnitude and variability of the subsidiary's returns is a strong indicator that the investor is acting as an agent. An investor is an agent if the remuneration for his services is commensurate with the services provided and the terms and conditions of the underlying service agreement are on an arm's length basis similar to comparable services.

- Exposure to variability of returns from other interests[4]

    In addition to rights, an investor may have other interests in a subsidiary. These interests may indicate that an investor is not acting as an agent but as a principal. The indications should be based on the relationships between returns from other interests and total returns. Both the amounts and variability of returns have to be assessed in absolute terms and by relationship. The higher the relative portion and variability of returns from other interests, the more likely the investor is a principal.

    Another indication is the spread of returns to investors. If an investor receives returns from other interests different to those of other investors, it is likely that this investor is a principal.

If the determination has unveiled that the investor is an agent, the extent of the delegation has to be assessed. The range of delegation can reach from selected items to full delegation. The delegation is primarily focused on decision-making rights granted by the ultimate investor. Rights can cover selected items and issues such as the use and distribution of profits or the appointment of key management personnel.

An investor does not necessarily act on behalf of one investor only. The extent of delegated power has to be determined individually for each investor. The determination has to include the extent of decision-making rights granted by each ultimate investor. This includes the rights individually exercisable for the investor as well as any limitations and aggregations of delegated rights as defined by the ultimate investor. An inquiry has to ensure that each investor that has delegated rights also has power. To fully understand the rights held by the investor, the combination and aggregation of rights held on behalf of several investors needs to be evaluated.

The definition of control, in IFRS 10 and supported by IFRS 3, relates to **how control is obtained**. Usually, control will be obtained in a business-acquiring

---

[4] See above explanation of other interests.

transaction. IFRS 3.B5 defines elements that might constitute control in case of business combinations. According to these definitions, control might be obtained:

- by transferring cash, cash equivalents or other assets (including net assets that constitute a business),
- by incurring liabilities,
- by issuing equity interests,
- by providing more than one type of consideration, or
- without transferring consideration, including by contract alone.

Detailed inquiry is required for each transaction to determine whether or not control is obtained. The inquiry can be executed in five steps.

Step	Task
1)	Identification of consolidation subject (the subsidiary)
2)	Identification of relevant activities
3)	Determination of power over relevant activities
4)	Determination of risks and variable returns
5)	Determination of the link between power and variable returns

Tab. C-2   Steps in determining control

In addition to these standard transactions, **special cases** exist that may constitute control. As these cases are rare compared to ordinary acquisition transactions, detailed investigation is necessary:

- Creep acquisitions
    Creep acquisitions are increases in voting rights through dividend reinvestment plans. Dividends are not distributed as cash or similar items. Instead, dividends eligible to shareholders are exchanged into equity instruments, preferably ordinary shares, that are distributed to shareholders.

- Potential voting rights
    Options, convertible instruments and similar financial instruments that become exercisable upon maturity are exchanged in equity instruments, increasing the voting rights in a company.

- Selective buy-back transactions
    Selective buy-back transactions of a company of the group reduce the number of shares outstanding. If a parent is not involved in such a buy-back transaction, its interest will increase the percentage of shares owned.

- Expirations between shareholders
    Agreements between shareholders that assign control to selected owners may expire by default or by termination. This may assign control to other shareholders based on the percentage of interests in the subsidiary held.

- Majority of voting rights at the annual general meeting

    Due to the non-presence of shareholders in the annual general meeting, the percentage of voting rights will change in favour to the shareholders present in the meeting. This may even give shareholders and investors the majority of voting rights. If such a situation occurs over several periods, control may be assumed. The shareholder or the investor that has control over several periods may be able to direct the decision making process at the subsidiary through the installation of their own key personnel at the subsidiary, forcing the company to become part of the group.

In addition to what it is and how it can be obtained, the question of **how control can be maintained** has to be answered. This is because control is not always as stable as it seems. Conditions that are out of scope and out of the control of the investor may change adversely. Therefore, continuous assessment of control is recommended. IFRS 10.8 requires an assessment at any time power changes occur, the exposure to variable returns or the link between power and returns. An individual check is required upon any changes. Typical events that may result in changes are:

- Changes in the exercising of power

    Other parties may enter into or terminate arrangements that establish or shift control. In such cases the type of power has been shifted from voting rights or a contractual arrangement towards other agreements. A shift of power may also arise if the subsidiary defaults or breaches defined conditions that have to be met so that a creditor is legally or contractually entitled to obtain power. In such cases, the creditor often has an enforceable position. A typical scenario is a loan agreement covered by covenants that are subsequently breached.

- Changes to the exposure of variable returns

    The right to receive variable returns subject to agreements with other investors of the subsidiary may cease upon the termination of these agreements.

- Changes to the status of an investor

    An investor's status may change between a principal and an agent depending upon the relationship between investors or the investor and other relevant parties.

As the reassessment is event-driven, there is no need for a regular reassessment of control, either at a defined date, such as the reporting date, or on defined items, such as control or potential control relationships.

2. JOINT CONTROL

The control concept, as explained before, is more or less designed in a way that an investor has control over a company (subsidiary). The scope is therefore on situations where one investor has control only and not on situations where control is obtained by more than one investor. To deal with situations where control is held by more than one investor, application of *IFRS 11 – Joint Arrangements* and *IAS 28 – Investments in associates and Joint Ventures* is mandatory. There is a division of work for these two standards. While the scope of IFRS 11 is on joint arrangements and therefore the definition of joint control is within this standard, the scope of IAS 28 is on the application of joint control (as a consequence of a joint arrangement) and the related accounting.

> IFRS 11 is the successor of IAS 31. Its definition of joint control is now embedded in the standards that deal with consolidated financial statements: IFRS 10, IFRS 12 and IAS 28 (rev. 2011). As a consequence, the determination of joint control, and particularly the steps necessary, has changed. The isolated definition as implemented in IAS 31 is now obsolete.

Joint control as defined in IFRS 11.7 is "...the contractually agreed sharing of control of an arrangement, which exists only when decisions about the relevant activities require the unanimous consent of the parties sharing control". Therefore, an arrangement has to exist that link parties with control together. This arrangement is a joint arrangement when the parties can only jointly execute control and the parties are linked together on a contractual base.

Step	Task
1)	Joint arrangement exists
2)	Control not given by one party only
3)	Joint control given

Tab. C-3   Steps in determining joint control

The **joint agreement**, as the underlying source of joint control, has to be contractually agreed – though not necessarily in writing. The form of the joint agreement and the contractual requirement can be implemented in several ways:

- In oral form (to be avoided as there is no common understanding in case of disputes);
- As part of the minutes of shareholder / investor meetings or another form of documentation;
- As a separate contract between shareholders / investors;
- As statutory mechanisms based on local law (with or without contracts);
- As an implied element in the articles or bylaws of a legal entity (if this entity is carrying the joint business).

Due to the contractual requirement, the enforceability of the agreement is assumed to be an implied element of the agreement.

> A written form is preferable as this will strengthen the position of all parties in case of a dispute and prevent any misinterpretation.

The content of a joint agreement depends on individual facts and circumstances considering the intended activities of a joint venture and the involvement of the parties. IFRS 11.B4 lists some matters that are dealt with by joint agreements:

- the purpose, activity and duration of the joint arrangement,
- the process of the appointment of members of the joint arrangement,
- the process of decision-making,
- the capital or other contributions required, and
- the sharing of assets, liabilities, revenues, expenses or profit & loss.

Evaluating joint agreements regarding **joint control** should be based on an overall consideration of the intention for the joint arrangement. The main requirements, control and a unanimous consent have to be assessed in determining joint control.

Due to the definition of control in IFRS 10.7, the process in determining joint control has to be expanded by considering the control definition of that standard. For each party that is involved in a joint arrangement, a detailed check of control has to be performed. If control can be assumed for each party involved, an assessment of the joint arrangement regarding joint control and any limitations or dependencies are applicable. This is because the arrangement binds all parties together and brings their control into a balanced relationship so that control can only collectively be executed. These requirements may involve detailed checks that have to be performed in determining whether or not joint control is given. These checks not only have to consider control aspects for each party involved but also an evaluation of the procedures of establishing a unanimous consent and the way on how to apply control over a joint arrangement. Depending on this outcome, a final decision on joint control can be made. Such checks have to be performed every time a change in the composition of investors in a joint arrangement or a contractual change of the joint arrangement occurs. The rationale for a check is based on the assumption that – depending on the type of change – joint control might either not be given any longer or will be newly established.

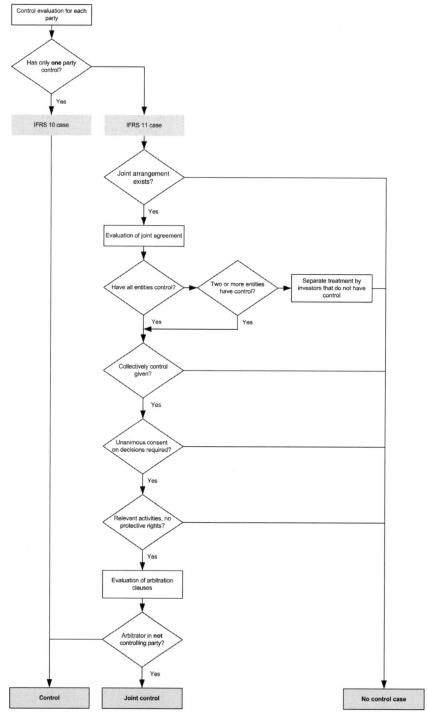

Fig. C-2   Workflow in determining joint control

> For accounting and compliance purposes, the documentation on the determination of joint control should be part of the permanent file that belongs to each arrangement.

Even if joint control is required, not all parties are requested to have control by default. It is sufficient if at least two parties exist that can collectively control the arrangement. Those **parties that do not have control** are excluded from a determination of joint control. They have to account for their stake in the arrangement by applying appropriate accounting standards. This is usually IAS 28 if their stake qualifies as an associate of IFRS 9 if their stake represents just a financial investment.

The parties that have control must be subject to **unanimous consent**. This means that all parties have to jointly agree on a decision subject to relevant activities. If at least one controlling party does not consent to a decision or uses veto rights, a unanimous consent is not given and therefore no decision has been made. Unanimous consent often involves thresholds. The threshold is designed in a way that all parties with control have to agree so that the threshold can be passed and a decision will be taken. Only by using such mechanisms will consent be ensured. By contrast, if it is sufficient that a majority of controlling parties is able to pass a defined threshold, no consent is given. This is because a majority can be built upon changing compositions of controlling parties, which assumes that not all controlling parties need to be involved to achieve consent.

The unanimous consent has to be subject to **relevant activities**.[5] This is because relevant activities affect variable returns of the arrangement and – as a consequence – also control. Therefore, it is important to understand the contractual arrangement and the way decisions are established upon relevant matters. In practice a decision hierarchy on relevant matters is often established. Depending on the matter and its impact on returns, all or selected parties or one party only is needed for approval. Such hierarchies focus on significant issues only. As the focus is on relevant activities, regulations that focus on protective rights are excluded. Consequently, if a party only needs to consent on issues that relate to protective rights, this party is not subject to joint control.

Decisions on relevant activities might end in a dispute between controlling parties. Joint agreements therefore often incorporate solutions regarding the **treatment of disputes**. A typical solution is the initiation of an arbitration process to solve a pending situation. If an arbitrator is chosen from the parties with control, the party who is an arbitrator has an advantage compared to the others and therefore has control because he can overrule other parties. As a consequence, control – and not joint control – is given: this requires an application of IFRS 10 and forces the inclusion of the company in consolidated financial statements as a subsidiary instead of a joint venture. On the other hand, if the arbitrator is independent of all parties, no one has an advantage and therefore joint control and non-control is given.

---

[5] This is similar to the definition of power as defined in IFRS 10.10 and 10.B11. See page 45 for further explanation.

Even if joint control is clearly defined, including a reference to the control concept defined in IFRS 10, there are special cases that may lead to some kind of **de facto joint control**.

• Agreements between shareholders

Shareholders may enter into agreements to vote together on all relevant activities of their company. Such an agreement may establish de facto joint control in the absence of any other major shareholders that have control over the company.

• Majority of voting rights at the annual general meeting

Joint control can also be given through annual general meetings. If two or more dominant shareholders are able to control the company, a de facto control can be established. This requires that these shareholders have contractually signed an agreement that binds them together to jointly execute their voting rights. If such a situation occurs over several periods, control may be assumed. The shareholders or the investors that have joint control over several periods may be able to direct the decision making process at the company through the installation of their own key personnel at the subsidiary. Therefore, the company is forced to become part of the group.

Example

In 2008, Flexing Cables entered into a joint venture with Shenzhen Enterprises to provide goods and services to the Chinese market. The joint venture was established through a purchase transaction, where Flexing Cables acquired a 50% share in Yao Tung Ltd from Shenzhen Enterprises. The purchase agreement included a set of appendices. One appendix included an agreement of changes to be performed to the articles of incorporation. The most important paragraphs are presented as an excerpt:

"...

§ 3 - Voting rights

(1) No party shall have the right to decide on transactions material to the company without the consent of the other party. Appropriate minutes shall be prepared on each decision made.

(2) Material transactions are:
• Appointments and removals of members of the board
• Appointments and removals of managing staff
• Changes to the article of incorporation
• Business transaction in excess of 500,000 USD or equivalents
• Distribution of any profit generated by the company

(3) Other transaction may qualify as material transactions if both parties agree on.

...

§ 6 - Disputes

```
   (1) In case of any disputes, an arbitration process
       has to be initiated. An external arbitrator shall
       be elected. The arbitrator shall hear the position
       and opinion of both parties in a hearing and find a
       solution that satisfies the concerns and interests
       of both parties. The decision of the arbitrator is
       final and binding to both parties.
   (2) The arbitrator will be …
...″
```

Due to the changes of the article of incorporation and the consideration of both parties, this document qualifies as a joint arrangement. Flexing Cables and Shenzhen Enterprises could not decide on material transactions without the consent of the other party. Therefore, collectively control had been given to both parties. The consent by both parties was unanimous. In the case of disputes, an external arbitrator would ensure that no party had an advantage. Under these conditions, joint control was given, with an assumption that protective rights did not exist.

3. LOSS OF CONTROL

A loss of control means that a parent no longer has control over its subsidiary. One or more of the criteria demanded in IFRS 10.7 is no longer being fulfilled: Power, the exposure to variable returns, the link between power and return – or a combination of these three elements. Such an event is a change in conditions and triggers a reassessment of whether or not a loss of control has to be assumed to be permanent or temporary. In case of a permanent loss, further control is not required. As a consequence, a set of accounting transactions has to be initiated because a deconsolidation is required. Even if a deconsolidation is required and the subsidiary is not any longer part of the companies of the group subject to consolidation, loss of control does not mean that the subsidiary does not belong any longer to the group. Upon the loss of control, the company may have a different status requiring a different type of consolidation, e.g. by applying the equity method.

Another topic that needs to be considered is the level where loss of control occurs. A loss of control can occur at:

- Parent level
    Loss of control at this level requires changes in the investment in subsidiaries. Such a change would assume that the parent has disposed of interests in the subsidiary so that control can no longer be given.

- Group level
    Loss of control at this level assumes no changes at parent level. Therefore, a loss of control can only occur if changes in the investor structure, contractual agreements or similar take place.[6]

---

[6] Please also refer to chapter C -1 The control concept on page 44 that discusses in detail requirements in having control.

Reasons for a loss of control are manifold. In practice the following transactions are often observed that may cause a loss of control:[7]

- Sale of a subsidiary by the parent

  This is not always subject to a disposal and therefore loss of control. Contractual agreements or obligations can force the parent not to account the sale as a disposal, particularly if a certain degree of continuing involvement is retained by the parent. It is necessary to check whether control is still present. Again, power, exposure to variable returns, and the link between power and return, have to be assessed. This has to include voting and similar rights. More important than these rights are other rights and interests that may constitute control. Typical items that may cause continuing involvement are:

  - the effective veto power over major contracts or customers by the parent,
  - the ability by the buyer to give the subsidiary back to the parent at an unfair value,
  - the ability by the parent to demand the subsidiary back from the buyer at other than a fair value,
  - the significant voting power of the parent on the subsidiary's board,
  - the continuing involvement of the parent in the subsidiary's affairs with risks and management authority similar to ownership,
  - the lack of any significant financial investment in the subsidiary by the buyer,
  - the buyer's repayment of debt (which is more or less the principal consideration in the acquisition) depends on future profitable operations of the acquired subsidiary, or
  - the parent's continuous guarantee of a debt or contract performance of the acquired subsidiary.

  These items are often part of the purchase agreement. Therefore, a thorough review of the underlying contract combined with careful judgement is recommended. Furthermore, additional items may arise – either standalone or in combination with the above-mentioned items – that may constitute a continuing involvement. It is dangerous to rely only on the listed items as substantial arrangements in the purchase agreement may be missed.

- Insolvency or liquidation of the subsidiary

  The insolvency of a subsidiary may not necessarily result in a loss of control. Depending on local laws and regulations regarding the treatment of insolvencies and liquidations control may still exist. A detailed review of the conditions required to retain control is mandatory. Such conditions often depend on the situation of the subsidiary, its business, the reasons for filing insolvency or liquidation and the involvement of its investors. This is not always the parent; other investors might be involved as well.

---

[7] This is not a final list. Other reasons may exist.

A loss of control is likely if administrators or liquidators are appointed that have the power by law to direct the activities of the subsidiary. The appointment of administrators or liquidators does not necessarily mean that they will take over all decision-making rights. It is important to investigate whether an administrator or liquidator is involved in the decision-making process. If a full take-over of these rights occurs and all decisions are made by the administrator or liquidator, or if the current management needs upfront approvals on the execution of business transactions, the power of the parent ceases even if the parent is able to maintain control due to voting rights.

- Seizure of assets or operations by local government
  This transfers possession to the local government or an institution or corporation that acts on behalf of the government; anyway, access to these items is no longer possible. As a consequence, the lack of access to assets and operations will result in a loss of power as decisions on activities cannot be made.

- Contractual agreements to transfer control
  Contractual agreements between investors may shift control to defined parties regardless of whether contractual agreements have terminated or lapsed.

Example

As a strategic decision, the management of Flexing Cables decided to dispose of the French production facilities. The decision was made because the products of these two factories had faced continuous decline in sales due to a technology shift towards other products and solutions. Management believed that such products would be available for three to four years until the substitution process had finished. The decision to dispose of the French production facilities had been made at the beginning of January. An investment bank had been hired to find potential buyers. The bank had identified potential buyers willing to have a closer look into the companies. Due diligence had started at the end of January. As a result of the due diligence, two potential buyers had continued to be interested in acquiring Cuivre Manufacture. The subsequent negotiation process had been finalized at the end of February and the sale and purchase agreement signed on February 28th. The most important items of this agreement were:

- The transaction is structured as a share deal where the buyer acquires directly all shares in Cuivre Manufacture held by Flexing Cables.
- Flexing Cables has the right to market the products of Cuivre Manufacture for the next two years.
- The transaction is backdated to 1.1.2013 so that the buyer would acquire Cuivre Manufacture as of the beginning of the period.
- The purchase price is due within 14 days by wire transfer.

> - A performance guarantee is not given by Flexing Cables due to the assumption of management regarding the future market decline.
> - The sales and purchase agreement is subject to the approvals of the French antitrust agency. Flexing Cables as well as the buyer assume that approval will be given.
>
> The structure of the sale of Cuivre Manufacture would result in a loss of control as of the date of signing the sale and purchase agreement. At that time the shares in Cuivre Manufacture would be transferred to the buyer who would take possession and would therefore control the acquiree due to its majority of voting rights. Backdating the purchase agreement towards the beginning of the period was irrelevant as control existed by Flexing Cables until the moment the agreement was signed. The backdating only impacted the accounting of the sales price as the profit (or loss) generated by Cuivre Manufacture had to be considered.
>
> A continuing involvement of Flexing Cables could not be observed. The right to market the products of Cuivre Manufacture would bring Flexing Cables into the role of commercial partner, though as a customer. This position was strengthened by the fact that no performance guarantees had been given.
>
> The missing approval of the French antitrust agency resulted in a conditional sales and purchase agreement. The agreement could be executed as intended. Once approval is given, the agreement becomes unconditional: subsequent actions are not necessary. If an approval is not given, the sale of the subsidiary has to be reversed in such a way that disposal has never occurred. This is an accounting issue that also has an impact on the management of the subsidiary.

A loss of control can occur in more than one transaction. These transactions are usually based on defined **multiple arrangements** that intend a planned disposal in several steps to achieve an overall advantage. Therefore, it is important to check whether these transactions and the underlying arrangements have been treated as one transaction only. An assessment of the terms and conditions of the underlying arrangements is required in such cases. The economic effects have to be kept in mind. To assess whether the transactions have to be accounted for as a single transaction, IFRS 10.B97 provides indicators that should be considered:

- Timing

  Are the transactions entered into at the same time or in contemplation of each other?

- Commercial effect

  Are the transactions designed to achieve an overall commercial effect?

  Are the transactions structured in a way that each transaction on its own is not economically justified?

- Dependency

  Do the transactions depend on each other?

Not all indicators have to be met. It is sufficient if some indicators are satisfied that prove the economic effects behind the structuring in several transactions.

If sufficient evidence is given that an overall economic advantage is expected to be achieved, an accounting as one transaction is required.

Loss of control can arise from **group-internal transactions**. Every time a subsidiary is sold or contributed to an associate or a joint venture, a loss of control for the subsidiary occurs. This is because the associate and the joint venture are included in consolidated financial statements by applying the equity method. The sale or contribution will move the net assets of the subsidiary to the associate or joint venture, which will result in an increase of the net assets of these companies and therefore an increase of the carrying amount of interests in associate or investments in joint ventures (depending on the chosen accounting method).[8]

4. GROUP COMPOSITIONS

The composition of a group depends on the companies that belong to the group and the extent and type of interest in these companies. These two elements define not only the composition; they also define the structure of the group required for the integration in preparing consolidated financial statements. As a general rule, all companies are subject to consolidation. Depending on the interest in **group companies** and the associated voting rights, each company is classified to one of four categories that rule how these companies are consolidated:

- Financial investment

   Financial investments are those investments where the stake in the company is less than 20%. The relevant accounting standard for this type of investment is *IFRS 9 – Financial Instruments*. Financial investments are usually not consolidated in preparing consolidated financial statements. Instead, interests in financial investments are presented as non-current financial assets in the consolidated statement of financial position. Income resulting from interests in financial investments is recorded as dividends or similar items in the consolidated statement of income.

- Associates

   Associates are those financial assets with a stake in the company of more than 20% but less than 50%. The relevant accounting standard for this type of investment is *IAS 28 – Investments in Associates and Joint Ventures*. Associates are integrated into consolidated financial statements by applying the equity method. The presentation is similar to financial investments as a non-current financial asset in the consolidated statement of financial position. Allocable profit and losses from interests in associates are recorded as financial income or similar items in the consolidated statement of income.

- Joint venture and joint operation

   Joint ventures are companies that are jointly controlled by several investors. Therefore, voting rights will be 50% (for two investors), 33% (for

---

[8] See chapter J -3.3.3 on page 600 for further details.

three investors) or less if more investors are involved combined with special agreements regarding the application of control. The relevant accounting standards for this type of investment are *IFRS 11 – Joint Arrangements* and *IAS 28 – Investments in Associated and Joint Ventures*. The presentation is identical to associated companies as the same accounting methods have to be applied.

In addition to joint ventures, joint operations may exist that require a separate treatment. Even if the accounting is based on the same standards than joint ventures, each investor recognized only his part of the joint operation in consolidated financial statements. Thus, a proportionate consolidation may be necessary depending on the form of joint operation.

- Subsidiary

Subsidiaries are companies where an investor has control and therefore can influence the activities of subsidiaries. Usually, voting rights are more than 50%. The relevant accounting standard for this category of companies is *IFRS 10 – Consolidated Financial Statements*. Subsidiaries are fully consolidated.

The dependency between the category, its voting rights and the types of control, the consolidation method to be applied will change. In general, a full consolidation based on the purchase method and an in-line consolidation based on the equity method are the methods to be applied in preparing consolidated financial statements. Only in rare situations, an application of a proportionate consolidation is appropriate.

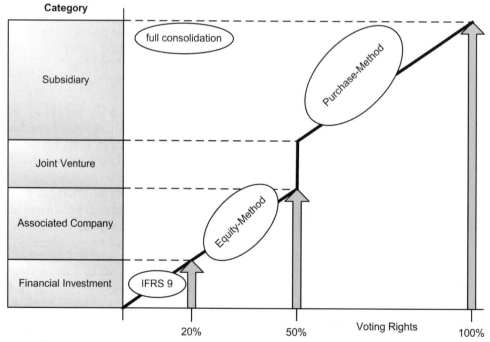

Fig. C-3   Dependency between types of investment and their control

In accordance with the status of a company in the group, the wording of the influence of the parent in its investment will change:

- Control is given every time a parent can direct its subsidiary without involving any other party.
- Joint control is given if the parent requires at least one other party to direct the joint venture in common.
- Significant influence is given, if the parent has a reasonable share in a company but other parties exist that may constitute control on their own or in joint arrangements or due to collaboration or any other reasons.

A second element that defines the group composition is the **extent and way of interest** in group companies. A group can be built on a set of companies that is directly held by the parent. Interests in a company can also be held indirectly through holding companies that are either held by the parent or by other companies of the group. A parent of a group can also hold subgroups. The composition and, in particular, the structure of the group is driven by management, taxation or acquisition reasons. Accounting usually has to consider these facts in preparing consolidated financial statements.

The group composition together with the status of a company in the group is not a static construction. Every time a company is acquired or disposed of the composition of the group changes. Changes in the group composition will always trigger accounting tasks as the changes in structure directly impacts consolidated financial statements in two ways: the process in preparing consolidated financial statements as well as the content to be considered during the preparation process (which is more or less the question, which companies are subject to consolidation). The acquisition and disposal does not necessarily refer to new companies. Also an increase or decrease of interests in existing companies may trigger a change in the group's structure.

A special case that has an impact on control is a **group-internal restructuring**. Restructurings are often initiated to improve the legal structure of a group, its overall tax position or the management of the group. These restructurings require a separate and a consolidated view of the group to understand the impact on control. A separate view is focusing on the separate financial statements of companies in the group. A restructuring might forward the interests in a company from one parent to another parent. As a consequence, a shift in control occurred where the company that "received" the investment in a company has to account this transaction as an acquisition and the company that "sent" the company has to account for the transaction as a disposal. From a consolidated view, a restructuring does not have an impact on consolidated financial statements as no group-external transaction occurred. The different views have to be aligned by accounting as all restructuring transactions have to be reversed to present the initial group structure.

The example discussed focused on a transfer of a company, thus of a legal entity. Group-internal restructurings also have different other forms like mergers (up-, down- or sidestream mergers), demergers and other forms. A consolidated view of these transactions is identical to a transfer of a legal entity, nothing has changed.

From a **parent's perspective**, investment in a company is always a non-current financial asset. Financial assets (in the context of group accounting, and as defined in *IAS 32 – Financial Instruments: Presentation*) are equity instruments of another entity (IAS 32.11, IAS 32.AG13). Therefore, all investments in companies which are part of a group have to be presented in that way, regardless of the amount of the investment. To differentiate between investment types, a separate presentation in the consolidated financial statements or in the fixed asset schedule (as part of the notes) is often maintained by the ultimate parent.

5. SPECIAL CASES

Groups are often defined and designed in a way to optimize the overall position of the group in terms of financial performance. Such optimizations often include:

- Tax minimization;
- Risk securitizations;
- Financing optimizations;
- Improved financial rations (like working capital management);
- Lean management structures.

In addition to these optimizations, business purposes drive the structure of the group. A typical example is the exploration of new markets without applying the full administration overheads to the group.

One way to achieve such efforts is the use of special companies or vehicles in the group that are merely used for selected issues. Due to the dedicated purposes they are designed for special treatment is required. Nevertheless, these companies and vehicles are also subject to consolidation like any other company of the group. Traditional, structured entities, limited partnerships and deemed entities are the preferred legal forms to be used in achieving the effects, management intends to achieve.

5.1. Structured entities

Structured entities (or special purpose entities as previously defined by SIC 12) are popular legal forms that are often used for off-balance-sheet financing or accounting purposes. They have a defined scope and are used for one dedicated purpose only. Traditionally, asset-backed securities, lease arrangements of defined assets, sale-and-lease-back arrangements and special funds are often realized by using structured entities. Depending on the design, structured entities record assets, liabilities or activities and therefore relieve the financial statements by these items. From the group's point of view, structured entities were also exempt from consolidation. As a consequence, improved financial statements (both, separate and consolidated) combined with improved (performance and balance sheet) ratios could be presented to auditors. In the light of the Enron scandal and the financial crisis, the accounting for structured entities has changed. As a consequence of the introduction of IFRS 10, all structured entities are now subject to consolidation. Groups are now forced to present their consolidated financial statements by considering structured entities and therefore providing a full picture about the financial position of a group. To integrate structured entities in consolidated financial statements and to determine control, an inquiry about the purpose and design is necessary to understand the behaviour of the structured entity.

> Due to the introduction of *IFRS 10 – Consolidated Financial Statements* and the revised definition of control, *SIC 12 – Consolidation – Special Purpose Entities* has now become obsolete.

Due to the application of structured entities, the **purpose and design** are most important to understand the way a structured entity works. Structured entities are entities "… whose activities are restricted to the extent that those activities are, in essence, not directed by voting or similar rights".[9] Therefore, few or no decisions are made in conducting the on-going activities of the structured entity as long as the structured entity is working in a predetermined way. This does not neglect that decisions may be made in extraordinary situations or circumstances arising from particular events. Typical cases where such decisions need to be made are failures in delivering a defined return, for example due to the damage of assets, default of receivables or decline in value. Even if decisions do not play an important role in the on-going activities of the structured entity, this does not mean that the activities of a structured entity are not relevant activities. In particular in extraordinary situations where additional decisions need to be made, the activities of a structured entity are always relevant activities as they have a significant impact on returns. Therefore, even contingent decisions have to be considered in the determination of power.

A common practice is to design structured entities by implementing an autopilot. Autopilots work in a way that seemingly no decisions are necessary on on-going and relevant activities. This requires more attention compared to the before mentioned "few or no decisions". Such autopilots demand a thorough evaluation and understanding of the purpose and design of the structured entity and the assessment of power. If there are no decisions on relevant activities necessary and observable, a fall-back to the initiation of a structured entity should be made as the relevant activity is the design of the structured entity. The more an investor is involved in the design of the structured entity and its autopilot mechanism and the more his interest is, the more decision-making for the benefits of the investor can be assumed. Power may be assumed in such situations depending on the level of involvement.

Depending on the design of the structured entity, the power and the exposure to variable returns as well as the link between them can directly be derived. Nevertheless, a formal investigation of the three elements mentioned combined with a proper documentation is recommended.

---

[9] Definition taken from *ED 10 – Consolidated Financial Statements* which is the predecessor of IFRS 10.

5.2. Limited partnerships

A limited partnership is a partnership that consists of general and limited partners. General partners usually take the full responsibility of the partnership including all risks and therefore are part of management. By contrast, limited partners benefit from a protection of liabilities and risks that arise in the ordinary course of the business. Due to limited liabilities, these partners are not entitled to be a part of management. To achieve such benefits, a form-driven structure is often chosen by considering legal and tax requirements.

The determination if an investor that acts as a partner has control over a limited partnership has to follow the same procedures as that for any other interest in a company. The application of the control concept is therefore mandatory.

- Purpose and design

    The structure of the partnership and, in particular, the legal and tax requirements are the core elements that need to be evaluated to understand the decision process of a limited partnership. Some partnerships are built in a way that the general partner is represented through another limited entity to protect partners against risks. Combined with an optimized tax structure benefits may directly forward towards the limited partners. This will include all activities as listed by IFRS 10.B11.

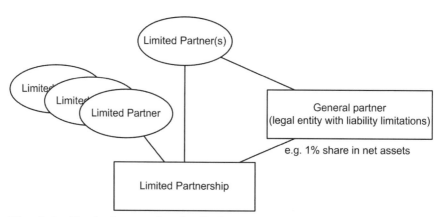

Fig. C-4   Typical example of a limited partnership structure

- Power

    General partners that direct the business of the partnership always have power. Consequently, limited partners that do not manage the business of the partnership do not have power. Nevertheless, partners that have the power to remove or replace a (sole) general partner by another one also meet the definition of power. Such a partner is not necessarily a general partner. A limited partner can fulfil this definition as well.

- Variable returns

    Similar to other partners, limited partners are also subject to benefit from variable returns. This criterion is fulfilled in most cases.

- Link between power and return

    The link between power and return does not necessarily exist. Under normal conditions, a general partner that directs the business of the partnership is also entitled to benefit from variable returns. Therefore, control might be constituted. Limited partners that benefit from variable returns only, without managing the business of the partnership, are not entitled to have control. Due to the missing link between power and return, a general partner who is managing the business without a beneficial interest in the partnership's net assets, also has no control (this is typical of 1% scenarios).

    Partners may also act as agents for other partners. Therefore, the standard procedure in determining the link between power and return has to consider an inquiry of any principal–agent relationships. Standard checks can be applied.

Due to legal structures, tax optimizations and risk minimizations, in limited partnerships it is difficult to determine whether or not control is established by a partner or joint control by a set of partners. Assessing such set-ups demands careful judgement considering all relevant facts and circumstances.

5.3. Deemed separate entities

A deemed separate entity is a portion of a company that consists of assets and liabilities and that is fully separated and isolated from the rest of the company.[10] Deemed separate entities are also known as "silos". A typical application of a deemed separate entity is when a parent wants to establish a new business in a foreign country. It may use an existing company that is separate from the group as a host to establish the new business by giving assets to them. The host company may be a related party or a business partner or customer or supplier that is willing to act as a host for a while until the new business is established preferably as a separate entity. Another example is a structured entity that acts as a lessor where each lease arrangement is treated, managed and financed separately.

To account for deemed separate entities and to consider the control over a deemed separate entity, the requirements as outlined in IFRS 10.B77 have to be cumulatively met:

- Specified (or defined or named or reserved) assets of the company are the only source for payments of specified (or defined or named or reserved) liabilities of the company. Instead of specified liabilities, specified assets may relate to specified other interests in the company.

---

[10] IFRS 10.B77 names the separate treatment of assets and liabilities as "ring-fenced".

- Specified liabilities (and therefore also the specified assets) relate to a particular party. No other party has rights or obligations to the assets and liabilities specified and their resulting cash flows.
- Any returns of specified assets cannot be used for other purposes of the company.
- Any payables of specified liabilities cannot be satisfied by other assets of the company.

If all conditions are met, an ordinary application of the determination of control over the deemed separate entity has to be initiated. This includes the determination of power (so how the activities in the deemed separate entity are directed), the determination of variable returns (do rights or the exposures exist?) and a determination if the power can be used to affect the investor's return. Once control is given, the deemed separate entity is subject to consolidation by the parent. Other parties, particularly the parties that control the rest of the company are required to exclude the deemed entity from their interests in the company.

D PREPARATION OF CONSOLIDATED FINANCIAL STATEMENTS AND ANNUAL REPORTS

About this chapter:

Preparing consolidated financial statements is a task that involves several people in several companies in several countries. Depending on the size of a group and its business (and, in particular, its internal relationships), the preparation can become a critical and time-consuming activity in the accounting department. This will even be enhanced if unusual stages of a subsidiary have to be considered that require special accounting attention. Therefore, it is important to define some rules regarding the preparation process. These rules have to be followed by each party involved in the preparation of consolidated financial statements. This does not necessarily stop at the border of the accounting department; other departments across the whole group may be affected as well.

This chapter discusses all organizational aspects around the preparation of consolidated financial statements that are necessary for an efficient preparation process. Based on the lifecycle of a subsidiary, required activities are discussed for each stage during the lifecycle by with different views of the subsidiary. The structure and the process in considering the subsidiary in consolidated financial statements are the two core elements discussed in detail based on a pure accounting view of groups. The main issue from an accounting perspective is the availability of accounting information in the group and how to structure them for consolidation issues by considering not only group requirements but also accounting requirements at a local level which a subsidiary has to fulfil. Another issue is to make use of this structured accounting information by with an appropriate reporting system in place that is able to capture accounting information in a structured way. The discussion on group structures is completed by providing an outlook on efficiency opportunities, particularly the use of shared services. While efficient structures are only one part of the game, a detailed view of the preparation process of consolidated financial statements is taken; in particular, of the definition of the closing process itself and of tasks and timing to ensure a fast close. It is accomplished by information on rules to be followed during the preparation process.

1. LIFECYCLE OF SUBSIDIARIES

Like any ordinary asset, investment in a parent company's subsidiary follows the same behaviour: it will be purchased, used and sold or trashed. The differences between these assets are that investments in subsidiaries usually have a much longer horizon than ordinary assets have and that their "use" is based on a business pattern rather than on an asset pattern for dedicated purposes. An investment also has the potential to generate profit and cash.

The asset pattern a company follows can be transferred into a lifecycle scheme. Such a lifecycle scheme is valid for all kinds of investment in subsidiaries. It usually consists of four major phases:

- Acquisition;
- Integration;
- Performance;
- Disposal.

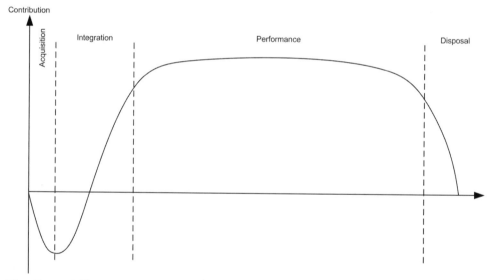

Fig. D-1   Lifecycle of a subsidiary in a group

During and for each phase of the subsidiary's lifecycle in the group, specific accounting requirements have to be applied.

The **acquisition** phase is marked by high uncertainty regarding the probability a company can be acquired. The uncertainty is based on the intention of the purchaser which risk to take if and how the company and its inherent risk are acquired. The uncertainty is also based on the attractiveness of the company and the competitor's intentions to acquire the company. This phase is also associated with high costs for advisors to become familiar with the company. To fully understand the risk exposure of the company and the impact on the group due diligence is required. The due diligence usually focuses on critical areas of the company and covers commercial, financial and operational aspects. In minimum, due diligence should include the following areas of a company:

- Market and market position;
- Financial;
- Tax and legal;
- Environmental.

In particular the financial and tax due diligence are important as they may unveil the potential risk exposure for the group. Typical elements of a financial due diligence are checks, queries and scenarios on net assets, financial status and performance of the company, planned investment and capital expenditures, plans, budgets and forecasts, impacts of accounting standards and other relevant financial information. The tax due diligence include checks and queries on the current tax position of the company, the tax structuring of the acquisition and often also tax impacts on the parent company as the acquirer.

Acquirers often use due diligence not only to become familiar with the company under acquisition, they will also use the results of the due diligence to find or optimize the quoted price for the company. The quoted price will be the basis for negotiations with the seller in determining the final purchase price.

In addition to due diligence, tendencies can be observed to prepare a so called "pre purchase price allocation". The purpose of this purchase price allocation is to simulate the effects on the group, such an acquisition would have. The allocation considers, in particular, the recognition and measurement of assumed non-accounted assets and liabilities, and step-ups of carrying amounts of assets and liabilities as well as their tax effects and the goodwill as the residual value. Based on the items identified, a simulation of changes in the group, particularly the net assets and the performance of the group, is carried out. Such a simulation covers not only the period the acquisition takes place but also subsequent periods.

An acquired company that has become a subsidiary of a group is subject to the **integration** in the group. The integration is based on a set of organizational tasks. These tasks are necessary for a seamless integration so that the new subsidiary fits into the group. Tasks span across all parts and functions of the subsidiary: logistics, sales and marketing, production, sourcing (purchasing), administration, IT, HR and finance & accounting. From a business perspective, the operation of the subsidiary has to be aligned to the group's business. Sharing knowledge, products and services offered to customers, customers and production capabilities is a mandatory task so generate synergies and reduce costs. A traditional area to generate synergies is administration. By centralizing functions like IT, HR, legal and similar departments, synergies are raised through cost reduction or business restructuring. Another important area of improvement is finance & accounting. This function has a double role to fulfil. On one side, synergies have to be raised similar to other administration departments. On the other hand, the subsidiaries have to be integrated into the group's accounting and reporting environment. The degree of integration of some or all departments of the new subsidiary depends on the management philosophy of the group. It can range from a loose integration where the subsidiary's management has substantial freedom to run the operations of the subsidiary to highly integrated subsidiaries where a subsidiary is more or less treated as another department in the group.

The finance and accounting integration into the group depends on the structures and processes of the group. Usually, the subsidiary will be aligned to the existing accounting and reporting systems in the group. This practice is preferred by most companies as it easier to align one company to the group rather than aligning the group to the subsidiary. Even if such a practice is often applied in practice, it is always recommended to scan the new subsidiary regarding structures, processes and practices that have the potential to improve the administration performance of the group.

Since the integration of the subsidiary is finished, the **performance** of the new subsidiary is subject to attention by finance & accounting. Typical tasks are the performance monitoring & analysis, optimization of accounting & reporting structures and processes, management of subsidiaries and similar tasks. Performance tasks can be divided into two sections: the on-going performance optimization of the operations and improvements of accounting & reporting structures and processes.

The on-going performance optimization is usually driven by management to ensure that market needs are fulfilled. Aligning the subsidiary to market needs includes activities like product portfolios optimizations, market penetration, cost reduction and similar ones. As the optimization is driven by management, this task is usually not a topic in preparing consolidated financial statements.

Improvements in accounting & reporting in the context of the preparation of consolidated financial statements have several dimensions. One dimension is the alignment of group accounting standards to new accounting standards issued by standard setters. The implementation of new accounting standards has to be executed by all companies of the group. Another dimension is process improvement in administration. The alignment to market needs of the subsidiary has to be adopted by finance & accounting. Accounting structures and accounting and reporting processes have to be aligned to the new structures. This involves the corporate centre and its functions as well as subsidiaries.

The **disposal** of a subsidiary from the group triggers several accounting tasks. The disposed subsidiary has to be removed from the accounting & reporting environment. Due to the disposal of one subsidiary the reporting volume decreases. The removal from the reporting processes is usually easy to realize. The removal of the subsidiary from consolidated financial statements is more complex. In addition to a deconsolidation, the total contribution of the subsidiary during the membership of the group as well as the expected gain or loss of the disposal is information often required by management. The gain or loss realized is calculated differently at parent and group level. The disposal also requires an update of the business plan in subsequent periods as a follow-up activity.

Different **views** are possible on the lifecycle of a subsidiary in a group. The views depend on who is looking at the subsidiary and on how the view is done.

An accounting view of the subsidiary and its purpose from a superior position depends on what level the view is taken from:

- Parent view

  From a parent's view, the investment in subsidiary is – like other assets – a non-current asset that reflects the share in the subsidiary held by the parent company. The carrying value of the investment usually reflects the purchase price unless no adjustments are made. These kinds of investments usually have an indefinite life. Due to IAS 39.58, depreciation is prohibited. Instead, an impairment test is required to ensure that the carrying amount of the investment in subsidiary is not overstated. An overstatement would require a write-down on the investment in subsidiary. The impairment test is required each period the subsidiary belongs to the group. Upon the disposal of the subsidiary (whether sold or "trashed"), a gain or loss is recorded based on the retirement of the investment's carrying amount and earnings realized.

- Group view

  Due to the one-entity theory, the group view differs from the parent view because it focuses on the assets of the subsidiary rather than on the share in the subsidiary. All assets and liabilities of the subsidiary are included in consolidated financial statements right from the date the acquired company becomes a subsidiary using its fair value. They consist of accounted-for as well as non-accounted-for assets and liabilities. This may cause valuation differences as the subsidiary may record or not record assets and liabilities in a different way. In subsequent periods, presentation and measurement of the subsidiary's assets and liabilities are subject to group accounting policies based on the use by the subsidiary.

  While the acquisition of a subsidiary is accompanied with payments that exceed the assets acquired and liabilities assumed, goodwill may arise as a residual value (purchase price less net assets acquired) that requires a dedicated treatment. Like the investment in subsidiaries by the parent company, goodwill has an indefinite life. Again, an impairment test is required to ensure that the carrying amount of the goodwill that is allocated to the subsidiary[1] is not overstated. An overstatement would require a write-down on the goodwill. Similar to the parent's view, the impairment test on goodwill is required each period the subsidiary belongs to the group.

  Upon disposal of the subsidiary from the group, all assets and liabilities including the allocated goodwill have to be removed from consolidated financial statements.

- Management view

  In contrast to the parent's and group's view of the subsidiary, the management view is purely functional and focused on the business. The subsidiary

---

[1] Be careful: Goodwill can also be allocated to a subsidiary due to cash generating units!

can have various units or departments that belong to one or more business units of the group. The subsidiary itself can also be allocated to one business unit only. It can have various functions like sales organization, production, research & development or corporate functions like service centres. From an accounting point of view, the management view is important if performances or assets have to be measured on a consolidated basis by business unit, department or other functional areas.

The lifecycle of a subsidiary in the group can be assigned directly to accounting tasks. Acquisitions are usually handled by management and – if required – supported by management accounting. The financial accounting department is not involved in most cases. The accounting's responsibility during the integration phase is linked to the initial consolidation covering all tasks necessary to prepare the subsidiary for the group's life. During the performance phase, subsequent consolidation will take place. Finally, the disposal requires a deconsolidation of the subsidiary from the group.

2. STRUCTURES

Groups – whether organically grown or formed through mergers & acquisitions – have implied structures. The structures follow, on the one hand, legal aspects and, on the other, management aspects. Legal aspects include aspects like the relationship between subsidiaries and the parent company or all consequences arising due to the place of incorporation and the domicile of a group company. Legal aspects have to be seen on a global basis where a dedicated view per country is required due to local accounting and reporting requirements, taxation and national compliance. Management aspects follow a business rationale and have an impact on strategic and operational decisions. Typical aspects are business units, product portfolios, production, markets to be penetrated or customer demands.

The accounting organization of a group has to consider these aspects to ensure that an efficient and timely preparation of reports and statements occurs. The challenge, the accounting organization has, is to structure their organization in a way that reflects the group. Therefore, an efficient accounting structure is required considering group structures, reporting structures and accounting environments.

2.1. Accounting in group structures

As already mentioned, group structures follow legal and management aspects and requirements. These structures have to be considered by the accounting function in the group. Due to the establishment of groups, an accounting function is located at every company of the group. In addition, the parent company has additional accounting functions for group accounting purposes; there is interaction between individual accounting functions. While different recipients have to be satisfied by the accounting function, a separation between local accounting that deals with the preparation of separate financial statements and group accounting that deal with the preparation of consolidated financial statements is often realized.

This is because separate financial statements have to be prepared by all companies of the group while consolidated financial statements are prepared only by the parent. Even if the preparation of financial statements is separated, they follow the same management.

A central element is the corporate centre of a group. This centre can host several functions of a group like accounting, human resources, IT, legal and other functions. Accounting is therefore only one element of the corporate centre. Nevertheless, the accounting part of the corporate centre has a broad responsibility as it directs the accounting of the whole group. Therefore, the chief accounting officer heads the accounting function of the group.

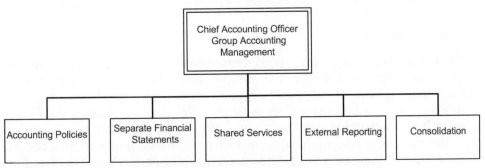

Fig. D-2 Typical structure of an accounting corporate centre

The corporate centre is usually organized in a set of departments that have dedicated purposes:

- Accounting policies and processes deal with the application of current and future IFRS and their impact on the group.
- Separate financial statements are often used as a supervisor for the accounting departments of subsidiaries. Compliance functions may be included.
- Shared services process tasks that are usually performed by subsidiaries.
- An external reporting may be part of the group if the reporting is not done by management accounting or by the investor relations department.
- Consolidation is responsible for preparing consolidated financial statements.

The preparation of consolidated financial statements is usually executed in a separate department of the corporate centre. The consolidation department has to serve different "clients" with consolidated data and analysis. In addition to the preparation of consolidated financial statements of the group, the department often also prepares consolidated statements for business or other units by performing management consolidations. The input the consolidation department will get depends – again – on the group structure. To ensure an efficient consolidation and preparation process, only one consolidation instance should exist in a group. This is the preferred solution while more than one consolidation instance produces additional workload and reconciliations. There are situations where more than one consolidation instance is unavoidable. This applies, in particular, to subgroups where non-controlling interests exist or when subgroups are publicly listed.

Such subgroups often have own consolidation department because they have to prepare consolidated financial statements as they are not exempt from preparation requirements. From the group's point of view, such consolidation tasks are treated as pre-consolidations of subgroups. The pre-consolidated financial statements are used in preparing consolidated financial statements. Such pre-consolidations have the disadvantage that information of subsidiary details gets lost and the consolidation process takes longer than necessary.

> It is recommended to have only one centralized consolidation department that prepares all kinds of statements and analysis.

2.2. Shared Services

Shared service centres are typical departments or separate legal entities in midsize and larger groups. The intention of using shared service centres is to bundle similar functions and tasks to achieve costs advantages. Such a bundling of similar functions and tasks does not only offer cost advantages, it will also ensure a better utilization due to the concentration on specific items. As a consequence, riding the experience curve in such a way additionally offers a pooling of knowledge so that tasks can be executed more efficiently. Due to the bundling of similar functions and tasks, shared service centres act as service providers for other departments or companies of the group. Usually, they belong to the corporate function of a group or subgroup. Based on the structure and composition of a group, shared service centres are either departments of the group or separate legal entities that are treated as subsidiaries for consolidations.

Depending on the intention to create a shared service centre, the centre can host various functions, departments and tasks of the group. Typical functions are administration tasks and, in particular, IT services, HR, legal and accounting services. In addition to these more traditional functions, operational tasks like order processing, logistics and contract management can be found. Other functions subject to integration in a shared service centre exist depending on the business of the group. As far as accounting is concerned, ordinary accounting tasks are often subject to shared services. These accounting tasks focus on the daily accounting of ordinary business transaction like the recording of sales, purchases and other earnings and expenses. Other typical tasks are cash management and selected management accounting tasks like reporting.

Group accounting functions are rarely part of shared services as these functions do not follow the typical patterns of functions and task that qualify for the integration in shared service centres. This is because group accounting functions usually exist only once in a group and are also part of the corporate centre. In such an environment, where the accounting of the companies of a group is executed fully or partially in a shared service centre, an interaction between the shared service centre and the corporate centre is obvious. While the accounting of the group companies is executed in the shared service centre, the centre has to report to the corporate centre data and other information required for preparing consolidated financial statements. Such a setup offers benefits as the reporting can be kept lean due to reduced reporting lines from group companies to the corporate centre. Within the shared service centre, accounting and reporting processes can be standardized and bundled so that communication between the corporate and shared service centres can be limited to a few persons only, which boosts efficiency in the reporting cycle.

An alternate structure is the combination of a corporate centre and a shared service centre within one organizational unit that hosts all accounting tasks of a group. As group accounting is a part of a shared service centre in such a configuration, synergies may arise due to short reporting lines and enhanced communication between group and local accounting, even if there are no scaling effects at group level achievable.

Regardless of whether the corporate centre is part of the shared service centre or not, an interaction of the shared service centre with other parts of the group and external parties is always necessary. Due to the provided services, an interaction with the served companies is always the case. This is not limited to pure accounting tasks; an interaction with other departments is always the case. One example is the sales department as this department generates sales invoices to be processed by the shared service centre. An interaction is also given with external parties. External parties can be customers and suppliers of the served company in the ordinary course of the business. Typical activities where the shared service centre is involved are cash collection, cash spending, reconciliation of outstanding balance and similar tasks. Other typical activities with external parties are preparation activities of financial statement that involve auditors.

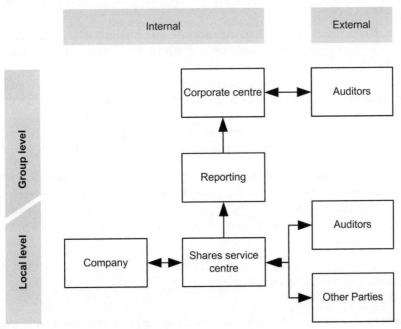

Fig. D-3   Environment of a shared service centre

A general topic is the handling of **costs** that arise with a shared service centre. From the customer's point of view, services charged are always costs. From the group's point of view, costs or profits can arise depending on the implementation of a shared service centre in a group. This will initiate different activities in preparing consolidated financial statements. The shared service centre can be either a department of the parent or any other company of the group that belongs to the corporate sphere or a separate legal entity.

- Cost allocation

  Cost allocation is a typical task if the shared service centre shall not generate any profits and cost coverage is sufficient. Costs are charged to the served companies depending on services agreed and volume consumed. The handling from the group's point of view is simple as costs are just distributed across the group.

  Using such an allocation method, the shared service centre is usually part of the parent company where the company does not intend to generate any profits. The shared service centre is then a department of the parent.

- Profit allocation

  Service rendered to group companies can also include a profit element. The shared service centre should make a profit; services and their prices are often similar to service that are offered in the market. The rationale to generate profits depends on the integration of the shared service centre in a group. If the shared service centre is a department of the parent, profits of the group companies can be forwarded to the parent. If the shared service centre is organized in a separate legal entity, profits are often mandatory to fulfil tax requirements.

  Regardless of the organization of the shared service centre, services charged to group companies require additional attention in preparing consolidated financial statements. While services provided to group companies can be cross-border activities, transfer pricing issues will arise from taxation requirements. This requires a solid cost calculation together with appropriate documentation.[2] The charging of profits in a group is also subject to consolidation activities. The consolidation requirement is a consequence because profits generated by the shared service centre are purely internal.[3]

To ensure an efficient preparation process, an acceptable cost allocation and a compliance with legal requirements, **service level agreements** are mandatory for shared service centres. Service level agreements (or SLAs) provide the basis of rendered services that all parties can rely on. As a minimum, the following topics should be covered in a service level agreement:

- List of tasks and activities including a description of them that have to be executed by the shared service centre.

---

[2] See chapter F -6.2 on page 316 regarding a more detailed explanation on transfer pricing.
[3] See chapter F -5 on page 286 regarding consolidation requirements.

- The intended quality and accuracy and the handling in case of failure or default by the shared service centre.
- Documentation to be prepared by the shared service centre and reporting processes and structures the shared service centre has to follow. This should include a treatment in case of changes in the reporting structures and processes.
- Tasks to be performed on a daily, weekly, quarterly or even annual basis.
- Priorities of tasks to be performed.
- Deadlines, response and lead times of tasks to be performed.
- Escalation and sanction procedures in case of non-performance, wrong performance, disputes, failures, defaults or any other unusual behaviour between the shared service centre and other group departments and functions or unusual behaviours of the shared service centre.
- Interface description that defines the content to be delivered by which party and the type and format of the contents. In other words: who delivers what item how and who is in charge of what.
- Costs charged by the shared service centre for the services rendered. The cost definition is usually based on one service or one transaction for each service category.

Even if a service level agreement covers a description of tasks that have to be executed by the shared service centre, the way that these tasks are executed is the responsibility of the shared service centre.

2.3. Accounting structures

An efficient preparation of consolidated financial statements depends not only on group structures but also on accounting structures. Based on the group structure, an appropriate accounting and reporting structure is required that considers all basic elements in gathering accounting data for preparing consolidated financial statements. Therefore, the structures define tasks that are necessary in the preparation process. At a minimum, the following elements should be considered in defining an appropriate accounting structure:

- The chart of accounts;
- Accounting standards (IFRS and local GAAP);
- Implementation in accounting systems;
- Reporting structures and cycles;[4]
- Organization of the group.

A central topic of group structures is the **chart of accounts**. It is the underlying basis of the reporting system within a group and therefore a key element in with efficient structures. Usually, the chart of accounts of a group is identical to the chart of accounts of the parent company. It is recommended that this chart of accounts is applied by all subsidiaries in the group. Such a solution has the advantage that all

---

[4] See next chapter.

subsidiaries can be easily integrated into the consolidation and preparation process. Difficult account mappings, reallocation of accounts and similar challenges can be avoided. While accounts follow local requirements (e.g. rules and regulations, business demands) the group's chart of accounts cannot cover all details of a group. To cope with this issue, several solutions are possible. One possible solution is the split account method. This method divides account IDs into two elements, a group and a local part. The group part is defined by the corporate centre and has a binding character for all subsidiaries. The local part acts as subaccounts a subsidiary can use for its own purposes. For reporting purposes, the balances of all subaccounts are mapped into the group account. The advantage of this method is that subsidiaries have the flexibility to align the chart of accounts to their individual requirements and fulfil group reporting requirements at the same time.

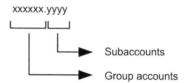

Fig. D-4   Example of an account structure of the split-account method

Account names and IDs are assigned in the ordinary way as before.

> Whenever possible define a group chart of account that has a defined structure which is only alterable by corporate centre and assign subaccounts to them that are changeable by subsidiaries as appropriate to reflect their local accounting environment.

Nevertheless, there might be situations where the application of the group's chart of accounts by a subsidiary is not possible. Typically, situations may arise in which local authorities require either a standardized account structure or standardized reporting. In these situations, a mapping of accounts of the local chart of accounts to accounts of the group's chart of accounts is required. The mapping has to ensure a defined relationship between the accounts:

* One to one
   A one to one relationship between local and group accounts is a simple definition that required no further attention.

* Multiple to one
   If a subsidiary maintains several accounts to trace details, these accounts have to be accumulated in one defined group account.

* One to multiple
   A subsidiary account that have to be allocated to several group accounts, require a manual assignment where the balance on the account

has to be split up into several balances that have to be assigned to group accounts. Such a practice is inappropriate and should be avoided due to potential errors that might evolve. If a subsidiary account has to be assigned to several group accounts, the subsidiary account has to be split up at local level into several accounts that are then mapped into the group accounts. The best solution in this scenario is that the subsidiary maintains in its ledger as many accounts as required to fulfil reporting purposes.

Whenever possible implement the group's chart of account at local level!

The application of a standardized chart of accounts across a whole group is based on the group management's intentions, on strategic and political reasons within the group. While large publicly listed groups often have efficient structures in place that are based on a standardized chart of accounts, smaller groups – regardless of publicly listed or private – often do not implement such standardized chart of accounts. There are manifold reasons for this behaviour: the historical evolution of a group, responsibilities of local management for their accounts and the treatment of subsidiaries as a pure investment are just a few reasons. Disadvantages like an additional workload for the preparation of consolidated financial statements are accepted in these cases.

Regardless how the charts of accounts on group and at local level are built up, they have to consider group requirements for consolidation. The easiest way is the integration of intercompany accounts so that group internal transactions can be separated from external ones by recording all intercompany transactions on these accounts. Intercompany accounts usually exist of all balance sheet items and items in the profit & loss statement. Non-present intercompany accounts bear the danger that an isolation of intercompany transactions from external ones cannot be managed without picking up all group internal transactions. This should only happen if the accounting systems are capable of identifying intercompany transactions on accounts by using additional criteria.

Always define separate accounts for intercompany purposes in all sections of the balance sheet and profit & loss statement and insist that all companies of the group record intercompany transactions on these accounts. It will significantly ease the consolidation process.

Charts of accounts used for reporting purposes are often enhanced by additional information required to prepare consolidated financial statements. The accounting view, that accounts belonging to the general ledger have to be reported only, is often not sufficient. Therefore, the chart of accounts is expanded for group purposes towards a reporting logic that covers additional elements. In practice, IDs are often expanded by a leading digit that classifies the type of reported item.

Account-ID	Description
0.xxxxxx	Balance sheet
1.xxxxxx	Profit & loss statement
2.xxxxxx	Cash-flow statement
3.xxxxxx	Segment information
4.xxxxxx	Fixed asset schedule
5.xxxxxx	Tax reporting
6.xxxxxx	Details for notes
7.xxxxxx	Ratios, key indicators
8.xxxxxx	Non-financials
9.xxxxxx	Other relevant information

Traditional chart of accounts. All accounts have to add to zero! *(bracket spanning Balance sheet and Profit & loss statement rows)*

Fig. D-5 Example of an enhanced group chart of accounts

Preparing consolidated financial statements by applying IFRS accounting standards often require a conversion of separate financial statements of subsidiaries as these companies may have to apply different (local) **accounting standards**. Avoiding local standards is not possible as dividend distribution rules, taxation and similar issues are based on local accounting standards. Therefore, an implementation of IFRS and various local GAAPs into one accounting framework is necessary. The implementation can occur on several accounting levels in the group:

- At group level

    A conversion of local GAAP to IFRS at group level is only appropriate if the parent company has to prepare consolidated financial statements by applying local GAAP. In such a scenario, the conversion towards IFRS is often based on two reasons: to fulfil reporting requirements of regulators, stock exchanges, investors or other stakeholders or as a courtesy of management in providing additional services. If subsidiaries apply different local accounting standards than the parent company, their separate financial statements have to be adjusted to the local GAAP of the parent company. The additional conversion to IFRS may result in a loss of detail information of subsidiary specific items that are required for IFRS accounting. To compensate this effect, additional information has to be gathered from subsidiaries as part of the overall reporting requirements.

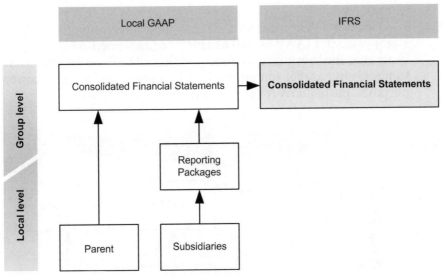

Fig. D-6   Accounting standard conversion at group level

• At reporting level

A conversion application at reporting level creates an accounting environment that offers full flexibility for subsidiaries. The subsidiary can apply local accounting standards as appropriate for their needs. The conversion towards IFRS will take place in the reporting package. Usually such a reporting package demands the population of a reporting balance sheet and a reporting profit & loss statement based on local accounts. The balances of all items have to be adjusted by valuations and reclassifications due to IFRS to arrive at reportable balances. Such a solution assumes a mapping of accounts to reporting items of the reporting package.

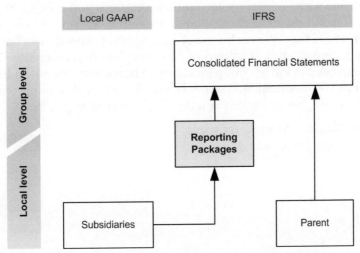

Fig. D-7   Accounting standard conversion on reporting level

- At local level

  A conversion at local level is the highest integration of a subsidiary in a group. Local GAAP as well as IFRS are implemented in the accounting systems of the subsidiary. The accounting will be done for both accounting standards in parallel so that the IFRS accounts can be used for reporting purposes, particularly for populating reporting packages.

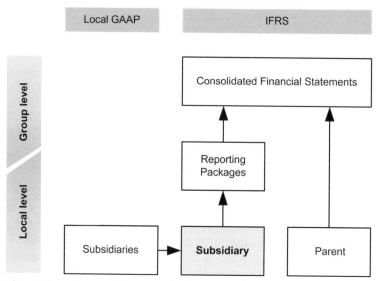

Fig. D-8   Accounting standard conversion at local level

The implementation of several accounting standards at reporting and local levels triggers additional auditing activities. To ensure that the conversion to IFRS is in line with the group's accounting standards and policies, the conversion is subject to auditing tasks at local level. Therefore, auditors of subsidiaries have to audit not only the separate financial statements of subsidiaries but also reporting packages based on instructions of the group's parent company.

The **implementation** of group structures, charts of accounts and the accounting standards **in accounting systems** is mandatory in designing efficient group structures. Two types of implementation are observed in practice:

- The "Mickey-Mouse" principle;
- The client principle.

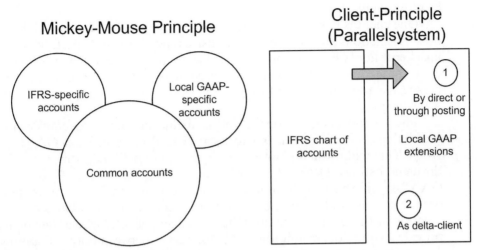

Fig. D-9 Implementation in accounting systems

The "Mickey-Mouse" principle combines two accounting standards in one system using one chart of accounts. All accounts can be sorted into one of three sections:

- Common accounts

  Common accounts are used under both accounting standards. There is no deviation regarding the measurement and recording of business transactions between IFRS and local GAAP.

- IFRS-specific accounts

  IFRS-specific accounts are used to account for business transaction by applying IFRS rules because the accounting for these transactions differs between IFRS and local GAAP.

- Local GAAP-specific accounts

  Local GAAP-specific accounts are used to measure the same business transaction from a local-GAAP perspective.

The advantage of this principle is an easily configured accounting system that handles two accounting standards within one accounting area. Nevertheless this principle is prone to errors. If business transactions are not recorded in a proper and consistent way or blindfold journal entries are recorded, a mixture of IFRS and local GAAP may result under both accounting standards. Such errors are difficult to find and often initiate an extensive workload of error correction. Accountants have to be aware of this danger and have to record business transactions carefully.

In contrast to the "Mickey-Mouse" principle, the client principle strictly separates both accounting standards. Typical errors of the "Mickey-Mouse" principle – in particular, the mixture of two accounting standards – are avoided. Nevertheless, the client principle requires a more complex configuration of accounting systems. For each accounting standard, there is a separate client or ledger.

- Leading client

  One client is based on the leading accounting standard where all business transactions are recorded. If extensive reporting duties exist, the leading client should be based on IFRS. If such reporting requirements do not exist, the leading system can also be based on local GAAP. From a group's perspective the leading client should be based on IFRS.
- Adjustment client

  The second client carries all adjustments necessary to convert the trial balance either from IFRS to local GAAP or from local GAAP to IFRS. These adjustments can be realized as pure delta adjustments or by through-postings. Delta adjustments correct only IFRS-specific or local GAAP-specific business transactions to arrive at the other accounting standard. The final trial balance of the "other" accounting standard is a combination of the leading client and the adjustment client. Delta adjustments provide a good documentation on all differences between both accounting standards and journal entries are easier to read. Through-postings work in a similar way. All transactions of the leading client are automatically recorded in the adjustment client. Again, adjustments are used to correct either IFRS or local GAAP balances to arrive at the other accounting standard. Due to through postings, the trial balance of the other accounting standard is directly taken from the adjustment client.

Having two clients available that record accounting standards in different clients provides timing opportunities regarding the closure of financial statements of subsidiaries. If the leading client is used for reporting purposes, it can be closed as appropriate for group demands considering the timing of the group. The adjustment client is not touched in this case. To prepare financial statements for statutory purposes of the subsidiary, the adjustment client has to be closed. This can be done at a later stage when group demands are fulfilled. The subsidiary has the freedom to account for additional transactions required by local GAAP.

Avoid mingling accounting standards in one accounting system! Try to set up a structure that separates the standards in different environments based upon the capabilities of your accounting software.

Which principle applies depends on several criteria: for example, the level of deviation between local GAAP and IFRS, the reporting complexity and range, the level of integration of a subsidiary in the group or the centralization of systems and procedures in the group, etc. If a principle is chosen, it should usually be applied across the whole group unless there are reasons to exclude selected subsidiaries.

The implementation of the principles described is based on the assumption that IT and accounting systems are used consistently by all companies of the group. Such tight integration is not always the case. Smaller groups or merged groups often have various IT and accounting systems in place. The implementation of efficient group structures requires either replacement of legacy systems by other accounting systems used or implementation of one of the principles in each accounting system.

Consolidated financial statements do not only cover the basic statements. The disclosure of accompanying information like segment reporting as required by IFRS 8 or selected analysis of balance sheet items, revenues and expenses is an integral part in the notes to the basic statements. Therefore, the **organization of the group** by segments, business units, entities, departments and cost centres plays an important role. Similar to the chart of accounts, cost centres have to be assigned to higher organizational units so that they roll up to business units and finally to segments. An allocation to more than one higher organizational unit has to be avoided. While several entities roll up into the structure, management consolidations may be required to retrieve information if intercompany transactions between companies exist that are part of the same reportable segment.

Example

Flexing Cables had run several improvement projects over recent years to increase reliability and performance and to better serve customers on deliverability of products and reduced response times on customer specific requests. Two of these projects had impacted the finance units of the group: the introduction of a new ERP system and a standardization and harmonization of the accounting infrastructure. These two projects had been initiated by the CFO in order to have one source of data only without any misinterpretation of financial results. Financial results were now available within two weeks after a close, which meant that management were supported by an improved database for their decisions, particularly if action became necessary due to deviations from planned performance. The results of the improvement projects are summarized as below:

- One ERP system in the whole group using centralized data storage.
- Two client model in finance where one client acts as the leading client that is used for reporting purposes based on IFRS and the other client acts as a delta-client that is used to adjust IFRS transactions to local accounting standards.
- Dual reporting structure. One set of reports is based on the leading client used to provide management (at all levels) with several reports containing relevant information to run the daily operation. These are standard reports often automatically provided to management. The other set of reports is just to satisfy local accounting and reporting requirements.
- Based on local (legal) requirements and group needs, one chart of accounts was developed to be applied by all group companies. Companies are free to add subaccounts if they are required for local purposes (e.g. for VAT reconciliations).
- Similar to the chart of accounts, there is only one chart of cost centres. This is combined with a cost centre hierarchy so that cost centres roll up into functions, business units and segments.
- Reporting packages are integrated into the ERP environment though an special extension ensuring that non-financial information are available next to financials of the group companies. A workflow system supports the timely submission, aggregation and analysis of non-financial data.
- To ensure flexibility in analyzing financial information relevant to run the business in the group, a centralized data storage using a data warehouse carries several data dimensions. All dimensions are based on three core elements: the entity, accounts and cost centres.

2.4. Reporting structures

Reporting is a topic each company and group is confronted with. This is because companies and groups are obliged to externally report their performance, financial positions and other relevant facts and circumstances. Companies also have an internal reporting to manage and control the business and performance of a company. Due to these activities, reporting means that some kinds of data and / or information have to be gathered from an organizational unit, prepared and brought into a condition that it can be used by another party. Based on these considerations, several reporting tasks can be derived for groups:

- An external reporting by the parent of the performance and financial position of the group based upon the activities of financial and management accounting.
- A group-internal reporting by affiliated and associated companies of their business performance for the management of the group and the preparation of consolidated financial statements.
- A company-internal reporting of the performance of departments, cost and profit centres.

While the group-internal reporting task is the important one for preparing consolidated financial statements, requirements for this task will be discussed in detail. Even if all other tasks are minor, there may be an overlap between all reporting tasks which requires appropriate consideration.

The reporting structure as the core element in each group is the backbone for all reporting tasks. It defines how and when information of subsidiaries are retrieved and reported to the corporate centre. Reporting structures are always based on the implementation of group structures in accounting systems. The more reporting content is defined and implemented in accounting systems, the less reporting activities are required in addition to the information in the accounting systems. In highly integrated accounting systems, most information is within the IT system itself. Financial details of subsidiaries are available as the subsidiary's local accounting is also covered by the systems. Even if financial details are available, much other information, such as non-financials,[5] is required by the corporate centre. For those types of information, reporting is still mandatory. By contrast, less highly integrated systems require more extensive reporting as more information has to be submitted manually to the corporate centre.

Regardless of the reporting systems used, reporting is the key task to be executed in groups. All kinds of financial data and information have to be retrieved from subsidiaries as they are needed at group level. The reporting may be used in managing and running the group, it is also used in preparing consolidated

---

[5] Non-financials are data and information that complement financial information (the balance sheet and profit & loss statement). A typical example for a non-financial is information about the number of staff sorted by various criteria like management, employees, trainees, temporary help and others calculated as full time employees (FTEs).

financial statements. Due to different reporting purposes, different types of report exist with different set-ups. Similarities and redundancies between these reports may exist as well. To reduce the reporting burden by subsidiaries, a well-designed reporting structure will consider such issues. Finally, an integrated reporting structure is required that systematically deals with all reporting requirements as well as the reporting process by reducing the reporting workload so that only essential topics have to be reported by subsidiaries. Therefore, two main reporting purposes exist, and their contents have to be aligned:

- Management reporting

    Management reporting is the reporting in the context of managing the daily business of the group. Companies have to report their current position and their current performance, combined with forecasts about the expected performance at the end of a month and supported by detailed analysis of selected items. In addition to the current balance sheet and the profit & loss statement (reporting actual figures, budget and forecast for both) information on several other business topics is often requested. Such information includes: A management commentary about the current activities combined with a discussion of the performance and an outlook on the remaining period, order-books, accounts receivable analysis, production metrics like rework, utilization, backlogs, current cash position, staff, research & development status and similar items. Reported items – financials as well as non-financials – have to be consolidated at different levels to provide figures and facts to business unit managers or group managers.

    Management reporting is often triggered by management accounting.

- Statutory reporting

    Statutory reporting is an annual task related to the closing activities of the group. Companies of the group have to report specific information that is required for the preparation of consolidated financial statements including the accompanying notes. Due to the different reporting purpose, the requested information will change. Two items are identical to management reporting: the balance sheet and the profit & loss statements; all other types of information differ. Typical items to be submitted to the corporate centre are: analysis of provisions, intercompany information of accounts receivable, accounts payable, inventory revenues and expenses, movement of fixed assets in groups, cash flow information, fixed asset schedule, financial instruments, number of staff, tax position, auditor fees and several other items. Due to this special information and its purpose, a consolidation occurs at group level only.

    Statutory reporting is a task initiated by financial accounting.

Management and statutory reporting demand the submission of several reports at the same time. These various reports are often combined into one set of reports that are also called reporting packages.

While different reporting purposes exist, the content of reporting structures changes depending on the information and data requested. In general, a reporting structure includes in minimum the reporting forms (the reports or set of reports) and ways used together with procedures applied to the reporting. An efficient reporting consists of standard reports prepared in standard procedures that are often also automated. These standard reports are enhanced by dedicated reports for user-specific requirements. While the standard reporting covers recurring items needed for group purposes, user-specific reports include selected collections of data and information and their analysis. These reports have dedicated recipients. The information reported is used for specific purposes, either once (so the reports are finally ad-hoc reports) or regularly. Irrespectively of standard or user-specific reports, all reports have to be defined in a consistent manner. Therefore, the following criteria should be considered in defining the reporting structure of the group:

- Which **types of report** are needed? The general assumption of (separated) management and statutory reports is often not sufficient. Several reports may be used that can be allocated to one of these general reports. Furthermore, reports may interact or have to be used for management and statutory purposes. Therefore, it is recommended to define reports in a consistent way so that redundancy is avoided. The definition of reports should be based on the reportable content. Due to the broad reporting demands, a tendency to modularize the reporting is observed. Based on the reportable content, reporting modules are defined that will be bundled to reports, regardless of which type of report is required.

- The **reportable content** may vary based on the reporting purpose. Standard items like balance sheets, and profit & loss statements as well as other financial information, classify as reportable content. Analysis of standard items, like details on intercompany receivables, payables, other assets and liabilities or intercompany inventory, are also typically reporting contents. In addition to financial information, non-financials are subject to reportable contents. Typical examples of these kinds of content are tax positions of subsidiaries, ratios, explanation for the notes and similar items. In theory the reportable content may cover all information within the group needed at a higher level.

- The **reporting form** has changed over the years. Today, four types of reporting form are applied in practice. Their use depends on the technological capabilities and their implementation within the system and on the client to be served.

    - The traditional paper format is more or less out-dated within groups and has been replaced by an electronic reporting form. Such forms are only used for the management and the board of a group or for external stakeholders.
    - A spreadsheet-based reporting form is applied in most small and medium-sized groups. As spreadsheets are a standard tool in accounting and

reporting, it is widely spread and accepted. Excel-based reporting forms often include full reporting packages considering all kinds of information required for one purpose (e.g. the preparation of consolidated financial statements). Due to the flexibility and the wide range of applications, spreadsheets should be customized for reporting purposes. The customization has to ensure that user can only enter data without performing any changes in the layout of report. The layout itself should be consistent across all spreadsheets and in line with the general layout rules of reports.

Spreadsheet-based reporting forms are also used if a group maintains different accounting systems. They have the potential to act as a bridge by retrieving reportable information out of local accounting systems, transforming them and providing them to the group. Such uses can be combined automatically with validations that help the user to ensure that data entered is appropriate and free of any material errors due to manual data entry.

- Web-based reporting forms have become more and more popular. They are the standard of large groups for information and data to be gathered from subsidiaries that are not present in the accounting systems. The advantage of web-based reporting forms is a centralized approach. Data can easily be entered via the internet by every reportable unit, then stored in a centralized system, often combined with a central database. Furthermore, complex communication when sending and receiving reporting packages is now obsolete. The group centre has an overview of the status of each subsidiary and therefore has the opportunity to interfere if necessary.

  Web-based reporting forms are also used if a group maintains different accounting systems. By uploading data from the local accounting system into the web-based reporting system, a conversion to group requirements is done automatically in the background without requiring manual adjustment of local data. Nevertheless, information that cannot be retrieved out of the local accounting systems has to be entered manually. Again, validations may help to improve the reporting quality by avoiding manual data entry errors.

- Integrated solutions are state of the art if a group applies one accounting system spread across the whole group. Local (accounting) data is already available in the system so that dedicated reporting is not any longer required. The group centre has always an overview of the current status of all subsidiaries. Integrated systems have their limitations on reportable information that cannot be integrated into the underlying accounting systems. In such cases, additional reporting forms like Excel's web-based solutions have to be used.

- The **reporting volume** is based on four items: The number of subsidiaries in a group, the reportable content, the degree of automation and the frequency of reporting. The reporting volume is a critical item as it defines the setup of the corporate centre in terms of staffing and resources required. To manage the volume in a timely manner, a high degree of automation is required in the corporate centre. All tasks and processes have to be analyzed regarding the improvement and automation potential. The same applies to data and information retrieved from subsidiaries. Only those data should be asked for which the group centre and its clients require. Group analysis can unveil unrealized performance potential particularly in these areas.

- The **reporting frequency** is aligned to the reporting type. The reporting intervals for management requirements are either on a monthly cycle for performances and financial positions to be reported or on a weekly cycle for cash and liquidity. Reporting intervals for statutory purposes are less frequent than for management purposes. Usually, a quarterly cycle is used for interim reporting to shareholders and investors and an annual cycle for preparing consolidated financial statements.
- In addition to the reporting frequency, the **timing of reporting** is a key element. Usually, the group centre issues reporting deadlines that have to be met by all companies of the group. Each subsidiary has to align its internal processes to meet group requirements. Depending on the integration of accounting systems in the group, reporting deadlines will produce a workload at the end of a reportable period (week, month, quarter or year). To be able to manage the timing and the deadlines, the group centre has to consider resources available at local level.

Like charts of accounts, reports tend to inflate over time. This usually results in the preparation of a bunch of reports by local and group accounting. Often it is not clear what the reports are used for and what the client intends to do with these reports. A strict reporting management is recommended ensuring that a minimum of reports offer a maximum in information.

The standardization of reporting within a group is also a potential threat. A standardized reporting set is favourable as it considers all potential circumstances of a subsidiary. Such a practice may be appropriate for the group and is also doable for larger subsidiaries; smaller subsidiaries may face a challenge in preparing these reports. The reason is that small subsidiaries do not have the resources or knowledge required or are often overstrained in preparing the reports. Therefore, it is worth considering simplification and a reduction of reporting requirements for small companies of a group. This rationale is based on the theory that small companies do not significantly contribute to the overall performance or assets of the group. A potential error due to improper reporting by these companies may not result in a material error of the group's overall performance. Smaller companies should be exempt from reporting the whole package. Instead, a context-sensitive report is preferred focusing on the most relevant reportable items only. In practice, groups often classify subsidiaries due to their size and nature of business and align the reporting requirements to the inherent risk of those subsidiaries.

> Minimize the reporting workload by asking only for the information you really need! Standardize them based on the classification, size and status of a subsidiary, associated company or joint venture.

The reporting system has to ensure a certain flexibility. This flexibility is needed to adjust the reporting to changes in the group. Changes in the group may have different reasons:

- Group structure

    Group structures, particularly the legal structure of a group, are often subject to change. These changes occur due to acquisitions or disposals of companies. The reporting system has to be flexible in adding new subsidiaries so that the new subsidiary will be easily integratable into the existing reporting environment. It also has to be flexible in case of a disposal of a subsidiary following defined procedures to eliminate the disposed unit from the group. The disposal not only covers the sale of a subsidiary, it also has to ensure to comply with *IFRS 5 – Non current Assets Held for Sale and Discontinued Operations* in case subsidiaries are held as discontinued units.

    Changes in structure are also initiated by restructuring activities. As a group-internal restructuring does not affect the external view of the group, all changes in the group structure have to be reversed for external reporting purposes. The reporting system has to consider restructuring activities by adding additional reportable information in these cases.

    Changes in the group structure also trigger additional effects for management reporting. All planning and forecasting systems have to be adjusted according to the changes that have occurred.

- Backward reporting

    As standard-setters frequently improve accounting standards, the introduction of new accounting standards is an on-going task. Some of these new standards require a retrospective application while others require a prospective application combined with pro-forma information of previous periods. In both cases, previous years will change. The reporting system has to be flexible in dealing with multiple figures of previous years (e.g. the closing numbers together with pro-forma numbers for the same period).

    A backward reporting is also required if errors of previous years are corrected. Error correction of previous years is defined in *IAS 8 – Accounting Policies, Changes in Accounting Estimates and Errors*. The reporting process is identical to changes in accounting standards. Nevertheless, pro-forma information has to be replaced by audited closing information.

- Currencies

    Reporting results of subsidiaries in multiple currencies is a standard requirement in groups. In addition to the reporting of results in the transaction or local currency of a company, results are reported using one or more reporting currencies of the group. The reporting requirement will even be enhanced, if the performance of an operation is also used for performance measurement by applying different currencies. The reporting system therefore has to include a multi-dimensional currency handling.

> Let subsidiaries report in their local currency and use tools at local or group level to convert reports to the currencies you demand!

A common method in group reporting is the use of **reporting packages**. Reporting packages are used for specific purposes, e.g. for liquidity reporting, the annual preparation of consolidated financial statements or the monthly performance reporting by subsidiaries. Regardless of which purposes they are used for, reporting packages consist of a set of reports that are required. Reports of the reporting package also interact. They are often combined with validations that are used to minimize errors or translations for converting local data into group reporting requirements.

To ensure that reporting packages and reported data is correct and consistent, **controls and checksums** are used in reporting packages. The intention is to force the reportable companies to prepare error-free packages the corporate centre can rely on. A quality check on consistent and complete data as a further step in preparing consolidated financial statements by the corporate centre can be dropped immediately.

3. THE PREPARATION PROCESS

Consolidated financial statements have to be published within a certain timeframe after the end of a period. The final deadline is often defined by commercial laws or – if the parent is listed at a stock exchange – by regulations of the stock exchange. Deadlines vary usually between two and six months, depending on legislations and stock exchanges. Large groups listed in prime standards often have a neck-and-neck race to publish their results (the consolidated financial statements) first. Some groups have their results available up to 30 days after the end of a period. To provide such a service to investors and shareholders, efficient processes have to be in place in preparing consolidated financial statements. They always have to consider the publishing date as defined by the board.

The process of preparing consolidated financial statements is based on two cornerstones: the adjusted financial statements of subsidiaries, and the consolidation. The consolidation includes eliminations of intercompany transactions as well as the preparation of all consolidated statements. While several companies and departments of the group at local as well as at group level are involved in preparing consolidated financial statements, a precise process and an appropriate communication between all parties are required. The overall preparation process has to be designed in a way that all issues arising on group and local level are covered. A set of elements has to be considered in designing the preparation process:

- Coordination of internal and external parties

    Preparing consolidated financial statements of a group is a task that involves several parties inside and outside of the group. The overall responsibility is with financial accounting of the group that has to co-ordinate all parties involved. External parties have to be integrated into the preparation process. External parties are those who provide accounting or taxation services to companies of the group. Accounting services are often consumed by small subsidiaries which are too small to have their own accounting department. Sometimes, even selected accounting services at group level are outsourced to service providers. Taxation services are usually provided by tax advisors or chartered accountants to small and midsize companies of a group if the group itself has no own tax department. Tax advisors have to be available at the end of the period to calculate income and deferred taxes. Like all internal parties, external parties have to be aware of the timing and the services to be rendered (so when and what to deliver).

    > Communicate upfront to your external service provider the timing and the services required.

    In addition to the integration of external parties, coordination with auditors is required. The coordination has to occur at local level for separate financial statements and reporting packages of the subsidiary and at group level for consolidated financial statements.

- Conflict management

    Preparing consolidated financial statements sometimes have to deal with unusual issues that can arise at several levels. Such issues may lead to conflicts, delays or other unexpected behaviour. Therefore, a conflict management solution combined with escalation procedures to deal with such issues should be available and communicated to all parties involved.

- The closure timing

    Based on the given publishing date, an agreed timing to close the accounts has to be derived for all parties involved. The overall responsibility is usually with the corporate centre. The centre has to define closure deadlines for the group and submission deadlines for subsidiaries. The submission deadlines may include several dates based on the information required to be submitted by subsidiaries. The corporate centre also has to agree the auditor's involvement in the timing.

    Based on the timing defined by the corporate centre, a fine-tuning may be necessary at group level between management, the accounting department and the tax department. Other departments like investor relations may be involved as appropriate.

At local level, the responsibility regarding the timing is with the subsidiary. The subsidiary has to align its timing to the submission deadlines as set by the corporate centre. This includes in particular:

- the timely closure of all accounts and the preparation of separate financial statements;
- the preparation of reporting packages after financial statements are prepared and audited;
- the auditing and submission of reporting packages.

- Fast closes

    The timing, particularly the submission of reporting packages to the group centre, requires that subsidiaries have to rethink their accounting processes. Often, the group centre is requiring the submission of reporting packages at an early stage. Large publicly listed companies, being part of a stock index, often race to see whose financial results and annual reports are published first. Some companies are even able to report their figures within 30 to 60 days after the end of the period. Rethinking the timing to publish the results, which includes not only the preparation of consolidated financial statements but also their auditing and approval by management and the board of the group, subsidiaries are often forced to apply fast close techniques. Only by the application of fast close techniques, a group will be able to report on time; delays are not acceptable.[6]

    Fast close techniques allow a company to have audited financial statements available soon after the end of a period. These techniques aim to move accounting tasks that are part of the annual preparation process to the month prior to the balance sheet date. Topics like the reconciliation of accounts receivable, accounts payable, calculation of provisions, tax reconciliation (in particular VAT and sales taxes), preparation of inventory valuation, supply management, notes and similar activities have to be processed in the months before the end of the period. This will leave only selected activities to be performed at the beginning of the new period. Such activities are sales recording (of last-minute sales), expense reconciliations, inventory finalization, income and deferred tax calculation and recording and similar tasks.

    In parallel, the auditor is performing a similar fast close process. This means that most auditing activities are done before the end of the period and only selected auditing activities are performed after the balance sheet date.

    To realize fast closes, a standard closing process is required. If necessary, the closing process has to be divided into sub-processes with each process with a detailed closing schedule. The process has to define which activities are due at which day before or after the balance sheet date. To speed up the closing of the accounts, wait times are of particular interest

---

[6] See figure Fig. D-10 on page 102 regarding a typical timing of a group closing process.

as these times slow down the closing process. Detailed planning and the consideration of dependencies between activities help to minimize wait times. This has to be combined with the automation of closing activities: whenever possible, manual activities should be avoided.

Another continuously discussed issue is the quality of data when applying fast close techniques. While the accounting department depends on information of other departments and external suppliers and customers, not all information and data might be available before the end of the period. Missing data and information force the accountants to accrue outstanding items. This is not an issue if the outstanding items are known; it becomes an issue if the amounts of outstanding items have a high volatility. In such cases it has to be decided if there is any material risk associated with accruing improper amounts due to the implied volatility. Another issue is the treatment of immaterial items. Even if they do not significantly contribute to the performance of a company or the group, accountants tend to consider these items to ensure completeness and good data quality. Thus, considering all immaterial items will slow down the closing process so that a cost benefit ratio may not be given. On the other hand, not considering these items may result in bad data quality. A careful decision is required regarding data quality, the omission of immaterial items and the risks accruals may bear by considering all pros and cons and their impacts on the preparation process and the quality of consolidated financial statements.

In particular in large groups, fast closes are often not fast enough; there is always room for improvement. Therefore, it is good practice to continuously review the processes regarding further automation of closing activities and any on-going improvements.

- Tasks to be executed

    Tasks in preparing consolidated financial statements are spread across the group involving different parties. At local level, financial accounting departments of subsidiaries have to prepare audited separate financial statements and report facts and figures to the corporate centre. Financial accounting at group level involves preparing consolidated figures that are used for consolidated financial statements and their accompanying notes. There is an interaction with taxation that has to ensure that tax effects of the group are properly considered. Some legislation requires that management reports or discussions are part of consolidated financial statements. Even if this is not a mandatory element by IFRS, the preparation of a management report has to be considered as a separate task to be executed by group management. Finally, management accounting is involved in that impairment tests and analysis of selected business transactions are demanded that have to be disclosed in the notes. Management accounting is also involved in preparing management reports by providing data and information about the business, its environment and the expected development to group management.

Due to the issues discussed before, the overall process in preparing consolidated financial statements is a challenging task at the end of each period which should be treated as a separate project. All tasks have to be arranged in a way that they meet group reporting deadlines and that the financial statements and reporting packages prepared are auditable and audited within the deadlines set.

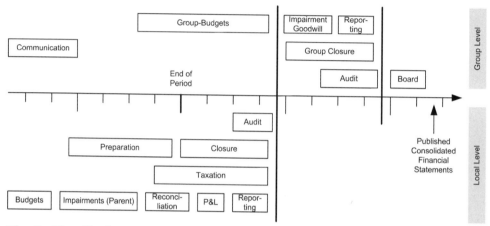

Fig. D-10   Closing process of the group

To better manage the preparation of consolidated financial statements, the overall process should be divided into sub-processes. These sub-processes consist of:

- Communication;
- Subsidiaries;
- Parent;
- Reporting;
- Group.

The advantage of dividing the overall process into these sub-processes is the simplified manageability of the preparation process as dedicated tasks can be assigned to selected parties in the group.

3.1. Communication

Communication is vital in preparing consolidated financial statements because the sharing of information ensures that all parties are aware of their tasks and the impact on other tasks. The overall responsibility is with the corporate centre. The preparation of consolidated financial statements usually starts with the communication of the corporate centre to all parties involved. It includes all relevant data and information necessary to prepare consolidated financial statements. This can also be understood as the road map of the preparation process. The communication acts also as an underlying instrument of all necessary sub-processes. It lasts until consolidated financial statements are prepared and published.

The **form** of communication depends on the topics to be communicated. Usually, a mixture between written and oral forms is used. The written form is a more formal form that includes general topics for all parties. Oral communication is only used upon special requests, for interaction between two parties and very often for clarification of selected issues.

To ensure proper communication, **tools** are used. The core instrument of the communication between the corporate centre and the companies of the group is a preparation manual. This manual includes instructions and descriptions for all companies of the group regarding the forms to be used, the timing of the group closure process and the process itself. The manual is often accompanied by an allocation of tasks and duties to organizational units and sometimes even to key personnel in the group. Such an allocation is often combined with responsibilities, obligations and rights of each party involved.

Like any other communication, a sender / receiver relationship will be established. To ensure that both parties have the same understanding of a topic, an **information context** is needed. Again, the preparation manual can help. To ensure that all parties involved in the preparation process have a common understanding, the manual should contain an introduction session giving basic information about the preparation process and explaining general items and definitions used. It is recommended to include an overview of the group so that all parties can identify their individual position and contribution to consolidated financial statements.

The communication in publicly listed companies often includes detailed regulations about the **external communication** and relationship during the preparation process. All staff involved in preparing consolidated financial statements are prohibited from communicating financial information externally before consolidated financial statements are officially published. This avoids insider information being used to trade shares. A good practice is to define a period where staff is prohibited from external communication of facts and figures of the group. As far as external service providers like tax advisors are involved in the preparation process, these parties have to comply with the communication rules of the group. This can be realized by non-disclosure agreements to be signed upfront. The period usually starts with a defined time by the corporate centre and ends with the official publishing of consolidated financial statements. This period is also called a quiet period.

3.2. Subsidiaries

Subsidiaries, as well as other affiliated and associated companies, are the foundation of the group. The financial statements of these companies are used for the preparation of consolidated financial statements. Therefore, the corporate centre has to be aware of the activities of all companies of the group and the progress in preparing financial statements. This **awareness** has to cover two topics that are from special interests for group purposes: the preparation of audited separate financial statements and the preparation of audited reporting packages.

- Separate financial statements
  As already discussed, separate financial statements are usually prepared by following local accounting policies combined with a conversion

to IFRS by applying group accounting policies. As far as group interests are concerned, the corporate centre is keen to ensure that financial statements are prepared without delay and that financial statements are based on IFRS by applying group accounting policies. Financial statements for local GAAP are only a by-product. Their relevance is limited to two items only: compliance with local laws and regulations and taxation matters.

To ensure that financial statements comply with group accounting policies, auditing activities have to be performed on these financials statements. While financial statements for local GAAP are also subject to audits, the audit for group purposes can be limited to IFRS adjustments based on the application of group accounting policies. This will often lead to a segregation of auditing tasks if the local auditor is not identical to the group auditor.

• Reporting packages

As also discussed, reporting packages reflect the financial statement of the company based on IFRS by considering group accounting policies. While the packages are not limited to financial information, non-financials have to be reported that will be needed for preparing notes to consolidated financial statements. Similar to financial statements, these reporting packages have to be prepared on time to ensure no delays at group level. Both, the financial statements and the reporting packages have to be available on or before the reporting deadline.

Usually, reporting packages have to reflect separate financial statements of a company or – if an IFRS conversion is required – adjusted separate financial statements. To ensure that the corporate centre can rely on reporting packages and that they reflect local financial statements combined with additional information, reporting packages have to be audited in the same manner as financial statements. This task is often combined with auditing activities on financial statements for group purposes.

Due to the requirements of the corporate centre to have reporting packages available that are prepared on time by considering group accounting systems and policies, the corporate centre has to define **auditing responsibilities**, requirements, engagements and relationships. This includes the selection of the local auditor of the subsidiary. The local auditor can be either identical to the group auditor (that is selected by the supervisory board) or different to the group auditor (if there is a policy in the group to stick to local auditors). Large companies with streamlined accounting structures, often in combination with shared service centres, prefer to have one auditor for the whole group only. The benefit is a simplified and more efficient audit, as local accounting issues have to be picked up by the auditor for local and group accounting procedures. This will often result in an efficiency improvement on the auditing side. By contrast, midsize companies often allow subsidiaries to pick their own auditors for local accounting purposes. These auditors sometimes have to perform group auditing tasks such as giving an opinion on reporting packages so that the group auditor can assume their work. The argument for such an auditing configuration is often cost driven as small local accounting firms are often cheaper than international auditing networks. Regardless of the auditor selected, the responsibility of an auditor does not change.

The **timing** of the preparation of consolidated financial statements allocates and assigns timeframes to each activity. As far as subsidiaries are involved, these companies usually will get dedicated deadlines on items they have to report. A subsidiary may have more than one deadline to follow if not all information is asked for at the same time or in the same reporting package by the corporate centre. While the subsidiary has been given a reporting deadline by the corporate centre only, it is often up to the subsidiary to derive their local timing on year-end closings. Based on the final reporting deadline, the subsidiary should execute a retrospective planning of its closing tasks and activities considering all items defined in the preparation manual. Special attention should be given to changes in the reporting structure and content compared to the previous period. Changes may require additional time that has to be spent to populate the reporting packages based on new reporting requirements.

Upon the initial communication of the group timing and the derived deadlines, a subsidiary shall immediately prepare its own timing and align this with the auditors to ensure meeting the reporting deadline.

A potential risk in preparing reporting packages is the **size and knowledge** of a subsidiary. As a general rule, the larger the subsidiary the more reliable the reporting packages. This is because larger subsidiaries often have more capacity and expertise in the accounting department to cope with accounting and reporting requirements of the group. By contrast, small subsidiaries, which have to submit exactly the same reporting packages, often do not have the resources required to prepare reporting packages. They also are unaware of specific accounting issues demanded by the corporate centre. Therefore, support is required from the corporate centre. A well-designed reporting system will consider scaling effects in the group.

Any **default** or delay in preparing audited reporting packages by the subsidiary will result in a delay at group level. The likelihood of such defaults depends on the experience a subsidiary has and on the capacity and quality of the preparation process of financial statements and reporting packages. The reasons for defaults and delays may have different origins: Improper requirements issued by the corporate centre, insufficient structures and processes of the subsidiary, errors in preparing separate financial statements, non-performance of auditors, disputes on auditor findings and several other reasons. To solve the underlying issues, additional time might be necessary. Therefore, a well-timed group preparation process has to consider such effects by with spare time available to capture any defaults. This requires some knowledge of the individual behaviour, knowledge and resources of the subsidiaries.

3.3. Reporting

One core element in preparing consolidated financial is the reporting of subsidiaries' results. The reporting is required for subsidiaries, joint ventures and associates. Nevertheless, the reporting content varies due to the status of the companies. Depending on the status of a group company, different reporting requirements exist that have to be satisfied by the reporting companies. As a general rule, the more interests in a subsidiary are given, the more reporting requirements have to be fulfilled. This is because separate financial statements of subsidiaries are not only integrated into the consolidated financial statements but their details have to be reflected in the notes as well.

The backbone of the reporting is based on reporting packages as outlined in chapter 2.4 – Reporting structures. Reporting packages used in the preparation of consolidated financial statements differ from reporting packages used by management. This is because of the focus on the packages and its intended use. The reporting and the application of reporting packages as part of the preparation process of consolidated financial statements depends on the implementation in IT systems. Traditional reporting packages (e.g. paper forms, data files, etc.) require manual data entry at corporate level and may bear the danger of mechanical errors due to the manual data transfer. It also slows down the preparation process as additional steps are required. An advanced application is the mixture of traditional reporting and IT-based reporting. Core information like the balance sheet and profit & loss statement as well as supporting financial information are already available in IT systems so that electronic data transfer is sufficient. If subsidiaries reside on the same accounting system as the parent, a simple check out notice to the corporate centre is sufficient. All other elements of the reporting package not electronically available, have to be submitted to corporate centre by using the traditional reporting packages. Such a reporting solution will significantly reduce the reporting volume.

While reports are demanded of all companies in the group and the submission is due at a defined date, the preparation and auditing of reporting packages is usually integrated into the closing process of each reportable company to ensure meeting the reporting deadlines. As far as **subsidiaries** are involved, a seamless transfer from financial statements to full reporting packages combined with an auditing activity of both elements is often common practice. Exemptions on reporting exist only for those companies which are not material to consolidated financial statements and therefore not considered in the group of companies subject to consolidation.[7]

Other companies of the group that have a different status like **associates** and **joint ventures** are often subject to modified reporting. These companies have to apply the same reporting package as subsidiaries but are exempt from populating all forms of the reporting package. Due to the consolidation method used for these companies – the equity method – not all details captured by the reporting

---

[7] See chapter E -6.7 on page 241 regarding further explanations on non-material subsidiaries.

packages are needed. Forms and reports not used are often kept blank. Typical data and information not asked for from associates and joint ventures are analysis of provisions, fixed asset schedules, revenue analysis, receivable analysis or taxation details. While reporting packages include checks to ensure good data quality, integrity and completeness, these checks have to consider the status of a reportable company. Either a level-based modification of reportable content in a reporting package or a modified (stripped-down) reporting package should be used.

Companies that are recorded as interests in **financial investments** are fully independent from any reporting requirements. Due to the missing influence of such companies, it cannot be expected that these companies prepare reporting packages. The only information a parent will get is the annual report including separate financial statements together with information on dividends distributed. Therefore, it is sufficient to handle all aspects of these investments at group level.

3.4. The parent

A slightly modified role in preparing consolidated financial statements applies to the parent. In general, the parent is obliged to report to the corporate centre in the same way as other companies and particularly in the same way as subsidiaries. While the parent record investments in subsidiaries, joint ventures and associates in its separate financial statements, the parent is obliged to execute impairment tests of these financial assets which may result in adjusted carrying amounts of financial assets. Therefore, the parent is subject to enhanced reporting which includes details of all investments and changes in investments that are typically integrated into a separate report.

If other companies in the group act as holding companies for investments, these companies are also subject to enhanced reporting.

3.5. The group

Based upon the work of the companies of the group, the activities at group level in preparing consolidated financial statements will start upon the receipt of reporting packages. It cannot be guaranteed that all reporting packages will arrive on time. However, the corporate centre usually supports and monitors subsidiaries – particularly those which are always late on submission – to encourage preparation improvement.

The processes at group level do not only focus on the preparation of consolidated financial statements. The processes include all tasks necessary to publish financial results and can be differentiated into two categories: the preparation of consolidated financial statements and the publishing of financial results. Both categories have their own sub-processes.

- Preparation of consolidated financial statements
    The preparation process at group level can be divided into a set of sub-processes. Each sub-process deals with a dedicated issue.

The initial sub-process deals with **data gathering & preparation**. The corporate centre has to ensure that all reporting packages are available within the expected timeframe. If no validation checks are implemented in reporting packages, these packages have to be reviewed and checked regarding their consistency, correctness and completeness. Even if automated checks are integrated into reporting packages, a quick manual inspection should be executed in search of any abnormal financial items that cannot be caught by automated checks. Any deviation – regardless of the reason – will trigger requests to be solved by the issuing company. Reporting packages that pass the inspection and fulfil all quality criteria have to be prepared for consolidation. Preparation means that data have to be taken from the reporting packages, expanded by level III adjustments, converted into the reporting currency of the group and imported into the consolidation tools. This is usually a highly automated activity.

Subsequent to the data gathering & preparation, the **consolidation** process will be initiated. The sole responsibility of this process is the elimination of all intercompany dependencies to arrive at consolidated figures, preferably at account level. Supporting data – intercompany balances of receivables, payables, earnings, expenses and inventory – need to be taken from the reporting packages. The output of the consolidation process is often a consolidated trial balance that will be used in the next step.

Having a consolidated trial balance available does not automatically assume with consolidated financial figures available. **Group-level transactions** have to be considered and added. Standard transactions are the execution of impairment tests for goodwill and selected intangible assets, recording of journal entries for adjustments of carrying amounts of selected assets and liabilities, reclassification and netting. Adjustments of carrying amounts might be necessary if adjustments taken by subsidiaries and already considered are not sufficient for group accounting purposes. Typical examples are bad debt reserves and provisions as these items often do not consider group-level policies and events.

If a group has prepared consolidated financial statements by applying local accounting rules and regulations, a **conversion to IFRS** might be necessary. A top-level conversion from local GAAP to IFRS might be useful in some cases which removes the conversion burden from all companies of the group. Nevertheless, an additional accounting task has to be performed at group level.

Based on an adjusted and consolidated trial balance, the **statement preparation** process will be initiated. All statements and the accompanying notes have to be derived from the trial balance and prepared. The consolidated statement of financial position and the consolidated statement of income are easily preparable. A more sophisticated approach is demanded for the consolidated statement of cash flows. Additional information of reporting packages are needed to understand changes in cash positions. The same applies to all figures in the notes that explain elements of the financial statements. Such tasks result in highly manual activities.

While consolidated financial statements and their accompanying notes have to be audited, good **documentation** on the preparation is required. The documentation should assume audited separate financial statements as a starting point and consider all transactions, adjustments and similar items performed in preparing consolidated financial statements.

The final step in preparing consolidated financial statements is not any longer under the control of the corporate centre as this step has to be performed by group auditors. Like any financial statements, the **auditing** of consolidated financial statements is a mandatory task due to national rules and regulations. As far as any audit findings exist, the corporate centre is obliged to adjust the financial statements to arrive at the final consolidated statements.

- Publishing of financial results

  This requires some kind of **workflow** at group level. Consolidated financial statements prepared by the corporate centre will flow through various other departments and governing bodies of the group before they can be published. The statements are usually embedded in an annual report that also hosts a management report and other important items to be disclosed. Therefore, other departments need the consolidated financial statements to prepare their parts for the annual report. Once the whole package is finalized, **approvals** have to be given upon the publishing of financial results. Approvals are needed by the group's management who have to sign and who are legally liable that a true and fair view is given in consolidated financial statements. Approvals may also be required by the board of directors or other supervisory bodies of the parent before financial results are published.

  In addition to the preparation of (audited) consolidated financial statements, some legislations require a **management report** to be part of the annual report which might be subject to auditing as well. Even if a management report is not a mandatory element of financial statements by IFRS, the IASB has issued an IFRS practice statement of management commentary which is non-binding. The preparation of a management report is usually the responsibility of the group's management. The management therefore requires consolidated financial information from financial accounting and detailed analysis of selected financial figures and the business from management accounting. The preparation of management reports involves intense interaction with management accounting at group level.

  Due to the reliance of investors on management reports, they are often subject to audit. This should ensure that the management report presents the business as it occurred and that the information disclosed ties to the consolidated financial statements.

  Another exercise is the preparation of an **annual report** (often referred to as the "glossy"). The annual report not only includes consolidated financial statements and the management report, other important information is also part of the annual report:

- A presentation of the company, its business units and activities;
- Letters from the board and / or management to investors and owners;
- Key figures for the group;
- Corporate governance and sustainability information;
- Independent auditor's report;
- Disclosures demanded by stock exchanges;
- Voluntary information as appropriate.

The overall responsibility in preparing an annual report is not a task of the finance department of a group. This task is often assigned to investor relations or marketing departments.

Some of the information in an annual report – particularly the corporate governance and the sustainability reports – are complex, combining financial facts and figures with other information of the group. The preparation of these reports is executed in sub-processes where the responsibility is often with other departments. Management accounting at group level is usually involved by providing the financial information.

4. ORGANIZATION

To execute the preparation of consolidated financial statements and to have a solid preparation process in place, organizational aspects cannot be ignored.[8] These aspects always have to be considered when preparing consolidated financial statements.

- Manuals
   To ensure that all parties of a group apply the same principles as the parent in a consistent manner, group manuals exist that summarize the most important group rules and regulations. The spread of rules and regulations cover not only relevant accounting topics but also general aspects of groups. Such general aspects are the group composition, business units, commercial and business roles and responsibilities, authorization and approval procedures and lines and similar topics.
   As far as accounting is concerned, roles and responsibilities for accounting procedures are not the only items in group manuals. The core contents of a group (accounting) manual are accounting policies and procedures, forms and reports to be used depending on individual accounting issues. It often contains a general section that deals with the accounting

---

[8] Most organizational topics have already been discussed in prior chapters, either implied or explicitly mentioned. Therefore, this chapter includes just a small summary on selected organizational aspects.

language and the definition of selected terms. The preparation of consolidated financial statements is another item of a group manual.

In any well-organized accounting organization there is an interaction between the group manual and the preparation manual (that includes guidelines on preparing consolidated financial statements). As the latter has to refer to the group, references to the group manual are standard.

- Roles & responsibilities

    While the preparation of consolidated financial statements is a project that involves several parties, the roles and responsibilities of all parties involved are an integral part of the closing infrastructure. Tasks and activities of the group's closing process have to be assigned to dedicated persons. If a task or activity cannot be assigned to a dedicated person, an allocation to an organizational unit has to occur. The organizational unit then has to nominate a person who is in charge of the task or activity. Such a practice is usually applied to subsidiaries as they have to nominate the person in charge of their activities (which is particularly the closing of the period, the preparation of separate financial statements and the preparation of reporting packages).

    Defining the role in the closing process is only part of the game. The person assigned a task has to be equipped with adequate responsibilities. This is necessary while decisions need to be made on issues arising when processing data or executing consolidation tasks or preparing statements. The person in charge needs to know if he has the responsibility to decide on that issue. If this responsibility is missing, an escalation to other parties is necessary assuming that sufficient escalation procedures exist.

- IT

    Midsize and large groups often have heterogeneous IT infrastructures, including different accounting and consolidation systems, various databases from which information has to be retrieved, various release levels of the same application and other topics. Such infrastructures may be a risk for the preparation process that may result in low data quality, loss of information or delays. The design and the timing of the closing process has to consider these infrastructure issues.

> Such infrastructures are typical candidates for improvement projects.

E   INITIAL CONSOLIDATION

About this chapter:

An initial consolidation is required any time a new company becomes part of a group. Several tasks need to be executed, depending on the way this happens. This chapter will pick up all issues that arise around the acquisition and integration of a company in a group. Based on a theoretical introduction regarding accounting levels and views of the acquired company, this chapter focuses on three important accounting issues:

- the preparation of an opening balance sheet,
- the valuation of assets and liabilities acquired, and
- the initial consolidation.

As the company acquired often applies accounting standards different to those of the group, an opening balance sheet is required as the starting point for the group. Therefore, it is necessary to account for all assets and liabilities acquired. As these asset and liabilities are not necessarily accounted for by the acquired company, a purchase price allocation is required to identify, measure and recognize all assets and liabilities. Based on the adjusted opening balance sheet, an initial consolidation integrates the new subsidiary in the group. This initial consolidation is discussed in detail providing also journal entries of each consolidation step. Acquisitions of companies do not follow the same procedure. Special effects are often the case resulting in enhanced accounting activities. The discussion on a set of special cases completes this chapter. Special cases discussed are reverse acquisitions, acquisitions achieved in stages, the accounting of multi-component contracts, pre-existing relationships and shares of the acquirer.

1. BASICS

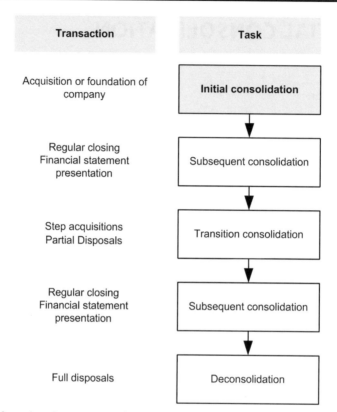

Fig. E-1   Lifecycle of a corporation: Initial consolidation

The initial consolidation of a subsidiary is the process that fully integrates a new subsidiary in consolidated financial statements. It will be executed in the moment when a company becomes a subsidiary of the parent or any other company in the group. This occurs either by acquisition of a corporation or by the foundation of a new company. Therefore, the initial consolidation is embedded in a process that includes other activities like the acquisition of a corporation. It is usually the final task that has to be performed for the integration of the new entity in the consolidated financial statements. The initial consolidation also acts as a starting point for the life of the subsidiary in the group. All subsequent consolidations are based on the initial consolidation, particularly the recognition and measurement of equity and selected assets and liabilities.

The relevant standards for an initial consolidation are *IAS 27 – Separate Financial Statements* and *IFRS 10 – Consolidated Financial Statements.*

While IAS 27 focuses on the preparation of separate financial statements, this standard is important if companies of the group apply IFRS as their local accounting standard. By contrast, IFRS 10 covers all accounting requirements for the preparation of consolidated financial statements. This standard does not care how separate financial statements of the group's companies are prepared. IFRS 10 does not differentiate between initial and subsequent consolidations. Therefore, the same accounting rules apply to both consolidations. As the initial consolidation depends on a new subsidiary in the group, an interaction with other standards is given. For acquisition of corporations, *IFRS 3 – Business Combinations* is the relevant standard. Both standards complement each other. While IFRS 3 focuses on the accounting of business combinations, IFRS 10 focuses on the integration in the group and its initial consolidation. The acquisition of a company is in this context just one case of a business combination. In general, IFRS 3 defines a business combination as "a transaction or other event in which an acquirer obtains control of one or more businesses. Therefore, transactions referred to as 'true mergers' or 'mergers of equals' are also business combinations as that term is used in this IFRS."[1] Furthermore, IFRS 3.A defines a business as "an integrated set of activities and assets that is capable of being conducted and managed for the purpose of providing a return in the form of dividends, lower costs or other economic benefits directly to investors or other owners, members or participants". Due to these definitions, other forms of business combinations than acquisitions may also trigger the need for an initial consolidation. Typical examples are all forms of mergers. Excluded from a business combination are all combinations of entities under common control according to IFRS 3.2c.

The initial consolidation has to consider all accompanying effects that arise in business combinations. In addition to IFRS 3's accounting rules, the different views of the new subsidiary from the parent and the group have to be considered. Even if accounting standards are applied consistently by the parent and the group, the enhanced group-wide view of subsidiaries may lead to additional activities during the initial consolidation. While the parent just records its investment in subsidiaries, the group has additional requirements to its new subsidiary:

- Application of the accounting standards of the parent (so the group's accounting policies);
- Uniform balance sheet day;
- Adjustments, reclassification and allocation of balance sheet items;
- Conversion between accounting standards.

All effects have to be considered within the initial consolidation.

---

[1] IFRS 3, Appendix A.

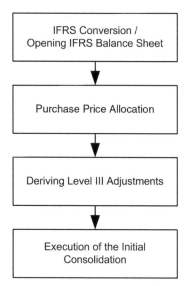

Fig. E-2 Accounting steps of the integration of a new subsidiary in the group

1.1. Valuation levels

To prepare consolidated financial statements, the accounting policies (standards and rules) of the parent have to be applied as stated by IFRS 10.19. This application is based on the fact that the parent has to apply the one-entity theory. This theory states that the group, so the parent including all subsidiaries, associates, joint ventures and other investments, has to present itself as if it is one company only. This requirement triggers a set of activities in the group to ensure that a consolidated financial statement can be prepared. Regardless of the group structure, an overall activity is to ensure that all subsidiaries are capable to deliver their "numbers" (so their separate financial statements) in a way that they comply with the parent's accounting policies. This implies that the accounting policies of the parent and the same balance sheet day are applied. While subsidiaries may use different accounting policies due to local standards and regulations, an adjustment of their separate financial statement is necessary due to IFRS 10.B87. These adjusted financial statements are used in preparing consolidated financial statements.

To ensure that subsidiaries comply with the parent's accounting policies, the theory has developed a valuation hierarchy that can be used in adjusting separate financial statements of subsidiaries. The hierarchy differentiates required adjustments by their nature. Depending on the applied accounting standards, a subsidiary can run through up to three levels of adjustments, as outlined in Fig. E-3.

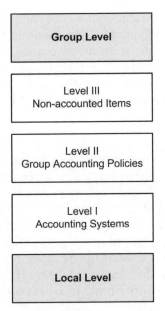

Fig. E-3   Accounting hierarchy in a group

All accounting transactions should be allocated to the levels using the following guidelines:

- Local level
  This is the level where all accounting transactions of the subsidiary are recorded by applying the accounting policies of the subsidiary. Separate financial statements are prepared based on the balances of local accounts.

- Level I
  Level I is the preferred level for adjustments necessary at local level without changing local accounts. Typical applications are adjustments due to different accounting systems and push-down entries of the group.
  Adjustments due to accounting systems are necessary when the subsidiary is applying a different account system to the parent company. To convert the subsidiary to the accounting system of the parent company, it is recommended to convert the financial statement "as it is". This means that all transactions at local level are remeasured by applying the accounting system of the parent company. The differences between both accounting standards are then recorded at this level. These differences are subject to a revaluation in subsequent periods. A typical scenario is the application of US-GAAP at local level and IFRS at group level. To adjust

the separate financial statements of the subsidiary, recorded transactions are remeasured by applying IFRS accounting rules.

Adjustments due to push-down entries are an appropriate method when preparing consolidated financial statements. These journal entries are initiated by the group centre that relate to transactions and assets / liability measures that have to be booked at local level in the subsidiaries' accounts.

- Level II

   Level II adjustments are used to transfer the separate financial statements based on the subsidiary's accounting policies to an adjusted financial statement based on the group accounting policies. The adjustments assume that the subsidiary applies the same accounting system as the parent company. Adjustments relate to all accounting areas where options, alternatives or similar possibilities exist in the measurement of assets, liabilities revenue or expenses. This is done by recording valuation differences at level II. If necessary, transactions recorded in local accounts have to be reversed and replaced by group-compliant journal entries.

   Typical examples of level II adjustments are different depreciation methods, useful life and residual values for long-lived assets (e.g. declining balance at local level and straight line at group level), bad debt allowances and valuation and discounting of provisions.

- Level III

   Level III adjustments relate to the measurement of the subsidiary's assets and liabilities from the group's point of view. This includes all accounted and non-accounted assets and liabilities. The different measurement from a group's perspective is often caused by an acquisition of a company combined with the application of the acquisition method as outlined IFRS 3.5. IFRS 3.18 requires measuring all assets and liabilities at its fair value, whether accounted for or not. Therefore, two scenarios occur:
   - Assets and liabilities may have different balances than recorded in local accounts. By recording the difference between local and group measures, hidden reserves and burdens are raised.
   - Additional assets and liabilities are recorded that are either prohibited for recording at local level or are not subject to recording due to missing recognition criteria.

Even if the theory differentiates between these three levels, differences between local and group level are often recorded in practice on one level only. They are so called level II adjustments.

To illustrate all effects of group accounting, this book will stick to the theory of separate levels and assigns all transactions to their appropriate levels.

Example

Flexing Cables uses a three-tier valuation system to cope with the different accounting standards group companies have to apply. The valuation system is harmonized with the IT accounting environment.

The bases – and therefore level one of the valuations system – are the local IFRS accounts of each group company as recorded in the leading client of the ERP system. These accounts are prepared based on group accounting policies. While compliance with local accounting standards is based on delta-clients, the accounting to comply with local accounting standards is the responsibility of each group company. Accordingly, level I and level II adjustments are recorded in the delta-client.

Level two of the valuation system is used for adjustments performed by the corporate centre. These adjustments are either level III adjustments or push-downs initiated during the closure.

Level three of the valuation system is the group level. Next to consolidation and elimination tasks, any adjustments to items of the aggregated trial balance are recorded at this level.

1.2. The opening balance sheet

The purchase price of an acquired company is usually the result of a negotiation process between the vendor and the purchaser. Even if the final purchase price is the result of an agreement between both parties, the purchaser often places his indicative offer based on the findings during a due diligence. The due diligence should obtain information about the net assets, financial position and results of operations and its accompanying risks. Therefore, the final purchase price does not only reflect net assets and a vendor's premium but also non-accounted assets, knowledge, market position and other facts that drive the value of a company. An integral element is the financial statement at the acquisition date as it reflects the net assets that are part of the purchase agreement. This financial statement has a special role as it acts as the starting point for the future life in the purchaser's group.

In most cases, financial statements of the acquired company are prepared by applying the accounting system of a nation. This may be IFRS or any other local accounting system. Typical examples of this kind of accounting systems are UK-GAAP applied in Great Britain, Swiss GAAP FER applied in Switzerland or US-GAAP applied in the United States. In such cases, a transition towards IFRS is necessary. Therefore, an opening balance sheet by applying IFRS standards has to be prepared based on the financial statements at the acquisition date.

Hence, the purchase generated two views of the acquired company:

- The acquirer's group view
  As the acquirer has not only acquired accounted net assets but also other assets, these additional assets and liabilities have to be considered as well. This task is based on the requirement of IFRS 3.

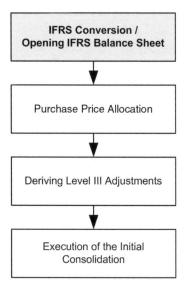

Fig. E-4   Accounting step: IFRS conversion to prepare the opening balance sheet

- The company's view
  From a company's point of view, the acquisition process results in a new ownership. The situation of the company, especially the net assets, financial position and results of operations and the applied accounting system and standards did not change. Therefore, any additional assets and liabilities are different in nature to the company and not accounted for by them.

In this area of conflict, the opening balance sheet has a special meaning. It acts as a bridge that transfers the local accounts to an IFRS accounting. Due to disclosure requirements as outlined in IFRS 3.B64 (q) (ii), the opening balance sheet has to be prepared at the beginning of the reporting period. This balance sheet has to be advanced to a balance sheet at the acquisition date by considering all the company's transactions during that period. This advanced opening balance sheet acts as the starting point in the group. The period between the (initial) opening balance sheet and the advanced opening balance sheet constitutes a pro-forma period that is required to derive information for disclosure as defined in IFRS 3.B64 and B67. The results of the pro-forma period are used for disclosure purposes only, they will not be considered as part of the group's result of the reporting period.

If the results of the pro-forma period do not deviate significantly from the results by applying local accounting standards and the differences are marked as non-material, an alternative way of preparing the opening balance sheet might be appropriate. Considering a cost–benefit ratio the opening balance sheet can be derived directly from the financial statement as of the acquisition date. The required disclosures are taken from local accounts.

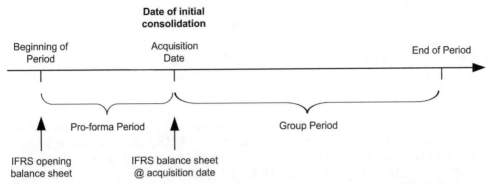

Fig. E-5 Timing of the IFRS conversion during the initial consolidation

The conversion towards the initial IFRS balance sheet at the acquisition date can be realized in different ways. In practice, two concepts are applied to provide the best conversion:

- Single-step transfer

    The single-step transfer method prepares the opening balance sheet directly from local accounts by considering the group's accounting policies. All transactions as recorded in the local accounts are remeasured by applying the group's accounting policy based on IFRS accounting standards. Differences between local and IFRS financial statements are recorded at level II only. This single step transfer requires excellent documentation because the preparation of subsequent financial statements is based on this documentation.

    Even if the single-step transfer is an advantage, the method also lacks transparency. A reconciliation between the local financial statements and IFRS financial statements is difficult to realize as the application of group accounting policies and the IFRS conversions are mingled in one set of accounting transactions.

- Multi-step transfer

    The application of a multi-step transfer method is more time-consuming as the conversion is realized in two steps. The first step converts local accounts to IFRS accounts "as they are". The second step adjusts the IFRS accounts towards the group's accounting policies. This method directly follows the valuation hierarchy as outlined in the previous chapter.[2] The advantage is a more transparent conversion process, particularly while it provides details of differences between local accounting standards and IFRS that may help in preparing subsequent IFRS financial statements.

---

[2] See page 117 for a detailed description of the levels involved.

Even if the group's accounting principles have to be applied in the preparation of IFRS financial statements by the subsidiary, the conversion towards IFRS offers a set of accounting options. These options may have an impact on the future performance of the subsidiary. Therefore, it is recommended to analyze future impacts by varying accounting options before deciding on the final conversion.

Regardless of which conversion method is chosen, the technical principles are still the same. Each balance sheet account has to be analyzed regarding transactions that qualify for a different treatment under IFRS accounting standards. If transactions are detected, the account is adjusted by the valuation difference at one or more levels. As required by IFRS 3.11, all adjustments are cumulated in retained earnings. It is recommended to use a separate account as part of retained earnings. This account will carry only the adjustments, nothing more, nothing less. As a consequence, this account will not be touched any longer until liquidation or sale of the subsidiary. The advantage of using a dedicated conversion account is a separation from retained earnings of on-going operation. This enhances transparency and structures the elements of retained earnings.

Record all initial IFRS on a dedicated equity account that is part of retained earnings. Close the account for further use if the job is done.

Example

Solenta GmbH was a producer of high-frequency and high-speed cables used in the telecommunication business. The company was founded in 1954 and had been family-owned since then. The heirs of the deceased owner had decided not to continue the business, so the company had been put up for sale. As of 1.4.2013, Flexing Cables acquired 80% of Solenta's shares, the remaining 20% staying with the heirs.

To comply with reporting requirements, a conversion of balance sheets and profit & loss statements towards IFRS had to be initiated. The conversion was executed in two steps:

- Conversion of the balance sheet as of the beginning of the period;
- Conversion of the balance sheet as of the acquisition date and the profit & loss statement of the period up to the acquisition date.

The **first step** was conversion of the balance sheet as of the beginning of the period (so the ending balance sheet of the previous period) to IFRS. The balance sheet was prepared according to German GAAP. The resulting balance sheet was used as the basis to prepare an opening balance sheet according to IFRS.[3]

---

[3] Para 266 of the German Commercial Code defines the layout of and the items presented in the balance sheet. As a consequence, the presentation of the balance sheet has to be adjusted as well.

Statement of financial position Solenta as of 31.12.2012 (k EUR)			
Assets		**Liabilities & Equity**	
Intangible assets	3,448	Share capital	2,500
Property, plant & equipment	52,660	Capital reserve	250
Financial assets	102	Retained earnings	19,720
Non-current assets	**56,210**	Profit carried forward	9,454
		Profit of the period	9,309
Inventory	54,800	**Equity**	**41,233**
Trade receivables	21,275		
Other assets	20,570	Pensions	6,330
Cash at hand & bank	2,880	Taxation	8,500
Current assets	**99,525**	Other provisions	8,560
		Provisions	**23,390**
Deferred items	42		
		Loans	56,000
		Prepayments	284
		Trade payables	18,383
		Other payables	16,487
		Liabilities	**91,154**
Total assets	**155,777**	**Total liabilities & equity**	**155,777**

All items of the balance sheet are subject to inspection whether or not any adjustments are necessary. The inspection unveiled the following issues:[4]

- Intangible assets and property, plant & equipment are depreciated using depreciation rates and useful lives as defined by tax rules. An application of real useful lives would result in an adjustment of 613 k EUR for intangible assets and 6,775 k EUR for property, plant & equipment.
- The company uses a bad debt allowance system that consists of individual and general allowances. An amount of 426 k EUR relates to general allowances.
- The company has accrued an amount of 5 k EUR that relate to interest cut-off issues.
- Provisions for pensions are understated by an amount of 870 k EUR due to the application of different underlying assumptions.
- Long-term liabilities and provisions are overstated by an amount of 336 k EUR.
- An amount of 5,632 k EUR presented in other provisions belongs to accruals.
- An amount of 4,500 k EUR of the loans are short-term.
- The company elected not to account for deferred taxation.

---

[4] Some remarks on the accounting under German GAAP:

- A common practice is to use specific and general allowances for trade receivables. By contrast, general allowances for financial instruments under IFRS are an unusual practice.
- Para 253 of the German Commercial Code requires companies to discount long-term liabilities using average interest rates of the past seven years which are calculated and published by the German Federal Reserve.
- Accounting for deferred taxes is subject to options and exemptions depending on the company's size and the actual balances of deferred tax assets and liabilities. Para 274 and 274a of the German Commercial Codes offers several accounting options.

- Financial assets are equity instruments of other companies that are held for strategic reasons. Accordingly the company is accounting for these financial assets by applying the cost model.
- Reclassification of selected items for a presentation according to IFRS is necessary.

Preparing the opening IFRS balance sheet, the initial balance sheet had to be adjusted by the following items:

Item	Carrying amount	Adjustment due to Valuation	Reclassification	IFRS carrying amount	Deferred tax impact Assets	Liabilities
Intangible assets	3,448	613		4,061		(183)
Property, plant & equipment	52,660	6,775		59,432		(2,019)
Trade receivables	21,275	426		21,701		(127)
Other assets	20,570		37	20,607		
Deferred items	42	(5)	(37)	0	2	
Pension provisions	(6,330)	(870)		(7,200)	259	
Other provisions	(8,560)	336	5,632	(2,592)		(100)
Accruals			(5,632)	(5,632)		
Loans	(56,000)		4,500	(51,500)		
Loans, short-term portion			(4,500)	(4,500)		
Deferred tax assets		261		261		
Deferred tax liabilities		(2,429)		(2,429)		
Retained Earnings				(5,107)		
Equity impact		(5,107)			261	(2,429)

The following balance sheet was the result of the IFRS conversion.

IFRS Statement of financial position Solenta as of 1.1.2013 (k EUR)

Assets		Liabilities & Equity	
Cash at hand & bank	2,880	Trade payables	18,383
Trade receivables	21,701	Tax liabilities	8,500
Inventory	54,800	Prepayments	284
Other assets	20,607	Accruals	5,632
Current assets	**99,988**	Loans	4,500
		Other payables	16,487
Property, plant & equipment	59,435	**Current liabilities**	**53,786**
Intangible assets	4,061		
Financial assets	102	Loans	51,500
Deferred tax assets	-	Pensions	7,200
Non-current assets	**63,598**	Other liabilities	2,592
		Deferred tax liability	2,168
		Non-current liabilities	**63,460**
		Share capital	2,500
		Capital reserve	250
		Retained earnings	43,590
		Equity	**46,340**
Total assets	**163,586**	**Total liabilities & equity**	**163,484**

The task to prepare an opening balance sheet has to be repeated as the **second step** at the acquisition date using the financial statements as of the acquisition date. Again, the statement of income and the statement of financial position as of the acquisition date (1.4.2013) according to German GAAP are needed.

Statement of income Solenta as of 1.4.2013 (k EUR)	
Revenues	35,210
Changes in inventory	(1,043)
Work performed and capitalized	
Other income	411
Total performance	**34,578**
Raw materials and consumables	(14,384)
Employee expenses	(8,068)
Depreciation and amortization expenses	(1,125)
Other expenses	(9,031)
Operating profit	**1,970**
Finance expenses	(579)
Profit before tax	**1,391**
Income tax expenses	(415)
Other tax expenses	(6)
Net profit for the period	**970**

Statement of income Solenta as of 1.4.2013 (k EUR)	
Revenues	35,210
Cost of goods sold	(27,193)
Gross margin	**8,017**
Sales & distribution expenses	(1,872)
Administration expenses	(1,618)
Research & development expenses	(1,051)
Other income	411
Other expenses	(1,923)
Operating profit	**1,964**
Finance expenses	(579)
Profit before tax	**1,385**
Income tax expenses	(415)
Net profit for the period	**970**

Statement of financial position Solenta as of 1.4.2013 (k EUR)			
Assets		**Liabilities & Equity**	
Intangible assets	3,153	Share capital	2,500
Property, plant & equipment	51,455	Capital reserve	250
Financial assets	102	Retained earnings	19,720
Non-current assets	**54,710**	Profit carried forward	18,763
		Profit of the period	970
Inventory	53,757	**Equity**	**42,203**
Trade receivables	22,023		
Other assets	19,966	Pensions	6,470
Cash at hand & bank	3,400	Taxation	8,300
Current assets	**99,180**	Other provisions	8,240
		Provisions	**23,010**
Deferred items	34		
		Loans	54,000
		Prepayments	280
		Trade payables	17,254
		Other payables	17,143
		Liabilities	**88,677**
Total assets	**153,890**	**Total liabilities & equity**	**153,890**

Preparing the IFRS balance sheet as of the acquisition date had required the execution of a set of activities. The IFRS profit & loss statement of the pro-forma period had had to be prepared to ensure an appropriate presentation of retained earnings. Furthermore, all items of the balance sheet had had to be checked and adjusted regarding the following issues:

- The initial identified adjustments needed to be advanced towards the acquisition date;
- The German GAAP balance sheet as of the acquisition date had to be observed regarding any transactions that required different treatment for IFRS.

The procedure to be executed was the same as in the first step. Accordingly, the following issues were unveiled:

- The step-up of the carrying amounts of intangible assets and property, plant & equipment were still valid. Accordingly, an amount of 18 EUR related to the depreciation of the step-up amount of intangible assets and 158 k EUR to the depreciation of the step-up amount of property, plant & equipment.
- The company used a bad debt allowance system that consisted of individual and general allowances. An amount of 440 k EUR related to general allowances.
- The initial adjustment of the interest accrual needed to be reversed as the accrued interest had been expensed.
- The company had accrued an amount of 8 k EUR that related to interest cut-off issues for the first quarter of the period.
- Provisions for pensions had been understated by an amount of 883 k EUR due to the application of different underlying assumptions.
- Long-term liabilities and provisions had been overstated by an amount of 314 k EUR. The difference from the initial IFRS balance related to interest effects.
- An amount of 5,104 k EUR presented in other provisions belonged to accruals.
- The short-term portion of loans was 5,000 k EUR.
- The company still elected not to account for deferred taxation.
- Reclassification of selected items for a presentation according to IFRS was necessary.

Preparing the IFRS balance sheet at the acquisition date, the German-GAAP balance sheet had to be adjusted by the following items:

Item	Carrying amount	Adjustments carried forward	Adjustment due to Valuation	Adjustment due to Reclassification	IFRS carrying amount	Deferred tax impact Assets	Deferred tax impact Liabilities
Intangible assets	3,153	613	(18)		3,748		(177)
Property, plant & equipment	51,455	6,775	(158)		58,072		(1,972)
Trade receivables	22,023	426	14		22,463		(131)
Other assets	19,966			26	19,992		
Deferred items	34	(5)	(3)	(26)	0	3	
Pension provisions	(6,470)	(870)	(13)		(7,353)	263	
Other provisions	(8,240)	336	(22)	5,104	(2,822)		(94)
Accruals				(5,104)	(5,104)		
Loans	(54,000)			5,000	(49,000)		
Loans, short-term portion				(5,000)	(5,000)		
Deferred tax assets		261	5	(266)	0		
Deferred tax liabilities		(2,429)	55	266	(2,108)		
Retained Earnings		(5,107)			(5,107)		
Profit & loss impact			140			266	(2,374)

The following balance sheet and profit & loss statements were the results of the IFRS conversion.

IFRS Statement of financial position Solenta as of 1.4.2013 (in k EUR)

Assets		Liabilities & Equity	
Cash at hand & bank	3,400	Trade payables	17,254
Trade receivables	22,463	Tax liabilities	8,300
Inventory	53,757	Prepayments	280
Other assets	19,992	Accruals	5,104
Current assets	**99,612**	Loans	5,000
		Other payables	17,143
		Current liabilities	**53,081**
Property, plant & equipment	58,072		
Intangible assets	3,748		
Financial assets	102	Loans	49,000
Deferred tax assets	-	Pensions	7,353
Non-current assets	**61,922**	Other liabilities	2,822
		Deferred taxes	2,108
		Non-current liabilities	**61,283**
		Share capital	2,500
		Capital reserve	250
		Retained earnings	44,420
		Equity	**47,170**
Total assets	**161,534**	**Total liabilities & equity**	**161,534**

This IFRS balance sheet acts as the starting point for the purchase price allocation.

IFRS Statement of income Solenta as of 31.3.2013 (k EUR)	
Revenues	35,210
Changes in inventory	(1,043)
Work performed and capitalized	
Other income	411
Total performance	**34,578**
Raw materials and consumables	(14,384)
Employee expenses	(8,081)
Depreciation and amortization expenses	(1,301)
Other expenses	(9,023)
Operating profit	**1,789**
Finance expenses	(604)
Profit before tax	**1,185**
Income tax expenses	(355)
Net profit for the period	**830**

IFRS Statement of income Solenta as of 31.3.2013 (k EUR)	
Revenues	35,210
Cost of goods sold	(27,369)
Gross margin	**7,841**
Sales & distribution expenses	(1,872)
Administration expenses	(1,615)
Research & development expenses	(1,051)
Other income	411
Other expenses	(1,922)
Operating profit	**1,789**
Finance expenses	(604)
Profit before tax	**1,185**
Income tax expenses	(355)
Net profit for the period	**970**

The statement of income is needed for disclosure purposes, for the results of the pro-forma period (1.1. to 31.3.).

2. MERGERS AND ACQUISITIONS

Acquisition and mergers of companies and groups, combination of businesses and any similar form of bringing businesses together are always discussed under the heading of mergers and acquisitions. Regardless of which transaction is executed, an increase in the size of the group will result at the end of the day. This increase will be realized by adding groups or companies to the companies subject to consolidation. It can also be realized by an increase of the size of existing companies due to the acquisition and integration of businesses into the purchasing companies. Mergers and acquisitions should not be confused with restructuring. A restructuring may also deal with merger and acquisition activities, but these activities occur in a group. The size of the group will either stay constant or can shrink. But an increase can never happen as restructurings are pure group internal transactions.[5]

---

[5] Restructurings are discussed in detail in chapter K -5 on page 693.

Mergers & acquisitions are often initiated by management to further grow the business. The intentions are as manifold as the ways the growth of a group is realized. Typical rationales of merger & acquisition activities are:

- The organic growth is less than the market or less than expected;
- Expansion with existing products in new markets or new regions / countries;
- Access to new technology;
- Enrichment of product portfolio;
- New sales channels;
- Securing the access to raw materials;
- Economies of scale;
- Utilization of factories;
- Performance optimization of the group.

Mergers & acquisitions are realized in various ways. The most popular form is the acquisition, realized either through share or asset deals, in a direct way or by using acquisition vehicles like "NewCo's". Other popular forms are formation of new groups realized through shell companies at shareholder level and selective acquisitions that cover selected businesses branches of parts of companies. Regardless of how mergers & acquisitions are realized, they all are all accounted for in a similar way.

The expansion of a group through an acquisition or similar activity is in the first instance a business issue that involves all business areas. This is because the acquisition is just the initial phase of the lifecycle of a company in a group. More important is a successful integration in the group as this is the critical phase where synergies and success potentials are realized. Therefore, several views are taken on the acquisition regarding a successful integration into the group. Such views can cover sales and sales channel optimizations, sourcing and purchasing, production allocation and utilization as well as centralization of functions. Acquirer and group each have their unique points of view. Depending on the topic to be viewed, different aspects may arise that are subject to discussion whether or not potential improvements are possible.

From a **general accounting perspective**, mergers and acquisitions is a discipline that requires special attention. The reason for this special attention is linked to the fact that such transactions are infrequent and expensive, combined with risks and uncertainties that impact consolidated financial statements. In addition to these dominating concerns, administration issues in accounting and related departments have to be mastered. Two dimensions are important: administration structures in accounting involving the corporate centre and the accounting department of the acquired company for their daily accounting and bookkeeping tasks in preparing separate financial statements and the structures and processes in preparing consolidated financial statements. Both dimensions have dedicated requirements to be fulfilled.

Mergers & acquisitions, in the context of group accounting, have high significance and relevance. This is because the accounting of an acquisition is – like the acquisition itself – often an infrequent and expensive task that faces special challenges. Some accounting literature describes this accounting as "high-level accounting" because the variety and complexity of issues to be considered in the accounting of acquisitions is not comparable to the accounting of an on-going business.

> If you are not sure you can do this or there is a lack of experience, involve consultants that support you on the accounting and integration!

While mergers & acquisitions impact and change the structure of the group the accounting for them is usually a task that belongs to an initial consolidation. This is because the "acquisition subject" has to be integrated into the group, which triggers the initial consolidation. This is also the starting point of life in the group.

From a more **specific accounting perspective**, mergers & acquisitions are only one case of how the composition of a group can change. Other cases exist as well that will result in a changed group composition even if management is not always fully aware of the facts and circumstances that trigger such changes. All these issues are treated as business combinations that have some impact on the accounting of groups. The relevant standard is – as already discussed – *IFRS 3 – Business Combinations*. The standard covers the accounting methods that have to be followed, gives guidance on the required steps and considers exceptions and special areas that usually occur in business combinations and of course in acquisitions.

As a prerequisite, one or more businesses have to be subject to mergers & acquisitions. Acquisitions that focus on assets or groups of assets are regular purchases that have to be accounted for in accordance with IAS 2 for inventories, IAS 16 for property, plant & equipment or IAS 38 for intangible assets.

2.1. The acquirer's view

The acquisition of a company that becomes part of the group is a process that involves several departments of the acquirer. It is not important if the acquisition will refer to an investment in subsidiaries, associates or joint ventures. All acquisitions are treated in a similar way by the acquirer. Therefore, management, accounting and administration departments are involved in a similar way for all kinds of acquisitions. Each department will have its individual view of the acquisitions as several tasks have to be executed.

- Management or commercial view
    The acquirer's management view of the acquisition is usually driven by strategic reasons. The intention to acquire the company is based on the growth expectations and on the strategic fit of the subsidiary in the group. How the business of the acquiree is used and how it interacts with the group's business is subject to the group's view.

- Accounting view

    The acquirers accounting view of the acquisition is limited to a few facts only. The acquisition is just an ordinary transaction that includes the acquisition of an investment in a subsidiary, associate or joint venture that is classified as a financial asset in the separate financial statements of the acquirer. The acquirer can be any company in a group. It is not important if the ultimate parent, a holding or any other company is carrying the investment in the acquiree. The company that carries the investment will be the parent for the acquiree.

    The main concern of the accounting view of the acquisition will be the initial recording (are all items that belong to the acquisition considered?) and the subsequent measurement (is a recoverability given?). In particular, the latter issue is linked directly to the performance of the acquiree. To ensure recoverability, regular impairment tests are mandatory. This requires access to management accounting information, particularly to the current and planned performance of the acquiree.

    Another primary issue is the financing of the acquisition. Even if the financing is a separate transaction, it should be ensured that the performance of the acquiree and therefore the generated profits (whether distributed as dividends or retained) are sufficient to cover interests associated with the financing of the transaction. In practice, holding companies often demand in minimum coverage of the interests due to the debt incurred in the first instance. On top of this minimum requirement, the performance measurement of the acquiree often considers the equity financing in addition to debt financing. Depending on the realization of the acquisition, the debt to finance the acquisition is often passed through to the acquiree.

    A secondary issue is the presentation in separate financial statements combined with appropriate disclosures in the notes. The acquisition has to satisfy the disclosure requirements of IAS 1 and IFRS 3, 7 and 9.

- Administration view

    The administration view of the acquiree is driven by formal aspects which each subsidiary of the group has to comply with. These aspects focus on the integration of the acquiree as a legal entity into structures and processes as well as on the compliance of the legal entity with group-internal and group-external rules and regulations. The primary issue in this context are integration issues. The acquiree has to implement the overall policies of the group. Typical elements of structures and processes that interact with group policies include regulations on:

    - Authorizations of transactions;
    - Risk policy and particularly on the segregation of duties;
    - Procedures to follow on escalating issues under dispute in the group and to corporate centre;
    - Processes for sales, purchasing and other functions.

A subset of integration issues is the reporting the legal entity has to fulfil. The reporting requirement includes reporting structures (so what form when to deliver to whom), reporting methods and contents.

Compliance requirements focus on the legal entity. From an acquirer's perspective, the legal entity has to comply with the group's policies as already outlined. Furthermore, the acquiree as a legal entity has to comply with local rules and regulations. This includes topics like the preparation of financial statements and tax returns based on local accounting and taxation policies, filing of documents on-time and in line with individual policies and application of laws and regulations like environmental protection, antitrust rules, bribery acts and similar items.

In addition to these primary issues administration has to consider, some secondary issues will arise when integrating the acquiree into the group: a typical issue is IT systems. Either the systems have to be aligned to satisfy group requirements or they have to be replaced. Satisfying group requirements means that additional functions have to be integrated, queries implemented or reports prepared so that the information necessary for reporting can be retrieved out of the IT systems. Replacing IT systems means that the current systems of the acquirer are either legacy systems that need to be replaced by new systems or the acquiree will be transferred to the group's IT systems to ensure a consistent IT infrastructure across the group.

Example

The acquisition of 80% of the shares in Solenta by Flexing Cables was driven by the intention of Flexing's management to improve the position of the copper cables business unit. Due to the acquisition, Flexing Cables had not only acquired an up-to-date manufacturing environment but also new sales channels and an enhanced customer base enabling the group to cross-sell their products.

From an accounting perspective, the acquisition of Solenta demanded the following activities:

- Recording an investment in a new subsidiary;
- Negotiating a new loan facility to finance the acquisition;

From an administration perspective, the following activities were necessary:

- Introduction of group policies to Solenta;
- Introduction of the group accounting system to Solenta (management and financial reporting) as an immediate activity;
- Transfer of Solenta to the group's IT system as a mid-term activity.

2.2. The group's view

Other than the purchaser's view, the group's view of the acquisition of a new company considers all effects the acquisition can have on a group. Effects arise not only from accounting issues but also from management and administration issues. These issues, particularly the management issues, play an important role in determining accounting effects due to mergers & acquisitions activities. While various parameters and management decisions influence the view of the acquisition, each acquisition has to be reviewed individually. Nevertheless, a set of common practices can be identified across all acquisitions and integrations in group structures, which should be considered whether or not they are important for the initial accounting of the acquiree.

- Management or commercial view

  The management view of the acquiree is driven by business purposes only. These business purposes interact with the original intention of the acquisition on what to achieve with the acquisition. The management view and the expected tasks management will execute to realize the initial intention will be based on the structure of the group from a business perspective and on the acquiree's business. Management will usually allocate the subsidiary to one or more business units. Furthermore, to raise synergies, the acquiree is often subject to a restructuring as one task of the integration in the group. Restructuring means, that resources of the acquiree and the group are shared or optimized, product and service portfolios are harmonized and functions centralized. Typical tasks that are observed in practice usually cover the following areas:

  - Cross-selling through an optimized use of sales channels;
  - Alignment and reconciliation of marketing activities in business units that relate to products, services and brands;
  - Improved product branding;
  - Allocation of production across the group depending on local markets, utilization of factories, production process optimization and similar rationales;
  - Allocation of products and services to product lines, and companies in the group;
  - Optimization of overhead costs by combining and / or centralizing similar activities like sourcing or corporate marketing;
  - Allocation of departments and business activities to similar business groups for an improved management.

  The impact of the initial accounting is driven by two aspects: The first aspect is the acquisition itself. The accounting is based on assets acquired and liabilities assumed, so on the items purchased. Any influences of the group do not play a role. Subsequent to the acquisition accounting, effects of management, and particularly the restructuring, have to be considered. This second aspect is focused on the allocation of parts of the acquiree to business units and to corporate functions. Goodwill as a residual value will follow the underlying asset allocation. Furthermore, management accounting has to integrate the new parts into their planning, budgeting and forecasting systems.

  Such tasks presume that the business of the acquiree and the group's business are comparable and have some overlap. If the business of the acquiree is totally different from the business of the group, synergies due to products and services, structures and processes may not be given. In such cases, the acquiree is often treated as an own business unit. Accounting tasks are less complex than in the other case.

The integration activities sometime will lead to a contractual conflict. Purchase agreements – particularly those agreements where payments are based on the determination of variable elements, such as earn-out options – often include clauses on calculation method, cost elements to be, or not to be, considered in the calculation and conditions used in determining any variable payments. A common condition in most purchase agreements is the composition of the acquiree's business that stipulates a continuing business without any major changes. Considering these clauses would require a postponed alignment of the acquiree's business with the group's business. By contrast, not considering those clauses will often result in a full payment of variable components. It is then up to the management to decide whether or not an increased purchase price is acceptable. An increased purchase price is usually acceptable if the excess payment is less than the synergies achieved.

- Accounting view

  The accounting view of an acquisition is primarily based on the need to prepare consolidated financial statements where the acquiree has to be integrated in. Therefore, accounting for an acquisition from a group's perspective combined with appropriate accounting and reporting structures are the major issues. Minor issues exist as well; these issues deal with the new or intended structure of the group, restructuring of the subsidiary for group purposes, group internal allocations and similar transactions.

  The accounting view interacts with the management view in terms of restructuring. Depending on the acquisition and the subsequent restructuring, the accounting manager has to determine the risks associated with the acquisition in terms of enhanced purchase prices, changes in the acquiree's business structure and the impact on accounting.

  Even if the merger & acquisition activities of the parent result in a new company, the accounting of the acquisition from the group's point of view is different to that from the parent's. Due to the one-entity theory, the group is not acquiring shares in the subsidiary or an investment in a subsidiary. Instead, assets are acquired and liabilities assumed. The transformation of investments in subsidiaries into assets acquired and liabilities assumed is a task of group accounting that requires the execution of a purchase price allocation. The purchase price allocation is a one-time activity, involving both the corporate centre and the acquiree in executing dedicated tasks.

  An appropriate accounting structure has to be in place. The group centre needs this structure to understand the accounting of business transactions at the acquiree and to identify such business transactions and balance sheet items that are material to the group. An efficient accounting structure will therefore focus on the application of group accounting policies, on the implementation and / or application of group structures like the group's chart of accounts, reporting tools and methods and on the compliance with local legal accounting requirements and group accounting requirements. Depending on the size, management and structure of a group, different levels of detail might be requested by the group centre.

- Administration view

    The administration view of the acquiree considers various aspects that are grouped around business and accounting views of the acquiree. In addition to the group's accounting policies, the acquiree has to fulfil and comply with other requirements that are mandatory to the subsidiaries of a group. These requirements deal with the application of group policies for each function (finance, sales, purchasing, manufacturing and other functions and sub-functions) in the group, for the application of group procedures and systems.

    The primary administration focus is on integration issues so that the acquiree will be a seamless integrated entity like all other companies of the group. Integration issues can arise on the transformation to and application of group policies and procedures. This is particularly important if existing systems and procedures of the acquiree do not match with the group's procedures. Reports – whether reports are used for management or finance purposes – are integral elements based on the reporting structure of the group. Typical issues that arise in addition to the handling and understanding of those reports are data source and the appropriate publication of those reports.

    Another administration focus is compliance with internal and external (local) rules and regulations. Larger groups usually have an internal audit department that ensures compliance while the responsibility in smaller groups is often with management or management accounting. In contrast to compliance issues arising from an acquirer's view, compliance issues arising from a group's view focus on the business and the accounting in the group rather than on a legal entity's perspective.

    While non-compliance may bear risk that can impact the group's risk position, an integration into the legal infrastructure of the group is a standard administration activity. The legal integration will not only focus on compliance, it covers all legal aspects starting with current and new contracts with customers and suppliers and ending with other business, restructuring, environmental or regulatory issues.

    To ensure a seamless integration, the acquiree's key personnel (and particularly its management) is often linked to management programmes and incentives of the acquirer. Such integration is often managed by the HR department.

Mergers & acquisitions of companies and the successful integration in a group can be achieved in various ways. How a company is integrated often depends on the culture and principles of the group, the management and the level of integration. Therefore, it can be up to the acquiree alone to adjust its systems, structures and processes without any involvement of the parent. Another scenario is an adjustment that is driven by the group where several integration projects – such as the switch to the group's accounting systems or a common IT infrastructure – are initiated. Such tasks are often executed by the group's personnel due to the knowledge required. The realization and the concept for transition finally depend on several factors that require an individual integration strategy.

Successful companies often use a "buddy-system" to speed up the integration. For each function of the acquiree, a counterpart in the group is available to help the managers of the acquiree during the transition to the group's standards. These buddies act as consultants regarding the application of group policies and procedures, which are not necessarily limited to accounting. They should give advice on selected group issues and on the set-up of a network in the group (e.g. contact persons for dedicated issues).

3. PURCHASE PRICE ALLOCATION

The accounting of business acquisitions follows a structure that is defined in IFRS 3. This standard requires that all assets acquired and liabilities assumed have to be measured at the acquisition date with their fair value. Any surplus of the purchase price above this fair value has to be recorded in goodwill. The allocation of the purchase price to the acquired assets and liabilities is embedded in the process of the initial consolidation of the new subsidiary. As the purchase price allocation is based on IFRS requirements, it is recommended to use the opening IFRS balance sheet as of the acquisition date.

Due to the fair value requirement of IFRS 3.18, any kind of adjustment – regardless of whether it is related to a step-up of the carrying amount of an asset or a non-accounted asset – has to be recognized for group accounting purposes. These adjustments are usually recorded at level III.

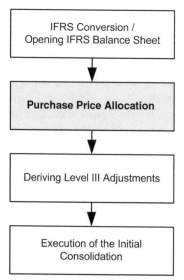

Fig. E-6   Accounting step: Purchase price allocation

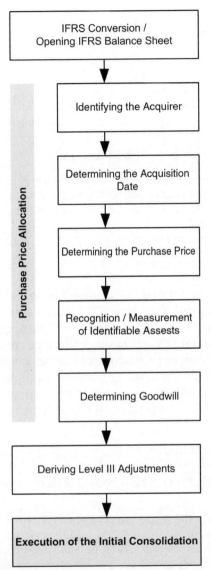

Fig. E-7 Embedded purchase price allocation as part of the initial consolidation

The purchase price allocation is realized by applying the acquisition method. This method defines the elements that are required in recognizing goodwill. Even if the acquisition method defines four steps according to IFRS 3.5, it is recommended to execute the acquisition method in six steps. This simplifies the application and ensures that all aspects of the acquisition method are considered.

Step	Task
1	Determining if the transaction is a business combination[6]
2	Identifying the acquirer
3	Determining the acquisition date
4	Determining the purchase price
5	Recognizing and measuring identifiable assets and liabilities
6	Recognizing and measuring goodwill and non-controlling interests

Tab. E-1   Steps of the purchase price allocation

> Considering the six steps combined with a proper documentation for each step will not only ease the purchase price allocation process but also supports the knowledge exchange with your auditor.

3.1. The acquirer

The first step to be performed is the identification of the acquirer according to IFRS 3.6 and 3.7. Regardless of how the business combination is designed, the acquirer is finally the one who obtains control of "the acquiree". Due to the reference to IFRS 10, the standard clearly indicates that the control concept of IFRS 10 has to be applied in determining what control is, when control is given and who has control.[7] Based upon this definition, the acquirer from an accounting perspective is not necessarily the one who legally acquires the company. Instead, an economic view of the business transaction is taken. As a consequence, the acquirer might be:

- the legal acquirer,
- the owners of the acquiree,
- the ultimate parent of the acquirer, or
- any other party that might be involved directly or indirectly.

> Due to the change of the definition of control in IFRS 10 compared to IAS 27 (and SIC12), movements in determining the acquirer occurs. As IFRS 10 has to be applied for periods beginning after 1.1.2013, only the new definition is mandatory. This will result in an adjustment of the determination process of the acquirer.

If an identification of the acquirer is not possible by applying the control concept of IFRS 10, IFRS 3.B13 to 3.B18 provide additional support in identifying the acquirer. Even if the criteria have a comprehensive character, they will be applied only in selected cases. An acquirer might be allocated by checking the criteria as outlined in Tab. E-2.

---

[6] This is already discussed in chapter E -3.6 on page 190.
[7] See chapter C -1 on page 44 for details of the control concept.

Criterion	Reference	Allocation of acquirer
Consideration transferred is primarily cash or cash equivalents.	3.B14	Acquirer is the one who transfers cash or cash equivalents.
Consideration transferred is either other assets of liabilities incurred.	3.B14	Acquirer is the one who transfers assets or incurred the liability.
Consideration transferred is based on equity interests (fall-back criterion if more specific criteria on equity interests do not apply).	3.B15	Acquirer is the one who issues equity interests. Exception: reverse acquisitions.[8]
• Relative voting rights in the combined entity after the business combination.	3.B15a	Acquirer is the one whose owners (as a group) retain or receive the largest portion of voting rights of the combined entity.
• Existence of large minority interests if no other significant voting interests exist.	3.B15b	Acquirer is the one whose owner or an organized group of owners holds the largest minority voting right in the combined entity.
• Composition of the governing body.	3.B15c	Acquirer is the one whose owners have the ability to elect, appoint or remove a majority of the members of the governing body of the combined entity.
• Composition of senior management.	3.B15d	Acquirer is the one whose (former) management (of the single entity) dominates the combined entity.
• Terms of the exchange of equity instruments.	3.B15e	Acquirer is the one who pays a premium over the fair value of the other entity.
Relative size.	3.B16	Acquirer is the one whose size is significantly greater than the other entity ones. Size can be measured in terms of revenue, profit, total assets, fair value or other items.
More than two entities.	3.B17	Acquirer is the one who initiated the combination in conjunction with its relative size.
New formed entity that issues equity interests.	3.B18	Acquirer is the one of the combined entities. The above-mentioned criteria have to be applied to this case to determine the acquirer.
New formed entity that transfers cash, other assets or incurs liabilities.	3.B18	Acquirer is the new entity.

Tab. E-2   Auxiliary criteria in determining an acquirer

The identification of an acquirer is elementary to the acquisition method. It has to be applied to all kinds of combinations without any exception. The above-mentioned tasks in identifying an acquirer (first the control concept then the detailed transaction criteria) provide an exhaustive tool for business combinations that is capable of covering all kinds of combination scenarios. Nevertheless, in most cases, business combinations are based on traditional acquisitions where the acquirer is easy to identify.

---

[8]   See chapter E -6.1 on page 217

> **Example**
>
> The acquisition of 80% of the shares of Solenta had been realized directly by Flexing Cables SE. The company is therefore acting as the parent of Solenta. It is also the ultimate parent of the group. In the absence of any specific regulation regarding the treatment of shares and any impairment of voting rights in the sales and purchasing agreement, Flexing Cables is entitled to benefit from its investment by receiving dividends. Furthermore, the company is able to govern the policy of Solenta through its voting rights. So, control is given. As long as the company is able to directly control Solenta, it will be regarded as the acquirer. Application of auxiliary criteria as outlined in IFRS 3.B14 to 3.B18 is not necessary.
>
> Nevertheless, a reverse acquisition could have been given. According to the sales and purchase agreement, Flexing Cables had to issue a volume of 6,300,000 shares to the shareholders of Solenta. These shares represent 8% of the outstanding shares in Flexing Cables. As the shares issued to Solenta shareholders are far fewer than the outstanding shares of Flexing Cables, Solenta shareholders will not be able to direct the business of Flexing Cables; a reverse acquisition is not given.

3.2. The acquisition date

IFRS 3.8 defines the acquisition date as that date on which the acquirer obtains control. The standard also assumes that the acquisition date is usually the closing date where all assets, liabilities (so the ownership) and considerations are transferred; honouring that there may be situations where the acquisition date deviates from the closing date. Others define the closing date as the date where all rights and obligations are assumed by the acquirer or the ownership is transferred to the acquirer. All definitions are based on a commercial condition and detach the acquisition date from a pure legal view. All legal activities around the acquisition are treated as follow-up activities to finalize the acquisition. This also includes the registration at commercial or company registers.

The separation of the commercial from a legal view may induce a pending situation where control is deferred. Such pending situations may arise when authorities have to approve the acquisition or the acquisition is linked to special conditions. Depending on the reasons and its releases, control may be transferred partially or in total at the dates when defined conditions are met.

The acquisition process and the negotiations between the acquirer and the vendor may include other legally binding forms of the transfer of control where control is transferred before the closing date. A typical example is an early application of control by signing a memorandum of understanding. If these kinds of binding form exist, an enhanced check is necessary. This check focuses on the rights of the acquirer to influence or control the company under acquisition. If control is given and agreed conditions are met, the acquisition date may be before the closing date.

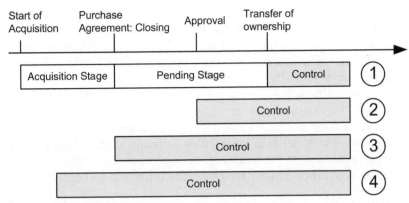

Fig. E-8   Possible acquisition dates

The acquisition and the purchase agreement are often linked to **defined conditions** or **preconditions**. They are usually part of the purchase agreement. If these conditions are not met or satisfied, the transfer of ownership is suspended until all conditions are met. The reasons for such conditions are manifold; they can be based on internal approvals (e.g. the board or shareholders' meeting) by the acquirer and the vendor, on external approvals from antitrust or competition authorities or the execution of defined tasks and transactions.

In this context, approvals of **antitrust or competition authorities** play an important role. Even if they belong to legal activities, they influence the commercial aspect of the acquisition. These authorities may give conditional approvals that suspend the acquisition date. In these cases, the acquirer is forced to execute defined conditions, e.g. selling parts of the business to avoid a dominant market position. The authorities even may give non-approvals that will lead to dissolving activities of the acquisition. The control, established meanwhile, has to be abandoned and the acquirer's financial statements have to be presented as if the acquisition never took place. If interim annual financial statements are prepared in the meantime, the initial consolidation has to be reversed. This includes all consolidation tasks performed during the initial and, if appropriate, subsequent consolidations combined with a restatement of the involved financial statements according to IAS 8. The prevailing view of this reversal is not to execute them as a deconsolidation. Such a deconsolidation would pretend that the company acquired would be part of the group even for a limited period of time, which is legally not permissible.

Companies are often acquired in stages. An **acquisition achieved in stages** has a similar effect on the acquisition date that defined conditions have. The acquisition date is deferred until that moment, when an acquisition of a further interest in the company constitutes control.

If acquisitions are realized through an **offer**, the acquisition date depends on the type of offer and on the acceptance of the offer. If the offer is a public offer, the acquisition date is that date where the offer becomes unconditional and a sufficient number of shares is collected that constitutes control. The number of shares collected has to pass a defined threshold (which is 50% plus one share in most cases). If the offer is a private offer, the acquisition date will be that date when the (unconditional) offer will be accepted.

In some cases, the acquisition date may depend on **other facts and circumstances**. A typical example is the pending stage where approvals to execute the acquisition are missing due to formal procedures, whether they relate to the vendor, the acquirer or competition authorities. Pending stages often require a joint control by the vendor and the acquirer. In such situations, the acquisition date might be determined individually based on the influence on control:

- the acquirer will be able to direct the operating and financial policies of the acquiree,
- the flow of economic benefits changes,
- the consideration transferred passes at defined dates, or
- the appointment of a majority of board members of the acquiree.

A common practice is to shift the acquisition towards the beginning of the period. This **backdating** simplifies complex contractual and accounting tasks and is often implemented in the purchase agreement. It often includes also regulations about the associated profit payout rights. These rights have no impact on the acquisition date; they only influence the purchase price. From the group's point of view, a backdating of the acquisition date is only appropriate to that date where ownership and control is obtained. If such a case cannot be proven, the acquisition date is equal to the closing date.

Purchase agreements may include conditions that the purchase price may be subject to a contingent or deferred consideration. A **deferred payment** is a separate transaction that has no influence on the acquisition date.

In addition to the above-mentioned issues on control and on determining the acquisition date, the acquisition date is important for a set of **accounting tasks** to be executed at the acquisition date:

- It acts as a cut-off point. It has to separate profits belonging to the vendor from profits belonging to the acquirer. The profit allocation is used for consolidation purposes, as old profits are considered during the initial consolidation while new profits are subject to subsequent consolidations.
- The measurement of acquired assets and assumed liabilities as well as contingent considerations is based on the acquisition date.
- The initial consolidation has to be executed at the acquisition date.

Example

The process of acquiring 80% of the shares in Solenta had the following milestones:

- 11/2011   Start research for investment opportunities;
- 2/2012   Identification of potential investment opportunities;

> - 3/2012   Start negotiations;
> - 11/2012   Start due diligence Solenta;
> - 2/2013   Finalization due diligence;
> - 3/2013   Negotiations purchase price;
> - 1.4.2013   Signing of sale and purchase agreement.
>
> Due diligence revealed that an acquisition of Solenta would not constitute a dominant market position by the Flexing Cables group. Therefore, approvals from antitrust agencies were not necessary.
>
> The sales and purchase agreement included the following regulations that had to be considered in determining the acquisition date: "... The seller sells 80% of the shares in Solenta with a nominal value of 2,000 k EUR including any profit distribution rights as of 1 January 2013 and any minor rights to the buyer. The sale of the shares and its associated rights will take place as of 1.1.2013 0:00h. ..."
>
> The acquisition date was 1.4.2013. This is because the date on which the sale and purchase agreement was signed was the earliest date on which Flexing Cables had access to govern the policies of Solenta, and therefore control. The backdating towards the beginning of the period was a pure economic decision to simplify the sale, which would be considered according to the purchase price only. Any other agreements to pass over the business responsibility to Flexing Cables (so that Flexing Cables would be able to influence the business) could not be identified. Furthermore, no other defined conditions were identified that might have altered the acquisition date.

3.3. Consideration transferred (purchase price)

As business combinations may have different forms, IFRS 3 has a broad approach regarding the compensation an acquirer has to give to obtain the desired subject. Therefore, IFRS 3 does not define the cost of an acquisition or a purchase price from the acquirer's point of view. Instead IFRS 3 defines a consideration that has to be transferred. This is a much broader definition than a pure purchase price and offers a wide collection of elements that qualify as a consideration transferred.

To measure the consideration transferred, IFRS 3.32a (i) and IFRS 3.37 require that all elements are measured at their fair value at the acquisition date. As elements incurred may require different methods for fair value measurement, thus each element has to be measured separately applying their individual measurement methods. The sum of all fair values equals the consideration transferred. A deviation from the fair-value principle exists only for employee share-based payment awards that are measured in accordance with IFRS 2.

As the standard does not provide any detailed guidance, but instead lists just some examples of what kinds of element qualify as a consideration, the following list may help in determining elements of considerations transferred:

- Cash
  All kinds of cash payment and payments of cash equivalents; measured by their nominal values.

- Stocks, shares and equity instruments

    Common and preferred stocks and other equity instruments like convertible bonds and debentures refer to the equity of the acquirer. These equity instruments are usually measured by their market values at the acquisition date. A deviation of the measurement principle might be necessary in selected cases. In such cases, adequate market values or equivalents have to be chosen or assumed. Typical cases are:

    - Shares traded in the market have a high volatility due to low trading volumes,
    - Shares traded in the market have significant and unusual fluctuations around the acquisition date,
    - Shares traded in the market have a low free floats,
    - Shares are not traded in a market, or
    - A market value cannot be derived from the market for new issued shares.

- Earn-out options

    Earn-out options usually refer to a certain period after the acquisition date and are therefore contingent considerations. They reflect the efforts of the vendor before the acquisition date to initiate or generate new business, new orders or projects and are linked to the performance, usually to EBIT or EBITDA of the acquired company. This assumes that the business of the company will not change for a defined period. As earn-out options become due up to several years after the acquisition, they are discounted and measured by their present or fair value. The form of payment (e.g. cash vs. shares) is not important for the calculation.

    The calculation model that is used to calculate earn-out options has to be agreed between both parties and takes the planned business development over the next few years as the basis for the earn-out calculation. Depending on the planned business development and its underlying assumptions, a large measurement bandwidth for the final recognition exists.

    To improve reliability, it is recommended to validate earn-out options by calculating best- and worst-case scenarios. Based on these results, an adjustment of the expected earn-out option might be appropriate.

- Exchange of non-monetary items

    Non-monetary items are all kinds of asset and liability that are not easily convertible into cash (so monetary items) in a short period of time. Typical examples are: non-current assets and liabilities like intangible assets, property, plant and equipment, investments and provisions.

    Non-monetary items given in exchange for the investment in a subsidiary to the vendor are always measured with their fair values according to IFRS 3.38 at the acquisition date. This implies that the non-monetary item has an intrinsic value. If these non-monetary items have different carrying balances in the accounts of the acquirer than its intrinsic values, the acquirer has to adjust the carrying amount through profit or loss before the items are transferred. If these items are given to the acquired company, any adjustments are not applicable while the items are measured by their carrying amounts. This is because the acquirer still remains in control of these items.

- Options, bonds and debentures

Options are either put or call options allowing the vendor or the acquirer to purchase / sell the shares of a company. The exercising of these options may force the transfer of ownership in the subsidiary. Therefore, the date options are exercised may be treated as the acquisition day if control is obtained. While options are within scope of IFRS 9 they are always financial instruments. The accounting of options starts upon the agreement with the vendor (so the signature of an appropriate contract) and ends either with an exercising or with an expiration of the option. The requirements of IFRS 9 of a fair value measurement will lead to an adjustment of options through profit & loss at each subsequent balance sheet date. Therefore, the accounting of options may start long before the acquisition finally takes place.

Bonds and debentures might be issued to the vendor. They follow from a commercial perspective the same rational than equity but are recorded as a liability instead of equity.

- Hidden elements

Considerations transferred can be not visible at first sight. These considerations are often embedded in "special" agreements with one or more vendors, either directly or indirectly via a third party. Reasons of hiding such considerations are manifold; they are usually the result of the negotiation process with the vendor and often initiated by the vendor. The identification of such hidden elements as part of the consideration transferred is often difficult to realize. It is recommended to scan all agreements that are signed in conjunction with the acquisition. The scanning has to focus on the purpose of the agreement and its contents in relationship to the acquisition. Any unusual findings should be observed during the measurement period. If evidence is given that the agreement has embedded considerations, these considerations have to be separated, measured and accounted as part of the consideration transferred.

Typical examples are consulting contracts with former owners. The acquirer fulfils its commitment; services of the former owners are often not rendered.

- Instalments and annuities

Regardless of which forms of instalment and annuity are agreed, they are always considered by their present values considering an adequate discount rate. Annuities for life have to consider also an adequate retention period based on an anticipated average life.

- Deferrals, delays and extensions

Payments that become due after the acquisition date have to be discounted on the acquisition date using a discount rate that meets market conditions. This applies to all kinds of deferrals, not only cash components. Typical examples are earn-out options.

- Foreign currency payments

   Payments made in a foreign currency have to be translated with the exchange rate of that date when control is given. In most cases, this is the acquisition date.

- Warranties

   Warranties are a subset of contingent considerations. They may be given by the acquirer as well as by the vendor. The purpose of these warranties is to compensate the other party in case of defined conditions will not be met. Typical examples are warranties for stock prices, profits and balance sheet items.

   - Stock price warranties are usually given by the acquirer in case of stocks as the consideration transferred. It is not important if stocks cover the whole consideration or just a part of it. Their purpose is to ensure that the stocks received by the vendor will equal a defined minimum price. Stock price warranties refer to the situation as of the acquisition date. They have to be accounted for and are treated as a financial liability (if compensation in cash occurs). Warranties often have the character of options. The fair value of such an option can be determined by the volatility of the share and the duration of the option. Therefore, warranties that relate to the period between the signature and the execution of the purchase contract (the acquisition date) are not subject to any warranties.
   - Profit warranties are often used in connection with earn-out options. Their purpose is to ensure a minimum profit that is subject to the earn-out calculation. Depending on the contractual agreement, warranties may constitute a deferral, a minimum payment or a repayment by the vendor.
   - Balance sheet warranties are given by the vendor. The vendor guarantees that the balances of balance sheet items are free from any material misstatements. Such kinds of warranties are usually given for equity and for selected balance sheet items and cover two levels: misstatements at the acquisition date and subsequent changes in carrying amounts. Misstatements often result in overstated or understated carrying amounts of balance sheet items. Reimbursements of purchase prices are often the case in such situations. Subsequent changes in carrying amounts refer to minimum values of assets to be guaranteed by the vendor for a defined period. A breach of such warranties often results in reimbursements or adjustments of contingent considerations to be paid at a later stage.
   - Warranties will lead to a (partial) repayment of the consideration transferred if warranties are used.

All kinds of warranty have one problem in common: a high uncertainty regarding the use of warranties. An accounting of these warranties would be possible only if statistical or historical data on occurrence probabilities is available that can be used as an underlying assumption. In most cases, an accounting of warranties is not applicable due to missing measurement feasibility. Nevertheless, if a measurement is given, warranties have to be measured by its fair value according to IFRS 3.39 in combination with IFRS 3.37. The recording is based on the type of warranty given. It is either a financial liability or an equity instrument.

- Indemnifications

    Indemnifications are payments of the vendor if outcomes of contingencies or uncertainties regarding selected assets or liabilities are outside given promises or contractually agreed conditions. The acquirer accounts for these indemnifications as assets or valuation allowances according to IFRS 3.27 and 3.B41. Future cash flows by the vendor will only apply if agreed conditions are not met. Due to the accounting as a (separate) indemnification asset, indemnifications are not part of considerations transferred.

- Other contingencies

    Any contingent consideration other than the ones listed above have to be considered with its fair value at the acquisition date as a liability.

The broad range of contingencies includes elements that are due for later payment or includes components where the payment is uncertain. IFRS 3.39 subsume these items as **contingent considerations**. Contingent considerations are always financial instruments and measured in accordance with IFRS 9. They include earn-out options, warranties, rights to return the subsidiary acquired and indemnifications. As already mentioned, accounting rules require the measurement with their fair values. Nevertheless, accounting rules regarding contingent considerations may be subject to abuses. The initial estimation of contingent considerations as part of the purchase price might be overstated at the acquisition date. As the initial recording increases goodwill and has no impact on profit & loss, adjustments of contingent considerations subsequent to the acquisition will result in a gain, usually recorded in profit & loss.

Excluded from the consideration transferred are all **acquisition-related costs**. IFRS 3.53 does not permit any exceptions. All costs allocable to the acquisition have to be expensed. The rationale behind this requirement is that acquisitions are based on fair-value exchanges where acquisition-related costs are neither part of the exchange nor do they meet the definition. Typical examples of acquisition-related costs are:

- Fees for lawyers, auditors and advisors;
- Costs of due diligence;
- Appraisals as part of purchase price allocations;
- Registering costs;

- Administrative costs;
- Staff bonus payments;
- Other internal costs directly allocable to an acquisition;
- Financing costs.

To mitigate any potential abuse, IFRS 3.51, 3.52c and 3.BC370 clarify that a routing of acquisition related costs via other parties – and particularly via the seller – to recognize these costs as acquisition costs is out of the scope of the acquisition. In such cases, transactions carrying acquisition related costs have to be treated as separate transactions apart from the acquisition. A similar interpretation can be taken on vendor due diligence to prepare a company for sale. Costs relating to activities of the seller fulfil the same criteria so that these costs are also handled in separate transactions.

Even if acquisition-related costs are recorded as an expense under IFRS, they are subject to capitalization under most tax rules. Therefore, quasi-permanent differences exist in the accounts of the parent that require recognition of deferred taxes.

An exception from the rule of recognizing acquisition-related costs is the handling of **financing costs** that relate to the issuing of debt or equity instruments. Costs relating to these transactions are recorded directly in equity in accordance with IAS 32 and IFRS 9. Depending on the acquisition type, financing costs may be difficult to separate from other acquisition related costs. Detailed analysis of the nature of these costs is required in such situations. To separate financing costs from acquisition-related costs, the following tasks should be applied in the following order:

Step	Task
1)	If costs would also be incurred in an ordinary acquisition or business combination, these costs are always acquisition related costs.
2)	If costs directly relate to the issuing of shares, these costs are always acquisition related costs.
3)	Any costs left have to be allocated based on the intention of the underlying objective.

Tab. E-3 Tasks to separate financing costs from acquisition-related costs

> Consider the above listed tasks as a mandatory activity of a purchase price allocation.

The non-recognition of acquisition-related costs always triggers an accounting of deferred taxes.

As a measurement of all consideration to be transferred is not possible at the acquisition date, a **measurement period** of 12 months is available to finalize and record all components of the purchase price allocation. The measurement period can end earlier if all information required to measure all assets and liabilities is available. During the measurement period, two adjustments are possible for

- Considerations recognized if new information obtained is available that will result in a remeasurement of those considerations, and
- Additional considerations not already recognized but should be recorded as of the acquisition date.

Both adjustments require that facts and circumstances have to be present at the acquisition date. The adjustments have an impact on goodwill and will result in a change in goodwill. Any information that is based on events after the acquisition date is excluded from being used for measurement and valuation purposes. If consolidated financial statements are prepared during the measurement period and the purchase price allocation is not finalized, provisional amounts have to be considered. These financial statements have to be adjusted retrospectively upon any adjustments made after the preparation and within the measurement period. Any facts on the acquisition that arrived after the end of the measurement period may require also an adjustment of the consideration. These adjustments have to be accounted for through profit & loss.

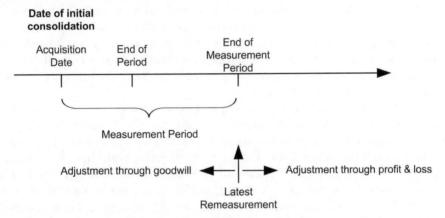

Fig. E-9 Measurement period and its related accounting

Transactions to acquire a company can have **legal forms** that result in a conglomerate of contracts. There may be also several transactions combined into contracts that have different purposes and sometimes even do not relate to an acquisition. As all these contractual forms may generate individual accounting effects that may contradict the acquisition, an economic view of the acquisition and its transactions is required. A fall-back to the framework might be appropriate to confirm the economic view of the transaction by considering the substance over form approach. In practice two major types of "contractual designs" are observed:

- Separate contracts

  The acquisition is split up into a set of contracts. These contracts may include the sale of selected items like the share in a company, intellectual property, the role of the former owners or warranties given. Even side letters are an appropriate tool to arrange details of the acquisition. Regardless of how contracts are designed, all separate contracts have to be treated as one for acquisition purposes and for the measurement and accounting of contingencies.

- Several transactions in one contract

  An acquisition contract may cover more than just the acquisition.

Special agreements are often included in a contract that may have a direct or indirect relationship with the acquisition. Nevertheless, from an accounting point of view, these agreements are not applicable for an acquisition accounting and require a separation between the acquisition-related element and all other elements.

Typical examples of such agreements are the employment of former owners as officers of the subsidiary, special bonuses upon the acquisition, retirement arrangements and similar issues. A detailed analysis of the purchase agreement is required to understand the accounting implications.

Another typical form of acquisitions is a combination of contracts that include the ultimate acquisition and accompanied transactions. These accompanied transactions relate to the acquisition but have different contents. They would not be signed if the acquisition as the underlying transaction would not be realized. Even if a link to the acquisition is given, a separate accounting is required. This is because these transactions are – like acquisition-related costs – outside fair-value exchanges. Typical examples are employment contracts of the former owners that serve as managers of the subsidiary.

Considerations are subject to **subsequent measurement**. These measurements apply to all contingent considerations recognized on the acquisition date, particularly to earn-out options, deferrals or warranties. As far as new information is available that refers to the acquisition date, initial estimations have to be adjusted or (future) events occurred, an update of considerations accounted for as a liability is necessary. If the update occurs within the measurement period and relates to the condition as of the acquisition date, an adjustment against goodwill is available. In most cases, subsequent measurements are due outside the measurement period. Any adjustments have to be recorded through profit & loss either as a gain or a loss. The same accounting applies to events after the acquisition date that have no dependencies to the acquisition date. Changes relating to these events have to be accounted for separately through profit & loss or other comprehensive income.

Another subsequent event is the **right to return**. Those rights are contractually agreed in most cases if defined conditions are not met. They are often linked to warranties or indemnifications. As the right to return triggers a full reversal of the acquisition, it is not subject to a subsequent measurement.

Example

The consideration Flexing Cables had to transfer for the acquisition of the shares in Solenta had several elements, as defined in the sale and purchase agreement:

"...

§4 Purchase price

    (1) The buyer has to pay an amount of 23,000,000 EUR in cash. The amount has to arrive on the bank account of the seller not later than four working days after signing this contract.

The seller immediately provides required bank details to the buyer after signing this contract.

(2) The buyer has to transfer a volume of 6,300,000 of its ordinary shares to the seller. The buyer indemnifies the seller in case shares will be traded as of 31.12.2013 below a price per share of 7 EUR. The indemnification will be calculated based on the difference between the market price per share as of 31.12.2013 and the guaranteed amount per share times the transferred volume.

(3) To consider the efforts of the seller in investing in new technology and new products, the buyer will pay the seller an additional amount that is based on the performance of the company. This amount is defined as follows:

   a. If the cumulative EBIT of the fiscal years 2013 and 2014 falls below the double of the EBIT as stated in the financial statement as of 31.12.2012, the seller indemnifies the buyer due to underperformance of the company based on the following rational.[9] The indemnification amount is calculated on a proportionate basis and may add up to 6,000,000 EUR in case the cumulative EBIT of the company is up to 3,000,000 EUR below the double EBIT as stated in the financial statement as of 31.12.2012. In any other case, the indemnification amount is limited to 6,000,000 EUR.

   b. If the cumulative EBIT of the fiscal years 2013 and 2014 exceed the double EBIT as stated in the financial statement as of 31.12.2012, the seller pays an additional amount to the seller based on the following rationale. If the cumulative EBIT exceeds the double EBIT as stated in the financial statements as of 31.12.2012 by an amount of 4,000,000 EUR, the buyer will pay an additional amount up to 12,000,000 EUR in proportion to the performance of the company.

   c. If the cumulative EBIT exceeds the double EBIT as stated in the financial statements as of 31.12.2012 and an amount of 4,000,000 EUR, the additional payment is limited to 12,000,000 EUR.

(4) The additional amount to be paid is due ten days after the approval of the audited financial statements as of 31.12.2014 by the shareholders but not later than 1.9.2015.

(5) EBIT will be calculated based on the accounting policy applied in the financial statement as of 31.12.2012 and a consideration of the following expense and revenue items:
   a. …
   …"

Based on the sales and purchase agreement, Flexing Cables had to determine the consideration transferred to record it in their separate financial statement. The determination may require additional information.

---

[9] According to the referred financial statement, the EBIT is 15,595 k EUR.

Item	Explanation and calculation	Amount
Cash	Nominal value as of the acquisition date and contractually agreed	23,000
Shares	As of the acquisition date, the closing price of the shares of Flexing Cables is fixed at 7.14 EUR per share. This information is retrieved from the stock exchange where Flexing Cables shares are traded. 6,300 * 7.14 (in '000s of shares)	44,982
Earn-out	Determining the variable payment, the planning of the business years 2013 and 2014 as of the acquisition date is needed. The planning forecasts an EBIT of 16,850 in FY 2013 and an EBIT of 18,200 in FY 2014. Based on the planning and the provisions of calculating the additional payment in the sales and purchasing agreement, an additional payment of 11,580 k EUR will be expected. As the payment is due not later than 1.9.2015, it has to be discounted by 883 days (1.9.2015 – 1.4.2013). The discount to be used is derived from a peer group of competitors and fairly considers the situation and risks of Flexing Cables. The discount rate is 6.2%.	10,000
Warranty	Even if the warranty given has to be accounted for as an option, management rejected to determine the fair value of the warranty and to consider an amount as of the acquisition date due to several reasons: • Due to the good performance of Flexing Cables, management does not believe that the share price will fall below 7 EUR. • The warranty will lapse at the end of the period, so within eight month. Therefore, in the unlikely event that the share price will fall below 7 EUR, the indemnification to be paid can be considered as an additional consideration element as this is within the 12 month period.	-
		77,982

3.4. Acquired assets – recognition and measurement

3.4.1. *General requirements on recognition and measurement*

From the group's point of view, the acquisition of a subsidiary is not an investment in a subsidiary but an acquisition of assets and an assuming of liabilities. Therefore, assets acquired and liabilities assumed have to be recognized and measured in addition to and separately from any non-controlling interests and goodwill. This requirement clarifies that new recognition and measurement have to be applied. Any recognition and measurement previously undertaken by the acquiree will be overwritten for group accounting purposes. For a proper handling for group purposes, four tasks have to be executed on those assets and liabilities in ensuring that asset or liability will be available for group purposes:

• Identification of an asset or liability;
• Recognition;
• Initial measurement;
• Subsequent measurement.

IFRS 3.10 explicitly mentions the recognition of all identifiable assets and liabilities. This definition is much broader than a focus on assets and liabilities recorded in the balance sheet as it also considers assets and liabilities that are not accounted for by the acquiree. In addition to the recognition requirements, IFRS 3.18 requires a measurement at the acquisition-date fair value for all assets acquired and liabilities assumed. This may involve a check of all accounted assets and liabilities regarding an appropriate measurement at the acquisition date and an **identification**, recognition and measurement of all not-accounted assets and liabilities. To ensure that assets and liabilities are properly accounted for at group level, the following steps should be executed:

Step	Task
1)	Inventorying and categorization of accounted balance sheet items
2)	Assessment of all recognized assets acquired and liabilities assumes regarding an IFRS recognition
3)	Identification of hidden reserves and burdens of all recognized assets acquired and liabilities assumed
4)	Identification of non-accounted assets acquired and liabilities assumed
5)	Identification of additional risks and charges
6)	Assessment of the reliability of an IFRS recognition
7)	Revaluation of accounted assets acquired and liabilities assumed
8)	Measurement of non-accounted assets acquired and liabilities assumed
9)	Estimation of tax effects and recognition of deferred tax assets or deferred tax liabilities

Tab. E-4 Steps of identifying and measuring acquired assets and assumed liabilities within purchase price allocations

The initial **recognition** of assets and liabilities at group level due to the acquisition of a new subsidiary is subject to defined conditions. All conditions have to be fulfilled to qualify for a recognition

- The definitions of assets and liabilities as defined in the framework in F4.4 have to be met. This means that assets
  - are resources,
  - that are controlled by the entity,
  - as a result of past events,
  - where future economic benefits will flow to the entity.

  Accordingly, liabilities
  - are present obligations of the entity,
  - as a result of past events,
  - that result in an outflow of economic resources,
  - for a settlement.

  The definitions are particularly important to those assets and liabilities that are not already accounted for. They will help in determining if assets and liabilities exist that have to be recognized. Usually such assets and liabilities are outside the accounting scope of the acquiree.

- The assets and liabilities have to be part of the acquiree or the business acquired. Any asset or liability that does not belong to the business combination has to be accounted for separately from the acquisition.

As a consequence, assets and liabilities that do not meet both recognition criteria have to be treated separately from the acquisition and its recognition policies.

Due to the recognition criteria, assets and liabilities recognized at group level will deviate from assets and liabilities on the acquiree's local level. The reason for this deviation is based on the fact that assets and liabilities may exist the acquiree is not permitted to account for. Typical examples are brands or trade names the acquiree has developed, introduced in the market and maintained over several years. Because of the acquisition, these assets and liabilities are subject to a purchasing transaction (which is the business combination) that requires an accounting at group level. As a consequence, a change in scope occurred for these assets and liabilities.

As already outlined, the **initial measurement** principle is the fair value as of the acquisition date. Exceptions to this guiding principle apply only to selected assets and liabilities. They are measured on an alternate base, usually according to their corresponding IFRS. Depending on the nature of assets and liabilities, different measurement bases are used in determining the carrying amount. The following list provides a comprehensive view of applicable measurement bases.

Assets / Liabilities	Measurement base
Securities, traded in stock exchanges	Actual market price
Securities, not traded	Expected or assumed fair value
Receivables, favourable contractual relationships and other assets	Cash values
Finished and traded goods	Net realizable value
Unfinished goods	Net realizable value less remaining production costs
Raw materials	Replacement costs
Property	Fair value
Technical and office equipment	Market values or fair value based on appraisals
Indemnification assets	Fair value based on contractually agreed indemnifications
Insurance contracts	IFRS 4
Intangible assets, traded on a market	IAS 38
Intangible assets, not traded	Fair value based on appraisals by considering the arms-length principle
Leasing contracts	IAS 17
Pensions	Cash values
Tax assets and liabilities	Nominal values
Payables, non-current debt and other liabilities	Cash values, either discounted or undiscounted
Onerous contracts	Cash values
Contingent liabilities	Fair value based on appraisals by considering the arms-length principle

Tab. E-5   Measurement bases of assets and liabilities

In some cases, **fair value** is difficult to estimate. In such cases, a measurement is based on the valuation techniques outlined in *IFRS 13 – Fair Value Measurement*. Such techniques can be based on a cost, income or market approach.[10]

---

[10] See Appendix I: Fair value on page 751 for fair value measurement.

Even if the above listed assets have a defined measurement base, their **future cash flows may vary** or are uncertain. As this behaviour is already considered in the fair value of the asset, an additional or separate valuation allowance is prohibited according to IFRS 3.B41. All kinds of receivable and inventory with uncertain cash flows are affected particularly by this rule. Balances have to be presented on a net basis. A strict application of this rule might lead to the opinion that an application to non-current assets with uncertain cash flows is mandatory. Therefore, these assets have to be presented on a net basis and not at its gross acquisition costs and cumulated depreciation.

A special handling is required for **assets that have no or less future use** or value to the acquirer. This may result in no use or a different use than originally intended. The accounting treatment is similar to all other assets in the first instance; it has to be measured by its fair value assuming a regular use (as usually intended by each market participant, so by a third party). The subsequent measurement is based on the useful life of an unused asset. This may include impairment testing. Typical examples are intangible assets that relate to research and development projects, brand and trade names of competing products and services and similar assets.

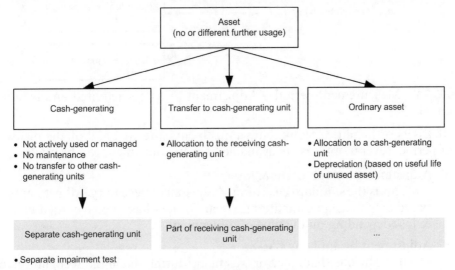

Fig. E-10 Treatment of asset with no further use

As measurement of all assets and liabilities acquired is not possible at the acquisition date, a **measurement period** of 12 months is available to finalize, recognize and measure all assets acquired and liabilities assumed during the purchase price allocation. The measurement period can end earlier if all information required to measure all assets and liabilities is available. During the measurement period, two adjustments are possible for:

* Recorded assets and liabilities if new information obtained is available on conditions at the acquisition date that will result in a revised measurement of those assets or liabilities, and
* Additional assets and liabilities not already recognized but should be recorded as of the acquisition date.

Both adjustments require that facts and circumstances have to be present at the acquisition date. Any information that is based on events after the acquisition date is excluded from being used for measurement and valuation purposes. If consolidated financial statements are prepared during the measurement period and the purchase price allocation is not finalized, provisional amounts have to be considered. These financial statements have to be adjusted retrospectively upon any adjustments made after the preparation and within the measurement period.

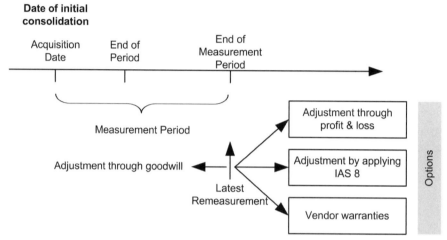

Fig. E-11   Measurement period – Adjustment of assets acquired and liabilities assumed

If assets or liabilities require any adjustments after the end of the measurement period, several options are available how an adjustment can be made.

- Adjustment through profit & loss
  This is the standard case of any adjustment necessary. Adjustments are based on change in estimations. A gain or loss has to be recorded in profit & loss depending on the type of adjustment.

- Adjustment by applying IAS 8
  If it obvious that an error was made during the initial recognition and measurement of assets and liabilities, an adjustment according to *IAS 8 – Accounting Policies, Changes in Accounting Estimates and Errors* is necessary. IFRS 3.50 directly requires the application of IAS 8 in such cases.

- Vendor warranties
  If the adjustments of assets and liabilities are necessary and a vendor guarantee was given to the carrying amounts of these assets and liabilities, any adjustments can be made against vendor warranties. The warranty can cover any valuation issue of assets. It can also cover any understatements of liabilities. Before executing the use of a warranty, an exhaustive check should be made to ensure a valid claim against the vendor.

The following journal entries are applicable upon the use of a warranty.

Journal entry
dr.   Vendor warranties
     cr.   (Intangible) Asset or liability

An alternate recording is an execution in two steps. The first step will adjust the asset or liability incurred. This is identical to an adjustment through profit & loss. The second step records the claim against the vendor.

Journal entry		Comment
dr.	Vendor warranties	This is the journal entry applicable on the first option
cr.	Profit & loss	
dr.	Profit & loss	
cr.	(Intangible) Asset or liability	

> IFRS 3 was amended by the *Improvements to IFRS* in May 2010. The standard now includes accounting specifications for the treatment of non-controlling interests in a business combination.

Due to the availability of the two options for each business combination, a selection can be made individually for each business combination. A consistent application of accounting purposes as required by IAS 8.13 is not necessary in this case.

Depending on the option chosen, the carrying amount of non-controlling interests will vary. This is because a fair value of an ownership interest is different from a proportionate share. As a consequence, goodwill as a residual value will also vary. While this measurement is taken at the acquisition date, the increase in goodwill is a permanent difference.

While the fair value principle at the acquisition date is the guiding principle, only limited **exceptions** to this principle regarding recognition and measurement are allowed. Depending on the item either recognition or measurement or both exceptions apply. The following list provides an overview about those exceptions.

Item	Explanation	Exception	Reference
Contingent liabilities	See chapter 3.4.3.4 – Non-accounted & contingent liabilities for explanation.	Recognition	IFRS 3.22
Income taxes	Deferred tax assets and liabilities that relate to assets acquired and liabilities assumed in a business combination are recognized and measured by applying the accounting requirements of *IAS 12 – Income Taxes*.	Recognition & Measurement	IFRS 3.24
Employee benefits	As far as any employee benefits are involved, liabilities covering employee benefits are recognized and measured in accordance with *IAS 19 – Employee Benefits*.	Recognition & Measurement	IFRS 3.26

(continued)

Item	Explanation	Exception	Reference
Indemnification assets	See page 147 for explanation.	Recognition & Measurement	IFRS 3.27
Reacquired rights	See chapter 6.5.1 – Reacquired rights for explanation.	Measurement	IFRS 3.29
Share-based payment transactions	See chapter 6.4 – Multi-component contract for explanation.	Measurement	IFRS 3.30
Assets held for sale	Assets held for sale that relate to non-current assets or disposal groups which are acquired in a business combination are measured in accordance with IFRS 5.15 to 5.18.[11] The measurement base is usually fair value less costs to sell.	Measurement	IFRS 3.31

Tab. E-6   List of exceptions to the fair value principle

In some cases, the initial recognition combined with an initial measurement will have an impact on the **subsequent measurement**. This might be the case if specific accounting rules have to be followed other than the ones that would normally be applied to assets and liabilities.

3.4.2 Existing assets and liabilities

The requirement to measure all assets acquired and liabilities assumed by their fair values, at the acquisition date and based on the accounting policies of the group, demands a revaluation of assets and liabilities which have deviating carrying amounts in the acquiree's accounts. While the acquiree may apply different accounting policies to the acquirer, a reassessment of the carrying amounts under IFRS has to consider the following topics:

- Accounting systems

     If the acquiree applies local accounting standards, a conversion to IFRS is mandatory. This conversion should already be done as one part of the opening balance sheet preparation. Conversions are level I adjustments.

- Accounting policies

     Like the handling of accounting systems, an application of the group's accounting policies should be applied as another part of the opening balance sheet. These are level II adjustments.

- Carrying amount of balance sheet items

     Carrying amounts of business transactions can be recorded with different carrying amounts and in different places compared to accounting to group level. This requires a reclassification.

- Different periods

     The fiscal year of the acquiree is different from the group's fiscal year. This may require the preparation of interim financial statements.

---

[11] See chapter J-4 on page 601 for details on the accounting of non-current assets and disposal groups held for sale.

While most of these tasks are already considered as part of the opening balance sheet, a few necessary adjustments remain. This is particularly the **identification** of accounted assets acquired and liabilities assumed regarding a proper measurement as of the acquisition date. Those assets and liabilities that have a deviating carrying amount from its fair value require further attention. A deviation of the carrying amount of an asset or liability from its fair value arises always on non-monetary items and on monetary items if changes in fair value occurred that are not already considered in the carrying amounts of monetary assets and liabilities. This will leave only a limited set of assets and liabilities subject to adjustment.[12]

In practice, the most observed deviations from fair value refer to hidden reserves and burdens that are inherent in selected assets and liabilities due to applied accounting rules. This is particularly the case for the following items:

Item	Issue
Intangible assets	Selected intangible assets are subject to impairment test. Depending on the parameters used, adjustments may be necessary. Other assets may be recorded at cost not considering its real or intrinsic value. Patents are a typical example for such intangible assets.
Property	Property recorded at historical costs not considering any increases in value.
Fixed assets	Fixed assets may be subject to decommissioning, restoration or similar obligations that are not considered.
Inventory	Market prices may have been changed so that an adjustment to the lower of cost or market is required.
Trade receivables	Bad debt allowances need to be adjusted to reflect the group's risk policy (that may be separated from any accounting policies).
Contingent liabilities	Due to different views of measurement of contingencies, a remeasurement might be required.

Tab. E-7   List of existing assets and liabilities subject to revaluation

A check regarding **recognition** of these assets and liabilities is not necessary as they are already recognized in the accounts of the acquiree.

Upon the identification of assets acquired and liabilities assumed subject to a revaluation, the **initial measurement** for group purposes has to occur on an asset-by asset base. As far as hidden reserves are involved, the estimation of fair value is often subject to the work of appraisers. Appraisals are a standard document in estimating the fair value of property and patents that can be used to align the carrying amount towards its fair value. Accounted liabilities with inherent risks are subject to be remeasured by applying the group's accounting policy considering management judgement about the probability of an economic outflow.

Any adjustments that lead to a step-up or step-down of the carrying amount due to the business combination have to be recorded at level III.

> Stick to the valuation hierarchy and record the valuation effects at each appropriate level. It will support you in analyzing the effects for disclosure purposes, particularly for the disclosure according to IFRS 1 (first time adoption of IFRS) and IFRS 3 (details on the business combination).

---

[12] See chapter K -1.8 on page 655 for a list of monetary and non-monetary balance sheet items.

Example

A scan of Solenta's accounted assets and liabilities regarding an appropriate measurement by applying IFRS unveiled the following issues:

- The fair value of property (the land) where the company resides and that it owns is 3,480 k EUR. The amount is determined by an appraiser.
- The fair value of financial assets is understated.
- The company is currently involved in an environmental pollution case. Due to leakage, oil polluted the underground. The company was forced by the local environmental agency to clean the underground. This cleaning started one year ago and the company expects that it will continue for two additional years. Even if the company already has built an appropriate provision for this task, it expects that total costs will exceed the provision. An additional amount of 3,176 k EUR will be needed to finish the cleaning of the underground. This amount was determined by the engineering company responsible for the cleaning.

Adjustments to the carrying amounts due to the above facts were:

Item	Explanation and calculation	Amount
Property	The carrying amount of the property is 2,580 k EUR. Accordingly, a step-up amount has to be recorded. 3,480 – 2,580	900
Financial assets	The adjustment of financial assets has to reflect the changes in the market price of the shares. 15,500 * (7.14 – 6.58)	9
Environmental pollution	The additional amount required qualifies as an additional provision due to the legal obligation to clean the underground. It has to be discounted towards the acquisition date. The market rate used for discounting was determined by 2.9% for a period of two years.	(3,000)

The **subsequent measurement** of any step up and step down of the carrying amount in local accounts has to follow the treatment of the underlying asset or liability for group purposes. If the carrying amount in local accounts is subject to depreciation and amortization, so is the carrying adjustment amount at level III.

Example

Identified assets and liabilities as of the acquisition date were subject to subsequent measurement:

- An adjustment of the step-up amount of the land is only applicable if there is an impairment of the land. IAS 16.58 prohibits a regular depreciation of land due to its unlimited useful life. Therefore, land is subject to an impairment test as defined by IAS 36 due to IAS 16.63.
- The step-up amount of the provision for environmental pollution has to be observed regarding its use. If a part of this additional provision has to be used by the end of the period, an appropriate adjustment (including an interest adjustment) is necessary. The remaining balance has to be compounded.

3.4.3. *Non-accounted assets and liabilities*

Non-accounted items are usually an integral part of the operation. An accounting of these assets and liabilities typically is not appropriate by the acquiree due to accounting regulations that prohibit a recording. Nevertheless, they have to be accounted for in a business combination because the consideration transferred covers also these assets and assumed liabilities. As the nature of non-accounted assets and liabilities varies due to the nature of the business, different types of presentation might appear. In most cases, non-accounted assets are recorded as intangible assets and liabilities are recorded as contingent liabilities.

While intangible assets can arise in different forms for different purposes, IFRS 3 is highlighting the treatment of selected intangible assets, particularly on lease arrangements, indemnification assets and reacquired rights in addition to the general treatment of intangible assets. Common to all these assets – if identified as an asset – is that they have to fulfil the asset definition requirement as outlined in the framework (F 4.4a and F 4.8 et seq.).

3.4.3.1 *Intangible assets*

The identification of intangible assets follows a process that is derived from IFRS 3 accounting requirement. In general, three steps are required for the accounting of an intangible asset:

- Identification;
- Recognition;
- Measurement.

All three steps are embedded in a workflow because specific activities in each step have to be performed to ensure that intangible assets match the accounting requirements of IFRS 3 (and related standards like IAS 16, IAS 37 and IAS 38).

To securely identify intangible assets, IFRS 3.IE16 to 44 provides a list of typical assets that may qualify for an additional recognition as intangible assets. Even if potential intangible assets are identified, the recognition of these identified assets depends on the general accounting requirements for assets and particularly on the measurability of those assets. The following list of potential **identifiable items** is based on the examples provided in the illustrative examples of IFRS 3 expanded by other assets types.[13]

---

[13] IFRS 3.IE16 mentions that some of the examples provided do not meet the intangible asset criteria and have to be recorded as other current or non-current assets. For simplicity reasons, all assets discussed in this chapter are treated as intangible assets. Nevertheless, a proper application is mandatory in practice to reflect the nature of the asset and its intended use.

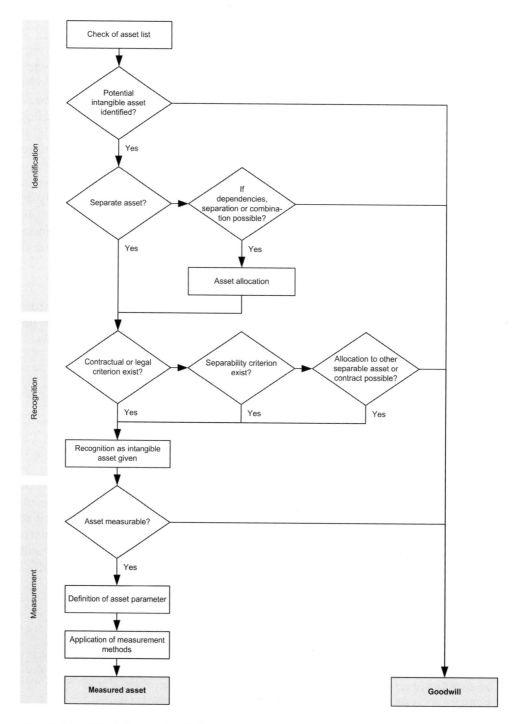

Fig. E-12 Workflow to initially account for intangible assets

Category	Type of asset	Additional explanation	Basis
Market related			
	Trademarks, trade names, service marks, collective marks and certification marks	All kinds of names, symbols or similar marks used in trading where a product, service or company can be associated with. If such an element is legally protected through registration, it always qualifies as an intangible asset in a business combination. Otherwise it has to be checked if it is separately measurable. This includes brands and brand names.	Contractual
	Trade dress (unique colour, shape or package design)	Similar to trademarks except that the association of a product or service is not linked to a name or symbol but to other facts like designs, packages, shapes and similar unique things. To qualify as an intangible asset, the same criteria like the ones for trademarks apply.	Contractual
	Newspaper mastheads	Mastheads are similar to trademarks as customers identify a newspaper masthead in the same way as a brand.	Contractual
	Internet domain names	A registered domain name links the presence in the internet with a corporation and is renewable. It therefore meets the contractual recognition criterion.	Contractual
	Non-competition agreements	Non-competition agreements create a market advantage that qualifies as an intangible asset if an underlying contract exists.	Contractual
Customer related			
	Customer lists or customer base	Customer lists comprise all kinds of information about customers, current ones as well as historic information. This includes not only general information about customers but also information about orders, order patterns and any type of sales and service activities rendered on customers. As customer lists are traded in specific markets, a customer list is separately marketable. Customer lists that include only information that can be obtained in the same volume and same quality from other sources usually do not provide any specific advantages. It is questionable if such lists qualify as assets. Customer lists do not qualify as an intangible asset if legal or contractual restrictions exist that limit the use (selling, leasing, exchanging information) of them. In such a situation the separability criterion is not met.	Non-contractual
	Order or production backlog	As order and production backlogs are usually based on placed orders by customers, they establish a contractual liability that has to be fulfilled. A termination or cancellation of an order does not prevent from recognition.	Contractual
	Customer contracts and related customer relationships	Contracts and relationships with customers may bind the customer to a corporation through which it will achieve future sales or services. Depending on the type of contract and nature of relationship, both items may constitute separate intangible assets. Contract renewals should be considered. A consideration of fluctuation rates might be appropriate if large volumes of customer contracts or relationships are grouped for valuation purposes.	Contractual

(continued)

Category	Type of asset	Additional explanation	Basis
	Non-contractual customer relationships	Even if customer relationships are not based on contracts, there might be a relationship due to historical patterns where future economic inflows are expected. Grouping non-contractual customer relationships in portfolios based on selected criteria that reflect the type of relationships does not disturb a measurement.	Non-contractual
		IFRS 3.IE31 assumes that non-contractual customer relationships are transferable and therefore meet the separability criterion. This depends on the type of business and the intention of the relationship. There might be business types where relationships are not transferable due to the nature of the business.	
		The question on reasons, events and circumstances that trigger the recognition of non-contractual customer relationships was rejected by the IFRIC due to missing guidance of IFRS 3.[14]	
Artistic related			
	Plays, opera and ballets	All kind or artistic related items may arise from contractual or legal rights. They qualify as intangible assets if they are subject to a legal protection, e.g. by copyright. Such a legal right can be sold, assigned, licensed or otherwise marketed.	Contractual
	Books, magazines, newspapers and other literary works		Contractual
	Musicals, such as compositions, song lyrics and advertising jingles		Contractual
	Pictures and photographs		Contractual
	Video and audiovisual material, including motion pictures or films, music videos and television programmes		Contractual
Contract based			
	General	Contract based relationships may qualify as assets and as liabilities depending on the nature of the underlying contract.	
	Licensing, royalty and standstill agreements	Licensing, royalties and standstill agreements offer a contractual advantage due to an exclusive use of products, knowledge, technology, services or intangible assets. As the contractual criterion is met, these contracts qualify as an asset.	Contractual
	Sales and purchasing contracts and agreements	Pending contracts may qualify as assets if favourable or unfavourable conditions compared to market conditions exist.	Contractual / non-contractual
	Advertising, construction, management, service or supply contracts		Contractual
	Lease agreements (whether the acquiree is the lessee or lessor)	Finance leases are always accounted for as assets (and may include liabilities as well). Favourable and unfavourable elements of operating leases qualify as intangible asset when the acquiree is a lessee.[15]	Contractual

[14] IFRIC Update March 2009.
[15] See chapter E‑3.4.3.3 on page 171 for details on lease arrangements.

(continued)

Category	Type of asset	Additional explanation	Basis
	Construction permits		Contractual
	Franchise agreements		Contractual
	Operating and broadcasting rights		Contractual
	Service contracts, such as mortgage servicing contracts	Usually services are integral part of financial assets and therefore not subject to a separate recognition. Only if services are agreed or purchased separately or are contractually separated, they may be capitalized as an intangible asset.	Contractual
	Employment contracts	Employment contracts usually do not qualify as an intangible asset because services of employees are rendered on arm-length base. If an employment contract becomes favourable to the company it qualifies as an asset due to the advantage the company has. The assumption of identifying favourable employment contracts has to consider the market situation, regional situations, productivity factors and company internal situations (e.g. workforce compared to workload).	Contractual
	Independent contractors	Even if independent contractors may perform the same services as employees, the nature of their services is different because they are engaged to perform specific tasks within a specific period under agreed conditions.	Contractual
	Use rights, such as drilling, water, air, timber cutting and route authorities	Use rights are often contractually agreed and therefore an asset. Depending on the nature of the underlying subject use rights qualify either as tangible or intangible assets.	Contractual
Technology based	Patented technology	Patented technology as part of products or services is separable and can be sold, licensed or otherwise marketed.	Contractual
	Computer software and mask works	Computer software and mask works (so software on a chip) are often legally protected by patents or copyrights.	Contractual
	Unpatented technology	Unpatented technology may qualify as an intangible asset if the separability criterion is met or if it is attached to another asset that fulfils this criterion.	Non-contractual
	Databases, including title plants	According to IFRS 3.IE42, databases are collections of information that are either protected by copyright or – if not protected – marketable in part or in total.	Non-contractual
	In-process research & development	In-process research & development might be an intangible asset if it has an implied fair value that can be measured and the recognition criteria of IFRS 3.B31 are met.	Non-contractual
	Trade secrets, such as secret formulas, processes and recipes	Trade secrets offer a market advantage due to knowledge that is not generally known.	Contractual

Tab. E-8 List of non-accounted assets

> Always checking the list of non-accounted assets in each acquisition will help to ensure that all assets are detected, measured and recorded.

The classification of identified intangible assets to contractual and non-contractual assets is a mandatory task of the identification process. It is used for the recognition criteria of the asset. Even if a pre-allocation to one of these two categories is given, some intangible assets may have different behaviours that will result in a deviating allocation.

The identification of potential intangible assets is usually the most time consuming task of a purchase price allocation as this task is often combined with the question of an appropriate recognition and measurement base. To identify such intangible asset, the application of **identification techniques** is necessary. Such techniques can be taken from professional auditing techniques auditors often apply:

- Analyzing the rationale of the business and identifying their value drivers,
- Analyzing sales, purchasing, production and employment activities, patterns and maintenances,
- Market analysis on competitors, products, service and the position of the acquiree in the market,
- Inventorying, scanning and analyzing of contracts in all business units, departments and other organizational units of the acquiree, and
- Further identification and analysis activities as appropriate.

In some cases, an identification of intangible assets will also identify **dependencies** between intangible assets. Such existing dependencies have to be considered as part of the identification because this has an impact on the measurement. The question arises, if identified intangible assets can be separated from each other or if they have to be treated as one intangible asset. To solve such situations, a qualitative analysis of the underlying business model is required. Typical situations where dependencies exist are:

- Non-contractual customer relationships and trademarks or trade name
  If a business model is driven by trade names and combined with technology or other lifestyle topics and customer purchase products due to the combination of these reasons, a separation is not possible in most cases. Due to the missing separation, an individual identification is not given and consequently recognition and measurement not possible. On the other hand, if a trade name dominates and other reasons are secondary, an allocation towards the trade name might be appropriate.

- Production secrets and trademarks or trade names
  Products that are sold under specific trademarks are often manufactured by using specific production processes and conditions that are kept secret. Under such conditions, it has to be checked if a trademark can be marketed separately from the production facilities and its secrets. The trademark may lose its value if the initial products associated with the trademark by the customers are not available any longer due to replacement by other or

similar products with different specifications that may prevent customers from purchasing those products.

- Merchandizing platforms
    On a merchandizing platform, affiliates and merchants are linked together. A separate treatment of affiliates and merchants as customer- or contract-related intangible assets is not given as both parties depend on each other and both depend on the merchandizing platform. Therefore, it is more appropriate to treat the merchandizing platform (that consists of hardware, software external and internally developed and affiliates and merchants that offer marketable space and content) as one asset only that generates cash flows.

Any **non-identifiable items** of the acquiree are subsumed into goodwill. That will include:

- All separate or mingled assets that do not meet the identification criteria,
- The assembled workforce that represents the acquiree's staff (even if human or intellectual capital of the staff has a different or defined value to the acquiree),
- Potential contracts if they do not qualify as assets (even if those contracts are signed at a later stage, the value of a potential contract resides with goodwill) and
- Any synergies derived from the business combination like future expansion opportunities, riding the experience curve, economies of scale or similar business reasons.

Upon the identification of intangible assets, these assets have to match the **recognition** criteria. The identification of an intangible asset does not necessarily include an automatic recognition of that asset. Instead an identified asset has to be checked, if it fulfils the recognition criteria as outlined in IFRS 3.B31. This requires that either the separability criterion or the contractual-legal criterion has to be met.

- The separability criterion
    The separability criterion of intangible assets is defined in IAS 38.12a. According to this definition, an intangible asset is separable if it can be separated or detached or divided from an entity and sold, transferred, licenced, rented or exchanged individually or in conjunction with another asset or contract. Therefore, an asset that is linked to an entity is usually not separable. It may become separable if it can be combined with or liked to a contract, an asset or liability that is separable and can be sold, transferred, leased, licensed, exchanged or otherwise marketed. Assets can also depend on each other. If an asset is sold that requires the use of another asset, then this other asset has to be sold as well. Regardless of the attribute of that other asset, it always meets the separability criterion. IFRS 3.B34 provides further explanation on the separability criterion.
- The contractual-legal criterion
    According to IAS 38.12b, if an intangible asset is based on a contract or a legal obligation or a legal right, it is always identifiable.

Due to the definitions and this differentiation, recognition is always given upon a contractual or legal nature of the intangible asset. A simple document like an underlying contract is sufficient in providing evidence. If this criterion is not given, a check regarding the existence of the separability criterion has to be executed next. The check has to consider if the asset directly satisfies this criterion or if an indirect cased is given (via another intangible asset). To prove that an identified asset is recognizable the group's accounting policies have to be applied. This is necessary because group accounting policies of the acquirer may have different criteria than the one used by the acquired; recognition occurs at group level rather than local.

The final step in considering an identified intangible asset is its measurability. Upon the **initial measurement** of an intangible asset, the general measurement requirements have to be applied. Therefore, intangible assets are measured by their fair value if not otherwise required. If the fair value of an intangible asset can be derived directly from active markets, such a value is always preferred. Due to the nature of intangible assets, an application of market values is possible only in rare cases. Therefore, valuation techniques have to be applied instead. Depending on the nature of the asset, a market approach, a cost approach or an income approach has to be used.[16] As the allocation of the intangible asset occurs at level III for group accounting purposes, it has to follow the group accounting policies. Accounts at local level will not be touched. If an intangible asset cannot be reliably measured through these approaches, a recognition as a separate asset is prohibited and an allocation to goodwill required.

Intangible assets are always non-current assets. They are therefore usually subject to amortization unless the asset does not have an indefinite useful life. This requires an estimation of its useful life based on the expected future use and its utilization, an amortization pattern and an estimation of a residual value if appropriate. The definition of these parameters required for subsequent measurement have to be a defined task upon the initial measurement. A direct estimation of the useful life of the original asset is often impossible because the asset and its purpose might be so special that knowledge of useful lives is not present. In such a situation it is appropriate to derive a useful life from intangible assets that have similar economical behaviour. An amortization pattern has to be defined that reflects the utilization of the intangible asset. In most cases, a straight-line amortization as mentioned in IAS 38.97 might be sufficient. Nevertheless, there are intangible assets that have different behaviours. A standard task is therefore the assessment of the economical behaviour to decide on the amortization pattern to be used. Typical examples of intangible assets are internet-driven databases. The user has to register on a website to attain their services, regardless of whether they are free-of-charge or associated with costs. The typical behaviour of a customer is that he will frequently come back to the website, followed by infrequent visits

---

[16] See Appendix I: Fair value on page 751 for the application of valuation techniques in accordance with IFRS 13.

then no visits at later stages. As a consequence, marketable data of the customer becomes out of date following a declining balance behaviour (if applied to all customers stored in the database). Therefore, it is appropriate to amortize the database by using a declining balance method. Evidence on the amortization pattern is delivered by the database itself, particularly by access information of customers to the website. Residual values may exist for selected assets. A consideration of a residual value is subject to the accounting requirements as defined in IAS 38.100. The residual value should always be assumed to be zero unless a third party has commited to purchase the asset at the end of its useful life, or there is an active market that will still exist at the end of the intangibles asset's useful life where a residual value can be determined by reference to that market.

Intangible assets that are identified and recorded at level III and that have to be amortized are also subject to taxation. The consideration of tax effects is based on the accounting requirements of *IAS 12 – Income Taxes*. Even if intangible asset are recognized at level III, they belong to the sphere of the acquiree. The tax base derived from separate financial statements is nil but the intangible asset will be depreciated at level III which triggers temporary differences qualifying as inside basis differences II. Due to the behaviour, deferred tax liabilities have to be recognized, again at level III. A similar approach is required on assets with an indefinite useful life. In this case, deferred tax liabilities have to be considered due to quasi-permanent differences.

Example

In identifying any assets Solenta owned but had not accounted for, the company had applied the IFRS checklist for non-accounted items and evaluated the Solenta's business. The evaluation unveiled the following items:

- A set of patents. These patents relate to technology as part of the products and the production process of cables.
- Existing orders. These orders arrived at the company before the acquisition date but are not already processed.
- Customer base.

To determine the fair value of the patents and the customer base, Flexing Cables hired an appraiser. The fair value of the existing orders was calculated by Solenta.

Item	Explanation and calculation	Amount
Patents	Patents identified were registered several years ago. They still offer protection until March 2021. Due to the technological background and the remaining protection period, the appraiser determined a fair value of these patents of 17,800k EUR.	17,800
Existing orders	Non-processed existing orders of customers include two large orders from retailers and a set of smaller orders. The expected total revenue to be achieved with these orders is 33,140k EUR. Based on historical information of similar sales and on product calculations, an average margin of 11.8% will be achieved with these orders. 33,140 *11.8%	3,900
Customer base	Depending on historical customer order patterns, the appraiser has determined a fair value of 22,500k EUR for the customer base. It is expected that the customer base will have a useful life of nine years.	22,500

The **subsequent measurement** of identified intangible assets is based on parameters defined at the initial measurement of the intangible asset. This measurement follows the ordinary accounting rules of IAS 38. If an indefinite useful life is given, intangible assets are subject to an impairment test where IAS 36 is applicable.

3.4.3.2 Indemnification assets

Warranties given by the vendor that are combined with reimbursements are often accounted for by the acquirer as indemnification assets qualifying as intangible assets. These assets are based on contractual obligations by the vendor that relate to defined conditions and the treatment of a deviation from these defined conditions. Subject to indemnifications can be all kinds of risk and uncertainty that are associated with business combinations. Typical examples of such risks and uncertainties are:

- Misstatements of balance sheet items that will result in a loss upon the adjustment of their carrying amounts. This can be applied to selected assets and liabilities or a group of them or even to parts of assets and liabilities,
- Debt risks that require additional payments by the acquirer,
- Legal risks due to pending litigations,
- Tax risks that relate to group restructurings, profit transfers in groups or local or international taxation (in particular to prior years) or any other tax commitment up to the acquisition date,
- Approvals from competitive authorities, or
- Other risks like customer defaults.

The indemnification is often combined with defined thresholds that have to be passed to trigger an indemnification. Common to this practice are arrangements that consider ceilings or floors of indemnification payments.

Even if indemnification clauses are part of the purchase agreement, the vendor is not necessarily the one who is in charge of indemnification payments. Therefore, a check is mandatory to identify who is contractually liable for such payments. In addition to the vendor, a third party that is related or not related to the vendor may indemnify the acquirer upon the default. An example of a third party related to the vendor might be the parent of the vendor if the vendor is a subsidiary in a group. An example of a non-related third party might be an insurance company that covers any defaults.

If indemnification clauses are part of the purchase agreement, an **initial check** of those clauses is mandatory. This check has to consider the underlying risk, conditions indemnifications are subject to and – particularly – the identification of those risks. Furthermore, an assessment should be made regarding the probability that an indemnification case may occur considering any recognition and measurement challenges. This should include whether or not an indemnification asset can be recorded by considering the underlying assumptions on assets. Once the initial check has been successfully passed, an accounting for an indemnification asset can start.

The **recognition** of an indemnification asset occurs at the acquisition date. Due to the contractual obligation and expected economic inflows upon a default, the indemnification assets will meet the asset specification. It has to be recorded at the acquisition date applying the following measurement principles.

The **initial measurement** of indemnification assets is based on the risk and the expected obligation that will arise upon a default and the contractual obligation regarding the indemnification expected. The amount has to mirror the expected risk of the indemnified item (the associated risk). Therefore, the measurement base is the same for both items, which is usually the acquisition date fair value. Nevertheless the carrying amount may be different. If a deviation from this measurement principle is mandatory that requires an application of other IFRS, the indemnification asset's measurement has to be based on that deviating base. Any uncertainties of the underlying risk are considered by the carrying amount of the indemnification asset. Therefore, valuation allowances or other kinds of adjustment are not necessary.

Indemnification can also be based on risks that are not related to any accounted item. To measure those risks on a fair value base, appropriate assumptions and estimation have to be used in combination with the application of fair value measurement and valuation techniques provided by *IFRS 13 – Fair Value Measurement*.[17]

Whatever the recognition scenario, contractual terms and limitations on indemnifications, as well as the collectability of an indemnification asset, have to be assessed and considered upon measurement.

The **subsequent measurement** of indemnified assets follows the same rationale than the measurement of other assets. Any adjustments in the expected risks in subsequent periods have to be reflected by the indemnification asset's carrying amount. Again the carrying amount of the indemnification asset has to be the same as the underlying indemnified item considering the contractual situation of indemnifications by the vendor.

A derecognition of the indemnification asset is required in four cases:

- A risk of the indemnified item is not any longer present that will lead to an indemnification.
- The indemnified item is sold or otherwise derecognized.
- An indemnification case occurred that utilizes the asset.
- The right to an indemnification is lost.

As long as no indemnification case occurred, a derecognition of the indemnification asset will always result in a loss to be recorded in profit & loss.

3.4.3.3. Leases

Specific guidance is also given on lease arrangements that are part of business transactions. As lease arrangements have an impact on future cash flows, it might be the case that such a lease arrangement has to be accounted for as part

---

[17] See Appendix I: Fair value on page 751 for fair value measurement in accordance with IFRS 13.

of the business combination. Therefore, lease arrangements have to be identified and checked whether or not an accounting adjustment is required. **Identification** is straightforward, as lease arrangements are always contract-based and a contract exists.

> Even if contracts are stored in central places like management, legal or purchasing departments, there is no guarantee that they cover all and everything. Some contracts might be stored at different places.

The **recognition** is based on IFRS 3.17 that requires that lease arrangements have to be classified according to *IAS 17 – Leases*. The conditions at the inception of the lease have to be applied.

Any accounting adjustments of the **initial measurement** depend on the classification of leases and on the role the acquiree has in these lease arrangements. Furthermore, items already recognized in the accounts of the acquiree have to be considered.

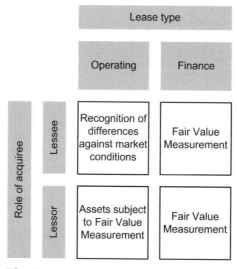

Fig. E-13   Lease matrix

- Operating lease / acquiree is lessee

    This combination might affect most lease arrangements. The general principle according to IFRS 3.B28 is that no assets and liabilities should be recognized upon operating leases. This is based on the assumption that the initial lease arrangements are based on market conditions. Two exceptions to this rule exist:

    - The lease arrangement is – compared to market conditions – favourable or unfavourable. This requires a determination of the current lease conditions and a determination of the market terms at the acquisition date. If the lease arrangement is favourable, an asset has to be recognized that presents the favourable element. This is the difference between the current conditions and the market terms, measured at fair value. If the lease arrangement is unfavourable, a liability has to be recognized. The measurement is similar to the corresponding asset.

A typical example for such a favourable situation is the rental of office space where the acquiree was granted a rent-free period. An asset has to be recognized that represent the rent-free period. This asset is independent from recognizing any deferrals relating to the rental.

- Some lease arrangements are – even if measured at market terms – attractive so that others are willing to pay a premium to step into the lease arrangement because they expect economic benefits. Such premiums are recorded as additional intangible assets.

The recognition criteria for intangible assets have to be met.

- Operating lease / acquiree is lessor
  Operating leases, where assets are leased out, are always measured by the fair value of the lease arrangement. These fair values are considered and incorporated as part of the fair value of the asset subject to a lease.
- Finance lease / acquiree is lessee
  No specific guidance is given by IFRS 3 on this combination. Therefore, the general recognition and measurement requirements apply: fair value measurement at the acquisition date.
- Finance lease / acquiree is lessor
  No specific guidance is given by IFRS 3 on this combination. Therefore, the general recognition and measurement requirements apply: fair value measurement at the acquisition date.

Lease arrangements may be subject to changes in the classification. If contractual changes subsequent to the inception of the lease occur, a reclassification at the acquisition date might be appropriate. Group accounting policies have to be considered when determining a reclassification. Otherwise, the initial classification should not change.

Upon the recognition of additional assets and liabilities, the **subsequent measurement** is based on the remaining contractual period of the lease arrangement. Assets have to be amortized over the remaining lease period; liabilities have to be released.

3.4.3.4. *Non-accounted & contingent liabilities*

Like assets acquired, liabilities assumed to be part of the business combination have to be accounted for. Due to the different handling of liabilities in business combinations, a recording might be necessary for selected or defined business transactions even if an accounting in the accounts of the acquiree is not allowed. In most cases, liabilities to be accounted for in business combinations relate to contingent liabilities of the acquiree. A recording at group level (more precisely at level III) is mandatory as they are part in the determination of considerations transferred due to the acquisition process. Therefore, contingent liabilities are subject to the deviating recognition criteria required by IFRS 3.22.

The **identification** of contingent liabilities is as time-consuming as the identification of tangible assets. This is because contingencies can arise in nearly every business transaction without being immediately identified. If such contingencies are identified, the question of an appropriate recognition and measurement basis arises. Therefore, as for intangible assets, the application of identification techniques is necessary to systematically scan the acquiree for any contingencies that require recognition as contingent liabilities. Such techniques can be taken from professional auditing techniques auditors often apply:

- Analyzing the rationale of the business and identifying their value drivers,
- Analyzing sales, purchasing, production and employment activities, patterns and maintenances,
- Inventorying, scanning and analyzing of contracts in all business units, departments and other organizational units of the acquiree, and
- Further identification and analysis activities as appropriate.

The search for and the identification of contingencies is often combined with the identification of intangible assets. This search for contingent liabilities should not be limited to the acquiree itself. In some situations the business combination itself initiates contingencies that require an appropriate accounting. Typical examples are the integration of the acquiree as a new subsidiary in the group or a restructuring of the acquiree because of its business performance. If assets are relocated due to commercial needs that are subject to grants, the business combination may trigger a repayment of such grants, either in full or in part. The following list will provide support on selected contingencies that may qualify for recognition, either as a contingent liability, an ordinary liability or a provision as a consequence of a business combination based on the accounting requirements of IFRS 3.22.

Category	Contingency	Additional explanation	Classification[18]
Legal			
	Insurance	Subject to IFRS 4 accounting.	/.
	Pending litigations, appeals and similar cases	Always require consideration as the outcome of these litigations is unclear. Recognition criteria are always fulfilled.	Contingent liability
	Settlements in process	Even if a future economic outflow is not certain, other criteria are fulfilled to recognize settlements in process. Depending on the stage of negotiations, settlements in process qualify as contingent liabilities or current / non-current liabilities.	Contingent liability
	Violation of legal requirements	Legal requirements that are not followed might be subject to fines and penalties. Recording of a contingent liability or provision required. Provision, if it is likely that payment occurs, otherwise contingent liability.	Contingent liability or provision
	Warranties	Legal obligations due to warranties given to customers may qualify as contingent liabilities. This depends on the type of warranties given: • Products: Defined or guaranteed attributes of products, use or similar conditions may qualify for contingent liabilities, provided that firm commitments are received by customers, either directly or indirectly. Measurement usually based on historical return rates of defect products or similar measureable conditions. Contingent liabilities will lapse at the end of the warranty period. • Sales: Extended warranties subject to contingent liabilities that lapse at the end of the warranty period. Inherent warranties are not subject to contingencies. • Others: Individual check, if any present obligations exist on past activities.	Contingent liabilities
Contractual	Onerous contracts	Onerous contracts are characterized as contracts where (unavoidable) costs to satisfy the contract exceed its economic benefit. The definition is very broad. In can include running costs allocable to the contract; it can also include any penalties or fines due to failure or performance in executing the contract. Recognition and measurement of onerous contracts follow a modified accounting approach according to IAS 37.67 and IFRS 3.22 that demand the consideration of the present obligation in conjunction without the requirement of economic outflows. Onerous contracts are measured by the lower of costs to fulfil the contract and any "compensation or penalties arising from failure to fulfil the contract" (or in other words: any costs to terminate or not executing the contract). The scope of onerous contracts can also cover assets if these assets are dedicated to the onerous contract. In such situations, additional allowances have to be recognized after the adjustment due to an impairment test if necessary.	Provisions

[18] The classification follows the ordinary behaviour of obligations: Provisions, liabilities, contingent liabilities, even if contingent liabilities are accounted for in business combinations.

(continued)

Category	Contingency	Additional explanation	Classification[18]
	Reimbursements	Reimbursements of funds or grants to any third party as a consequence of a contractual obligation have to be accounted for provided that contractual obligations are not met that trigger such a reimbursement. The past event usually violates contractual terms, so if there is an obligation it has to be checked against the contract and the type of violation.	Liability or provision
Commercial			
	Future operating losses	Usually no consideration due to the missing past event.	./.
	Late delivery penalties	Late deliveries are no past events. Instead they are current events. No consideration. But: check if the underlying contract becomes onerous due to the penalty.	./.
	Maintenance, repair and overhaul	Except for repairs and maintenance obligations under leases, IAS 37 does not permit any recognition of such obligations. In business combination, the recording of an obligation might be appropriate if it relates to required maintenance, repair or overhaul activities of assets that are due and not conducted before the acquisition date. This does not apply to future commitments or obligations.	Liability or provision
	Redundancies	Even if IFRS 3.22 is referring to IAS 37 regarding the handling of contingent liabilities, redundancy payments are not covered by that standard. Instead, measurement principles of *IAS 19 – Employee Benefits* have to be applied.	./.
	Refunds	If a published policy is applied and the acquiree sticks to this policy, a recognition is required whether there is an economic outflow. Measurement is based on historical refunds.	Provision or liability
	Repayments	Either triggered by special events (if these events are likely to occur) of the acquiree or as a consequence of the business combination. Relates often to government grants.	Liabilities or contingent liabilities
	Restructuring	Provisions for restructuring are permissible only if a restructuring would already have been required before the business combination took place and the vendor was entitled to record such provisions. Requirements of IAS 37.72 need to be considered. Restructuring does not qualify as a contingent liability due to the probability of restructuring needs > 50%.	Provision
	Vouchers, campaigns and similar items	Vouchers and campaigns are used to stimulate the market to purchase goods and services by offering discounts for a defined period. The issue of a voucher confers an obligation even if there may be no economic benefit. This is different to IAS 37.	Contingent liability

Category	Contingency	Additional explanation	Classification[18]
Environmental	Decommission & restoration	A use of public infrastructure, use of land or activities of the extractive industries like oil, gas or other natural resources are often combined with obligations to remove or dismantle all assets associated with the use. Often this includes the requirement, to restore land and public infrastructure and bring it into the original condition.	Provision
		If a direct allocation of these obligations to defined non-current assets is possible, a netting and a presentation as net assets is appropriate at the acquisition date. This is because the obligations will perform a part of the net asset according to IAS 16.18. If obligation relate to a portfolio of assets, a separate presentation and measurement might be appropriate. A typical example is the obliged restoration of public ground by a gas utility company. The gas net in the ground consists of different types of tube to ensure that a constant supply under defined conditions (e.g. pressure) is given. Such a net cannot be split up into individual assets but it can be grouped depending on the supply and distribution characteristic. Therefore, a separate treatment of decommission and restoration obligations following the underlying asset portfolio is recommended.	
	Environmental pollution, contaminations and similar issues	Cleaning either subject to legal requirements that are certain or widely published clean-up policy.	Provision or contingent liability
Others	Guarantees	Guarantees are often provided for another entity. In groups, the parent often provides guarantees or indemnification for its subsidiaries to third parties. Guarantees are treated as financial guarantee contracts that are subject to IFRS 9 accounting.	

Tab. E-9 List of potential contingent liabilities that may arise in business combinations

There are situations where risks associated with contingent liabilities are covered by other instruments such as insurances, indemnifications and warranties. In most cases, the coverage will lead to a reimbursement. It is important to check for non-accounted liabilities. The instrument that provides that coverage has to be accounted for as an indemnification asset.[19]

The **recognition** of all kinds of liability, and particularly contingent liabilities in a business combination, is exempt from regular recognition rules. Contingent liabilities acquired in a business combination can be recognized even if it is not probable that an economic outflow occurs in accordance with IFRS3.22.[20] Never-the-less, all other criteria have to be fulfilled:

- Past event;
- Present obligation.

The rationale for this exception is based on the idea that the risk of a potential outflow is measured by its fair value and the acquirer is willing to remove the risk by payment. To account for contingent liabilities requires a determination of a past event and a present obligation. The past event has to refer to events before the acquisition date. If this obligation exists, it is appropriate to recognize a liability, if it can be measured and found to be reliable.

Even if the recognition is exempt from applying the recognition standards according to IFRS 3.22, the **initial measurement** has to comply with the requirements of IFRS 3.18. Therefore, all liabilities assumed have to be measured in accordance with their fair values. That will be the cash value in case of payables and provisions, either undiscounted or discounted, or fair value in the case of any contingent liabilities. Again, the fair value measurement principles of IFRS 13 have to be applied if necessary.[21]

Other than the initial measurement, **subsequent measurement** is subject to a mixture of the application of IFRS 3 and IAS 37. While contingent liabilities are recognized as part of the purchase price allocation, a pure application of IAS would immediately require an elimination at the end of the period because IAS 37.36 requires to use " [...] the best estimate of the expenditure required to settle the present obligation at the end of the reporting period". This is contrary to the requirement of IFRS 3.22 to account for contingent liabilities. Therefore, the subsequent measurement is based in IFRS 3.56. According to this standard, provisions, liabilities and contingent liabilities that arise from a business combination are measured: by the higher of the amount recognized in accordance with IAS 37 and the initial amount recognized (less cumulative amortization recognized in accordance with IAS 18 if appropriate). Excluded from this application are all liabilities that are measured in accordance with IFRS 9 (so financial liabilities, instruments, trade payables and similar items). Whether a contingent liability is subject to further recognition and measurement depends on the underlying business transaction that needs to be assessed at the end of every period.

---

[19] See chapter E -3.4.3.2 on page 170.

[20] This is contrary to IAS 37 that requires the probability of an economic outflow.

[21] See Appendix I: Fair value measurement on page 751.

Example

In search of any risks Solenta might have been exposed to, all past business transactions and events had been evaluated. The evaluation unveiled one contingent liability only, a patent infringement: Solenta had made use of a competitor's patent. At the time, negotiations between the lawyers of both parties were continuing. Whatever progress was made, Solenta's lawyer expected that an agreement regarding the patent infringement was not likely: litigation was. Even if the patent infringement qualified as a contingent liability it had to be considered part of the purchase price allocation.

Item	Explanation and calculation	Amount
Patent infringement	Based on the current stage of negotiations with the competitor's lawyer, Solenta lawyer expects that litigation is likely. Based on the experience of the lawyer in similar cases, a court decision can be expected within five years from the acquisition date. The maximum exposure due to this litigation is assumed by the lawyer:	(8,000)
	• Penalty payment 8,000 k EUR • Lawyer fees 1,200 k EUR • Court and other fees 120 k EUR	
	In total, the maximum exposure could reach an amount of 9,320 k EUR. The present value of this exposure is 8,000 k EUR based on a market rate of 3.1% for a period of five years.	

3.4.3.5. *Tax assets and liabilities*

Taxation is always part of a business combination. Usually, it starts with a tax due diligence to obtain any risks or uncertainties associated with the acquiree. Taxes are also an integral part of purchase price allocations as the initial accounting of tax effects arising in business combinations will be executed during the initial consolidation. Furthermore, post business combination activities are required to optimize the tax position in the group by considering tax effects and opportunities through the acquiree.

In the context of a purchase price allocation, tax effects have to be analyzed and initially accounted for. Here, the accounting for taxes is limited to those effects that are not already considered (like the conversion from local GAAP towards IFRS at level I and valuation adjustments for recognized asset acquired and liabilities assumed at level II to align with the group's accounting policies).[22] Tax effects that are not already recognized usually cover three large areas:

- Temporary differences that result from the recognition of previously not-accounted for assets acquired and liabilities assumed;
- Tax assets that relate to any unused tax credits and tax losses;
- Tax assets and liabilities that relate to tax rules of the jurisdiction where the acquiree resides.

Like all other assets and liabilities, tax assets and liabilities, whether they refer to current or deferred taxes, need to be identified, recognized and measured.

---

[22] These topics are discussed in other chapters.

The **identification** of taxation issues that result in the recording of tax assets and liabilities is primarily subject to the tax due diligence and therefore not necessarily an issue for the purchase price allocation. Nevertheless, some situations exist in which identification is required during a purchase price allocation. Such situations are always follow-ups of issues arising during the purchase price allocation.

The **recognition** of tax assets and liabilities depends on the underlying tax effects. A determination depends on the three large areas of tax effects.

As far as non-accounted assets acquired and liabilities assumed are involved, temporary differences for these assets have to be estimated. While these items are recorded at level III and therefore outside the scope from taxation, temporary differences exist that equal the carrying amount of these assets. The carrying amount for tax purposes is always nil. As these temporary differences are allocable to the sphere of the acquiree, the tax rate of the acquiree has to be applied in measuring deferred tax assets and liabilities resulting from non-accounted assets acquired and liabilities assumed. Deferred tax assets and liabilities follow the underlying items. They are therefore also recorded at level III.

Unused tax credits and tax losses, as part of a business combination, always have two aspects: tax effects that relate to the acquiree and those that relate to the acquirer. Accounting for both effects is treated in different ways. If the acquiree has unused tax credits and tax losses, an opportunity-check of these items as assets is a mandatory task. This presumes that the tax rules of the jurisdiction where the acquiree resides allows further utilization. Some tax jurisdictions do not accept the utilization of unused tax credits and tax losses if the "environment" of an entity changes. This may include changes in business purpose or shareholder structure. Unused tax credits and tax losses are not only subject to non-recognition but may also be destroyed. The intention of such tax rules is not to allow new shareholders to benefit from tax reliefs for their business that relate to old taxation issues that might be allocable to the old ones. Despite these taxation basics, recording unused tax credits and tax losses as deferred tax assets is mandatory, if the acquiree can prove that utilization is given. The measurement of unused tax credits and tax losses is subject to the underlying planning of the acquiree.[23]

A different scenario exists, if unused tax credits and tax losses are available to the acquirer. If the new subsidiary is used for utilization of unused tax credits and losses through a tax unity or another tax vehicle, then this transaction is a separate transaction that has to be accounted for separately from the business combination. A capitalization of these unused tax credits and losses by recording of a deferred tax assets has to be accounted for through profit & loss. As the capitalization requires evidence that use is given by forecasting the profits of future periods through an appropriate plan, a revised plan is required taking the performance of the acquiree into account as a further element. This requires the involvement of management accounting as they have to prepare the revised plan.

---

[23] See chapter K -2.3.2 on page 668 for detailed explanations regarding the accounting of unused tax credits and tax losses.

The starting point is the acquisition date to consider the effects of the first period the acquiree contributes to the performance of the group.

Tax assets and liabilities sometimes relate to specific tax rules of jurisdictions. Some jurisdictions grant special tax exemptions and reliefs to companies and investors for investments that are in the interest of that jurisdiction, e.g. for economic reasons.[24] Such exemptions and reliefs may even result in non-payment of taxes. As this is an advantage, it might be appropriate to account as a separate asset – either current or deferred. In such a case it is important to differentiate the origin:

- If the advantage relates to specific assets of the acquirer and its tax base, a recording of the advantage is given. Any future economic benefits that arise from this tax advantage have to be considered in determining the fair value of the (underlying) asset.
- If the advantage relates to the acquiree and its business (and hence the taxable net profit), recognition is not appropriate.
- If the advantage is based on an individual contractual agreement between the acquiree and tax authorities, the advantage is eligible to be recognized as a separate intangible asset.

The existence and accounting of specific tax rules is usually part of the tax due diligence that needs to be considered at this stage.

The **recognition** of deferred tax asset and liabilities is usually limited to temporary and quasi-permanent differences only. Therefore, an estimation of the appropriate tax rate of the acquiree in conjunction with the tax type is required as the acquiree might be subject to different types of income tax. Some tax assets and liabilities will need to be presented as current; this may be the case if they relate to specific tax rules of the jurisdiction. A separation from deferred tax assets and liabilities is necessary in such cases.

The **initial measurement** of deferred tax assets and liabilities follows the ordinary accounting rules as defined in *IAS 12 – Income Taxes*.[25] IFRS 3.24 defines an exception from the overall fair value principle by reference to IAS12. Accordingly, the **subsequent measurement** is based on the same accounting rules.

> **Example**
>
> Solenta's tax due diligence, performed by an external auditor, did not reveal any unusual tax exposures. No tax audit was running at the time, all taxes had been paid, tax returns had been filed on time, and, due to the successful past business performance, no unused tax losses or credits existed. Therefore, the only topics to be considered were deferred tax items that related to non-accounted assets and liabilities. The tax base of these items was nil. Solenta had to apply a tax rate of 29.8%.
>
> The following tax effects had to be accounted for:

---

[24] Sometimes also called "tax holidays".
[25] See chapter K -2 on page 656 regarding the accounting of deferred taxes in groups.

Item	Carrying amount	Deferred tax impact	
		Assets	Liabilities
Patents	17,800		(5,304)
Customer base	3,000		(6,705)
Pending orders	22,500		(1,162)
Property (land)	900		(268)
Financial assets	9		(3)
Bad debt allowances	220		(65)
Environmental pollution	(3,000)	894	
Patent infringement	(8,000)	2,384	
		3,278	(13,507)

3.5. Goodwill and non-controlling interests

As IFRS 3 is a standard that is jointly established by the FASB and IASB as a result of the business combination project phase II, it combines different views of underlying theories. This gives the opportunity to account for business transactions by choosing between several options for an accounting of goodwill and non-controlling interests. The overall philosophy of measuring all items involved at acquisition by their fair value (with the exception of items on a different base), will generate differences that have to be caught. This is because an acquisition will never result in an equal exchange as the vendor usually expects a profit to be made upon the sale of "his" company. From an acquirer's point of view, the consideration he gave to acquire a new subsidiary has to be allocated to all identified assets acquired and liabilities assumed. While it is not possible to allocate the full consideration to all assets and liabilities involved, a difference is left that has to be allocated to goodwill. To be more precise, goodwill is the residual amount between the consideration transferred and the remeasured net assets (that consists of assets acquired and liabilities assumed by their fair values).

Depending on the acquired company and the negotiation process between the acquirer and the vendor, **goodwill** usually includes several components:

- Intangible assets excluded from a separate accounting

  Selected assets are not subject to recognition due to IFRS 3 rules. In addition, items that do not meet the definition of an asset but have some kind of value to the acquirer are subsumed into goodwill. Examples of such items are human capital, assembled workforces or potential customer contracts.

- Assets and liabilities that cannot be measured reliably

  This applies particularly to intangible assets that are not separable from the acquiree, have uncertain cash flows or do not provide a reliable measurement base.

- Expected synergies

  Synergies are often expected by the acquirer for various commercial reasons. Typical expectations are economies of scale, to complement one another, new markets or market access and similar reasons. Such synergies can only be created by successful transitions of both – the acquirer and the acquiree – to new integrated structures. Surveys have shown that expected synergies are overestimated by management in most acquisitions.

- Excess payments necessary to acquire the target company
  Excess payments are often paid just to own the target company, whether or not the excess payment reflects future economic benefits.

Separate treatment of these components is not appropriate. Goodwill will be measured, due to its residual nature, as one amount only.

If an interest in the acquiree existed before the acquisition date, the acquisition is treated as a step-acquisition or acquisition achieved in stages. Special accounting rules apply to such situations. Interests previously held in the acquiree have to be remeasured to reflect the fair value as of the acquisition date. This requires an application of appropriate measurement techniques. These cases are discussed in detail in chapter I-3.

Goodwill is also affected by the percentage of shares acquired. If not all shares have been acquired, minority shareholders have a non-controlling interest, which has to be considered. IFRS 3 (rev. 2008) introduced alternatives to account for goodwill by considering non-controlling interests. This option can be applied individually to each business combination as stated in IFRS 3.32.

Two options are available to preparers for the presentation and measurement of goodwill:

- Purchased goodwill method
  The purchased goodwill method recognizes only the goodwill that is attributable to the acquirer.

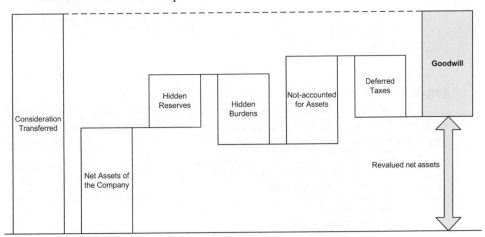

Fig. E-14   Goodwill calculation, purchased goodwill method

The following calculation scheme will help in determining the goodwill attributable to the acquirer:

	Consideration transferred
+	Fair value of any previously held interest in acquire
−	Net assets of the company
−	Hidden reserves
+	Hidden burdens
−	Not-accounted for assets
+/−	Deferred taxes
=	Goodwill / badwill attributable to the acquirer

Tab. E-10   Goodwill calculation scheme, purchased goodwill method

All assets and liabilities have to be considered on a proportionate basis to determine the good- or "bad"-will attributable to the acquirer.
- Full goodwill method

The full goodwill method recognizes the full goodwill of the acquiree and assigns the portion attributable to non-controlling interests to them. As a consequence, the goodwill recognized is increased compared to the goodwill of the purchased goodwill method.

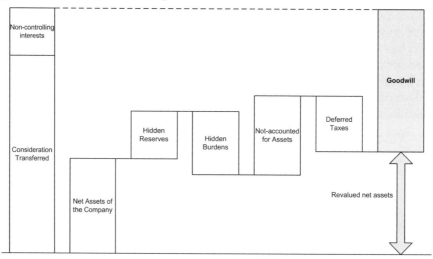

Fig. E-15   Goodwill calculation, full goodwill method

The following calculation scheme will help in determining the goodwill (which is attributable to the acquirer and the non-controlling interests):

	Consideration transferred
+	Fair value of any previously held interest in acquire
+	Fair value, attributable to non-controlling interests
−	Net assets of the company
−	Hidden reserves
+	Hidden burdens
−	Not-accounted for assets
+/−	Deferred taxes
=	Goodwill / badwill

Tab. E-11   Goodwill calculation scheme, full goodwill method

As a consequence, increased goodwill is recorded that includes not only the goodwill attributable to the acquirer but also the goodwill that is attributable to non-controlling interests.

Involving **non-controlling interests** in the determination of goodwill by applying the full goodwill method stipulates that non-controlling interests are measurable by their fair values. Therefore, general measurement principles apply not only to assets acquired and liabilities assumed but also to non-controlling interests as outlined in IFRS 3.19. The non-controlling interest is measured by its fair value or by the non-controlling interest's percentage (the proportionate share of the present ownership's instruments) in recognized net assets. The fair value of non-controlling interests can be derived from the quoted price in active markets or by valuation techniques, in the absence of active markets.[26] Premiums or discounts related to control should be considered similar to the consideration by market participants. An appropriate documentation has to provide evidence to the auditors.

If the acquiree accounts for (pre-existing) goodwill in its investments, goodwill is excluded from the calculation of the proportionate share of the non-controlling interest as goodwill is a residual amount and not an asset that meets the definition of an asset as defined in the framework.

Due to the option of an individual measurement of non-controlling interests in each business combination as stated in IFRS 3.19, either the purchased goodwill or the full goodwill method can be applied. This is contrary to the consistent application of accounting policies as demanded by IAS 8.13.

Non-controlling interests are presented in the consolidated statement of financial position as part of equity but below all equity categories of the acquirer that are attributable to its shareholders. The carrying amount reflects the underlying method chosen (purchased- or full-goodwill method) and all measurement effects that arise during the initial recognition and measurement including such items as share-based payments.[27]

In rare cases, the acquisition of a subsidiary will result in a **bargain purchase**. The acquired net assets exceed the consideration transferred. While such situations are not usual in business transactions with third parties at arms-length, IFRS 3 requires a reassessment of the purchase price allocation. This reassessment has to ensure that an over- or under-statement of the carrying amounts of acquired assets and liabilities due to improper calculations or assumptions is not given. IFRS 3.36 demands a review of the following items:

- Correct identification of all assets acquired and liabilities assumed;
- Correct identification and measurement of non-controlling interests (if fair value option is applied);
- Recognition of additional assets identified during the review;
- Correct measurement of considerations transferred;
- Measurement of previously held equity interest in the acquiree;
- Review of measurement processes.

---

[26] IFRS 13 may hold in determining the fair value of non-controlling interests. See also chapter N -3 on page 753 for fair value measures.

[27] See chapter E-6.4.2. on page 229 for details.

Based on the given requirements, the following checklist can be used for the reassessment of the purchase price allocation. The reassessment should not be seen as a formal task that confirms the initial calculation. It is more or less an assessment that has to consider also the reasons for a bargain purchase and the effects arising in a purchase price allocation. IFRS 3.BC371 – 3.BC381 explain the rationale behind the reassessment.

No.	Check
1)	Are all assets and liabilities accounted for properly measured?
2)	Are all non-accounted assets, liabilities and risks identified and measured?
3)	Are all parameters used for valuations and measurement explainable and consistent to the market? Do they fit into the company's environment? Are assumptions made by management consistent to the market and to the development of the acquiree and acquirer?
4)	Are those IFRS rules considered that may explain the negative differences in subsequent periods (e.g. deferred taxes)?
5)	Are all components of the purchase agreement considered?
6)	Are all pre-existing relationships identified and considered? Are they considered by the purchase price?
7)	Are all elements of the consideration transferred observed regarding potential compensations or multi-component contracts or their elements?
8)	Are all elements of the consideration transferred that are based on future events identified and measured reliably without any omissions?
9)	Is the range where future events may realize properly assumed by management?
10)	Are any mechanical errors avoided (e.g. calculation of sums, application of formulas)?

Tab. E-12   Checklist for bargain purchases

If the reassessment still unveils a negative difference (badwill), an immediate gain has to be recorded through profit & loss. Due to the adjustment of consideration transferred through profit & loss, it is obvious that the bargain purchase does not affect an involvement of non-controlling interests. The allocation of the gain attributable to the acquirer due to measurement or other issues of the business combination is confirmed in IFRS 3.34.

Goodwill is also subject to an allocation to **cash-generating units**. A cash-generating unit represents "… the smallest identifiable group of assets that generates cash inflows that are largely independent of the cash inflows from other assets or group of assets".[28] Due to this definition, a commercial, rather than legal, view is taken on goodwill for the purpose of impairment testing. As a consequence, an allocation of goodwill established during the business combination has to be allocated to cash-generating units. IAS 36.84 provides a gratuitous period up to the end of the subsequent period following the period where the acquisition took place. This is a maximum period of 24 months. Coverage of the purchase price allocation's measurement period is always given so that any effects arising as part

---

[28] Definition in IAS 36.6.

of an adjustment during the measurement period can be considered for the allocation of goodwill. Depending on the type of acquisition, goodwill may be:

- Allocated to one cash-generating unit,
- Allocated separately to two or more cash-generating units,
- Allocated to two or more cash-generating units in total (if goodwill cannot be separated), or
- Form a new cash-generating unit.

Which case has to be applied depends on the businesses of the acquiree and the acquirer as well as the intended group structure after the business combination took place.

While IAS 36.80 demands an allocation of goodwill to one cash-generating unit from the acquisition date, this task should be executed immediately even if this is not part of an ordinary purchase price allocation. The type of allocation is not specified in IAS 36. Therefore, any method that reflects a fair allocation can be used. In selecting an appropriate method, some considerations have to be borne in mind:

- Fair value of identifiable assets or the cash-generating unit.
- Consistency between the method selected and already disclosed facts on goodwill.
- The underlying purchase price allocation.
- Level where assets are tested for impairments should be the same where the operation is managed.

Examples of proven methods for goodwill allocation are:

- Relative fair values of identifiable net assets,
- Relative fair values of the cash-generating unit, or
- Proven reserves in each cash-generating unit.

If all considerations are taken into account and an appropriate allocation method is applied, goodwill has to be allocated to a cash-generating unit. While a cash-generating unit can consist of goodwill allocations from several subsidiaries, the composition of that goodwill, as well as any movements and adjustments, should be subject to an auxiliary calculation. This calculation becomes important if goodwill is established in a currency other than the functional currency of the group. Foreign exchange effects arise that will follow goodwill and that need also a proper documentation for recording.[29]

> Document the allocation of goodwill in an auxiliary calculation that includes goodwill allocation of all subsidiaries. This auxiliary calculation should also include any movements, adjustments due to impairment losses, allocations and disposals. It will help in executing the impairment test at each subsequent period.

---

[29] See chapter K -1.7.1 on page 650 regarding the dependency between goodwill and foreign exchange effects.

As it is possible to measurements of considerations transferred and all assets and liabilities acquired during the twelve month **measurement period**, adjustments of non-controlling interests and goodwill are also possible. Adjustments that relate to non-controlling interests may arise either by an incomplete or inappropriate initial fair value measurement that is derived from the market or adjustments due to an erroneous application of the proportionate share of the non-controlling interest.

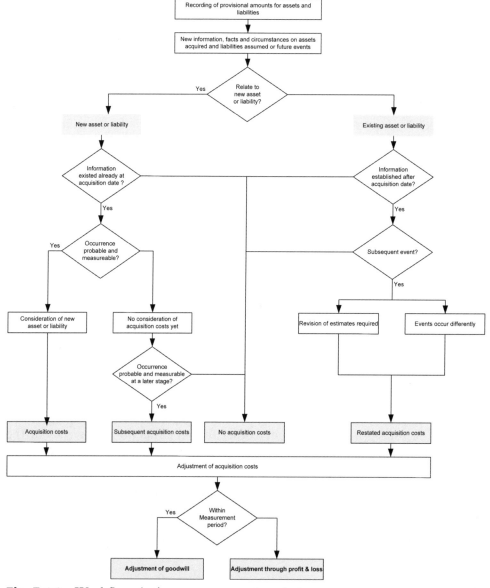

Fig. E-16   Workflow during measurement period

Adjustments of non-controlling interests may also arise upon changes of assets acquired and liabilities assumed in combination with the application of the proportionate share of the non-controlling interests. Adjustments of non-controlling interests are against goodwill during the measurement period or through profit & loss after the measurement period. Goodwill adjustments during the measurement period occur for every change made on assets acquired and liabilities assumed, or non-controlling interests in the acquire, due to the residual character of goodwill. Once the measurement period lapses, changes to goodwill are no longer possible.

The **initial measurement** of goodwill and non-controlling interests is based on an equity consolidation and is the result of purely technical activity. This is because all measurement tasks that have an impact on goodwill are executed before. The expected goodwill as calculated for the business combination should be confirmed by the equity consolidation. This assumes a correct measurement and recording of non-controlling interests.

Example

In determining the goodwill that would result from the acquisition of Solenta, Flexing Cables had elected to apply the purchased goodwill method. Based on the identified and measured assets and liabilities, goodwill allocable to the group was calculated by the following scheme:

	Consideration transferred		77,982
	IFRS net assets of the company as of 1.4.2013		47,170
+	Hidden reserves property		900
+	Patents		17,800
+	Customer orders		3,900
+	Customer base		22,500
+	Fair value adjustment financial assets		9
−	Patent infringement provisions		(8,000)
−	Environmental pollution provisions		(3,000)
+	Pre-existing relationships		220
+	Deferred tax assets		3,278
−	Deferred tax liabilities		(13,507)
=	Total assets Solenta		71,269
−	Assets allocable to the Flexing Cables	80% of 71,269	57,015
=	Goodwill attributable to Flexing Cables		21,967

The **subsequent measurement** of goodwill is fully based on the initial equity consolidation and an impairment test that depends on the allocation of the goodwill to cash-generating units.[30] If an impairment test passed successfully, goodwill established at the initial consolidation is kept untouched. Other than goodwill, the carrying amount of non-controlling interests is subject to an ordinary recording of profits & losses of the current period as well as any transactions at shareholder level.

---

[30] See chapter F -8.2 on page 348 for a detailed discussion on goodwill.

3.6. Business vs. assets and liabilities

According to IFRS 3, it has to be checked upfront if a business combination is present and if the acquisition covers a business or just a collection of assets and liabilities.

IFRS 3.B5 defines a **business combination** as a transaction or event that constitutes control over an acquiree. Control and its constitution can be obtained in various ways; a specific method in obtaining control is not required.[31] The underlying transaction and its understanding are therefore important as the knowledge of how the business combination is structured can help to assess control. Transactions of business combinations are often based on legal, tax and shareholder requirements, so assessment of control – and who finally obtains control – is not easy to identify. Typical examples of transactions applied in business combinations are:

- Acquisition of a business as a new subsidiary. This can include a single business or company. This can also include the acquisition of a company acting as a parent of a group of businesses,
- Merger of the acquired net assets of a business into the acquirer's business,
- Transfers of net assets from a company to another one. Alternatively, the owner can transfer their equity in a similar way.
- Transfers of net assets of all involved companies into a new entity. Again, the owner can transfer their equity in a similar way.
- Obtaining control by owners of a company over another company,
- Equalization arrangements between companies,
- Contractual agreements between companies to bind them to each other,
- Pass-through arrangements where a third party is the beneficiary to all economic returns, or
- Arrangements involving trustees.

Even if IFRS 3.B6 has the focus on net assets, transactions might be realized either by an asset deal or a share deal.

Upon a positive check of a business combination, a **business** has to be identified that meets the definition of business according to IFRS3.A.[32] To clarify how to identify a business, IFRS 3.B7 has made use of old definitions of a business (or operation). According to these definitions, a business is some kind of black box that requires an input, then processes that input so that an output will result.

- Input
    The traditional definition of economic resources focuses on materials, labour and capital. IFRS 3.B7a has adopted that definition slightly to cover all types of asset and liabilities required for processing. Accordingly, inputs are all economic resources that are used for processing. This includes the

---

[31] See chapter C -1 on page 44 regarding the definition of control and the ways, how control can be obtained.

[32] See previous chapter regarding the definition.

ability to obtain access to materials and rights (a synonym for materials), employees (labour) and non-current assets and intellectual property (capital). Depending on the industry, the mixture and weighting of all three components can vary. Production companies require more materials and fixed assets. By contrast, contracts with employees and customers are the core for service and consulting companies.

- Processes

    A process is an activity or a system of movements that transfer an input into an output and creates (additional) value. It is usually based on a documented structure that describes how and when the process has to be executed by skilled and experienced employees and management in a structured way. Such value-adding processes are often supported by management processes that focus on sourcing, operations and strategy. Administrative processes like accounting, HR, IT and legal are not inside the scope of these processes as they do not add value.

    IFRS 3.B7b has changed the original definition by allocating the underlying activities to systems, standards, protocols, conventions or rules applied to inputs. Even if the definition of the process is different, the overall understanding of a process as part of a business does not change.

- Output

    This is the result of a process applied to inputs. As the process is intended to create value, an economic benefit should be expected. This economic benefit will arise in different forms: dividends, lower costs or competitive advantages are just some examples. The benefit accrues to owners, investors, members or other participants.

Even if these three items represent a business, their presence and behaviour can change depending on the industry, the structure of the business and the stage of the business. Common for all types of business, inputs and processes are mandatory. Outputs may change depending on the stage of a business. If such businesses include goodwill, a business always can be assumed. Newly established businesses and development stage entities may even have no output. Therefore, IFRS 3.B7 does not necessarily demand an output as a mandatory element in defining a business. Nevertheless, it defines an "integrated set of activities and assets" that is "capable of being conducted and managed" as a business. Other or additional characteristics have to be considered in conducting if all activities focusing on becoming a business qualify as a business.

A business subject to a business combination or acquisition does not necessarily have to include all activities, inputs and processes. It is sufficient if the only part of the business that is subject to the business combination fulfils this requirement. Best evidence is given, if such a (partial) business can be managed and operated by a third party, e.g. a further market participant. Neither is it important if this partial business was treated as a business by the vendor nor if the acquirer treats it as a business.

Because of the complex dependencies, the interaction with the industry, the structure and set-up of the business, assessment of whether the business is a business or not is sometimes difficult to realize. Therefore, a consideration of all facts and circumstances, including the environment the business operates in, is required. This should include an acclamation and judgement of the whole business context.

Due to the nature and definition of a business, some acquisitions will not meet the criteria of being a business. Typical examples of such acquisitions are:

- Shell companies

    Shell companies are "empty" companies that have no business. The acquisition has to be accounted for like the formation of a new corporation.

- Asset-holding companies

    In some businesses, it is common practice to have companies that just hold defined assets for legal purposes. Typical examples are the holding of intellectual property, exploration and evaluation rights, investment properties and similar assets. A transfer of these assets is often based upon the sale of the asset-holding company. Due to the nature of this company, the business is located elsewhere. By contrast, if asset-holding companies have a set of assets that are managed actively by the company, a business case is given.

- Group of financial assets or liabilities

    A group of financial assets and liabilities will never qualify as a business even if those assets and liabilities are traded on the market. Active management (the portfolio management and the trading in the market) is handled by other parties.

- Tax assets

    In some jurisdictions it is still possible to acquire shell companies which carry tax losses and can be utilized by other companies. Again, the business is missing: tax assets due to former losses have to be accounted for individually.

If identification fails and a **business is not given**, all assets and liabilities have to be identified, measured and recorded individually. The purchase price and any other form of consideration transferred or to be transferred have to be allocated to the assets and liabilities; goodwill will not exist. This approach, as defined in IFRS 3.2b, will generate some conflicts for the measurement of selected assets and liabilities:

- Monetary items

    An allocation of a fraction of the purchase price to monetary items like cash, loans or similar assets and liabilities (e.g. tax payables or receivables) does not make any sense. Such items are always measured by their nominal values.[33]

---

[33] For a list of all monetary items refer to chapter K -1.8 on page 655.

- Financial instruments

  As financial instruments – whether instruments are assets or liabilities – are usually recorded at fair value in conjunction with IAS 39 or IFRS 9, the allocation practice of IFRS 3.2b will result in a deviating carrying amount of the financial instruments from its fair value. This requires an immediate adjustment, either through other comprehensive income or as day-one gains or losses.

- Share based payments

  If contributions transferred are based on equity instruments, a measurement of the equity instruments with its fair value is applicable due to the requirements of IRS 2.10. Again, this may result in a deviating measurement base.

- Taxes

  Deferred tax assets that are based on tax losses of prior periods have to be accounted for in accordance with IAS 12.34 based on their recoverable amounts.

This regulatory gap will offer to account for identified assets and liabilities by applying either IFR3 or other standards.

The accounting for individual assets and liabilities will trigger further activities. In the absence of a business combination, all acquisition related costs and all financing costs have to be allocated to assets according to their individual standards. Furthermore, accounting requirements of deferred taxes according to *IAS 12 – Income Taxes* have to be considered.

4 OTHER ASPECTS OF PURCHASE PRICE ALLOCATIONS

The initial acquisition, together with the purchase price allocation, not only impacts the statement of financial position and the statement of income, it also impacts the cash flow statement and the notes. The cash flow is impacted because acquisitions of investments in subsidiaries, joint ventures and associates are presented as separate line items as part of the investing category. Notes are impacted because exhaustive information has to be given upon acquisitions due to the disclosure requirements in IFRS 3.

4.1 Cash flow statements

The acquisition of a new subsidiary not only impacts on the consolidated statement of financial position but also on the consolidated statement of cash flows. This is because a cash outflow usually occurs upon acquisition. While the acquisition of a subsidiary represents an investment in financial assets at parent level and an increase in assets and liabilities at group level that have a long-term effect, acquisitions have to be presented as a line item in the category of investing activities. IAS 7.39 through 7.42B include all relevant accounting and disclosure requirements.

Due to the consolidation techniques in preparing consolidated financial statements and the derived movements in cash, a direct presentation is not given. Adjustments are necessary that reclassify movements in balance sheet items towards its appropriate position in the cash flow statement.[34]

4.2 Disclosures

Disclosures of acquisitions should provide the user of financial statements with information about the nature and financial effect as well as decisions and changes in the group that might impact the financial position of the group. IFRS 3.59 and 3.60 in combination with IFRS 3.B64 to 3.B67 provide all requirements that have to be incorporated into consolidated financial statements. Disclosures of acquisitions belong to changes in the group and the information on companies subject to consolidation. In addition to information of group companies to be consolidated, disclosures relating to acquisitions and disposals often are combined in a separate subtopic. The disclosure information of the group is placed directly behind the general accounting policies and principles.

IFRS 3 demands a long list of details to be disclosed. All details can be grouped into three categories: general information, financial details and additional information. Depending on the type of acquisition, some disclosures may not apply that belong to additional information. Furthermore, there may be situations in which the level of detail is impracticable for disclosure.[35] In such situations, an explanation is demanded that lists the facts and impracticabilities regarding the non-disclosure.

- General information

    General information shall provide information about the acquiree and the rationale behind the acquisition. Therefore, information will focus on the following mandatory items:

    - the name of the acquired company,
    - the acquisition date,
    - the percentage of voting equity,
    - the rationale of the business combination (the intention of management to acquire the company), and
    - a brief explanation about how control is obtained.

    The qualitative descriptions about factors that constitute goodwill have to include aspects that are derived from the business combination and the expectations of management. Typical aspects are synergies due to the business combination by sharing products, resources, reducing overheads, non-recognized intangible assets, non-accountable items like staff knowledge and similar items.

---

[34] Techniques for adjusting the cash flow statement are described in detail in chapter K -3.2.1 on page 682.

[35] According to the definition in IAS 8.5, impracticable means that an accounting requirement cannot be applied after the preparer made every reasonable effort in trying an application.

- Financial details

    Financial details of the acquiree have to cover the fair value at the acquisition date as well as the amounts recognized. Due to the exhaustive disclosure requirements on cash, and each class of assets and liabilities, it is recommended to present net assets for fair value and amounts recognized together with a reconciliation. Furthermore, fair value net assets acquired have to be reconciled with the consideration transferred by including goodwill as a residual item. This includes a qualitative description of the factors that constitute goodwill. Therefore, most of the financial disclosures required can be put together in a reconciliation schedule representing all financial information. This reduces the burden to describe the numbers and offers an improved, easily readable format.

Item	Carrying amount	Adjustment to fair value	Fair value @ acquisiton date
Non-current assets			
Intangible assets	xxx	xxx	xxx
Goodwill	xxx	xxx	xxx
Property, plant & equipment	xxx	xxx	xxx
Financial assets	xxx	xxx	xxx
Other assets	xxx	xxx	xxx
Current assets			
Inventory	xxx	xxx	xxx
Receivables	xxx	xxx	xxx
Other assets	xxx	xxx	xxx
Cash & cash equivalents	xxx	xxx	xxx
Total assets	**xxx**	**xxx**	**xxx**
Non-current liabilities			
Pensions	xxx	xxx	xxx
Debt	xxx	xxx	xxx
Other provisions & liabilities	xxx	xxx	xxx
Current liabilities			
Prepayments	xxx	xxx	xxx
Debt	xxx	xxx	xxx
Payables	xxx	xxx	xxx
Accruals	xxx	xxx	xxx
Cu rent taxes	xxx	xxx	xxx
Other liabilities	xxx	xxx	xxx
Total liabilities	**xxx**	**xxx**	**xxx**
Net assets	**xxx**	**xxx**	**xxx**
Goodwill			xxx
Considerations transferred (purchase price)			**xxx**

Fig. E-17 Example of a reconciliation schedule

If the consideration transferred includes more than cash, the composition of the consideration has to be disclosed. This includes the following items:

- Cash;
- Equity instruments (typically common or preferred shares including the number of shares and the method of fair value measurement);
- Tangible and intangible assets;
- A business or subsidiary of the acquirer;
- Liabilities.

These disclosures have to be combined with further details if contingent considerations are involved. IFRS 3.B64g requires in minimum a description of the arrangement and the calculation base.

- Additional information

In addition to general and financial information, selected financial details have to be disclosed that complement financial information. These details cover various issues:

- Receivable analysis (including the fair value and gross amounts, sorted by major classes of receivables like loans, leases, trade and other receivables).
- Contingent liability analysis for those liabilities recognized (nature of obligations, uncertainty information and expected reimbursement as required by IAS 37.85) and additional information for contingent liabilities not recognized (in particular the reasons for the non-recognition).
- Goodwill deductible for tax purposes. Such goodwill positions can only arise for taxation purposes.
- A description of transactions recognized separately from the business combination. This description has to include the accounting by the acquirer and amounts recognized. These amounts have to include acquisition-related costs and the amounts expensed together with a reference to the line item in the statement of comprehensive income where expenses are recorded. For pre-existing relationships the calculation method used to determine the settlement amount is subject to disclosure.
- A description of the reason of gains in bargain purchases together with the gain recognized and a reference to the line item in the statement of comprehensive income.
- The amount and the measurement basis of non-controlling interests. If the full goodwill method is applied and non-controlling interests are measured at fair value, this disclosure has to include the valuation techniques together with significant inputs used.
- In step acquisitions, the fair value and the adjustment to fair value of those equity interests have to be disclosed that are held directly

before the acquisition of the interests that constitute control. A reference to the line item in the statement of comprehensive income where adjustment gains or losses are recorded is part of this disclosure.

- In the period the acquisition takes place, the contribution of the acquiree to the group's performance has to be disclosed. This includes revenues and profit or loss allocable to the acquiree.
- Pro-forma information of revenues and profit or loss for the group if the acquisition had taken place at the beginning of the period.

While not all business combinations will be finalized in the period involved, reporting obligations arise that relate to **business combinations of previous periods**. Issues subject to disclosure are often variable payments due that relate to earn-out options or similar agreements or subsequent adjustments (due to new facts and circumstances that refer to the acquisition date). It is recommended to provide the same prominence to these old business combinations as to acquisitions of the current period.

The volume of disclosure details is not always necessary for each acquisition. If acquisitions are treated as **immaterial business combinations**, reduced disclosure information applies. General information – like the name and description of the company acquired, the acquisition date, the percentage of voting equity acquired and a description of the acquisition intention combined with information on the acquisition process – has to be incorporated in the notes for each immaterial acquisition. All other information is subject to disclosure only if the sum of all immaterial business combinations are material. In this case, an aggregated disclosure of all business combinations is required.

The above listed disclosure details are mandatory for each acquisition during the period. If acquisitions are completed **after the end of the period** but before consolidated financial statements are authorized to be published, special disclosure is required. Like every other acquisition, mandatory disclosure details have to be incorporated in the notes. Such detailed disclosures are often hard to realize as acquisitions are either complex and demand a time-consuming purchase price allocation or necessary information is often not immediately available. Therefore, incomplete business combinations are exempt from full disclosure. Instead, a statement in the note should describe the missing disclosures and the reasons why disclosures cannot be made. Groups often use this exemption and provide only general information about the acquisition. Details are disclosed in the consolidated financial statements of the following financial statements.

5. CONSOLIDATION TECHNIQUES

The recording of the acquisition and the initial consolidation are the final stages of the acquisition accounting for new subsidiaries. Up to this moment and based on the purchase agreement, the financial statements of the new subsidiary are transferred to IFRS accounting standards – if appropriate – and the purchase price allocation is finished. As a result, all assets acquired and liabilities assumed are known and measured based upon IFRS as applied by the parent company.

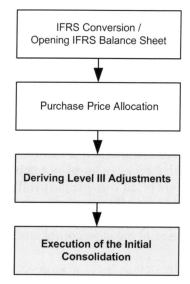

Fig. E-18 Accounting step: Adjustments and consolidation

To finalize the initial recognition of a new subsidiary, the recording and the initial consolidation of the new subsidiary have to be executed. Both tasks have to be performed at both parent and group level, resulting in different activities.

5.1. The parent's view

The acquisition of a subsidiary is an ordinary transaction like an acquisition of any current and non-current asset. There is no difference in a purchase of fixed assets, raw materials or shares of subsidiaries. At the acquisition date, the investment in a subsidiary has to be recorded. It has to include all elements of the contractually agreed considerations. These elements have to be taken from the purchase price allocation, particularly from the estimation of the purchase price.[36] Depending on the type of consideration either an immediate cash transfer or a liability has to be recorded. The type of presentation as a current or non-current liability in the consolidated financial statement depends on the nature of the liability. Long-term liabilities are initially recorded at their present value and have to reflect the conditions affecting the purchase price. This applies particularly to contractual obligations that include variable elements. They are recorded based on the expected and discounted future cash flows using an appropriate discount rate that reflects the current market condition.

Due to the accounting requirements of IFRS 3 and the structure of the acquisition, journal entries will vary. Therefore, only some journal entries are presented that reflect the **initial accounting** of standard acquisitions (without considering special effects). These journal entries have to be executed as of the acquisition date.

---

[36] See chapter E -3.3 on page 143 for details.

- Standard journal entry for an acquisition

    The standard journal entry for an acquisition, that is cash based, consists of all elements of the consideration either transferred or due for transfer:

Journal entry		Comment
dr.	Investment in subsidiaries	
	cr. Cash or bank	For immediate payment
	cr. Liabilities	For short-term items
	cr. Non-current liabilities	For earn-out options and similar long-term items
	cr. Debt	Either current or non-current, depending on type of debt

- Debt-financing of acquisition

    If the acquisition is financed in part or fully by debt, an additional transaction – the funding by the financing institution – has to be accounted for separately. The payment may be routed via the acquirer, which requires a separate journal entry or transferred directly to the vendor. If the latter is the case, the debt can be included into the standard journal entry.

Journal entry		Comment
dr.	Cash or bank	Only if the funding is routed via the acquirer
	cr. Debt	Either current or non-current, depending on type of debt

- Equity-financing of acquisition

    If equity instruments of the acquirer are involved, the standard journal entry to record the acquisition is slightly different:

Journal entry		Comment
dr.	Investment in subsidiaries	
	cr. Cash or bank	For immediate payment
	cr. Liabilities	For short-term items
	cr. Non-current Liabilities	For earn-out options and similar long-term items
	cr. Share capital	Par value of issued shares
	cr. Capital reserve	Excess value to arrive at the agreed value or market value as of the acquisition date

- Acquisition-related costs

    As acquisition-related costs are not subject to be capitalized but expensed instead, one or more separate journal entries are necessary for each invoice received that relate to the acquisition.

Journal entry	
dr.	Other expenses
	cr. Cash or bank or liabilities

- Bargain purchases

    In bargain purchases, effects of purchase price allocations are recorded at group level. The parent will record its investment in subsidiaries similar to any other acquisition of a subsidiary. Therefore, the above-mentioned journal entries will also apply to acquisitions that result in bargain purchases.

Example

The acquisition of 80% of the share in Solenta would result in a transfer of 77,982 k EUR to the former owners of Solenta in two stages: one immediately and one when the variable payment becomes due. Flexing Cables SE financed this amount through the issuing of its own shares, a loan and the use of its own cash. The acquisition would be recorded in the separate financial statement of Flexing Cables.

Item	Explanation and calculation	Amount
Shares	The issuing of shares relate to new shares with a par value of 1 EUR per share. As of the acquisition date, shares of Flexing Cable are traded at the stock market with a market value of 7.14 EUR per share.	44,982
Bank loan	The bank loan was arranged before the negotiations with the former owners of Solenta have started. The bank provides an amount up to 25,000 k EUR upon the date the sale and purchase agreement will be signed.	23,000
Liability	The liability represents the obligation of Flexing Cables due to the variable payment to be due in 2015 for the earn-out.	10,000
Cash	Any cash to be paid by Flexing Cables's is not yet due.	-
		77,892

The amount to be paid in 2015 could be taken from the remaining bank loan and Flexing Cables's own cash.

Journal entries

				Comment
dr.	Cash	23,000		
	cr. Bank loans		23,000	
dr.	Investment in subsidiaries	77,892		
	cr. Cash		23,000	
	cr. Non-current liabilities		10,000	Present value of earn-out
	cr. Share capital		6,300	Par value 1 EUR * no. of shares issued
	cr. Capital reserve		38,682	Excess amount: (7.14 EUR - 1 EUR) * no. of shares issued

---

Depending on the nature of the recorded liabilities, a **subsequent accounting** might be necessary. This includes adjustments to consideration transferred during the measurement period, payments of short-term items and recording of interests for long-term liabilities. Adjustments may be necessary during the current period or in subsequent periods until all obligations are settled.

- Adjustments during the measurement period

    Any adjustments necessary to the consideration transferred will also lead to an adjustment of the carrying amount of the investment in subsidiaries. This can either be a reduction of the carrying amount of investments in subsidiaries due to repayments of the vendor or an increase in the carrying amount of investments in subsidiaries. The latter case is often caused by contractual extensions subsequent to the original purchase agreement. A typical example of the recording of an additional consideration is the exercise of a call option that was initially not planned to be executed.

Journal entry	Comment
dr. Liabilities	Depending on the nature of the adjustment. Can also be a non-current liability.
cr. Investment in subsidiaries	

or

Journal entry	Comment
dr. Investments in subsidiaries	Depending on the nature of the adjustment. Can also be a non-current liability.
cr. Liabilities	

- Payments of short-term items
  Regular payments at the maturity date regardless of which reason.

Journal entry	Comment
dr. Liability	Depending on the nature of the adjustment. Can also be a non-current liability.
cr. Cash or bank	Only if the payment is directly made by the funding bank.
cr. Debt	

- Interests
  Long-term liabilities are not due for payment at the acquisition date. Therefore, an interest element has to be added at the end of each subsequent period to increase the liability to arrive at the payment obligation at the maturity or payment date.

Journal entry	Comment
dr. Interests	An application of the discount rate is required.
cr. Non-current liabilities	Adjustment to arrive at the amount due at the expected payment date.

- Adjustments due to over- or under-performance of subsidiary
  If, in subsequent periods, a further payment becomes due that is related to any earn-out options, adjustments may be necessary if payments due do not reflect the initial estimation of future cash-flows. Payments due can be made by the acquirer or the financing institution on behalf of the acquirer. If the subsidiary underperforms in relation to the initial estimation, either fewer payments are due or a refund by the vendor can be expected. On the other hand, if the subsidiary overperforms compared to the initial estimation, an additional payment becomes due unless there is no limitation on variable payments incorporated in the purchase agreement.

The following journal entry applies to situations where the subsidiary underperforms and less payment to the vendor is due.

Journal entry		Comment
dr.	Non-current liabilities	
	cr. Other earnings	
	cr. Cash or bank	
	cr. Debt	Either current or non-current, depending on type of debt

The following journal entry applies to situations where the subsidiary overperforms and an additional payment is due. The amount recorded as an expense reflects the additional payment that is not covered by the initial estimation of expected earn-out options or other variable payments.

Journal entry		Comment
dr.	Non-current liabilities	Either current or non-current, depending on type of debt
dr.	Other expenses	
	cr. Cash or bank	
	cr. Debt	

5.2. The group's view

From the group's point of view, the acquisition of a new subsidiary as recorded by the parent is just an increase in assets and liabilities. The acquisition is not directly recorded at group level. Instead, assets acquired and liabilities assumed are recorded indirectly through the acquisition of the investment in the subsidiary combined with the initial consolidation. The initial consolidation of the acquiree to prepare consolidated financial statements is a two-step process:

- Step one: preparation of subsidiaries for consolidation;
- Step two: consolidation and finalization of group figures.

Defined tasks have to be executed at each step before consolidated financial statements are available.

An important role is the **timing** of the initial consolidation. Usually, the initial consolidation of the acquired subsidiary has to occur at the acquisition date to properly reflect the conditions as of that date. It is also necessary to estimate the profit or loss achieved during the period by considering the contribution of the acquiree to that profit or loss. From a purely technical point of view, the initial consolidation does not necessarily need to be executed at the acquisition date. It can also be executed during the remaining period or at the end of the period. All three alternatives are available and they will generate the same results. This is more or less an administration issue of the corporate centre when subsidiaries are due for an initial consolidation. In practice, a general tendency when initial consolidations are executed is not observed. Some companies initially consolidate an acquiree during the period when the effects of the purchase price allocation are known, others initially consolidate the acquiree at the end of the period. Both practices consider the situation as of the acquisition date. Initial consolidations as of the acquisition date or shortly after the acquisition date are executed only in business combinations that have clear and simple structures without any significant non-accounted assets acquired or liabilities assumed.

Depending on the timing chosen, **tasks** and activities of the initial consolidation will change. Even if tasks change, their final result will always be the same.

- At acquisition date

    The carrying amounts of all assets and liabilities have to be adjusted to reflect their fair values. Differences are recorded at their appropriate levels combined with an equity consolidation as of the acquisition date.

- During period

    Tasks performed to execute the initial consolidation during the period are substantially the same tasks as the one as of the acquisition date. The only difference from the first option is its time offset. This is more or less an administration issue and does not impact the initial accounting of the acquisition.

- At end of period

    At the end of the period, two transactions fall together: the initial consolidation and its first subsequent consolidation. For consolidation purposes, effects as of the acquisition date as well as all changes during the remaining period have to be considered. This can be realized by using the closing carrying amounts of all assets and liabilities of the subsidiary and adjust them according to the group's accounting policies. The then adjusted balances are finalized by the initial equity consolidation of the acquiree.

    An alternate option is the execution of the initial consolidation as of the acquisition date and a development of all adjustments at all levels towards the end of the period. Both methods will generate the same results for the consolidated statements of income and financial position.

If possible, try to execute the initial consolidation as of the acquisition date, regardless at which date of the period it is executed. This ensures that a proper cut-off between the pro-forma and group period is achieved. It will deliver the information required for disclosures of changes in the group composition in the notes.

5.2.1. Step one – preparation for consolidation

The purpose of step one is to prepare the acquiree for consolidation. This requires coordination with all tasks of the preparation of the opening balance sheet. If this is not already done, all tasks of the opening balance sheet (so the level I adjustments for a conversion towards IFRS, level II adjustments for a consideration of the group accounting policies and the translation towards the functional currency if appropriate) have to be executed. Preferably, this should be done per account on its corresponding level to achieve a direct allocation to the underlying transaction. Once the opening balance sheet is available, all effects of the purchase price allocation have to be incorporated. These effects include the recording of considerations transferred – if not already done – and the adjustments of assets acquired and liabilities assumed towards its fair value and are then recorded at level III. The incorporation of the purchase price allocation has to consider two tasks:

- Determination of the effects of the purchase price allocation

  While the purchase price allocation has measured all assets acquired and liabilities assumed by its fair value only, all differences between fair value and carrying amounts have to be retrieved.

- Recording of effects of the purchase price allocation

  Upon the availability of all differences between the carrying amount and their fair values, a recording of these differences at level III is required.

If the business combination includes pre-existing relationships, reacquired rights or elements of multi-component contracts that are not part of the business combination, these transactions have to be recorded as well. The recording can either occur at level III as part of the preparation procedure or at group level next to the initial equity consolidation. Both tasks will deliver the same results.

Recording these effects at group level may bear the danger of a lack of transparency and allocation to the subsidiary caused these effects. Therefore, it makes more sense to record them at level III as a direct relationship between these effects and the subsidiary is always given.

As far as all adjustments are made, a currency translation towards the group's currency is usually the final task in preparing the acquiree for its initial consolidation. This translation is based on the application of the translation towards the presentation currency of the group.

For an efficient preparation of the subsidiary, the following tasks should always be checked if appropriate and then executed in the proposed order (these tasks assume that the acquiree has a functional currency, otherwise an additional step is required to convert the acquiree's balance sheet from a foreign currency towards a functional currency):

Step	Task	Activity	Level
1)	IFRS conversion of all assets and liabilities of the acquiree's balance sheet as of the beginning of the period	Opening Balance Sheet	(Pro forma only)
2)	IFRS conversion of all assets and liabilities of the acquiree's balance sheet as of the acquisition date	Opening Balance Sheet	I
3)	Application of group accounting policies on the converted balance sheet as of the beginning of the period	Opening Balance Sheet	(Pro forma only)
4)	Application of group accounting policies on the converted balance sheet as of the acquisition date	Opening Balance Sheet	II
5)	Purchase price allocation	Initial consolidation	-
6)	Determination of differences between fair value and carrying amounts of assets acquired and liabilities assumed	Initial consolidation	-
7)	Recording of deviating balances of selected assets and liabilities	Initial consolidation	III
8)	Recording assets and liabilities identified by the purchase price allocation	Initial consolidation	III
9)	Recording of pre-existing relationships	Initial consolidation	III or group
10)	Currency translation into the presentation currency of the group	Initial consolidation	III
11)	Any other transaction as appropriate	Initial consolidation	III or group

Tab. E-13   Steps in preparing the initial equity consolidation

Preparing the acquiree for its initial consolidation is not just an execution of the above-mentioned tasks, it is more or less a process where several parties are involved. The IFRS conversion and the alignment towards the group's accounting policies are activities that are usually executed by the acquiree. At local level, are all detailed information for a conversion and alignment available? As the adjustments deal with an initial preparation of a balance sheet, the cumulative effects are recorded against retained earnings for both adjustments. This includes the step-up or step-down of assets and liabilities as well as any deferred taxes (either assets or liabilities). Adjustments to be recorded at level I can be executed by the following journal entry.

Journal entries			Comment
dr.	Asset		This journal entry assumes a step-up in assets and liabilities. Step-downs may also apply (dr. instead of cr. and vice versa).
	cr.	Liabilities	
	cr.	Retained earnings	
dr.	Deferred tax asset		Follow-up activity, consideration of tax effects (follow underlying asset / liability).
	cr.	Deferred tax liabilities	
	cr.	Retained earnings	

If selected assets are measured by applying a revaluation model, changes have to be recorded in a revaluation reserve.

Similar to the journal entry of the IFRS conversion is the journal entry to apply the accounting policies of the group. Other than the conversion that may cover a set of accounts subject to a conversion, the application of group accounting policies is limited to selected assets and liabilities only. Adjustments are recorded at level II follow the same rationale as other journal entries.

Journal entries			Comment
dr.	Asset		This journal entry assumes a step-up in assets and liabilities. Step-downs may also apply (dr. instead of cr. and vice versa).
	cr.	Liabilities	
	cr.	Retained earnings	
dr.	Deferred tax asset		Follow-up activity, consideration of tax effects (follow underlying asset / liability).
	cr.	Deferred tax liabilities	
	cr.	Retained earnings	

As group accounting policies may treat selected items differently than a pure IFRS application, reclassification may apply that require additional journal entries. A proper documentation for each journal entry for auditing purposes is assumed.

Based on the work of the acquiree, the effects of the purchase price allocation have to be accounted for. This task is usually executed by the corporate centre. Effects of the purchase price allocation are recorded at level III. Two different sets of journal entries accompanied by tax journal entries have to be recorded: Those where fair value adjustments of recorded assets and liabilities are necessary; and those that initially record assets and liabilities. The first set of journal entries deal again with the same assets and liabilities that are already adjusted before. Consequently, the same journal entries as outlined before have to be executed.[37] The second set will record all assets and liabilities identified by the purchase price allocation.

Journal entries			Comment
dr.	Asset		
	cr.	Liabilities	
	cr.	Retained earnings	
dr.	Deferred tax asset		Follow-up activity, consideration of tax effects (follow underlying asset / liability).
	cr.	Deferred tax liabilities	
	cr.	Retained earnings	

While the initial recognition of all remeasured assets acquired and liabilities assumed, as well as the initial recognition of assets and liabilities identified through the purchase price allocation, are fully recorded in the balance sheet only, a more detailed view of the opposite entry is required. All steps so far have created an IFRS balance sheet based of group accounting policies that reflects the fair value of the acquiree's business. Accordingly, the opposite entries are one or more items in equity. As assets and liabilities are subject to a subsequent adjustment, either through profit & loss or other comprehensive income, it is important to differentiate between the positions in equity to achieve some kind of transparency

---

[37] Please refer to the journal entries provided above.

for accounting purposes. Separate accounts are therefore mandatory in retained earnings that are able to cope with initial and subsequent effects. The following list provides a **recommendation on accounts** feasible for such purposes. The purpose of these accounts is to carry differences between local GAAP applied by the acquiree and IFRS applied at group level only.

Account	Explanation
IFRS opening balance	The default account for all adjustments at all levels. This account carries all differences in arriving at the opening IFRS balance sheet and any adjustments necessary to align with the group accounting policies and fair value measurements.
	This account will never be touched again in subsequent periods.
Revaluation reserve (assets)	Used for any assets that are subject to a revaluation due to the application of a revaluation model or other fair value adjustments recorded through other comprehensive income. The carrying balance represents step-ups and -downs in fair value compared to the initial carrying amount.
Deferred taxes (assets)	Deferred taxes that relate to the revaluation of assets.
Revaluation reserve (financial instruments)	Used for any financial instruments subject to a revaluation due to fair value measurement requirements recorded through other comprehensive income.
Deferred taxes (financial instruments)	Deferred taxes that relate to the revaluation of financial instruments.
IFRS profit & loss of the period	This account carries all differences between local GAAP and IFRS recorded through profit & loss of the current and prior periods.
Foreign exchange differences	Plug-account to cover differences arising in the translation from the functional currency of a subsidiary to the presentation currency of the group. This account will be adjusted at each reporting date (which is either the end of the period or the end of a quarter if a quarterly reporting cycle is required).

Tab. E-14 Recommendation of additional IFRS accounts

Example

Applying the preparation order as outlined in Tab. E-13, the following steps had to be executed to prepare Solenta for the initial consolidation.[38]

Step 2 – Recording all adjustments to the carrying amount of balance sheet items

Solenta had opted to record all adjustments to the carrying amount of balance sheet items in a two-step approach. In the first step, all adjustments as of the beginning of the period would be recorded. In the second step, these adjustments had to be advanced towards the acquisition date. All adjustment of balance sheet items would be recorded against retained earnings at level I. This treatment has the advantage that it follows the preparation process of the opening balance sheet and that it reconciles with the determination of the profit or loss achieved in the pro-forma period. Alternatively, all adjustments to balance sheet items can be realized in one step.

The following journal entry is used to adjust the carrying amount of those balance sheet items subject to valuation adjustments as of the beginning of the period.

---

[38] See page 205.

Journal entry

dr.		Intangible assets	613
dr.		Property, plant & equipment	6,775
dr.		Trade receivables	426
dr.		Other provisions	336
dr.		Deferred tax assets	261
	cr.	Deferred items	5
	cr.	Pension provisions	870
	cr.	Deferred tax liability	2,429
	cr.	Retained earnings	5,107

The following journal entries can be used for subsequent adjustment of the affected balance sheet as of the acquisition date (1.4.).

Journal entry

dr.		Accounts receivable	14
dr.		Deferred tax asset	5
dr.		Deferred tax liabilities	55
dr.		Retained earnings	140
	cr.	Intangible assets	18
	cr.	Property, plant & equipment	158
	cr.	Deferred items	3
	cr.	Pension provisions	13
	cr.	Other provisions	22

Step 4 – Alignment to group accounting policies

In the absence of any specific application and group accounting policies, no specific valuation adjustments have to be recorded at level II.

Step 7 – Recording of deviating balances

Any adjustments to already accounted assets and liabilities have to be recorded at level III, again against retained earnings. Journal entries have to consider deferred tax assets and liabilities.

Journal entry				Comment
dr.		Property, plant & equipment	900	Fair value adjustment property
dr.		Financial assets	9	
dr.		Deferred tax assets	894	
dr.		Retained earnings	1,468	
	cr.	Other provisions	3,000	Environmental pollution
	cr.	Deferred tax liabilities	271	

Step 8 – Recording of identified assets and liabilities

Identified and measureable assets and liabilities including their tax effects have to be recorded next, again at level III.

Journal entry				Comment
dr.		Intangible assets	44,200	Patents: 17,800; Existing orders: 3,900; Customer base: 22,500
dr.		Deferred tax assets	2,384	
	cr.	Deferred tax liabilities	13,172	
	cr.	Other provisions	8,000	Patent infringement
	cr.	Retained earnings	25,412	

Step 9 – Recording of pre-existing relationships

The identified pre-existing-relationship will be recorded at level III considering its tax effects. While the reversal of the bad debt allowance will increase the carrying amount of the trade receivables, a deferred tax liability amounting to 66 k EUR (29,8% of 220) has to be recorded.[39]

Journal entry

dr.	Trade receivables	220
cr.	Deferred tax liabilities	65
cr.	Retained earnings	155

Step 11 – Other transactions

While all transactions consider an appropriate treatment of deferred tax assets and liabilities, these items have to be offset according to IAS 12.74. It is recommended to offset these items at group level leaving the carrying amounts at each level untouched.

- Deferred tax asset: $261 + 5 + 894 + 2,384 = 3,544$
- Deferred tax liability: $2,429 - 55 + 271 + 13,172 + 65 = 15,882$

As the carrying amount of the deferred tax liability is larger than the carrying amount of the deferred tax asset, the amount to be offset is therefore 3,544 k EUR.

Journal entry

dr.	Deferred tax liability	3,544
cr.	Deferred tax asset	3,544

Furthermore, the transfer of financial assets to Flexing Cables has to be considered.[40]

For presentation purposes, reclassification similar to the opening balance sheet should also be executed at group level:

- Short-term portion of loans 5,000 k EUR;
- Accruals 5,104 k EUR;
- Deferred items 26 k EUR.

Having executed all steps, the adjusted statement of financial position for group purposes and subject to consolidation is:

Adjusted IFRS Statement of financial position Solenta as of 1.4.2013 (in k EUR)

Assets		Liabilities & Equity	
Cash at hand & bank	3,400	Trade payables	17,254
Trade receivables	22,683	Tax liabilities	8,300
Inventory	53,757	Prepayments	280
Other assets	20,103	Accruals	5,104
Current assets	**99,943**	Loans	5,000
		Other payables	17,143
Property, plant & equipment	58,972	**Current liabilities**	**53,081**
Intangible assets	47,948		

---

[39] See exercise in chapter E -6.5 on page 231 for details.
[40] See exercise in chapter E -6.6 on page 240 for details.

Financial assets	-	Loans		49,000
Deferred tax assets	-	Pensions		7,353
Non-current assets	106,920	Other liabilities		13,822
		Deferred taxes		12,338
		Non-current liabilities		**82,513**
		Share capital		2,500
		Capital reserve		250
		Retained earnings		68,519
		Equity		**71,269**
Total assets	206,863	**Total liabilities & equity**		206,863

As far as **pre-exiting relationships** are involved, assets and liabilities have to be adjusted for further transaction. The further transaction might be a settlement, a consolidation or the presentation of an asset or a liability. The adjustment in this context has to ensure that all assets and liabilities that belong to pre-existing relationships are recorded.[41] Corresponding journal entries may be recorded through profit & loss or other comprehensive income as demanded by applicable IFRS.

- Recording through other comprehensive income

Journal entry			Comment
dr.		Asset	
	cr.	Liability	
	cr.	Other comprehensive income	Can also be a debit.

- Recording through profit & loss

Journal entry			Comment
dr.		Asset	
	cr.	Liability	
	cr.	Other earnings / other expenses	Can also be a debit.

Example

As identified pre-existing relationships between Solenta and the Flexing Cables group qualify as contractual relationships that existed before the acquisition date; the adjustment has to be recorded through other comprehensive income.[42]

5.2.2 Step two – consolidation

Having prepared the adjusted accounts for consolidation, the second step initially consolidates the acquiree becoming a subsidiary of the group. The initial consolidation is an equity consolidation that will be executed based on the option chosen to account for goodwill either as purchased or full goodwill. The equity

---

[41] This adjustment does not care about the further accounting of pre-existing relationships. The accounting of pre-existing relationships, its adjustments and required journal entries are discussed in detail in chapter E -6.5 on page 231.

[42] See step 9 of the previous example for details.

consolidation might be accompanied by additional effects based on pre-existing relationships that require a reclassification and debt consolidation and by transactions next to the business combination that may generate profit & loss effects or be recorded in other comprehensive income. For a better illustration, the initial equity consolidation is presented for both methods.

- Purchased-goodwill method

    The purchased-goodwill method records only the goodwill that belongs to the parent and ignores other effects. This requires that the carrying amounts of all assets and liabilities are based on level III adjustments. If the subsidiary is a wholly-owned one, one journal entry is sufficient. If non-controlling interests are involved, two journal entries might be recorded; one that reflects the journal entry of the parent and one that reflects the journal entry of the non-controlling interests. It is recommended to execute the following steps for consolidation purposes.

Step	Task
1)	Pro rata elimination of the subsidiary's equity against the investment in subsidiaries account of the parent company.
2)	Pro rata elimination of hidden reserves and burdens, non-accounted assets and liabilities and deferred taxes at level II against the investment in subsidiaries account of the parent company.
3)	Reclassification of the remaining investment in subsidiaries to goodwill.
4)	Pro rata elimination of the subsidiary's equity against non-controlling interests.
5)	Pro rata elimination of hidden reserves and burdens, non-accounted assets and liabilities and deferred taxes at level II against non-controlling interests.

Tab. E-15 Steps of the initial equity consolidation applying the purchased goodwill method

The **standard journal entry** to consolidate the acquiree if it is a wholly-owned subsidiary can be realized in one step.

Journal entry		Company	Comment
dr.	Goodwill	Group	
dr.	Share capital (common stock)	Subsidiary	
dr.	Retained earnings	Subsidiary	
dr.	Profit / losses carried forward	Subsidiary	
dr.	Revaluation reserve	Subsidiary	Only the portion that relates to fair value adjustments and the recognition of non-accounted assets and liabilities. Can also be a credit.
dr.	IFRS opening balance	Subsidiary	Only the portion that relates to fair value adjustments and the recognition of non-accounted assets and liabilities. Can also be a credit.
cr.	Investment in subsidiaries	Parent	
cr.	Deferred taxes revaluation reserve	Subsidiary	Elimination in proportion to the elimination of the revaluation reserve and the IFRS opening balance sheet. Can also be a debit.
cr.	Foreign exchange differences	Group	Can also be a debit.

The journal entry presented can be split up into separate journal entries if required. It is different from the steps of the initial equity consolidation to be performed. The reason for this is the handling of carrying amounts of assets and liabilities and allocation to different levels. While assets and liabilities are adjusted at levels I to III and recorded against retained earnings, it is sufficient to eliminate this opposite entry of the original journal entry. Therefore, the journal entry incorporates those equity accounts that carry any IFRS-adjustments of the purchase price allocation.

The journal entry becomes more complex or has to be split up into two journal entries, if **non-controlling interests** are involved. To ensure a proper allocation to the parent and the non-controlling interests, the standard procedure should focus on separate journal entries for each party.

Journal entries			Company	Comment
dr.		Goodwill	Group	
dr.		Share capital (common stock)	Subsidiary	Pro-rata parent.
dr.		Retained earnings	Subsidiary	Pro-rata parent.
dr.		Profit / losses carried forward	Subsidiary	Pro-rata parent.
dr.		Revaluation reserve	Subsidiary	Pro-rata parent. Only the portion that relates to fair value adjustments and the recognition of non-accounted assets and liabilities. Can also be a credit.
dr.		IFRS opening balance	Subsidiary	Pro-rata parent. Only the portion that relates to fair value adjustments and the recognition of non-accounted assets and liabilities. Can also be a credit.
	cr.	Investment in subsidiaries	Parent	
	cr.	Deferred taxes revaluation reserve	Subsidiary	Pro-rata parent. Elimination in proportion to the elimination of the revaluation reserve and the IFRS opening balance sheet. Can also be a debit.
	cr.	Foreign exchange differences	Group	Can also be a debit.
dr.		Share capital (common stock)	Subsidiary	Pro-rata non-controlling interests.
dr.		Retained earnings	Subsidiary	Pro-rata non-controlling interests.
dr.		Profit / losses carried forward	Subsidiary	Pro-rata non-controlling interests.
dr.		Revaluation reserve	Subsidiary	Pro-rata non-controlling interests.
dr.		IFRS opening balance	Subsidiary	Pro-rata non-controlling interests.
	cr.	Non-controlling interests	Group	
	cr.	Deferred taxes revaluation reserve	Subsidiary	Pro-rata non-controlling interests.
	cr.	Foreign exchange differences	Group	Can also be a debit

The first journal entry is similar in its structure to the journal entry of a wholly-owned subsidiary. The only difference is an application of a pro-rata elimination. All accounts of the subsidiary are eliminated by the percentage of interests of the parent in its subsidiary. The second journal entry eliminates the remaining balances of the subsidiary by establishing the equity attributable to non-controlling interests on a pro-rata basis.

As an alternate treatment, both journal entries can be combined into one journal entry. This requires an upfront calculation of the portion attributable to non-controlling interests.

Journal entry		Company	Comment
dr.	Goodwill	Group	
dr.	Share capital (common stock)	Subsidiary	
dr.	Retained earnings	Subsidiary	
dr.	Profit / losses carried forward	Subsidiary	
dr.	Revaluation reserve	Subsidiary	Only the portion that relates to fair value adjustments and the recognition of non-accounted assets and liabilities. Can also be a credit.
dr.	IFRS opening balance	Subsidiary	Only the portion that relates to fair value adjustments and the recognition of non-accounted assets and liabilities. Can also be a credit.
	cr. Investment in subsidiaries	Parent	
	cr. Non-controlling interests	Group	
	cr. Deferred taxes revaluation reserve	Subsidiary	Elimination in proportion to the elimination of the revaluation reserve and the IFRS opening balance sheet. Can also be a debit.
	cr. Foreign exchange differences	Group	Can also be a debit.

- Full-goodwill method

  The full-goodwill method assumes that non-controlling interests are present. Like the purchased-goodwill method, it requires that the carrying amounts of all assets and liabilities are based on level III adjustments. It is recommended to execute the following steps for consolidation purposes.

Step	Task
1)	Pro rata elimination of the subsidiary's equity against the investment in subsidiaries account of the parent company.
2)	Pro rata elimination of hidden reserves and burdens, non-accounted assets and liabilities and deferred taxes at level II against the investment in subsidiaries account of the parent company.
3)	Reclassification of the remaining investment in subsidiaries to goodwill.
4)	Recording of the fair value on non-controlling interests against goodwill.
5)	Pro rata elimination of the subsidiary's equity against non-controlling interests.
6)	Pro rata elimination of hidden reserves and burdens, non-accounted assets and liabilities and deferred taxes at level II against non-controlling interests.

Tab. E-16 Steps of the initial equity allocation applying the full goodwill method

The **standard journal entries** to consolidate the acquiree are split into three. The first two journal entries are similar to the purchased-goodwill method. They eliminate the equity interest of the parent and the non-controlling interest separately, based on their pro-rata portions. The third one then increases goodwill by the portion attributable to the non-controlling interests. Again, the handling and allocation of assets and liabilities at the various levels has to be considered for elimination. The opposite entries of the original journal entries at each level are used.

Journal entries		Company	Comment
dr.	Goodwill	Group	
dr.	Share capital (common stock)	Subsidiary	Pro-rata parent.
dr.	Retained earnings	Subsidiary	Pro-rata parent.
dr.	Profit / losses carried forward	Subsidiary	Pro-rata parent.
dr.	Revaluation reserve	Subsidiary	Pro-rata parent. Only the portion that relates to fair value adjustments and the recognition of non-accounted assets and liabilities. Can also be a credit.
dr.	IFRS opening balance	Subsidiary	Pro-rata parent. Only the portion that relates to fair value adjustments and the recognition of non-accounted assets and liabilities. Can also be a credit.
	cr. Investment in subsidiaries	Parent	
	cr. Deferred taxes revaluation reserve	Subsidiary	Pro-rata parent. Elimination in proportion to the elimination of the revaluation reserve and the IFRS opening balance sheet. Can also be a debit.
	cr. Foreign exchange differences	Group	Can also be a debit.
dr.	Share capital (common stock)	Subsidiary	Pro-rata non-controlling interests.
dr.	Retained earnings	Subsidiary	Pro-rata non-controlling interests.
dr.	Profit / losses carried forward	Subsidiary	Pro-rata non-controlling interests.
dr.	Revaluation reserve	Subsidiary	Pro-rata non-controlling interests.
dr.	IFRS opening balance	Subsidiary	Pro-rata non-controlling interests.
	cr. Non-controlling interests	Group	
	cr. Deferred taxes revaluation reserve	Subsidiary	Pro-rata non-controlling interests.
	cr. Foreign exchange differences	Group	Can also be a debit
dr.	Goodwill	Group	Based on fair value measurement of non-controlling interests.
	cr. Non-controlling interests	Group	

The journal entries can be combined into one journal entry, if a calculation on the carrying amount of non-controlling interests is available.

Journal entry		Company	Comment
dr.	Goodwill	Group	
dr.	Share capital (common stock)	Subsidiary	
dr.	Retained earnings	Subsidiary	
dr.	Profit / losses carried forward	Subsidiary	
dr.	Revaluation reserve	Subsidiary	Only the portion that relates to fair value adjustments and the recognition of non-accounted assets and liabilities. Can also be a credit.
dr.	IFRS opening balance	Subsidiary	Only the portion that relates to fair value adjustments and the recognition of non-accounted assets and liabilities. Can also be a credit.
cr.	Investment in subsidiaries	Parent	
cr.	Non-controlling interests	Group	
cr.	Deferred taxes revaluation reserve	Subsidiary	Elimination in proportion to the elimination of the revaluation reserve and the IFRS opening balance sheet. Can also be a debit.
cr.	Foreign exchange differences	Group	Can also be a debit.

Example

Based on the adjusted IFRS statement of financial position as of 1.4.2013, the initial consolidation could be performed. While pre-existing relationships existed, the initial consolidation consisted of an equity consolidation and a debt consolidation.

- Equity consolidation

  To eliminate the interests in Solenta and the equity of Solenta, non-controlling interests had to be calculated first:

	Share capital Solenta	2,500
+	Capital reserves Solents	250
+	Retained earnings Solenta	68,519
+	Goodwill allocable to Flexing Cables	20,967
–	Carrying amount of investment in Solenta recorded by Flexing Cables	(77,982)
=	Non-controlling interests	14,254

The journal entry to eliminate Solenta's equity:

Journal entry			Company
dr.	Goodwill	20,967	Group
dr.	Share capital	2,500	Solenta
dr.	Capital reserves	250	Solenta
dr.	Retained earnings	68,519	Solenta
cr.	Investment in subsidiaries	77,982	Flexing Cables SE
cr.	Non-controlling interests	14,254	Group

- Debt consolidation

    Pre-existing relationships had to be eliminated as part of the initial consolidation. This elimination had to consider each company of the Flexing Cables group.[43]

Journal entry			Company
dr.	Trade payables	453	Flexing Cables SE
dr.	Trade payables	834	Cable Systems
dr.	Trade payables	147	Flexing Cables Belgium
dr.	Trade payables	766	Wilmington
cr.	Trade receivables	2,200	Solenta

5.2.3. Bargain purchases

In case of a bargain purchase transaction or otherwise resulting badwill, no goodwill will be recognized. Instead a "consolidation profit" has to be recorded. Therefore, the journal entry to be recorded upon the initial consolidation is slightly different.

Journal entry		Company	Comment
dr.	Share capital (common stock)	Subsidiary	
dr.	Retained earnings	Subsidiary	
dr.	Profit / losses carried forward	Subsidiary	
dr.	Revaluation reserve	Subsidiary	Only the portion that relates to fair value adjustments and the recognition of non-accounted assets and liabilities. Can also be a credit.
dr.	IFRS opening balance	Subsidiary	Only the portion that relates to fair value adjustments and the recognition of non-accounted assets and liabilities. Can also be a credit.
cr.	Investment in subsidiaries	Parent	
cr.	Non-controlling interests	Group	
cr.	Deferred taxes revaluation reserve	Subsidiary	Elimination in proportion to the elimination of the revaluation reserve and the IFRS opening balance sheet. Can also be a debit.
cr.	**Other income / other earnings**	**Subsidiary**	**Gain from initial consolidation.**
cr.	Foreign exchange differences	Group	Can also be a debit.

---

[43] We assume that all balances of all companies involved are reconciled. While Cables Systems is an American and Wilmington a British company, foreign exchange differences usually arise upon the elimination. We will ignore this fact in this example.

Like the other journal entries presented, this journal entry can be split into two or more journal entries considering each item separately.

6 SPECIAL CASES

Acquisitions of companies are never standard transactions. Acquisitions are manifold in their appearance, with individual arrangements between vendors and acquirers, including or excluding defined items and transactions, considering various businesses in different countries or coping with external regulations and requirements. As manifold as the acquisition is, as manifold is the related accounting. This is because the accounting has to consider all agreements and side-effects of acquisitions. When there are numerous acquisitions, issues often arise. While the details may vary, the rationale behind the issues is often the same. Therefore, a dedicated view is required for those issues that are often observed in acquisitions. The most important ones will be discussed in this chapter:

- Reverse acquisitions;
- Acquisitions achieved in stages;
- Obtaining control in special situations;
- Multi-component contracts;
- Pre-existing relationships;
- Shares of the parent company;
- Non-material subsidiaries.

6.1 Reverse acquisitions

This is a special version of an acquisition. A reverse acquisition takes place if a smaller company (the legal acquirer) acquires a larger company (the legal acquiree) by issuing shares so that the former shareholders of the legal acquiree taken over are able to control the legal acquirer. From a business perspective, the (new) subsidiary has taken over the parent company. These kinds of transactions are very popular if a company wants to get access to stock markets without running through a complete IPO or issuing own shares or generating unnecessary expenses.

To account for reverse acquisitions, IFRS 3.B19 to B27 in combination with IFRS 3.IE2 et seq. requires a business-related view of this transaction. Therefore, all steps of a purchase price allocation have to be applied. Nevertheless, some specialities have to be considered:

- The acquirer from an accounting perspective is the legal acquiree, not the legal acquirer.
- The purchase price is determined by a fictitious acquisition of shares. Based on the relationship between shares issued to the former owners of the legal acquiree and the old shares of existing owners of the legal acquirer an acquisition rate is determined. This rate is valued by the fair value of shares the former owners had in the legal acquiree.

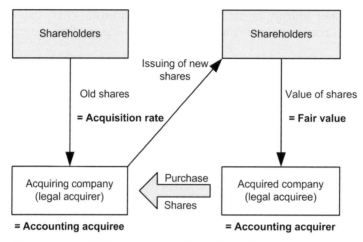

Fig. E-19   Reverse acquisitions: accounting allocations

Further specialities do not exist. All remaining tasks of the reverse acquisition are handled by a purchase price allocation as described before.[44]

Due to the situation with a company that legally is the acquiree but treated as an acquirer from an accounting perspective, special effects arise that need to be considered for the preparation and presentation of consolidated financial statements and its accompanied disclosures. Due to this situation, consolidated financial statements published are legally the ones of the legal parent while the content is based on the business of the legal acquiree considering the capital of the legal parent.

Even if the reverse acquisition was realized as intended, there is no guarantee that all shareholders of the legal acquiree will accept the offer of the legal acquirer to exchange their shares in the acquired company. The rationale of such decisions is often driven by the assumption not to benefit from the results and net assets of "their" company (the legal acquiree) as they differ from the results of the legal acquirer and are often better than the results of the legal acquirer.[45] These shareholders are treated as non-controlling interests and are accounted for accordingly. Non-controlling interests reflect the proportionate share of the carrying amount of net assets of the legal acquiree before the business combination.[46]

The following list provides support on the handling of selected items:

---

[44] See chapter E -3 on page 136 for details of the purchase price allocation.

[45] A different situation would exist if the transaction would be managed as a merger. Then, an access to the results and net assets would be ensured.

[46] This is a deviation from the measurement of non-controlling interests in other situations which would normally be measured by their fair values.

Item	Who	Recognition, measurement and presentation in consolidated financial statements
Assets & liabilities	Legal acquiree	Recognized and measured at their carrying amounts before the business combination
Assets & liabilities	Legal acquirer	Recognized and measured in accordance with IFRS 3. They are subject to the purchase price allocation and have to be adjusted to arrive at their fair values.
Non-accounted assets & liabilities	Legal acquirer	Recognized and measured in accordance with IFRS 3. They are also subject to the purchase price allocation as they belong to assets acquired or liabilities assumed.
Share capital	Legal acquirer	Issued equity interests before the business combination plus fair value of issued shares to shareholders of legal acquire
Other equity items issued	Legal acquiree	Recognized and measured at their carrying amount before the business combination plus the fair value of the legal acquirer
Retained earnings	Legal acquiree	Recognized and measured at their carrying amount before the business combination
Non-controlling interests	Legal acquiree	Proportionate share of retained earnings and other equity interests before the business combination (no fair value treatment!)
Equity structure	Legal acquirer	Reflects number and types of equity instrument issued. This requires a restatement of the equity structure of the legal acquiree using the exchange ratio as of the purchase agreement.

Tab. E-17 Accounting treatment of selected balance sheet items in reverse acquisitions

If the reverse acquisition results in a **bargain purchase**, the goodwill / badwill is determined by the transferred consideration less the identified net assets of the legal acquirer.

To be consistent with the application of the equity allocation, **earnings per share** have to be adjusted accordingly as required by IFRS 3.B25. To compute the earnings per share for the current and the previous (restated) period, the following parameters have to be used.

Calculation of	Acquisition date		Comparative periods
	Before	After	
Average number of shares outstanding	Weighted average number of ordinary shares outstanding of the legal acquirer multiplied by exchange ratio	Actual number of ordinary shares outstanding of the legal acquirer	Historical weighted average number of ordinary shares outstanding multiplied by exchange ratio
Profit of the period	Profit or loss by legal acquiree	Profit or loss by legal acquiree	Profit or loss by legal acquiree

Tab. E-18 Parameter required in computing earnings per share

Other **comparative information** of previous periods in consolidated financial statements has to be adjusted as well. This applies particularly to equity as the equity of the legal acquiree is subject to reporting, adjusted by capital of the legal acquirer.

6.2 Acquisitions achieved in stages

Acquisitions achieved in stages (or step acquisitions) are those transactions where the investment in a company is acquired step by step. It may start with a small investment that is increased with every additional purchase transaction of an investment in that company until control is given. The company therefore will run through all classifications of a company: from an ordinary financial investment according to IAS 39 or IFRS 9 via an associate according to IAS 28 to a subsidiary according to IFRS 10. The transaction of acquiring investments in the company may continue even after control is given until a full ownership is established.[47]

From an accounting point of view the transaction that establishes control is the relevant one. Transactions before control is given are accounted differently to those where control is already established.

- Before control is given

   In principle, IFRS 3 does not care about what happened before control. Some transactions before the transaction that establishes control are considered as an element of the consideration transferred. Other transactions, like pre-existing relationships subject to the status of the company in the group, may be adjusted depending on the specific accounting rules of their particular status.

Example

Ehrlicher is a manufacturer of optical and electronic connectors. The company is highly specialized and serves the market for high frequency, ultrafast data transmitting. Flexing Cables has held a 10% investment in Ehrlicher for several years to ensure access to Ehrlicher products. Flexing Cables's management has often tried to extend the investment in Ehrlicher but, until now, the founding family has rejected all attempts.

As the next generation of the founding family is not willing to continue the business in its current condition, an agreement with Flexing Cables was made in 2011 to ensure a going concern for Ehrlicher. The agreement consisted of the following elements:

- The members of the founding family concentrate all their shares in Ehrlicher in a family office that is arranged as a holding company.
- As of 1.1.2012, Flexing Cables would acquire 15% of Ehrlicher shares by paying an amount of 37,500 k EUR in cash.

---

[47] This chapter discusses only general topics of step acquisitions. For details on the accounting of step acquisitions see chapter I-3 on page 505.

> - As of 1.5.2013, Flexing Cables would acquire 45% of Ehrlicher shares by transfer of 16,100,000 ordinary shares of Flexing Cables.
> - As of 1.10.2013, Flexing Cables would acquire 30% of Ehrlicher shares by transfer of 10,700,000 ordinary shares of Flexing Cables.
> - A member of the family office would be nominated as a member of the Flexing Cables board.
>
> Flexing Cables board approved the agreement.
> The acquisition of an additional 15% shares in Ehrlicher as of 1.1.2012 would change the status of the company. While the investment in Ehrlicher had been recorded as a pure investment before, it would then qualify as an associated company. Accordingly, the investment would have to be remeasured and reclassified, requiring a purchase price allocation and a one-line consolidation.

- During establishment of control

  The transaction that establishes control triggers the acquisition and purchase price allocation. Some relationships may exist before control, so additional tasks may be necessary. Such pre-existing relationships are subject to an initial consolidation.

> **Example**
>
> According to the original agreement with the founding members, the next step would be due as of 1.5.2013. Flexing Cables had to transfer a volume of 16,100,000 ordinary shares in return for a 45% stake in Ehrlicher. The acquisition of this share would constitute control as Flexing Cables would then own 70% of Ehrlicher shares (10% + 15% + 45%). Ehrlicher would then have the status of a subsidiary, which required a purchase price allocation in combination with an initial consolidation. All previously acquired shares would have to be remeasured by fair value as of 1.5.2013. Furthermore, effects of the equity accounting would have to be reversed.
>
> While Flexing Cables and its subsidiaries are customers of Ehrlicher, all trading relationships have to be treated as pre-existing relationships as part of the initial consolidation.

- After control is given

  Additional step acquisitions after control is established are treated as transactions between shareholders / investors. An additional equity consolidation and an adjustment of goodwill is not necessary.

> **Example**
>
> Obtaining the remaining 30% shares in Ehrlicher as of 1.10.2013, the company would become a wholly-owned company of Flexing Cables. While Flexing Cables already had control of Ehrlicher, this transaction was treated as an

> equity transaction. Accordingly, all costs associated with the acquisition had to be recorded in equity, other balance sheet items were not involved.
>
> Special attention was required as obtaining control and increasing investment in Ehrlicher both occurred in the same reporting period. During the period 1.5.2013 to 30.9.2013, the founding family still owned a 30% stake in Ehrlicher. Accordingly, the profit generated by Ehrlicher during this period had to be assigned to the group and to non-controlling interests. The increase of the carrying amount of non-controlling interests is important in executing the equity transaction as non-controlling interests have to be reclassified.[48]

6.3 Obtaining control in special situations

6.3.1 *Obtaining control without an acquisition or consideration*

In some situations, a business combination may occur without any consideration transferred. This is the case when a company obtains control over another company without performing any acquisition or business combination activities. Control is only achieved because there was a change in voting rights that brings the company that obtains control into a favourable position. The initial events and transactions for a change in voting rights are often out of scope of the company that obtains control. Reasons for changes in voting rights are manifold. Typical examples are:

- selective buy-back transactions of shares from selected owners by the acquiree that increase the percentage of shares (and so of voting rights),
- lapsing of minority veto rights,
- changes in the article of incorporation regarding the handling of voting rights, and
- termination or formation of contractual agreements between shareholders that assign control to selected owners.

Like any other business combination, such a case initiates the same accounting activities as an ordinary acquisition of a company. The acquisition method has to be applied, requiring an execution of a purchase price allocation. As no consideration is transferred, a modified application of the acquisition method will take place:

- The company that obtains control will be treated as an acquirer while the other company is the acquiree.
- The consideration transferred is based on the fair value of the acquirer's interest in the acquiree.

---

[48] Some argue that while both transactions take place in the same period, a 100% consolidation can be realized. This is because non-controlling interests are reclassified to retained earnings which has the same impact as the execution in two steps. Such a practice would result in a non-appropriate presentation of the profit achieved and allocable to non-controlling interests.

To measure the consideration transferred, an appropriate valuation technique has to be applied that reflects the market conditions of the equity instruments of the acquiree. This can either be deductions from observed market transactions or a measurement technique.

> IFRS 3.B46 provides support on the fair value measurement until *IFRS 13 – Fair Value Measurement* is not effective.[49] Upon the effective date, an application of IFRS 13 is mandatory.[50]

All other items of the acquisition method are applied as appropriate.

6.3.2 Exchange of equity interests

Business combinations may be realized without a transfer of cash or similar forms of payment. Instead, equity instruments, particularly shares, are exchanged as consideration transferred. Such transactions are also called share-for-share exchanges. All transactions and the corresponding accounting of a purchase price allocation are executed like transactions in any other purchase price allocation. The challenge of share-for-share transactions is the determination of the fair value of shares given as consideration. This is because in some business combinations, shares of companies are either not publicly traded or do not provide a reasonable measurement basis. Therefore, measurement of the acquisition date fair value of the acquirer's shares is hard to achieve. In such situations, IFRS 3.33 requires using the fair value of the acquiree's shares instead of using the fair value of the acquirer's shares.

The requirement mentioned in IFRS 3.33 is a fall-back method to estimate the fair value at the acquisition date of the consideration transferred. This does not automatically presume that a measurement is always based on the acquiree's shares. Any check of whether it is possible to base the measurement on the acquirer's shares, has to occur before using the alternate measurement method.

6.3.3 Mutual entities

According to the definition in IFRS 3.A a mutual entity is "an entity [...] that provides dividends, lower costs or other economic benefits directly to its owners, members or participants". Typical examples mentioned in this definition are insurance companies, credit unions and co-operative entities. Their members benefit from the membership itself as mutual entities offer reduced fees charged for goods and services, patronage dividends or similar benefits.

Mutual entities involved in business combinations have to apply the same accounting rules and regulations. An exception is not given as explicitly mentioned

---

[49] IFRS 3.B46 refers to the old version. The current version of IFRS 3.B46 is already adjusted reflecting an application of IFRS 13.

[50] IFRS 13 has to be applied for periods beginning on or after 1 January 2013.

in IFRS 3.BC104. Therefore, all steps of the purchase price allocation have to be applied.

- Identification of the acquirer
  The identification of an acquirer has to follow the normal rules. If an identification is not possible, the criteria outlined in IFRS 3.B14 – 3.B18 have to be applied. An application may be mandatory if the business combination involves two mutual entities.

- Estimation of consideration
  Business combinations involving mutual entities are often realized by issuing member interests instead of cash. Due to the absence of a market dealing with such member interests, their fair value is difficult to measure. IFRS 3 proposes to derive the fair value from the member interest of the acquiree in such situations as this is more reliably measurable than the member interests of the acquirer. This guidance on the estimation of the consideration transferred is equal to share-for-share exchanges.
  The measurement of consideration is only described very vaguely in the standard. Future membership benefits and other relevant assumptions should be considered in determining a fair value. Such a fair value can be derived from discounted cash flow models that are based on cash flow comparisons of fees due to goods and services between a membership and regular market conditions.

- Net assets of the acquiree
  Net assets of the acquiree are directly recognized as an addition in equity of the acquirer according to IFRS 3.B47. The position where the addition is recorded in equity is not explicitly defined. Additions can be recorded at every position in equity unless it is not recorded in retained earnings. Even if an initial recording is prohibited in retained earnings, a subsequent reclassification to retained earnings is not prohibited. Such a reclassification might be necessary to comply with local requirements.
  The measurement of assets acquired and liabilities assumed in a business combination with mutual entities is similar to the measurement of assets and liabilities in ordinary transactions.

Recording an acquisition of an entity by another entity is in principle the same as recording an investment in a subsidiary. Instead of a transfer of cash, the acquirer records an increase in equity. Any fair value adjustments of assets acquired and liabilities assumed are recorded at the appropriate levels. The consolidation follows the same procedures as other initial consolidations. The following standard journal entries illustrate the accounting:

- The acquiring mutual entity

Journal entry		Company
dr.	Investment in subsidiaries	Parent
cr.	Member interests issued	Parent

- Subsidiary adjustments

  Adjustments of accounted-for assets and liabilities as well as unrecognized assets and liabilities follow the same principles as for other acquisitions. The execution of specific journal entries is not necessary.

- Initial equity consolidation

  The consolidation journal entry is identical to the journal entries presented, except that the equity account of the subsidiary subject to consolidation is different.

Journal entry		Company	Comment
dr.	Goodwill	Group	
dr.	**Member interests issued**	**Subsidiary**	
dr.	Retained earnings	Subsidiary	
dr.	Profit / losses carried forward	Subsidiary	
dr.	Revaluation reserve	Subsidiary	Only the portion that relates to fair value adjustments and the recognition of non-accounted assets and liabilities. Can also be a credit.
dr.	IFRS opening balance	Subsidiary	Only the portion that relates to fair value adjustments and the recognition of non-accounted assets and liabilities. Can also be a credit.
cr.	Investment in subsidiaries	Parent	
cr.	Non-controlling interests	Group	
cr.	Deferred taxes revaluation reserve	Subsidiary	Elimination in proportion to the elimination of the revaluation reserve and the IFRS opening balance sheet. Can also be a debit.
cr.	Foreign exchange differences	Group	Can also be a debit.

6.4. Multi-component contracts

Acquisitions of subsidiaries are sometimes accompanied by or bundled with other transactions. For each transaction (including the acquisition of investments in the subsidiary) there is a separate agreement or contract. Each agreement would also be executed as agreed. Nevertheless, from a commercial or business point of view, those agreements belong together as they are integral elements of the acquisition. They would never be signed as standalone contracts and therefore qualify as multi-component contracts.

This pattern is often observed in practice regardless of the purpose for which the agreements were established. One typical reason is driven by the acquirer. The success of a company is often linked to key personnel – management or owners – who push the business. These people should often be encouraged to stay for a defined period to ensure that their knowledge, their business contacts and their ideas, visions and approaches of technologies, products and services are transferred into the acquirer's environment. In order to prevent harm to the business and the newly acquired subsidiary, protection regulations, such as non-competition, are often agreed between the acquirer and the former owners. Another intention is to ensure access to technology, patents, property and similar assets that rest with the former owners. They often are needed in the ordinary course of the business by the subsidiary. The acquirer therefore is willing to enter into additional agreements that support the acquisition of a subsidiary. Another reason is driven by the former owners. Their intention is to maximize profit on sale of their business. As the initiated activities may realize a profit in the future, the former owners will be keen to ensure that the profit is realized in a way they expect. Therefore, they not only accept earn-out options as one compensation element, but are also willing to support the company to realize this profit, at least for a defined period, which may be subject to another consideration. While not all assets are easily transferable to the acquirer, agreements that result in additional compensation, by providing exclusive access and use, are common practice. This not only includes access to those assets which are similar to the acquirer's, it may also include the transfer of intangible assets, such as knowledge. For each asset and each issue, a separate agreement is often established, including separate compensation.

IFRS 3.51 picks up the multi-component contract issue in a broader context. All agreements made between the acquirer, acquiree and the former owners before or during the acquisition may constitute an integral part of the acquisition. In determining which agreement or contract is part of the acquisition, three important aspects have to be considered.

- The reason for the agreement

  The substance, intention or reason of that agreement has to be assessed. They are the best sources available. If it can be proven that the intention to enter into an agreement refers or belongs to the acquisition, the agreement is part of the acquisition and has to be considered. If not, the agreement has to be accounted separately by applying appropriate IFRS. To prove that the agreement is part of the acquisition itself, benefits of the agreement either have to be balanced equally between the parties involved or for the advantage of the former owners or the acquiree. If the agreement is established for the benefit of the acquirer, it can be assumed that the whole or the excess benefit unlikely belongs to the acquisition. It has to be accounted for separately.

  Typical examples of separately accounted items as listed in IFRS 3.52 are pre-existing relationships, remuneration of employees (and therefore also of former owners) and reimbursement on acquisition related costs. IFRS 3.B50 – B62 provide guidance regarding the treatment of these special items.

- The initiator

  An agreement initiated by one party may indicate if the agreement is subject to consideration transferred or not. It is more likely that the agreement belongs to the acquisition if it is initiated by the former owner or the acquiree rather than by the acquirer. The acquirer as the initiator often proves that the agreement has to be accounted separately.

- The timing

    Agreements signed shortly before, after or even during negotiations often indicate a connection to the acquisition. This will even be enhanced if the timing aspect is combined with one of the other aspects.

Identified agreements as part of multi-component contracts that belong to the acquisition have to be recorded and measured by applying the same valuation approach that is used for the other elements of the acquisition method; all items have to be measured by their fair value. Even if there are interconnections between all elements of the acquisition, agreements should be measured separately. Based on the nature of the agreement an appropriate valuation technique has to be chosen and applied.[51]

Even if agreements have to be checked if they qualify as part of acquisitions, IFRS 3.52 list some agreements that are not subject to acquisitions: remunerations of employment contracts and reimbursements to the acquiree and its former owners. It is always recommended to verify that these agreements have to be accounted separately from acquisitions.

> Always add a check regarding potential multi-component contracts in the purchase price allocation process!

Example

In addition to the sales and purchase agreement, a side letter between the management of Flexing Cables and one owner of Solenta was signed. This owner was also the managing director of Solenta. The intention of the side letter was to ensure that the managing director would remain with Solenta for the next few years, so the initiator of this side letter was Flexing Cables. The letter includes a commitment from the managing director to serve Solenta, and was arranged as a remuneration contract.

Even though the letter was initiated by Flexing Cables, had a direct link to the sales and purchase agreement and had been signed at the same time as that agreement, it did not qualify as part of the acquisition and therefore had to be treated separately.

6.4.1. Regular employment contracts

In addition to its remuneration, employment contracts often cover complex and extensive agreements. The intention to add such items to employment contracts, particularly in the context of business combinations and acquisitions, is to attract former management of the company to stay. The arrangement can have multiple elements like incentives, contingent payments or non-financial elements. While these items are not so obvious at first sight, an assessment is always required whether or not the elements of employment contracts qualify as additional consideration as part of acquisitions. IFRS 3.B55 lists a set of criteria that can be used to determine whether an employment contract has to be considered as an

---

[51] See Tab. E-5 on page 154 for measurement bases of agreements.

element of transferred consideration. These employment contracts usually refer to the former owners or top management of the acquiree who should be attracted to continue their engagement under the new owner of the acquiree due to their knowledge about the acquiree, the market and market behaviours, as well as the contacts they have in the market.

No.	Criterion	Description
1)	Continuing employment	Any contingent payments not affected by the termination of a continuing employment are additional considerations.
2)	Duration of employment	If the employment period is equal to or less than a contingent payment period payments may qualify as considerations. A detailed relationship is not necessary. It is sufficient if the periods coincide.
3)	Level of remuneration	Unusual levels of remuneration may indicate additional considerations. IFRS 3.B55 (c) also suggests contingent payments to be treated as considerations if remunerations are at a reasonable level compared to the remuneration of other key employees in the group.
4)	Incremental payments	Contingent payments (on a per-share base) to former owners who will be employed may be higher than payments to the ones that will not be employed. Such incremental payments have to be treated as remuneration.
5)	Number of shares owned	Depending on the relative number of shares and the awards and compensations assigned to these shares, contingent payments either qualify as considerations or profit sharing agreements if the former owners are employed.
6)	Linkage to valuation	Contingent payments may qualify as considerations if the underlying earn-out model assumes an aquiree's value at the lower end of a valuation range contractually agreed and considerations transferred are based on that value.
7)	Formula for determining consideration	The earn-out model[52] itself may also be used in determining the allocation of contingent payments as consideration or remuneration. If the model supports the fair value of the acquiree contingent payments may qualify as considerations.
8)	Other agreements and issues	Other agreements may cover issues such as:
		Non-competition agreements
		Executory contracts
		Consulting contracts
		Lease agreements
		Exclusive forms of usage rights
		Depending on the original intention, these agreements may qualify as contingent considerations. The arms-length principle should be used in determining what belongs to consideration.

Tab. E-19   Checklist of employment contracts subject to business combinations

Often, employment contracts have to be split up due to terms negotiated. The remuneration is treated as an ordinary cost element separately from the acquisition as the staff provides contractually agreed services. By contrast, contingent payments are often subjects to be included as considerations transferred of the acquisition. To avoid unexpected effects, a pre-agreement check is recommended to ensure a proper treatment as originally intended.

---

[52] IFRS 3.B55 (g) describes the calculation or earn-out model to determine any contingent payments as "the contingent formula".

> **Example**
>
> As the side letter had been arranged as a remuneration contract, it contained the typical elements of an employment contract, tailored to the position of a managing director:
>
> - The fixed salary was in the same range as the remuneration of other managing directors of subsidiaries.
> - A variable payment based on the performance of the managing director would be part of the remuneration. Payment depended on the achievement of liquidity, profit and personal targets and would be agreed on a quarterly basis.
> - The managing director would be integrated into the Flexing Cables employee share programme.
> - The managing director would serve Solenta for a minimum of three years. If the employment contract was terminated earlier by the managing director, an appropriate penalty would have to be paid to the company.
> - The contract included a non-competition agreement covering the period of employment plus two additional years, starting with the last day of service by the managing director. The company would pay appropriate compensation in return for the non-competition agreement.
>
> The arrangement of the contract assumed that an ordinary employment contract was present and that no hidden considerations existed. Any payments were on an arm's-length principle and similar to the compensation of other managing directors. While the duration of employment was larger than the earn-out period, a hidden consideration could not be assumed. The same applied to the non-competition clause.
>
> All in all it can be assumed that the side letter regarding the remuneration was an ordinary employment contract that would be handled separately to the sales and purchase agreement.

6.4.2 Share-based payments as non-controlling interests

A special type of multi-component contract is the share-based compensation, either as part of the regular employment contract (and therefore a share-based payment) or as part of bonus of stock plans for selected or all employees of the acquiree. These compensations will impact not only on the presentation and measurement during the acquisition, but also on the initial and subsequent consolidations.

Whether shares are granted due to services provided by staff or as an attractive method for the employer, an increase in the shareholder structure is always the case. This is independent from the access to the shares by the parties the shares were granted to. While these shares follow special rules and are often restricted in access, an acquisition of the acquirer is not possible. Therefore, shares subject to share-based payments have to be presented as non-controlling interests.

The measurement of non-controlling interests subject to share-based payments varies depending on whether the payments are vested or not. If vested, the share-based payments are measured by market-based "measures" at their grant dates. If unvested, IFRS 3.B62A in conjunction with IFRS 3.30 and *IFRS 2 – Share-based Payment* assumes that the grant date is the acquisition date. In this case, an allocation is necessary. The portion of the vesting period completed at the acquisition date is subject to non-controlling interests measured with their fair values at the acquisition date whilst the remaining portion will be subject to regular personnel expenses in future periods. The allocation of the appropriate amount to non-controlling interests is based on the ratio between the vested period and the vesting period (so the greater of the original vesting period and the total vesting period).

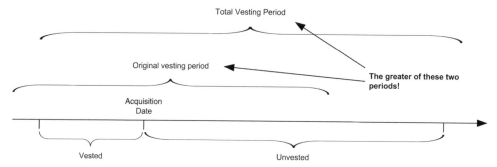

Fig. E-20   Allocation scheme for unvested share-based payment

6.4.3 Share-based payment exchanges

A different situation occurs if the acquirer eliminates all share-based payments awards[53] of the subsidiary and replaces them with the acquirer's own share-based payments. The intention of such an exchange transaction is based on various intentions of the acquirer:

- Non-controlling interests due to share-based payments should be avoided;
- Only one uniform system in the group should exist;
- The measurement of the subsidiary's shares in subsequent periods would be difficult to realize;
- Other intentions as appropriate by the acquirer.

The ability to exchange share-based payment awards is based on the original terms of the acquiree's share-based payment agreement and local laws and regulations on employment matters. The accounting for exchange transactions is independent from these underlying legal issues and has to be realized by considering IFRS 3. B56-62, in conjunction with IFRS 2. In general, exchange transactions are treated as modifications of existing share-based payment agreements. This is whether payments are vested or not. While the underlying share-based payment agreements may have different options, different situations exist requiring different types of accounting:

- Plain replacement
    A replacement without any other obligations and conditions is always subject to an additional consideration transferred as the acquirer is initiating such a transaction on his free will.

- Expiring due to an acquisition
    Share-based payment awards of acquirees may contractually retire due to an acquisition or business combination. An accounting for such a

---

[53] In this context, awards relate to and summarize all share-based payments that are subject to future payment where the employees have some kind of right to.

retirement is not subject to any considerations transferred. Instead, if the acquirer is replacing these awards by his own ones without an obligation to do so, all share-based payments under the new system are treated as remuneration items to be expensed.

- Enforcements

   If the acquirer is contractually obliged to replace awards or employees have the right to enforce a replacement, the acquirer has to initiate an exchange of awards. These kinds of enforcements are again based on the original terms of the acquiree's share-based payment agreement and local laws and regulations on employment matters.

The measurement of an exchange transaction is based on IFRS 2.16, 2.35 or 2.41 using either a fair value base derived from market prices or a cash base depending on the nature of the share-based payment agreement.[54] Both, the awards of the acquiree, as well as the awards of the acquirer, have to be measured using these principles at the acquisition date. The measurement of the acquiree's award has to consider also the portion that belongs to any pre-acquisition services. The same measurement principle has to be applied as when measuring share-based payments which are part of a non-controlling interest.[55] To determine the transferred consideration, the portion of the acquirer's award has to equal the portion of the acquiree's award belonging to services before the acquisition date. The difference between the fair value of the acquirer's award and its pre-acquisition portion are treated as post-acquisition expenses. The calculation of the valuation of the acquirer's awards should be based on those awards expected to vest.

While the accounting requirements on share-based payments according to IFRS 2 and 3 will deviate from the treatment for taxation purposes, deferred taxes have to be considered as well.

6.5 Pre-existing relationships

Pre-existing relationships are usually relationships between the acquirer and the acquiree that already exist before the acquisition date. They may even involve a business combination. In most cases, these relationships are commercially based for different purposes:

- trading with each other,
- use of assets, knowledge or rights,
- sharing resources like production facilities, sales channels or research and development or
- competition that may result in lawsuits regarding patent violations, competitive regulations or monopoly situations.

Other reasons might be applicable as well. Pre-existing relationships are embedded in the determination of what is part of the business combination. This is necessary because not all transactions and issues of pre-existing relationships

---

[54] Other conditions and measurement requirements of IFRS 2 have to be considered as well but are not discussed in this context.
[55] See previous chapter.

are subject to consideration as part of a business combination. If a relationship with a business combination is not given, a separate accounting is required. On the other hand, if a relationship is given, the pre-existing relationships may be subject to dedicated accounting requirements of the business combination.

Whether a pre-existing relationship is or is not part of a business combination, it cannot be compared with multi-component contracts. This is because pre-existing relationships between an acquirer and acquiree can exist without an acquisition while multi-component contracts have a direct relationship with the acquisition.

In general, pre-existing relationships can be divided into two main areas: contractual and non-contractual. Both areas require the same attention as a commercial background is often the case. Contractual relationships are usually established in a vendor-customer or licensor-licensee or franchisor-franchisee or lessor-lessee relationship or any similar relationship. The focus is on commercial or trading transactions. By contrast, non-contractual relationships may arise in situations where two parties are involved in an issue or transaction that does not belong to the ordinary course of the business. Typical examples are lawsuits.

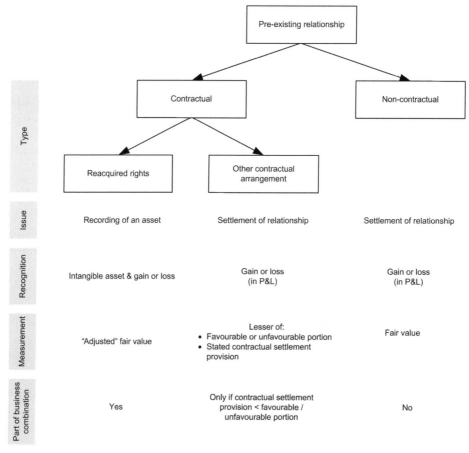

Fig. E-21 Classification of pre-existing relationships

Contractual relationships include a subset of relationships that deal with rights that are reacquired due to the business combination. Such transactions are part of the business combination and subject to specific accounting rules.[56] If a contractual relationship that is not a reacquired right is subject to settlement according to IFRS 3.52a, a gain or loss might be recorded if the relationship is not part of the business combination. The criterion whether or not the contractual obligation is part of the business combination is based on IFRS 3.B52.

Non-contractual relationships are always assumed to be separate transactions that do not belong to business combinations. Their settlement is always recorded through profit & loss.

Due to the relationship between the acquirer and the acquiree as parent and subsidiary after the establishment of control, it will be stipulated that as many pre-existing relationships will be settled as possible. This settlement assumes that no balances are present in consolidated financial statements. In fact, the settlement is a combination of adjusting balances in separate financial statements of acquirer and acquiree combined with the elimination as a group internal transaction. This involves all transactions before the acquisition date that are not settled at this date. Consequently, a debt consolidation is required as part of the initial consolidation. Some pre-existing relationships may involve third parties. A full settlement might not be possible if third parties are involved. Only in such cases, a carrying amount has to be recorded and presented in consolidated financial statements.

An **identification** of pre-existing relationships is a task that is very similar to the identification of non-accounted-for assets acquired and liabilities assumed to be part of the purchase price allocation. In most cases pre-existing relationships can be easily identified as there is a commercial history between the acquirer and the acquiree. This history is either based on contracts that link the companies together or on collaborations over a period of time. Due to the history, accounting information might be available that supports the identification. Nevertheless there might also be situations where a history is not given or is very vague. An exhaustive check may result in determining pre-existing relationships in such situations.

The identification of pre-existing relationships might be as time-consuming as the identification of potential intangible assets during a purchase price allocation. Similar to intangible assets, this task is also combined with the question of an appropriate recognition and measurement base. Therefore, the same **identification techniques** can be applied to items that represent pre-existing relationships as necessary. Such techniques can be taken from professional auditing techniques auditors often apply: [57]

- analyzing the accounts of the acquiree and perhaps also the accounts of the acquirer regarding any pending and accounted business transaction,

---

[56] See next chapter.
[57] See chapter E -3.4.3.1 on page 161 regarding identification techniques available.

- scanning and analyzing the business relationships with customers and suppliers,
- inventorying, scanning and analyzing of contracts in all business units, departments and other organizational units of the acquiree and
- further identification and analysis activities as appropriate.

> To avoid multiple identification tasks, a single identification activity should take place after the closure of the acquisition. This identification tasks should inventorying all underlying contracts, transactions, relationships, facts and circumstances important for the initial consolidation.

The **recognition** of pre-existing relationships depends on the type of relationship. In general, such relationships are represented by assets and liabilities. Those items are either recorded by the acquirer and the acquiree or by one party only. The recognition follows the usual recognition practices of similar transactions in separate financial statements of the acquirer and acquiree. From a group's perspective, pre-existing relationships are either non-existent or require third party treatment. Non-existent relationships are due to elimination or settlement during the consolidation process (and consequently do not require recognition). However, pre-existing relationships are recognized as assets or obligations against third parties, whether those parties are involved directly or indirectly.

The **initial measurement** of pre-existing relationships is summarized in IFRS 3.51 to 3.53 and its application guidance. Depending on the type of relationship, either a fair value measurement or a measurement based on contractual obligations is required for assets and liabilities representing the pre-existing relationships. In addition to the recognition criteria, an allocation of pre-existing relationships to a business combination and therefore achieving a consideration as a part of goodwill is subject to the initial measurement.

Contractual relationships are measured according to IFRS 3.B52b which requires a market comparison. The underlying contract has to be measured and compared to market conditions as of the acquisition date from an acquirer's point of view. This is the first measurement and it requires that the terms and conditions of the current relationship have to be applied to same or similar market transactions with the same or similar content. If the current contract offers an advantage compared to the market transaction, it is a favourable contract, otherwise the contract is unfavourable. The difference between the fair value of the market transaction and the value of the underlying contract has to be determined as this difference is needed in the further calculation. The second measurement is a determination of the settlement provision that is stated in the underlying contract. As a general rule, all adjustments are recorded as a settlement gain or loss. Only if the settlement provision is lower than the favourable or unfavourable amount, the difference between the favourable or unfavourable amount and the settlement provision has to be accounted for as part of the business combination.

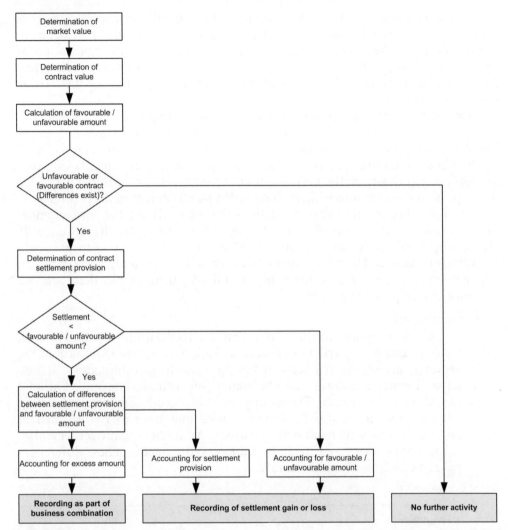

Fig. E-22 Calculation scheme for the accounting of contractual pre-existing relationships

Even if this measurement model sounds reasonable, there might be situations, where a market or a market value is hard to estimate. Furthermore, a set of questions has to be solved before entering in the calculation of the adjustment amount:

- Is there a market?
- Can items that relate to the underlying contract be traded in the market?
- Are the same or similar contractual items or transactions traded in the market?
- Can a market value be derived from those contractual items or transactions?
- Are market participants (so third parties) willing to enter in such a transaction?

A positive answering of these questions combined with appropriate evidence should be part of the documentation of the initial consolidation. This documentation will act as the underlying parameter and evidence for the calculation of favourable or unfavourable elements of the contractual relationship. The calculation itself follows the ordinary valuation of contracts and the benefits arising from such contracts.

Non-contractual relationships are measured according to IFRS 3.B52a. The standard requires a full fair value measurement. Exceptions are not given. The determination of the fair value of a non-contractual relationship is based on the usual valuation methods.[58] Necessary fair value adjustments due to a step-up or step-down of the carrying amount of assets or liabilities recorded that represent those relationships are recorded as settlement gains or losses.

The **recording** of pre-existing relationships depends on the measurement as well as on the items already recorded by the acquirer and the acquiree. If pre-existing relationships are not accounted by one party or by both parties, a recording of assets and liability is required depending on the underlying contract. This presumes that an accounting is not prohibited. In principle, there are two scenarios that require recording:

- Collaboration

   A collaboration scenario is based on relationships that deal with trading, uses and sharing of resources. Both parties, the acquirer and the acquiree, are obliged to account for the underlying transactions. If one party has not accounted for the underlying transaction, an additional recording is necessary. Depending on the accounting as pre-existing relationships, elimination differences arise that have to be recorded in profit & loss as settlement gains or losses. An intercompany settlement in subsequent periods may again be subject to differences. These differences have to be adjusted against equity.

Example

Solenta and Flexing Cables, and some other companies of the group, had been engaged in ordinary trading relationships for several years in which Solenta provided its products to the Flexing Cables companies. Accordingly, as of the acquisition date, the following receivables were recorded by Solenta:

- Flexing Cables SE   453 k EUR;
- Cable Systems   834 k EUR;
- Flexing Cables Belgium   147 k EUR;
- Wilmington   766 k EUR.

---

[58] See Appendix I: Fair value measurement on page 751 for the application of valuation methods.

> Flexing Cables had negotiated an "umbrella agreement" with Solenta that included special conditions for all companies of the group. These conditions consisted of an extended payment period of 60 days and a bonus system that defined bonus payments to Flexing Cables depending on the volume purchased from Solenta. These payments were calculated and paid annually at the end of the calendar year. An extended payment period of 60 days had always been used by Flexing Cables, with a historical average of 59 days.
>
> Solenta had accounted for its receivables by applying a bad debt allowance system depending on the age of its receivables. All receivables with ages between 30 and 60 days were given a 10% bad debt allowance. Accordingly, Solenta considered a bad debt allowance of 220 k EUR for the receivables of the Flexing Cables group (453 + 834 + 147 + 766 = 2,200 and thereof 10%).
>
> In determining this pre-existing relationship, a regular check was executed during the purchase price allocation. The results of this check are that receivables related to goods which Solenta had sold for adequate market prices. While bonuses are measured and calculated at the end of the calendar year, they do not have an impact on pre-existing relationships. So, this left the bad debt allowance as the only subject for consideration.

- External commitments

    External commitments arise if third parties are involved. Commitments are subject to the measurement as a pre-existing relationship, usually a non-contractual relationship. The original transaction does not require both parties to account for it but one party has to record its consequences. This party usually is required to adjust the balances recorded to arrive at their fair values. Typical applications are lawsuits e.g. due to patent infringements. The party being sued will usually record a provision covering court and lawyer fees and potential penalties. The other party does not record anything at all.

Similar to the scenarios of pre-existing relationships, different journal entries have to be applied depending on whether the pre-existing relationship is part of the business combination or a separate transaction.

- Part of business combination

    Two journal entries are only necessary if there is a contractual relationship and a business combination has been recorded: the portion to be considered as a settlement gain or loss and the portion which is part of the business combination. While the pre-existing relationships are triggered by the acquisition, it is recommended to record the adjustment in the acquiree's environment at level III. The valuation adjustment can be recorded as another element of hidden reserves or burdens against the opening balance account. While this account is subject to the initial consolidation an appropriate adjustment of goodwill will be achieved.

Journal entries		Company	Comment
dr.	Assets	Acquiree	Can also be a credit.
	cr. Other earnings	Acquiree	Level III adjustment. Portion belonging to settlement gain / loss.
	cr. IFRS Opening balance	Acquiree	Level III adjustment. Portion belonging to offset against goodwill upon the execution of the initial consolidation.
dr.	IFRS Opening balance	Acquiree	Level III adjustment. Portion belonging to offset against goodwill upon the execution of the initial consolidation.
dr.	Other expenses	Acquiree	Level III adjustment. Portion belonging to settlement gain / loss.
	cr. Liabilities	Acquiree	Can also be a debit.

- Separate transaction

 Whether the pre-existing relationship is part of the business combination or a separate item, the recording of the adjustment in profit & loss follows the same pattern for contractual and non-contractual relationships. The gain or loss determined will generate a consolidation that dilutes the operation profit of the group.

Journal entries		Company	Comment
dr.	Assets	Acquiree	Can also be a credit.
	cr. Other earnings	Acquiree	
dr.	Other expenses	Acquiree	
	cr. Liabilities	Acquiree	Can also be a debit.

While pre-existing relationships are presented as assets and liabilities in the accounts of the acquirer and acquiree, an additional debt consolidation is mandatory. A debt consolidation as part of an initial consolidation is only required if pre-existing relationships are not settled at the acquisition date. Therefore, assets and liabilities, either current or non-current have to be eliminated. Assuming that the balances on both sides are reconciled, either due to an adjustment of the favourable or unfavourable portion of the relationship or due to ordinary business transactions, the standard journal entry for debt consolidation can be applied.

Journal entry		Company	Comment
dr.	Liabilities	Receiving company	Either acquirer or acquire
	cr. Assets	Sending company	Either acquirer or acquire

Example

 The bad debt allowance recorded by Solenta related to contractual relationships. Accordingly, a consideration as part of the initial consolidation was required. The bad debt allowance had to be reversed and recorded against retained earnings.

Journal entry

dr.	Bad debt allowance	220	
	cr. Retained earnings		220

The **subsequent measurement** of pre-existing relationships is defined in IFRS 3.55. As contractual and non-contractual relationships are settled at the acquisition date in most cases, a subsequent measurement only applies to reacquired rights (which are discussed in the next chapter in detail). In some cases, the settlement generates a follow-up effect in the subsequent period. Even if the settlement occurs in the period of the acquisition at group level, a settlement may be realized in the separate financial statements of the acquirer and acquiree in subsequent periods. Therefore, reversals of the settlement transactions are necessary at group level to establish the old state. As far as external commitments against third parties are still given and settled in subsequent periods, an ordinary accounting applies.

6.5.1 Reacquired rights

Reacquired rights are rights that were initially granted by the acquirer to the acquiree. This is more or less a subset of pre-existing relationships as reacquired rights are based on business transactions that are entered in before an acquisition or other form of business combination took place. The right brings the acquiree into a position to make use of selected assets of the acquirer, whether these assets are tangible or intangible, recognized or unrecognized. Typical examples are the use of trade names, brands, technologies. They can also include franchise agreements, construction permits and other rights. As the reacquired right is based on a contractual agreement between the acquirer and the acquiree, it is identifiable and therefore also measurable.

As a general rule, reacquired rights are recognized separately from goodwill as an intangible asset. Their **initial measurement** is based on the fair value principle, applied in two steps. In the first step, a measurement is made based on the remaining contractual terms and conditions of the underlying contract in accordance with IFRS 3.29. In other words, the measurement is based on historical costs and not on any fair value measurements during this step. The second step tries to determine fair value for the required rights. The determination is based on the required right as it is without any consideration of contractual items like renewals or other options. A true fair value measurement would probably generate a higher value as other contractual conditions like renewals, options and other items would be considered in deriving it. Hence, it is sufficient to derive a value from the same or similar contracts that are available in the market.

The difference between the market price and the assumed value of the remaining contractual life is recorded as a settlement gain or loss. This depends on the value of the remaining terms and conditions of the contract against the market price. It may either be favourable or unfavourable. If the value of the contract is less than the market price, the contract is favourable, because the acquiree has invested less than a third party would invest to acquire the same rights. Consequently, a gain has to be recorded to adjust the carrying amount to market conditions (step-up of the carrying amount). On the other hand, if the contract is unfavourable, a loss has to be recorded through a step-down transaction. Settlement gains or losses on required rights due to favourable or unfavourable conditions are recorded separately from the business combination according to IFRS 3. B53. This means that goodwill will not be affected by the settlement.

Settlement gains and losses of reacquired rights as part of a business combination are special items. While a business combination and its initial consolidation is usually a pure equity transaction that is accounted for only in the balance sheet, and therefore profit neutral, settlements will produce an initial impact of profit & loss. These settlements are comparable to lucky buys or bargain purchases that have similar effects.

The **subsequent measurement** of reacquired rights follows the same pattern as any other non-current intangible asset. It has to be amortized over the remaining contractual period. If the right is sold to a third party, the carrying amount of the required right has to be expensed like any sale of non-current assets.

6.6. Shares of the parent company

The acquisition of a new company is sometimes accompanied by special effects. The company acquired may hold shares of the parent either as financial or short-term investments. A consolidation would then present own shares as assets in the consolidated financial statements. Own shares are always treated as treasury shares according to IAS 32.33. It is not important which company of the group carries the shares as long as that company is subject to consolidation. Therefore, reclassification from assets to equity is necessary. This reclassification is presented as a reduction of equity of the parent. The fact that a newly acquired subsidiary is holding shares of the parent may trigger undesirable equity effects. This is particularly important if the parent has to maintain a defined level of equity due to financing agreements with banks.

Shares of the parent should always be the subject of special regulations in the group. To avoid negative impacts, no company of the group that is subject to consolidation should be allowed or able to acquire and hold shares of the (ultimate) parent. If a newly acquired company is holding such shares, these shares should immediately be transferred to the parent. It is up to the discretion of the parent to keep these shares as treasury shares, to distribute them to shareholders as dividends, to reissue or retire them.

> If shares of the (ultimate) parent are identified, they should immediately be transferred to the parent by compensating the new subsidiary to avoid complex equity reporting and accounting. If group policies allow subsidiaries to carry shares of the ultimate parent, consider an appropriate information gathering in reporting packages.

The journal entries presented assume that the shares held by the acquiree are transferred to the parent and kept as treasury shares before they are subject to a different treatment.

Journal entries		Company	Comment
dr.	Other receivable	Subsidiary	Handling as an intercompany item subject to elimination.
	cr. Financial asset	Subsidiary	Can be current or non-current.
dr.	Treasury shares	Parent	
	cr. Other payable	Parent	Handling as an intercompany item subject to elimination.

Example

The financial assets in Solenta's statement of financial position referred solely to shares in Flexing Cables. Solenta had purchased an amount of 102,000 shares in 2011 at a price of 6.58 EUR per share. As the company was treating these shares as a long-term investment, it had applied the cost model for measuring the carrying amount of this investment.

As the group policy of Flexing Cables did not permit any subsidiary to hold equity instruments of Flexing Cables SE, Solenta was forced to transfer its shares to the parent. The transfer was realized as part of the acquisition in order to avoid any accounting specialities as part of the initial consolidation.

The following journal entries were executed upon the initial accounting:

a) Solenta

Journal entry				Comment
dr.	Other receivables, Intercompany	102		Carrying amount in Solenta's accounts, Level I
	cr.	Financial assets	102	
dr.	Other receivables, Intercompany	9		Fair value adjustment, Level III
	cr.	Financial assets		9

b) Flexing Cables

Journal entry				Comment
dr.	Treasury shares	111		
	cr.	Other payables, Intercompany		111	Recorded in separate financial statements

6.7. Non-material subsidiaries

The **materiality concept** as defined in the *framework* is not only mandatory for business transactions, balance sheet and profit & loss items, it also covers consolidated financial statements and even legal entities that are part of the group. Under the materiality concept as defined in F.30, an item is classified as non-material if the omission or misstatement is not relevant to the economic decision of users of financial statements. This concept is picked up by IAS 8; IAS 8.8 explicitly confirms the material concept of the framework.

Applying the materiality concept to the group, particularly to the companies to be consolidated, a subsidiary may not be subject to consolidation if the profit and total net assets of that subsidiary are not material to the group. Both criteria have to be considered in determining the materiality of a subsidiary. Even if the profit of a subsidiary does not significantly contribute to the profit of the group, and is therefore treated as non-material, the subsidiary may record assets or liabilities that are material to the group. A subsidiary may also have profits that are material to the group whereas their assets and liabilities are marked as non-material. If a subsidiary qualifies as a non-material subsidiary, and is therefore not consolidated, the investment in that subsidiary, recorded by the parent company, is also presented in consolidated financial statements.

Changes in the current condition of a **non-material subsidiary** require a check if that change results in different treatment of the subsidiary. If such a change is given and the subsidiary is treated as a material subsidiary it has to be considered in the consolidated financial statement to be a fully consolidated subsidiary. Neither IAS 27 nor IFRS 3 provide guidance regarding the accounting for these kinds of changes. To fill this regulatory gap, the prevailing opinion is to include the subsidiary in two steps into the consolidated financial statements. The first step is the first time adoption of IFRS for the subsidiary by applying IFRS 1. This step converts separate financial statements, based on local GAAP of the so far non-material subsidiary, into the consolidated financial statements, based on IFRS. The second step integrates the adjusted financial statements through an initial consolidation into the group's accounting environment.

The initial consolidation is required in accordance with IFRS 10 at the date when the company became a subsidiary. This is also the date of the first-time adoption of IFRS for that subsidiary. If the company was acquired by the parent, a purchase price allocation is required. Any items that are identified and recorded at level II or level III, due to the purchase price allocation, have to be developed towards the date when the change in the status of the subsidiary occurs. The same applies to goodwill. Subsequent effects like depreciation and deferred taxes have to be considered as well. They cover the period from the fictitious initial consolidation date to the actual balance sheet date. By contrast, if the company was founded by the parent company, the purchase price allocation task can be omitted.

> Most companies tend to integrate all subsidiaries into the list of companies to be consolidated, even if they are classified as non-material to the group. This avoids unexpected future effects if the status of the subsidiary should change.

In rare situations, even parent can be treated as **non-material parents**. Such situations occur if shareholders bundle their shares in the parent of a group by using a holding company. A further purpose does not exist. Normally, consolidated financial statements have to be prepared by the ultimate parent, not by the parent of the group. Due to the handling of the ultimate parent as a non-material parent (upon the discretion of the shareholders), consolidated financial statements are prepared at the parent's level in the group. The holding company only records investment in the subsidiary and dividends received that may be distributed to shareholders.

If a change in condition is detected, it is necessary to check in a similar way as for non-material subsidiaries. If a change in condition is confirmed, consolidated financial statements have to be prepared by the ultimate parent. This requires two steps. The first step is the first time adoption of IFRS by the parent in applying IFRS 1. The conversion of separate financial statements prepared by applying local GAAP towards IFRS accounting standards impact also the preparation of consolidated financial statements by the ultimate parent. Accounting policies chosen and applied in the preparation of separate financial statements by the ultimate parent, using IFRS, will also become the group accounting policies. The second step required is a purchase price allocation, combined with an initial consolidation of the parent. The problems regarding purchase price allocation are the same as for subsidiaries. In particular, if the structures are maintained over a long period, information required for purchase price allocations might no longer be available.

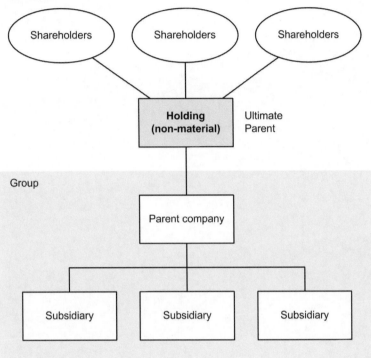

Fig. E-23   Non-material parent company

Other than the above described situation, non-material parent companies do not exist. Even if the parent qualifies as a non-material company, it has to prepare consolidated financial statements, because a group cannot exist without a parent as long as the subsidiaries are treated as material. Only if subsidiaries are also non-material to a group is the parent exempt from preparing consolidated financial statements. But this is a different situation.

F   SUBSEQUENT CONSOLIDATION

About this chapter:

The subsequent consolidation of a group is that recurring task that has to be executed at the end of each period. It has to be arranged in a way that external deadlines to publish consolidated financial statements have to be met. To ensure smooth and timely preparation, special attention is given in practice to the subsequent consolidation, as this is the core process in preparing consolidated financial statement.

This chapter discusses the whole subsequent consolidation process. Its focus is on all the necessary consolidation steps, particularly equity, debt and profit consolidation. It also deals with presentation issues, particularly for non-controlling interests and group transactions such as the impairment test. For all consolidation steps, detailed explanation is given on intercompany relationships, consolidation techniques and the treatment of consolidation problems and errors. This includes journal entries of each consolidation step. The chapter also covers the accounting of special intercompany business transactions like transfer pricing, dividend payments, non-current asset sales and the consolidation of multi-level groups.

The consolidation process is explained for subsidiaries. The subsequent handling of associates and joint ventures are discussed in chapters G - Associated companies and H - Joint Ventures.

1. BASICS

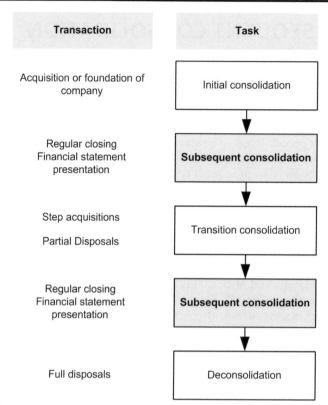

Fig. F-1 Lifecycle of a corporation: Subsequent consolidation

Consolidated financial statements need to be prepared at the end of each period during the lifecycle of a group. The lifecycle – and therefore, subsequent consolidation – will continue until the last subsidiary is sold, liquidated, or otherwise no longer part of the group's companies. Consolidation of the subsidiary is the process that prepares consolidated financial statements based on the various financial statements of all companies which are subject to consolidation.

The relevant standards for the subsequent consolidation are *IAS 27 – Separate Financial Statements* and *IFRS 10 – Consolidated Financial Statements*. While IAS 27 focuses on the preparation of separate financial statements, this standard is important if companies of the group apply IFRS as their local accounting standard. By contrast, IFRS 10 covers all accounting requirements for the preparation of consolidated financial statements. This standard does not care how separate financial statements of the group's companies are prepared. IFRS 10 does not differentiate between initial and subsequent consolidations. Therefore, the same accounting rules apply to both consolidations.

The preparation of consolidated financial statements is embedded in a set of accounting requirements defined by IFRS 10.B86 to 10.B99. According to these requirements, the following items need to be considered when preparing consolidated financial statements:

- Consolidation procedures

  In general IFRS 10.B86 requires elimination of all group-internal transactions. The elimination is discussed in detail in this chapter.

  Even if it is not explicitly mentioned, consolidation procedures assume an application of the group's currency. Therefore, any currency conversions necessary for subsidiaries that qualify as foreign investments are tasks that indirectly belong to the application of consolidation procedures.[1]

- Uniform accounting policies

  Uniform accounting principles (so the group accounting policies) have to be applied across the whole group. Any accounting treatments that differ will result in adjustments due to group accounting policies.[2]

- Measurement

  IFRS 10.B88 refers to the period the subsidiary belongs to the group (so from the date control is gained up to the date control ceases). Income and expenses of the subsidiary refer to the corresponding assets and liabilities that are recognized in consolidated financial statements.

- Potential voting rights[3]
- Reporting date

  As a general rule, the last available separate financial statements of all subsidiaries have to be included in the consolidated financial statement. IFRS 10.B92 proposes that the parent and all subsidiaries have to use the same reporting date. Nevertheless, there might be situations where deviating balance sheet dates exist. A typical example is the application of a balance sheet date of the parent during the calendar year, which results in an offset fiscal year. A subsidiary might have a deviating reporting date due to local requirements. In such situations, the subsidiary has to prepare additional financial statements at the balance sheet date of the parent. If the reporting dates deviate by less than three months, an alternate treatment is possible. In such situations, the most recent financial statements of the subsidiary have to be adjusted by significant transactions. These adjustments relate to the period between the balance sheet date of the subsidiary and the reporting date of the group.[4] If the subsidiary has a deviating balance sheet date of less than three months and a decision is made to adjust the last available financial statements for consolidation, special attention is required about significant transactions. Application of the alternate treatment is based on a few requirements:

  - The balance sheet date of financial statements is consistent over the periods.
  - The length of the reporting periods is consistent over the periods.

---

[1] See chapter K -1 on page 632 regarding currency conversions.
[2] See chapter F -2 on page 253 regarding the handling of adjustments.
[3] See chapter C -1 on page 44 regarding the consideration of potential voting rights.
[4] See chapter F -4.3 on page 278 regarding further details on significant transactions that have to be adjusted. These adjustments are discussed as part of cut-off differences.

- It has to be impracticable for the subsidiary to prepare additional financial statements for consolidation purposes (which is a flexible interpretation).
- Loss of control[5]

1.1. Preparation mechanics

Subsequent consolidated financial statements are prepared based on separate financial statements of each company of the group that are subject to consolidation. These are usually all companies of the group unless they are marked as non-material.[6] The separate financial statement of each company has to be adjusted to comply with the group's accounting policies, the reporting date of the group and its currency. The adjustment will be based on a mix of the advancement of previous period adjustments and on new adjustments. In addition to any adjustments of separate financial statements, transactions at group level have to be advanced.

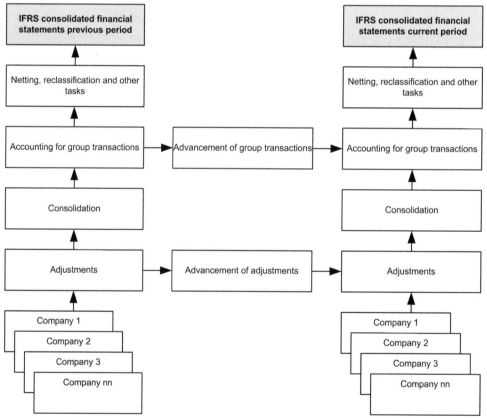

Fig. F-2   Preparation mechanics of consolidated financial statements

---

[5] The accounting in case of a loss of control is discussed in general in chapter C -3 Loss of control, in detail in chapters I -4 (Decrease in investments) for the loss of control by retaining an interest in the subsidiary and J -1.1 (Transitional consolidation without external involvement) for a full loss of control.

[6] See chapter E -6.7 on page 241 regarding the treatment of non-material subsidiaries.

Consolidated financial statements can be prepared at different data levels. These levels reflect the availability of data for consolidation as well as its preciseness. In practice, two data levels are applied for the preparation of consolidated financial statements.

- Account level

    Preparing consolidated financial statements at account level offers the opportunity of using detailed data. A direct relationship between accounts can be established that are subject to elimination. The consolidation therefore can focus only on those pairs of accounts that carry balances that equal each other. All accounts that do not have any intercompany balances can be ignored for consolidation. Offset differences can be detected much easier, as carrying amounts of intercompany accounts are separated from carrying amounts with third parties.

    This consolidation should always be the preferred solution as it is more precise and less risky. Accounting systems that offer consolidation solutions are always based on consolidations at account level.

- Presentation level

    Preparing consolidated financial statements at presentation level means that the consolidation occurs to an abstract (presentation) layer. Such a consolidation will work but it requires more information of the composition of the carrying amount of balance sheet items. Furthermore, there is uncertainty:

    - Regarding the identification of balance sheet items that may carry intercompany transactions that need to be eliminated, and
    - The volume and mixture of intercompany and external transactions of balance sheet items.

    Therefore, an auditor will pay more attention to eliminations and the supported evidence that all intercompany transactions are identified and eliminated.

    This consolidation is often prepared by small groups where the details of subsidiaries are easily available.

1.2. Tasks & timing

Due to consolidation's requirements and extent, a structured process for preparing consolidated financial statements is necessary. The design of the closing process is influenced by general considerations of the preparation process, as discussed in chapter D - Preparation of consolidated financial statements and annual reports. Based on these more general thoughts, the technical process in preparing consolidated financial statements follows the execution of dedicated activities that relate to defined consolidation steps. An efficient preparation will always execute the consolidation steps in the proposed order.

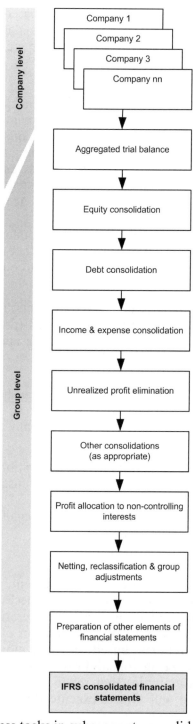

Fig. F-3 Required process tasks in subsequent consolidations

Consolidation of financial statements is always based on the separate financial statements of each company in the group. Therefore, these financial statements have to be available at a defined deadline. Depending on availability of the statements, the consolidation process will start with the following steps:

- Adjustments

    The separate financial statements (to be more precise, the reporting packages that are based on the separate financial statements) have to run through an adjustment process, which aligns the separate financial statements of each subsidiary to the group's accounting policies. The statements also need to reflect the group's currency, should the subsidiary be using a different currency to the group.

- Aggregated trial balance

    All adjusted separate financial statements have to be added up to arrive at an aggregated trial balance. This trial balance has to be adjusted by applying defined consolidation procedures. This step executes the requirements of IFRS 10.B86a.

- Equity consolidation

    The first consolidation step is to eliminate the carrying amount of the parent's investments in its subsidiaries and the equity of the subsidiary as of the acquisition date, combined with reckoning any goodwill. This step executes the requirements of IFRS 10.B86b.

    Any changes in the carrying amount of the parent's investments in subsidiaries due to acquisitions or disposals of subsidiaries are subsets of the equity consolidation. They can be processed as part of equity consolidations or other consolidations.

- Debt consolidation

    The debt consolidation eliminates intercompany balances in assets and liabilities. This step is one of the requirements of IFRS 10.B86c.

- Income & expense consolidation

    The income & expense consolidation eliminates intercompany transactions that are recorded in profit & loss, particularly: revenues, other earnings and expenses like cost of goods sold and other expenses. This step is the other part of the requirements of IFRS 10.B86c.

- Unrealized profit elimination

    As far as balance sheet items like non-current assets or inventory result from any intercompany transactions, it has to be assumed that these items carry profits generated by a selling company. These – from the group's perspective – unrealized profits have to be eliminated as the next step.

- Other consolidations

    These are consolidation tasks outside the regular consolidations; they occur infrequently and / or relate to special events. An example is a change in the group's structure. Recording them as other consolidations should improve transparency of the consolidation process by separating regular from exceptional consolidations.

- Profit allocation to non-controlling interests

    If not already executed the profit of subsidiaries attributable to minority shareholders have to be reclassified to non-controlling interests.

- Group adjustments

    Even if the parent and all the subsidiaries have prepared their "adjusted" separate financial statements in line with the group's accounting policies, it can happen that further adjustments become necessary due to valuation issues. Such a demand may arise in the interaction of related transactions which are spread across several companies of the group. Group adjustments may also arise from adjustments on balance sheet items that exist only at group level: A typical example is the write-down of goodwill.

- Netting & reclassifications

    Nettings and reclassifications relate to a proper presentation of selected items only. They do not have an impact on or rely on any valuations.

- Preparation of other elements of financial statements

    Once the final trial balance is available, all the requisite statements have to be derived. Depending on the statement this may require additional activities. A typical example is the preparation of the consolidated statement for cash flows requiring elimination of a non-cash transaction.

Consolidation tasks have to consider the **intercompany transactions** as they occur. This implies that at least a sending and a receiving company are involved in every transaction. Based on the individual intercompany case, sending and receiving companies have different duties to fulfil. Furthermore, follow-up activities may arise due to the elimination of intercompany transactions. These activities can relate to one company only. A typical example is accounting for deferred tax assets or liabilities upon the elimination of unrealized profits at the receiving company. Therefore, the differentiation between sending and receiving companies is important as consolidation and elimination tasks vary depending on the type of company.[7]

The overall **timing** of preparing consolidated financial statements is influenced particularly by two cornerstones: the publishing date of consolidated financial statements as part of the annual report and the availability of reporting packages of the subsidiaries to be consolidated. The consolidation task that is handled by the corporate centre at group level is therefore just one in a set of processes.[8] The

---

[7] We will stick to the differentiation between a sending and receiving company throughout the book.

[8] See chapter D -3 on page 98 for a description of the whole preparation process of consolidated financial statements and annual reports.

corporate centre – and in particular the consolidation department – has to ensure that all reporting packages of the subsidiaries are available on time so that there is no delay. If there is a delay the corporate centre will have to allocate additional resources to ensure the statements are on time as the publishing date cannot be changed.

Preparing consolidated financial statements by applying the recommended technical process strongly depends on the tools used in preparing these statements. Those activities that are potential candidates for automation should be automated and any spare time should be allocated to activities that cannot be automated.

2. SUBSIDIARY PREPARATION

Before a consolidation can start, subsidiaries have to be prepared so that they apply the group's accounting policies and procedures. This preparation can be executed either by the subsidiary or the corporate centre. There is a strong preference for the first option as the subsidiary will be in charge of subsidiary preparation.[9] This is because the subsidiary has all the necessary details to align their accounts with the group's policies. As the separate financial statements and the subsidiaries' reporting packages are audited, the corporate centre can rely on these financial figures.

Some **adjustments** are always subject to handling at corporate level. These adjustments relate to transactions that are out of scope for the subsidiary and are therefore recorded at group level: for example, acquisitions of new subsidiaries where purchase price allocations are necessary.

All adjustments that may arise can be allocated into one of the following categories:

- Conversions from local accounting standards towards IFRS;
- Application of the group's accounting policies and principles;
- Accounting for business transactions that occur at group level;
- Currency conversions.

Similar to the initial consolidation, adjustments are recorded at different levels.[10] As the concept of valuation levels is consistently applied during the whole life-cycle of a group, subsequent consolidations have to consider the levels and the adjustments that are carried out at each level. The levels reflect adjustment categories as already discussed.

- Level I
    Any changes in accounting standards and push-down entries of the parent are recorded on this level.

- Level II
    Adjustments due to the application of group accounting policies are recorded on this level.

---

[9] See chapter D -3.2 on page 103 for timing and responsibility details.
[10] See chapter E -1.1 on page 116 regarding a detailed discussion and application of valuation levels.

- Level III

     This level carries all adjustments that relate to a different handling of assets and liabilities at group level. This is typically caused by purchase price allocations due to the acquisition of subsidiaries.

Due to a subsequent preparation of consolidated financial statements, adjustments of prior periods that are recorded at their appropriate levels need to be considered. Two cases are important:

- One-time effects

     Adjustments due to one-time effects are often necessary to consider an item, to reclassify an item, to cut-off transactions or to consider a transaction that had not been accounted for under local GAAP. They relate to a dedicated period and are only used as part of the closing process. These adjustments are established at the end of the previous period and have to be reversed in the current period. Typical examples are the netting of VAT with input tax if they are recorded as assets and liabilities, reclassification of tax payables from provisions to liabilities or the recording of unbilled intercompany invoices as accruals.

     One-time effects are heavily used if the subsidiary has a different balance sheet date than the parent has. In such situations, one-time effects are applied in aligning the subsidiary's reporting packages to the conditions as of the reporting date of the group.

     Special cases are effects of purchase price allocations that have a short-term nature. A typical example is the accounting of the order book. Orders received have to be accounted for as an asset at group level due to the acquisition and the consideration transferred whilst these orders are pending at local level. If orders recognized as of the acquisition date are processed in the meantime, the corresponding asset has to be expensed.

     Other special cases are push-downs of the corporate centre. Push-down entries are used in transferring assets and liabilities from the parent's accounts to the subsidiary accounts. Although this is an acceptable method under some local accounting rules, it is rather unknown in the IFRS world.[11] It might also be in conflict with taxation rules. Therefore, push-downs can be captured at a higher level. Their treatment follows all other adjustment procedures.

     In general, all adjustments due to one-time effects have to be checked if the underlying transaction is either solved or otherwise processed. An elimination or reversal of the adjustment is required in this case. It is standard practice to check the status of adjustments that relate to one-time effects.

---

[11] E.g. Push-down entries are required under US-GAAP as demanded by the Securities and Exchange Commission for selected transactions (SEC Staff Accounting Bulletin No. 73).

- Long-term effects

    Some adjustments may have long-term effects. These effects relate either to valuation or to recognition issues that arise from different treatments at local and group levels. Valuation issues arise every time the measurement for IFRS is different to local GAAP measurement rules. Recognition issues arise either due to different recognition criteria of IFRS and local GAAP or due to the accounting of assets and liabilities that are out of scope by the subsidiary.

    Typical adjustment reasons are the application of different depreciation methods and useful lives of non-current assets, discounting of provisions using different discount rates, or the capitalization of self-constructed assets, which is not allowed under local GAAP.

    Similar to one-time effects are adjustments that relate to purchase price allocations. These adjustments refer to the accounting of acquired items at group level. Typical examples are intangible assets like a customer base or contingent liabilities. Items have to be accounted for in the same manner as any other assets and liabilities.

    Push-downs from the parent company may have long-term effects if debt due to the acquisition process of a subsidiary is moved to them. The accounting is similar to any other asset or liability.

    In general, adjustments that relate to long-term effects require extra attention. The first action is to check whether or not the conditions of recognizing the adjustment are still given or if any correction of the carrying amount is necessary. A correction of the adjustment follows the ordinary accounting procedures, e.g. by recording an impairment loss, a disposal, a use or an addition. If the carrying amounts of the adjustments are still reasonable, a regular alignment to reflect the carrying amounts as of the balance sheet date is necessary. As far as non-current assets are concerned, adjustments have to be depreciated; provisions and other long-term liabilities have to be compounded.

Having considered and aligned all adjustments of the previous period, adjustments of the current period have to be accounted for. These adjustments can relate to one-time effects that arise again at the end of the current period, similar to the previous period or to an allocation of valuation adjustments to the current period.

In addition to all kinds of adjustments that are caused by recognition, valuation and presentation issues, the so-adjusted separate financial statements of the subsidiary have to be translated into the presentation currency of the group if the subsidiary maintains a functional currency that is different to the group's currency. **Currency translation** is usually the final task in preparing the subsidiary for consolidation.[12]

---

[12] See chapter K -1 on page 632 regarding a detailed description of the conversions.

Due to the above issues, an efficient preparation of the subsidiary can be realized if the following steps are executed in the mentioned **execution order**:

Step	Task	Responsibility
1)	Preparation of audited separate financial statements of the subsidiary (audited financial statements are more or less the starting point for the subsidiary preparation).	Subsidiary
2)	Level I adjustments: Roll-forward / advancement of all previous period adjustments to convert financial figures from local GAAP to IFRS. This activity relates to valuation and recognition adjustments.	Subsidiary
3)	Level II adjustments: Reversals of all one-time adjustments of the previous period which are solved, lapsed or otherwise not any longer necessary. This step implies a check before the adjustments are corrected.	Subsidiary
4)	Level II adjustment: Check and recording of any one-time adjustments which are necessary at the end of the current period.	Subsidiary
5)	Level II adjustments: Check whether or not a recognition or valuation adjustment is necessary for the carrying amount of already recorded non-current adjustments that relate to the application of group accounting policies.	Subsidiary
6)	Level II adjustment: Roll-forward / advancement of non-current adjustments which relate to the application of group accounting policies (this step relates to the activities of the previous step).	Subsidiary
7)	Level III adjustments: Check whether or not a valuation or recognition adjustment is necessary for the carrying amount of assets and liabilities recorded at group level.	Corporate centre
8)	Level III adjustments: Roll forward / advancement of all assets and liabilities recorded on this level.	Corporate centre
9)	Currency conversion from the functional (local) currency to the reporting currency of the group.	Corporate centre

Tab. F-1   Execution order of subsidiary preparations

All above explained adjustments and currency translations have to be executed for each subsidiary. If all subsidiaries have been adjusted, an **aggregated trial balance** can be prepared. This trial balance – whether prepared at account or reporting level – is a simple summation. The summation is based on the carrying amounts of each balance sheet or profit & loss item across all reporting subsidiaries.

Example[13]

Applying the preparation order as outlined in Tab. F-1, the following steps have to be executed to prepare Solenta for the subsequent consolidation.[14] As Solenta was purchased during the period, an additional task is necessary, a profit cut-off. This profit cut-off is required to reflect only the profit for the period from the acquisition date to the end of the reporting period.

Step 1 – Preparing audited financial statements

The standard procedure for preparing consolidated financial statements of the group is to use audited reporting packages that are derived from separate financial statements of subsidiaries. Flexing Cables had refrained from Solenta preparing reporting packages in the first period due to the alignment of IT and reporting systems. Preparing the local accounts of Solenta for the first subsequent consolidation required a series of activities. The starting point now was the audited financial statement of Solenta as of 31.12.2013 prepared under local GAAP.

Statement of income Solenta as of 31.12.2013 (k EUR)		
Revenues	140,910	
Changes in inventory	3,130	
Work performed and capitalized		
Other income	2,307	
Total performance		**146,347**
Raw materials and consumables		(56,244)
Employee expenses		(33,402)
Depreciation and amortization expenses		(4,575)
Other expenses		(38,723)
Operating profit		**13,403**
Finance expenses		(2,516)
Profit before tax		**10,887**
Income tax expenses		(3,245)
Other tax expenses		(12)
Net profit for the period		**7,630**

Statement of income Solenta as of 31.12.2013 (k EUR)	
Revenues	140,910
Cost of goods sold	(108,837)
Gross margin	**32,073**
Sales & distribution expenses	(7,440)
Administration expenses	(6,496)
Research & development expenses	(4,200)
Other income	2,307
Other expenses	(2,853)
Operating profit	**13,391**
Finance expenses	(2,516)
Profit before tax	**10,875**
Income tax expenses	(3,245)
Net profit for the period	**7,630**

---

[13] This example does not consider any allocations due to non-controlling interests as the view is on the subsidiary and not on the group. See the example in chapter F -7.2 on page 343 regarding this task.

[14] See page 256.

Statement of financial position Solenta as of 31.12.2013 (k EUR)			
Assets			**Liabilities & Equity**
Intangible assets	2,813	Share capital	2,500
Property, plant & equipment	49,359	Capital reserve	250
Financial assets	-	Retained earnings	19,720
Non-current assets	**52,172**	Profit carried forward	18,763
		Profit of the period	7,630
Inventory	58,973	**Equity**	**48,863**
Trade receivables	26,767		
Other assets	17,358	Pensions	6,690
Cash at hand & bank	3,951	Taxation	7,800
Current assets	**107,088**	Other provisions	8,730
		Provisions	**23,220**
Deferred items	39		
		Loans	49,000
		Prepayments	300
		Trade payables	18,534
		Other payables	19,343
		Liabilities	**87,177**
Total assets	**159,260**	**Total liabilities & equity**	**159,260**

Step 2 – Level I adjustments

All level I **adjustments** as of the acquisition date had to be advanced. This task is similar to the task performed at the acquisition date. Accordingly, the following issues are identical to the ones as of the acquisition date. They cover the period from 1.4. to 31.12.:

- The step-up of the carrying amounts of intangible assets and property, plant & equipment were still valid. Accordingly, an amount of 72 EUR related to the depreciation of the step-up amount of intangible assets and an amount of 632 k EUR related to the depreciation of the step-up amount of property, plant & equipment.
- The company used a bad debt allowance system that consisted of individual and general allowances. An amount of 535 k EUR related to general allowances.
- The accrued interests as of 31.3.2013 were expensed in the meantime.
- Provisions for pensions were understated by an amount of 890 k EUR due to the application of different underlying assumptions.
- Long-term liabilities and provisions were overstated by an amount of 248 k EUR due to the application of different interest rates.
- An amount of 5,320 k EUR presented in other provisions belonged to accruals.
- The short-term portion of loans was 6,000 k EUR.
- The company still elected not to account for deferred taxation.
- Reclassification of selected items for a presentation according to IFRS was necessary.

Due to the above-mentioned adjustments, the German-GAAP balance sheet had to be adjusted by the following items:

Item	Carrying amount	Adjustments carried forward	Adjustment due to Valuation	Adjustment due to Reclassification	IFRS carrying amount	Deferred tax impact Assets	Deferred tax impact Liabilities
Intangible assets	2,813	595	(72)		3,336		(156)
Property, plant & equipment	49,359	6,617	(632)		55,344		(1,784)
Trade receivables	26,767	440	95		27,302		(159)
Other assets	16,882			39	16,921		
Deferred items	39	(8)	8	(39)	0		
Pension provisions	(6,690)	(883)	(7)		(7,580)	266	
Other provisions[15]	(8,730)	314	(66)	5,320	(3,162)		(74)
Accruals				(5,320)	(5,320)		
Loans	(49,000)			6,000	(43,000)		
Loans, short-term portion				(6,000)	(6,000)		
Deferred tax assets		266		(266)	0		
Deferred tax liabilities		(2,374)	201	266	(1,908)		
Retained Earnings		(4,967)			(4,967)		
Profit & loss impact			(473)			266	(2,173)

Recorded on accounts:
- Personnel expenses — 7
- Depreciation — 704
- Other expenses — (95)
- Interest expenses — 58
- Tax expenses — (201)

Journal entries to be executed:[16]

Journal entries				Comment
dr.	Accounts receivable	95		
	cr. Other expenses		95	
dr.	Depreciation expenses	72		
	cr. Intangible assets		72	
dr.	Depreciation expenses	632		
	cr. Property, plant & equipment		632	
dr.	Deferred items	8		
	cr. Interest expenses		8	
dr.	Personnel expenses	7		
	cr. Pension provisions		7	
dr.	Interest expenses	66		
	cr. Other non-current liabilities		66	
dr.	Deferred tax liabilities	201		
	cr. Tax expenses		201	Also tax earnings possible.

---

[15] Remaining balance presented as other non-current liabilities.

[16] This is a comprehensive summary only! In practice, a journal entry would be executed for each transaction.

Having prepared a level I profit & loss statement and balance sheet, the mentioned **profit cut-off** has to be executed. The profit for the period from 1.1. to 31.3. has to be eliminated as this profits relates to pre-group activities. The easiest way to perform this cut-off is to remove revenues and expenses from the profit & loss statement and assign them to retained earnings. The pro-forma results of the pro-forma period can be used for this purpose. This will be realized using the following journal entry:

Journal entry

dr.		Revenues	35,210
dr.		Other income	411
	cr.	Changes in inventory	1,043
	cr.	Raw materials and consumables	14,384
	cr.	Employee expenses	8,081
	cr.	Depreciation and amortization expenses	1,301
	cr.	Other expenses	9,023
	cr.	Finance expenses	604
	cr.	Income tax expenses	355
	cr.	Retained earnings	830

Step 3 to 6 – Level II adjustments

As no level II adjustments had initially been recorded, no subsequent adjustments were necessary. Accordingly, these steps could be skipped.

Step 7 to 8 – Level III adjustments

A review of all assets and liabilities, recorded as a result of the purchase price allocation regarding any unusual events that may alter the carrying amount due to measurement or recognition, did not unveil any unexpected results. Accordingly, adjustments to the carrying amounts were not necessary. Therefore, a roll forward of the carrying amounts, combined with a regular adjustment of the carrying amounts, was the only task to be performed.

Item	Explanation and calculation	Amount
Patents	Patents have to be depreciated over the remaining protection period. As the protection period lapses in March 2021, the recorded amount of 17,800 k EUR have to be depreciated over a period of eight years. 17,800 / 8 * 9 / 12	(1,669)
Existing orders	A scan of the existing orders unveiled that 80% of the orders are processed and revenue recorded. The remaining 20% will be executed within the next two months. 3,900 *80%	(3,120)
Customer base	The carrying amount of the customer base 22,500 k EUR has to be depreciated over its useful life of nine years. 22,500 / 9 * 9 / 12	(1,875)
Fair value property	As there are no reasons identified that may impair the carrying amount of the property, a write-down is not necessary.	-

Item	Explanation and calculation	Amount
Financial assets	As the shares held by Solenta are transferred to Flexing Cables SE, the recorded adjustment has to be reversed.	(9)
Pre-existing relationships	Bad debt allowances on receivables of group companies are not any longer necessary and have to be reversed.	(220)
Environmental pollution	Accrued interests have to be added to the other non-current liabilities recorded for the environmental pollution. The interest rate of 2.9% has to be used. The remaining period will be 15 months (two years less than the life of the group). Carrying amount: 3,065 3,065 – 3,000	(65)
Patent infringement	Accrued interests have to be added to the other non-current liabilities recorded for the patent infringement. The interest rate of 3.1% has to be used. The remaining period will be 51 months (five years as estimated by the lawyers less the life of the group). Carrying amount as of 31.12.2013: 8,186 8,186 – 8,000	(186)
Deferred tax asset	Deferred tax assets are calculated based on the following scheme. 3,353 – 3,278	75
Deferred tax liability	Deferred tax liabilities are calculated based on the following scheme. 11,454 – 13,508	2,054

Item	Level III initial amount	Adjustment due to Valuation	Adjustment due to Reclassification	Level III carrying amount	Deferred tax impact Assets	Deferred tax impact Liabilities
Intangible assets	44,200	(6,664)		37,536		(11,186)
Property, plant & equipment	900			900		(268)
Trade receivables	220	(220)		0		-
Other assets	9	(9)		0		-
Other non-current liabilities	(11,000)	(251)		(11,251)	3,353	
Deferred tax assets	3,278	75		3,353		
Deferred tax liabilities	(13,508)	2,054		(11,454)		
Retained Earnings	(24,099)			(24,099)		
Profit & loss impact		5,015			3,353	(11,454)
Recorded on accounts:						
• Depreciation		6,664				
• Other expenses		229				
• Interest expenses		251				
• Tax expenses		(2,129)				

All level III adjustments were recorded using the following journal entries:

Journal entries   Comment

dr.		Depreciation expenses	1,669		Patents
	cr.	Intangible assets		1,669	
dr.		Depreciation expenses	3,120		Existing orders
	cr.	Intangible assets		3,120	
dr.		Depreciation expenses	1,875		Customer base
	cr.	Intangible assets		1,875	
dr.		Other expenses	220		Pre-existing relationship
	cr.	Trade receivables		200	
dr.		Other expenses	9		Shares held in Flexing Cables SE
	cr.	Other assets		9	
dr.		Interest expenses	65		Environmental pollution
	cr.	Other non-current liabilities		65	
dr.		Interest expenses	186		Patent infringement
	cr.	Other non-current liabilities		186	
dr.		Deferred tax assets	75		
	cr.	Tax expenses		75	
dr.		Deferred tax liabilities	2,054		
	cr.	Tax expenses		2,054	

Step 9 – Group transactions

The final step in preparing Solenta for the subsequent consolidation is to offset deferred tax assets and deferred tax liabilities. Like all other offsettings, it is recommended to execute them at group level.

Journal entry

dr.		Deferred tax liability	3,353	
	cr.	Deferred tax asset		3,353

Having executed all adjustments at all levels, the adjusted statements of income and financial position were:

Adjusted IFRS Statement of income Solenta as of 31.12.2013 (k EUR)		Adjusted IFRS Statement of income Solenta as of 31.12.2013 (k EUR)	
Revenues	105,700	Revenues	105,700
Changes in inventory	4,173	Cost of goods sold	(89,012)
Work performed and capitalized Other income	1,896	**Gross margin**	**16,688**
Total performance	**111,769**		
		Sales & distribution expenses	(5,568)
Raw materials and consumables	(41,860)	Administration expenses	(4,885)
Employee expenses	(25,341)	Research & development expenses	(3,149)
Depreciation and amortization expenses	(10,818)	Other income	1,896
Other expenses	(29,832)	Other expenses	(1,064)
Operating profit	**3,918**	**Operating profit**	**3,918**
Finance expenses	(2,246)	Finance expenses	(2,246)
Profit before tax	**1,672**	**Profit before tax**	**1,672**
Income tax expenses	(500)	Income tax expenses	(500)
Net profit for the period	**1,172**	**Net profit for the period**	**1,172**

Adjusted IFRS Statement of financial position Solenta as of 31.12.2013 (in k EUR)			
Assets		**Liabilities & Equity**	
Cash at hand & bank	3,951	Trade payables	18,534
Trade receivables	27,302	Tax liabilities	7,800
Inventory	58,973	Prepayments	300
Other assets	17,397	Accruals	5,320
Current assets	**107,623**	Loans	6,000
		Other payables	19,343
Property, plant & equipment	56,244	**Current liabilities**	**57,297**
Intangible assets	40,872		
Financial assets	-	Loans	43,000
Deferred tax assets	-	Pensions	7,580
Non-current assets	**97,116**	Other liabilities	14,413
		Deferred taxes	10,009
		Non-current liabilities	**75,002**
		Share capital	2,500
		Capital reserve	250
		Retained earnings	69,690
		Equity	**72,440**
Total assets	**204,739**	**Total liabilities & equity**	**204,739**

3. EQUITY CONSOLIDATION

As part of subsequent consolidations, equity consolidation is a task that is strongly connected to the initial consolidation of a subsidiary. The primary purpose of the equity consolidation is to eliminate investments and equity in the subsidiary as this represents a group-internal transaction. Furthermore, the equity consolidation has to deliver the contribution of the subsidiary to the group's performance since its initial integration into the group.

3.1. Consolidation requirements

To realize the equity consolidation, two elements are required: the equity position of the subsidiary as of the reporting date and details of the initial consolidation. This is because the initial consolidation of a subsidiary is carried forward and has to be advanced and – if appropriate – adjusted due to new facts and circumstances. Furthermore, the subsequent consolidation of equity has to consider in addition to the initial consolidation any other changes in the subsidiary's equity. Due to these requirements, the equity consolidation has to fulfil several tasks, which usually include:

- Tracking subsequent effects arising from different recognitions in local accounts,
- Adjustments at levels I to III,
- Impairment tests,
- Reclassifications, and
- The equity consolidation itself.

The relevant tasks can be laid out in four sections:

- Initial consolidation

  Subsequent consolidations depend strongly on the purchase price and the initial consolidation of the subsidiary. At the end of each period, the initial consolidation has to be repeated. If there are no changes other than retained earnings and other comprehensive income in the equity of the subsidiary, and the parent records its investment in subsidiaries without any adjustments or changes, the subsequent equity consolidation is equal to the initial consolidation. In practice, there are two methods of realizing the subsequent equity consolidation:

  - The consolidation journal entries of the initial consolidation are carried forward.
  - The initial consolidation is executed again.

  Both practices have their advantages and disadvantages. Nevertheless, they will deliver the same results.

- Preparation of local accounts

  Both the parent and its subsidiaries are subject to a preparation before an equity consolidation can take place. It is recommended to follow the preparation procedures explained in the preceding chapter to ensure that the equity accounts of the subsidiary, as well as the investment in subsidiaries account by the parent, carry their appropriate balances.

  - Parent

    Preparing the local accounts of the parent requires that the carrying amount of investment in subsidiaries is consistent with the carrying amount at the end of the previous period. As far as any changes occurred between the reporting dates that changes the investment in subsidiaries, consolidation activities due to an increase or decrease in the investment should have been executed. This applies particularly to a decrease or an increase of the proportionate share in the subsidiary that triggers transitional consolidations.[17]

    A special issue will arise if the carrying amount of investments in subsidiaries is written down at parent level. Such a write-down may occur as a result of the failure of an impairment test for financial assets or due to ongoing losses of the subsidiary. For consolidation purposes, this write-down has to be reversed. Nevertheless, reasons remain to write down the investment in subsidiaries and should be considered when preparing consolidated financial statements typically by integrating the reasons into the goodwill impairment test of the subsidiary.

    An investment in subsidiaries may also be subject to a write-down for tax purposes. Such a write-down does not necessarily demand a write-down in the accounts of the parent. The deviating tax base of the

---

[17] See chapter I - on page 501 regarding the accounting and the interaction with subsequent consolidation.

investments in subsidiaries will result in a recording of a deferred tax liability in the accounts of the parent that has to be considered during the equity consolidation.

- Subsidiary

    Preparing the local accounts of the subsidiary requires a consideration of equity in separate financial statements of the subsidiary as well as all level II and level III adjustments. Transactions that impact equity at one or all of these levels should have been executed and all carrying amounts advanced so that they are updated. These activities will usually be performed during the subsidiary preparation.

    Any changes in the equity of the subsidiary that caused an adjustment of the equity consolidation have to be repeated as well. This repetition can be realized in the same manner as for the initial consolidation. If there are differences compared to the previous period that are not caused by retained profit or other comprehensive income of the previous period, such changes in equity require further investigation. In most cases, the differences are due to historical exchange rates, changes of equity in local accounts due to local legal requirements, non-executed level II or level III adjustments, dividends paid, or similar reasons.

- Equity consolidation

    Applying the initial consolidation on the reported equity of the subsidiary will always leave a residual value of the subsidiary's equity. This residual amount:

    - Can belong to non-controlling interests,
    - Is retained earnings or other comprehensive income that belongs to the group, or
    - Is a difference that needs to be eliminated.

    As far as non-controlling interests are involved, a simple reclassification from equity to non-controlling interests is sufficient. This reclassification has to consider equity attributable to non-controlling interests as of the initial consolidation as well as any changes in equity from the date of the initial consolidation to the current reporting date on a proportional base.

    Retained earnings, and other changes in the subsidiary's equity, are the items that belong to the group. There is no adjustment necessary.

    Any other equity balances that do not relate to the above-mentioned categories are differences that need to be resolve and eliminated. Reasons for these differences relate to transactions by the parent or by the subsidiary, and require detailed investigation.

- Group transactions

    Goodwill is the residual amount of the purchase price allocation established through the initial consolidation. This asset is a group item that does not qualify for regular depreciation; an impairment test is demanded instead. Such a test occurs at group level for goodwill, tangible and intangible assets that are either not subject to depreciation or amortization or have an indefinite useful life.[18] As far as goodwill is concerned, any adjustments due to a failure of the impairment test are subject to amortization at group level. The standard journal entry for the recording of any goodwill adjustments is:

Journal entries			Company
dr.		Depreciation / Amortization	Group
	cr.	Goodwill	Group

3.2. Consolidation techniques

Whether the consolidation journal entries are carried forward or the initial consolidation is again executed, repetition is always required. The repetition has to consider the journal entries of the initial consolidation. Repeating the initial consolidation and any subsequent adjustments will not only eliminate the equity of the subsidiary and the investment in subsidiaries of the parent, it will automatically leave that equity of the subsidiary which has contributed to the group's performance since its integration into the group. This activity has to be performed by each company of the group subject to consolidation.

As already mentioned, the **initial consolidation** has to be repeated. It is therefore sufficient to execute the original journal entry. The following journal entry represents a standard journal entry of the initial consolidation that has to be repeated. Similar journal entries might be applicable as well if they relate to the initial consolidation.

Journal entry			Company	Comment
dr.	Goodwill		Group	
dr.	Share capital (common stock)		Subsidiary	
dr.	Retained earnings		Subsidiary	
dr.	Profit / losses carried forward		Subsidiary	
dr.	Revaluation reserve		Subsidiary	Only the portion that relates to fair value adjustments and the recognition of non-accounted assets and liabilities. Can also be a credit.
dr.	IFRS opening balance		Subsidiary	Only the portion that relates to fair value adjustments and the recognition of non-accounted assets and liabilities. Is usually part of retained earnings. Can also be a credit.
	cr.	Investment in subsidiaries	Parent	
	cr.	Deferred taxes revaluation reserve	Subsidiary	Elimination in proportion to the elimination of the revaluation reserve and the IFRS opening balance sheet. Can also be a debit.
	cr.	Foreign exchange differences	Group	Can also be a debit.

---

[18] The impairment test itself will be discussed in detail in chapter F -8.2 on page 348.

The journal entry to be applied can deviate from the standard journal entry depending on the conditions and circumstances of the subsidiary at the initial consolidation. If the parent does not own all the subsidiary's shares, the allocation of equity to non-controlling interests has to be repeated as well. This repetition can be realized by the following journal entries (which consist of a modified standard journal entry of the initial consolidation in addition to the allocation of equity to non-controlling interests).

Journal entries		Company	Comment
dr.	Goodwill	Group	
dr.	Share capital (common stock)	Subsidiary	Pro-rata parent.
dr.	Retained earnings	Subsidiary	Pro-rata parent.
dr.	Profit / losses carried forward	Subsidiary	Pro-rata parent.
dr.	Revaluation reserve	Subsidiary	Pro-rata parent. Only the portion that relates to fair value adjustments and the recognition of non-accounted assets and liabilities. Can also be a credit.
dr.	IFRS opening balance	Subsidiary	Pro-rata parent. Only the portion that relates to fair value adjustments and the recognition of non-accounted assets and liabilities. Can also be a credit.
cr.	Investment in subsidiaries	Parent	
cr.	Deferred taxes revaluation reserve	Subsidiary	Pro-rata parent. Elimination in proportion to the elimination of the revaluation reserve and the IFRS opening balance sheet. Can also be a debit.
cr.	Foreign exchange differences	Group	Can also be a debit.
dr.	Share capital (common stock)	Subsidiary	Pro-rata non-controlling interests.
dr.	Retained earnings	Subsidiary	Pro-rata non-controlling interests.
dr.	Profit / losses carried forward	Subsidiary	Pro-rata non-controlling interests.
dr.	Revaluation reserve	Subsidiary	Pro-rata non-controlling interests.
dr.	IFRS opening balance	Subsidiary	Pro-rata non-controlling interests.
cr.	Non-controlling interests	Group	
cr.	Deferred taxes revaluation reserve	Subsidiary	Pro-rata non-controlling interests.
cr.	Foreign exchange differences	Group	Can also be a debit

If any subsequent **adjustments** to the initial consolidation occurred, these adjustments have to be carried forward as well. This can be realized by two alternatives:

• Separate balances
    Separate balances differentiate between the initial consolidation and any adjustments occurring between the initial consolidation date and the

current reporting date. Both items are carried forward separately. Therefore, there is more than one journal entry: one for the initial consolidation and at least one for adjustments. The extent of adjustments carried forward depends on the level of detail desired.

For the consolidation and each adjustment, standard journal entries can be used. Which items of these journal entries have to be used depends on the original transactions and their recordings.

- Integrated balances

  Integrated balances do not differentiate between the initial consolidation and any subsequent adjustments. The full history of the initial consolidation, together with all adjustments, is forwarded in one step by using one journal entry only. Even if this forwarding is an often applied practice, it lacks transparency and richness of detail. This is acceptable as long as subsequent consolidations do not necessarily require this level of detail. It becomes a problem if changes in the equity structure of the subsidiary or changes in control, deconsolidations or disposals occur. In such cases, details of previous periods are required which demands additional activities to retrieve the historical information required.

  The journal entries required do not differentiate from the above presented standard journal entries. The only differences to the presented journal entries are the deviating amounts.

A proper repetition of the original journal entries should leave **no differences**. This can be checked through an equity comparison. The equity at the end of the reporting date has to be compared to that of the previous reporting date and any changes that occurred between these two dates. This reconciliation can be applied by using the following calculation:

	Equity of the group @ previous reporting date
+	Group profit / loss of the period
−	Dividends distributed by the parent
+/−	Changes in treasury shares
+/−	Other shareholder transactions (e.g. share-based payments)
+/−	Pension valuation gains or losses
+/−	Unrealized gains and losses
+/−	Currency translation adjustments
+/−	Deferred taxes
=	Equity of the group @ current reporting date

Tab. F-2 Equity reconciliation

Any differences have to be evaluated and adjusted as appropriate: individual assessment for each difference of a subsidiary in a group is required. Typical reasons for differences are changes to the shareholder structure of subsidiaries, improper accounted shareholder transactions at subsidiaries or the parent, and similar transactions. To allocate the differences an analysis of equity by equity categories is necessary. Share capital has always to be eliminated in full. Additional paid-in capital (or capital reserves) may carry an amount that only relates to changes during the lifetime of the subsidiary in the group. The same applies to retained earnings and other components of equity.

Example

Executing the subsequent equity consolidation of Solenta, three tasks were necessary:

- Reparation of parent
  The investment in subsidiaries account of Flexing Cables still showed the carrying amount as of the acquisition date. Accordingly, no additional activities were necessary to prepare Flexing Cables for consolidation.

- Preparation of subsidiary
  The preparation of Solenta followed a standard procedure which had to be applied to all companies of the group.[19]

- Repetition of the initial consolidation
  The following journal entry had to be recorded. This is the journal entry of the initial consolidation.

Journal entry				Company
dr.	Goodwill	20,967		Group
dr.	Share capital	2,500		Solenta
dr.	Capital reserves	250		Solenta
dr.	Retained earnings	68,519		Solenta
	cr.	Investment in subsidiaries	77,982	Flexing Cables SE
	cr.	Non-controlling interests	14,254	Group

3.3. Special cases

Reciprocal interests represent situations where two companies hold interests in each other. IFRS 10 does not provide specific accounting guidance for such situations. In the absence of any guidance, two solutions are applied in practice:

- Subsidiaries holding shares in each other[20]
  The mutual dependency will be solved by the equity consolidation, as all equities of subsidiaries have to be eliminated anyway. The standard techniques of equity consolidation apply. The type of subsidiary is irrelevant:

---

[19] See the example in the previous chapter.

[20] See chapter F -9.3.3 on page 415 regarding the treatment and accounting of reciprocal interests at subsidiary level.

ordinary companies, holding companies, etc. Consolidation will be complicated, as non-controlling interests need to be considered. In such cases, a determination of the effective shares in subsidiaries involved is required before a consolidation can be executed.

- Subsidiary and parent holding shares in each other[21]
  From an external view of this situation, shares held by a subsidiary in its parent are just handled as treasury shares. Therefore, IAS 32.33 applies: present the shares held as a reduction of equity in combination with an appropriate disclosure. The equity consolidation of shares held in the subsidiary therefore follows standard procedure, while shares held in the parent are treated as reclassifications from investments in subsidiaries to treasury shares.

Journal entry		Company
dr.	Treasury shares	Parent
cr.	Financial investments	Subsidiary

Another special case is an equity consolidation of **partnerships**. Partnerships usually do not have the equity structure of a company and instead maintain capital and withdrawal accounts for each partner. The equity consolidation of a partnership always follows the same logic as for every other company. The equity accounts of the subsidiary have to be replaced by the partnership account instead. Therefore, a standard journal entry for an equity consolidation of a partnership would be:

Journal entry		Company	Comment
dr.	Goodwill	Group	
dr.	Capital account partner	Subsidiary	
dr.	Profit / losses carried forward	Subsidiary	Only if appropriate.
dr.	Revaluation reserve	Subsidiary	Only if appropriate. Can also be a credit.
dr.	IFRS opening balance	Subsidiary	Only if appropriate. Can also be a credit.
cr.	Withdrawal account partner	Subsidiary	
cr.	Investment in subsidiaries	Parent	
cr.	Deferred taxes revaluation reserve	Subsidiary	Only if appropriate. Can also be a debit.
cr.	Foreign exchange differences	Group	Can also be a debit.

4. DEBT CONSOLIDATION

Debt consolidation belongs to the consolidation tasks that eliminate intragroup balances in the balance sheet. This task is defined in IAS 27.20, which requires a full elimination of all intragroup balances. The origin of the requirement is derived from IAS 27.18 which defines the aggregated balance sheet as the

---

[21] See chapter E -6.6 on page 240 for the application during the initial consolidation.

sum of line items line by line. Any instructions regarding the consolidation itself are not provided by the accounting rule. Therefore, an elimination should be performed by applying good accounting practices.

A debt consolidation usually includes a set of tasks to be executed:

- Identification of intercompany items;
- Consolidation;
- Clearance of any differences.

4.1. Intercompany relationships

Knowing relationships within a group is a basic requirement to identify the underlying eliminable transactions. The relationships cover all kinds of activity. They can be allocated to one of the following categories:

Trading relationships are based on commercial activity, so the ordinary business of a company within the group. Products and services offered do not differ between group-internal and external customers. There may be special arrangements regarding price and payment terms within the group but there are no special arrangements regarding all other business aspects. Trading relationships are presented in the statement of financial position as trade receivables or payable.

Financing relationships are usually built up to ensure that companies within the group are sufficiently financed to run the operations on a daily basis. They also include all kinds of dividend flows towards the parent company and similar capital movements within the group. Often, larger groups also run financing service centres that bundle cash and loans in one hand to minimize capital and financing costs. As financing relationships in a group usually exist between companies without the involvement of an internal bank, they are presented in the statement of financial position as other assets and liabilities. If there is a group internal bank, a presentation of financial assets and liabilities is appropriate. Due to the nature of these relationships, presentation as non-current items with a current portion is required.

More extensive relationships are **collaboration** relationships. They not only cover intragroup collaboration but also management issues. Their origins are derived from the structure of a group, the allocation of resources across the companies in the group and their management. Typical examples of transactions belonging to collaboration relationships are the use of shared or centralized resources, lending of personnel and equipment, joint projects and forwarding of expenses, management charges or use of supporting activities. These relationships are presented as other current assets and other current liabilities in the statement of financial position.

Some relationships are not allocable to one of the above-mentioned categories and are therefore grouped under the category **others**. One type of relationships belonging to this category is tax-driven to optimize the tax position of the group. Typical applications are VAT and income tax groups. VAT groups minimize the number of taxpayers and tax creditors to only one, or a few. As a consequence, VAT paid or received by the tax reporting entity has to be allocated in the group to the affected companies, often realized by intercompany loans.

Income tax groups work similarly to VAT groups. They should help to minimize tax payments on the profit of the period by offsetting profits of companies with losses of other companies. Another type of relationship in this category is non-trade: for example, asset exposures of non-financial items. This kind of relationship is treated the same as collaboration relationships. This includes also the presentation in the statement of financial position. All other relationships are presented as other current asset and other current liabilities.

Regardless of which category is involved, the underlying business transactions triggers several accounting activities:

- The treatment of contractual relationships under the law of obligations;
- The way of recording the business transactions;
- The presentation in separate financial statements.

From a group perspective, intercompany relationships have at least two sides that need to be considered. Each side has an obligation that needs to be accounted for. One side is the sending company – the company that sells goods, renders services or acts as a service provider in the group. The other side is the receiving company (the counterpart) – this is the company that consumes goods and services of the sending company. Like ordinary business transactions that are executed on an arms-length basis, intercompany relationships, and therefore intercompany transactions, follow the same procedure.

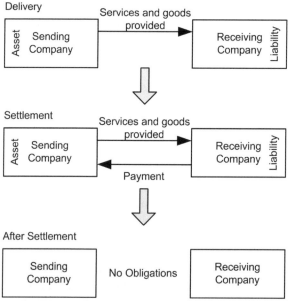

Fig. F-4 Timing of business transaction

The nature of intragroup balances of assets and liabilities follows the corresponding relationship. With the exception to financing relationships, all balances are of a short-term nature, presented as current items, and settled within

12 months. Even if financing relationships are of a long-term nature, they are also subject to consolidation like current intragroup balances.

4.2. Consolidation techniques

Debt consolidation is a purely technical task that is independent from any accounting regulations and standards. Even if a dependency is not given, the consolidation always follows the intercompany relationships. Therefore, a differentiated view of consolidation techniques is necessary as different balance sheet items are involved. Even if a differentiated view is required, all intercompany relationships, and their underlying transactions, follow the same elimination mechanics. Each party involved has to record at least one side of the business transaction via the journal entry in the balance sheet. The other side of the journal entry can vary: a recording in the balance sheet as well as in the profit & loss statement is allowed. While both parties record at least one side of the journal entry in the balance sheet, a simple debt consolidation is suitable for an elimination. All relationship eliminations are based on a standard consolidation journal entry involving assets and liabilities. If it is uncertain which items to eliminate, an analysis of the underlying business transaction, together with the standard journal entry, may help to solve the elimination requirements. The standard journal entry for debt consolidation always is:

Journal entry		Company
dr.	Liabilities	Receiving company
cr.	Assets	Sending company

To apply the standard journal entry on the intercompany relationships, assets and liabilities have to be replaced by the appropriate detailed balance sheet item. The replacement depends on the type of relationship:

- Trading relationships
  An elimination of ordinary trading relationships refers to payables and receivables. The journal entry assumes that goods are delivered or services rendered and each company has recorded its obligation.

Journal entry		Company
dr.	Intercompany trade payables	Receiving company
cr.	Intercompany trade receivables	Sending company

Example

MPG had sold various cabling equipment products to Flexing Cables Belgium and Chorunta Cables during the relevant period. At the end of the period, there were a trade receivable of 365 K EUR belonging to Flexing Cables Belgium and 248 k EUR belonging to Chorunta Cables. While intercompany items were reconciled in the group, Flexing Cables Belgium and Chorunta

Cables had similar balances recorded as trade payables. Accordingly, the following journal entry eliminates the intercompany balances.

Journal entry   Company
dr.   Trade payables, intercompany   365   Flexing Cables Belgium
dr.   Trade payables, intercompany   248   Chorunta Cables
    cr.   Trade receivables, intercompany   613   MPG

As an alternative, the elimination can be realized by two journal entries.

A slightly different journal entry has to be chosen if good are delivered or services rendered but the receiving company has not received the corresponding invoice. In such cases, an accrual is needed for outstanding invoices.

Journal entries   Company
dr.   Accruals   Receiving company
    cr.   Trade receivables   Sending company

Example

At the end of the period, a last minute order was processed by the group. A customer had ordered goods from Chorunta Cables and, while the goods were not in stock, Chorunta Cables had ordered the goods from Ehrlicher and instructed Ehrlicher to ship the goods directly to the customer. The order had been processed at the end of December by Ehrlicher, so the goods would reach the customer before the end of the month. The invoice of 125 k EUR arrived at Chorunta Cables at the beginning of the subsequent period in January. To properly account for the sales transaction, the following journal entries are required to record the transaction by Chorunta Cables.[22]

Journal entry
dr.   Trade receivables   xxx
    cr.   Revenue   xxx
dr.   Material expenses   125
    cr.   Accruals   125

To eliminate the intercompany transaction, the following elimination journal entry has to be recorded.

Journal entry   Company
dr.   Accruals   125   Chorunta Cables
    cr.   Trade receivables, intercompany   125   Ehrlicher

• Financing relationships
    Loans, asset exposures and other forms of lending or borrowing that have a long-term character are recorded as non-current items – either as

[22] Sales tax will be ignored for this example.

financial assets or other non-current assets. While loans given by other group companies are an intragroup related issue, the receiving company usually will present these loans as other liabilities.

Journal entry		Company
dr.	Other liabilities	Receiving company
cr.	Financial assets	Sending company

Those loans, lending and borrowing that have a short-term character have to be presented as current items. Therefore, the sending company will record short-term loans as other liabilities. A typical application for these loans is the use of cash pools.

Journal entry		Company
dr.	Other liabilities	Receiving company
cr.	Other assets	Sending company

If loans are granted by a group internal bank, the receiving company may present the obligations as long-term debt instead of other liabilities.

Example

A centralized treasury function was installed at Flexing Cables SE. The purpose was to finance all companies of the group without involving subsidiaries in arranging loan facilities. Accordingly, all loans arranged with banks were solely negotiated by Flexing Cables SE and forwarded to subsidiaries through intercompany loans. An exception to this rule existed only for acquired subsidiaries that already had a loan at the acquisition date; these loans were maintained by the subsidiary until the loan was settled.

As of 30.11., Flexing Cables had issued a loan to MPG to finance a new assembly line in production amounting to 3,500 k EUR. The conditions of this loan were: an interest rate of 2.8% charged quarterly by Flexing Cables SE and repayment within five years, starting as of 1.1.2014 (also on a quarterly basis). These conditions were market adequate. Both companies had properly recorded the loan and the related interests (expenses and earnings) for the period. To eliminate the financing relationship, the following journal entry had to be recorded.

Journal entry			Company
dr.	Other non-current liabilities, IC	3,500	MPG
cr.	Other non-current assets, IC	3,500	Flexing Cables SE

- Collaboration relationships

  As collaboration relationships are outside the ordinary scope of the business, a recording of receivables and payables that belong to this kind of relationship are classified as other assets and other liabilities and not as trading.

Journal entry		Company
dr.	Other liabilities	Receiving company
cr.	Other assets	Sending company

Example

Part of the transfer pricing system that Flexing Cables maintained was the charging of management and other services to all group companies. The charging was based on an activity-based allocation of consumed management activities and services. Services provided to group companies were extensive:

- Accounting and financing;
- IT;
- Legal;
- Trademark use;
- Other (as demanded by group companies).

The management charges relating to these services were forwarded at the end of every quarter to group companies, who were obliged to settle their liabilities within 30 days. The liabilities of those companies which were part of the cash-pool and netting arrangement were automatically settled after 30 days. Accordingly, management charges as of December had not been settled and therefore needed to be removed. As one part of the charging activities in the fourth quarter, Flexing Cables SE had charged 55 k EUR to Flexing Cables Belgium and 42 k EUR to Flexing Cables Austria.[23] The consolidation journal entry was:

Journal entry				Company
dr.	Other non-current liabilities, IC	55		Flexing Cables Belgium
dr.	Other non-current liabilities, IC	42		Flexing Cables Austria
cr.	Other non-current assets, IC		97	Flexing Cables SE

- Other activities

    All other activities are treated in the same way as collaboration relationships. As these other activities are also outside the ordinary course of the business they are recorded as other assets and other liabilities.

Journal entry		Company
dr.	Other liabilities	Receiving company
cr.	Other assets	Sending company

Example

In the Netherlands, MPG and Chorunta Cables are members of a tax group for value added tax. MPG acts as the controlling company that prepares tax returns and forwards all group VAT payments to the Dutch tax office. VAT payments that are attributable to Chorunta Cables are reimbursed by Chorunta Cables on a monthly basis in an invoice issued by MPG. The invoice itself is based on a VAT reporting of Chorunta Cables to MPG. The settlement of all

---

[23] We will pick up only two companies in this example.

payables is subject to the ordinary group requirements (30 days). At the end of the period, an amount of 67 k EUR relates to VAT reimbursements:

Journal entry			Company
dr.	Other current liabilities, intercompany	67	Chorunta Cables
cr.	Other current assets, intercompany	67	MPG

Debt elimination can become complex (as errors, currency conversions and other effects creep in), so a reconciliation matrix will help. The matrix always includes corresponding balance sheet pairs like receivables and payables or other assets and other liabilities. The consolidation matrix can be used for double checks of reconciling intercompany balances and any differences due to improper accounting. The matrix enables both sending and receiving companies to have a view on the transaction. If both views do not match, there are differences that need to be fixed. If the reporting company is the sending company, a receivable should be reported against a contra company which is the receiving company. On the other hand, if the reporting company is the receiving company, a payable should be reported against the contra company, which is the sending company. If the two reported balances do not match, a difference exists that needs to be analyzed. These differences can relate to real and unreal differences.[24]

A reconciliation matrix can be implemented easily by using pivot tables.

Fig. F-5 Intercompany reconciliation matrix for debts

---

[24] See next chapter for a detailed explanation of differences.

4.3. Differences

In a well-organized group environment, a debt consolidation should be performed without any problems. Nevertheless, there are cases in practice where differences occur. Reasons for these differences vary due to the manifold potential sources. To eliminate differences, an understanding of typical differences is necessary as there are many reasons for their appearance. The theory has developed a model that systematically differentiates between three types of difference. All types will be summarized under the definition of so called offset differences.

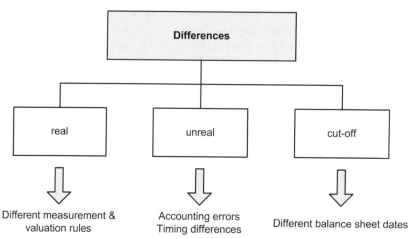

Fig. F-6   Structure of offset differences

Types of offset difference are:

- Real offset differences

    Real offset differences result from divergent measurement & valuation rules in the group. In this scenario, subsidiaries apply other accounting rules than the rules required by the parent company. As a consequence, business transactions will be valued individually by each subsidiary so that differences arise. Another reason for real offset differences is the application of local accounting standards without any adjustments to the parent's accounting standards. Depending on the nature of the business transaction, differences can trigger follow-up activities so that adjustments in subsequent periods are necessary.

    Typical examples of real offset differences are:

    - Foreign exchange differences;
    - Discounting of payables;
    - Application of the lower of cost or market principle.

In these cases, it is recommended to have documentation available that covers all affected periods. This ensures correct treatment of differences in subsequent periods.

A special treatment is required for foreign exchange differences. Even if these differences belong to real offset differences, the treatment is different compared to other differences. Based on the translation method used, foreign exchange differences are either recorded as a profit or loss or a change in other comprehensive income.[25] A profit or loss will be recorded if foreign operations are translated. If translation into a presentation currency takes place, all foreign exchange differences are recorded as a separate line item in other comprehensive income.

> Most real offset differences can be caught at level II due to the adjustment towards the group's accounting policies. Special attention should be given to this task as it eases debt consolidation.

- Unreal offset differences

    Unreal offset differences cover all kinds of differences that result from an erroneous recording of business transactions. The reason why this erroneous recording occurred is not important. Nevertheless, as there are always two parties involved, it is important to know on which side the error occurred. This as well as the underlying business transactions rule the way the error has to be fixed. As a general rule, a correction of errors follows the underlying business transaction. It is recommended to adjust errors at the level where the business transaction resides. This is either the local level or level II. If correction is impossible (e.g. because error identification is impossible) differences have to be expensed impacting the group's profit. There are no follow-up activities as unreal offset differences are eliminated during the consolidation process.

    Typical unreal differences arise from these errors:

    - Wrong journal entries (wrong accounts used, no intercompany accounts used);
    - Improper reconciliation of intercompany balances;
    - Wrong presentation of intercompany balances and transactions;
    - Timing differences (one company records business transaction in the current period while its counterpart records the business transaction in the next period);
    - Wrong foreign exchange rates and methods used.

---

[25] See chapter K -1 on page 632 for a detailed description of translation methods.

> Unreal offset differences can be avoided by applying dedicated defined accounting rules during the closing process.

Example

During the period, Solenta sold products to Flexing Cables Austria. At the end of the period, Solenta reported an amount of 36 k EUR as an intercompany trade receivable against Flexing Cables Austria. Flexing Cables Austria did not report any intercompany trade payables. Accordingly, there was a consolidation difference of 36 k EUR. As such a difference is not acceptable, both companies were forced to reconcile their carrying amounts. The reconciliation unveiled that intercompany trade payables had been recorded as ordinary trade payables by Flexing Cables Austria. Reclassification of Solenta from the category "external supplier" to "group supplier" was not easy to reconcile in the IT systems of Flexing Cables Austria, so a deviating consolidation journal entry was necessary to adjust the initially incorrect journal entries.

Journal entry				Company
dr.	Trade payables		67	Flexing Cables Austria
	cr.	Trade receivables, intercompany	67	Solenta

- Cut-off differences

    This is the third category of offset differences. Cut-off differences occur if a subsidiary's financial statement has a different balance sheet date to that used in the consolidated financial statement. IFRS 10.B92 and IFRS 10.B93 require that, if the dates differ by more than three months, the subsidiary must prepare additional financial statements with the parent's balance sheet date. This is mandatory. Therefore, this case is not subject to cut-off differences, which occur only when no additional financial statements are prepared. IFRS 10.B93, in combination with IFRS 10.B92, requires an adjustment of significant transactions that occur between the balance sheet dates of the parent company and its subsidiaries. These transactions cover third-party and also intercompany transactions. Even if significant transactions are considered in adjusting subsidiaries financial statements, they do not cover all differences of intercompany balances.

> Intercompany transactions are always significant transactions as they are needed for consolidation.

To eliminate cut-off differences, a more detailed view of types of difference is necessary. In general, two types of intercompany balance impact not only the current, but also the following period. Lapsed balances exist at the subsidiary's balance sheet date and are settled before the group's balance sheet date. Established balances are established between the balance sheet dates and exist at the group's balance sheet date.

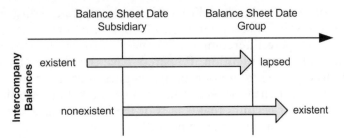

Fig. F-7 Types of cut-off differences

To simplify the consolidation procedure, an adjustment of all intercompany balances is recommended. These adjustments should occur either at local level or at level II. The adjustments should be executed by considering the following issues:

- Intercompany revenues should be adjusted against intercompany receivables.
- Intercompany expenses (whether costs of goods sold or other expenses) should be adjusted against intercompany payables.
- Intercompany receivables and payables that are settled in the meantime should be adjusted against cash or bank (if no netting systems are in place).[26]

As balance sheet items and their adjustments roll forward, a further balance sheet adjustment in the subsequent period is required. The reason for this second adjustment is that it reverses the original adjustments (of the then previous period). As a result, the on-going intercompany balances will be available, recorded and reconciled on a daily business by the subsidiary. A pragmatic approach is the execution of the reversal at the next date when consolidated financial statements have to be prepared. Adjustments that relate to profit & loss items (so intercompany revenues and expenses) have to be reversed against retained earnings. Based on the reversal adjustments, the whole adjustment process will start right from the beginning for the next close.

> Force all subsidiaries to have the same balance sheet date, if permitted by local law (of the subsidiary involved)!

Derived from the IFRS framework, consolidated financial statements should contain all material information (F.29). In other words, the omission of non-material items should not lead to misstated financial statements. It is up to the

---

[26] Including subsidiaries with deviating balance sheet dates will always result in a misleading cash position of the group. By charging adjustments of intercompany transactions against cash, the cash position will be adjusted by intercompany transactions so that the misleading cash position only refers to group external transactions that occurred between the balance sheet date of the subsidiary and the reporting date of the group.

discretion of prepares and auditors to decide on materiality. This materiality concept also covers offset differences which, consequently, are not material. In this case, there were intercompany balances on intercompany accounts which require an additional attention. Preparers have the choice of associating intercompany accounts with an appropriate balance sheet item (no manual involvement, one-time activity), or reclassification of the balance on the intercompany account to another account that is part of the balance sheet structure (recurring manual activity at the end of each period).

4.4. Preventative activities

To avoid offset differences, preventative activities are necessary. These activities focus on organizational aspects in a group. By ensuring a well-defined structure, relationships between companies in a group will have the transparency required for a debt consolidation. Usually, groups tend to combine this enhanced transparency with an improved handling on cash to minimize cash flows within the group.

4.4.1. Organizational aspects

> Follow the hints given below. You will benefit.

Organizational aspects in the context of debt consolidation focus on the handling of intercompany receivables and payables of all kind. The targets are reconciled intercompany balances in each company of the group to ensure error-free consolidation. To achieve these balances, a framework has to be defined that each company of the group has to follow. This framework is often a part of the group manual and consists of a formal documentation of the processes implemented in the group. The core of this documentation is a description of the process itself, particularly the definition, the timing and the parties involved. It is recommended to include at least the following elements into the documentation:

- Recording
  A relationship or transaction based description of accounts to be used to record the business transaction in the ledgers.

- Reconciliation
  Instructions regarding the execution of intercompany balance reconciliations. These instructions should contain timing and deadline information. It is recommended to reconcile balances on a monthly basis.

- Reporting
  A description of forms and methods to be used for the reporting of intercompany balances to the group centre.

- Settlement

    A description of methods and procedures to be used to settle intercompany balances. The most common methods used are a simple settlements and netting mechanisms.

This framework should be accompanied by general organizational aspects that help to improve the consolidation process:

- All companies in the group should have the same balance sheet date.
- All companies in the group should implement a group chart of accounts with dedicated intercompany accounts.
- A group manual should exist that includes accounting guidelines.
- A group-wide settlement system should be in place.

In addition to these improvements, additional tasks may help:

- Definition of foreign exchange rates by the group centre.
- Guidelines regarding the treatment of business transactions at the end of the period to avoid timing differences.
- Continuous checks regarding the recording of business transactions on intercompany accounts.
- Continuous reconciliation of intercompany balances between involved companies.

Only limited real offset differences should occur if these recommendations are applied. All other differences (unreal and cut-off) will then be avoided.

4.4.2. Simple settlement

If no cash flow optimization in a group is required, a simple settlement is the preferred way to settle intercompany balances. The settlement consists of a cash payment between affected companies only and is therefore comparable to ordinary third party transactions. The payment is often combined with a deadline, so as not to inflate the intercompany ageing on trade receivables or trade payables.

Fig. F-8 Simple settlement process

Even if this form of payment is easy to manage and very comfortable for the companies concerned, it is an inefficient and expensive settlement type from the group's point of view. The parent has no control of the cash flows within the group. Detailed information on the group's cash position is not given because cash is distributed across all companies not to mention cash in transit. To know the exact cash position in the group, either regular or ad-hoc reporting have to be used. Furthermore, due to the nature of the payment, fees are levied for each transaction to the bank, making the simple settlement method expensive. Fees will increase even more if there are any cross-border payments in foreign currency. Next to these measurable effects, the group will suffer another disadvantage due to the unbundled cash that also may be stored at different banks. Such a heterogeneous cash position will weaken the bargaining power of the group in negotiating higher interest rates with financing banks.

4.4.3. Netting

Improved cash flow management in a group is often realized by using netting methods. The advantage of netting methods is that the cash flow between companies is minimized and limited to selected transactions at defined dates. Netting methods are often combined with cash pool systems to virtually reduce group internal cash flows to zero. These systems – cash pooling combined with netting – are implemented at special locations in the group. If not run at the parent, group centres or clearing houses are the preferred institutions. They often act as internal banks providing additional services to group companies.

By implementing a netting system, groups can choose between several netting methods, the most common being:

- Settlement netting

   A settlement netting offsets several receivables and payables of two companies so that only one final balance exists. This method belongs to bilateral netting methods. It is often the basis for cash management or cash pooling systems.

- Close-out netting

   Close-out nettings are used in the liquidation of business transactions due to termination, passage of time or similar reasons. This method also belongs to the bilateral netting methods.

- Novatran netting

   A novatran netting is similar to a settlement netting: receivables and payables are offset. The remaining balance is converted into a loan arrangement by novation. This netting is most common in Anglo-Saxon environments but can be found nowadays also in European environments.

The netting process is a mechanism that involves a group or corporate centre. Receivables of one company and payables of another company are transferred to this centre. At the same time, receivables and payables are converted into a loan arrangement. As this process will be executed for all relationships between group companies, each group company will have only one loan arrangement with the group centre after the netting process is completed. Therefore, a reduction of intercompany relationships has occurred.

To execute this kind of netting, all group companies have to report their intercompany balances together with the corresponding counterpart to the group centre. The group centre will calculate company specific balances and instruct the group companies about the journal entries to be executed. The remaining balance of each group company can be eliminated by one settlement payment only. These activities are usually performed on a monthly basis giving it the advantage that all intercompany balances are reconciled and differences will either not occur or be fixed over a short period of time.

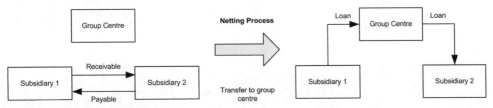

Fig. F-9 Netting process

As intercompany balances are based on intercompany relationships, a relationship-specific view is necessary. For each relationship, the following journal entries have to be executed:

Journal entry		Company
dr.	Other assets	Subsidiary 1, against group centre
	cr. Trade receivables	Subsidiary 1
dr.	Trade payables	Subsidiary 2
	cr. Other liabilities	Subsidiary 2, against group centre

As the loan arrangement between group companies and the group centre is the sum of all intercompany relationships, the group centre has to execute one journal entry only:

Journal entry		Company
dr.	Other assets	Group centre, against subsidiary 2
	cr. Other liabilities	Group centre, against subsidiary 1

Example

The centralized treasury function Flexing Cables SE had introduced several years before would now be expanded by a novatran[27] netting scheme. The treasury function included a cash-pooling system and a financing service where Flexing Cables SE acted as an internal bank for long-term loans. The netting scheme implemented would convert trade receivables and payables into a loan arrangement. To test the new netting scheme, a dry run with two subsidiaries of the group was scheduled in the current period before a global roll-out in the following period.

Flexing Cables chose to use MPG and Flexing Cables Belgium for the dry run. MPG was reporting an intercompany trade receivable with a balance of 365 k EUR whereas Flexing Cables Belgium was reporting an intercompany trade payable of

---

[27] This is a netting scheme where receivables and payables are offset and transferred in to debt due to novation (the word novatran is derived from novation).

the same amount. Based on the reported figures, the following journal entries were executed:

- MPG

Journal entry				Contra company
dr.	Other assets, intercompany		365	Flexing Cables SE
	cr.	Trade receivables, intercompany	365	Flexing Cables Belgium

- Flexing Cables Belgium

Journal entry				Contra company
dr.	Trade payables, intercompany		365	MPG
	cr.	Other liabilities, intercompany	365	Flexing Cables SE

- Flexing Cables SE

Journal entry				Contra company
dr.	Other assets, intercompany		365	Flexing Cables Belgium
	cr.	Other liabilities, intercompany	365	MPG

The real strength of netting systems is revealed in multi-currency intercompany relationships. In this case, the group centre will establish a loan arrangement with every group company, using the local currency of that company and thus transferring the currency risk to the group centre, which can minimize them as it aggregates all transaction specific risks of the original transactions.

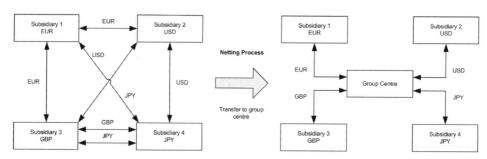

Fig. F-10   Example of multi-currency netting

Try to implement netting systems to minimize intercompany cash flows and bank fees even if netting systems require an increased accounting awareness. If possible combine them with a cash pooling system.

5. CONSOLIDATION OF INCOME AND EXPENSES

Like equity and debt, income and expenses have to show third party transactions only. Therefore, all group-internal transactions have to be eliminated, in line with IAS27.20 that explicitly requires this elimination. The accounting rule only states that an elimination is required. It does not include any instructions on how to perform the elimination. Therefore, an elimination can be achieved by:

- Reclassification,
- Adjustment, or
- Transferral.

The need for elimination is also a consequence of the preparation process of consolidated financial statements. As all subsidiaries considered are included in the aggregated balance sheet, internal as well as external income and expenses are already part of it. Thus, the internal income and expenses have to be eliminated to show the external side only.

5.1. Intercompany relationships

The elimination of group-internal transactions covers all transactions that have an impact on the profit and loss statement. To identify these transactions, an understanding of intercompany relationships that have a profit impact is necessary. These relationships usually focus on trading, financing and collaboration within the group.

Trading relationships are those relationships that are based on the original business of a company within the group. Products and services offered do not differ between group-internal and external customers. There may be special arrangements regarding price and payment terms within the group but there are no special arrangements regarding all other business aspects. Therefore, core transactions are the sale of goods and rendering of services.

Financing relationships are usually built up to ensure that companies within the group are suitably financed to operate on a daily basis. They also include all kinds of dividend flows towards the parent company and similar capital movements within the group. Often, larger groups also run financing service centres that bundle cash and loans in one hand to minimize capital and financing costs. As far as companies are involved in these relationships the core transactions are interest recording, either as expenses or earnings and recording of dividends due to profits of subsidiaries.

More extensive are **collaboration** relationships, which cover not only intra-group collaboration but also management issues. Their origins are derived from the structure of a group, the allocation of resources across the companies in the group and their management. Core transactions of these relationships vary as they depend on the group structure. Common to all transactions are cost allocation, charges and similar expense recordings. Typical examples of transactions belonging to collaboration relationships are use of shared or centralized resources, lending of personnel and equipment, joint projects and forwarding of expenses, management charges or use of supporting activities.

Regardless of which intercompany relationships exist, all kinds of underlying intercompany transactions can be allocated to one of **four basic transactions.** From a receiving company's point of view:

- For immediate sale;
- For later sale;
- For own use;
- For own consumption.

Transactions **for immediate sale** are those transactions where goods or services are purchased from another company (the sending company) within the group and immediately sold to a customer outside the group. Both transactions – the purchase and the sale – occur in the same period. Inventory balances at the end of the period do not exist. The use of goods and services by the receiving company is also not important. The receiving company can use the goods purchased for trading as well as for manufacturing purposes. The same applies to services.

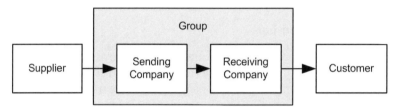

Fig. F-11   Base transaction for immediate sale by external supply

Like the treatment of goods at the receiving company, the treatment at the sending company is also not important. The sending company can purchase the goods from an external supplier or take them out of their inventory, usually finished goods. How the inventory is built up is not important as this is a separate transaction that has to be valued independently from the intercompany sale. Goods can be manufactured on request or taken from inventory previously ordered from the supplier.

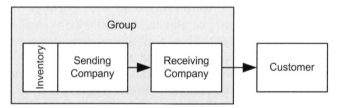

Fig. F-12   Base transaction for immediate sale by inventory use

The typical context of transactions for immediate sale is a manufacturer–sales combination. The sending company usually is the manufacturer that supplies sales companies, outlets or similar facilities as receiving companies with their goods.

Transactions for immediate sale can span more than one intercompany relationship (one sending–receiving company pair). Therefore, each relationship has to be valued individually.

Transactions **for later sale** differ from transactions for immediate sale in that the intercompany purchase and the sale to the customer occur in different periods. Therefore, the purchase of goods from the sending company will result in an inventory increase at the receiving company. If goods purchased are used in a manufacturing process, these goods may be part of other products and recorded as raw materials, unfinished or finished goods, depending on its use. As a consequence, the use of goods by the receiving company has to be considered to decide on elimination requirements. Goods purchased for trading are always recorded as finished goods. Due to the nature of this transaction, the focus is on goods only. Services are not subject to this type of transaction and not considered because services received cannot be stored as inventory and then delivered to the customer in the following period.

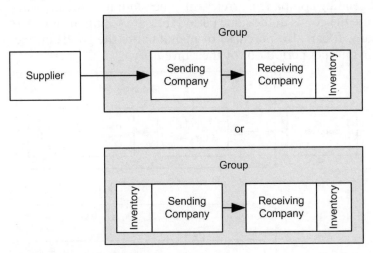

Fig. F-13 Base transaction for later sale

Unlike the treatment of goods at the receiving company, the treatment at the sending company is not important. The sending company can purchase the goods from an external supplier or take them out of their inventory, usually finished goods. It is not important how the inventory is built up as this is a separate transaction that has to be valued independently of the intercompany sale. Goods can be manufactured on request or taken from inventory. Increases in inventory are followed by subsequent decreases with sales to customers.

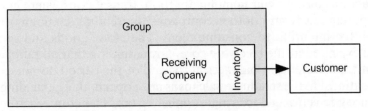

Fig. F-14 Base transaction for later sale in the subsequent year

Transactions **for own use** are purchases from another company within the group with the intention of long-term use. These goods are capitalized by the receiving company as non-current assets – either fixed or intangible. Treatment at group level depends on the activities of the sending company. If the sending company has purchased the capitalized goods from an external supplier the capitalization is also treated as a purchase transaction at group level. If the sending company has manufactured the capitalized goods the capitalization is treated as a manufacturing transaction of a self-constructed asset. This needs to be recognized and measured at group level.[28] IAS 16 and IAS 38 give additional guidance regarding measurement.

Whether goods are purchased from a supplier or self-constructed, the timing of the sending company is irrelevant. The sending company can purchase or manufacture the goods in the same period they are selling the goods to the receiving company. It can also purchase or manufacture the goods in one period and sell them in another period out of their inventory.

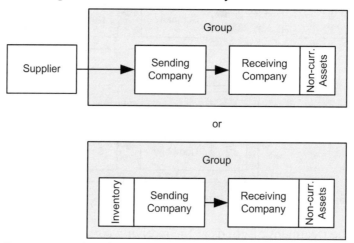

Fig. F-15   Base transaction for own use

Transactions for own use are common in larger groups with heterogeneous structures. The sending company benefits from a sale and the group benefits from an internal transaction at reduced cost without an accompanying cash outflow from the group.

Transactions **for own consumption** are those transactions where goods or services are purchased from another company (the sending company) within the group with the intention to consume them. Therefore, goods and services purchased are expensed at the receiving company assuming that all purchased items are consumed, so inventory balances at the end of the period do not exist.

The treatment at the sending company is not important. The sending company can purchase goods from an external supplier or take them out of their inventory, usually finished goods. How the inventory is built up is not important as this is a separate transaction that has to be valued independently from the intercompany

---

[28] The measurement depends on the accounting principles used. Some accounting systems like the German GAAP prohibit the capitalization of selected self-constructed intangible assets for example.

sale. Goods can be manufactured on request or taken from inventory from previous years of orders from the supplier. By contrast, services rendered by the sending company are always recorded in the same period by the receiving company.

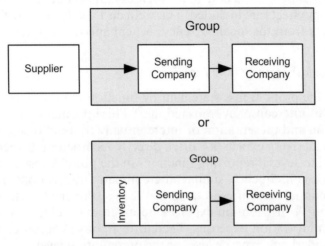

Fig. F-16 Transactions for own consumption

Like transactions for own use, transactions for own consumption are also common in larger groups. While the sending company benefits from the sales transaction the group will benefit from group-internal transactions at reduced cost without the accompanying cash outflow from the group.

From a consolidation point of view, the four basic transactions will provide information of the relationship between sending and receiving companies, the intended use of goods and services and their origins. Depending on the type of transaction, some or all information is required to eliminate intercompany transactions.

5.2. Consolidation techniques

The consolidation of income and expenses is a purely technical task that is independent from any accounting regulations and standards. The consolidation techniques depend only on two items that have a strong interdependence: The structure of the profit & loss statement and the four basic transactions. Both control the way consolidation is to be performed.

The structure of the profit & loss statement decides the extent of consolidation tasks. These tasks not only include the elimination of intercompany transactions but also any reclassifications required for a proper presentation. As the preparer has the choice between two presentation formats according to IAS 1.99, consolidation tasks will vary depending on the chosen format.

The four basic transactions rule the lines in the profit & loss statement that have to be used for elimination. Depending on the type of transaction, it has to be decided which line items are involved in the intercompany transaction on the sender's and the receiver's side. Furthermore, the basic transactions have an influence on profit adjustments due to balance sheet adjustments that are required for group internal assets.

The consolidation of income and expenses can become more complicated if foreign currency effects are included. These effects usually occur if the transaction currency differs from the local currency. An enhanced consolidation is required in these cases.[29]

5.2.1. Profit & loss statement by function

Applying the profit & loss statement by function requires information about the recording of intercompany transactions.[30] This information is needed to identify the position and presentation of intercompany transactions in the statement because the underlying expenses – often directly recorded on dedicated accounts – are allocated to several reporting functions in the profit & loss statement simultaneously. As a consequence, similar intercompany transactions may be spread across all functional categories in the profit & loss statement: cost of goods sold, sales, marketing & distribution expenses, research & development expenses and general & administration expenses. Therefore, a consolidation can be achieved either at the underlying expense level or the presentation level.

If the consolidation takes place at the expense level, an assignment of all consolidation journal entries to the presentation level is necessary. Information required in this case is not only information on intercompany transactions but also the assignment to the position in the profit & loss statement. Cost centres are often used for this assignment task. The consolidation itself is identical to the consolidation procedures for the profit & loss statement by nature.[31]

If the consolidation takes place at the presentation level, information about the assignment of the intercompany transaction is required. In this case, an allocation of consolidation journal entries to reported functions is not necessary.

Regardless of which kind of consolidation takes place, it is easier to consolidate a profit & loss statement by function than by nature. As all raw materials, work in progress, finished and unfinished goods are recorded in the balance sheet, consolidation tasks on changes in inventory and capitalized assets are not required. This leads to simplified consolidation tasks that will be discussed in this chapter.

Consolidation at the presentation level varies depending on the type of intercompany transaction. The starting point of all consolidation tasks is the aggregated balance sheet. Therefore, all four basic transactions have to be considered:

• For immediate sale;
• For later sale;
• For own use;
• For own consumption.

---

[29] See chapter K -1 on page 632 for the theoretical background on currency effects.
[30] We will use the structure of the profit & loss statement as defined in IAS 1.103.
[31] See next chapter.

As goods are already sold in transactions **for immediate sale** a simple consolidation takes place by eliminating internal sales and cost of goods sold only. This consolidation is required for each relationship between companies within the group. It is not important if there is only one or more than one transaction. All transactions can be included into one consolidation task that considers revenue and expenses only. The standard journal entry to eliminate transactions for immediate sale is:

Journal entry		Company
dr.	Sales	Sending company
cr.	Cost of goods sold	Receiving company

Example

During the period, MPG had sold products amounting to 4,288 k EUR to Flexing Cables Belgium. Flexing Cables Belgium had used these products in two projects with customers. The products were used as they were without any modifications. The projects were all finished during the period and properly invoiced. To eliminate the sale of the products, the following journal entry had to be recorded:

Journal entry			Company
dr.	Revenues, intercompany	4,288	MPG
cr.	Cost of goods sold, intercompany	4,288	Flexing Cables Belgium

---

A more complex consolidation is required for transactions **for later sale**. As goods are in stock at the receiving company at the end of the year, the consolidation consists of two parts:

- An elimination of entries in the profit & loss statement of the sending company;
- An elimination of unrealized profit in the inventory of the receiving company.

By executing both consolidation tasks, goods in stock at the receiving company will have the same value they would have had if they had been in stock at the sending company. The only difference at this stage is – from the group's point of view – the place of storage. The movement of goods opens a wider measurement opportunity in preparing consolidated financial statements. All handling and transportation costs can be considered as other costs for bringing the inventory to their present location according to IAS 2.15. If these costs are expensed – whether this occurs by the sending or receiving company – a write-up of inventory is possible.

The first part, the elimination of entries in the profit & loss statement, applies to the sending company only: the receiving company just records an increase in inventory. Therefore, the sales transaction, as well as the recording of accompanying cost of goods sold, have to be reversed. While the sales transaction will have a higher value than costs of goods sold, the profit realized by the sending company has to be eliminated, which is the task of the second part. From the group's point of view, this profit is unrealized because the goods are still in stock. As a consequence, the profit of the selling company, as well as the overstated inventory value, have to be adjusted. Both tasks can be integrated into one journal entry:

Journal entry			Company
dr.	Sales		Sending company
	cr.	Cost of goods sold	Sending company
	cr.	Inventory	Receiving company

The unrealized profit elimination at the end of the period will trigger a follow-up activity in the period the goods are sold. While the receiving company will record the sale using their inventory value as cost of goods sold at local level, an adjustment is necessary because the inventory at group level has a different value. This adjustment represents the unrealized profit that is realized at the date of sale. The following journal entry is required at the date of sale:

Journal entry			Company
dr.	Inventory		Receiving company
	cr.	Cost of goods sold	Receiving company

The value represents the unrealized profit that was eliminated at the end of the period. It can be taken from the other journal entry, it is the inventory credit.

The elimination discussed did not consider any capitalization of handling and transportation costs. If these costs should be considered, two additional journal entries have to be executed:

- At year end, the capitalization of other costs

Journal entry			Company
dr.	Inventory		Receiving company
	cr.	P&L[32]	Receiving company

- At the date of sale the release of other costs as an expense

Journal entry			Company
dr.	P&L		Receiving company
	cr.	Inventory	Receiving company

Example

During the period, Chorunta Cables had ordered products from MPG for a value of 7,847 k EUR. At the end of the period, products with a value of 527 k EUR remained in stock. These products were manufactured by MPG.

Flexing Cables used a transfer pricing system for all intercompany transactions. Group policy for trading activities was to apply the cost plus method for manufacturing facilities using a mark-up rate of 8.2% on production costs. Accordingly, the items in stock at Chorunta Cables included unrealized profit of 40 k EUR (527 – 527 / (1 + 0.082)). The elimination was based on the use at Chorunta Cables.

---

[32] P&L is a synonym for the appropriate category where the expenses are recorded.

- Products sold

Journal entry				Company
dr.	Revenues, intercompany		7,320	MPG
	cr.	Cost of goods sold, intercompany	7,320	Chorunta Cables

- Products in stock

Journal entry				Company
dr.	Revenues, intercompany		527	MPG
	cr.	Cost of goods sold	487	MPG
	cr.	Inventory	40	Chorunta Cables

The consolidation requirements for transactions **for own use** are very similar to transactions for later sale. As the goods purchased are now used in the ordinary business of the receiving company, different positions in the balance sheet have to be used. The follow-up activities in the following periods are also different. Nevertheless, the consolidation technique is identical to transactions for later sale:

- An elimination of entries in the profit & loss statement of the sending company;
- An elimination of unrealized profit in the non-current assets of the receiving company.

Again, by executing both consolidation tasks, non-current assets at the receiving company would have the same value they had if they were in stock at the sending company. The difference at this stage – from the group's point of view – was the place of storage. Directly attributable costs for bringing the asset into its current location and condition have to be capitalized according to IAS 16.16 (b) for property, plant and equipment or according to IAS 38.27 (b) for intangible assets. If these costs are expensed – whether by the sending or the receiving company – a write-up is possible.

The elimination of entries in the profit & loss statement applies to the sending company only as the receiving company records an increase in long-term assets only. As for inventories, sales, as well as the accompanying cost of goods sold, these have to be reversed. The sending company's realized profit from this transaction would have to be eliminated as the profit was unrealized from the group's point of view. As a consequence, the profit of the selling company, as well as the overstated non-current asset value of the receiving company, had to be adjusted:

Journal entry		Company
dr.	Sales	Sending company
cr.	Cost of goods sold	Sending company
cr.	Non-current asset	Receiving company

The unrealized profit elimination at the end of the period would trigger a follow-up activity in all periods that the non-current asset was used. Regardless of which depreciation method was used – assuming a useful life or existing residual value – the initial cost of the non-current asset would differ between local and group level due to the eliminated unrealized profit and other capitalized costs. Therefore, the depreciable amount would differ, as would the depreciation expenses. If these differences have not already been considered in the level II adjustments, an additional depreciation adjustment is necessary. The annual adjustment is calculated by unrealized profit and capitalized other costs divided by the useful life. Depending on the total amount, the adjustment of depreciation expenses would result in either a gain or a loss.

Example

    To supply the sales organization with product information and cable models for exhibitions, Solenta had prepared special demonstration models for the sales companies of the Flexing Cables group.[33] The various models were combined into demonstration model sets, which were sold on 1.7.2013 for 24 k EUR per set. While the models related to new products, it was expected that the models would be used for the following four years. Solenta applied the group policy for trading activities using a mark-up rate of 8.2% on production costs.

    The sales companies had depreciated the demonstration model sets over a period of four years from 1.7.2013 using straight line depreciation. Accordingly, an amount of 3 k EUR was charged to depreciation expenses (24 / 4 * 6 / 12) by each sales company.

    Elimination of these transactions required adjustment of two transactions: The sales transaction and the subsequent depreciation.

- Sales transaction

    The sales transaction had to eliminate the profit & loss effects of Solenta and to adjust fixed assets of Flexing Cables Austria by unrealized profit of 2 k EUR (24 – 24 / (1 + 0.082)).

Journal entry			Company
dr.	Revenues, intercompany	24	Solenta
cr.	Cost of goods sold	22	Solenta
cr.	Property, plant & equipment	2	Flexing Cables Austria

- Subsequent depreciation

    The depreciation at local level by Flexing Cables Austria also included unrealized profits at group level, which would have to be eliminated. The unrealized profit attributable to the current period was 0.25 k EUR (2 / 4 * 6 / 12).

Journal entry			Company
dr.	Property, plant & equipment	0.25	Flexing Cables Austria
cr.	Depreciation expenses	0.25	Flexing Cables Austria

---

[33] Here we will demonstrate the consolidation task for one sales transaction only, Flexing Cables Austria.

Transactions **for own consumption** require detailed review, necessary due to the consumption itself. The receiving company can record the purchase at various positions depending on the type of transaction and the intended use. This information is required for consolidation. The consolidation itself is as simple as the consolidation for immediate sale, as long as all purchases are expensed. Therefore, no unrealized profits exist. Accordingly, the journal entry for this kind of elimination is:

Journal entry		Company
dr.	Sales	Sending company
cr.	P&L	Receiving company

The disadvantage of this journal entry is a transaction-specific orientation. Journal entries cannot be combined on a relationship specific basis. To simplify the consolidation of transactions for own consumption, a two-step approach is recommended. This approach consists of a standard elimination journal entry and a reclassification of expenses:

Journal entry		Company
dr.	Sales	Sending company
cr.	Other expenses	Receiving company
dr.	Other expenses	Receiving company
cr.	P&L	Receiving company

The first journal entry is used for a relationship-specific elimination where all transactions can be bundled. The second journal entry reclassifies the expenses of each line in the profit & loss statement to other expenses.

Example

Due to several changes in the group and also in the product portfolio, new product manuals, which included technical specifications of all the group's products, had been prepared by Flexing Cables SE. These manuals were used by resellers, application engineers and other parties and given free to these parties. The costs for the manuals were borne by the relevant sales organizations and other parties requiring technical information about Flexing Cables' products. The production cost of a manual was 23 EUR, and the price charged to the sales companies 25 EUR.

As Flexing Cables Austria served not only the Austrian market but also the whole East European market, the company had ordered 1,000 manuals. To eliminate the purchase of manuals by Flexing Cables Austria, the following journal entry was required.

Journal entry				Company
dr.	Revenues, intercompany	25		Flexing Cables SE
cr.	Marketing expenses		25	Flexing Cables Austria

While all transactions are based on different transaction types, the following chart presents all consolidations at a glance:

Category	Transaction type	Transaction for			
		immediate sale	later sale	own use	own consumption
Goods	**External procurement** by sc[34]	Sales sc with CoGS rc	Sales sc with CoGS sc and unrealized profit	Sales sc with CoGS sc and unrealized profit	• Sales sc with CoGS rc • Reclassification between expense categories rc
	External procurement by sc and processing by rc in current period	Sales sc with CoGS rc	Sales sc with CoGS sc and unrealized profit	Sales sc with CoGS sc and unrealized profit	• Sales sc with CoGS rc • Reclassification between expense categories rc
	External procurement by sc and processing by rc in next period	n/a	Next period: CoGS rc with (un)realized profit	n/a	n/a
	In-house production by sc	Sales sc with CoGS rc	Sales sc with CoGS sc and unrealized profit	• Sales sc with CoGS sc and unrealized profit • Depreciation adjustment rc with unrealized profit	• Sales sc with CoGS rc • Reclassification between expense categories rc
	In-house production by sc and further processing by rc in current period	Sales sc with CoGS rc	Sales sc with CoGS sc and unrealized profit	• Sales sc with CoGS sc and unrealized profit • Depreciation adjustment rc with unrealized profit	• Sales sc with CoGS rc • Reclassification between expense categories rc
	In-house production by sc and further processing by rc in next period	n/a	Next period: CoGS rc with (un)realized profit	n/a	n/a
	From stock sc	Sales sc with CoGS rc	Sales sc with CoGS sc and unrealized profit	• Sales sc with CoGS sc and unrealized profit • Depreciation adjustment rc with unrealized profit	• Sales sc with CoGS rc • Reclassification between expense categories rc

[34] Sc = sending company, rc = receiving company

Category	Transaction type	Transaction for			
		immediate sale	later sale	own use	own consumption
	From stock sc and further processing by rc in current period	Sales sc with CoGS rc	Sales sc with CoGS sc and unrealized profit	• Sales sc with CoGS sc and unrealized profit • Depreciation adjustment rc with unrealized profit	• Sales sc with CoGS rc • Reclassification between expense categories rc
	From stock sc and further processing by rc in next period	n/a	Next period: CoGS rc with (un)realized profit	n/a	n/a
Services	External procurement by sc	Sales sc with CoGS or similar expenses rc	n/a	Sales sc with CoGS or similar expenses sc and unrealized profit	• Sales sc with CoGS or similar expenses rc • Reclassification between expense categories rc
	Internal services by sc	Sales sc with CoGS rc	n/a	Sales sc with CoGS sc and unrealized profit	• Sales sc with CoGS rc • Reclassification between expense categories rc
Allocations	By sc	Earnings sc with expenses rc	n/a	n/a	Earnings sc with expenses rc
Other	By sc	Earnings sc with expenses rc	n/a	n/a	Earnings sc with expenses rc

Tab. F-3   Summary of consolidation entries applying P&L by function

5.2.2. Profit & loss statement by nature

Even though it is prohibited in some legislations and accounting standards – such as the US-GAAP – the profit & loss statement by nature is an accepted form of presentation according to IAS 1.102. Compared to the profit & loss statement by function, less information is needed for the identification of positions and presentations of intercompany transactions in the statement. The reduced need for information is opposed by the structure of the profit & loss statement by nature. The separate disclosure of sales, changes in inventory and capitalized assets require enhanced consolidation tasks that combine elimination and reclassification activities, depending on the type of transaction.

The profit & loss statement by function focuses on the corporation, but the profit & loss statement by nature focuses on the underlying business model and its operation. This focus was induced by business economic theories that assume that the operation is the core of the business whereas the corporation acts only as a legal shell that can cover more than one operation. Based on this understanding, an operation can have more than one output depending on its intended use. The sum of all outputs equals the total performance of an operation. While this behaviour applies equally to a single company or a group, appropriate consolidation tasks are necessary, not only to eliminate intercompany transactions of each output type but also to reclassify transactions between output types of an operation.

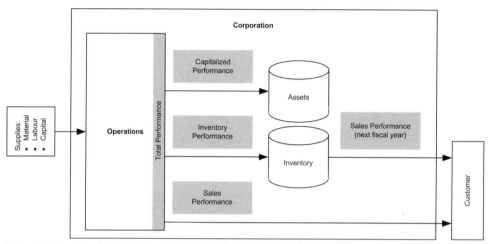

Fig. F-17   Underlying business model of profit & loss statement by nature

Again, the consolidation varies depending on the type of intercompany transaction. The starting point of all consolidation tasks is the aggregated balance sheet. Therefore, all four basic transactions have to be considered:

- For immediate sale;
- For later sale;
- For own use;
- For own consumption.

Transactions **for immediate sale** are treated in the same way in both profit & loss statements. A simple consolidation by eliminating internal sales and material expenses is sufficient for each type of relationship. If the nature of expenses distinguish between goods and services, different journal entries are required. The standard journal entry to eliminate transactions for immediate sale of goods is:

Journal entry		Company
dr.	Sales	Sending company
cr.	Material expenses	Receiving company

The journal entry for services consumed is slightly different:

Journal entry		Company
dr.	Sales	Sending company
cr.	Services consumed	Receiving company

A follow-up activity may arise for incidental acquisition costs. The receiving company will record these costs as material expenses. These costs have to be reclassified to other expenses to fully revert the internal sales transaction. The rationale behind this reclassification is the group-internal transportation from one site to another site before the goods are sold. These logistical costs are treated as other expenses from the group's point of view.

Example[35]

During the period, MPG had sold products amounting to 4,288 k EUR to Flexing Cables Belgium. Flexing Cables Belgium had used these in two projects with customers without any modifications. The projects completed within the period and had been properly invoiced. To eliminate the sale of the products, the following journal entry has to be recorded:

Journal entry				Company
dr.	Revenues, intercompany		4,288	MPG
	cr.	Material expenses, intercompany	4,288	Flexing Cables Belgium

---

Transactions **for later sale** require a detailed analysis regarding the consolidation. The treatment of goods at the receiving company has to be considered. The receiving company can either put the goods purchased directly in stock or use goods purchased in the further production process and put the then finished goods in stock. This criterion rules the consolidation process because different tasks are necessary:

- Goods put in stock

   Reclassifying the entries in the profit & loss statement at both sending and receiving companies, and eliminating unrealized profit in the inventory of the receiving company, ensures that goods at the receiving company have the same value as if they were in stock at the sending company. The difference is – from the group's point of view – the movement of goods. The movement of goods opens a wider measurement opportunity in preparing consolidated financial statements. All handling and transportation costs can be considered as other costs for bringing the inventory to their present location according to IAS 2.15. If these costs are expensed – whether this occurs by the sending or receiving company – a write-up of inventory is possible.

   Putting goods in stock directly by the receiving company is treated as a change in inventory at group level. Therefore, a reclassification of the sales transaction in the profit & loss statement is necessary. Profit realized by the sending company has to be eliminated as it is unrealized from the group's point of view. The profit of the selling company as well as the overstated inventory have to be adjusted. All tasks can be integrated into one journal entry:

Journal entry		Company
dr.	Sales	Sending company
	cr. Changes in Inventory	Receiving company
	cr. Inventory	Receiving company

---

[35] To demonstrate the accounting mechanics we will use the same case for transactions for immediate sales as in the previous chapter.

If a write-up of inventory should occur the amount that relates to handling and transportation costs has to be recorded using the following journal entry:

Journal entry		Company
dr.	Inventory	Receiving company
cr.	Changes in Inventory	Receiving company

- Goods used in the further production process

  If goods are used for further production, the goods purchased from the sending company becomes part of another product. The receiving company records the finished product as a change in inventory. Therefore, an elimination of sales and material expenses is necessary. As the purchased goods include a profit realized by the sending company, an elimination of unrealized profit is necessary to adjust the overstated inventory. The standard journal entries are:

Journal entries		Company
dr.	Sales	Sending company
cr.	Material expenses	Receiving company
dr.	Changes in inventory	Receiving company
cr.	Inventory	Receiving company

The unrealized profit elimination at the end of the period will trigger a follow-up activity in the period the goods are sold. While the receiving company will record the sale using their inventory value at local level, an adjustment is necessary because the inventory at group level will have a different value. This adjustment represents the unrealized profit as well as handling and transportation costs that will be realized at the date of sale. The following journal entry is required at the date of sale:

Journal entry		Company
dr.	Inventory	Receiving company
cr.	Changes in inventory	Receiving company

Example[36]

During the period, Chorunta Cables had ordered products from MPG for a value of 7,847 k EUR. At the end of the period, products to a value of 527 k EUR were still in stock. These products had been manufactured by MPG.

Flexing Cables used a transfer pricing system for all intercompany transactions. Group policy for trading activities was to apply the cost plus method for manufacturing facilities using a mark-up rate of 8.2% on production costs. Accordingly, the items in stock at Chorunta Cables included unrealized profit of 40 k EUR $(527 - 527 / (1 + 0.082))$.

Journal entries				Company
dr.	Revenues, intercompany	7,487		MPG
cr.	Material expenses, intercompany		7,487	Chorunta Cables
dr.	Inventory	40		Chorunta Cables
cr.	Changes in inventory		40	Chorunta Cables

---

[36] To demonstrate the accounting mechanics we will use the same case for transactions for later sales as in the previous chapter.

Transactions **for own use** are very similar to transactions for later sale from an accounting perspective. The receiving company capitalize items (inventory or non-current assets) in both transactions. The difference between both transactions is the presentation in the balance sheet as well as the treatment in the following periods. From a commercial perspective, transactions for own use require a dedicated analysis involving both the sending and the receiving company. This analysis focuses on the question "How are the assets prepared at the sending company?" as it rules the consolidation process. Two scenarios are important:

- Third party purchase

  In a third party purchase, the sending company acts as an agent and forwards the goods purchased directly to the receiving company. It is not important whether the receiving company records its purchase directly as a non-current asset or uses it in a production process to build a new non-current asset that will be capitalized.

  If directly capitalized, the receiving company's profit & loss statement is not involved. If the new non-current asset created by the receiving company is capitalized the receiving company will already have accounted for this via the assets capitalized entry in the profit & loss statement. So, no adjustment is necessary.

  A recording as a non-current asset requires an elimination of all tasks of the sending company because a profit & loss statement involvement is not given from the group's point of view. While the sending company will realize a profit, this profit has to be eliminated too as it is again unearned from the group's point of view. The elimination occurs in the non-current assets of the receiving company:

Journal entry		Company
dr.	Sales	Sending company
cr.	Material expenses	Sending company
cr.	Non-current assets	Receiving company

- Manufacturing by sending company

  A different consolidation is required when the sending company manufactures the non-current assets that will be capitalized by the receiving company. It is irrelevant whether the items are manufactured in the current or past periods. The purchase by the receiving company will always be treated as a capitalization of assets from the group's point of view. Here, the unearned profit in the capitalized asset has to be eliminated as well:

Journal entry		Company
dr.	Sales	Sending company
cr.	Capitalized assets	Receiving company
cr.	Non-current assets	Receiving company

Like transactions for later sales, handling and transportation costs can be capitalized. These costs are treated as directly attributable costs for bringing the asset into their present location and condition (IAS 16.16 (b) for property, plant and equipment or IAS 38.27 (b) for intangible assets). If these costs are expensed – whether this occurs by the sending or receiving company – a write-up is possible.

Having executed the consolidation tasks the non-current asset will have different values at local and group levels. This triggers follow-up activities in subsequent periods due to different depreciation bases. The annual adjustment is calculated by non-realized profit plus directly attributable costs divided by the useful life.

Example[37]

To supply the sales organization with product information and cables models for exhibitions, Solenta had prepared special demonstration models for the sales companies of the Flexing Cables group.[38] The various models were combined into demonstration model sets. The sets were sold on 1.7.2013 for a price of 24 k EUR per set. While the models related to new products, it was expected that they would be in use for the following four years. Solenta applied the group policy for trading activities using a mark-up rate of 8.2% on production costs.

The sales companies depreciated the model sets over a period of four years from 1.7.2013 using straight line depreciation. Accordingly, an amount of 3 k EUR was charged to depreciation expenses (24 / 4 * 6 / 12) by each sales company.

Elimination of these transactions required an adjustment of two transactions: The sales transaction and the subsequent depreciation.

- Sales transaction

  The sales transaction had to eliminate the profit & loss effects of Solenta and to adjust fixed assets of Flexing Cables Austria by unrealized profit of 2 k EUR (24 – 24 / (1 + 0,082)).

Journal entry			Company
dr.	Revenues, intercompany	24	Solenta
cr.	Capitalized assets	22	Flexing Cables Austria
cr.	Property, plant & equipment	2	Flexing Cables Austria

- Subsequent depreciation

  As the depreciation at local level by Flexing Cables Austria also included unrealized profits at group level, these unrealized profits had to be eliminated. The unrealized profit attributable to the current period was 0.25 k EUR (2 / 4 * 6 / 12).

Journal entry			Company
dr.	Property, plant & equipment	0.25	Flexing Cables Austria
cr.	Interest expenses	0.25	Flexing Cables Austria

---

[37] To demonstrate the accounting mechanics we will use the same case for transactions for own use as in the previous chapter.

[38] Here we will demonstrate the consolidation task for one sales transaction only, Flexing Cables Austria.

Transactions **for own consumption** require detailed review, due to the consumption itself. The receiving company can record the purchase at various positions depending on the type of transaction and the intended use. This information is required for consolidation because this rules the line items in the profit & loss statement to be used. The consolidation itself is as simple as the consolidation for immediate sale as long as all purchases are expensed. Therefore, no unrealized profits exist. Accordingly, the journal entry for this kind of elimination is:

Journal entry		Company
dr.	Sales	Sending company
cr.	P&L	Receiving company

The consolidation may require a reclassification of expenses between categories due to the consumption, particularly between material expenses and other expenses. This reclassification depends on the use by the receiving company:

Journal entry		Company
dr.	P&L	Sending company
cr.	P&L	Sending company

Example[39]

Due to several changes in the group, and also in the product portfolio, new product manuals that included technical specifications of all products of the group had been prepared by Flexing Cables SE. These manuals were used by resellers, application engineers and other parties and given for free to these parties. The costs for the manuals were borne by the sales organizations that had given the manuals to their customers and other parties requiring technical information of Flexing Cables products. The production cost of a manual was 23 EUR; 25 EUR was charged to the sales companies.

As Flexing Cables Austria served not only the Austrian market but also the whole East European market, the company had ordered 1,000 manuals. To eliminate the purchase of manuals by Flexing Cables Austria, the following journal entry was required.

Journal entry				Company
dr.	Revenues, intercompany	25		Flexing Cables SE
cr.	Other expenses		25	Flexing Cables Austria

---

[39] To demonstrate the accounting mechanics we will use the same case for transactions for own consumption as in the previous chapter.

While all transactions are based on different transaction types, the following chart presents all consolidations at a glance:

Category	Transaction type	Transaction for			
		immediate sale	later sale	own use	own consumption
Goods	**External procurement by sc**[40]	Sales sc with material expenses rc	Sales sc with changes in inventory rc and unrealized profit	Sales sc with material expenses sc and unrealized profit	• Sales sc with material expenses rc • Reclassification material expenses sc with other expenses rc
	External procurement by sc and processing by rc in current period	Sales sc with material expenses rc	• Sales sc with material expenses rc • Changes in inventory with unrealized profit	Sales sc with material expenses sc and unrealized profit	• Sales sc with material expenses rc • Reclassification material expenses sc with other expenses rc
	External procurement by sc and processing by rc in next period	n/a	• Changes in inventory with material expenses rc and unrealized profit • Next period: material expenses rc with (un)realized profit	n/a	n/a
	In-house production by sc	Sales sc with material expenses rc	• Sales sc with changes in inventory rc and unrealized profit • Depreciation adjustment rc with unrealized profit	• Sales sc with capitalized assets rc and unrealized profit	Sales sc with material expenses rc Reclassification material expenses sc with other expenses rc
	In-house production by sc and further processing by rc in current period	Sales sc with material expenses rc	• Sales sc with material expenses rc • Changes in inventory with unrealized profit	• Sales sc with capitalized assets rc and unrealized profit • Depreciation adjustment rc with unrealized profit	Sales sc with material expenses rc Reclassification material expenses sc with other expenses rc
	In-house production by sc and further processing by rc in next period	n/a	• Changes in inventory with material expenses rc and unrealized profit • Next period: material expenses rc with (un)realized profit	n/a	n/a

---

[40] sc = sending company, rc = receiving company

Category	Transaction type	Transaction for			
		immediate sale	**later sale**	**own use**	**own consumption**
	From stock sc	Sales sc with material expenses rc	Sales sc with changes in inventory rc and unrealized profit	• Sales sc with capitalized assets rc and unrealized profit • Depreciation adjustment rc with unrealized profit	• Sales sc with material expenses rc • Reclassification material expenses sc with other expenses rc
	From stock sc and further processing by rc in current period	Sales sc with material expenses rc	• Sales sc with material expenses rc • Changes in inventory with unrealized profit	• Sales sc with capitalized assets rc and unrealized profit • Depreciation adjustment rc with unrealized profit	• Sales sc with material expenses rc • Reclassification material expenses sc with other expenses rc
	From stock sc and further processing by rc in next period	n/a	• Changes in inventory with material expenses rc and unrealized profit • Next period: material expenses rc with (un)realized profit	n/a	n/a
Services	External procurement by sc	Sales sc with services consumed rc	n/a	Sales sc with capitalized assets rc and unrealized profit	• Sales sc with services consumed rc • Reclassification services consumed rc with other expenses rc
	Internal services by sc	Sales sc with services consumed rc	n/a	Sales sc with capitalized assets rc and unrealized profit	• Sales sc with services consumed rc • Reclassification services consumed rc with other expenses rc
Allocations	By sc	Earnings sc with expenses rc	n/a	n/a	• Earnings sc with expenses rc
Other	By sc	Earnings sc with expenses rc	n/a	n/a	• Earnings sc with expenses rc

Tab. F-4   Summary of consolidation entries applying P&L by nature

5.2.3. Consolidation differences

In an ideal world, all consolidations are easily executed to achieve a "clean" profit & loss statement without any intercompany relationships. However, reality is more complicated. Consolidations often uncover differences that need to be adjusted. Even well-managed companies cannot avoid differences that result from improper transactions, arising from the same background as those in debt consolidation:[41]

- Errors

    Due to the underlying business transaction, consolidation differences on income and expenses have the same origin as unreal offset differences during debt consolidation. If these differences are adjusted in the context of debt consolidation, income and expense consolidation differences will not be present. However, differences must be adjusted – or logged as profit reduction. Regardless of which activities are necessary, adjustments will always follow the methods of unreal offset differences in debt consolidation.

- Foreign exchange effects

    Foreign exchange differences require special treatment depending on the translation method used for the conversion of a subsidiary's financial statement prepared in a foreign currency.[42] Translation differences are recorded in profit and loss, with foreign exchange differences being allocated to a separate line in the statement. If financial statements are translated in a presentation currency, translation differences are reported as other comprehensive income. Therefore, foreign exchange differences have to be allocated to other comprehensive income as well.

> Apply the procedures of debt consolidation in dealing with consolidation differences! Both often have the same origins.

Errors, currency conversions and other effects can complicate profit elimination: a reconciliation matrix will help. The matrix always includes corresponding profit & loss pairs – revenue / cost of sales, other earnings / other expenses, and interest revenues / interest expenses. The consolidation matrix can be used to double check reconciliations of intercompany balances and any differences due to improper accounting. The matrix enables a view from both sending and receiving companies. If both views do not match, there are differences that need to be fixed. If the reporting company is the sending company, revenues should be reported against a contra company which is the receiving company. On the other hand, if the reporting company is the receiving company, expenses should be reported against the contra company which is the sending company. If both reported balances do not match, the difference needs to be analyzed. These differences can relate to real and unreal differences.

---

[41] See also chapter F -4.3 on page 278 for a detailed description on differences.
[42] See chapter K -1 on page 632 for a detailed description of translation methods.

A reconciliation matrix can be implemented easily using pivot tables.

Contra company Company ID	Reporting company Company ID	xx1	xx2	xx3	xx4	xx5	xx6	xx7	xx8
Revenues									
xx1		-			yyy				yyy
xx2			-				yyy		
xx3				-		yyy			
xx4		yyy			-			yyy	
xx5		yyy				-			
xx6						yyy	-		
xx7	The same transaction		yyy	yyy				-	
xx8						yyy			-
Expenses									
xx1		-			yyy	yyy			
xx2			-					yyy	
xx3				-		yyy			
xx4		yyy			-				
xx5				yyy		-	yyy		yyy
xx6							-		
xx7			yyy		yyy			-	
xx8		yyy							-

Fig. F-18 Intercompany reconciliation matrix for profit & loss

Example

At the end of December (22.12.), Flexing Cables SE had sold fibre cables to Flexing Cables Norway amounting to 178 k EUR. The exchange rate at that date was 8.4268. Accordingly, Flexing Cables Norway recorded an expense of 1,500 k NOK. Flexing Cables had to apply an average exchange rate of 7.8084 to convert the profit & loss statement into EUR, which then reported an amount of 192 k EUR – a difference of 14 k EUR. This difference had to be eliminated as well, in this case against foreign currency translation effects. The accompanying journal entry is:

Journal entry				Company
dr.	Revenues, intercompany	178		Flexing Cables SE
dr.	FX translation effects	14		Group
cr.	Material expenses		192	Flexing Cables Norway

6. UNREALIZED PROFITS

Unrealized profits arise in transactions between group companies where goods and services of the sending company are capitalized by the receiving company: the capitalization results in an overstated balance of assets that needs to be eliminated. Unrealized profits can only relate to selected current and non-current assets. Typical examples of unrealized profit-bearing assets are:

- Intangible assets like patents, software and capitalized projects;
- All type of fixed assets;
- Inventories.

In rare situations unrealized profits can occur within the restructuring of groups. A typical example is the sale of investments in subsidiaries between group companies.

As the elimination of unrealized profit belongs to balance sheet items only, two types of **transaction** are relevant: Transactions for later sales and transactions for own use. Both transactions are subject to valuation at different levels, which requires – in addition to the elimination of unrealized profits – adjustments due to different accounting rules. These activities are usually executed in combination with the consolidation of income and expenses. The whole consolidation process is therefore based on three consecutive steps:

- Consolidation of income and expenses;[43]
- Elimination of unrealized profit;
- Adjustments (reallocation, additions and contraction of cost components) due to group accounting standards.

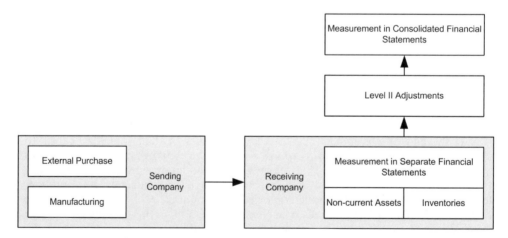

Fig. F-19   Unrealized profit scheme

---

[43] As outlined in the previous chapter.

The **elimination** of unrealized profits requires detailed knowledge of the cost composition of assets (e.g. items in stock). Based on the available information, assets or items in stock at the receiving company (volume and product mix) and group companies involved in the sales and manufacturing process, the elimination can be based on either reported positions or transfer prices:

- Reported positions

  The elimination by reported positions is based on products or product groups if appropriate. For each product or product group, costs of goods manufactured have to be calculated. The calculation is usually based on a standard costing system considering the normal capacities of manufacturing facilities involved in production. These costs are compared with the carrying balances of items in stock to determine the amounts to be eliminated.

- Transfer prices

  A different approach is based on transfer prices. A transfer pricing system is often built on a standard costing system combined with defined mark-ups for selected costs and profit margins for products and product groups. The carrying balances of items in stock are adjusted by mark-ups of the transfer pricing system.

The final step in the measurement and presentation of assets at group level is **adjustments** that relate to group accounting policies. Even if the receiving company is applying the same accounting policies as the parent, assets may have a different value. The reason for this effect is a different view of the measurement of the asset due to the consideration of all activities within the group. These adjustments can occur at level II if different accounting policies are applied and at group level if additional measurements are necessary.

The elimination of unrealized profit often faces **practical problems** which have their origins in the nature and use of the assets involved, as well as the structure and processes in the group. Typical problems that may arise are;

- The identification of assets carrying unrealized profits;
- The initial and subsequent measurement of assets;
- Obtaining information on cost structures;
- The tracking of all measurement effects as long as the asset rests in the group;
- Handling issues due to the volume of group internal transactions and products, their complexities and logistics.

Like the ordinary consolidation process, the elimination of unrealized profit requires a detailed structure and process that – together with an appropriate documentation and forms needed – guides through the elimination process. The process has to consider the sending and receiving company as well as the group centre. The level of preciseness of the process description depends on the group itself, and the chosen elimination methods. At the end of the day, the elimination of unrealized profits is a task that has to be aligned individually to the group.

> The best way to eliminate unrealized profits is the application of a standard costing system combined with a transfer pricing system. The larger a group is the more important is such an application.

6.1. Profit calculation

Information on profit calculation is required to attain knowledge about cost composition and the items to eliminate. It is not important if the items are purchased or self-constructed, both have to be considered. This classification (purchased vs. self-constructed asset) is based on the transaction of the sending company. Nevertheless, the latter requires more attention as additional effects arise that need to be considered.

Depending on the nature of the asset that carries the unrealized profit, several underlying standards apply to the calculation and measurement of assets.

- Inventories

    Inventories are measured by applying IAS 2. IAS 2.9 to IAS 2.33 provide guidance regarding cost composition and measurement. In general, inventories are valued at the lower of cost or net realizable value. All costs of purchase, conversion and allocation have to be considered. Excluded are any abnormal, storage, selling and administration costs, as laid out by IAS 2.16, as well as any (expected or unrealized) profits. Selected costs can be assigned to either conversion costs or excluded. This depends on the nature of these costs. Typical examples are financing and borrowing costs; they can be considered as a cost element if they are directly attributable to the asset according to IAS 23.8.

- Fixed assets

    IAS 16 is the relevant standard this case. IAS 16.15 to IAS 16.28 provide guidance regarding the measurement of costs of a fixed asset. In general, all directly attributable costs for purchase, conversion and allocation of the asset have to be considered again excluding abnormal, selling and administration costs. As fixed assets are used for the business, additional costs like dismantling have to be considered as well. For profit calculation, these kinds of costs are gratuitous as they do not arise as part of a group-internal transaction.

- Intangible assets

    Covered by IAS 38. As intangible assets can arise for a variety of reasons, this standard includes detailed regulations regarding recognition and measurement. Intangible assets as part of group-internal transactions usually consist of purchased or internally generated intangible assets. For these kinds of assets, similar costs to costs of inventories can be considered according to IAS 38.65 to IAS 38.67. Nevertheless, there are additional requirements for internally generated intangible assets. They limit the capitalization to selected assets where it can be demonstrated that they will meet the general requirements of assets as defined in the framework (F.89) and defined conditions that prove to have "useable" assets (IAS 38.57).

Regardless of the detailed regulations, there are similarities in all group-internal assets. Differences are rare as they depend on the nature of the assets only.

6.1.1. Purchased assets

The profit calculation of purchased assets can be realized without any obstacles. As the sending company purchases goods from an external supplier and sells them to the receiving company, a profit calculation is easy to determine. Information needed:

- The profit mark-up on the sale of goods;
- Accompanying costs that relate to the sale of goods to the receiving company. Such costs are shipping and packaging costs, import duties and any handling and other costs of the selling company that belong to the sales transaction.

6.1.2. Self-constructed assets

To determine the costs of an asset that are eligible to be capitalized, detailed analysis of its cost components is required. This is necessary because of the different levels (local at the receiving company and group) at which assets are recorded. While some cost components may be identical at both levels, other cost components may be subject to elimination, extension or contraction depending on the level and the applied accounting rules.

Referring to IAS 2.12, mandatory costs components to be capitalized as costs of goods manufactured in all situations always include:

- Direct materials;
- Direct labour;
- Variable manufacturing overheads as part of production overheads;
- Fixed manufacturing overheads as part of production overheads.

Production overheads are based on normal production capacity. As already outlined, borrowing costs may qualify as an additional cost component. They have to be considered either as part of overhead costs or as a separate cost item enhancing the manufactured goods cost. Capitalization as cost of goods manufactured is limited to these costs components only. Other costs are subject to a capitalization prohibition. This applies particularly to administration overheads that cannot be applied to production overheads, sales & storage costs as well as any abnormal production (overhead) costs. To determine the amounts to be eliminated, any information on profit mark-ups of the sending company is required in addition to the cost component ones.

Subject to elimination are sales and administration overhead costs and any profit mark-ups. While the sending and receiving companies are part of the group, the items charged to the receiving company are – from the group's point of view – also part of the unadjusted carrying balance at group level. The sales transaction by the sending company represents a group-internal transaction so that the mentioned cost components are prohibited for capitalization, which triggers the elimination requirement. This elimination requirement applies to all self-constructed and capitalized assets, whether they belong to transactions for later sale or transactions for own use.

- Transaction for later sale
    These refer to inventories (all categories, raw materials, unfinished and finished goods) of the receiving company where components of another group company (the sending company) are used or intended to be used. The elimination has to consider sales and administration overhead costs and profit mark-ups to be stripped from inventories. This requires an identification of the location of intercompany goods in inventory.

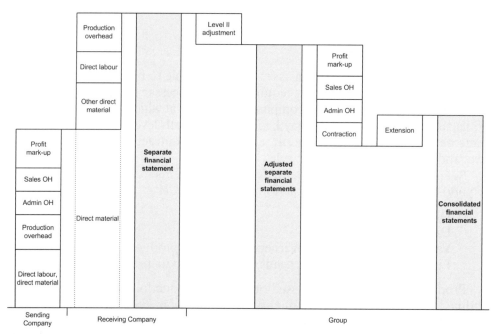

Fig. F-20   Cost allocation scheme for transactions for later sale

- Transactions for own use
    Transactions for own use refer to fixed and intangible assets the receiving company capitalizes. The elimination of sales and administration overhead costs and profit mark-ups result in an adjusted balance of fixed and intangible assets.
    The elimination can also cover discounts if these items directly refer to the purchase by the receiving company. This is because the cost of

goods manufactured is the measurement base for capitalization that does not consider discounts due to group internal transfers of assets. Directly allocable costs and incidental acquisition costs that are attributable to the assets and that are initiated by the sending company may qualify for elimination and recognition depending on the intention. As long as these cost components relate to the activity to bring the asset into its present location and condition, such costs can be capitalized. Consideration as contraction or extension costs is not necessary.

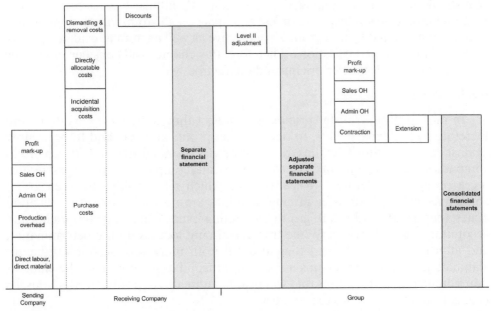

Fig. F-21 Cost allocation scheme for transactions for own use

In addition to the elimination of overhead costs excluded from capitalization and unrealized profits, valuation adjustments are necessary to comply with the group accounting policies. These valuation adjustments have to consider two elements, a pure measurement alignment for group purposes and a consideration of additional cost components. These additional components are either contractions or extensions that are created due to the different view of the assets from a group perspective. A typical example for a contraction is the inclusion of borrowing costs as defined by *IAS 23 – Borrowing Costs*. The inclusion of borrowing costs of a subsidiary may be different than the inclusion of borrowing costs at group level due to accounting policies or the calculation of costs that are eligible to be included. A typical example for an extension is the handling of logistic costs. While logistic costs (e.g. selling and storage costs of finished goods) of the sending company are excluded from capitalization (for example inventories: IAS 2.16b and 2.16d), these costs qualify as group-internal logistic costs to bring the goods from one location to another location, so in their present location and condition (for example inventories: IAS 2.15).

6.2. Transfer pricing

Transfer pricing is a method that simplifies intercompany transactions in groups, particularly if these transactions are cross-border transactions. Group companies and the corporate centre benefit from this simplification by a leaner reporting system and an improvement in consolidation procedures. While transfer pricing is a continuously and recurring discussion topic particularly with taxation issues, a lot of aspects have to be considered when implementing and running transfer pricing systems. In particular, the implementation of a transfer pricing system is a project that should not be underestimated. It does not only influence the accounting systems and procedures, it has more or less an impact on all group transactions as they have to be measured from a group's perspective as well as from a local perspective involving various tax legislations. Therefore, this chapter will consider only some basic issues around transfer pricing and interaction with groups.

6.2.1. Basics

In most groups, transfer pricing is a subject that is driven by taxation, and therefore by tax departments, to optimize net profits after tax and to be secured against any tax authority claims due to improper profit allocation between group companies. As a result, tax issues impact intercompany transactions requiring a proper consideration. Regardless of which relationships between group companies exist, all transfer pricing activities are not only subject to taxation issues, they are also subject to group accounting issues. Thus, transfer pricing and accounting share activities. While transfer pricing focuses on the determination and allocation of profits and therefore on profit mark-ups, accounting has to eliminate these profit mark-ups as part of consolidation activities. The elimination is limited to transactions that will result in unrealized profits: transactions for later sale and transactions for own use.

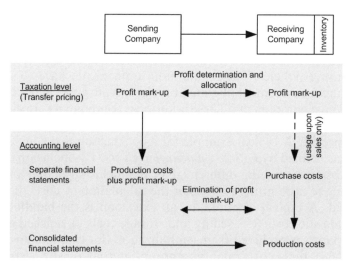

Fig. F-22 Dependency between transfer pricing and group accounting

The determination of profit mark-ups and the allocation of profits are tasks that are usually handled by the tax department at group level. Based on the guidelines issued by the tax department (which are valid for the whole group), all group companies have to account for intercompany transactions applying those tax guidelines. The outcome of applying group tax guidelines can be measured in separate financial statements as the profits of individual group companies, and include allocated profits as far as they relate to intercompany transactions. Consolidated financial statements again require the application of group tax guidelines. In this context, profit marks-ups are used to eliminate unrealized profits. All other tax issues around transfer pricing – particularly for immediate sale transactions – are not important and can therefore be ignored.

The underlying issue of transfer pricing systems is **profit allocation** within groups, which depends on the structure of the group and the products and services offered. As more than one company is often involved in the sale of products or the rendering of services, the question often arises where profits have to be recorded. This is because each company involved would like to record a certain profit for their activities. Often, these profits are also subject to management bonuses to encourage local management to improve the performance of their organizational unit (this can be a group company, a department of a group company or a set of group companies organized in a business unit). From the group's point of view, profits can be allocated to more than one company. Such allocation may be appropriate at local level but they do not ensure that the overall maximum profit in the group can be realized. The maximum profit depends on the view of the group's performance as there is not only one ultimate maximum. There is one profit maximum if a pure commercial view is taken, ignoring any tax effects, whereas with tax effects, the profit maximum will shift due to the application of various tax rules. The determination of the extent of profit shift depends on the value chain in the group and its structure in combination with its taxation. The issue management needs to solve is to decide which profit maximum is preferred – commercial or tax. Furthermore, the consequences, if a decision for one application is taken, have to be considered. The consideration of tax consequences is always mandatory.

Groups often try to optimize their profits after tax to offer shareholders a distributable maximum.

The art of profit allocation is to ensure that maximum profit is realized for group purposes while minimizing tax expenses and ensuring at the same time that each state involved gets its portion of taxes, based on the activities of group companies in each state.

An integral part of transfer pricing systems is the **group structure**. The structure is often the result of a management decision on how to design the group to have a competitive position in markets and on how to serve markets.[44] This becomes of particular interest if groups serve more than one market due to their

---

[44] See chapter L -2 on page 714 for further aspects on group structures.

different business activities and / or products offered, either per branch or per region. Such management decisions include strategic as well as operational aspects and consider the available resources of the group and the expected economies of scale and economies of scope. Considerations regarding economies of scale and scope are important in the design of the value chain that impact more or less all group companies regarding their functions and contributions to the overall value creation along the value chain. Traditional group structures differentiate between sourcing, production / servicing and sales activities where companies are often assigned to one or more of these areas. Production / servicing activities can even be allocated to more than one company where companies have defined roles.

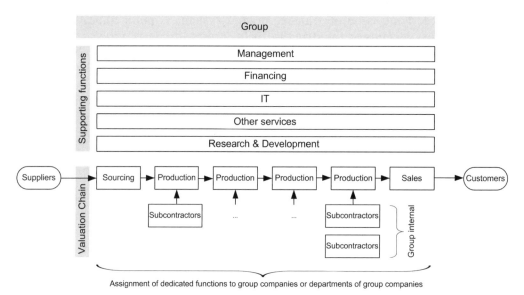

Fig. F-23   Valuation chain in groups

To understand the impact on transfer pricing structures, a functional and risk **analysis** is required. The intention of a functional analysis is to identify and allocate functions and their tasks to dedicated companies based on their structure and organization within the group, as well as the allocation of assets in the group. Assets are important as they are required for some functions. This applies particularly to intangible assets, which are often not accounted for but required to fulfil a function. Examples are product names or marketing slogans that sales functions use to sell their products. The risk analysis will determine the risks associated with each company. This determination not only has to consider the individual risk each company is confronted with, it also has to consider any indemnifications of risks. A sales organization, for example, might be confronted with the risk of non-payment by the customer, and therefore will incur bad debt risk while indemnified from any product warranty risk from the manufacturing company. Due to the variety of individual risks that exist, the risk analysis demands consideration of functional analysis to categorize and prioritize associated risks. The type and extent of risks associated with a function have a direct impact on the profit contribution of the company.

> The higher the risks of a dedicated function, the higher the profit contribution to the company.

The functional and risk analysis is complemented by an analysis of the value creation processes and the portion each company is contributing. The value creation process in a group is not limited to pure manufacturing or servicing activities. Underlying activities such as research & development have to be considered as they enable the value creation process. They have to be allocated along the valuation chain. Furthermore, outsourcing and subcontracting activities in the manufacturing process have to be considered. The risks and contribution of these (sub-) functions might have less impact due to lower risk; nevertheless a certain allocation has to be performed.

The requirements demanded by all analysis, and particularly by valuation chain analysis, demand involvement of **management accounting**. Their duty is to provide appropriate calculations, particularly on the value creation of each instance in the valuation chain. Furthermore, management accounting has to ensure that risks for each function and the dependency with profits are detected, allocated and documented. The duties often demand an involvement of management accounting at local level for details and at group level for the overall calculations. Details at local level often include profit calculation for selected functions in the valuation chain: so, the contribution of departments, subsidiaries or business units in total or individually, determination of functions and calculations about the dependency between risks and profits. Group management accounting's primary task is to compile all details to provide a reconciled set of calculations, often adjusted by additional aspects at group level. Even if tax departments are the main driver for transfer pricing issues, there is a strong interaction between the tax department, management and financial accounting. Their interaction is more or less driven by requirements of tax authorities in all tax jurisdictions involved.

In line with the previously discussed analyses, all companies of a group that are involved in a valuation chain fall into three categories. The **categorization of companies** is important as they carry different risks and therefore different profit margins. The categorization is transaction based, meaning that a company may have different roles at the same time depending on the underlying transactions. Tax authorities often use a company's category to determine the appropriate transfer pricing system, particularly the use of proper and accepted transfer pricing methods (which means acceptance by tax authorities).

- "Routine" companies

    These companies are limited and have minimal risk; their functions are straightforward and might be provided also by third parties. Their assets are not unique to the group's value proposition. Due to the character of these companies, profits are low but stable. Typical examples are subcontractors or logistic companies in groups.

- Enhanced "routine" companies

    A more sophisticated classification is the "enhanced routine company". This company is embedded in the valuation chain providing important tasks and is therefore responsible for value creation. Selected risks are associated with such companies. They also use or generate tangibles which are important to the valuation chain, although they only contribute to, but do not control, the valuation chain. Accordingly, their assets are only important to the function they have in the valuation chain. Typical examples are fully-fledged manufacturers, fully-fledged distributors or factories in a larger group specializing in parts or subparts (e.g. a manufacturing facility that produces engines that are installed in trucks, the core product of a group, but are also sold externally to other manufacturers to be used in tractors).

- Entrepreneurs
    Entrepreneurs are that instances in a group (or a business unit) that control the whole valuation chain. They are responsible for the overall strategy, the design of the valuation chain, the corresponding processes and any supporting functions. They also own assets that are important for value creation. As a consequence they not only earn (residual) profits but also bear any losses.

Subject to transfer pricing all are **intercompany transactions** that deal with cross-border activities between group companies. Therefore, these transactions can be allocated to one of the four basic intercompany relationships (which are trading, financing, collaboration and others) and also to one of the four basic intercompany transactions (for immediate sale, for later sale, for own use, for own consumption).

As **trading** relationships deal with commercial activities of the group, transactions that belong to this type are part of the value chain, and hence core profit-generating activities.

- Goods
    A common practice by manufacturing companies is to separate manufacturing and sales activities in the group. These activities are often arranged in one or more separate legal entities with defined duties. While manufacturing itself may have complex structures, an arrangement in separate production units is not an exception. Therefore, dedicated views are necessary in determining transfer pricing on goods.

    - Manufacturing
        Manufacturing activities can be organized in various ways. They can be performed by companies who are in charge of a product or business; they can also be outsourced to another production facility. Furthermore, a combination with subcontracting activities like production of parts is also possible. As there are various combinations possible in arranging the manufacturing process, transfer pricing activities focus on an appropriate profit allocation to each company involved in the production of goods unless the manufacturing activities are not concentrated on one company. To determine allocated profits, an analysis of the processes in the manufacturing environment is necessary. This analysis will be used in allocating profits to each unit or company involved using appropriate allocation methods. Preferred methods are

cost plus or similar methods assuming that market access is not given to determine comparable profit mark-ups.[45]

- Sales

    Sales activities assume that goods sold by the sales organization have to be purchased from the manufacturing units. The sales organization acts as a merchant that has to cover its sales and related costs together and an appropriate profit. The determination of profits allocable to the sales organization is preferably based on the resales price method as this method is based on comparable arm's length transactions of similar competitors.[46] Nevertheless there might be situations where other methods are more appropriate. This has to be checked in each individual case.

- Services

    Services performed to customers differ from goods that services have more or less an intangible character. Depending on products and services offered to customers, services to customers can be rendered by the staff of the sales organization directly or the sales organization can purchase additional resources from affiliates to complement their own service capabilities. A group structure that hosts one or more group-internal service organizations, that deliver services to the customers, might also be possible. A typical example is the support organization of a software manufacturer that delivers software updates and offers hotline support based on maintenance contracts with customers. Services are then comparable to goods, where the sales organization might receive a profit mark-up due to the acquisition and group-internal forwarding of such services.

    As long as services are comparable to goods, the same profit allocation methods can be applied. If services are ordered in the group to complement own services provided to customers, cost plus-, net margin- or profit split methods might be more appropriate depending on the group-internal handling of such services.[47] Profit mark-ups, and their allocation to the companies involved, therefore vary.

Collaboration relationships comprise all kinds of transactions that are required to run the group. These transactions usually do not directly relate to the value creation process. They support the value creation process more or less indirectly.

- Subcontracting

    Subcontracting is a group-internal service where the subcontractor manufactures goods or part of goods according to the instructions and specifications of the purchaser. The subcontractor is treated as a routine manufacturing company with limited risks only. Subcontracting activities

---

[45] See OECD Transfer Pricing Guidelines, chapter D.

[46] See OECD Transfer Pricing Guidelines, chapter C, paragraph 2.21.

[47] The application of appropriate methods does not only depend on an intercompany treatment. The application might also vary across businesses. A common practice in the software and consulting business for example is to apply profit split methods while other businesses prefer the application of net margin methods.

can also be cascaded depending on the products, its complexities and the desired value creation process. Transfer prices are therefore based on either the costs of goods manufactured or the pure manufacturing activity as a service provided considering appropriate profit mark-ups.

• Transfers of assets

These have to be treated like any transfer of goods. Tax legislations demand that assets transferred are sold with an appropriate profit mark-up identical to sales transactions on arm's-length basis with third parties. This implies that a market value has to be determined which might be difficult for selected assets. In such cases, valuation methods have to be applied to determine a fair value of the asset. As a simplification, tax authorities often accept a profit mark-up on the net book value or the historical costs of the transferred asset. The profit mark-up accepted by tax authorities will vary. A range of 10% to 20% is often accepted.

• Transfer of business

A transfer of a business is – from a group's perspective – more or less the same as the transfer of an asset. A business can consist of a legal entity, a part of a legal entity or a set of legal entities. Their transfer can consist of a transfer of the ownership without a physical relocation of the business or a physical transfer of the whole business. The latter is seen as a business restructuring by tax authorities due to the transfer of a function of the group. Reasons for business restructurings vary and can be sorted into the following categories:[48]

Category	Reason
Economic	• Access to markets (sales, purchasing, capital) • Place of operation and availability of resources (personnel, qualifications, logistics) • Competition (market presence and visibility) • Costs (employment costs, infrastructure costs, energy and other costs) • Taxation
Regulatory	• Pricing • Capital requirements • Obligations and qualifications to run a business
Environmental	• Shareholders, strategies • Legal (employment conditions, unions, competitive laws, etc.)
Internal	• Management and changes in management • Management strategies • Changes in the group due to acquisitions and disposals • Organizational aspects

Tab. F-5   Reasons for business restructurings

The treatment of business restructuring differs. From a commercial perspective, the transfer is valued like any ordinary restructuring activity of a group.[49] From a tax perspective, the measurement of the transfer

---

[48] Taken from Renz / Wilmanns and adjusted for own purposes.
[49] See chapter K -5 on page 693 regarding details.

follows a double view approach by considering a seller's and a buyer's view of the transaction. Prices can be determined by the price a buyer is willing to pay and the price a seller expects to achieve. Furthermore, prices have to be determined on an arm's-length basis, especially as market transactions are often not available for real transactions. These requirements demand a set of calculations that determine present values of mid-term plans combined with appropriate profits and discount rates. The calculations have to consider the situation as of the date of transfer. The final transfer price used is taken from the average of the calculated present values.

• Employee secondment

A common practice in large groups is to send staff to other companies of the group for a limited period of time to support their operations. Depending on the duration and on the reason, several cases are possible that demand individual treatments. Typical reasons can either be the work on a project, rendering of services or ordinary work in the subsidiary (which assumes a full integration in that company). Common to all cases is the determination of the employment situation. Does the employment relationship rest with the sending company or does it transfer to the receiving company? Typical indicators to determine the allocation are the type of work or service to be performed, the company responsible for salary payments and all obligations arising from the employment contract, the integration of the employee in the group and similar reasons. A very broad categorization can be based on the following timing:

- Secondments up to three months, regardless of the reason, assume an employment relationship with the sending company.
- Secondments of more than three months may assume an employment relationship with the sending company providing that some organizational aspects are considered. The sending company is still acting as the employer including all aspects that arise from the employment, the employee is reporting to the sending company and is not integrated into the organization of the receiving company.
- Secondments of more than six months often involve the previously mentioned organizational aspects: it may be assumed that a branch or commercial unit will be established which will result in additional tax issues. To avoid such effects, secondments of employees should be limited to a maximum of six months.

> Be careful! Employee secondments of less than six months can also assume a commercial unit in some jurisdictions if several employees are sent to perform services or execute work that lasts more than six months.

- Secondments of more than six months, where the employee is integrated into the organization of the receiving company, transfer the employment responsibility usually to the receiving company. These employee secondments are often managed in expatriate programmes.

In addition to these categorizations, the underlying contractual conditions between the companies have to be considered. Employee secondments of more than six months transfer the employer duties to the receiving company for the time the employee is assigned to that company even if the underlying employment contract will not change. Therefore, all personnel costs have to be carried by the receiving company. Costs have to be determined individually for each employee. A profit mark-up is not allowed.

All other employee secondments establish a contractual relationship between the sending and receiving company like any other business transaction as long as no commercial unit is established. These activities have to be charged with an appropriate profit mark-up. The determination of the profit mark-up follows the same procedure that the determination of mark-up's for goods and services based on benchmark studies or similar methods.

A special case is knowledge transfer. An employee secondment that intends to establish and transfer an operation from one entity to another one in a group is subject to a business restructuring (or transfer of functions) and therefore a business transfer. Costs that are associated with this employee secondment are subject to the business transfer.

- Services

To enhance efficiencies in the group, selected activities and functions are often centralized and arranged in shared service centres. These centres provide their services to all companies of the group. Typical examples of such services are management, financing and administration functions, IT and HR-services. These services are often not externally available. Therefore, services have to be rendered in groups including an appropriate profit mark-up. The profit mark-up can be determined by benchmark studies.[50] The profit mark-up accepted by tax authorities vary. A range of 5% to 10% is often accepted.

Financing relationships combine all activities and transactions that aim to allocate cash within the group according to its needs. The allocation supports all companies and departments that are part of the value chain to ensure that they have the resources to fulfil their duties. Financing relationships therefore belong to supporting relationships. While they vary depending on their needs, only the most important ones are listed. They are a mixture of traditional financing forms and more sophisticated allocations.

---

[50] E.g. The benchmark study by the EU Joint Transfer Pricing Forum is a typical example for such a study.

*   Loans

    Loans are the most important and popular financing relationship in groups. Using an internal financing institution, financing activities can be centralized. This financing institution can be the ultimate parent of the group or any other company in the group, either designed for such purposes or as part of a shared service centre of any ordinary company that only hosts such a function. Bundling loans at one instance offers several advantages: The parent has better control of loans, conditions of external loans can be improved due to an improved negotiation volume, and subsidiaries benefit from better conditions than the market offers. These advantages exist for short-term and long-term loans.

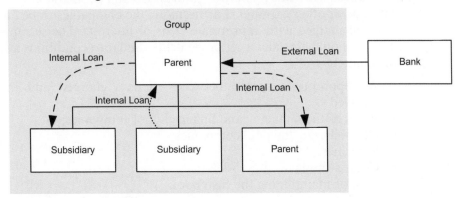

Fig. F-24   Group loans

    Issuing loans by a financing institution is not the only option. Excess cash of subsidiaries can also be transferred to the financing institution as a loan to reduce the need for external loans.

    The measurement of interest charged is often based on a reference interest rate (e.g. LIBOR, EURIBOR or similar interest rates) and an interest mark-up. The interest mark-up should reflect market conditions including an appropriate rating. Even if the estimation of the interest mark-up should not be a problem, the complexity increases with the volume of intercompany loans. Therefore, large groups intend to switch to standard loan agreements using a set of defined interest rates. These rates usually reflect credit risk classes and are easier to maintain.

*   Netting schemes

    As already discussed, netting schemes help to minimize cash flows in groups.[51] The conversion of receivables and payables into loans and the transfer to a corporate centre will establish a loan relationship with a financing institution of the group. The then established loan can be of either short-term or long-term nature depending on financing and

---

[51] See chapter F -4.4.3 on page 284 regarding details of netting schemes.

liquidity needs. These loans are – like any other loan – subject to interest. Interest charged and received is calculated in the same way as ordinary intercompany loans, as discussed before.

Netting schemes are often combined with cash-pooling systems. In such a case, it is important to separate interests of the loans from interests due to cash pooling.

- Cash Pools

  The improvement and the advantages of applying cash-pooling systems require a detailed analysis. This is because several aspects have to be considered. In general the benefits achieved by concentrating cash at one instance have to be forwarded to the financing companies of the pool as interests or other earnings. Furthermore, the companies to be financed have to be charged with appropriate costs or interests. The set-up of the cash pool should consider a set of elements similar to conditions available in the market:

  - An appropriate spread between interests charged and interests received;
  - Risks of the financing and financed pool companies;
  - Credibility of the pool companies;
  - Securities;
  - Country and currency risks;
  - Cost of maintaining the cash pool.

  In practice, uniform ratings are applied for all pool companies and – if necessary or appropriate – adjusted by individual facts for pool companies.

- Factoring

  Factoring is an instrument to improve liquidity by selling receivables to a factorer. In groups, such an instrument can be used for an improved liquidity management if tools like cash pools are not available. Two factoring types are available that differentiate in the handling of the associated risks of failure (the non-payment of the debtor).

  - Traditional factoring assumes a transfer of risk to the factorer. This risk is considered to be a part of the factoring fee.
  - The risk rests with the factoree. Due to the missing risk transfer, the nature of the factoring agreement is more a (short term) loan arrangement than a factoring.

  Depending on the factoring type, the fees charged include three components:

  - An interest component. This component can be derived from quotes of the finance market. A common practice is to use a reference rate (e.g. LIBOR, EURIBOR or similar short-term reference rates) combined with an appropriate interest mark-up.

- A risk component. The determination of the risk component can be derived from historical failure rates of debtors.
- A service fee component. This fee is for the administration and management of receivables. It can be determined by their activities.

Even if the factoring fee is based on the three components, the practice to charge only a flat or all-inclusive fee is often not accepted by tax authorities. Therefore, a separate determination of each component of the factoring fee is strongly recommended. This will result in customer specific fees that are also subject to consolidation.

- Guarantees

    A common practice in groups is the use of guarantees to secure financial and other transactions and relationships. Securing transactions can either reduce the risk associated with the underlying transaction or to achieve advantages like reduced costs. Like other financing relationships, a certain measurement base has to be allocated to guarantees. This measurement base used is often derived from the difference between the cost of the underlying transaction without any guarantees and the costs of the underlying transaction considering guarantees.

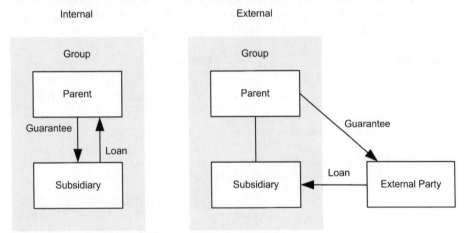

Fig. F-25   Basic guarantee applications

Guarantees can either be used group-internally or group-externally. An internal use might be appropriate to secure transactions; it is not always accepted by tax legislations. The argument due to the non-acceptance is the control concept and therefore the control of the subsidiary combined with the ability to direct and influence risks of the underlying transactions. An external application is a widely accepted scenario. The advantage the subsidiary achieves will establish a tax relationship between the parent (or any other company of the group providing the guarantee) and the subsidiary benefiting from the guarantee. Depending of the implementation in the group, subsidiaries might also be charged by the issuing institution for commercial purposes. Charges should be based on the measurement base described before.

There may be other forms of financing relationships in groups. They depend on the extent of financing activities of the group. Typical examples are hedging and foreign currency management. Such advanced financing activities require more or less the same attention and application of tools as the above listed financing relationships.

Group-internal transactions can sometimes be so unique that they cannot be allocated to one of the above categories of relationships. These transactions will be subsumed under **other relationships**. One of these transactions is use of charges in groups to transfer profits to the parent, which is a common practice in groups. As with other transactions, a business case is required to justify such charges. Often the use, leasing or otherwise assignment of intangible assets are used for such business cases. Brands, logos, patents and other forms of rights are typical examples of intangible assets to be used. The measurement follows the same procedure as the measurement of those assets subject to transfer pricing.

All intercompany transactions can be allocated to one or more of the four **basic intercompany transactions**. The accounting and particularly the consolidation and profit elimination for these transactions is similar to all other transactions. The following matrix provides a comprehensive summary.

Transaction for	Relationships			
	Trading	**Collaboration**	**Financing**	**Other**
Immediate sale	Goods and services rendered to customers	Subcontracting of manufacturing activities		
Later sale	Goods in stock	Subcontracting of manufacturing activities		
Own use		• Transfer of assets, businesses and similar transactions within the group • Leasing of assets • Knowledge transfer	• Providing loans • Netting schemes • Cash Pooling • Factoring • Guarantees • Hedging • Other	• Use of intangible assets • Leasing of intangible and fixed assets
Own consumption		• Services rendered within the group • Employee secondment • Providing of resources	See above	Group charges

Tab. F-6 Allocation of business transaction subject to transfer pricing to relationships and group transactions

6.2.2. *Profit and cost determination*

All intercompany cases follow one underlying rationale: is a **cost and profit allocation** possible and which basis is used for this allocation? Cost and profit allocations are always based on the underlying business transactions between two group companies (a sending and a receiving company) which may allow direct and indirect profit allocations. Both methods are accepted by tax authorities. Direct allocation is best as it allocates profits on an individual transaction. This requires detailed recording of all activities of the transaction to prove that only those activities are charged that are consumed or ordered. An application is often limited to defined business transactions only. Typical transactions can be found in trading relationships where goods or services are ordered by a group company that are charged to customers. Most intercompany transactions are not able to measure individual activities. An indirect profit allocation using charges is therefore applied. The intention is to charge costs from a sending to several receiving companies using allocation keys. Determining these allocation keys is a responsibility of management accounting as it has to reflect the underlying transaction and allocation base. In parallel to direct and indirect cost and profit allocations that are based on individual transactions, or classes of transactions, pool concepts allocate costs and profits based on additional criteria.

To allocate cost and profits, appropriate allocation method have to be applied that reflect the intention of the underlying business transaction. There is a set of **methods**, accepted by the tax authorities, for allocation of costs and profits. The allocation is realized by determining the transfer prices that include cost and profit elements. The application of the appropriate method depends on the underlying business transaction, particularly its nature and its uniqueness compared to the market the group or its business units operate in. From a tax perspective, all methods can be assigned to two sets of methods: traditional transactions methods and transactional profit methods.

Traditional transactions methods combine a set of methods that always consider similar transactions at arm's length. The application of the arm's length principle is the underlying intention of all transactions.

- Comparable uncontrolled price method (CUP method)

    This method compares prices charged in controlled transactions (so transactions between related parties) with prices charged in comparable uncontrolled transactions (so transactions between unrelated parties on an arm's length base). Differences between these two prices might indicate a non-arm's length transaction that demands a price substitution. These comparisons can be realized applying an extrinsic approach (so a pure market comparison) or an intrinsic approach (so involving group companies in market transactions).

    The issue of this method is the identification of comparable transactions as transactions are often unique. Therefore, an application of this method is often not given due to the uniqueness of transactions.

- Resale price method

  This method takes a different approach as it determines accepted prices of intercompany transactions for goods and services that are derived from the market. The determination of accepted intercompany prices follows a retrospective application. Based on the price that can be realized in the market on sale to an unrelated party in an arm's length transaction, market-obligatory profit mark-ups are deducted, as well as those costs associated with the handling and sale, as well as other related expenses (that consider the use of tangible and intangible assets and risks associated with the sales transaction). The determined intercompany price is then compared to charged intercompany transactions.

  Such methods are often applied in groups where manufacturing units sell goods and services to sales organizations. The method faces two issues: what is the appropriate profit mark-up and which uses of assets have to be considered? This is because the involvement of the reseller might add a certain value to the transaction that needs to be taken into account.

- Cost plus method

  A different approach is maintained by using the cost plus method. While the resale price method uses a retrospective price allocation scheme, the cost plus method applies a prospective price allocation, starting with costs incurred and adding an appropriate mark-up. Traditionally, the cost plus method is used in groups where parts, subparts and unfinished goods are moved and sold between production facilities before the final product is available. The method faces some issues: Which costs have to be considered?, What is the cost base?, and What is the appropriate mark-up?

  Generally, the cost basis has to consider those costs that also would be charged to third parties on an arm's length base. A strict interpretation might come to the conclusion that – depending on the cost accounting system applied – various costs have to be included or excluded. Cost allocation is not an issue as long as a consistent application is given that does not differ between external or internal customers. The determination of costs does not differ between separate legal entities and groups; an application has to ensure consistency. OECD requirements of the application of an appropriate mark-up include two dimensions: an internal comparable mark-up and an external comparable mark-up. The internal one is derived from transactions if products are sold with this mark-up to unrelated parties. The external one is assuming mark-ups that are usual between external independent parties. While the internal mark-up can be derived from similar transactions with customers, the determination of external mark-ups is more sophisticated, particularly due to the availability of such information and the limited comparability of cost structures. Competitors or comparable companies rarely disclose such information. In addition to all mentioned items, the cost base used has an impact on the cost plus method. Appropriate cost bases can be actual and planned costs. The latter requires appropriate mid-term planning which considers the product mix to be manufactured and sold (sale-cost-volume relationships) in combination with appropriate product margins. The determination of all discussed aspects is subject to management accounting.

Even if high hurdles are given to apply the cost plus method, this method is the most used method in practice as companies often have sufficient experience in cost calculation and management.

Transactional profit methods follow a different approach. These methods try to approximate an arm's length condition in given transactions by allocating profits to all parties involved. This is because a direct determination of an allocation by using transactions between independent parties is not possible. Instead, benchmark studies are used to establish some kind of arm's length principles.

*   Transactional net margin method (TNMM)
    The transactional net margin method determines transfer prices based on net margins. The net margin is the operating profit to be achieved at the end of the period (which more or less equals the EBIT) in relation to an appropriate base (e.g. costs, sales or assets). Indicators used to determine the net margin have to be applied consistently across all transactions, so for group internal as well as external transactions. While the method is based on net margins, it is also based on actual costs and not on planned costs. This requires an annual adjustment of the transfer price. The practice often uses standard transfer prices that are derived from previous period transfer prices throughout the whole current period that are adjusted at year-end when the net margin of the period is known.

    This method is often used in combination with other methods, as net margins and EBITs are publicly available. Furthermore, the application of this method as a standalone method is often not accepted by tax authorities or accepted only if certain criteria are met.

*   Transactional profit split method
    The transactional profit split method follows a different approach. The profit achieved by a transaction has to be allocated to all parties involved. A similar treatment is required for losses. The allocation therefore is based on actual costs and has to consider the contribution and function of each party involved as well as their risk profile. Because of the underlying rationales used in allocating profits, a good documentation of the functional and risk analysis is vital. Furthermore, contribution analyses and residual analyses might be applied to prove an appropriate allocation of profits.

    The application of the profit split method is often found in global acting groups that have highly integrated structures that are more or less function driven ignoring any local or legal requirements. The legal shell of a company is only fulfilling local duties and carrying some functions.

Even if every method is accepted by the tax authorities, this does not mean that each method will be accepted in each case. Tax authorities more or less have their own understanding which methods are appropriate for which business case. Some even demand a method application in a defined order subject to the application feasibility. Another proven demand by tax authorities is a comparability analysis of the method applicable and applied to one intercompany transaction. Others may demand a simple explanation why the method selected is chosen (both are best method rules). Some tax legislations do not accept all the methods mentioned. Here it is important to find an agreement with the tax authorities in accepting certain methods as they may impact several countries and legislations.

6.2.3. Documentation and compliance

Transfer pricing, like other accounting and taxation subjects, is subject to compliance requirements. These compliance requirements have their origins in the legal environment of each country group members reside, particularly in national and international tax rules and regulation and commercial codes. Even if commercial codes are involved, the primary focus of compliance regarding transfer pricing is on tax rules and regulations. While transfer pricing is subject to cross-border activities, OECD Transfer Pricing Guidelines are the underlying subject that act as the basis for bilateral taxation agreements between countries. These bilateral taxation agreements are realized in double tax treaties which are also implemented in local tax rules and regulations e.g. as part of foreign transaction tax acts. Even if dependencies exist, national tax rules and regulations are not necessarily identical to the proposed OECD guidelines. So, it's important to know the national regulations.

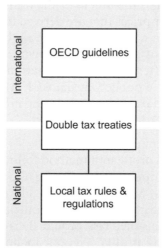

Fig. F-26 Tax dependencies

Based on tax rules and regulations, many tax legislations and jurisdictions have developed principles and regulations to be followed by taxpayers that are often refined by tax administrations and also forwarded to tax payers. As a result, companies are obliged to enhanced duties, particularly to enhanced duties to cooperate and documentation duties.

- Enhanced cooperation duties
    Tax legislations often demand cooperation duties in all tax matters from taxpayers. Such duties include timely submission of tax returns,

appropriate documentation of tax relevant transactions, explanation of transactions on the request of tax authorities and other duties important to determine taxes. Such duties consist of formal and material obligations as defined by tax authorities. Even if these are general duties, they may change from tax legislation to tax legislation depending on local needs and requirements. A general attribute to these duties is that they apply to all kinds of taxation issues.

These general cooperation duties are enhanced every time transactions are involved that are out of reach for tax authorities. Such transactions typically include foreign operations and cross-border business transactions. Taxpayers are obliged in such situations to support tax authorities by collecting and providing documents and information relevant to taxation issues, even if they belong to the foreign operation. Documents and information are manifold, they can consist of contracts relating to cross-border transactions, plans, calculations, benchmark studies and other documents. The data gathering to provide tax authorities with sufficient information has to consider the role of the taxpayer and its ability to collect the demanded documents:

- Tax authorities expect appropriate documents and information in outbound cases (so a parent holding interests in foreign operations is taxpayer).
- Only limited documents and information can be expected by tax authorities in inbound cases (so subsidiary belonging to a foreign group is taxpayer).

The extent of cooperation duties, the ability to collect documents and the detail level of documents requested from foreign operations should be agreed with tax authorities in the case of tax audits if possible. A proactive behaviour is in favour.

- Documentation duties
  Documentation duties are expanded over the past 15 years obliging companies to have appropriate documents available to be delivered to tax authorities on their request. This is because some tax legislations provide only short lead time to taxpayers to deliver requested documents and information. Preparation of appropriate documentation is then not possible.

  The core documentation is a transfer pricing documentation. This documentation has to be available to each party involved, sometimes even locally available as a hardcopy. This has to be with each subsidiary and the parent of the group as long as they belong to more than one tax legislation. Groups may run different strategies in providing transfer pricing documentations. Some prefer a centralized storage and management, others prefer a decentralized solution as local tax requirements cannot be ignored. Another proven practice is a mixture of both centralized storage and management of the general transfer pricing documentation, combined with local enhancements for specific tax issues or documentation requirements.

Most tax legislations demand more or less similar contents of a transfer pricing documentation. The documentation should include in minimum the following items:

- General information about the group, its structure, subsidiaries, its business and an analysis of the industries they are engaged in.
- A description of transactions and transaction groups in the group. A bundling of transactions in appropriate groups can be based on the transaction types and relationships as outlined before and refined if necessary. To minimize the documentation requirement, it is recommended to arrange groups according to intercompany relationships.[52]
- A functional and risk analysis, combined with an analysis of the valuation chain in the group.
- A transfer pricing analysis that includes a description and explanation of the applied methods and their appropriateness.
- Exceptional events and transactions. They should be treated and documented separately. Typical items that belong to this section are business restructurings, material changes in the business model and the group structure including their functions and risks, material changes in underlying or new contracts and extraordinary business transactions.
- A collection of special cases like agreements with other tax authorities material to the own tax authority, pending tax law suits, price changes of transfer prices and similar cases.

The documentation should be updated at regular intervals to ensure an up-to-date status. As already mentioned, this is a minimum requirement. Tax legislation may have additional requirements that need to be included in the documentation.

A further issue is the language. Tax authorities often demand a transfer pricing documentation to be available in local language. An alternate language is either not allowed or allowed after a prior approval of the tax authority. Even then the tax authority may demand a translation in local language for selected documentation elements.

> To minimize documentation activities and to improve flexibility in adjusting documentation of changes in the group, a modular approach should be used in preparing the transfer pricing documentation. It is strongly recommended to consult the tax advisor when preparing the documentation to ensure nothing is omitted.

All legal compliance aspects are more or less driven by tax regulations. Also, groups often have their own compliance systems in place. Group compliance systems are a mixture of local compliance requirements combined with dedicated compliance issues that relate to group accounting policies and further group requirements. The enforcing body to ensure compliance is often internal audit.

---

[52] See Tab. F-6 on page 328 as a basic template for grouping transactions.

Example

Due to the large amount of international transactions and past difficulties with tax authorities, Flexing Cables SE had installed a transfer pricing system for the group considering all group internal transactions. The company had chosen the master file approach to document the transfer pricing system. It consisted of a master document that included all relevant components plus local addendums for each country in which the group had some kind of business installed.

The master file includes the general documentation valid for all subsidiaries. It includes:

- The group's structure, its subsidiaries, the role of each party and a description of the functions of the group;
- An allocation of companies to functions in the group;
- A risk analysis of group functions;
- A definition of applied profit allocation methods.

Local addendums cover only those issues that are unique to a country and that do not have a substantial influence on the transfer pricing system.

The documents are updated annually to always reflect the current status of transfer pricing regulations.

Flexing Cables SE had implemented a "mark-up system". All group-internal transactions, whether they related to goods or services were subject to defined mark-ups, which had to be applied either to a single transaction on the date of occurrence (which applies particularly for goods and services finally rendered to customers) or on a monthly basis (for group-internal services only). To cover all costs, an adjustment procedure was to be initiated every December that charges additional costs or reliefs from servicing to consuming units. For the current period, the following mark-ups had to be applied:

Transaction	Mark-up	Interval
Trading (goods and service in the ordinary course of the business)	8.2%	Transaction
Subcontracting (group-internal trading on products and services charged to customers)	7.8%	Transaction
IT		
• Infrastructure (Backbone, communication, e-mail and similar items)	6.0%	Monthly
• Customer specific services (storage, applications and similar items)	7.2%	Transaction or monthly
Human resources		
• Payroll	5.5%	Monthly
• Recruiting, training & education	7.2%	Transaction
Accounting & Financing		
• Loans	2.1% on loan margin	Quarterly
• Cash pool	0.2% on cash balance	Quarterly
• Other services	6.0%	Transaction or monthly
Management	7.2%	Monthly
IP charges (Use of corporate design, logo, use of software and similar items)	9.6%	Monthly
General administration and other services not listed above	6.0%	Transaction or monthly

> Upfront approval for any other group internal transaction was required but not listed in the above-mentioned transactions. Furthermore, any planned or intended changes in the group structure, the composition and allocation of its functions (in particular changes in the production environment) needed upfront approval by the tax department of the corporate centre.

6.2.4. *Application in group accounting*

The detailed requirements on the determination of transfer prices and the influence of tax regulations on the determination of transfer prices demand a dedicated application. Due to the transaction specific determination of transfer prices, the application of one standard procedure only is not appropriate. Instead, a transaction specific treatment as part of subsequent consolidations is necessary for regular activities. This requires some general preparation activities: an inventorying and classification of all intercompany transactions subject to transfer pricing and a determination of standardized profit mark-up rates for each type of intercompany transaction. Profit mark-ups for each intercompany transaction may consist of more than one mark-up if necessary.

An application of transfer pricing in subsequent consolidations is based on a reporting system that differentiates between the different types of intercompany transaction. For each type of intercompany transaction that belongs to one class of transaction and for each type of profit mark-up, a separate reporting is required. This reporting requirement can be realized by detailed line entries in the reportable profit & loss statement or by using a reporting matrix:

Intercompany P&L Item	Profit mark-up category				
	Cat. 1	Cat. 2	Cat. 3	Cat. 4	Cat. 5
Revenues					
Goods	yyy		yyy	yyy	
Services	yyy				
Other earnings					
Services		yyy	yyy		
Personnel secondment				yyy	
Fees	zzz				
Group charges		zzz			
Interest earnings					
Loans					yyy
Cash pooling					yyy
Guarantees				yyy	

Fig. F-27 Reporting structure for transfer pricing purposes

Based on the reported figures, an elimination of unrealized profits can be executed by the corporate centre by applying the standardized profit mark-up rates. Any reporting activities on profits achieved are not necessary any longer. This will reduce the reporting needs by subsidiaries.

6.3. Consolidation techniques

The elimination of unrealized profits is a purely technical task that is independent from any accounting regulations and standards. The consolidation techniques depend only on two items that have a strong interdependence: The structure of the profit & loss statement and the basic transactions that capitalize assets. Both control the way eliminations have to be performed. While the elimination of unrealized profits is not a stand-alone task, it is often combined with the elimination of income and expenses.

The structure of the profit & loss statement is needed to decide on the extent of consolidation tasks. These tasks not only include the elimination of intercompany transactions but also any reclassifications required for a proper presentation. As the preparer has the choice between two presentation formats according to IAS 1.99, consolidation tasks will vary depending on the chosen format.

- P&L by function

  As the P&L by function presents only items that are sold, a full reversal of all items of the sending company that belong to intercompany transaction is required as the receiving company carries all acquired assets in its balance sheet. This applies to transactions for later sales as well as for transactions for own use. The profit implied in these transactions is adjusted in the balance sheet.

  - Transactions for later sale

    As transactions for later sale deal with the sale of goods, the elimination of unrealized profits has to adjust the carrying amount intercompany inventories. This adjustment occurs in the current period by executing the following journal entry:

Journal entry			Company
dr.	Sales		Sending company
	cr.	CoGS	Sending company
	cr.	Inventory	Receiving company

    If the goods are sold in the next period, the elimination journal entry has to be reversed by the receiving company:

Journal entry			Company
dr.	Inventory		Receiving company
	cr.	CoGS	Receiving company

- Transactions for own use

  Transactions for own use permanently carry the assets acquired by the receiving company as fixed or intangible assets in the balance sheet. Therefore, the elimination of unrealized profits in the current period occurs against the position of the acquired assets.

Journal entry		Company
dr.	Sales	Sending company
cr.	CoGS	Sending company
cr.	Fixed assets / intangible assets	Receiving company

The unrealized profit that is included in the carrying amount of the asset at group level has to be adjusted over the lifetime of the asset. Therefore, unrealized profits in the carrying amount of the asset at group level are adjusted against depreciation expenses in all subsequent periods.

Journal entry		Company
dr.	Fixed assets / intangible assets	Receiving company
cr.	Depreciation expenses	Receiving company

- P&L by nature

    As the P&L by nature presents the output of the operation and not of the corporation, extended consolidation tasks are necessary. A pure elimination of intercompany transactions as executed for the P&L by function is not sufficient. The elimination of intercompany transactions and the elimination of unrealized profits have to consider also reclassifications to reflect the proper presentation in the group. This applies to transactions for later sales as well as for transactions for own use.

    - Transactions for later sale

        Transactions for later sale consist of two basic treatments. Goods received can be put directly in stock or can be used in the further production process. The elimination of unrealized profits in both cases is closely linked to the consolidation of income & expenses.

        The journal entry for goods received in the current period and put directly in stock consists of a reclassification from sales to changes in inventory. The profit that is part of sales has to be credited to inventory as it reflects the unrealized profit.

Journal entry		Company	Comment
dr.	Sales	Sending company	
cr.	Changes in inventory	Receiving company	
cr.	Inventory	Receiving company	This is the unrealized profit.

Goods used in the further production process are charged to the profit & loss statement as material expenses. Therefore, one + one = two journal entries are required, one that eliminated the sales – expense relationship and one that capitalize the goods. Both journal entries have different balances. The difference between both balances represents the unrealized profit. In other words, a direct adjustment of the carrying amount of inventory for unrealized profits did not take place. Instead, a capitalization of the goods using the amount applicable to group needs is made.

Journal entries		Company	Comment
dr. Sales		Sending company	
	cr. Material expenses	Receiving company	
dr. Changes in inventory		Receiving company	This includes the
	cr. Inventory	Receiving company	unrealized profit.

If the goods are sold in the next period, the elimination journal entry has to be reversed by the receiving company:

Journal entry		Company
dr. Inventory		Receiving company
	cr. Changes in inventory	Receiving company

- Transactions for own use

    Similar to transactions for later sale, transactions for own use have to be divided into two treatments to execute the elimination of unrealized profits.

    The journal entry for assets manufactured by the sending company consists of a reclassification from sales to capitalized assets. The profit that is part of sales has to be credited to non-current assets as it reflects the unrealized profit.

Journal entry		Company	Comment
dr. Sales		Sending company	
	cr. Capitalized assets	Receiving company	
	cr. Fixed assets / intangible assets	Receiving company	This is the unrealized profit.

Third party purchases by the sending company are identical to transactions for own use of the P&L by function. Transactions for own use permanently carry the assets acquired by the receiving company as fixed or intangible assets in the balance sheet. Therefore, the elimination of unrealized profits in the current period occurs against the position of the acquired assets.

Journal entry		Company
dr. Sales		Sending company
	cr. Material expenses	Sending company
	cr. Fixed assets / intangible assets	Receiving company

The unrealized profit that is included in the carrying amount of the asset at group level has to be adjusted over the lifetime of the asset. Therefore, unrealized profits in the carrying amount of the asset at group level are adjusted against depreciation expenses in all subsequent periods. This journal entry is again identical to the corresponding transaction of the P&L by function.

Journal entry		Company
dr. Fixed assets / intangible adjustments		Receiving company
	cr. Depreciation expenses	Receiving company

The elimination of unrealized profits also impacts **non-controlling interests** of subsidiaries. A certain portion of these unrealized profits is attributable to non-controlling interests. The allocation is limited to profits of the sending subsidiary with non-controlling interests that are included in inventories or non-current assets of the receiving company. As a consequence, profits are eliminated in the accounts of the sending company applying regular elimination procedures. Unrealized profits attributable to non-controlling interests have to be allocated in the second step by considering the percentage held by other shareholders in the sending subsidiary.

An allocation of unrealized profits to non-controlling interests is a task necessary to properly present profits. Even if this is necessary for a proper presentation, the allocation of unrealized profits to non-controlling interests is often not exercised in practice. The reason for this practice is the complexity in identifying transactions that include unrealized profits in combination with subsidiaries having non-controlling interests. Unrealized profits attributable to non-controlling interests are therefore assigned to the group.

Example[53]

During the period, Chorunta Cables had ordered products from MPG to a value of 7,847 k EUR. At the end of the period, products with a value of 527 k EUR were still in stock. These products were manufactured by MPG.

Flexing Cables used a transfer pricing system for all intercompany transactions. Group policy for trading activities was to apply the cost plus method for manufacturing facilities using a mark-up rate of 8.2% on production costs. Accordingly, the items in stock at Chorunta Cables included unrealized profit of 40 k EUR (527 – 527 / (1 + 0.082)). The elimination was based on Chorunta Cables' methodology.

Applying the P&L by function, cost of goods sold and the corresponding revenue of MPG had to be eliminated. While the unrealized profit was included in MPG's revenue, the elimination of unrealized profits had to consider not only the inventory account of Chorunta Cables but also the revenue account of MPG. This would result in the recording of the following journal entry:

Journal entry				Company
dr.	Revenues, intercompany	487		MPG
	cr.	Cost of goods sold	487	MPG
dr.	Revenues, intercompany	40		MPG
	cr.	Inventory	40	Chorunta Cables

In practice, both journal entries were combined.
Variance:
A different consolidation is required if Chorunta Cables is applying the P&L by nature. In this case, not the revenue account but the changes in inventory account has to be used. All other conditions stay the same.

Journal entry				Company
dr.	Inventory	40		Chorunta Cables
	cr.	Changes in inventory	40	Chorunta Cables

---

[53] This example is the same example used in chapters F -5.2.1 on page 292 and F -5.2.2 on page 299 to demonstrate the elimination tasks transactions for later sale. Even if the example is the same, the focus has changed to unrealized profits.

7. NON-CONTROLLING INTERESTS

One of the final tasks in preparing consolidated financial statements is the allocation of profit and loss in the group to non-controlling interests. This allocation is necessary because shareholders of subsidiaries that hold only a minority stake in the subsidiaries have the same rights like the parent company on their portion of the realized profit or loss.

As non-controlling interests have an equity character, the presentation of this item follows the presentation of group's equity. IAS 27.27 requires a presentation on non-controlling interests in the equity section of consolidated financial statements. To distinguish between equity of the group and non-controlling interests, the presentation has to occur separately from the equity that belongs to the owners of the parent. In practice, non-controlling interests are disclosed separately below all other equity items of the group.

Another disclosure requirement applies to the statement of comprehensive income. As the profit or loss of the period is attributable to the owners of the parent and any non-controlling interests, the portion attributable to non-controlling interests has to be presented separately. IAS 1.83 provides instructions about the presentation in the statement. Usually, the separate disclosure occurs at the end of the statement providing information about the pro-rata profit or loss as well as the portion of total comprehensive income. In rare cases, preparers adopt an alternate presentation by providing information about non-controlling interests in a separate disclosure as defined in IAS 1.84.

7.1. Allocation of profit and loss

The **allocation** of profits and losses to non-controlling interests includes all profit elements of all levels in the group whether they are classified as comprehensive or other comprehensive income. The underlying rule for the allocation is IAS 27.28. The standard mentions the profit and loss of total comprehensive income as the item to be allocated. Therefore, any profits and losses and each element of other comprehensive income have to be considered. Nevertheless, the standard is silent about the exact definition of profit and loss. Therefore, the prevailing opinion is to consider profits and losses at all levels in the group and not only at company level. The rationale behind this opinion is that profits and losses realized at other levels than company level refer to unaccounted hidden reserves and contingencies that are accounted for for group purposes. Even minority shareholders have a right to possess their share in these items which implies that profits and losses at all group levels have to be considered.

In summary, the following items that are distributed across several levels and positions of the group should be considered in determining the non-controlling interest's portion:

- The ordinary profit or loss of the period achieved by the company (local level);
- Any accounting and valuation adjustments to adjust the results of the company to the group's accounting policies (level I adjustments);
- The recognition of any items subsequent to the initial consolidation through profit & loss (12 month deadline exceeded due to IFRS3.45, level III adjustments);

- Any depreciation and other adjustments to items that are recorded due to the acquisition and initial consolidation (level II and level III adjustments);
- Write-downs of goodwill (level II);
- Adjustments to deferred taxes at all levels;
- Actuarial gains and losses of pension plans (IAS 19.93a), unrealized gains and losses of financial assets and liabilities (e.g. IAS 39.55) and foreign exchange differences (e.g. IAS 21.39) that are recorded as other comprehensive income.

For accounting purposes, the allocation of profits and losses is not sufficient. A proper **presentation and accounting** of non-controlling interests as part of consolidated financial statements does not only consider profits, losses and elements of other comprehensive income but also any changes in the capital base of the subsidiary. Changes in the capital base can occur due to:

- Capital reduction;
- Dividends paid;
- Any increases in the capital stock.

All changes in the capital base have to be accounted for on a pro-rata basis for the non-controlling interest. The pro-rate basis depends on the actual stake of the minority shareholder in the subsidiary and on any planned changes in the relationship between the shareholders. If changes occur because the parent acquired additional shares from the minority shareholder (or vice-versa), a reallocation of the non-controlling interest presented in the consolidated financial statements is required.[54] This reallocation is a pure equity transaction where a calculated amount has to be transferred from the non-controlling interest to other equity elements (usually retained earnings).

To estimate the expected closing balance of the non-controlling interests account, the following calculation may help. This calculation considers all previously taken thoughts regarding the allocation of profits and losses to non-controlling interests.

	Profit / loss of subsidiary
−	Depreciation on hidden reserves
+	Disclosure of hidden reserves
−	Goodwill write-downs
+/−	Deferred taxes
=	Overall result
	Thereof, a percentage allocation to non-controlling interests
+	Opening balance of the non-controlling interests account
+/−	Elements of other comprehensive income
−	Pro-rata dividends
+	Pro-rata increase in equity
−	Pro-rata decrease in equity
=	Closing balance of the non-controlling interests account

Tab. F-7 Calculation scheme for balances of non-controlling interests

---

[54] These kinds of activities are usually part of stock or capital transactions that may constitute a change in control. Please refer to chapter I - on page 501 for a detailed description of accounting tasks in these cases.

It is important to mention that this calculation scheme is valid for goodwill accounting applying the purchased-goodwill and full-goodwill method. In case of the application of the purchased goodwill method any goodwill adjustments are obsolete.

7.2. Consolidation techniques

The allocation of profit and loss to non-controlling interests can be realized at different levels in the group. It depends on the structure of the group, the type of equity consolidation – particularly in multi-level groups, the levels involved and the number of subsidiaries with minority shareholders.

The standard consolidation technique for a proper allocation of non-controlling interests can be realized in two ways. The first way is allocation at all levels. The advantage is an increased transparency where the net profit of the group is visible for each company with non-controlling interests at all levels. Nevertheless, more journal entries have to be executed to achieve this kind of transparency. The second way is the allocation at group level only, which is easier to realize. The price of this simplification is a loss of transparency. Regardless of which way is chosen, journal entries have to be executed for each company in the group with minority shareholders.

The standard journal entry is based on a calculation of the portion that belongs to non-controlling interests. The journal entry debits the profit & loss statements and credits the appropriate equity account of the consolidated financial statement. It is recommended to have a structure (either on account or at presentation level) in the profit & loss statement available that distinguish between profit attributable to the group and profit attributable to non-controlling interests. The following excerpt fulfils this requirement:

	Profit before taxes
–	Income taxes
=	Net profit for the period
–	Profit attributable to non-controlling interests
=	Net profit attributable to the group

Tab. F-8   Profit allocation in profit & loss statement

The standard journal entry to be executed in a profit situation:

Journal entry
dr.   Profit non-controlling interests
    cr.   Non-controlling interests

The journal entry will be executed depending on the realized way. If an enhanced transparency is required, this journal entry has to be executed at local level as well as at level II for each company. If a transparency is not necessary, it is sufficient to execute the journal entry at group level. Furthermore, the journal entry can be executed for each company at group level as well as for all companies as a whole.

In loss situations, the journal entry revolves, using the same accounts:

Journal entry
dr.   Non-controlling interests
    cr.   Profit non-controlling interests

Example

Flexing Cables's corporate centre is applying a dedicated profit allocation policy at all levels of the group to provide management with details on consolidated financial statements if necessary and required. Accordingly, profits are either allocated to the group or to non-controlling interests for each subsidiary at each level. During the fiscal year an initial profit allocation is executed for Solenta. Based on the performance of the company and the transactions recorded at each level, the corporate centre has compiled the following break-up to be used for profit allocation:

	Separate financial statement	Level I – IFRS conversion	Level III – Purchase price allocation	Total
Net profit of the period	6,660	(473)	(5,015)	1,172
— Profit attributable to non-controlling interests	1,332	(95)	(1,003)	234
= Net profit attributable to the group	5,328	(379)	(4,012)	937

While the allocation to non-controlling interests has to be accounted for, the following journal entries have to be recorded:

- Separate financial statement

    While an allocation to non-controlling interest is impossible in separate financial statements, the allocation is accounted on level II to comply with group accounting policies.

- Level I adjustments

    Journal entry
    dr.   Non-controlling interests   95
        cr.   Profit non-controlling interests   95

- Level II adjustments

    Journal entry
    dr.   Profit non-controlling interests   1,332
        cr.   Non-controlling interests   1,332

- Level III adjustments

    Journal entry
    dr.   Non-controlling interests   1,003
        cr.   Profit non-controlling interests   1,003

Due to the application of assigning non-controlling interest separately at each level, an allocation at group level is needless.

A more complex accounting is required in multi-level groups. Due to the existence of non-controlling interests in the group hierarchy on various levels, the equity consolidation method has to consider the hierarchy when allocating non-controlling interests.[55]

7.3. Special cases

Special treatment is required if the company generates on-going **losses**. These losses may result in a negative non-controlling interests account (deficit balance). IAS 27.28 confirms that in such cases the presentation of a negative value in the statement of financial position is mandatory. This type of accounting has been introduced as part of the amendment of IAS 27 in 2008 due to part two of the business combinations project. Before that time, a deficit balance was not allowed. In such cases, the balance of the non-controlling interests account stated a balance of zero combined with an offside auxiliary calculation of the development of losses. Beside the negative account, the loss situation triggers an additional activity that needs to be considered. On-going losses are a typical indicator for the need of impairment tests.[56] These impairment tests are necessary at parent level; they focus on the carrying balance of the investment in the subsidiary as well as at group level for the goodwill that is associated with the subsidiary due to the equity consolidation. While the first impairment test does not affect the non-controlling interests account the latter one does if the full-goodwill method is applied. In such cases, the non-controlling interest account will be charged with a pro-rata portion of any goodwill write-downs.

Another special treatment is required in **multi-level groups**. Non-controlling interests have to be presented in multi-level groups in the same manner than in every other group. Due to the hierarchy of a group, the presentation requires special attention which is discussed in chapter 9.3.2.[57]

8. GROUP-LEVEL TRANSACTIONS

In addition to consolidations and eliminations, group-level transactions are subjects that have to be executed to prepare consolidated financial statements. These transactions have their origins in measurement and presentation requirements of IFRS. Both areas complement each other. Other than consolidations and eliminations that are renewed with every preparation of consolidated financial statements, group-level transactions deal with balances that are carried forward from period to period. Group-level transactions combine a set of tasks:

- Valuation adjustments and remeasurements;
- Impairments;

---

[55] See chapter F -9.3.2 on page 391 for the treatment in multi-level groups.
[56] See chapter F -8.2 on page 348 for the mechanics of impairment tests.
[57] See page 158.

- Reclassifications;
- Nettings.

Depending on the group's structure and their intercompany transactions, group-level transaction can unfold long-term and complex effects.

8.1. Valuation adjustments and remeasurements

Valuation adjustments and remeasurements of assets and liabilities are transactions at group level that require an individual treatment. This is because assets and liabilities of consolidated financial statements have to fulfil the same measurement and presentation requirements than separate financial statements. While assets and liabilities at group level might have a different composition than at local level, an application of the asset-carrying subsidiary measurement is not sufficient even if group accounting policies are applied. The composition of an asset at group level can be based on a pure addition of the same assets by several subsidiaries at local level (including appropriate level I to level III adjustments) and on optional additional transactions required at group level. To ensure an appropriate recording and measurement of all assets and liabilities at group level, a review of these items is required. Typical measurement issues that need to be considered are summarized in the following list.

Asset / Liability	Measurement issue
Goodwill	Write-down of goodwill as a result of an impairment test.
Intangible assets	Contractions and extensions of selected cost components.
Fixed assets	Contractions and extensions of selected cost components.
Inventory	Contractions and extensions of unfinished and finished goods.
Trade receivables	Bad debt allowances for a uniform measurement of receivables of the same customers recorded by several subsidiaries.
Provisions & accruals	Uniform application for similar transactions.

Tab. F-9 List of assets and liabilities subject to valuation adjustments at group level

The accounting of valuation adjustments and remeasurements is always executed at group level. The accounting follows ordinary accounting patterns as demanded by the appropriate IFRS. An allocation to a dedicated subsidiary is not possible and not required. Therefore, ordinary journal entries are sufficient. Due to the forwarding of the carrying amounts at group level, valuation adjustments not only have to consider measurements of assets and liabilities at the current reporting date but also valuation adjustments carried forward. These carried forward balances have to be checked regarding any subsequent adjustments or reversals. Final adjustments can be calculated by considering the carrying amounts recorded by subsidiaries, adjustments carried forward and any adjustment demands.

	Calculated carrying amount demanded at group level
–	Valuation adjustment carried forward
–	Aggregated balance of the carrying amounts at local level
=	Adjustment to be recorded

Tab. F-10 Calculation of valuation adjustment demand

Special attention is given, if the carrying amounts of assets and liabilities changes, if disposals are recorded at subsidiary level or if assets are established the first time.

- Disposal at subsidiary level

  A disposal of asset or a settlement of liabilities at subsidiary level during the period will result in a nil balance in the aggregated trial balance. If an adjustment is carried forward, the carrying amount of that adjustment has to be removed resulting in a gain or loss to be recorded in profit & loss unless a recording in other comprehensive income is required. The removal is not limited to group level only; all further adjustments at level I to level III are affected as well. Such clean-up activities are a standard procedure at group level.

- Changes of the carrying amounts

  Any changes in the carrying amount triggers a new calculation of the required carrying amount at group level. Considering the carrying amount carried forward, the adjustment to be recorded will either result in a profit or loss at group level.

- Movements

  Assets and sometimes also liabilities can be moved between group companies in the ordinary course of the business. A typical example is the transfer of equipment to the place where it is permanently needed. Even if there is no change in the carrying amount at local level, the corporate centre needs to be informed about such changes as adjustments might be reclassified or follow-up activities like a new calculation of deferred taxes at group level need to be performed. A good reporting will pick up such movements.

- Initial recognition at subsidiary level

  If an asset is recognized the first time by a subsidiary or a parent, a simple measurement adjustment will be recorded on the appropriate valuation level to comply with group accounting policies. Further activities are not necessary. If such an asset is recorded by more than one group company, each group company may apply appropriate adjustments at levels I to III. The carrying amount of the aggregated trial balance has to be reviewed in determining any additional adjustments. These adjustments are calculated and recorded at group level only.

Based on the calculation of any valuation adjustments, a journal entry for each type of adjustment has to be recorded at group level. Journal entries are identical to similar journal entries at local level.

A good documentation should track the development of each adjustment of each asset or liability separately!

8.2. Impairments

8.2.1. *Basics*

The phrase "Impairments" is often used to describe the procedure and the accounting of adjusting the carrying balance of an asset towards a lower value. In fact, the relevant standards *IAS 36 – Impairment of Assets* defines an impairment as a situation where the carrying balance of an asset is above its recoverable amount. An impairment loss is recorded when the carrying balance of an asset has to be adjusted to that recoverable amount. The procedure to adjust carrying balances is called an impairment test. This test is the core element in determining whether or not an adjustment is necessary. IAS 36 provides detailed requirements in executing impairment tests.

Due to the scope of IAS 36, the impairment is limited to selected assets only. Assets subject to an impairment test are non-current assets, particularly property, plant and equipment (as defined in IAS 16), intangible assets (as defined in IAS 38), selected financial assets (as defined in IAS 39 and IFRS 9) and goodwill (as defined in IFRS 3). IAS 36.4 clarifies that subsidiaries, associates and joint ventures are always financial assets that are subject to impairments even if they are defined in other standards.

Applying the impairment philosophy to group accounting, different views are necessary to fully capture all aspects on impairment of assets in groups. The first one is the parent's view. The primary view of the parent is on its financial assets, particularly the "group" ones. Investments in subsidiaries, associates and joint ventures are the assets to be determined. If their dividends are sufficient in justifying the carrying amount in these investments, an impairment is not given. The other view is the group one's. The focus at group level is not only on all assets that qualify for impairments but also on goodwill and on those assets that have either an indefinite useful life or are not available for use yet. The nature of the assets defines when and how impairment tests have to be performed. The impairment test at group level might be supported by impairment tests at subsidiary level. If the subsidiary performs impairment tests at local level due to local requirements, the results of these tests might be used at group level as well presuming that assumptions and parameters used are identical. In most cases, assets recorded at level II and level III are subject to impairment tests at group level. While these assets are identified as part of the acquisition of a company, special attention – particularly for intangible assets that are based on valuation techniques – has to be given. If the profit generated by these assets is sufficient to justify the carrying amount of the assets, an impairment is – again – not given.

The concept of IAS 36 is based on the idea that there may be a reason to diminish the value of an asset. Due to the reason, the nature of an asset and the timing of the impairment test during the period, different approaches are given in dealing with impairments.

- The one-step approach

    The one-step approach is mandatory for goodwill and for intangible assets with an indefinite useful life or are not available for use yet. Regardless of any indication, an impairment test has to be performed. The test can be performed any time during the period. If a date for the impairment test is chosen, is has to be applied consistently across all subsequent periods. If different assets are subject to an impairment test, the tests can be executed individually for each asset. The advantage of this approach is that the workload in the accounting department can be allocated across the period.

    Even if there is some kind of freedom regarding the date for the impairment test, it is recommended to schedule impairment tests towards the end of the period. The rationale behind this recommendation is the assumption that an impairment situation might occur at any time between the impairment testing date and the end of the period that requires for an additional impairment test at the end of the period.

    > Schedule impairment tests towards the end of a period before the closing processes start.

- The two-step approach

    Other than the one-step approach, the two-step approach is used if management becomes aware of a potential declining in the carrying amount of an asset. This information is obtained at the end of a period when – according to IAS 36.9 – an assessment of indicators occurs that represent the "behaviour", use or market environment of an asset. Only if indications are given will an impairment test be triggered.

The impairment concept is not limited to selected assets. It has to be understood and applied in a broader context. As a general rule the impairment concept applies to all individual assets as described before. Nevertheless, there might be situations, where an impairment test is not applicable for an individual asset. This is particularly the case if a recoverable amount of an asset cannot be estimated reliably. In such situation, an impairment test can be executed at a higher level. This is in most cases the cash generating unit the asset belongs to. The impairment test covers the whole cash-generating unit including all assets. Cash generating units may also be members of business units or other cash generating units. Depending on the ability to perform an impairment test on a lower cash generation unit level or not, impairment test may also be executed at higher levels. Which level is subject to an impairment test finally depends on the structure and management of a group and the ability to generate cash flows.

8.2.2. Impairment steps

Whether a one-step or two-step approach is required, the impairment test always follows the same procedure. Based on the nature of the asset subject to an impairment test, an assessment of indications is required. If such an indication is given, the recoverable amount of the asset has to be calculated. If the recoverable amount cannot be measured reliably, the test has to be repeated on a cash-generating unit level. In this case, net assets of the cash generating unit have to be identified. The impairment test itself is based on these net assets. Both, the impairment test of an asset and the impairment test of a cash generating unit compare the recoverable amount with the carrying amount of an asset. Only if the carrying amount exceeds the recoverable amount, an impairment loss is recorded.

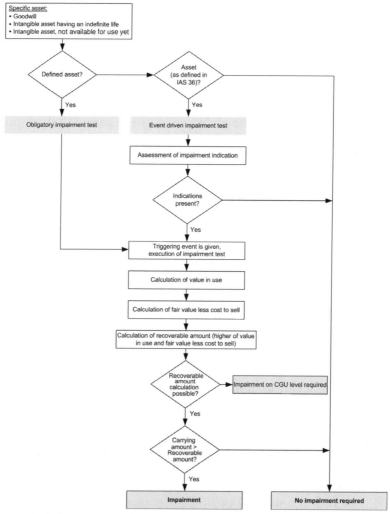

Fig. F-28　Workflow of the impairment test

8.2.2.1 Indications for impairment

The initial task is the assessment whether or not indications are present that require a full execution of an impairment test. This task has to be aligned to the business and structure of the group and performed either by the parent and any other holding companies or at group level. It is recommended to have consistent guidelines regarding the assessment throughout the group if more companies than the ultimate parent are involved. This is because the assessment and its results are also subject to documentation requirements.

Indications that an asset might be impaired may have different origins. In general, indications should be distinguished between external and internal ones. External indications usually refer to the market and the environment the group operates in and cannot be influenced by the group. Internal indications are group-specific. Which indications are more reliable – external or internal ones – depend on various factors, the business environment, the current situation of the group and many more. A case-by-case review may be required to determine which indications can – or will have to – be used. Consistent application is recommended.

IFRS 36.12 provides a list of typical external and internal indications that may be used in determining whether or not signs of a potential impairment appear (see Tab. F-11 Indicators for the execution of an impairment test). The standard mentions these indicators as the minimum to be considered. Due to the wording "… an entity shall consider, as a minimum, the …")[58] indications as provided by IAS 36 have a non-binding character. While this list is non-exhaustive, it is up to the discretion of management to change, enhance or adopt the indications proposed. Regardless of which indicators are used, it is important that these indicators are consistently applied and matches the business of the group and its market environment. The opportunity to define its own indications opens a wide range for accounting policies and the demand to record impairment losses. Therefore, indications should be chosen carefully.

No.	Category	Criterion	Description
1)	External	Value of asset	The asset's value declines more rapidly during the period than it would do under normal circumstances.
2)	External	Carrying amount of net asset	The carrying amount of (all) net asset is higher than the market capitalization of the group.
3)	External	Significant market changes	Significant changes have an adverse impact on the group. This may impact various environments the group operates: • Economic; • Market; • Technology; • Legal. These changes may occur during the period. If it is observable by management that these changes occur within the near future, an indication is also given.

(continued)

---

[58] Extracted from IAS 36.12 – Impairment of Assets.

No.	Category	Criterion	Description
4)	External	Market interest rates and other rates of return	Increasing market interest rates may impact the carrying value of an asset as long as these rates impact discount rates used in determining the asset's value in use. The impact on the carrying amount of an asset has to be material.
5)	External	Government	The interference of government in a market by e.g. regulating prices or behaviours might be a strong indication.
6)	Internal	Obsolescence of asset	The physical condition of the asset has changed in a way that it is not anymore available for its intended use.
7)	Internal	Physical damage of asset	The physical condition of the asset has changed in a way that it is not anymore available for its intended use.
8)	Internal	Significant business changes	Significant changes have an adverse impact on the group. These may be triggered by market demands and have a direct impact on the asset. IAS 36.12 (f) lists a set of examples: • Asset becomes idle. • Discontinuing and restructuring of the operation the assets belongs to (even plans are sufficient). • Disposal of asset before the expected date (even plans are sufficient). • Reassessment of useful life (asset becomes finite rather than indefinite). These changes may occur during the period. If it is observable by management that these changes occur within the near future, an indication is also given.
9)	Internal	Performance of asset	The economic performance of the asset is or will be worse than expected (this is not necessarily linked to profits generated by the asset).
10)	Internal	Cash flows	Cash flows for acquiring, operating and maintaining an asset are significantly higher than initially budgeted. Or in other words: cash flows generated by the asset are worse than initially budgeted. Even a significant decline of cash flows may be an indicator.
11)	Internal	Restructuring of groups	Restructurings are typically indications that the business model has changed. Reasons for restructurings may be: • Turning a company or group back into a profitable area. • Alignment to market trends, technology, customer demands or other reasons. • New strategic focus, new business areas, products, services or similar events.
12)	Subsidiaries	Dividends	Dividends exceed total comprehensive income of the subsidiary, joint venture or associate in the period the dividend is declared.
13)	Subsidiaries	Carrying amount	The carrying amount of the investment in a subsidiary, joint venture or associate in separate financial statements exceed the net assets (including goodwill) in consolidated financial statements of that company.

Tab. F-11   Indicators for the execution of an impairment test[59]

[59] This list is a combination of indications as proposed by IAS 36 combined with other indications.

Indications can occur in two ways, either as one-time events or as trends. One-time events are easy to identify while they are unusual, infrequent and non-comparable. More challenging are trends. A creeping evolution is hard to identify as indications are often not given or obvious. Indications of such trends will often be detected by a passage of time. Therefore, the quality of indications is important to understand trends and the impact on impairments. Often, a combination of several indications is required for an assessment. They have to be interpreted in the light of a potential impairment. This interpretation is recommended not only for detecting trends, it should be used anytime an impairment may be given.

The types of indication are not specified by the standard. Therefore, quantitative and qualitative criteria may be used in assessing an indication. Quantitative criteria – either absolute or relative to a reference – may be preferred in situations where a measurement is given. By contrast, qualitative criteria might be preferred in situations where detailed information is not available or inherent uncertainty exists.

Assessing indications is also subject to the materiality concept as confirmed in IAS 36.15. Indications have to be significant and an obvious impairment loss is expected. Nevertheless indications may have an impact on the carrying amount of an asset even if they are not material. If an adjustment of the asset is required, IAS 8 has to be followed. Typical examples of these adjustments are:

- Remaining useful life changes;
- The depreciation method does not reflect the economic behaviour of the asset;
- Expected residual values may have changed.

If an indication is given, a triggering event requires the execution of a full impairment test. This requires a determination of the fair value less cost of disposal of the asset and the determination of the value in use.

8.2.2.2 *Fair value less cost of disposal*

The fair value less cost of disposal assumes that the asset can be sold or otherwise disposed of.[60] This assumption is based on the idea that there is a market and a buyer would generate cash flows due to the use of the asset. As the standard now is silent about the measurement of its fair value, the "old" valuation hierarchy is still applied in most cases.[61] The hierarchy suggests deriving the fair value by using the following steps:

1) Using the price of a binding sales agreement.
2) Using the current bid price or the price of a most recent transaction in an active market the asset is traded in.

---

[60] In previous versions of IAS 36, the name was "fair value less costs to sell".
[61] IAS 36.25 – 27 is now deleted.

3) Using a price that is based on the best information available derived from similar transactions of similar assets.
4) Assuming hypothetical prices between unrelated parties.

Disposal costs have to be deducted from the fair value of the asset. Typical disposal costs are:

- Legal costs;
- Stamp duties and similar taxes;
- Removal costs;
- Costs required bringing the asset into sales or disposal conditions.

8.2.2.3 Value in use

Other than the fair value less cost of disposal, the value in use assumes that the asset will be used and has the ability to generate future cash flows. Even if these assumptions sound reasonable, the true issue is whether or not the asset is able to generate cash flows. Cash flows have to relate to the asset itself without the involvement or support of other assets. This requirement is a hurdle at which most assets fail so that the impairment test will be subject to cash generating units.

Deriving the value in use from future cash flows requires the use of present value concepts. The most common method used in this context is the discounted cash flow method. The standard expects that discounted cash flows will be used as it defines a set of requirements that are based on present value models. Therefore, IAS 36.30 defines five criteria that have to be considered in calculating the value in use:

- Future cash flows;
- Variations in amount or timing of future cash flows;
- Time value of money;
- Inherent uncertainties;
- Other relevant factors.

All outlined criteria will result in two questions: What is the appropriate future cash flow and which discount rate is appropriate? Therefore, two dedicated steps have to be performed, a determination of the future cash flows to be used for the impairment test and a determination of the appropriate discount rate.

- Future cash flow

  Future cash flows should represent the expected business condition and its management **assumptions** that are derived from the asset subject to the impairment test. These assumptions should consider the economic conditions of the market and cover all expected cash flows. Due to this requirement, it is recommended to derive cash flows from the planning and **budgets** of the expected development of the company or the group. Therefore, several items have to be considered, particularly the product and service portfolio combined with the quantity structure of products / services expected to be sold or served, as well as the pricing of products and services. As the planning has to reflect the asset only, a break-down of the corporate plan towards an asset's plan is required. The planning should consider the current capacity of the asset and the asset as it is. Any changes in subsequent periods that relate to adjustments due to restructuring, capacity increases, cost savings, performance enhancement or a reconfiguration of the asset have to be eliminated.

The **planning horizon** should not exceed a period of five years. The rationale behind this five year period is that most companies are planning the near future as part of their mid-range plans that usually cover a period of three to five years. Such a period can be maintained with managing inherent risks. A planning horizon of more than five years usually inflates the risk on revenues, expenses and cash flows as the increasing uncertainty may lead to wrong cash flow projections. Reliability is often not given. Nevertheless, there are businesses producing constant and reliable cash flows over a longer period. Only in such cases is an expansion of the planning horizon to more than five years appropriate. Typical examples of such businesses are extractive industries like oil, gas and other natural resources. The planning period is also called the detail phase. By contrast, all cash flows beyond the detail phase should be based on the projection of current cash flows by an extrapolation. The extrapolations should consider appropriate growth rates but is limited to the average long-term growth rate of a product, industry or country (or countries if the group operates in more than one country). The growth rate should not be kept constant. A steady decline of the growth rate in subsequent periods is expected unless business patterns of products, industries or countries prove a different behaviour (like an increase or constant development). While expenses and revenues may have different growth rates, more than one growth rate can be appropriate and has to be applied. The extrapolation is limited to the expected remaining useful life of the asset. While assets deteriorate, growth rates do not necessarily increase. Therefore, no growth rates or even negative growth rates are also applicable. Zero or negative growth rates can also result from the competition in the market, e.g. because new competitors enter the market.

There are two **types of cash flow** an asset can generate. The first type considers cash flows arising due to the use of the asset in the ordinary course of the business. This is the standard case where cash inflows as well as cash outflows (due to the maintenance and use of the asset) exist. In addition, an asset may also generate one-time cash flows at the end of its useful life. Even if these cash flows relate to the disposal, they have to be considered as well due to the requirement of IAS 36.39(c). Cash flows from the disposal of an asset have to be assumed using the same arm's length principle than used in the ordinary course of the business.

As the overall plan of a company or a group as well as the derived plan for the asset include all kinds of cash flows, appropriate **adjustments** are required. Unusual events and circumstances have to be eliminated.

Restructurings, one-time effects – such as lay-offs of staff and similar items – are typical unusual events and circumstances. All cash flows that relate to financing activities and taxation have to be eliminated as required by IAS 36.50. Therefore, cash flows have to be calculated on a pre-tax basis. As a calculation does not interfere with discount rates that are often based on a post-tax basis, it is also appropriate to calculate cash flows on a post-tax basis to have a consistent planning model in use.[62]

The planning of future cash flows has to be **reasonable and consistent**. There are two dimensions that need to be considered in verifying a reasonable application. One dimension is alignment to the capacity of the asset. Revenues and expenses have to fit to the available capacity of the asset. The other dimension is a consistent cash flow over several periods. Future cash flows have to correlate to past and actual cash flows of the asset. A consistent cash flow requires an environment that provides the same conditions over several periods. Unusual events and circumstances have to be eliminated. This applies to all periods involved. Both dimensions have to ensure a consistent application and a consistent use of management assumptions.

For **documentation and audit requirements**, it is not sufficient to present the planning of future cash flows, even if this plan is supported by reasonable assumptions or is consistent in all matters. Additional evidence is required, where external evidence in estimating cash flows has priority before internal evidence. This means that all parameters and assumptions made should be supported or proved by external documents.

Even if a plan is consistent, reliable and logical, inherent risks exist because a plan for the asset is usually based on selected assumptions. But assumptions may change due to market or other reasons. Therefore, it is recommended to "play" with the impairment model to identify **critical parameters and assumptions**. The best way to detect critical parameters and assumptions is by using scenarios. Due to the uncertainty of the future behaviour of markets and the competition within the market, a set of potential scenarios should be defined that reflect at least best and worst cases regarding the expected market behaviour and the utilization of the asset because of the market behaviour. Therefore, the focus should be on those parameters and assumptions that have small changes but produce the highest changes of value in use: regular monitoring is recommended.

IAS 36.40 demands a consideration of the general **inflation** in determining cash flows. Inflation can be included in the cash flow models in two ways, either through real rates or through nominal rates. If real discount rates are applied, the plan subject to discounting has to be based on real cash flows, assuming appropriate increases and decreases of revenues and expenses at the dates when cash flows occur. Applying nominal rates, the plan is based on the current situation, again assuming appropriate increases and decreases of revenues and expenses as of the

---

[62] See also IAS 36.BC94 and BCZ85.

current date (so without an inflation impact). The real rate can be derived from the nominal and inflation rate.

$$\text{Real rate} = \frac{1 + \text{nominal rate}}{1 + \text{inflation rate}}$$

Fig. F-29 Dependency between nominal rate and real rate

Considering real and nominal rates is not the only concern with inflation. Future cash flows can be subject to various inflation rates. If the testing asset serves various markets that are subject to individual inflation rates, cash flow streams from each market have to be treated individually. This is particularly important if revenues and expenses are subject to different inflation rates or any restrictions e.g. by regulators.

To determine the **composition of future cash flows** that relate to the asset, selected revenues and expenses have to be considered in preparing cash flows. This may result in a reconciliation of the underlying plans regarding which cost elements to include and exclude. The whole lifecycle of the asset, as well as any changes in conditions of the use of the asset, is subject to an identification of cash flow items.

Subject	Description	Status	Reference
Preparation of asset	Preparing an asset so that it will be able to generate cash flows is always is a prerequisite and therefore mandatory. Activities and related costs are limited to those ones that are directly allocable to the asset. Costs to be considered are all direct costs as well as related overhead costs.	Included	IAS 36.39b in combination with IAS 36.41
Cash inflows of continuing use	All projections of cash inflows attributable to the assets under test due to the output of the asset.	Included	IAS 36.39a
Cash flows independent from the asset	Cash inflows of other assets which are largely independent from the asset's directly allocable cash-flows.	Excluded	IAS 36.43a
Running costs	As assets require an input to create an output, all costs associated with the ordinary use of the asset have to be considered. This includes all direct allocable costs like utilities, rental and other costs.	Included	IAS 36.39b
Asset maintenance	The day-to-day servicing of an asset as well as its maintenance. The day-to-day servicing includes costs like personnel expenses and related overhead costs.	Included	IAS 39.41
Cost savings	Testing an asset for impairment requires a testing at its current condition. Accordingly, all future cost savings that are already included in plans and budgets have to be reversed.	Excluded	IAS 36.45a
Performance improvements	Similar to costs savings, any future performance improvements, e.g. through a changed configuration of the assets, have to be excluded.	Excluded	IAS 36.45b

(continued)

Subject	Description	Status	Reference
Restructurings	Cost savings and performance improvements are only two areas of restructuring. Any other restructuring activities – particularly the business where the asset is used – that have an impact on the asset and its cash flows have to be considered and reversed accordingly.	Excluded	IAS 36.46
Disposal of asset	Disposing an asset at the end of its useful life may result in cash inflows due to the sale of the asset (if any exist) and outflows (costs associated with the removal of the asset). The net cash flow of those inflows and outflows has to be considered requiring an estimation of prices at the disposal date adjusted by general and specific future price increases and decreases.	Included	IAS 36.39c, IAS 36.53
Further disposal obligations	In some cases, the disposal of an asset is complemented by additional dismantling and removal costs demanding a restoration of the site as it was before the use of the asset. Such obligations may result from legal obligations or other commitments that have a direct dependency with the asset and its use. A consideration as a separate item is required to that extent provided that it is not already accounted for with the initial recognition of the asset according to IAS 16.16c.	Included	IAS 36.29c
Obligations already recognized	Any obligations that directly relate to the assets that are already recognized have to be excluded to avoid double-counting.	Excluded	IAS 36.43b
Corporate overheads	If an impairment test is run at cash-generating unit level, corporate overhead costs have to be considered.	Included	
Internal charges	If an impairment test is run at cash-generating unit level, any internal charges have to be eliminated if the cash-generating unit is carrying corporate assets. A double-counting of corporate cost would result otherwise.	Excluded	
Financing activities	As the time value of money is considered in the discount rate, any financing activities are excluded. If financing elements, particularly borrowing costs, have been capitalized as part of the asset, these costs have to be excluded for the impairment test.	Excluded	IAS 36.50a
Incomes taxes	As the impairment test is based on a pre-tax basis considering a pre-tax discounting rate, any income tax items have to be eliminated from the underlying plans.	Excluded	IAS 36.50b

Tab. F-12   List of cash flows subjects

If an asset generates cash flows in **foreign currencies**, IAS 39.54 demands that these foreign currency cash flows are discounted first before translating them into the base currency, using an appropriate discount rate for each currency. A spot exchange rate should be used, as at the impairment test.

Having considered all the above-mentioned aspects in determining future cash flows, the future cash flows should be free from any unrelated factors and bias. This includes two dimensions: the amount as well as the timing when cash-flows occur. The final cash flows are the ones of the asset and therefore not comparable with cash flows of the (planned) business.

*   Discount rate
    The determination of an appropriate discount rate is based on a set of requirements as defined by IAS 36.55 and 36.56. Therefore, a market rate has to be determined which represents the time value of money as well as the asset's specific risks. In other words, the discount rate reflects the expectations of the market that can be observed in **market transactions** of assets with similar risks. Such a discount rate reflects an asset's behaviour at best. The practical problem of this requirement is to identify companies and assets with similar risks. This would require similar and comparable products and services, similar transactions and uses of assets and similar risk profiles. As each company has more or less unique features due to their individual business approaches and appearances in the market, similar discount rates are rarely available. Therefore, a discount rate has to be derived from other or similar comparable rates.

    The determination of an appropriate discount rate as a **surrogate** is an accepted alternative. IAS 36.A17 accepts three different dates as a starting point:

    *   The entity's weighted average cost of capital (usually based on an capital asset pricing model);
    *   The entity's incremental borrowing rate;
    *   Market borrowing rates.

    Regardless of which rate is chosen as a starting point, it has to be adjusted by asset specific risks and excluded by risks that do not relate to the asset. IAS 36.A18 also highlights that country, currency and price risks should be kept in mind in adjusting the rate determined as a starting point.

    As the planning is based on cash flows before tax, a **pre-tax** rate has to be applied. If a post-tax rate is available only, it has to be converted into a pre-tax rate. The conversion can be realized by a simple gross-up.

$$\text{Pre-tax discount rate} = \text{Post-tax discount rate} * \frac{1}{100\% - \text{tax-rate}}$$

Fig. F-30   Discount rate gross-up

Determining the value in use is usually based on a single discount rate. Nevertheless, an application of **multiple discount rates** is acceptable if the value in use is sensitive to differences in risks for different future periods or to the term structure of interest rates.

Both the preparation of future cash flows and the discount rate are subject to estimations and assumptions. Such estimations and assumptions are important when deciding how much level of detail is desired and required and about where to consider risks. This is because risks can be considered either in the underlying plan (so in the cash flows) or in the discount rate. IAS 36.A4 – 36.A14 have picked up this issue and provide support on **risk consideration**.

- Traditional approach

     The traditional approach adopts a single set of cash flows derived from the plans that represent the cash flow expectations at best. If expected cash flows are determined on expected business scenarios, the best scenario with the highest probability has to be chosen. These cash flows are discounted using a discount rate that reflects risks.

- Expected cash flow approach

     This is a more effective method of determining cash flows. It will consider not only the ultimate cash flow as derived from plans, but also probabilities on how likely this cash flow occurs. Therefore, additional facts and information have to be kept in mind in determining the expected cash flow. While cash flows are adjusted based on their expectations, the risk associated with the probability that these cash flows occur is already included. Therefore, a consideration of these risks in the discount rate is not appropriate as a double counting of risks might otherwise be the result.

Calculating the **present value** of the asset under test requires a discounting of each cash flow of each period. Cash flows subject to discounting are: the current cash flows, the cash flows of the planning horizon and cash flows after the planning horizon. The current cash flow and the cash flow of the planning horizon can be calculated using the standard discounting formula. The cash flows after the planning horizon is presented as a term value. This term value usually assumes a steady growth rate and considers inflation. Therefore, an adjusted discount rate has to be applied.

The following formula calculates present values based on the application of nominal rates.

$$PV = \left(\sum_{n=1}^{m} CF_n * \frac{1}{(1 + i_{nom})^n} \right) + CF_m * \frac{1}{(1 + i_{nom})^m} * \frac{(1 + g)(1 + r)}{i_a}$$

Fig. F-31 Discount formula of value in use

Where:

CF_n	Cash flow of the n-th period
n	Period subject to discounting
m	No. of periods of the planning horizon
i_{nom}	Nominal pre-tax discount rate
i_a	Adjusted nominal pre-tax discount rate (due to growth rate and inflation rate)
g	Growth rate
r	Inflation rate

8.2.2.4 Net realizable value and impairment losses

Having done all calculations, the carrying amount will be either confirmed or adjusted to a **recoverable amount** at the end of the day by a simple comparison. The then (un-)adjusted amount represents the net realizable value. The recoverable amount is defined as the higher of the value in use or the fair value less cost of disposal of an asset in IAS 36.6. It is sufficient to calculate in the first instance only one item, either the value in use or the fair value less cost of disposal. If one of them exceeds the carrying amount of the asset, a calculation of the other item is redundant as an impairment of the asset is not given. Otherwise, the other item needs to be determined to decide whether or not an impairment loss has to be recorded.

This approach is contradicted by observed practice. In most cases, the calculation either of the value in use or the "fair value less costs" will fail. The reason is based on the intention of impairment tests, to align future cash flows to an asset or to obtain information about the expected price in case of a disposal of the asset. Furthermore, the initial recognition of assets was historically based on higher interest rates. Due to the financial crisis and its consequences, lower interest rates are observed in practice that either demand a recording of impairment losses or again result in a failure of the impairment test. Therefore, the lack of measurement abilities requires the execution of the impairment test at the next level up, cash-generating units.

Assuming that an impairment test failed and an **impairment loss** has to be recorded, the carrying amount will be adjusted through profit & loss to the recoverable amount by executing one journal entry only.

Journal entry		Comment
dr.	Depreciation expenses	
cr.	Non-current asset	Applies equally to intangible assets, property, plant & equipment and financial assets

If the impairment loss is higher than the carrying amount of the asset, a liability has to be recognized. This practice is mandatory for all types of asset unless a revaluation model is applied to the asset in accordance with another standard. In such cases, the adjustment is usually recorded in other comprehensive income.

Recording an impairment loss triggers a set of **follow-up activities**:

- As the carrying amount is adjusted, an adjustment of depreciation charges is necessary. In this context a review of the adequacy of the depreciation method, the residual value and the estimated useful life is recommended.[63]
- As the tax base of the asset is usually left untouched, an adjustment of deferred tax assets or liabilities is required.

---

[63] This practice is in line with the provisions of other standards (e.g. with IAS 16 which require an annual review anyway).

8.2.3. Cash-generating units

8.2.3.1 Composition

Often, single assets do not fulfil the demand of generating cash flows. This is because other assets are required to generate cash flows. All assets involved to generate cash flows are then grouped together in a separate unit, cash-generating, unit. Therefore, the impairment test has to be executed at the next level up, the cash generating unit.

According to IAS 36.6, a cash generating unit is defined as "the smallest identifiable group of assets that generates cash inflows that are largely independent of the cash inflows from other assets or groups of assets". Due to this "open" **definition**, cash-generating units can be applied to a set of assets, to products and product groups, to production facilities, business units, geographical areas or reportable segments. Nevertheless it has to be the smallest group which results in a bottom-up approach. Criteria to define a cash generating unit vary. Typical items to be considered in defining cash-generating units are:

- Products and services are tradable on separate markets (whether they are really traded);
- Cash inflows and outflows are based at arm's length principles;
- Cash inflows are based on own customer bases.

Such an approach demands an investigation of cash flows from the individual asset to a set of assets where the collaboration and use of these assets will result in cash flows externally induced. It requires an active market where goods and services as the output of the cash-generating unit are traded.[64] If external cash flows can be proved, a second check is required if these cash inflows are largely independent from other cash inflows. If not, more assets have to be added to determine the cash-generating unit. Common practice defines cash-generating units as slightly larger than they really need to be.

The concept of the cash-generating unit, as laid out in IAS 36, allows also a grouping and stacking of cash-generating units. Regardless how a cash-generating unit is defined and applied, a cash-generating unit cannot exceed a reportable segment and is therefore limited to that segment according to IAS 36.80b. Furthermore, a change in the composition of the cash-generating unit is only acceptable if a change can be justified. Otherwise, consistent application is required.

To qualify for an impairment test at cash-generating unit level, the recoverable amount of an individual asset cannot be determined. IAS 36.67 demands two **conditions** to be fulfilled cumulative in such cases:

---

[64] See Appendix I: Fair value measurement on page 751 regarding the definition of an active market.

- The value in use of an individual asset cannot be estimated close enough to its fair value less cost of disposal.
- Cash inflows of the individual asset are not largely independent from those of other assets.

If a cash-generating unit is defined, all assets (and debt) that belong to the cash-generating unit have to be identified and allocated to the cash-generating unit. As an **allocation of asset** can only occur once, it can never belong to another cash-generating unit. Assets allocated to a cash-generating unit are those assets that are directly involved in generating cash inflows. Exempt from the allocation are liabilities, provided the carrying amount of the cash-generating unit can be determined without these liabilities.[65] Typical examples are a provision for the removal and dismantling of an asset and liabilities mandatory for the sale of a cash-generating unit. A further exemption applies to those assets that are outside the scope of IAS 36.

> If liabilities need to be included in the carrying amount of an asset, it should be done consistently to avoid comparing unlike items: In the carrying amount of the cash-generating unit and in the estimation of the recoverable amount (so in fair value less cost of disposal and in the value in use)!

Considering the options available in determining the carrying amount of a cash-generating unit, the following assets and debts have to be kept in mind in defining a cash-generating unit.

Item	Consideration in carrying amount	Consideration in cash flow
Intangible assets	Yes	Yes
Fixed assets	Yes	Yes
Financial instruments / financial assets	Only if necessary asset	Only if necessary asset
Inventory	Yes	Yes
Trade receivables	Yes	Yes
Other assets	Yes, without taxes	Yes, without taxes
Cash	Yes	Yes
Deferred items	Yes	Yes
Deferred tax assets	No	No
Pension provisions	Only if allocation possible	Only if part of carrying amount
Tax liabilities	No	No
Other provisions and accruals	Yes	Yes
Bonds	No	No

(continued)

---

[65] In other words: Liabilities are not always part of the carrying amount of the cash-generating unit. They will be considered only if the carrying amount cannot be determined without them.

Item	Consideration in carrying amount	Consideration in cash flow
Loans and similar financial liabilities	No	No
Interest bearing liabilities	No	No
Prepayments received	Yes	Yes
Trade liabilities	Yes	Yes
Other liabilities	Yes, without taxes	Yes, without taxes
Deferred tax liabilities	No	No
Deferred revenue	Yes	Yes

Tab. F-13   Table of assets and debts allocable to cash-generating units

The carrying amount of a cash-generating unit might require a consideration of **corporate assets**. Corporate assets are assets other than goodwill jointly used by several cash-generating units and contributing to them but do not generate cash flows independently. IAS 36.100 lists some examples of corporate assets:

- Buildings of headquarters or divisions;
- EDP equipment;
- Research centre.

Other assets like brands, trademarks or licences may qualify for corporate assets as well, provided they are allocable to more than one cash-generating unit. This depends on the current set-up of the group, its business units, divisions and the allocation of products, product groups and services to them.

The allocation of corporate assets to cash-generating units has to be based on a reasonable and consistent basis. The standard is silent about how to allocate the assets. In practice, the allocation is therefore based on weighted ratios (e.g. a percentage of book values weighted by their absolute values). Once a decision regarding the allocation method is taken, a consistent application is required. The impairment test will be executed similar to the execution of an impairment test for an individual asset considering allocated corporate assets. If a determination on a reasonable and consistent basis is not ensured, a multi-step testing as required by IAS 36.102 has to be initiated. The first step will test the cash-generating unit without the allocated corporate asset for impairment. The next step is an identification of those cash-generating units to which an allocation of the carrying amount of corporate assets is reasonable. Identified cash-generating units are grouped including the cash-generating unit to be tested. An impairment test has to be performed for that group and, if necessary, an additional impairment loss to be recorded.

If corporate assets are not allocated to cash-generating units on a reasonable and consistent basis, an impairment test at corporate, business unit or group level is likely to result.

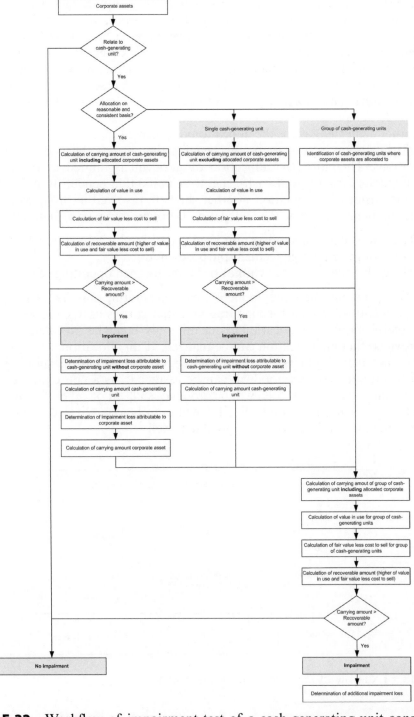

Fig. F-32 Workflow of impairment test of a cash-generating unit considering corporate assets

A consideration of corporate assets as part of group charges is a common practice to ensure a certain refinancing of the corporate centre for services performed to group companies. These charges have to be adjusted due to the consideration of corporate assets as part of the cash-generating unit to avoid a double-counting. The adjustment is limited to those elements that consider a use (return of) and refinancing (return on) of the corporate assets. A full elimination of group charges is not necessary and not necessary as charges may include other considerable elements.

Another dedicated task is the allocation of **goodwill** to cash-generating units. Goodwill represents future economic benefits that are established in business combinations. Therefore, the allocation of goodwill is limited to those cash-generating units (or groups of cash-generating units) that benefit from the synergies of the business combination whether they are involved in or subject to the business combination or not. The allocation is bound to a pair of requirements:

- The lowest cash-generating unit level is that level where goodwill is monitored for internal management purposes, and
- The cash-generating unit cannot be larger than an operating segment.

Due to the management requirement, a cash-generating unit that carries goodwill is not identical to a cash-generating unit that carries assets. Goodwill does not necessarily require an allocation to one unit only. It can be allocated to several units provided that an allocation can be realized. If an allocation is not possible but the cash-generating units are identified to benefit, these cash-generating units have to be grouped so that goodwill can be assigned. As a consequence, cash-generating units (carrying assets) will be grouped, stacked or otherwise arranged to enable an allocation of goodwill. This will even be complicated if corporate assets are present that have to be considered as well.

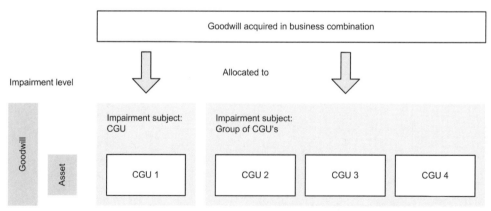

Fig. F-33   Example of cash-generating units structure

When allocating goodwill to cash-generating units, an **identification** of the cash-generating units eligible to carry goodwill is necessary. IAS 36 does not provide any guidance on identifying those units. The identification more or less has to be based on an economic management approach by considering the following criteria:

- Intention and purpose of the business combination;
- Intended synergies by management;
- Structure of the group before and after the business combination.

Further criteria may exist.

Upon identification of the relevant cash-generating unit, a goodwill **allocation** is required. Again, IAS 36 is silent about the allocation, demanding allocation on a non-arbitrary basis only. Allocation could be realized based on the relative fair values of the cash-generating units, provided such an allocation reflects the economic satiation.

A **disposal** of a part of a cash-generating unit impacts goodwill allocated to that cash-generating unit. Disposing a part of the cash-generating unit requires an adjustment of the allocated goodwill. The adjustment is based on the relative fair values as demanded by IAS 36.86:

$$\text{Goodwill disposed asset} = \text{Goodwill of CGU} * \frac{\text{Carrying amount disposed asset}}{\text{Carrying amount of CGU}}$$

Fig. F-34 Calculation of disposed goodwill

Using relative fair values is the default method of adjusting goodwill of a cash-generating unit upon (partial) disposal. Other methods are acceptable as well provided these methods ensure a better measurement of the disposed goodwill. Such a case might be given, if assets that drive the cash inflow of the cash-generating unit are disposed and replaced by less valuable surrogates or restricted use rights.

The goodwill associated with the disposed assets has to be expensed which can be realized by the following journal entry.

Journal entry
dr.   Loss (other expenses)
    cr.   Goodwill

Any **restructuring**s or reorganizations that impact cash-generating units and their compositions trigger a new setup of cash-generating units. If the composition of assets and liabilities of impacted cash-generating units is known, goodwill allocated in the old structure can be rearranged to the new structure based on relative fair values of the cash-generating unit's. This approach is identical to the disposal of parts of a cash-generating unit.

The **carrying amount of a cash-generating unit** is therefore built up on:

- Identified and allocated assets (and debt);
- Goodwill associated with the cash-generating unit;
- Corporate assets.

8.2.3.2 *Testing for impairment*

Testing a cash-generating unit for impairment is – like any other impairment test – a recurring activity. The impairment test has to be executed in each subsequent period. As the focus is on cash-generating units, the impairment test has to be executed at group level. Accordingly, any impairment losses are recorded also at group level. Due to the composition of cash-generating units, some specialities have to be considered:

- Corporate assets

   Corporate assets are treated the same way as any other assets of the cash-generating unit. Even if an allocation is done, any write-downs of the carrying amount will often be handled at group level.

- Goodwill

   Goodwill is the preferred object for impairments. Every time, goodwill is allocated to a cash-generating unit, it has to be adjusted first.

- Non-controlling interests

   Impairment tests may require an adjustment of goodwill if non-controlling interests are involved. This adjustment depends on the initial accounting of goodwill. If the full-goodwill method is applied, adjustments are not required. If the purchased-goodwill method is applied, goodwill has to be grossed up (to 100% or to full goodwill). This is necessary to bring goodwill in line with the other assets (which are already recognized by 100%) to have a consistent treatment of the carrying amount and the related cash flows of the cash-generating unit. Once the impairment volume is calculated on a 100% basis, it has to be adjusted again to arrive at the impairment loss to be recorded. This adjustment is based on the relationship between the recorded (purchased) goodwill and the full goodwill. Grossing up goodwill is an explicit requirement of IAS 36.C4.

The procedure of an **impairment test** in determining an impairment loss of a cash-generating unit is identical to the procedure applied for individual assets. The carrying amount of a cash-generating unit has to be compared with the recoverable amount. IAS 36.74 defines the recoverable amount of a cash-generating unit as the higher of its fair value less cost of disposal and its value in use.

Even if the procedure is the same as for individual assets, **problems and challenges** arise when determining the fair value less cost of disposal and the value in use. Determining the fair value less cost of disposal may assume that there is an active market in which similar transactions can be observed. In most cases, such a market does not exist, so other valuation techniques are needed (if such fair values can be measured at all). Determining the value in use requires the availability of an appropriate plan of the cash-generating unit. Assuming that such plans exist (which is not necessarily a given), issues arise on how to deal with growth that is initiated by improvements due to technology, efficiency and capacity expansion. Additional aspects like the handling of taxation have to be solved (a purchase price allocation includes tax effects and records deferred tax assets and liabilities that are covered by goodwill as the residual value but the impairment test requires a pre-tax execution! Do we have to adjust goodwill in that case or is an impairment loss required in the first subsequent period?). IAS 36 is silent about such issues. Therefore, individual solutions are observed in practice on how to cope with these issues.

> If you are running into such problems find a pragmatic solution and discuss this with your auditor upfront!

If the impairment test of a cash-generating unit (or a group of units) unveils a recording of an **impairment loss**, the impairment loss will be recorded based on a two step-approach. The first step demands a reduction of the carrying amount of goodwill allocated to the cash-generating unit. If the impairment loss to be recorded is fully absorbed by the goodwill, no further action is required. If any excess amount remains, or no goodwill is present, the second step has to be executed. This step demands a pro-rata reduction of the carrying amounts of all assets allocated to the cash-generating unit. The basis used to calculate the amounts assigned to each asset is their carrying amounts. Even if the carrying amounts of all assets are reduced equally, their carrying amounts cannot be reduced below a minimum amount. This minimum amount is the higher of:

- the fair value less cost of disposal,
- the value in use, or
- zero.

If an excess amount of the impairment loss to be recorded still remains, a liability has to be recognized.

> Only assets that are in the scope of IAS 36 have to be considered!

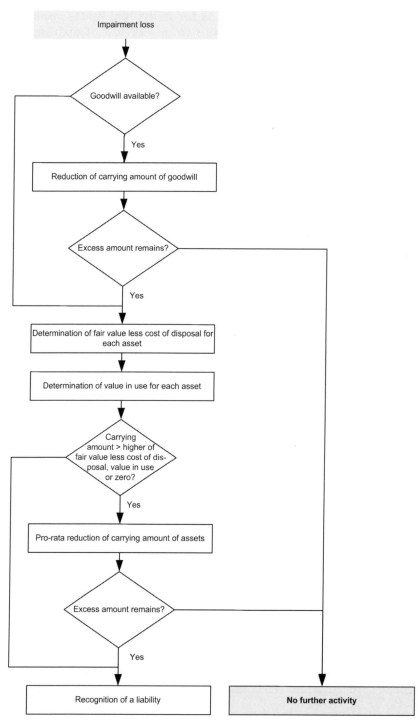

Fig. F-35 Workflow of recording an impairment loss of a cash-generating unit

Impairment losses are recorded in the same way as for individual assets, either in profit & loss as a default or in other comprehensive income if required by IFRS.

8.2.4. Other issues

Similar to the assessment of any indication for impairments, an assessment regarding a potential **reversal of impairment losses** is required in each period according to IFR 36.110. The assessment is based on the same external and internal rationales as outlined in IAS 36.12 (for impairments) and IAS 36.111 (for reversals of impairments). It has to be applied equally to assets and cash-generating units but not to goodwill.

No.	Category	Criterion	Description
1)	External	Value of asset	The asset's value increased more rapidly during the period than it would do under normal circumstances.
2)	External	Significant market changes	Significant changes have a favourable impact on the group. This may impact various environments the group operates: • Economic • Market • Technology • Legal These changes may occur during the period. If it is observable by management that these changes occur within the near future, an indication is also given.
3)	External	Market interest rates and other rates of return	Decreasing market interest rates may impact the carrying value of an asset as long as these rates impact discount rates used in determining the asset's value in use. The impact on the carrying amount of an asset has to be material.
4)	Internal	Significant business changes	Significant changes have a favourable impact on the group. These may be triggered by market demands and have a direct impact on the asset. IAS 36.12 (f) lists a set of examples: • Costs incurred to improve performance of asset • Restructuring of the operation the assets belongs to (even plans are sufficient) • Recycling of asset (even plans are sufficient) • Reassessment of useful life (asset becomes indefinite rather than finite) These changes may occur during the period. If it is observable by management that these changes occur within the near future, an indication is also given.
5)	Internal	Performance of asset	The economic performance of the asset is or will be better than expected (this is not necessarily linked to profits generated by the asset).
6)	Internal	Cash flows	Cash flows for acquiring, operating and maintaining an asset are significantly less than initially budgeted. Or in other words: cash flows generated by the asset are better than initially budgeted. Even a significant increase of cash flows may be an indicator.

(continued)

No. Category	Criterion	Description
7) Internal	Restructuring of groups	Restructurings are typically indications that the business model has changed. Reasons for restructurings may be: • Turning a company or group back into a profitable area • Alignment to market trends, technology, customer demands or other reasons • New strategic focus, new business areas, products, services or similar events
8) Subsidiaries	Dividends	Dividends do not exceed total comprehensive income of the subsidiary, joint venture or associate in the period the dividend is declared.
9) Subsidiaries	Carrying amount	The carrying amount of the investment in a subsidiary, joint venture or associate in separate financial statements is less than the net assets (including goodwill) in consolidated financial statements of that company.

Tab. F-14   Indicators for the reversal of an impairment loss

Again, indications can occur in two ways, either as one-time events or as trends. Both have to be considered in deciding about whether or not an impairment loss shall be reversed, either in full or in part. These indications trigger another activity, a review of the useful life and the depreciation (amortization) method. This review shall ensure that the accounting for the asset reflects its future use.

If an impairment loss of an **asset** has to be reversed, the reversal is limited to a maximum of the amount that would have been recorded if no impairment had been realized. In other words, an adjustment due to the original depreciation has to be considered when reversing the original impairment loss.

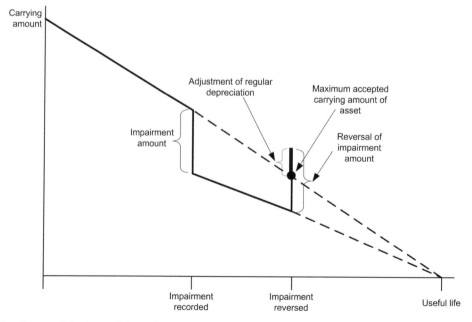

Fig. F-36   Timing of impairment loss and its reversal

As a consequence of the reversal, the depreciation (amortization) charge has to be adjusted to reflect the depreciation (amortization) pattern of the remaining useful life. By default, a reversal has to be recorded in profit & loss unless an IFRS requires valuation adjustments to be recorded in other comprehensive income.

A more sophisticated approach is the reversal of an impairment loss of a **cash-generating unit**. The reversal method is the same as for individual assets but the maximum accepted carrying amount is different. The carrying amount is limited to the lower of the recoverable amount and that amount that would have been recorded if no impairment had been realized. The requirement of IAS 36.123 to consider the recoverable amount as one limitation will result in a "quasi-impairment" calculation as the value in use and the fair value less cost of disposal of the cash-generating unit. The reversal amount determined has to be allocated pro-rata to all assets of the cash-generating unit except for goodwill.

Recording impairment losses and reversals is accompanied by several **disclosures**. In addition to the amounts recorded in profit & loss and other comprehensive income, information about the facts and circumstances of material impairments, the underlying assets and related information, such as segment information, are required. IAS 36.126 to 36.133 include extended disclosure details.

8.3. Netting

Netting is an activity to offset items in the balance sheet or profit & loss statement with other items in these statements. Assets, for example, can be offset with liabilities or revenues with expenses.

By default, an offsetting or netting is prohibited according to IAS 1.32. Assets and liabilities and revenues and expenses have to be presented separately. An exception to this rule is given, if other standards explicitly demand such an offsetting. Standards that consider an offsetting of assets and liabilities and revenues and expenses are limited. The ones that explicitly allow or demand an offsetting are:

- *IAS 12 – Income Taxes*;
- *IAS 19 – Employee Benefits*;
- *IFRS 9 – Financial Instruments* regarding the application of hedge accounting and the offsetting of receivables and payables.

Items that apply to a netting have to fulfil a set of requirements. There has to be some kind of contractual agreement or a legally enforceable right to offset or settle items. Furthermore, the settlement has to occur on a net basis. These rules have to be applied equally to separate and consolidated financial statements.

The application of netting activities to group accounting has to be carefully evaluated. The evaluation has to consider the companies involved, contractual agreements or enforceable rights. Therefore, a **two-step approach** should be chosen to decide on the extent of netting activities.

The first step is the determination of netting activities for each company of the group. The netting has to consider all valuation levels. It is recommended to offset items only on the level at which they are recorded. Typical netting candidates are deferred tax assets and tax liabilities if they relate to the same tax type and the same tax authority. They can occur at local level due to local accounting requirements and on all valuation levels to adjust local accounts for group purposes. Therefore, an offsetting should be done at those levels where the initial recording and the valuation adjustments take place.

The second step is the determination of any netting opportunities across companies. Again, the same rules have to be applied. In practice, the netting across companies occurs only in rare cases. Netting of deferred tax assets and liabilities often fails due to different tax types or tax authorities. Only tax groups are entitled for such a practice. The same applies to employee benefits while the accounting often rests with the subsidiary where employees are employed. Nevertheless, financial instruments, particularly hedge accounting activities are a typical candidate for netting activities at group level. Such a practice arises if the group maintains a centralized financing and cash-management system that supports commercial activities of subsidiaries. It is up to the underlying contractual arrangement in the group and with banks to decide about the extent on netting opportunities and activities.

Example

In its separate financial statements, Flexing Cables Norway is presenting deferred tax assets and deferred tax liabilities separately. Deferred tax assets are amounting to 76 k NOK or 9 k EUR, deferred tax liabilities to 168 k NOK or 20 k EUR. While group accounting policies require an offsetting of balance sheet items every time a standard offers an offsetting opportunity, the separate presentation of deferred tax items in the separate financial statements is subject to netting. While deferred tax assets and deferred tax liabilities related to a deviating tax base as required by the Norwegian tax authority, Flexing Cables Norway has the right to offset both items according to IAS 12.71 and 12.72. Accordingly, the following journal entry has to be executed at group level:

Journal entry				Company
dr.	Deferred tax liability	9		Group
cr.	Deferred tax asset		9	Group

8.4. Reclassifications

The consolidation process so far has focused on the elimination of intercompany transactions, a measurement to ensure that assets are not overstated and liabilities not understated and an allocation of transactions to its appropriate position. This applies to the balance sheet as well as to the profit & loss statement. To finalize the preparation process, the proper presentation in the consolidated statements of financial position and the consolidated statement of income, as demanded by IAS 1.54 et seq., is necessary. Therefore, all items have to be checked regarding presentation. If necessary, a reclassification to the appropriate position in the statements is necessary. This reclassification should be done – if possible – at account level.

Reclassification can occur at local as well as group level. Both have to be considered when preparing the final statements. While reclassifications at local level focus on the allocation of financial items to its proper position to one entity only, the reclassification at group level consider transactions at group level. If necessary, reclassification at group level can override reclassifications at local level. Such reclassifications can become necessary if transaction and its reclassification at local level are subject to eliminations and valuation adjustments at group level.

Example

As Solenta is presenting its separate financial statements according to the provisions of German GAAP, a set of reclassifications is necessary to comply with group requirements:

No.	Subject	Solution
1	Prepaid expenses amounting to 39 k EUR are presented separately	A reclassification of prepaid expenses to other assets is necessary.
2	The German GAAP does not differentiate between accruals and provisions and present both in one balance sheet item. The carrying amount as of 31.12. of 19,733 k EUR includes an amount of 5,320 k EUR that is attributable to accruals.	5,320 k EUR have to be reclassified from provisions to accruals.
3	Para. 266 of the German Commercial Code requires companies to present liabilities to banks as one item.	A reclassification of 6,000 k EUR from non-current liabilities to banks to current liabilities to banks has to be performed.

---

9. SPECIAL CASES

Subsequent consolidations have to deal with all kinds of transactions in groups. Some of these transactions are often outside the ordinary intercompany relationships. They are for example caused by the structure of the group, by the composition of the group or by investing or trading relationships that are rather unusual or infrequent. Even these transactions have to be considered in preparing consolidated financial statements. Therefore, a dedicated view is required for those transactions. The most important ones will be discussed in this chapter:

- Intercompany dividends;
- Sale of non-current assets;
- Consolidations of multi-level groups;
- Handling of interdependencies.

9.1. Intercompany dividends

9.1.1. Basics

The distribution of dividends is closely linked to **legal requirements**, to local laws and regulations, particularly to corporate law and commercial law. Material to dividends are the rules regarding the distribution of profits. They often depend on the legal form of a corporation.

- Partnerships
  A simple decision of the partners regarding the appropriation of profits is sufficient.

- Privately held corporations
  The income determination and the distribution of profits are subject to the resolution by shareholders during a shareholder's meeting.

- Publicly listed corporations
  The income determination is subject to the board and the annual general meeting of shareholders. The decision about the distribution of profit is solely the privilege of the annual general meeting. Nevertheless, the board can provide a proposal about the disposition of profits.

Another issue of intercompany dividends is **timing**. Due to the dependency of profit distributions on the legal form of a corporation, dedicated steps are required in enabling the company to be able to distribute profits. These steps vary depending of the form of incorporation. The steps have to be followed by all companies whether they belong to groups or not. These steps require, not only an income determination and a decision of profit distributions, but also formal steps like the filing of annual reports and the invitation and the execution of an annual general meeting. These formal steps vary depending on local laws and regulations. If all formal steps have been passed and a decision of profit distributions is made, dividends can be distributed.

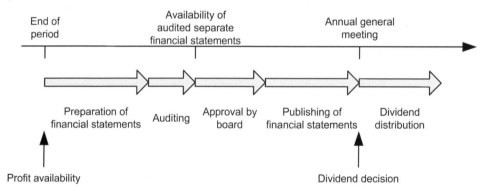

Fig. F-37 Timing of profit distribution

Fulfilling legal requirements may defer the profit distribution in groups, if the company is not a wholly owned subsidiary. While other shareholders are present, complying with formal and legal requirements has a special significance. Any disregarding may give minority shareholders an option in raising a plea or filing a lawsuit that may result in a further deferral of profit distributions.

Some arrangements, like profit transfer agreements, have an impact on whether the distribution timing allows recognition of the profit by the parent in the same period where the subsidiary has generated those profits. Some legal forms like partnerships follow the same behaviours by assigning the profits to the partner in the period those profits were generated. Dedicated contractual agreements are not required. Such a practice is available in some legislations and even confirmed by court decisions.[66] Considering these thoughts, the following matrix represents available options for profit transfers.

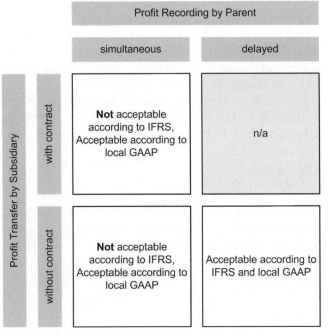

Fig. F-38   Profit transfer options

Recording intercompany dividends based on an **IFRS** accounting follows different rules and regulations. IAS 18.30c requires a dividend recognition only if the shareholder has a right to receive dividend payments and this right is established. Furthermore, IAS 10.12 requires a recording of liabilities that relate to dividends only if there is an obligation of payment. Therefore, there can never be a dividend payment liability at the end of a period as a consequence of missing approval from shareholders regarding dividend distribution. Because of these two accounting rules, simultaneous recognition of dividends by the parent and recording of the profit in the same period is not possible. Profits are always reported in the appropriate period while the profit distribution is subject to subsequent periods.

In addition to the legal form of a company, the **status within the group** is also important. In general, dividends can be received by subsidiaries, associate and joint ventures. While interests in companies vary and control is not always given, different principles apply to the recording of dividends and profit transfers. The

---

[66] E.g. the Tomberger-decision in the European Union (EuGH as of 27.6.1996, C-234/94) has confirmed that a simultaneous profit generation by the subsidiary and the recognition by the parent in the same period is an acceptable practice.

principles are based on the underlying accounting methods. As far as subsidiaries are concerned, the application of the purchase method requires the recording of dividends and profit transfers when an enforceable right exists. The profit recording of associates and joint ventures is based on the application of the equity method.

9.1.2. Ordinary profit distributions

An ordinary profit distribution is the standard case for subsidiaries if no limitations, contractual agreements or other constraints exist. Assuming that all formal steps are taken and the shareholders have approved a dividend distribution, the accounting cycle on dividend distribution starts. Shareholders are the parent and any minority shareholders.

Profits distributed are presented in separate financial statements as a decrease in equity. Upon the date of the shareholder's resolution that the company has to pay a dividend, the distribution becomes a liability by reducing equity.

Journal entry
dr.		Retained earnings
	cr.	Liability to shareholders

This journal entry is valid for the distribution of dividends to all shareholders. As far as minority shareholders are involved, the profit of the period allocated to non-controlling interests has to be allocated to liabilities as well.

Journal entry
dr.		Retained earnings
dr.		Non-controlling interests
	cr.	Liability to shareholders

At the same date, the parent that is entitled to receive the dividend has to record a receivable and a profit due to the expected payments in its separate financial statements.

Journal entry
dr.		Receivables
	cr.	Profit from financial investments

The recording of dividends by the companies will create an intercompany transaction that has to be eliminated in consolidated financial statements. The characteristic of these consolidation journal entries is the elimination against equity: from a group's perspective, dividends are just the movement of profits within the group without any external impacts. These transactions therefore have to be eliminated. Liabilities against non-controlling interests are exempt from eliminations. The portion belonging to minority shareholders is reflected by the remaining carrying amount on the liability account.

Journal entry
			Company
dr.		Liabilities to shareholders	Sending company
	cr.	Receivables	Receiving company
dr.		Profit from financial investments	Receiving company
	cr.	Retained earnings	Sending company

Example

The shareholders general meeting of Flexing Cables Belgium took place on 15.4.2013. The management of it's sole shareholder, Flexing Cables Holding decided that 50% of the prior period's profit of 2,860 k EUR had to be distributed as a dividend. Flexing Cables Belgium management instructed a wire transfer as of 22.4.2013 enabling Flexing Cables Holding to record the dividend payment the next day.

While the shareholder resolution of paying a dividend and the payment of the dividend were executed in the same period, no receivables by Flexing Cables Holding and no payables to shareholders by Flexing Cables Belgium existed at the balance sheet date. Therefore, no debt consolidation tasks were necessary.

Nevertheless, the Flexing Cables Holding recorded the dividends received in its profit & loss statement and Flexing Cables Belgium a reduction of retained earnings. Accordingly, a consolidation task was necessary to eliminate the changes of both companies. The following journal entry was executed:

Journal entry				Company
dr.	Profit from financial investments	1,430		Flexing Cables Holding
cr.	Retained earnings		1,430	Flexing Cables Belgium

9.1.3. *Profit transfer agreements*

A common practice in groups is the signing of profit transfer agreements. Such agreements require a company to transfer all generated profits to its parent. If a company has generated a loss, these losses have to be carried also by the parent. Profit transfer agreements are not limited to dedicated legislations. Some states also allow cross-border profit transfers. Such agreements may include specific arrangements, depending on the involvement of the parent in the company. Profit does not necessarily have to be transferred in full. A transfer in part is also possible. In some situations, even the management of the company through its parent may have the same prominence than a profit transfer agreement.

The establishment of a profit transfer agreement is linked to a set of **requirements**. These requirements may change depending on local laws and regulations. Typical requirements to establish a profit transfer agreements are:

- Filing of the agreement with a commercial register.
- Shareholder resolution to accept the agreement. The approval of the shareholders is often linked to a defined threshold that has to be passed.
- The agreement has to be in written form.

A valid profit transfer agreement that is applied in groups does not only assign profits and losses to parent, it will also result in a non-presentation of profits by the company. The application will result in a profit transfer in the same period. If the profit transfer is also applicable under IFRS, it is subject to a detailed assessment of the profit transfer agreement. The agreement has to be in line with the accounting regulations of IAS 10.12 and IAS 18.30c.

A common practice is to link profit transfer agreements with **tax groups** to optimize the overall tax position. The linkage to tax groups requires separate contracts. Even if a link between profit transfer agreements and tax group exist, both contracts follow their own accountings.[67]

Profit transfer agreements in **multi-level groups** require special attention: stacked transfer hierarchies pass profits from subsidiaries directly to the ultimate parent. Such hierarchies demand an elimination of profit transfers individually at each level.

> Prepare a documentation regarding profit transfers. This enables tracing profit distributions in multi-level groups and simplifies consolidations.

The accounting of profit transfer agreements is similar to the accounting of ordinary dividend distributions. The subsidiary is not entitled to present its own profits, so the whole profit of the period has to be forwarded to the parent. A limitation to the amount of profit transfers as a consequence of shareholder decisions does not exist. Furthermore, the profit has to be taken from profit & loss. Equity is left untouched. The profit transferred is a separate line item in the statement of income. The following journal entry is used for profit transfers.

Journal entry
dr.   Net profit of the period
    cr.   Liabilities to shareholders

The recording of profit transfers by the parent under a profit transfer agreement is identical to any other recording of dividends.

Journal entry
dr.   Receivables
    cr.   Profit from financial investment

Due to the recording of profit transfers in profit & loss, equity adjustments are not necessary. The elimination journal entries follow the ordinary scheme as for debt consolidations and consolidations of income and expense.

Journal entry		Company
dr.	Liabilities to shareholders	Sending company
cr.	Receivables	Receiving company
dr.	Profit from financial investments	Receiving company
cr.	Net profit of the period	Sending company

9.2. Intercompany sale of non-current assets

The intercompany sale of non-current assets is a business transaction that requires special attention due to their origin in the sales process and the triggering of complex accounting tasks. The transfer of non-current assets within a group can be initiated either by subsidiaries due to operational reasons or by the parent company or the group due to optimizations of the group. A typical example of

---

[67] See chapter K -2.3.4 on page 670 regarding tax groups.

the latter is a restructuring in the group to create a dividend distribution potential. Here, investments in financial assets are sold.

> Consider a section in your reporting environment to ask your subsidiaries for such transactions!

The sale of non-current assets by one subsidiary and the purchase by another subsidiary are separate business transactions for each company. While the selling company records a divestiture of assets that generates a profit or loss or is profit neutral, the receiving company records an ordinary purchase transaction. From the group's point of view, the asset has only been relocated to another entity within the group. Therefore, the recording in the subsidiaries at local level is opposed to no changes at group level. This requires several accounting adjustment, particularly for the receiving company. The adjustments may last until the asset belongs to the group.

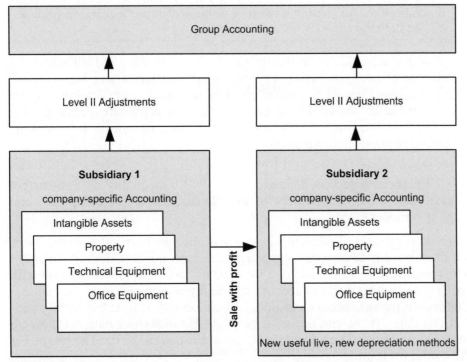

Fig. F-39   System of group internal sale of non-current assets

Non-current assets are those **assets**, which are used for the ordinary business. According to IAS 1.66 and IAS 1.67 non-current assets are all items that do not classify as current assets, particularly tangible, intangible and financial assets.

IAS 16.6 and IAS 38.8 refine this definition. According to these standards, non-current assets consist of these items:

- Property, plant and equipment
    Property, plant and equipment are tangible or fixed assets with a definite or indefinite life. Accordingly, land, buildings, technical and office equipment are summarized under this balance sheet position.

- Intangible assets
    Intangible assets are all kinds of assets without any physical substance. IAS 38.9 lists a set of examples that classify as intangible assets: licenses, trademarks, franchises, intellectual property, patents and many more. The standard does not care about the origin of these assets. Therefore, intangible assets include externally purchased assets as well as internally generated intangible assets unless specific reasons prohibit recognizing internally generated items as assets.

> The capitalization of internally generated items as intangible assets depends on the accounting legislation. Some accounting legislations prohibit this capitalization.

A special case is the treatment of goodwill. As goodwill meets the criterion of intangible asset, it belongs to non-current assets. Nevertheless, it is common practice to present goodwill separately from other intangible assets in the statement of financial position. An exception to the recognition of goodwill is defined in IAS 38.48 that prohibits accounting for internally generated goodwill as an asset.

- Financial assets
    Financial assets as defined in IAS 39.9 that qualify as non-current assets are usually investment in subsidiaries, associated companies and joint ventures.

Intercompany sales of non-current transactions may have a long-term effect. Even if the sales transaction occurs in one period, subsequent periods are involved as well. This involvement depends on the type of asset and the association with the group. The starting point to account for the intercompany sale is the transaction date when the sale occurs. An initial valuation adjustment has to be calculated at this date. At the end of any subsequent balance sheet date, a follow-up adjustment is required. The adjustments stop at the disposal date. The reason for the disposal is irrelevant.

As already mentioned, the sale of non-current assets may generate a profit at the sending company. From the group's point of view, this profit is treated as an unrealized profit because of the group-internal relocation of the asset. As a consequence, the carrying amount in the balance sheet of the receiving company is overstated by the unrealized profit. Therefore, an adjustment of the carrying amount is required.

The accounting of the intercompany sales at all parties involved, particularly the valuation and measurement, depends on the company involved, the related timing and the view of this business transaction. At the **transaction date**, an accounting at both the sending and the receiving company is necessary.

- Sending company

    The sale of non-current assets by the sending company requires the recording of a disposal of assets. This disposal is based on local accounting policies as applied by the sending company. If the sale occurs during the period, the carrying amount of the asset sold has to be adjusted to reflect the book value at the transaction date. Any depreciation or amortization is recorded as an ordinary expense.

    If local accounting policies of the sending company differ from group accounting policies, level II adjustments are present. These adjustments have to be adjusted as well to reflect the book value at the transaction date. At the transaction date, the remaining book value has to be eliminated which will result in a gain or loss on this level. Gains or losses depend on the actual differences due to accounting policies.

    Any further adjustments at the sending company are not necessary.

- Receiving company

    A more complex accounting treatment is required at the receiving company. The receiving company records an acquisition of assets measured at cost according to IAS 16.15. Based on an assumed useful life and a residual value, an appropriate depreciation pattern has to be chosen. The recording and measurement is based on the applied accounting policies by the receiving company.

    The simple recording of the purchase at local level is accompanied by a set of adjustments to ensure that the net book value of the asset at group level has not changed. Usually three adjustments have to be considered:

    - Level II adjustments of the sending company that have been eliminated and expensed jump over to the receiving company (from the group's point of view). The receiving company records a corresponding level II item.
    - If the receiving company applies different accounting policies than defined by the group, additional level II adjustments have to be considered.
    - The profit of the sending company has to be eliminated requiring an additional level II adjustment.

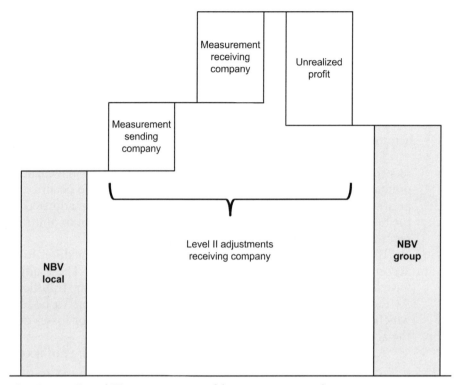

Fig. F-40   Level II components of intercompany sales

A further adjustment applies to directly attributable costs of the receiving company. These costs (e.g. for site preparation, delivery, handling, installation or assembly) follow the underlying asset according to IAS 16.16 and have to be considered as costs of the asset by the receiving company. From the group's point of view the asset was in use at the sending company and then relocated to the receiving company. Therefore, costs incurred for this relocation do not belong to directly attributable costs according to IAS 16.20. These costs have to be expensed as part of level II adjustments of the receiving company.

All adjustments are also subject to adjustments in subsequent periods.

- Group
  At group level, the carrying amount of the non-current asset held by the receiving company has to be identical to the amount held by the sending company at the transaction date. Any additional tasks at group level are not necessary as long as all adjustments are executed at level II of the receiving company.

All initial level II adjustments are subject to further adjustments in the **subsequent periods**. These adjustments apply to the receiving company and – if necessary – to the group. The sending company is not affected.

- Receiving Company

    The receiving company will depreciate the asset following the initial defined pattern. This depreciation will usually not comply with group accounting rules. Therefore, all level II adjustments have to be depreciated as well to reflect the carrying amount at group level. The depreciation of all level II adjustments have to be repeated in each subsequent period until the asset has ended its useful life or is disposed of.

- Group

    At group level, the asset should have a carrying amount that complies with group accounting rules. If no additional tasks at group level were taken, the carrying amount of the asset at group level is the sum of the carrying amount at local level plus any carrying level II amounts at the end of each subsequent period. But if additional tasks at group level were taken, valuation adjustments based on these tasks have to be depreciated as well to end up with the carrying amount at group level.

The above-mentioned explanations assume that the non-current asset has been purchased by the sending company from third parties. If in contrast the asset is purchased from another group company, an enhanced level II adjustment is necessary. In this case, a **transaction for own use** triggers a follow-up activity, eliminating unrealized profit as part of the consolidation of expenses and earnings.[68] The net value of non-depreciated unrealized profit of the original sales transaction (to the selling company) at the transaction date becomes another level II item. Accordingly, this item has to be depreciated in subsequent periods as well.

All valuation adjustments and the elimination of unrealized profit have an impact on the expected group profit and on the carrying amount of the non-current asset at group level. As the carrying amount is a result of level II adjustments, the carrying amount at group level differs from the carrying amount for tax purposes. This triggers the recording of a **deferred tax item** (either asset of liability). These deferred tax items belong to so called "inside basis differences II".[69]

Due to the complex accounting of intercompany sales of non-current assets, an extended **documentation** is recommended. The documentation acts, on one hand, as a proof of accounting for auditors and, on the other, as accounting instructions of the business transaction. The documentation should have at least a minimum content of the following items:

- The treatment together with its parameters (Net book value @ transaction date, useful life, depreciation pattern, residual value) at local level;
- The treatment together with its parameters (Net book value @ transaction date, useful life, depreciation pattern, residual value) at group level;
- The calculation of all level II adjustments together with the carrying amount @ transaction date and any underlying information necessary.

---

[68] See chapter F -5.2 on page 291 for the treatment of this transaction.

[69] See chapter K -2 on page 656 for a detailed description of inside basis differences.

Because of the inherent long-term effect of the intercompany sale the documentation should also cover the time horizon that ends with the expected disposal date. During this timeframe, all journal entries at all levels for each period have to be included. Even if today's IT systems will calculate depreciation of various accounting systems in parallel, level II adjustments are often based on manual tasks. Therefore, the documentation supports the calculated balances of the IT system at local and group level.

In case of an intercompany sale of non-current assets, perform the calculation of and document all effects at all levels immediately. It will help you in subsequent periods.

Usually, intercompany sales of non-current assets are rare transactions that occur not that often. Therefore, each transaction can be documented separately without any problem. If, by contrast, extensive transactions of this kind exist, a separate treatment of each transaction may be difficult to realize. The solution to this problem is a consistent application of group accounting policies at all levels within the group combined with the requirement to sell at net book value (so without any profit or losses). Nevertheless such a solution requires special consideration of the group structure, particularly if cross-border transactions are involved. It has to be checked whether group accounting policies can be implemented at local level in each company of the group and sale at net book value is permitted. National regulations and taxation often complicate the introduction of IFRS-based accounting regulations at local level. Therefore, accounting and tax advisors should be asked upfront before implementing such a system.

Example

Subsequent to the acquisition of Solenta, Flexing Cables management started to streamline the production facilities in the group to remove redundant production units and to reassign products to production facilities. The aim was to ensure efficiency in production. Part of this task was the transfer of a small production line from MPG to Solenta as the products manufactured on the production line were only a by-product for MPG, whereas Solenta's core activities focused on such products. Solenta would use the production line for custom-specific orders and as a spare-capacity for their ordinary products.

MPG purchased the production line in 2007 for an amount of 1,600 k EUR. The line became available for production as of 2.1.2008 and had depreciated since then. MPG had assumed a useful life of 12 years and applied the sum-of-digits method. Group accounting policies demanded a straight line depreciation over a period of 10 years by considering a residual value of 5% of the initial purchase price.[70]

---

[70] We will ignore deferred tax issues in this example.

The transfer of the production line was realized in June 2013, allowing Solenta to use the production line from 1.7.2013. Solenta paid 540 k EUR for the production line, and a further 20 k EUR, incurred for transportation and installation to the new premises, was also paid by Solenta. Solenta would depreciate the production straight line over a period of eight years without any residual value.

Even if the accounting at local level for the disposal and the purchase was treated like any other ordinary business transaction, the transfer of the production line at group level triggered extensive accounting tasks, since there was no change at group level. The production line was still within the group and therefore had to be treated as before. To properly manage the transfer of the production line at group level, a dedicated view had to be taken of each of the companies involved:

- MPG

    As MPG had depreciated the production line by applying a different method than required by group accounting policies, level II adjustments were needed on disposal by MPG. Level II adjustments for the production line are outlined in the following table:

Date	MPG		Level II adjustments		Group	
	Carrying amount	Depreciation	Carrying amount	Depreciation	Carrying amount	Depreciation
2.1.2008	1,600		0		1,600	
31.12.2008	1,354	246	94	(94)	1,448	152
31.12.2009	1,128	226	168	(74)	1,296	152
31.12.2010	923	206	221	(53)	1,144	152
31.12.2011	738	185	254	(33)	992	152
21.12.2012	574	164	266	(12)	840	152
30.6.2013	503	72	261	5	764	76

The transfer of the production line to MPG was properly accounted at local level by MPG:

Journal entries				Comment
dr.	Receivables		540	Sales price
	cr.	Proceeds from sale on non-current assets	540	
dr.	Proceeds from sale on non-current assets	503		Net book value of production line
	cr.	Property, plant & equipment	503	

While the production line was disposed by MPG, level II adjustments have to be disposed as well. The following journal entry has to be executed at level II:

Journal entry				Comment
dr.	Proceeds from sale of non-current assets	261		Level II MPG
	cr.	Property, plant & equipment	261	

The whole transaction generates the following loss:

At local level

	Proceeds from the sale of the production line	540
−	Net book value of the production line as of 30.6.2013	(503)

On level II

−	Derecognition of carrying adjustment amount	(261)
=	Total loss	(224)

This loss "jumps over" to level II of Solenta.

- Solenta, initial measurement

Solenta records the purchase of the production line like any other purchase of non-current assets in its separate financial statements:

Journal entries				Comment
dr.	Property, plant & equipment		540	Purchase price
	cr.	Accounts payable	540	
dr.	Property, plant & equipment		20	Transportation and installation costs
	cr.	Accounts payable	20	

Furthermore, on Solenta's level II, two transactions have to be recorded. The first transaction is the loss that jumped over from MPG. This loss is an adjusting amount that ensures that the proper starting point at group level is given so that no deviations from its previous handling occurs. The second transaction is the elimination of transportation and installation costs as such costs have to be expensed according to IAS 16.20. IAS 16.20 explicitly prohibits the capitalization of any relocation and reorganization costs. The following journal entries consider both facts:

Journal entries				Comment
dr.	Property, plant & equipment	224		
	cr.	Proceeds from sale on non-current assets	224	We have to use this account to ensure that no proceeds will be left in the consolidated statements of income.
dr.	Property, plant & equipment		20	Transportation and installation costs
	cr.	Other expenses	20	

Having prepared the starting point for the initial amount, the depreciation table can be prepared:

Date	Solenta		Level II adjustments		Group	
	Carrying amount	Depreciation	Carrying amount	Depreciation	Carrying amount	Depreciation
1.7.20013	560		204		764	
31.12.2013	525	35	163	41	688	76
31.12.2014	455	70	81	82	536	152
31.12.2015	385	70	(1)	82	384	152
31.12.2016	315	70	(83)	82	232	152
31.12.2017	245	70	(165)	82	80	152
31.12.2018	175	70	(95)	(70)	80	0
31.12.2019	105	70	(25)	(70)	80	0
31.12.2020	35	70	45	(70)	80	0
30.6.2021	0	35	80	(35)	80	0

- Solenta, subsequent measurement

    Once the transfer is finished, regular depreciation has to be recorded.

    In Solenta's accounts:

    Journal entry
    dr.   Depreciation expenses   35
         cr.   Property, plant & equipment   35
    On Solenta's level II:

    Journal entry
    dr.   Depreciation expenses   41
         cr.   Property, plant & equipment   41

9.3. Consolidation of multi-level groups

Regardless of the legal structure of a group, all companies that are part of the group have to be consolidated. While the legal structure is often driven by tax decisions or by acquisitions, a group can also include subgroups. Therefore, special attention is required to deal with these structures that are called multi-level groups.

9.3.1. Characteristics of multi-level groups

Multi-level groups are defined as groups with one or more subgroups. From a legal point of view, a parent holds a majority investment in a subsidiary so that control is given. This subsidiary itself acts as a parent that holds a majority investment in another subsidiary. Control is given as well. Even the "another subsidiary" can hold a majority investment in a subsidiary. In this scenario, three groups exist. Each company that acts as a parent has to have sufficient voting rights to ensure control is given. A full share in the subsidiary is not necessary. The following figure represents a typical multi-level group structure.

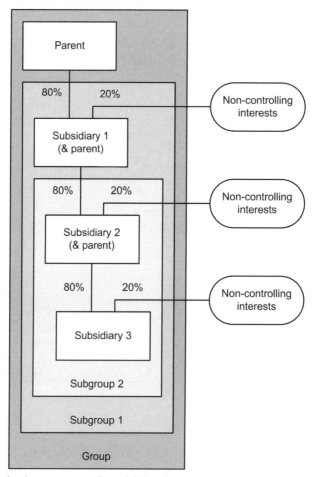

Fig. F-41 Typical structure of multi-level groups

In such a structure consolidated financial statements for the ultimate group and all subgroups have to be prepared. As this does not add any benefits because of the control of the ultimate parent, IFRS 27.10 defines exemptions to prepare consolidated financial statements for subgroups. Therefore, only the ultimate parent has to prepare consolidated financial statements.

The reasons to build multi-level groups vary. Each parent has its specific reasons to build these kinds of groups. Nevertheless, most reasons can be allocated to one of these three areas:

- Acquisitions

    An acquisition of a company that acts as a parent of a group initiates a multi-level group. In fact, an acquisition of a group occurred.

- Holding structures

    Holding structures are popular for investment in subsidiaries and for optimizing the group tax position, particularly for the use of tax havens and double tax treaties.

- Management requirements

    Groups are often structured to reflect management functions, to allocate companies to business units or divisions and for other reasons.

Regulations regarding the accounting treatment of multi-level groups are not covered by any IFRS standards. To fill this gap, the theory uses the historical formation of groups.

A special consideration requires the accounting of non-controlling interests of subgroups. As non-controlling interests are present on a specific level, this external stake in the equity of a subsidiary has to be presented at the highest group level as well. A pro rata presentation that is based on the percentage of shares in the subsidiary is prohibited as it falsifies the external requirement. This has to be considered in the consolidation process.

Similar to the treatment of non-controlling interests is the treatment of level II adjustments and the goodwill in subsidiaries. As non-controlling interests also hold a share in these items, it has to be ensured that – from the ultimate parent's point of view – these items are not over- or understated. This may require a recording of deferred items in the consolidated financial statements.

9.3.2. Consolidation techniques

The consolidation process of multi-level groups is similar to the consolidation of ordinary groups. In both cases, equity, debt and income / expense-consolidations are required. The difference between both groups is the handling of equity and its associated items (non-controlling interests and goodwill). Therefore, the focus is solely on equity. Debt, income and expense, unrealized profits and all other consolidations are identical to ordinary consolidations and do not require a special consideration or treatment.

Multi-level groups can be arranged in structures where non-controlling interests reside at every level in the group. This requires a special treatment. As a general rule, non-controlling interests have to be presented in consolidated financial statements with the amount that reflects the portion of the minority shareholder. This is also valid in multi-level groups. Nevertheless, there might be situations where subsidiaries also act as parents. If these companies also have non-controlling interests associated, a pro-rata recognition of the share of the ultimate parent in the "lowest" group member is an improper accounting. Instead, non-controlling interests of all subsidiaries in the group have to be added and presented on the group level of the ultimate parent as outlined in Fig. F-42. The portion of the minority shareholder has to be presented as initially calculated by the parent of the subgroup. Such calculations have to be repeated at all levels where non-controlling interests are present. The non-controlling interests as presented in the statement of financial position are finally an aggregation of all non-controlling interests spread across the group.

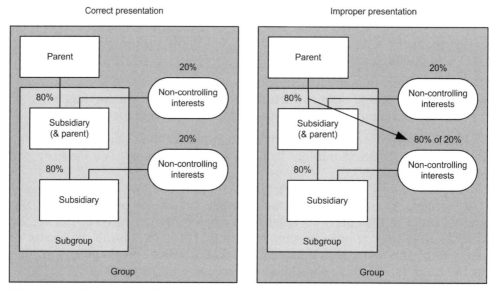

Fig. F-42   Treatment of non-controlling interests in multi-level groups

The handling of non-controlling interests is closely related to the consolidation methods applied for multi-level groups. Two consolidation methods are usually applied: chain consolidation and simultaneous consolidation. Both methods generate the same results.

- Chain consolidation

  The chain or intermediate consolidation consolidates a group by preparing consolidated financial statements for each subgroup as the default **consolidation procedure**. The processing direction is from the lowest subgroup to the group that is headed by the ultimate parent. Groups are therefore prepared along a chain where the consolidation of the group at the next level up uses the consolidated financial statements of the subgroup as a virtual company that will be integrated to arrive at consolidated figures of the consolidating group. As this practice requires the complete preparation of a subgroup, a full consolidation set is required (so equity, debt, income & expenses, unrealized profits), including the allocation of non-controlling interests. The activities have to be repeated for each (sub-)group until the final group will be consolidated.

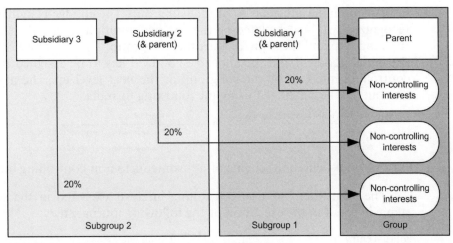

Fig. F-43 Structure of a chain consolidation

The parent of a subgroup always consolidates its subsidiaries by considering all valuation levels up to level III for each subsidiary. The parent itself uses its level II balances that are based on the ultimate group's accounting policies. If a subgroup prepares its consolidated financial statements using different accounting policies than the one of the ultimate group, additional adjustments for this subgroup are necessary.

Non-controlling interests that belong to subgroups require a special treatment. Depending on the foundation type of the subgroup (acquisition or simple foundation) and the options available to account for non-controlling interests (partial or full goodwill), hidden reserves and burdens, non-accounted items and goodwill have to be allocated to non-controlling interests. The allocation is based on accounting procedures applied during the initial consolidation. As the allocated non-controlling interests represent an external share in a subsidiary, they have to be presented in the consolidated financial statements of the ultimate parent. Therefore, non-controlling interests that relate to a subgroup have to be isolated from consolidation activities on the next higher group level. Special attention is required to properly reflect goodwill and non-controlling interests. Due to the consolidation method to consider all assets and all liabilities and to reclassify equity to non-controlling interests in proportion of its share in the subgroup, additional adjustments are necessary. The subgroup at the lowest level can prepare consolidated financial statements as usual including the allocation to non-controlling interests. The subgroup at the next level performs the same activities in the first step. While the parent of this subgroup only holds a defined share in the other subgroup and consequently also a reduced stake in the subsidiaries of that subgroup, an adjustment of goodwill of the other subgroup is necessary for the investment in the subsidiaries of that subgroup. The goodwill eligible to be recognized will be calculated by the goodwill multiplied with the share in the subgroup and the share of the other subgroup. The difference between the initial goodwill and the allocable goodwill has to be assigned to non-controlling interests of the subgroup at the next level up. The assigned amount will be calculated using the following formula:

Subsidiary	Calculation of Non-controlling Interests	Remarks
2	Goodwill Subsidiary 2 * (1-Share Subgroup 2)	First step: Regular consolidation of subgroup 2
3	Goodwill Subsidiary 3 * Share Subsidiary 3 * (1 - Share Subgroup 2)	Second step: Adjustment of interest in subsidiary 3 of subgroup 2

Fig. F-44 Calculation scheme of adjustments to non-controlling interests

The adjustment of non-controlling interests executed in the second step will result in the execution of the following journal entry:

Journal entry		Comment
dr.	Non-controlling interests	Group or subgroup level
cr.	Goodwill	Group or subgroup level

This procedure has to be repeated until the final group will be consolidated. Along this consolidation chain, a continuous assignment of goodwill to non-controlling interests has to be performed. Such an assignment can be calculated using the following table:

		lowest						highest			
	Goodwill / Level III	Subgroup 2			Subgroup 1			Group			Totals
Subsidiary	adjustment	Share	Allocated to Group	NCI	Share	Allocated to Group	NCI	Share	Allocated to Group	NCI	Group	NCI
3 (lowest)	x3	y3	x3*y3	x3*(1-y3)		x3*y3*y2	x3*y3*(1-y2)		x3*y3*y2*y1	x3*y3*y2*(1-y1)		
2	x2				y2	x2*y2	x2*(1-y2)		x2*y2*y1	x2*y2*(1-y1)		
1 (highest)	x1							y1	x1*y1	x1*(1-y1)		
Group			xxx			xxx			xxx		zzz	
NCI				xxx			xxx			xxx		zzz

Fig. F-45 Calculation scheme of goodwill and level III adjustments

This calculation will not only be performed for goodwill. If there are level III adjustments at lower levels, a similar assignment to non-controlling interests has to be performed.

The **advantage** of a chain consolidation is the availability of detailed information on other group levels. This availability is useful when subgroups are required to publish consolidated financial statements. Such a requirement is given, if the subgroup is publicly listed even if the majority of shares is with another group.

Details are not always needed, particularly if the ultimate parent has to prepare consolidated financial statements only. In such a situation, the application of a chain consolidation is a **disadvantage** compared to the simultaneous consolidation. This is because the preparation of consolidated financial statements of subgroups along the consolidation chain is a time consuming task that repeats similar tasks on each group level.

Applying the chain consolidation will be complicated if multi-level groups are established through **acquisitions of subgroups** and these subgroups have a requirement to publish consolidated financial statements. Each acquisition demands a purchase price allocation according to IFRS 3.

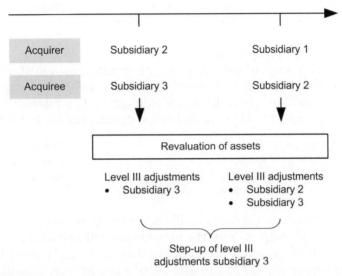

Fig. F-46 Timing of acquisitions in multi-level groups

The acquisition activities of the lower subgroup's parent acquired usually includes the accounting of hidden reserves and burdens and non-accounted assets of their subsidiaries as one part of its purchase price allocation. The acquisition of the subgroup at the next level up demands again an execution of a purchase price allocation. The extent of this purchase price allocation includes all companies of the lower subgroup, so the parent of the subgroup and all of its subsidiaries that have to be measured by their fair values. As a consequence, the subsidiaries at the lowest level have to go through a valuation process every time an acquisition at a higher level occurs. This will result in several measurements for the same assets and liabilities, but at different times. The preparation of consolidated financial statements along the chain has to consider these different measurements of the same assets and liabilities. Appropriate adjustments are necessary, which will be treated as step-up adjustments that are recorded at level III of the subgroup. The technical handling can be realized using two types:

• Separate level III adjustments
  For each subsidiary where different measurements of the same assets exist, an individual advancement will be calculated. Assets and its adjustment on the lower subgroup will be replaced by those adjustments that belong to the higher level.

Journal entry			Comment
dr.	Revaluation reserve		Historical amounts.
dr.	Non-controlling interests		
	cr.	Assets	Can also be liabilities.
dr.	Assets		Can also be liabilities.
	cr.	Revaluation reserve	Remeasured amounts.
	cr.	Non-controlling interests	

- Step-up adjustments

  Step-up adjustments do not require any adjustments of consolidated statements of lower subgroups. Instead, a step-up amount is derived from the different measurements. This amount acts as a level III adjustment to the consolidated statements of the lower subgroup.

Journal entry			Comment
dr.	Assets		Can also be liabilities.
	cr.	Revaluation reserve	Step-up amount only.
	cr.	Non-controlling interests	

Both adjustment types will deliver the same results.

The step-up of level III adjustments will impact also non-controlling interests of the lower subgroup. As additional amounts of hidden reserves and burdens as well as non-accounted assets are now recorded, a fraction of these step-up adjustments has to be allocated to non-controlling interests. The allocation is based on the consolidation procedures described above.

Depending on the needs to prepare consolidate financial statements of a subgroup that have to be published, several **methods** are available for a chain consolidation:

- Historical method

  The historical method consolidates subgroups based on the procedures described above. The consolidation of subgroups is executed in the first instance using historical measurements. This includes an allocation of goodwill of subsidiaries of lower subgroups to non-controlling interests. In the second instance, the step-up towards the new measurement base is executed at level III of the subgroup. All further consolidation procedures at higher levels are based on the remeasured assets and liabilities.

  At the end of the day, the subgroup has prepared two sets of consolidated financial statements, one using the historical measurements for publishing needs and one using current measurements for group purposes. This activity has to be performed in all subsequent periods.

- Remeasurement method

  The remeasurement method ignores any historical measurements and uses the remeasured assets and liabilities at the last acquisition date instead. Like the historical consolidation, this consolidation follows the procedures described above which are now based on remeasured assets and liabilities instead of their historical values. While the remeasured assets and liabilities relate to the acquisition of a group, the remeasurement can be recorded at subgroup level and at subsidiary level. Regardless of which group level is involved, the recording will always occur at level III.

Recording any valuation adjustments at subgroup level keeps the step-up amount in one central place. The consolidation of all lower subgroups will be executed without any changes. The consolidation at higher levels will consider the subgroup's consolidated financial statements (level II) and the step-up amounts (level III). An allocation to the subsidiaries carrying the assets and liabilities that cause the valuation adjustments will not occur. The advantage of a central recording will be contradicted by a recording of valuation adjustments in more than one place.

An alternate treatment is a push-down of the step-up amounts to subsidiaries. The assignment on a subsidiary level ensures that each subsidiary will carry its individual valuation adjustments, asset by asset. The advantage of this treatment is a consistent fair value handling of assets across the whole group.

At the end of the day, only one set of consolidated financial statements exists for group purposes. The step up is a one-time activity that is executed upon acquisition of the subgroup.

If there is no need to prepare consolidated financial statements at lower levels that are published externally, the chain consolidation can be executed at the highest group level. In such a case, all subsidiaries of the group are summed up to arrive at the aggregated trial balance. The consolidations of all subgroups and the ultimate group are executed step by step as a chain consolidation.

Regardless of which consolidation method is used, all methods will deliver the same results.

Example[71]

The Flexing Cables group has several subgroups. Traditionally, all sales subsidiaries and sales associates are held by Flexing Cables Holding, which is a wholly-owned subsidiary of Flexing Cables SE, unless there are reasons for a deviating investment. Flexing Cables Holding was founded for this purpose only. One exception is the Cable Systems group. This group combines sales and production activities. Flexing Cables has had the chance to acquire an interest in the group as of 1.1.2002. The acquisition was realized through Flexing Cables Holding, which acquired 80% of the shares of Cable Systems Holding Inc.

---

[71] This example covers equity consolidation only! Please refer to the appropriate chapters for the other consolidation tasks as these tasks are identical to ordinary consolidation techniques.

The Cable Systems group was established 1.1.2000 by a company split. The original company, Cable Systems (founded 1995) was split into a holding company (Cable Systems Holding Inc.) and an operating company (Cable Systems USA Ltd), responsible for sales and production. Cable Systems USA's equity was limited to the share capital at that date. Due to the founders' discretion, and for U.S. tax reasons, the founders of Cable Systems not only owned a 100% stake in Cable Systems Holding, but also a "20% minus one share" stake in Cable Systems USA.[72] At the same time, Cable Systems Mexico was founded by Cable Systems Holding together with a local partner which held a 25% stake in Cable Systems Mexico. Cable Systems Holding recorded its appropriate share in the companies based on the participation quota.

This acquisition was Flexing Cables Holding's largest acquisition so far. The company had paid a purchase price of 12,000 k EUR for 80% of the shares of Cables Systems Holding. Referring to the original purchase price allocation, the purchase price included net assets of 3,293 k EUR, level III net assets of 3,800 k EUR, foreign currency translation effects of -16 k EUR and a group goodwill of 4,923 k EUR. Level III net assets related to customer bases, customer orders and patents of Cables Systems USA and Cable Systems Mexico. All level III net assets had been fully depreciated so far. Accordingly, no balance remained at level III as of the current balance sheet date. As the group goodwill was not subject to an impairment, it was still recorded as it was.

The companies reported the following financial information as of the balance sheet date (all figures had already been converted to EUR and IFRS):

	Flexing Cables Holding	Cable Systems Holding	Cable Systems USA	Cable Systems Mexico
Cash at hand & bank	14,272	10,474	13,520	836
Trade receivables	12,301	7,585	12,457	1,207
Inventory			9,689	939
Other assets	76		4,964	268
Current assets	**26,649**	**18,059**	**40,630**	**3,250**
Property, plant & equipment	68		38,924	719
Intangible assets	24	1	5,245	106
Financial assets	29,950	596		
Non-current assets	**30,042**	**597**	**44,169**	**825**
Total assets	**56,691**	**18,656**	**84,799**	**4,075**
Trade payables	5,433		6,368	753
Tax liabilities	752	182	2,826	14
Prepayments				146
Accruals		18	2,067	244
Loans			1,453	112
Other payables	128		5,072	472
Current liabilities	**6,313**	**200**	**17,786**	**1,741**
Loans	4,400		8,717	
Provisions	167		328	

---

[72] The dividends received deduction (DRD) under the U.S. federal income tax law allows a 100% deduction if the receiving company owns more than 80% of the shares in the distributing company. This regulation was established to avoid a triple taxation of profits. Accordingly, an investment of the receiving company in the distributing company of 80% plus one share fulfils this requirement.

Pensions			1,415	
Deferred tax liabilities				
Non-current liabilities	**4,567**	**0**	**10,460**	**0**
Share capital	100	112	1,121	31
Capital reserves	3,000			
Retained earnings	42,711	19,587	60,380	2,886
Foreign currency translation		(1,243)	(4,948)	(583)
Equity	**45,811**	**18,456**	**56,553**	**2,334**
Total equity & liability	**56,691**	**18,656**	**84,799**	**4,075**
Revenues			84,078	10,076
Other income	114		1,191	210
Total performance	**114**	**0**	**85,269**	**10,286**
Raw materials & consumables			(27,032)	(6,525)
Employee expenses			(17,381)	(2,031)
Depreciation & amortization	(14)		(2,106)	(72)
Other expenses	(97)	(19)	(13,438)	(1,237)
Operating profit	**3**	**(19)**	**25,312**	**421**
Financial result	(157)	120	(705)	(28)
Dividend income	14,610	7,871		
Income tax expenses	(173)	(41)	(9,843)	(118)
Net profit for the period	**14,283**	**7,931**	**14,764**	**275**

To consolidate these companies using the chain consolidation, two subgroups had to be consolidated before the final group could be consolidated. We will go bottom-up, the first subgroup is the Cable Systems Holding group, followed by the Flexing Cables Holding group and then finally the Flexing Cables SE group. As already mentioned we will focus in this example on equity only. Therefore, all other balance sheet items and the profit & loss statement will be aggregated only. Furthermore, acquisitions occurred on Flexing Cables Holding level only. This will allow a simplified consolidation as any level III step-ups do not apply.

- Step 1 – Consolidation Cable Systems Holding group

a) Cables Systems USA

The equity consolidation for Cable Systems USA consists of two tasks: An allocation of equity to non-controlling interests and an elimination of the carrying amount of interests in subsidiaries as recorded by Cable Systems Holding. The amounts to be allocated to non-controlling interests and recorded are:

		Carrying amount	20%	80%
	Share capital	1,121	224	897
+	Retained earnings (carried forward)	45,616	9,123	36,493
+	Retained earnings (current period)	14,764	2,953	11,811
+	Foreign currency translation	(4,948)	(990)	(3,958)
=	Equity	56,553	11,310	45,242

Journal entries			Company
dr.	Share capital	224	Cable Systems USA
dr.	Retained earnings	9,123	Cable Systems USA
dr.	Foreign currency translation	990	Cable Systems USA
cr.	Non-controlling interests	8,357	Group
dr.	Profit allocable to non-controlling interests	2,953	Group
cr.	Non-controlling interests	2,953	Group

The profit of the current period presented in retained earnings is not reclassified in equity. Instead, the amount belonging to non-controlling interests is recorded through profit & loss. This ensures that the profit allocable to the group is properly stated in the consolidated statement of income. As the profit allocable to the group rolls-up in retained earnings, a proper presentation of retained earnings is also given.

The elimination of the carrying amount of interests in subsidiaries recorded by Cable Systems Holding is limited to share capital only. This is because Cable Systems USA was established through a split from the parent with an allocation of share capital only. Having executed the allocation of share capital to non-controlling interests, a balance of 897 k EUR remains in share capital. This balance represents 800 k USD, the stake of Cable Systems Holding in Cable Systems USA using the historical exchange rate of 0.8920 USD/EUR. At the same time, Cable Systems Holding is reporting a balance of 581 k EUR for its interest in Cable Systems USA. This is because IAS 21.39 requires a translation of assets using the closing rate instead of the historical rate. Accordingly, a foreign currency item has to be considered. That item can be calculated in the following way:

		USD	FX-rate (USD/EUR)	EUR
	1.1.2000	800	0.8920	897
−	31.12.2013	800	1.3766	581
=	Difference	0		316

Journal entry			Company
dr.	Share capital	897	Cable Systems USA
cr.	Foreign currency translation	316	Group
cr.	Investment is subsidiaries	581	Cable Systems Holding

b) Cable Systems Mexico

The equity consolidation of Cable Systems Mexico follows the same procedure as the consolidation of Cables Systems USA. The only difference is a double currency translation at the date, Cable Systems Mexico was founded. A translation from MXN to USD is applied by Cable Systems Holding to record the stake in Cable Systems Mexico by using the historical exchange rate. Furthermore, the historical exchange rate for the translation from USD to EUR is applied at the same date. Accordingly, translation difference can occur between USD and EUR for the carrying amount of investments is subsidiaries only.[73]

---

[73] Recorded by Cables Systems Holding: 75% of 250 k MXN = 188 k MXN

		Carrying amount	25%	75%
	Share capital	31	8	23
+	Retained earnings (carried forward)	2,611	653	1,958
+	Retained earnings (current period)	275	69	206
+	Foreign currency translation	(583)	(146)	(437)
=	Equity	2,334	584	1,750

Journal entries | | | Company
dr.	Share capital	8	Cable Systems Mexico
dr.	Retained earnings	653	Cable Systems Mexico
dr.	Foreign currency translation	146	Cable Systems Mexico
cr.	Non-controlling interests	515	Group
dr.	Profit allocable to non-controlling interests	69	Group
cr.	Non-controlling interests	69	Group

	MXN	FX-rate (MSN/USD)	USD	FX-rate (USD/EUR)	EUR
1.1.2000	188[73]	9.475	20	0.8920	23
− 31.12.2013	188	9.475	20	1.3766	14
= Difference			0		9

Journal entry | | | Company
dr.	Share capital	23	Cable Systems Mexico
cr.	Foreign currency translation	9	Group
cr.	Investment in subsidiaries	14	Cables Systems Holding

Having consolidated the Cable Systems Holding group, the adjusted balance sheet used for further consolidation purposes is presented below.[74] This balance sheet is used for the consolidation at the next level.

Adjusted IFRS Statement of financial position Cable Systems Holding group as of 31.12.2013 (in k EUR)

Assets		Liabilities & Equity	
Cash at hand & bank	24,830	Trade payables	7,121
Trade receivables	21,249	Tax liabilities	3,021
Inventory	10,628	Prepayments	146
Other assets	5,232	Accruals	2,328
Current assets	**61,939**	Loans	1,565
		Other payables	5,545
Property, plant & equipment	39,643	**Current liabilities**	**19,726**
Intangible assets	5,352		
Non-current assets	**44,995**	Loans	8,717
		Provisions	328
		Pensions	1,416
		Non-current liabilities	**10,461**
		Share capital	112
		Retained earnings	70,055
		Foreign currency translation	(5,314)
		Non-controlling interests	11,894
		Equity	**76,747**
Total assets	**106,934**	**Total liabilities & equity**	**106,934**

---

[74] We name the balance sheet "adjusted balance sheet", because equity is consolidated only while all other items are aggregated.

- Step 2 – Consolidation Flexing Cables Holding group

Having consolidated Cable Systems Holding group for equity purposes, Flexing Cables Holding group has to be consolidated now. From Flexing Cables Holding perspective, the adjusted financial statement of Cable Systems Holding group is treated like any other investment. Accordingly, all investments in subsidiaries of Flexing Cables Holding have to be consolidated now.[75]

Based on the shareholder relationships and the initial consolidation, the equity can be allocated to the group and non-controlling interests:

	Carrying amount	20% Initial consolidation	80% Initial Consolidation	20% Subsequent consolidation	80% Subsequent consolidation
Share capital	112	22	90		
+ Retained earnings (carried forward)	50,106	801	3,203	9,220	36,882
+ Retained earnings level III	0		3,800		(3,800)
+ Retained earnings (current period)	19,949			3,990	15,959
+ Foreign currency translation	(5,314)	8	34	(1,071)	(4,285)
+ Non-controlling interests	11,894				
= Equity	76,747	831	7,127	12,139	44,756

Other than the consolidation of the first step, this consolidation is based on a purchase price allocation. Therefore, the consolidation procedure is slightly different than the application in the first step. To consolidate Cable Systems Holding group, the initial consolidation has to be repeated:

Journal entry			Company
dr.	Share capital	90	Cable Systems Holding group
dr.	Retained earnings	7,003	Cable Systems Holding group
dr.	Foreign currency translation	34	Cable Systems Holding group
dr.	Goodwill	4,873	Group
cr.	Investment in subsidiaries	12,000	Flexing Cables Holding

Retained earnings consist of 3,203 k EUR that relates to local accounts and 3,800 k EUR that relates to level III items. Share capital and retained earnings represent 80% of the equity as of the original equity. Accordingly, the remaining equity has to be allocated to non-controlling interests. Furthermore, non-controlling interests are entitled for a pro-rata share of retained earnings of all subsequent periods, the current period and all foreign currency translation adjustments. The allocations will be realized by the following journal entries:

---

[75] To demonstrate the multi-level consolidation of equity, we will focus on the equity consolidation of Cables Systems Holding group only. All other interests in subsidiaries are kept untouched. They have to be consolidated by a separate task. Again, all other consolidations activities (debt, earnings and expenses, unrealized profits) are also not touched. They are also subject to a separate consolidation task.

Journal entry				Company
dr.	Share capital		22	Cable Systems Holding
dr.	Retained earnings		10,021	Group
	cr.	Foreign currency translation	1,063	Cable Systems Holding group
	cr.	Non-controlling interests	8,980	Group
dr.	Profit allocable to non-controlling interests		3,990	Group
	cr.	Non-controlling interests	3,990	Group

Again, the profit of the current period presented in retained earnings is not reclassified in equity. Instead, the amount belonging to non-controlling interests is recorded through profit & loss. This ensures that the profit allocable to the group is properly stated in the consolidated statement of income. As the profit allocable to the group rolls-up in retained earnings, a proper presentation of retained earnings is also given.

Having consolidated the Flexing Cables Holding group, the adjusted balance sheet used for further consolidation purposes is presented below.[76] This balance sheet is used for the consolidation at the next level.

Adjusted IFRS Statement of financial position Flexing Cables Holding group as of 31.12.2013 (in k EUR)

Assets		Liabilities & Equity	
Cash at hand & bank	39,102	Trade payables	12,554
Trade receivables	33,550	Tax liabilities	3,773
Inventory	10,628	Prepayments	146
Other assets	5,308	Accruals	2,328
Current assets	**88,588**	Loans	1,565
		Other payables	5,673
Property, plant & equipment	39,711	**Current liabilities**	**26,039**
Intangible assets	5,376		
Financial investments	17,952	Loans	13,117
Goodwill	4,873	Provisions	495
Non-current assets	**67,912**	Pensions	1,416
		Non-current liabilities	**15,028**
		Share capital	100
		Capital reserves	3,000
		Retained earnings	91,752
		Foreign currency translation	(4,284)
		Non-controlling interests	24,864
		Equity	**115,432**
Total assets	**156,500**	**Total liabilities & equity**	**156,500**

---

[76] We name the balance sheet "adjusted balance sheet", because equity is consolidated only while all other items are aggregated.

- Step 3 – Consolidation of Flexing Cables SE

  The final step is the consolidation of the ultimate parent's group. On this level, all companies subject to consolidation will be included. This includes not only the companies where Flexing Cables Holding is carrying a controlling investment in but also all subsidiaries which investment is held by Flexing Cables SE including another subgroup, Flexing Cables USA group.

  As far as Flexing Cables Holding is concerned, the consolidation to be applied is simple straightforward. Flexing Cables Holding was founded by Flexing Cables SE, is a wholly-owned subsidiary and uses the same currency. Therefore, only a simple share capital consolidation is required.

Journal entry				Company
dr.	Share capital		100	Flexing Cables Holding group
	cr.	Investment in subsidiaries	100	Flexing Cables SE

  Even if this simple journal entry is sufficient to consolidate Flexing Cables Holding group, special attention to capital reserves is required. While capital reserves in a group are only those of the parent, no other company can contribute to this equity category. Therefore, Flexing Cables Holding's capital reserves have to be reclassified to another equity category which is usually retained earnings.

Journal entry				Company
dr.	Capital reserves		3,000	Flexing Cables Holding group
	cr.	Retained earnings	3,000	Group

No further tasks are necessary to consolidate the multi-level group.

- Simultaneous consolidation

  Besides chain consolidation, simultaneous consolidation consolidates the equity of all companies in one step. Due to its mathematical background, the simultaneous consolidation is more flexible than a chain consolidation and has the ability to consolidate more group structures. Typical examples are multi-parent structures and reciprocal interests.

  The **advantage** is the immediate availability of consolidated figures for the ultimate parent. A longer consolidation period than usual for chain consolidation can be avoided. Furthermore, simultaneous consolidation also supports, due its mathematical application, complicated group structures that cannot be solved through chain consolidation.

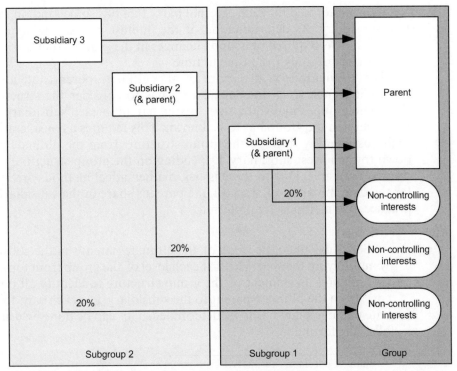

Fig. F-47 Structure of a simultaneous consolidation

The strength of this consolidation method to have the final financial figures immediately available is also a **disadvantage**. While the consolidation takes place at the highest level, detailed information of lower levels get lost or will not be available. They can only be established by another consolidation that considers the appropriate levels only. This will result in a double execution of consolidations.

The **consolidation procedure** follows a two-step approach based on the aggregated trial balance of the group. All separate level III financial statements of the group's subsidiaries are therefore considered in the aggregated trial balance. The relationships between the subsidiaries are ignored. Having an aggregated trial balance available, the two-step approach will be applied. The first step calculates the share in a subsidiary. This share is used for the execution of all consolidation tasks, which will be the second step.

The **first step** calculates the share in a subsidiary. This calculation has to occur for the ultimate parent to determine its share in each subsidiary. To estimate the level of non-controlling interests in subsidiaries, a calculation has to be performed for each external party that has some kind on interest in a subsidiary. As determination of the interest in a subsidiary and its related share is required only upon changes in the group structure, it needs to be performed only from time to time.

The calculation of the share of the ultimate parent and all non-controlling interests in the subsidiaries has to consider the structure of the whole group. Finally, the share of the parent in each subsidiary at the lowest level in the group has to be known. This requires a consideration of each possible way through the group structure, from the ultimate parent down to the lowest subsidiary. Depending on the group structure, several ways are possible. Due to these issues, mathematical methods are applied for the determination of the ultimate parent's share in the subsidiaries. In practice, two methods are preferred:

- Series

  Series calculate the share of the ultimate parent's in the subsidiary by multiplying the shares held at each level of the group from top down. This requires assessment of the group structure to identify all possible ways, from the ultimate parent to the subsidiary. For each way, the ultimate parent's share has to be determined. This can be done by using the following formula:

	Share of parent in subsidiary 1
*	Share of subsidiary 1 in subsidiary 2
*	Share of subsidiary 2 in subsidiary 3
*	…
=	Effective share of parent in subsidiary

Tab. F-15 Calculation scheme of shares in subsidiaries using series

> Take your time in identifying all ways through the group. Not all ways are obvious at first sight.

The above calculation of the share in a subsidiary follows one route only. But there is not always only one route. If several ways to the subsidiary exist, the share of each has to be calculated: the shares are then summed up to determine the final share in the subsidiary.

	Effective share of parent in subsidiary 3 using way #1
+	Effective share of parent in subsidiary 3 using way #2
+	…
+	Effective share of parent in subsidiary 3 using way #n
=	Effective share of parent in subsidiary 3

Tab. F-16 Calculation scheme of shares in subsidiaries with multiple ways

In some cases, subsidiaries record interests in each other. This will result in a reciprocal situation. To solve such a situation, series are expanded by another element of the geometric series using the following formula:

$$\sum_{i=0}^{\infty}(Share\,Subsidiary1 * Share\,Subsidiary2)^{i}$$

While the shares in the subsidiaries are always less than 100%, the geometric series converges so that a simplified formula can be applied instead:[77]

$$\frac{1}{1-(Share\,Subsidiary1 * Share\,Subsidiary2)}$$

Again, the above-mentioned elements are applied to determine the effective share of the ultimate parent in a subsidiary.

The disadvantage of using series is the uncertainty of full identification of all ways, from the parent through the group to all subsidiaries. In particular in complex group structures, a full discovery of all possible ways through the group cannot be guaranteed.

> To check if all ways through the group are detected, the sum of all effective shares of all parents and of all non-controlling interests (so the sum of their percentages), divided by 100%, has to equal the number of subsidiaries.

• Matrices

A more sophisticated approach is the use of matrices. A matrix represents the relationship between all companies subject to consolidation of the group. This obviates the need to find ways through the group. The matrix has to include all companies of the group – the ultimate parent and all subsidiaries, as well as all non-controlling interests. All entities and non-controlling interests have to be included in the columns and rows of the matrix so that the number of columns and rows equal each other. Within that matrix, the various interests for each subsidiary (the shares in that subsidiary) have to be inserted, whether they are held by companies of the group or by external parties. A typical matrix is presented by the following figure:

---

[77] The formula can be used because i will go to infinity. It will converge as the sum of shares of the subsidiaries will never be larger than 1 (which represents 100% or a full ownership).

Shareholder	Share in						
	Parent	Subsidiary 1	Subsidiary 2	Subsidiary 3	Non-controlling interests 1	Non-controlling interests 2	Non-controlling interests 3
Parent	-	xxx					
Subsidiary 1		-	xxx				
Subsidary 2			-	xxx			
Subsidiary 3				-			
Non-controlling interests 1		xxx			-		
Non-controlling interests 2			xxx			-	
Non-controlling interests 3				xxx			-

Fig. F-48   Shareholder matrix

The shareholder matrix has to be solved in a way that the interests of the ultimate parent and all external parties in the subsidiaries can be derived. Solving the matrix requires transfer in a mathematical matrix and determination of an inverse matrix.[78]

$$\text{Matrix} = \begin{pmatrix} 0 & 0.8 & 0 & 0 & 0 & 0 & 0 \\ 0 & 0 & 0.8 & 0 & 0 & 0 & 0 \\ 0 & 0 & 0 & 0.8 & 0 & 0 & 0 \\ 0 & 0 & 0 & 0 & 0 & 0 & 0 \\ 0 & 0.2 & 0 & 0 & 0 & 0 & 0 \\ 0 & 0 & 0.2 & 0 & 0 & 0 & 0 \\ 0 & 0 & 0 & 0.2 & 0 & 0 & 0 \end{pmatrix}$$

Tab. F-17   The shareholder matrix in a matrix formula (the initial matrix)

$$\text{Matrix}^{-1} = \begin{pmatrix} 0 & 0.8 & 0.64 & 0.512 & 0 & 0 & 0 \\ 0 & 0 & 0.8 & 0.64 & 0 & 0 & 0 \\ 0 & 0 & 0 & 0.8 & 0 & 0 & 0 \\ 0 & 0 & 0 & 0 & 0 & 0 & 0 \\ 0 & 0.2 & 0.16 & 0.128 & 0 & 0 & 0 \\ 0 & 0 & 0.2 & 0.16 & 0 & 0 & 0 \\ 0 & 0 & 0 & 0.2 & 0 & 0 & 0 \end{pmatrix}$$

Tab. F-18   The inverse matrix

---

[78] Several methods can be used to solve the matrix depending on the underlying complexity of the group structure. The methods used here to determine the inverse matrix considers complex group structures. For those who would like to know the determination of the inverse matrix: The initial matrix has to be subtracted from the identity matrix. The new matrix has to be transformed in an inverse matrix by augmenting it by the identity and by applying the Gauß-Jordan algorithm. From this new matrix, the identity matrix has to be subtracted to arrive at the inverse matrix.

The inverse matrix provides details of the shares in a subsidiary. The share of a parent in its subsidiaries at all levels can be directly retrieved from the matrix. Each row of the matrix represents the share of a parent in all of its subsidiaries, directly as well as indirectly. The sorting order of the parents and their subsidiaries is based on the initial shareholder matrix.

Regardless of which mathematical algorithm will be used to solve the determination of the share in subsidiaries, series and matrices will always deliver the same results. Comparing these results with a chain consolidation will unveil again the same results presuming that the group structure can be solved by a chain consolidation.

Having calculated the share of the ultimate parent in all subsidiaries, the **second step**, the execution of all consolidation tasks, can be performed. As far as multi-level groups are concerned, only the equity consolidation is the one that requires special attention. The equity consolidation has to follow a few rules to ensure a proper consolidation and presentation of goodwill:

- The determined shares of the first step have to be applied.
- The equity of the subsidiaries has to be eliminated using the determined shares.
- The carrying amount of the investment in subsidiaries has to be eliminated using either the share or the determined share in the subsidiary.
- Distortions may occur if the equity does not equal the relationships between shareholders. Such a distortion can occur by applying the partial goodwill method. Balancing items have to be considered in such a case.
- Foreign currency effects on lower subgroup levels have to be reclassified.
- A journal entry for each calculated share has to be executed.

These rules do not apply exclusively to the group and the ultimate parent, they are also mandatory for non-controlling interests. All journal entries have to be executed at group level and therefore consider all adjustments up to level III.

The standard journal entry for each consolidation concerning the **group** is:

Journal entry		Company	Comment
dr.	Equity	Subsidiary	Carrying amount * determined share
dr.	Goodwill	Group	Residual amount
	cr. Investment in subsidiaries	Parent	Carrying amount

This journal entry might be modified if the initial consolidation is based on a purchase price allocation that uses the partial goodwill method. In such a case, equity items have to be adjusted considering the journal entry of the initial consolidation. Another issue is the handling of foreign currency effects at lower levels that may require a modification of the journal entry.

The standard journal entries for **non-controlling interests** are:

Journal entries		Company	Comment
dr.	Equity	Subsidiary	Carrying amount * determined share
	cr. Non-controlling interests	Group	Residual amount (can also be a debit).
	cr. Investment in subsidiaries	Parent	Carrying amount
dr.	Equity	Subsidiary	Carrying amount * determined share
	cr. Non-controlling interests	Group	

The first journal entry has to be applied if there are non-controlling interests in the parent of a subgroup (which is also a subsidiary of the group) and the parent does not fully control its subsidiary. The second journal entry has to be applied in all other cases.

In addition to the equity consolidation, **other consolidations** have to be performed to eliminate intercompany transactions. These consolidations are applied particularly for debt, income & expenses and unrealized profits. The standard procedures of subsequent consolidations can be applied without any exceptions.[79] The advantage of these consolidations using a simultaneous consolidation is the availability of all intercompany balances of all balance sheet and profit & loss items at group level. Therefore, all relationships can be eliminated in one step.

Example[80]

This example complements the previous example! It consolidates the same companies to the Flexing Cables SE group by applying a simultaneous consolidation using matrices. Starting point like the other consolidation method are the reported financial statements of the companies as of the balance sheet date (all figures are already converted to EUR and IFRS).[81] Two steps have to be performed for consolidation.

- Step 1 – Determined share calculation

  To calculate the determined shares held by the Flexing Cables SE in each subsidiary, matrices are used. This table represents the relationship between the companies which is used to feed the matrix.

Shares held in	Shares held by			
	Flexing Cables SE	Flexing Cables Holding	Cable Systems Holding	Non-controlling interests
Flexing Cables Holding	100%			
Cable Systems Holding		80%		20%
Cable Systems USA			80%	20%
Cable Systems Mexico			75%	25%

---

[79] See chapter F -4 on page 270 for debt consolidation, F -5 on page 286 for income & expense consolidations and F -6 on page 310 for the elimination of unrealized profits.

[80] This example covers equity consolidation only! Please refer to the appropriate chapters for the other consolidation tasks as these tasks are identical to ordinary consolidation techniques.

[81] Please refer to the previous example regarding the financial statements.

The following matrix is the output that reflects the transformed relationships between the companies.

$$\text{Matrix}^{-1} = \begin{pmatrix} 1 & 0.8 & 0.64 & 0.6 \\ 0 & 0.8 & 0.64 & 0.6 \\ 0 & 0 & 0.8 & 0.75 \\ 0 & 0.2 & 0.16 & 0.15 \\ 0 & 0 & 0.2 & 0 \\ 0 & 0 & 0 & 0.25 \end{pmatrix}$$

According to this matrix, the following shares are determined:

	Determined shares held by	
Shares held in	Flexing Cables SE	Non-controlling interests
Flexing Cables Holding	100%	-
Cable Systems Holding	80%	20%
Cable Systems USA	64%	36%
Cable Systems Mexico	60%	40%

- Step 2a – Equity elimination, non-controlling interests

  Non-controlling interests are built up by allocating a fraction of the carrying amount of the equity amounts to non-controllling interests. Again the portion that belongs to the current period has to be recorded through profit & loss. The underlying formula in calculating the amounts that have to be allocated to non-controlling interests is: carrying amount of equity account * determined interest rate. This has to be done for each company.

  a) Cable Systems USA

		Carrying amount	36%
	Share capital	1,121	404
+	Retained earnings (carried forward)	45,616	16,422
+	Retained earnings (current period)	14,764	5,315
+	Foreign currency translation	(4,948)	(1,781)
=	Equity	56,553	20,360

Journal entry				Company
dr.		Share capital	404	Cable Systems USA
dr.		Retained earnings	16,422	Cable Systems USA
dr.		Profit allocable to non-controlling interests	5,315	Group
	cr.	Foreign currency translation	1,781	Cable Systems USA
	cr.	Non-controlling interests	20,360	Group

b) Cable Systems Mexico

		Carrying amount	40%
	Share capital	31	12
+	Retained earnings (carried forward)	2,611	1,044
+	Retained earnings (current period)	275	110
+	Foreign currency translation	(583)	(233)
=	Equity	2,334	933

Journal entry				Company
dr.	Share capital	12		Cable Systems Mexico
dr.	Retained earnings	1,044		Cable Systems Mexico
dr.	Profit allocable to non-controlling interests	110		Group
cr.	Foreign currency translation		233	Cable Systems Mexico
cr.	Non-controlling interests		933	Group

c) Cable Systems Holding

		Carrying amount	20%
	Share capital	112	22
+	Retained earnings (carried forward)	11,656	2,331
+	Retained earnings (current period)	7,931	1,586
+	Foreign currency translation	(1,243)	(249)
=	Equity	18,456	3,690

Journal entry				Company
dr.	Share capital	22		Cable Systems Mexico
dr.	Retained earnings	2,331		Cable Systems Mexico
dr.	Profit allocable to non-controlling interests	1,586		Group
cr.	Foreign currency translation		249	Cable Systems Mexico
cr.	Non-controlling interests		3,690	Group

d) Flexing Cables Holding

While Flexing Cables is a wholly-owned subsidiary, no allocation of equity to non-controlling interests applies.

- Step 2b – Equity elimination, group

The elimination of investments in subsidiaries against equity demands a consideration of items of the original journal entries as foreign currency translations as well as purchase price allocations are involved. The general principle of charging any residual amounts to non-controlling interests will not be changed.

a) Cable Systems USA

		Carrying amount	64%
	Share capital	1,121	718
+	Retained earnings (carried forward)	45,616	
+	Retained earnings (current period)	14,764	
+	Foreign currency translation	(4,948)	
=	Equity	56,553	

Journal entry			Company
dr.	Share capital	718	Cable Systems USA
cr.	Investment in subsidiaries	581	Cable Systems Holding
cr.	Non-controlling interests	137	Group

b) Cable Systems Mexico

	Carrying amount	60%
Share capital	31	18
+ Retained earnings (carried forward)	2,611	
+ Retained earnings (current period)	275	
+ Foreign currency translation	(583)	
= Equity	2,334	

Journal entry			Company
dr.	Share capital	18	Cable Systems Mexico
cr.	Investment in subsidiaries	14	Cable Systems Holding
cr.	Non-controlling interests	4	Group

c) Cable Systems Holding

	Carrying amount	80%
Share capital	112	90
+ Retained earnings (carried forward)	11,656	
+ Retained earnings (current period)	7,931	
+ Foreign currency translation	(1,243)	
= Equity	18,456	

Journal entry			Company
dr.	Share capital	90	Cable Systems Holding
dr.	Retained earnings	7,003	Cable Systems Holding
dr.	Foreign currency translations	34	Group
dr.	Goodwill	4,873	Group
cr.	Investment in subsidiaries	12,000	Flexing Cables Holding

d) Flexing Cables Holding

Because Flexing Cables Holding is a wholly-owned subsidiary, of the ultimate parent, Flexing Cables SE, the consolidation journal entries are the same for both consolidation methods. They can be executed unchanged.

Journal entry			Company
dr.	Share capital	100	Flexing Cables Holding group
cr.	Investment in subsidiaries	100	Flexing Cables SE
dr.	Capital reserves	3,000	Flexing Cables Holding group
cr.	Retained earnings	3,000	Group

e) Other allocations

All consolidation tasks so far focused on the elimination of the carrying amount of investments in subsidiaries and the allocation to non-controlling interests. To ensure that non-controlling interests are properly stated, foreign currency allocations to / from non-controlling interests are necessary. These allocations are initiated by foreign currency translations of subgroups.

Allocations of foreign currency translations by Cable Systems Holding relate to the translation of investments in subsidiaries (in Cables Systems Holding). An amount of 253 k EUR (80% of 316 k EUR) has to stay in the group. The following journal entry adjusts non-controlling interests.

	USD	FX-rate (USD/EUR)	EUR	Group 80%	Non-controlling interests 20%
1.1.2000	800	0.8920	897		
− 31.12.2013	800	1.3766	581		
= Difference	0		316	252	63

Journal entry				Company
dr.	Non-controlling interests	252		Group
cr.	Foreign currency translations		252	Group

The allocation that relates to Flexing Cables Holding has to reflect foreign currency effects of non-controlling interests of Cable Systems Holding. An amount of 8 k EUR (20% of 42 k EUR) has to be adjusted.

Journal entry				Company
dr.	Non-controlling interests	8		Group
cr.	Foreign currency translations		8	Group

Just to verify that the recorded journal entries of this example reconcile with the recorded journal entries of the other example, the non-controlling interest account will be reviewed in detail. This account is of particular interests as all residual amounts of all equity consolidations are charged against this account.

dr.	Non-controlling interests			cr.
Cable Systems Holding, foreign currency translation adjustment	252	Cable Systems USA, non-controlling interests	20,360	
Flexing Cables Holding, foreign currency translation adjustment	8	Cable Systems Mexico, non-controlling interests	933	
		Cable Systems Holding, non-controlling interests	3,690	
		Cable Systems USA, group	137	
		Cable Systems Mexico, group	4	
	260		25,124	
		Balance	**24,864**	

This account presents the same balance as if the chain consolidation had been applied.

Having executed the simultaneous consolidation, the adjusted balance sheet is presented below.[82] This balance sheet is an incomplete snapshot of the consolidated balance sheet of the ultimate group while the figures of Flexing Cables SE are missing and the equity of Flexing Cables Holding is still present. Nevertheless, this balance sheet is identical to the one presented for the chain consolidation.

---

[82] We name the balance sheet "adjusted balance sheet", because equity is consolidated only while all other items are aggregated.

Adjusted IFRS Statement of financial position Flexing Cables Holding group as of 31.12.2013 (in k EUR)			
Assets		**Liabilities & Equity**	
Cash at hand & bank	39,102	Trade payables	12,554
Trade receivables	33,550	Tax liabilities	3,773
Inventory	10,628	Prepayments	146
Other assets	5,308	Accruals	2,328
Current assets	**88,588**	Loans	1,565
		Other payables	5,673
Property, plant & equipment	39,711	**Current liabilities**	**26,039**
Intangible assets	5,376		
Financial investments	17,952	Loans	13,117
Goodwill	4,873	Provisions	495
Non-current assets	**67,912**	Pensions	1,416
		Non-current liabilities	**15,028**
		Share capital	100
		Capital reserves	3,000
		Retained earnings	91,752
		Foreign currency translation	(4,284)
		Non-controlling interests	24,864
		Equity	**115,432**
Total assets	**156,500**	**Total liabilities & equity**	**156,500**

9.3.3. Special cases

Structures of groups are often driven by local (national) and tax requirements to achieve certain legal effects or to minimize tax expenses of the group. Such requirements may result in complicated multi-level group structures that are often arranged cross-border. These structures are subject to consolidation like each other structure. Due to their special arrangements, a sophisticated application of consolidation techniques is demanded. To solve these arrangements, a simultaneous consolidation is often applied because chain consolidations do not always support such group structures.

There are plenty of configurations of groups available where dedicated problems arise on how to handle them. The most important group structures are discussed here by using a default configuration of each group structure.

- Multi-parent structures

   A typical case is a multi-parent structure. Such structures are sometimes required to establish subsidiaries in new countries where dedicated commercial rules regarding ownership structures exist. Multi-parent structures are often combined with non-controlling interests if local partners have to be integrated.

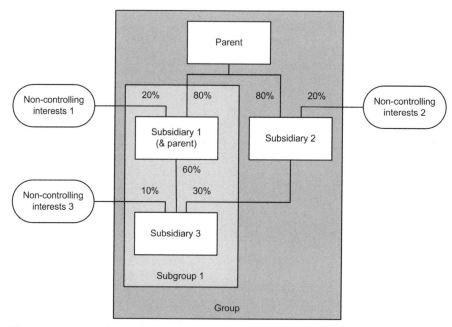

Fig. F-49   Multi-parent structures in groups

From the ultimate parent's perspective, there are several ways to subsidiary 3 that need to be considered for consolidation purposes. Consolidating such a structure by applying a chain consolidation would be possible but subject to additional adjustments. The preparation of consolidated financial statements of the subgroup 1 could be executed without any issues or serious problems. The shares of the external party and the affiliated company (subsidiary 2 that holds interests in subsidiary 3) are presented as non-controlling interests. The ultimate parent has to reverse the presentation as non-controlling interests of subsidiary 3 while – from a group's perspective – the profit of all subsidiaries is a regular element of the profit & loss statement of the group. Furthermore, subsidiary 2 will record its share of subsidiary 2's profits as financial income due to the application requirement of equity accounting. This reversal, as well as any related adjustments due to the recording of subsidiary 2, will result in a set of accounting tasks at group level to properly reflect the profits of subsidiary 3.

Therefore, the consolidation of such a structure by applying a simultaneous consolidation is the more elegant way as extensive adjustments can be avoided.

a) Calculation using series

The determination of the share of the ultimate parent and all external parties in the group's subsidiaries should be arranged in a matrix where the columns represent the subsidiaries and the rows the parents and external parties. For each parent–subsidiary combination, the ways from the parent to the subsidiary have to be determined and the effective share of the ultimate parent in the subsidiary has to be calculated using the previously explained formula. The following series are the standard series for multi-parent structures of groups.

Shareholder	Share in		
	Subsidiary 1 (S1)	Subsidiary 2 (S2)	Subsidiary 3 (S3)
Parent (P)	Ways to S1: • Direct: 80% Total: 80%	Ways to S2: • Direct: 80% Total: 80%	Ways to S3: • P → S1 → S3: 80% * 60% = 48% • P → S2 → S3: 80% * 30% = 24% Total: 72%
Non-controlling interests 1 (NCI1)	Ways to S1: • Direct: 20% Total: 20%		Ways to S3: • NCI1 → S1 → S3: 20% * 60% = 12% Total: 12%
Non-controlling interests 2 (NCI2)		Ways to S2: Direct: 20% Total: 20%	Ways to S3: • NCI2 → S2 → S3: 20% * 30% = 6% Total: 6%
Non-controlling interests 3			Ways to S3: • Direct: 10% Total: 10%

Tab. F-19   Series for multi-parent structures

b) Calculation using matrices

The determination of the share of the ultimate parent and all external parties in the group's subsidiaries will deliver the same results if using matrices. An analysis of the dependencies between the ultimate parent and the subsidiaries is not necessary. A simple use of the shares held in a subsidiary is sufficient. The following matrix represents a typical multi-parent structure.

$$
\text{Matrix} =
\begin{pmatrix}
0 & 0.8 & 0.8 & 0 & 0 & 0 & 0 \\
0 & 0 & 0 & 0.6 & 0 & 0 & 0 \\
0 & 0 & 0 & 0.3 & 0 & 0 & 0 \\
0 & 0 & 0 & 0 & 0 & 0 & 0 \\
0 & 0.2 & 0 & 0 & 0 & 0 & 0 \\
0 & 0 & 0.2 & 0 & 0 & 0 & 0 \\
0 & 0 & 0 & 0.1 & 0 & 0 & 0
\end{pmatrix}
$$

Tab. F-20   Initial matrix for multi-parent structures

$$
\text{Matrix}^{-1} = \begin{pmatrix}
0 & 0.8 & 0.8 & 0.72 & 0 & 0 & 0 \\
0 & 0 & 0 & 0.6 & 0 & 0 & 0 \\
0 & 0 & 0 & 0.3 & 0 & 0 & 0 \\
0 & 0 & 0 & 0 & 0 & 0 & 0 \\
0 & 0.2 & 0 & 0.12 & 0 & 0 & 0 \\
0 & 0 & 0.2 & 0.06 & 0 & 0 & 0 \\
0 & 0 & 0 & 0.1 & 0 & 0 & 0
\end{pmatrix}
$$

Tab. F-21 Inverse matrix for multi-parent structures

The equity consolidation can be executed by a set of journal entries typical for multi-parent structures. The parent will record the following consolidation journal entries:

Journal entries			Company	Comment
dr.	Equity		Subsidiary 1	0.8 * carrying amount
dr.	Goodwill		Group	Residual amount
	cr.	Investment in subsidiaries	Parent	Carrying amount
dr.	Equity		Subsidiary 2	0.8 * carrying amount
dr.	Goodwill		Group	Residual amount
	cr.	Investment in subsidiaries	Parent	Carrying amount
dr.	Equity		Subsidiary 3	0.72 * carrying amount
dr.	Goodwill		Group	Residual amount
	cr.	Investment in subsidiaries	Subsidiary 1	0.8 * carrying amount
	cr.	Investment in subsidiaries	Subsidiary 2	0.8 * carrying amount

The journal entries for non-controlling interests are:

Journal entries			Company	Comment
dr.	Equity		Subsidiary 1	0.2 * carrying amount
	cr.	Non-controlling interests	Group	NCI1
dr.	Equity		Subsidiary 3	0.12 * carrying amount
	cr.	Non-controlling interests	Group	NCI1
	cr.	Investment in subsidiaries	Subsidiary 1	0.2 * carrying amount
dr.	Equity		Subsidiary 2	0.2 * carrying amount
	cr.	Non-controlling interests	Group	NCI2
dr.	Equity		Subsidiary 3	0.06 * carrying amount
	cr.	Non-controlling interests	Group	NCI2
	cr.	Investment in subsidiaries	Subsidiary 1	0.2 * carrying amount
dr.	Equity		Subsidiary 3	0.1 * carrying amount
	cr.	Non-controlling interests	Group	NCI3

- Reciprocal interests

    Reciprocal interests exist every time a subsidiary has an interest in another subsidiary, and vice versa. Such a group structure is one of the most complicated set-ups in a group. These structures are even more complicated if non-controlling interests exist. The intentions to establish these structures vary:

    - Tax benefits by using tax laws and regulation of different states;
    - Creating additional shareholder value;
    - Legal and commercial aspects relating to acquisitions;
    - Acquisition of groups that have relationships to the acquirer;
    - Cross-border transactions.

    There may be other reasons for establishing such structures.

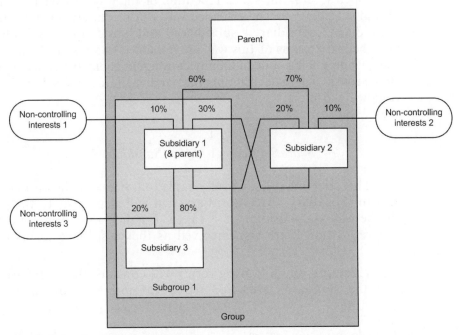

Fig. F-50 Reciprocal interests

The challenge to consolidate a group with such a structure is to solve the reciprocal interest. At this stage, the application of a chain consolidation does not really make sense. This will leave a simultaneous consolidation as the preferred solution method. As already discussed, the share of the ultimate parent in each subsidiary has to be calculated using either series or matrices.

a) Calculation using series

The determination of the share of the ultimate parent and all external parties in the group's subsidiaries should again be arranged in a matrix where the columns represent the subsidiaries and the rows the parents and external parties. For each parent–subsidiary combination, the ways from the parent to the subsidiary have to be determined and the effective share of the ultimate parent in the subsidiary has to be calculated using the previously explained formula. The calculation will be complicated due to the reciprocal behaviour. Some ways from the ultimate parent to the lowest subsidiary (subsidiary 3) will result in a dilemma that needs to be solved.

The way from the parent to subsidiary 3 will go via subsidiary 1, subsidiary 2 and subsidiary 1 to subsidiary 3. This way can be even expanded several times by a repetition of the ways between subsidiary 1 and subsidiary 2. The extended way will be parent via subsidiary 1, subsidiary 2, subsidiary 1, subsidiary 2 and subsidiary 1 to subsidiary 3. Further expansions of this way are possible. As a result, the described behaviour will result in an infinite convergent geometric series. This has to be considered in determining the parent's share in subsidiary 3 by the following formula:

$$\frac{1}{1-\left(Share\,Subsidiary\,1 * Share\,Subsidiary\,2\right)}$$

This dilemma does not only apply to the way of the ultimate parent to subsidiary 3 via subsidiary 1, it will also apply to the parent if the way via subsidiary 2 is taken. Furthermore, non-controlling interest 1 and 2 are also involved as they also have to take these ways.

Therefore, the following series will consider these effects. They are the standard series for reciprocal interests for such group structures.

b) Calculation using matrices

The determination of the share of the ultimate parent and all external parties in the group's subsidiaries will deliver the same results when using matrices. An analysis of the dependencies between the ultimate parent and the subsidiaries is not necessary. A simple use of the shares held in a subsidiary is sufficient. The following matrix represents a typical reciprocal interest structure.

Shareholder	Share in		
	Subsidiary 1 (S1)	Subsidiary 2 (S2)	Subsidiary 3
Parent (P)	Ways to S1: • Direct: 60% • P → S2 → S1 and ⌐S1S2: 70% * 30% / (1 - 20% * 30%) = 22.4% • P → S1 → S2 → S1 and ⌐S1S2: 60% * 20% * 30% / (1 - 20% * 30%) = 3.8% Total: 86.2%	Ways to S2: • Direct: 70% • P → S1 → S2 and ⌐S1S2: 60% * 20% / (1 - 20% * 30%) = 12.8% • P → S2 → S1 → S2 and ⌐S1S2: 70% * 30% * 20% / (1 - 20% * 30%) = 4.4% Total: 87.2%	Ways to S3: • P → S2 → S1 → S3 and ⌐S1S2: 70% * 30% * 80% / (1 - 20% * 30%) = 17.8% • P → S1 → S3: 60% * 80% = 48% • P → S1 → S2 → S1 → S3 and ⌐S1S2: 60% * 20% * 30% * 80% / (1 - 20% * 30%) = 3.1% Total: 68.9%
Non-controlling interests 1 (NCI1)	Ways to S1: • Direct: 10% • NCI1 → S1 → S2 → S1 and ⌐S1S2: 10% * 20% * 30% / (1 - 20% * 30%) = 0.6% Total: 10.6%	Ways to S2: NCI1 → S1 → S2 and ⌐S1S2: 10% * 20% / (1 - 20% * 30%) = 2.1% Total: 2.1%	Ways to S3: • NCI1 → S1 → S3: 10% * 80% = 8% • NCI1 → S1 → S2 → S1 → S3 and ⌐S1S2: 10% * 20% * 30% * 80% / (1 - 20% * 30%) = 0.5% Total: 8.5%
Non-controlling interests 2 (NCI2)	Ways to S1: • NCI2 → S2 → S1 and ⌐S1S2: 10% * 30% / (1 - 20% * 30%) = 3.2% Total: 3.2%	Ways to S2: • Direct: 10% • NCI2 → S2 → S1 → S2 and ⌐S1S2: 10% * 30% * 20% / (1 - 20% * 30%) = 0.6% Total: 10.6%	Ways to S3: • NCI2 → S2 → S1 → S3 and ⌐S1S2: 10% * 30% * 80% / (1 - 20% * 30%) = 2.6% Total: 2.6%
Non-controlling interests 3 (NCI3)			Ways to S3: Direct: 20% Total: 20%

Tab. F-22 Series for reciprocal interests

$$
\text{Matrix} =
\begin{pmatrix}
0 & 0.6 & 0.7 & 0 & 0 & 0 & 0 \\
0 & 0 & 0.2 & 0.8 & 0 & 0 & 0 \\
0 & 0.3 & 0 & 0 & 0 & 0 & 0 \\
0 & 0 & 0 & 0 & 0 & 0 & 0 \\
0 & 0.1 & 0 & 0 & 0 & 0 & 0 \\
0 & 0 & 0.1 & 0 & 0 & 0 & 0 \\
0 & 0 & 0 & 0.2 & 0 & 0 & 0
\end{pmatrix}
$$

Tab. F-23   Initial matrix for reciprocal interests

$$
\text{Matrix}^{-1} =
\begin{pmatrix}
0 & 0.862 & 0.872 & 0.689 & 0 & 0 & 0 \\
0 & 0.064 & 0.213 & 0.851 & 0 & 0 & 0 \\
0 & 0.319 & 0.064 & 0.255 & 0 & 0 & 0 \\
0 & 0 & 0 & 0 & 0 & 0 & 0 \\
0 & 0.106 & 0.021 & 0.085 & 0 & 0 & 0 \\
0 & 0.032 & 0.106 & 0.026 & 0 & 0 & 0 \\
0 & 0 & 0 & 0.2 & 0 & 0 & 0
\end{pmatrix}
$$

Tab. F-24   Inverse matrix for reciprocal interests

The equity consolidation can be executed by a set of journal entries typical for reciprocal interests. The parent will record the following consolidation journal entries:

Journal entry			Company	Comment
dr.		Equity	Subsidiary 1	0.862 * carrying amount
dr.		Goodwill	Group	Residual amount
	cr.	Investment in subsidiaries	Parent	0,6 * carrying amount
dr.		Equity	Subsidiary 2	0.872 * carrying amount
dr.		Goodwill	Group	Residual amount
	cr.	Investment in subsidiaries	Parent	0,7 * carrying amount
dr.		Equity	Subsidiary 3	0.689 * carrying amount
dr.		Goodwill	Group	Residual amount
	cr.	Investment in subsidiaries	Subsidiary 1	0.862 * carrying amount

The journal entries for non-controlling interests are:

Journal entries		Company	Comment
dr.	Equity	Subsidiary 1	0.106 * carrying amount
cr.	Non-controlling interests	Group	NCI1
dr.	Equity	Subsidiary 2	0.021 * carrying amount
cr.	Non-controlling interests	Group	NCI1
cr.	Investment in subsidiaries	Subsidiary 1	0.1 * carrying amount
dr.	Equity	Subsidiary 3	0.085 * carrying amount
cr.	Non-controlling interests	Group	NCI1
cr.	Investment in subsidiaries	Subsidiary 1	0.106 * carrying amount
dr.	Equity	Subsidiary 2	0.106 * carrying amount
cr.	Non-controlling interests	Group	NCI2
dr.	Equity	Subsidiary 1	0.032 * carrying amount
cr.	Non-controlling interests	Group	NCI2
cr.	Investment in subsidiaries	Subsidiary 2	0.3 * carrying amount
dr.	Equity	Subsidiary 3	0.026 * carrying amount
cr.	Non-controlling interests	Group	NCI2
cr.	Investment in subsidiaries	Subsidiary 1	0.032 * carrying amount
dr.	Equity	Subsidiary 3	0.2 * carrying amount
cr.	Non-controlling interests	Group	NCI3

- Associates as parents

    Group structures may have configurations where shares in an associate are held by the parent and the associate belongs to another group. If that associate holds an investment in a company that is again part of the group, issues arise on how to treat such configurations. The following figure provides an illustration of such a group structure.

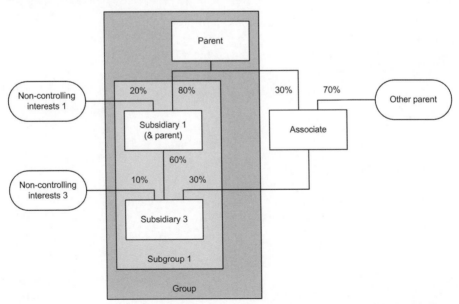

Fig. F-51 Associates as parents

The first question that arises is how to treat the investment in the associate and the investment of the associate. While IFRS 10.B86 requires to prepare consolidated financial statements by considering subsidiaries only, the associate itself is not part of the group and therefore not subject to consolidation. A consideration in the determination of the ultimate parent's in the subsidiary is therefore not appropriate.

Both the ultimate parent and the associate will record the profits of their investment in associates by applying the equity method. Because of this application the associate will record a portion of the profit of the subsidiary as financial income in its profit & loss statement. The ultimate parent will execute the same transaction and record its portion of the profit of the subsidiary as financial income in its separate profit & loss statement. Such a recording is consistent with the accounting rules for associates, as defined in *IAS 28 – Investments in Associates and Joint Ventures*. Nevertheless, this accounting will result in a strange presentation from a group's perspective. Some profits of the subsidiary will be part of the group's regular profit while other profits will be presented as financial income in the consolidated financial statement of income. This behaviour reflects the application of accounting standards even if a different presentation from an economic view would be more appropriate. Such presentation would demand a reclassification of a defined profit from financial income (of the parent's share in the associate which reflects the associate's share in the subsidiary) towards the regular profit of the group.

G ASSOCIATED COMPANIES

About this chapter:

Investments in associated companies do not constitute control; however, there is significant influence. Therefore, associated companies are treated differently than subsidiaries in preparing consolidated financial statements. While subsidiaries are subject to a full consolidation, associated companies are included in consolidated financial statement through the equity method.

This chapter discusses all aspects of associated companies and their treatment for group purposes. This includes not only general characteristics but also the initial and subsequent consolidations, treatment of losses and other specific items attributable to associated companies. The focus is on the consolidation process, including all effects that arise due to the status of the associated company.

1. BASICS

Associated companies or associates are a common occurrence in groups. The accounting for associates is defined in *IAS 28 – Investments in Associates and Joint Ventures*. This standard has to be applied for the accounting of associates in separate and consolidated financial statements.

IAS 28.3 defines associates as entities in which investors have significant influence. Significant influence is assumed if the investor holds more 20% but less than 50% of the voting rights in an associate. The investment in the associate can be held either directly or indirectly, through subsidiaries or trustees. They can also be split across other subsidiaries. To determine if a company of the group classifies as an associate, all investments held by the parent, and any subsidiaries, have to be considered in total. While voting rights and significant influence are the only criteria in determining an associate, the legal form of the associate is irrelevant.

Voting rights are usually based on the shares held in the associate expanded by potential voting rights. Convertible instruments like call options, warrants, debt or equity instruments – that can be exchanged for ordinary shares upon exercise – have to be considered in determining effective voting rights, provided that the instruments are currently exercisable. "Currently exercisable" means that the instruments are currently convertible and not convertible at or before a future date. Furthermore, they do not depend on the occurrence of a future event. The determination of voting rights has to consider other facts:

- Convertible instruments of other parties;
- Exercising conditions;
- Other contractual arrangements.

Not to be considered are management intentions and financial ability when exercising these voting rights.

Significant influence is expressed by the influence an investor has on the associate. This influence can be realized in several ways:

- Representation on the board of directors;
- Representation on another governing body;
- Participation in policy-making processes including decisions about dividends or other distributions;
- Material transactions between the associate and its shareholders;
- Interchange of managerial personnel;
- Provision for essential technical information.

Such influence might also be given even if there is an investment of less than 20%. In these cases, the financial investment has to be treated as if it were from an associate. Consequently, an equity consolidation is necessary. To comply with IAS 28, evidence is required that proves the existence of significant influence. Evidence can be based on written agreements with other shareholders, minutes of meetings of the board of directors, supporting papers on material transactions, employment contracts of staff or similar documents.

Even if an appropriate share in an associate is owned, there may be reasons that prevent significant influence. Typical examples of such reasons are contractual arrangements with other shareholders. Again, evidence is required supported by an appropriate documentation.

There is no significant influence if there is no power to participate in financial and operating policy decisions.

1.1. The equity method

In general, the application of an accounting of associates is mandatory for all IFRS preparers. The method to be applied is the equity method. This is an accounting method in which all changes in the equity of the associate are reflected by an appropriate accounting at shareholder level of any investments in the associate's account. In other words, the investment in the parent's associates account mirrors the proportionate share the parent has in the associate. This share changes each time profits are recorded, dividends paid or transactions require a recording in other comprehensive income. The starting point is always the initial purchase on an investment in the associate.

The carrying amount of investments in associates can be calculated by the following scheme:

	Carrying amount as of the acquisition date
+	Proportionate share of the profit or loss of the period
−	Proportionate dividends declared and paid
+/−	Proportionate changes in other comprehensive income
=	Carrying amount as of the end of the period

Tab. G-1 Calculation of the carrying amount of an investment in associates

Only a few preparers are **exempt** from applying the equity method. The definition of exemptions as outlined in IAS 28.17 is identical to the exemptions of IFRS 10.4.[1] In addition to these exemptions, venture capital organizations, mutual funds, unit trusts, and similar organizations can opt to account for the investments in associates by either applying the equity method or by measuring them at fair value through profit & loss in accordance with IFRS 9. Due to these alternatives, an investment can be treated either as an associate or a financial investment.

1.2. Preparation of and presentation in financial statements

The presentation of investments in associates is different compared to investments in subsidiaries. Associates are not considered in the same way as subsidiaries are considered due to the application of the equity method. A full

---

[1] See chapter B -2 on page 35 for the list of exemptions.

consolidation like it is applied for subsidiaries is therefore inappropriate. Instead, associates are presented as investments in associates and consequently as financial assets, based on their carrying amounts. The carrying amount accumulates all effects that arise from the application of the equity method. The application of the equity method is also called a "one-line consolidation". Depending on the intention why investments in associates are held, a presentation as non-current assets is mandatory. The presentation as current assets is applicable only in cases where the associate is classified as held for sale.

Due to the one-line consolidation, investments in associates are presented in separate financial statements of the parent and in consolidated financial statements of the group as one line item in the statement of financial position only. Nevertheless, the accounting requirements to record interests in associates differ between separate and consolidated financial statements so that the carrying amounts differ as well. This will demand separate views and handlings on associates.

The accounting of investments in associates in **separate financial statements** is defined in IAS 28.44 in combination with IAS 27.10. According to the available options, the investment in an associate can be recognized either at cost or in accordance with IFRS 9. This treatment is identical to all types of investment.

- If a recognition at cost occurs, all costs that relate to the acquisition of investments in associates have to be considered. These costs consist of the purchase price as well as any acquisition-related costs. While the standard itself is silent about purchase prices, the elements that qualify as a consideration transferred according to IFRS 3 can be considered in determining the purchase price. Typical elements are cash, shares, equity instruments, options, bonds, exchange of assets and many other items.[2] The purchase price can consist of a combination of one or more of these elements.

  The accounting requirements to consider all costs are often identical to taxation rules. Therefore, no differences should exist between the carrying amount of investments in associates and its tax base.

- A recognition in accordance with IFRS 9 is based on fair values that have to be assumed. The fair value requirement is derived from IFRS 9.4.1.4. as an investment in an associate is always a financial asset and from IFRS 9.5.1.1. that demands a fair value measurement plus transaction costs. Therefore, acquisition-related costs have to be considered. The subsequent measurement of investments in associates is also measured a fair value.

While all costs that relate to the acquisition of investments in associates have to be considered, **acquisition-related costs** cannot be ignored. In addition to the requirements of IFRS 3, which prohibit the consideration of acquisition-related costs and demand expensing instead, the consideration of acquisition-related costs for associate acquisitions is mandatory. As there is substantially no difference between IAS 28 (2003) and IAS 28 (2011), the old definitions can be used in determining acquisition-related costs. The IFRIC has decided on the

---

[2] See chapter E -3.3 on page 143 for a full list of purchase price elements and their measurements.

consideration of acquisition-related costs as an agenda rejection as of July 2009 pointing out that the cost definition of IAS 28.11 (2003) also covers acquisition-related costs. Therefore, acquisition-related costs are an integral part of the initial costs of investments in associates covering all types of cost. Typical examples of acquisition-related costs are:

- Fees for lawyers, auditors and advisors;
- Costs of due diligence;
- Appraisals as part of purchase price allocations;
- Registering costs;
- Administrative costs;
- Staff bonus payments;
- Other internal costs directly allocable to an acquisition;
- Financing costs.

Other than the accounting of investments in associates in separate financial statements, the accounting of investments in associates in **consolidated financial statements** includes activities that are also common for subsidiaries. Due to the one-entity theory, the carrying amount of investments in associates includes the net assets of the associate adjusted by consolidation tasks and other group transactions. The underlying rationale that applies to subsidiaries has also to apply to associates:

- Application of the accounting standards of the parent (so the group's accounting policies) as demanded by IAS 28.35. This requirement is identical to the requirements subsidiaries have to follow.
- The associate has to prepare its financial statements at the same balance sheet date than the parent to comply with the uniform balance sheet day within the group. A deviation of the group's balance sheet date may occur if the associate is preparing its financial statements at a different date. In such situations, IAS 28.33 requires the use of the last available financial statements of the associate adjusted by significant transactions, if the balance sheet date does not deviate more than three months from the group's reporting date. Otherwise, the preparation of interim financial statements for consolidation issues is required. If the preparation of an interim closure can be prepared is questionable as the associate cannot be forced to prepare such a statement. Either a support of the associate or agreements between shareholders is required to ensure a preparation of interim closures. The requirements are identical to the requirements for subsidiaries.
- Adjustments, reclassification and allocation of balance sheet items of the associate to comply with the accounting set-up of the group.
- Conversion between accounting standards if the subsidiary is applying different accounting standards than the group standards.

Due to these underlying rationales, the recognition of a carrying amount of investments in associates in consolidated financial statements is neither comparable with the purchase price nor with any fair value.

The presentation of investments in associates in consolidated financial statements demands application of the equity method. As the equity method is used just for the consolidation of equity, other consolidations are required as well: particularly, debt consolidation and an elimination of unrealized profit.

2. CONSOLIDATION TECHNIQUES

The one entity theory of consolidated financial statements applies to all companies of the group that are subject to consolidation, therefore also to associates. Even if the associate is considered by a one-line-consolidation in consolidated financial statements, it has to run through consolidation processes like any other company. In fact, an associate follows the same lifecycle as a subsidiary. Due to the lifecycle of an associate, various consolidation tasks are necessary:

- An initial consolidation upon the acquisition of an interest (shares or similar equity instruments) in the associate;
- A subsequent consolidation at the end of each period;
- A deconsolidation upon the disposal (sale) of all interests in an associate.

In addition to these standard consolidation tasks, other variables need to be considered: Interest in associates can be acquired in more than one step and also sold in small portions.[3]

2.1. Initial consolidation

The initial consolidation is a mandatory task when interests in associates are acquired by the parent company. At the acquisition date, a significant influence will be established that requires the application of the equity method. The **acquisition** can be realized in one or several steps.

- Acquisition in one step
  Acquiring a sufficient interest in a company in one step will immediately establish a significant influence at the acquisition date. The parent will recognize the acquisition at the acquisition date.

  <u>Journal entry</u>
  dr.   Investments in associates
       cr.   Liabilities

At group level, the initial consolidation will be triggered.

- Acquisition in several steps
  Step acquisitions increase the interest in a company over a period of time. Significant influence is deferred to that moment where the 20% threshold has been passed. This will also defer the application of the equity method. Interests in a company are presented as financial investments up to the moment where significant influence is given. At this stage a

---

[3] See chapter I - on page 501 for the accounting of step acquisitions and partial disposals.

reclassification to investments in associates is required in the parent's accounts in addition to the last acquisition.

Journal entry		Comment
dr.	Investments in associates	
dr.	Other comprehensive income	Valuation adjustment
cr.	Financial investments	These are the investments in associates of previous acquisitions

The accounting for step acquisitions is discussed in detail in chapter I -3.1.[4]

In addition to the establishment of significant influence by acquisitions, significant influence can be established by the **sale of interests** in companies so that a subsidiary or a joint venture becomes an associate.[5]

Having established a significant influence, the initial consolidation at group level has to be executed which requires several **tasks** to be executed. IAS 28.26 to 28.39 include some general guidelines about the accounting of associates but is otherwise silent about dedicated requirements to and the application of the initial consolidation. Therefore, it is acceptable to apply the methods used for the initial consolidation of subsidiaries as specified in IFRS3 in a modified way for the initial accounting of associates at group level. An efficient initial consolidation can be realized in five steps starting with the accounting of the investments in associates by the parent. As investments in one associate can be held by various companies of the group, all investments have to be added to determine the total acquisition costs in an associate.

Step	Task
1)	Recording of the acquisition of interest in associates by the parent
2)	Execution of a purchase price allocation
3)	Consolidation
4)	Search and accounting for any pre-existing relationships
5)	Execution of impairment tests

Tab. G-2   Steps of the initial consolidation of associates

While acquisition of shares in the associate may occur within the period, the **timing** of all tasks of the initial consolidation requires special attention. The initial consolidation has to occur at the acquisition date to reflect the conditions as of that date. It is also needed to estimate the profit or loss achieved from the acquisition date to the end of the period by considering the contribution of the profit or loss realized by the associate. From a purely technical point of view, the initial consolidation does not necessarily need to be executed

---

[4] See page 506.
[5] See chapter I -4 on page 527 regarding the accounting in such situations.

at the acquisition date. It can also be executed during the remaining period or at the end of the period. All three alternatives are available and will generate the same results. This is more or less an administration issue of the corporate centre when associates are due for an initial consolidation. In practice, a general tendency when initial consolidations are executed is not observed. Some companies initially consolidate an associate during the period when the effects of the purchase price allocation are known, others initially consolidate the associate at the end of the period. Both practices consider the situation as of the acquisition date. Initial consolidations as of the acquisition date or shortly after the acquisition date are executed only in business combinations that have clear and simple structures without any significant non-accounted assets acquired or liabilities assumed. Depending on the timing chosen, tasks and activities of the initial consolidation will change. Even if they do, the final result will always be the same:

- At acquisition date
  The carrying amounts of all assets and liabilities have to be adjusted to reflect their fair values. Differences are recorded in an off-site calculation by applying the equity method as of the acquisition date.

- During the period
  Tasks performed to execute the initial consolidation during the period are substantially the same tasks than the one as of the acquisition date. The only difference from the first option is its time offset. This is more or less an administration issue and does not impact the initial accounting of the associate.

- At end of the period
  At the end of the period, two transactions fall together: the initial consolidation and its first subsequent consolidation. For consolidation purposes, effects as of the acquisition date as well as all changes during the remaining period have to be considered. This can be realized by an execution of the initial consolidation as of the acquisition date and a development of all adjustments towards the end of the period.

A similar handling like the initial accounting of subsidiaries at the end of the period is not appropriate due to the different consolidation methods applied.

2.1.1. Purchase price allocation

Due to the one entity theory and the presentation of assets and liabilities at group level instead of investments in companies, the acquisition costs have to be allocated to all assets acquired and liabilities assumed on a pro-rata base. This allocation has to occur in two steps that interact. The required purchase price allocation focuses on the associate in total. All accounted and non-accounted assets and liabilities have to be considered and measured based on the assumption of a full acquisition of the associate. This is subject to the purchase price allocation.

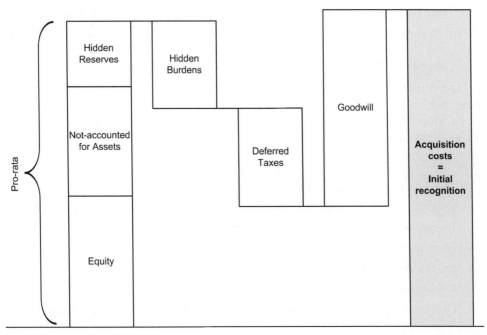

Fig. G-1 Purchase price allocation scheme of the initial consolidation of associates

The next step is the "drill-down" to the conditions of the associate by considering the absolute stake in the associate. This step can be realized as one part of the consolidation.

The purchase price allocation is subject to a set of **requirements**, estimates, assumptions and rules. They have to be considered in executing the purchase price allocation:

- Carrying amount
  The carrying amount of the investment in associates acts as the ceiling of all assets and liabilities.

- Accounting policies
  The underlying assumptions in preparing consolidated financial statements apply to all companies that are subject to consolidation and therefore also to associates.[6] IAS 28.26 explicitly confirms their application. By the application of group accounting policies adjustments are necessary if the local accounting of the associate differs from the parent's accounting policies upon the initial recognition.

---

[6] Remember: Uniform balance sheet day, accounting policies of the parent and functional currency of the parent.

- Pro-rata base

    The purchase price allocation has to consider all assets acquired and liabilities assumed on a pro-rata basis based on net assets. This requires the consideration of liabilities and any other contingencies.

The purchase price allocation required for associates can be based on a purchase price allocation as demanded by IFRS 3 adjusted by associate specific issues. **Steps** to be executed for the purchase price allocation of an investment in an associate can be realized in the following order:

Step	Task
1)	Definition of the acquisition date
2)	Determination of the acquisition costs
3)	Identification and measurement of hidden reserves and burdens
4)	Identification and measurement of non-accounted assets and liabilities
5)	Pro rata recognition of hidden reserves and burdens
6)	Pro rata recognition of non-accounted assets and liabilities
7)	Calculation of deferred tax assets and liabilities on identified and recognized assets acquired and liabilities assumed
8)	Calculation of the difference between the purchase price and assets acquired and liabilities assumed
9)	In case of negative differences: Optional reassessment of assets and liabilities[7]

Tab. G-3 Steps of the purchase price allocation of associates

The first step of a traditional purchase price allocation, the identification of an acquirer, is obsolete as control is not given due to significant influence only.

The determination of the **acquisition date** is more or less a formal step if a simple acquisition takes place by the parent as the acquirer. In such cases, the acquisition date is the date of the closing when the purchase agreement is signed by the parties involved. Nevertheless, the acquisition date may be deferred if the acquisition of the interests in an associate is subject to further tasks to be fulfilled by the parent as the acquirer. The following topics should be considered in determining the acquisition date:

- Approvals

    Approvals by governing bodies of the parent (as the acquirer) might be necessary that may defer the closing of the acquisition.

- Defined conditions

    The purchase agreement may include defined conditions that have to be met or satisfied before the ownership of the shares in the associate can be transferred and the corresponding accounting is possible.

---

[7] This step is mandatory for subsidiaries but not explicit required by IAS 38.32b. To ensure any assets and liabilities are measured accordingly, it is recommended to apply this step.

- Antitrust or competition authorities

    Acquisitions are often subject to approvals by antitrust or competition authorities. This may also occur to acquisitions of associates even if the probability is low that an acquisition of a significant influence of an associate will result in a market dominance. Missing or pending approvals of antitrust or competition authorities do not defer the acquisition date as there are no dedicated accounting rules to follow. Nevertheless decisions by these authorities have the power to reverse the acquisition at a later stage.

- Other facts and circumstances

    There may be other facts and circumstances that postpone the transfer and accounting for investments in associates. An individual check is necessary for each of these items.

The determination of the **acquisition costs** is the next step of the modified purchase price allocation. The acquisitions costs – often seen as the purchase price only – are usually based on the recording in the parent's accounts. The purchase price itself can consist of various elements depending on the agreement between the purchasing and selling party.[8] Nevertheless, three issues have to be considered when determining the purchase price: Allocation of interests across the group, acquisition-related costs[9] and alternatives in accounting of variable elements.

Investments in an associate can be held by other companies of the group and not necessarily by the parent only. These investments can even be established before the subsidiary carrying these investments became a subsidiary. So there is a step acquisition that requires an appropriate accounting of the purchase price. Furthermore all investments in the associate have to be summed-up to determine the total purchase price. Investments in associates held by other associates or joint ventures are not considered in determining acquisition costs and the significant influence according to IAS 28.27.

An unsolved item in IAS 28 is the consideration of variable elements based on contingent considerations as part of the purchase price. This regulatory gap can be filled by two alternatives, the application of IFRS 3 and an accounting that considers only reliable purchase price elements. If the application of IFRS 3 is in favour, variable elements like earn-out options have to be considered by their present values based on the expected future cash outflows and discounted by an adequate interest rate that reflects market conditions. Any differences between the expected and the actual payments are recorded in future periods through profit & loss. The concept of recognizing considerations (either transferred or to be transferred) is different to using pure purchase prices; it is valid to account for those acquisition costs if the purchase price can be reliably estimated. But

---

[8] See chapter E 3.3 on page 143 regarding examples of purchase price elements. Even if these elements relate to the acquisition of subsidiaries, they can be applied to associates as well.

[9] Other than IFRS 3 that prohibit a capitalization of acquisition-related costs, these costs can be considered as part of the purchase price for interests in associates.

only reliable payments should be considered. Any additional payments in future periods will result in an adjustment of the acquisition costs in those periods where payments are due. The adjustments will be recorded through other comprehensive income. Other solutions are acceptable if they provide a reasonable accounting basis.

The next two stages of modified purchase price allocation are of particular interest. They deal with the identification, measurement and presentation of **hidden reserves and burdens** and **non-accounted assets and liabilities**. The rules and requirements of IFRS 3 can be applied without any adjustments or modifications.[10] Therefore, the measurement of all discussed items depends on the accounting systems used and the accounting policies of the parent. These technical issues can easily be handled, but a bigger concern is the access to detailed information. Details are required for measuring the assets and liabilities from an acquirer's perspective and are needed to calculate the step-up amounts to be considered in the purchase price allocation. All details of assets and liabilities are with the associate, but full access is not always given. If the associate does not cooperate, only rough estimations can be made of necessary adjustments. They are derived from available general information, from financial statements of the associate and from secondary sources. A typical example of a secondary source is the estimation of property value. The value can be derived from public registers and statistical information either directly or indirectly or by using an appraiser's services. Even if the associate will not provide sufficient detail, sources are available that may help in determining fair values. All tasks are subject to cost-benefit considerations. Due to the accounting of the pro-rata net assets of the associate in one line only and the contribution of the associate to the total group performance, not every detail will be required in determining fair values of all assets and liabilities of the subsidiary.

Hidden reserves and burdens relate to assets and liabilities already recorded by the associate. They will be established according to the fair value requirements of the underlying assets and liabilities and the development of market values compared with the book values in the accounts of the associate.

A more complex issue is identification and measurement of non-accounted assets and (contingent) liabilities. This follows the same procedures and methods that are applied for subsidiaries. The biggest issue regarding the accounting of non-accounted assets and liabilities is the identification and measurement of these items. This requires – again – access to information from the associate.

> Try to ensure that an access to the information required is given by adding appropriate paragraphs to the sales and purchase agreement.

Having identified and measured all assets acquired and liabilities assumed on a pro-rata base, the calculation of any **deferred tax assets and liabilities** is the next

---

[10] See chapter E -3.4 on page 152 regarding all details of the accounting of these assets and liabilities.

step. The calculation follows the ordinary procedures for any deferred items; there are no special procedures for purchase price allocations of associates in place.

> If it is not possible to get tax information (in particular the tax base of all assets and liabilities) from the associate, the accounting for deferred tax asset and liabilities should be limited to non-accounted assets and liabilities and to hidden reserves and burdens. The tax base of these items can be assumed to be zero.[11]

While the identification, measurement and presentation is similar to acquisitions of subsidiaries by applying IFRS 3, the calculation schemes in determining goodwill for associates and subsidiaries are comparable. The difference between both schemes is the pro-rata consideration of all items when measuring goodwill of associates.

	IAS 28, pro-rata based on participation quota (associate)	IFRS 3 calculation scheme, partial goodwill (subsidiary)
	Carrying amount of investment in associates (acquisition costs)	Consideration transferred
−	Pro-rata carrying amount of net assets of the associate	Carrying amount of net assets of the associate
−	Pro-rata hidden reserves	Hidden reserves
+	Pro-rata hidden burdens	Hidden burdens
−	Pro-rata non-accounted assets	Non-accounted assets
+	Pro-rata contingent liabilities	Contingent liabilities
+/−	Pro-rata deferred taxes	Deferred taxes
=	Goodwill	Goodwill

Tab. G-4 Comparison of calculation schemes between subsidiary and associate

Similar to an ordinary purchase price allocation, positive and negative differences may result in the calculation. Dedicated accounting guidance is given in both cases.

- Positive difference
  A positive difference is always treated as goodwill according to IAS 28.32a. No separate presentation of goodwill occurs due to the one-line consolidation. Goodwill will be maintained in an auxiliary calculation. While this goodwill is kept separately from goodwill of subsidiaries, it is subject to an impairment test as demanded by IAS 28.40 to 28.42.

- Negative difference
  A negative difference does not impact the carrying amount of the investment in an associate. Instead, the negative difference is immediately recorded as income in profit & loss according to 28.32b. A reassessment in case of a negative difference as demanded by IFRS 3.32 for subsidiaries is not required for associates. Nevertheless such a task is recommended.

---

[11] In most purchase price allocations, the tax base of these items is often zero. Therefore, it is appropriate to assume such a tax base in these cases.

Example

To expand its operations in the Netherlands, Flexing Cables acquired an interest of 24.9% in Kijba, a Dutch retailer specialized in complex cabling solutions. The acquisition was negotiated between April and June, resulting in a sale and purchase agreement that was signed by the end of June. It gave Flexing Cables the right to benefit from Kijba's profits as of 1 July. The acquisition was accompanied by a set of detailed regulations demanded by Flexing Cables and the owner of Kijba, a publicly listed investment company:

- The purchase price consisted of a fixed amount and a variable component.
- The fixed amount of 2,000 k EUR was payable seven days after the signature of the sales and purchasing agreement.
- The variable amount that was based on the performance of Kijba in the fiscal years 2013 and 2014 was calculated on the realized EBIT. It would be ten percent of the cumulative EBIT of both periods but should not exceed 2,500 k EUR. The amount was due 10 days after the approval of Kijba's 2014 financial statements but not later than 1.7.2015.
- The official acquirer was Flexing Cables Holding.
- Flexing Cables would be granted the unconditional right to inspect the accounts of Kijba regarding the determination of the realized EBIT.
- The acquisition base was the financial statement as of 30.6.2013 listed in Annex 1 to the sales and purchasing agreement:

IFRS Statement of financial position Kijba as of 30.6.2013 (in k EUR)

Assets		Liabilities & Equity	
Cash at hand & bank	1,209	Trade payables	2,144
Trade receivables	4,965	Tax liabilities	1,482
Inventory	4,731	Prepayments	35
Other assets	1,338	Accruals	1,530
Current assets	**12,243**	Loans	600
		Other payables	1,078
		Current liabilities	**6,869**
Property, plant & equipment	2,695		
Intangible assets	855	Loans	1,400
Non-current assets	**3,550**	Pensions	267
		Deferred tax liabilities	120
		Non-current liabilities	**1,787**
		Share capital	100
		Retained earnings	7,037
		Equity	**7,137**
Total assets	**15,793**	**Total liabilities & equity**	**15,793**

IFRS Statement of income Kijba as of 30.6.2013 (k EUR)		IFRS Statement of income Kijba as of 30.6.2013 (k EUR)	
Revenues	20,968	Revenues	20,968
Changes in inventory		Cost of goods sold	(15,433)
Work performed and capitalized			
Other income	131	**Gross margin**	5,535
Total performance	**21,099**		
		Sales & distribution expenses	(1,127)
Raw materials and consumables	(7,685)	Administration expenses	(921)
Employee expenses	(4,275)	Research & development expenses	
Depreciation and amortization expenses	(416)	Other income	131
Other expenses	(5,183)	Other expenses	(78)
Operating profit	**3,540**	**Operating profit**	**3,540**
Finance expenses	(27)	Finance expenses	(27)
Profit before tax	**3,513**	**Profit before tax**	**3,513**
Income tax expenses	(896)	Income tax expenses	(896)
Net profit for the period	**2,617**	**Net profit for the period**	**2,617**

In addition to the sales and purchasing agreement, management of Flexing Cables expected either the following assumptions or information:

- Acquisition related costs would be 5% of the total (gross) acquisition price. This amount would cover all external costs for consultants, auditors, fees, taxes due and other items. No invoices had arrived at the company so far.
- Management expected that the variable portion would be paid in full.
- The interest rate used for discounting purposes was 6.2%.
- Due diligence had already uncovered issues that were relevant for the purchase price allocation: The company had a solid customer base that ensured substantial income in future periods; for the fiscal year 2013, Kijba's order intake was performing better than expected.
- The historical business relationship with the company was minor. There were currently no trading relationships or outstanding balances.
- The fixed amount was paid directly on the acquisition date by wire transfer.

Using the information of the due diligence as one aspect for the purchase price allocation, the purchase price allocation may be simplified even if it has to follow the same guideline as other purchase price allocations as outlined in IFRS 3.[12] Accordingly, the acquirer was Flexing Cables SE as the ultimate parent even if the acquisition

---

[12] See chapter E -3 on page 136 et seq. for details of purchase price allocations.

was realized by Flexing Cables Holding. The total purchase price was 4,442 k EUR as determined in the following calculation:

	Fixed amount	2,000
+	Present value variable amount	2,217
	(Present value of 2,500 k EUR, discounted over a period of 2 years using a discount rate of 6.2%)	
+	Acquisition related costs	225
	(5% of 4,500 k EUR)	
=	Purchase price	4,442

Assets acquired and liabilities assumed during the purchase price allocation consisted of the following items:

Item	Explanation and calculation	Amount
Property	Due to the attractive place where Kijba is residing, a strong increase in property, particularly the land could be observed over the past years. Based on the report of an independent appraiser, the property is 280 k EUR more worth than recorded in Kijba's accounts.	280
Customer orders	While Kijba's order intake is better than expected, the company now has an order backlog of 120 days. Based on cost accounting details, these orders will generate a net profit of 1,730 k EUR before taxation.	1,730
Customer base	Depending on historical customer order patterns, the appraiser has determined a fair value of 5,220 k EUR for the customer base. It is expected that the customer base will have a useful life of eight years.	5,220
Deferred tax liabilities	As confirmed in the tax due diligence, the above listed items are not subject to taxation. Accordingly, their tax base is zero. Applying Kijba's individual tax rate of 25.5%, the deferred tax liability to be recognized is 1,844 k EUR.	(1,844)

Considering all previously mentioned circumstances, goodwill amounting to 1,323 k EUR and allocable to Flexing Cables was calculated based on the following scheme:

			Pro-rata value (24.9%)
	Consideration transferred	4,442	
	IFRS net assets of the company as of 1.7.2013	7,137	1,777
+	Hidden reserves property	280	70
+	Customer orders	1,730	431
+	Customer base	5,220	1,300
−	Deferred tax liabilities	(1,844)	(459)
=	Total assets Kijba	12,523	
−	Assets allocable to the Flexing Cables 24.9% of 12,523	3,118	
=	Goodwill attributable to Flexing Cables	1,323	

2.1.2. Consolidations

The output of the purchase price allocation, the remeasured assets and liabilities, are used for consolidation purposes. The carrying amount of the investment in associates is replaced by the equity value that consists of the proportionate book value of equity of the associate, any adjustments to the carrying amount of assets and liabilities of the associate, non-accounted assets as well as the related deferred tax assets and liabilities and goodwill as the residual value. While some of these items are subject to depreciation and further adjustments, the equity value has to be developed in an auxiliary calculation. The initial items of the auxiliary calculation are derived from the following allocation of the equity value:

	Goodwill
+	Pro-rata hidden reserves
−	Pro-rata hidden burdens
+	Pro-rata non-accounted assets
−	Pro-rata contingent liabilities
+/−	Pro-rata deferred taxes
+	Proportionate book value of investment
=	Equity value (equals acquisition costs, the purchase price)

Tab. G-5   Initial allocation of the auxiliary calculation scheme

At the acquisition date when the initial consolidation has to be executed, the equity value is identical to the carrying amount of the investment in associates as recorded by the parent (and other companies of the group if appropriate). This is the only date where both balances are identical. Due to the application of accounting rules on the items implied in the equity value, both balances will develop in different ways. Consequently, the auxiliary calculation has to be advanced in subsequent periods to determine the carrying amounts of all items in subsequent periods.

Description	Goodwill	Hidden reserves & burdens	Non-accounted assets	Deferred taxation	Book value Investment	Equity value
Balance @ initial recognition	yyy	yyy	yyy	yyy	yyy	yyy
Other comprehensive income					yyy	yyy
Impairments	yyy					yyy
Depreciation & Amortization			yyy	yyy		yyy
Up- & downstream transactions					yyy	yyy
Unrealized profits					yyy	yyy
Profits					yyy	yyy
Dividends					yyy	yyy
Balance @ end of period	zzz	zzz	zzz	zzz	zzz	zzz

Fig. G-2   Auxiliary calculation for the investments in associates

As the equity value at group level and the acquisition costs of parent level are identical in case of a positive difference at the initial consolidation, no journal entries are necessary. Only in the case of a negative difference is a journal entry required that represents the negative difference. Thus, the carrying amount at group level deviates from the carrying amount by the parent.

<u>Journal entry</u>

dr.   Investments in associates
    cr.   Other earnings

Additional journal entries can arise from the consideration of other tasks.

Example

This example continues the example of the previous chapter!

As the acquisition of shares in Kijba was realized through Flexing Cables Holding, the acquisition had to be accounted for by Flexing Cables Holding. The following journal entries needed to be recorded:

<u>Journal entries</u>				<u>Comment</u>
dr.	Investment in associates	2,000		Fixed amount
cr.	Bank		2,000	
dr.	Investment in associates	2,217		Present value of variable amount
cr.	Liabilities, long-term		2,217	

Acquisition related costs are usually recorded as they occur. If not all invoices that relate to acquisition related costs arrived at the end of the period, outstanding invoices are accrued as a standard closing procedure. For this example we will accrue all expected invoices on acquisition related costs.

<u>Journal entry</u>			<u>Comment</u>
dr.	Investment in associates	225	Acquisition related costs
cr.	Accruals	225	

Having performed all tasks by Flexing Cables Holding, the auxiliary calculation could be prepared:

Item	Goodwill	Hidden reserves	Non-accounted assets	Deferred taxation	Book value investment	Equity value
Balance @ initial recognition	1,323	70	1,731	(459)	1,777	4,442
Depreciation & amortization						
Unrealized profits						
Profits						
• Cumulative						
• Current period						
Dividends						
Balance @ end of period						

No further tasks were necessary at the acquisition date.

2.1.3. Issues around the initial consolidation

The initial consolidation can include other tasks that arise from application of other IFRS or the business environment the associates and the group operate in. Therefore, the purchase price allocation for an associate has to be executed in the same exhaustive manner as for a subsidiary. The most important items that often arise in acquisitions of associates are pre-existing relationships and impairment tests.

Pre-existing relationships with associates are similar to those with subsidiaries. The associate is engaged in business transactions with the parent or other companies of the group. The detection of such transactions is similar to subsidiaries. The same tools and methods can be applied.[13] The accounting of pre-existing relationships can also be aligned to the accounting for subsidiaries unless intercompany transactions are involved that will result in the recording of assets and liabilities that include unrecognized profit. Depending on the type of transactions (either upstream or downstream), accounting methods of subsequent consolidations have to be used.[14]

The execution of **impairment tests** is a standard procedure as demanded by IAS 28.40. The test itself has to be executed even upon initial consolidation.[15]

Another issue is the way the parent establishes a significant influence in the subsidiary. It can be established either directly by the parent or indirectly through a subsidiary the parent controls. In such cases, an **aggregation of interest** in the associate is required to execute the purchase price allocation.

An **associate that is a parent** of a group has to prepare consolidated financial statements. These consolidated financial statements then have to be used in executing the purchase price allocation as demanded by IAS 28.27.

2.2. Subsequent consolidation

Subsequent to investment in an associate, consolidation is required at the end of each period, to properly reflect the investment in consolidated financial statements. The consolidation includes the same areas that an ordinary consolidation has to consider:

- Equity;
- Income and expenses (in limited portions only);
- Unrealized profits.

As with level II and level III items of the purchase price allocation need to be adjusted.

2.2.1 Adjustments

"Adjustments" is a generic term for all those corrections necessary to comply with group requirements. So, they cover a set of tasks like those which are

---

[13] See chapter E -6.5 on page 231 for details on pre-existing relationships.
[14] See the following chapter for details.
[15] See chapter G -4 on page 470 regarding its details and options.

valid in level I to level III adjustments of subsidiaries. While subsidiary adjustments are accounted for directly for each balance sheet item, adjustments for associates are used for off-balance sheet purposes, particularly for the calculation and derivation of any adjusted financial statements of the associate. This may lead to different profits compared to the one the associate has declared, and may be distributed. Adjustments are always executed before any consolidation takes place.

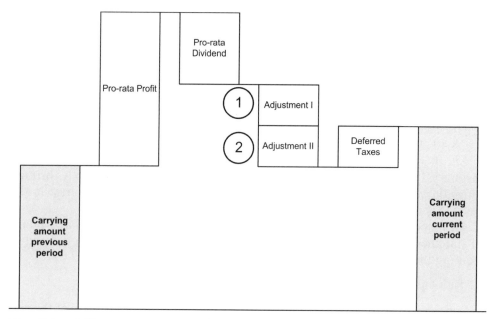

Fig. G-3 Adjustments as part of the subsequent consolidation of an associated company

In general, adjustments always relate to one or more of the following **categories**:

- Uniform accounting policies
    IAS 28.35 refers to the application of uniform accounting policies for like transactions and events in similar circumstances. Therefore, the application of group accounting policies is mandatory. If different accounting policies are applied by the associate, IAS 28.36 requires the adjustment of accounting policies of the associate as if the associate had prepared its financial statements by using group accounting policies. This will result more or less in a restatement of the financial statements of the associate. Consequently, a restatement of the profit of the associate might result if the restatements have a profit impact.
    Adjustments that relate to the application of uniform accounting policies are comparable to level I and level II adjustments of subsidiaries.

- Purchase price allocations

    Purchase price allocations have a direct relationship with accounting policies. The measurement is based on group accounting policies and covers those assets and liabilities that are identified, measured and recorded upon the initial consolidation the associate does not record or is prohibited from recording. All assets and liabilities that are part of the equity value have to be advanced to the carrying amount at the end of the period. This requires the following adjustments:

    - Tangible and intangible assets that have a definite useful life have to be depreciated or amortized;
    - Intangible assets and goodwill are subject to an impairment test that may result in the recording of an impairment loss;
    - Contingent liabilities and provisions have to be checked whether the conditions of recording such items is still given. If such conditions are not given, the carrying amounts have to be released. If conditions are given, liabilities and provisions may be subject to recording compound interests.

    Adjustments that relate to purchase price allocations are comparable to level III adjustments of subsidiaries.

Example

This example continues the example of the previous chapter!

In preparing the equity value of the investment in Kijba for consolidated financial statements of Flexing Cables, all assets and liabilities recognized during the initial consolidation had to be advanced to the reporting date. A dedicated investigation of each component initially recognized was necessary:

Item	Explanation and calculation	Adjustment amount
Property	There are no indicators present that the property will lose its value. Accordingly, no action required.	0
Customer orders	All orders are fully executed. The order backlog now includes only orders that arrived after the acquisition date. The carrying amount representing customer orders has to be expensed.	431
Customer base	A regular amortization over the useful life of eight years is necessary. The amount that relates to the fiscal year is: 483 k EUR / 8 years * 6/12	81
Deferred tax liabilities	Deferred tax liabilities have to be adjusted according to the new balances of the above-mentioned items. New deferred tax liability: $(70 + 1,218) \times 25.5\% = 315$	(144)

In addition to the adjustments of all components, an impairment test was executed. The test did not demand a recording of an impairment loss. Accordingly, the balance of the equity value that is attributable to goodwill was left unchanged.

- Balance sheet dates

    IAS 28.33 and 28.34 require the application of the balance sheet date of the parent. Therefore, the most recent available financial statements of the associate have to be considered in preparing consolidated financial statements. If the associate prepares its financial statements at a different balance sheet date: either, interim financial statements have to be prepared; or, the financial statements have to be adjusted by material transactions if the balance sheet date of the associate deviates by less than three months from the balance sheet date of the parent.

    Adjustments that relate to different balance sheet dates are comparable to level II adjustments.

- Foreign currencies

    If the associate is a foreign operation that uses a currency different from the functional currency of the parent, its financial statements have to be translated into the functional currency of the parent. The translation mechanism and its accounting are based on the accounting rules of *IAS 21 – The Effects of Changes in Foreign Exchange Rates*.[16]

Adjustments may impact the equity value and the profit & loss the associate has declared. Therefore, two types of adjustment exist that require dedicated handling. They are accounted for at group level.

- Adjustments type I

    These are recorded through profit & loss. They will directly influence the profit the parent is recognizing in its consolidated financial statements. Adjustments that qualify for recognition through profit & loss relate to all of the above listed categories. The only exception to this list is a foreign operation that has to translate its financial statements into the group's currency.

    Typical examples of adjustments that refer to this type are:

    - Depreciation on hidden reserves and identified assets of the initial recognition (the results of the purchase price allocation);
    - Adjustment of hidden burdens;
    - Deferred taxes on depreciation and adjustments;
    - Alignment of the associate's balance sheet items to the group's accounting policies.

    All adjustments are calculated on a proportionate basis unless a different handling is applicable.

- Adjustments type II

    These are recorded through other comprehensive income. This applies always to foreign currency translations (from the functional currency of

---

[16] See chapter K -1 on page 632 regarding details.

the associate to the reporting currency of the group) as demanded by IAS 21.39c. Adjustments that relate to this type are also defined in IAS 28.10. Accordingly, the following transactions always qualify as type II adjustments:

- Revaluations and adjustments of property, plant & equipment that are recorded by the associated company through other comprehensive income. They have to be recorded at group level as well to reflect the capital portion in the associated company.
- Changes in the participation quota that result from any under- or over-proportionate increases or decreases in capital.
- Tax effects resulting from the above described transactions.

Due to the variety of effects that impact the carrying amount in an associate, a tracking of all effects in an off-side documentation is recommended.

> Reconcile all effects in your documentation with the carrying amount in your accounts.

The above adjustments relate to the ordinary business of the associate. Nevertheless, there might be events and circumstances out of the scope of the parent that also require adjustment: typical examples are changes in the capital of the associate without any changes of the status of the associate that require adjustments in the carrying amount.[17]

Example

This example continues the example of the previous chapter!

Finalizing the carrying amount of investments in associates and to consolidate Kijba, all adjustments had to be recorded. While all adjustments related to the performance of Kijba and its carrying amount for group purposes, all journal entries had to be recorded at group level using that account where the profit of Kijba was recorded.

Journal entries				Comment
dr.	Share of profits of associates	483		Customer orders
	cr. Investment in associates		483	
dr.	Share of profits of associates	81		Amortization customer base
	cr. Investment in associates		81	
dr.	Investment in associates	123		Release of deferred tax liability that
	cr. Share of profits of associates		123	relates to customer orders
dr.	Investment in associates	21		Adjustment of deferred tax liability
	cr. Share of profits of associates		21	that relates to customer base

---

[17] See chapter I -5.2 on page 548 regarding such cases.

Recording all adjustments, the auxiliary calculation required an update:

Item	Goodwill	Hidden reserves	Non-accounted assets	Deferred taxation	Book value investment	Equity value
Balance @ initial recognition	1,323	70	1,731	(459)	1,777	4,442
Depreciation & amortization			(81)	21		(420)
			(483)	123		
Unrealized profits						
Profits						
• Cumulative						
• Current period						
Dividends						
Balance @ end of period						

2.2.2. *Equity accounting*

The core activity of the parent for each associate is equity accounting – recording profits and dividends. The recording will take place at parent level in its separate financial statements. It will be passed through at group level for consolidation purposes.

The equity methods demand that earnings and dividends of the associate are recorded pro-rata according to the investment in the associate. Pro-rata recognition is the default practice. However, if there are arrangements that allocate profits on different bases, profit recognition always follows these arrangements. Dividends distributed by the associate to shareholders also consider such arrangements. They have to be recorded as received.

Earnings recognized and dividends paid by the associate may occur in different periods and not necessarily in the same subsequent period.

Example

This example continues the example of the previous chapter!

At the end of the period, Kijba reported the following financial statement for its fiscal year:

IFRS Statement of financial position Kijba as of 31.12.2013 (in k EUR)

Assets		Liabilities & Equity	
Cash at hand & bank	3,550	Trade payables	2,373
Trade receivables	5,658	Tax liabilities	1,531
Inventory	5,063	Prepayments	21
Other assets	1,674	Accruals	1,211
Current assets	**15,945**	Loans	1,200
		Other payables	1,184
Property, plant & equipment	2,469	**Current liabilities**	**7,520**
Intangible assets	665		
Non-current assets	**3,134**	Loans	200

		Pensions		271
		Deferred taxes		114
		Non-current liabilities		**585**
		Share capital		100
		Retained earnings		10,874
		Equity		**10,974**
Total assets	**19,079**	**Total liabilities & equity**		**19,079**

IFRS Statement of income Kijba as of 31.12.2013 (k EUR)			IFRS Statement of income Kijba as of 31.12.2013 (k EUR)	
Revenues	45,485		Revenues	45,485
Changes in inventory			Cost of goods sold	(32,418)
Work performed and capitalized				
Other income	276		**Gross margin**	**13,067**
Total performance	**45,761**			
			Sales & distribution expenses	(2,463)
Raw materials and consumables	(16,634)		Administration expenses	(2,004)
Employee expenses	(8,812)		Research & development expenses	(4,200)
Depreciation and amortization expenses	(832)		Other income	276
Other expenses	(10,776)		Other expenses	(159)
Operating profit	**8,717**		**Operating profit**	**8,717**
Finance expenses	(53)		Finance expenses	(53)
Profit before tax	**8,664**		**Profit before tax**	**8,664**
Income tax expenses	(2,210)		Income tax expenses	(2,210)
Net profit for the period	**6,454**		**Net profit for the period**	**6,454**

Two tasks were required to determine Flexing Cables Holding's profit:

- Profit calculation group period

    While Flexing Cables Holding was entitled to benefit from Kijba's profits as of the acquisition date onwards only, the profit for the period of the acquisition date to the end of the period had to be determined first.

	Net profit for the period	6,454
−	Net profit from the beginning of the period to the acquisition date	2,617
=	Considerable net profit	3,837

- Profit calculation to be recorded

    The profit Flexing Cables Holding was entitled to benefit from was calculated by multiplying the considerable net profit with the participation quota:

3,837 k EUR * 24.9% = 955 k EUR. This amount would be recorded by Flexing Cables Holding applying the following journal entry:

Journal entry

| dr. | Investment in associates | 955 | |
| cr. | Share of profits of associates | | 955 |

By using this journal entry, the carrying amount of investments in associates would be increased. The entry would be forwarded to group level via the aggregated trial balance. Accordingly, an update of the auxiliary calculation was necessary.

Item	Goodwill	Hidden reserves	Non-accounted assets	Deferred taxation	Book value investment	Equity value
Balance @ initial recognition	1,323	70	1,731	(459)	1,777	4,442
Depreciation & amortization			(81)	21		(420)
			(483)	123		
Unrealized profits						
Profits						
• Cumulative						
• Current period					955	955
Dividends						
Balance @ end of period	1,323	70	1,167	(315)	2,732	4,977

2.2.3 Debt consolidation

The handling of intercompany transactions that involve associates are not explicitly defined in IAS 28. Due to referencing in IAS 28.26 to IFRS 10, consolidation procedures required by IFRS 10 can be applied to intercompany transactions with associates as well. Intercompany transactions always have a debt element (receivable or payable) and a profit element. Equity methods only focus on profit and its recording and are silent about the handling of the related debts. This relates particularly to any receivables and payables a group company has against the associate. The general consensus regarding the handling of debt is a presentation of these receivables and payables group companies have against the associate as if they relate to an unassociated third party. This consensus is based on two considerations:

- Due to the status of the associate, the associate is not part of the group that is subject to elimination of all group-internal transactions. Therefore, all receivables and payables of the group companies against the associate are presented as receivables and payables against third parties.
- As investments in associates are financial assets, presentation rules for financial assets have to be considered which are defined in *IAS 32 – Financial Instruments: Presentation*. While the conditions required by IAS 32.42 are not met, offsetting – and therefore elimination (from a group's perspective) – is not appropriate.

2.2.4. *Unrealized profits and income & expense consolidations*

The handling of intercompany transactions also impacts the profit of the associate and the group. Therefore, adjustments of profits may be necessary in dedicated cases where the profit is unrealized. Adjustments can relate to the profit of the group and / or profits the associate has generated. Which profit (associate or group) is involved depends on the underlying transaction. Due to the status of the associate, the profit elimination of an associate differs from the elimination practice of a subsidiary. As a general rule, the profit elimination always follows its type:

- Associate
  Profits of the associate are eliminated against the carrying amount of investments in associates. The base journal entry has to be used in all cases.

  Journal entry
  dr.   Share of profits of associates
       cr.   Investments in associates

- Group
  The elimination of profits of the group varies depending on the nature of the underlying transaction. As a general rule, the consolidated balance sheet and the consolidated profit & loss statement of the group are used to eliminate any unrealized profits. Journal entries are based on these transactions.

IAS 28 has a few dedicated instructions on selected transactions impacting profit that involve the profit & loss statement. It is silent about any other dedicated consolidation instructions. Therefore, the referencing of IAS 28.26 to IFRS 10 can be used again to decide about any consolidation tasks that relate to **income & expense consolidation**. It is up to the discretion of management to decide on the extent of consolidation tasks in such situations. Nevertheless, if a decision is made about the application of consolidation tasks on income & expenses, consistent application of that accounting policy is demanded.

Other than the consolidation of income and expenses is the treatment of **unrealized profits**. There are dedicated accounting rules that deal with unrealized profits (IAS 28.28, IFRS 10.B86c): their elimination is demanded for all relevant assets. Those are in particular:

- Non-current assets like fixed assets and intangible assets;
- Inventory;
- Foundation of associates using non-current assets as contributions in exchange for equity interests.

The elimination has to occur pro-rata based on the participation quota of the parent in the associate (with the exception for the foundation of associates, this has to occur in full). IAS 28.28 therefore differentiates between two transaction types: upstream and downstream transactions.

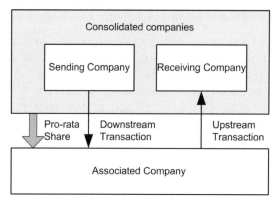

Fig. G-4 Upstream and downstream transactions

Intercompany transactions that deal with the sale of goods and assets require special attention if goods are not fully sold by the receiving company at the end of the period (so transactions for later sale). The result will be intercompany **inventories** with unrealized profits that are subject to consolidation. Depending on the location of inventories, an elimination has to occur either on inventory presented in consolidated financial statements if held by a subsidiary or on the investment in associates if held by the associate.

- Upstream

    In an upstream transaction, goods are delivered by the associate (the sending company) to any companies of the group that act as the receiving company. This will include the ultimate parent and any subsidiary of the group. In fact, the unrealized profit bearing inventory resides with the group.

    The elimination of unrealized profits requires knowledge about the implied profit that has to be disclosed by the associate. It is also influenced by the parent's portion in the associate. Special attention is required regarding the elimination entries. While the share of profit of the associate presented in the consolidated statement of income is a post-tax item, the elimination entry has to consider tax impacts on the profit of the associate. Therefore, the unrealized profit subject to elimination can be calculated in the following way:

Unrealized profit allocated in inventory
− Unrealized profit attributable to external party: $(1 - \text{investment rate}) \times$ Unrealized profit
= Unrealized profit attributable to group (subject to elimination)
− Deferred tax asset (Unrealized profit attributable to group $\times$ tax rate)
= Adjustment of share of profit of associate

Tab. G-6 Calculation of unrealized profit in upstream transactions

The elimination together with the tax adjustment can be recorded in one combined journal entry.

Journal entry
dr.   Deferred tax assets
dr.   Share of profit of the associate
    cr.   Inventory

The adjustment of the associate's profit is the preferred solution. Nevertheless, deviating opinions can be found in literature that prefer an adjustment of the carrying amount of investments in associates.

The elimination requires certain knowledge about the profit mark-up that is included in inventory. The elimination of unrealized profits is difficult to the realized one if the associated company does not provide sufficient information about the cost structure and their profits.

> Try to arrange reporting requirements the associated company has to fulfil upfront (e.g. as part of the shareholder contract or as shareholder resolutions).

* Downstream

    In downstream transactions, goods are delivered by companies of the group, acting as the sending company, to the associate which is acting as the receiving company. In this case, the unrealized profit-bearing inventory resides with the associate.

    The calculation of the amount to be eliminated is identical to the calculation of the upstream transaction.

	Unrealized profit allocated in associate
−	Unrealized profit attributable to external party: (1 − investment rate) × Unrealized profit
=	Unrealized profit attributable to group (subject to elimination)

Tab. G-7 Calculation of unrealized profit in downstream transactions

While the inventory is with the associate, the investment in associates account has to be adjusted instead of inventory. Furthermore, the unrealized profit has to be adjusted in the consolidated statement of income. The position where this adjustment is necessary depends on the type of P&L and the origin of the goods.[18]

Journal entry

dr.	Profit & loss	
	cr.	Investment in associates

There is a regulatory gap if the amount to be eliminated is higher than the carrying amount of the interest in the associate. IAS 28 is silent about the accounting in such cases offering no guidance. In practice, several solutions can be observed:

* No elimination
    An elimination of unrealized profit should not take place.[19]
* Deferred income / equity
    The amount that is subject to elimination is "parked" in a separate item, either as a component of equity or as a deferred income. The amount

---

[18] See chapter F -6 on page 310 regarding the accounting in such cases. The consolidation technique of the associate is identical to consolidation technique of a subsidiary.

[19] KPMG, Insights into IFRS, 2010/11

remains here until a profit is recorded on the investment in associates account. At that point, the "parked" amount is transferred to the investment in associate account. This transfer depends upon the parking amount in relationship to the profit recorded. Releasing this amount therefore can last several periods, if the inventory is still in stock.

The initial journal entry in this case would be:

Journal entry
dr.   Profit & loss
      cr.   Deferred income (or equity)

The transfer is realized using this journal entry:

Journal entry
dr.   Deferred income (or equity)
      cr.   Investment in associates

* Loss recording
   The elimination of unrealized profits follows the same logic as the recording of losses. The remaining carrying amount of investments in associates will be reduced to zero. Any unrealized profit left will be adjusted against financial commitments of the parent, recorded as a liability or simply documented without any accounting. This application is in line with the requirement of loss accounting according to IAS 28.39.[20] As this practice is in line with the accounting of losses, this solution should be the preferred.

The moment intercompany inventory is sold, a reversal has to be recorded. The reversal of the initial journal entry depends on the original journal entry.

Journal entry
dr.   Investment in associates
      cr.   Profit & loss

The elimination need of unrealized profits can also result from transactions for own use. If goods are sold by or to the associate that are capitalized as fixed or intangible **assets**, the handling of the elimination of unrealized profits is similar to that of the inventory, depending on the type of transaction (upstream or downstream).

* Upstream
   Upstream transactions require adjustments of fixed or intangible assets in the consolidated statement of income. Therefore, this transaction and its recording are identical to transactions of subsidiaries.[21]
   Journal entry for the elimination of unrealized profits:

Journal entry
dr.   Deferred tax assets
dr.   Share of profit of the associate
      cr.   Fixed assets / intangible assets

---

[20] See chapter G -3 on page 469 regarding the accounting.
[21] See chapters F -6 on page 310 and F -9.2 on page 380 regarding further details.

Journal entry for the subsequent adjustment of unrealized profits:

Journal entry
dr.   Fixed assets / intangible assets
    cr.   Depreciation expenses

* Downstream

    Downstream adjust the carrying amount of the investment in associates. The calculation of profit to be eliminated and the journal entries are similar to the ones dealing with inventory. There is a small exception for the release of unrealized profits as depreciation expense accounts have to be used.

    Journal entry
    dr.   Investment in associates
        cr.   Depreciation expenses

    The handling in case the unrealized profit exceeds the carrying amount of the investment in associates is identical to the handling of inventory.

A third area where unrealized profits can occur is the **foundation of an associate** by using non-monetary assets as the contribution of the parent. IAS 28.30 provides guidance regarding the treatment and accounting of unrealized profits in this situation.

> SIC 13 used to deal with these issues and was replaced by IAS 28 (rev. 2011).

The consolidation procedures described above are the only ones that are necessary to be performed. Any activities that deal with **sidestream** transactions (so business transactions between associated companies of the group) are out of scope of this standard. Therefore, the elimination of profits arising from business transactions between associates is not required. Furthermore, there are no additional consolidation tasks of earnings and expenses necessary due to the status of the associate.

Example

This example continues the example of the previous chapter!

As Kijba was a new sales channel for the Flexing Cables group, business activities had been started to transfer knowledge on Flexing Cables products and services to the Kijba staff. Furthermore, marketing campaigns had started to boost sales through this sales channel. To be deliverable, Kijba had ordered a set of standard products from Flexing Cables's production sites. At the end of the period, an amount of 524 k EUR of the inventory reported in the statement of financial position belonged to these ordered products.

While the inventory purchased from Flexing Cables's production sites represented a downstream transaction, an elimination of unrealized profits was required by applying the transfer pricing policies of Flexing Cables. These policies demanded application of an 8.2% profit mark-up on the carrying intercompany balance.[22] Accordingly, 43 k EUR (524 k EUR × 8.2%) had to be eliminated for unrealized profits, altering

---

[22] See example in chapter F -6.2.3 on page 332 regarding further details.

the carrying amount compared to the tax base, and recognizing a deferred tax asset of 11 k EUR (43 k EUR * 25.5%) as a consequence. Both subjects are considered by the following journal entries:

Journal entries

dr.		Revenue	43	
	cr.	Investment in associates		43
dr.		Investment in associates	11	
	cr.	Share of profit of the associate		11

Again, the auxiliary calculation requires an update.

Item	Goodwill	Hidden reserves	Non-accounted assets	Deferred taxation	Book value investment	Equity value
Balance @ initial recognition	1,323	70	1,731	(459)	1,777	4,442
Depreciation & amortization			(81)	21		(420)
			(483)	123		
Unrealized profits				11	(43)	(32)
Profits						
• Cumulative						
• Current period					955	955
Dividends						
Balance @ end of period	1,323	70	1,166	(326)	2,690	4,923

As there are no further transactions to be considered, an amount of 4,923k EUR represents the equity value of Kijba in the consolidated financial statement of Flexing Cables.

2.3. Disposals / Deconsolidation

Associates do not necessarily continue their status as an associate in the group throughout their entire life, there may be situations in which this will change. As a general rule, life as an associate ceases if the condition of IAS 28.22 are met. According to these definitions, the discontinued status will also result in a discontinued application of the equity method. There are three cases that qualify for a ceasing of the status of an associate:

• Acquisition of further interest in associates resulting in a change of control;[23]
• Partial sale of interest in associate;[24]
• Full disposal.

The partial sale of interests in an associate will trigger a change of the status only if the percentage of interests in the associate falls below the 20% threshold as defined in IAS 28.5.

---

[23] See chapter I -3.5 on page 515 regarding the accounting in such situations.
[24] See chapter I -4.1 on page 527 regarding the accounting in such situations.

Full disposal, of course, does not leave any interests in the associate. Such a disposal involves various levels where adjustments are necessary. Accordingly, the disposal has to be viewed from the parent's and the group's perspective. These views also reflect the development of the carrying amount of the investment in associates as the account will have different balances at parent and at group level.

2.3.1. The parent's view

The sale of all interests in an associate is a simple transaction to be executed in the accounts of the parent company. To ensure a proper profit, the proportionate share of the associate's profit and any dividend payments applicable to the parent have to be recorded upfront. The profit share has to cover the range from the beginning of the period to the disposal date. The following journal entries have to be applied for the preparation.

Journal entries		Comment
dr.	Investments in associates	Recording of the profit.
cr.	Share of profit of the associate	Can also be a debit in case of a loss situation.
dr.	Bank	Recording of the dividend.
cr.	Investments in associates	

The accounting of the disposal is similar to the sale of interests in subsidiaries where a gain or loss due to the sales transaction is recorded. At the purchase date, the interest in the associate has to be expensed. In parallel, the parent records earnings based on the agreed sales price. Earnings have to include any other contractual contribution in excess to cash to be received, measured by their fair values at the purchase date. Usually, a receivable will be recorded in the balance sheet until payment. If the contractual obligation includes variable elements, they are recorded based on the expected and discounted future cash flows using an appropriate discount rate that reflects the current market condition.

The gain or loss realized can be estimated by applying the following calculation:

	Proceeds from the sale of interests in associates
−	Carrying amount of the interests in associates
=	Realized gain / loss

Tab. G-8 Gain / loss of the sale of an associate, the parent's view

- Gain

    A gain due to the sale of a non-current asset is usually presented as other income or other earnings in the profit & loss statement.

Journal entry		Comment
dr.	Gain on sale of associate	Derecognition of investment which
cr.	Investments in associates	is a part of financial assets
dr.	Trade receivables (or other receivables)	Recognition of the sales transaction
cr.	Gain on sale of associate	

- Loss

    A loss due to the sale of a non-current asset is usually presented as other expenses in the profit & loss statement.

Journal entry		Comment
dr.	Loss on sale of associate	Derecognition of investment which
	cr. Investments in associates	is a part of financial assets
dr.	Accounts receivables (or other receivables)	Recognition of the sales transaction
	cr. Loss on sale of associate	

If expected cash flows that are based on variable elements deviate from the initial expected cash flows, an adjustment is required in the year the variable element becomes due for payment. In such a situation, an additional gain or loss has to be recorded. The journal entry to be executed is again subject to gains or losses.

- Gain

Journal entry		Comment
dr.	Cash	Payments exceed the initial expectation.
	cr. Accounts receivables (or other receivables)	
	cr. Gain on sale of associate	

- Loss

Journal entry		Comment
dr.	Cash	Payments fall below the initial expectation.
dr.	Loss on sale of associate	
	cr. Accounts receivables (or other receivables)	

The accounts "gain on sale of associate" and "loss on sale of associate" are to be disclosed in a separate line items according to IAS 1.82aa as the sale of interests in associates is a sale of financial assets. They are often part of the financial income and not disclosed as other earnings.

2.3.2. *The group's view*

A more sophisticated view of the sale of the interest in an associate is the group's view. The One-line consolidation could make identification of deconsolidation items easy. However, there are other items in consolidated financial statements that also need to be adjusted. These items are the subsequent result of the accounting for investments in associates. Compared to subsidiaries, items subject to adjustment exist at group-level only. Adjustments at other levels are not necessary.

The disposal includes a set of various activities; they do not exclusively relate to investment in associates. Some of the listed tasks may be obsolete depending on the current situation of the associate and its interaction with the group. The accounting of the disposal and its activities has to follow a dedicated **timing** to ensure that the contribution of the associate to the group's performance is properly recorded and presented.

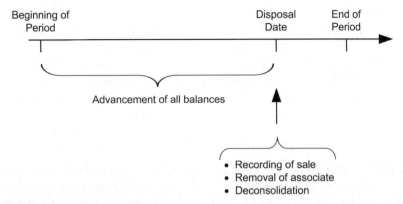

Fig. G-5 Timing of associate disposal

The timing, so the date of the sale, is important in determining the realized gain or loss of the sale of the associate. If the sale happened during the period, the "investment in associates"-account has to be advanced to the purchase date. The account has to be adjusted by all transactions as it would be done at the end of the period. Due to the one-line consolidation, the auxiliary calculation has to be advanced as well. The adjusted carrying amount of the investment in associates will then be used for the disposal.

The **preparation** and advancement of all balances consists of regular accounting activities: investment in associates and valuation tasks to be executed at the disposal date. Most of these adjustments are regular accounting activities at parent and group level, although there might be situations where not all adjustments are executed as demanded. Therefore, a check is required to ensure that the carrying amount of the investment in associates and all related items of the group are updated at the disposal date. The check and the related adjustment activities should consider the following issues that will arise:

- Advancement of the equity value of the investment in associates towards the disposal date

  This requires the application of the equity method, so the pro-rata recording of profits of and dividends declared and distributed by the associate. Furthermore, the advancement of the carrying amount towards the purchase date has to consider all adjustments to the equity value, as identified during the initial consolidation and maintained in the auxiliary calculation.

- Adjustment and reclassification of selected items that are changed

  Any items of the consolidated statement of financial position that are adjusted due to the accounting of investments in associates have to be reviewed. The review has to ensure that appropriate carrying amounts are recorded for these items. This applies particularly to inventories, non-current assets, other assets and other liabilities as these balance sheet items are often impacted due to the relationship with the associate, either through intercompany business transactions or long-term investments in the associate.

  If the associate's local accounting policies deviate from the group's, level II adjustments will also have to be considered.

• Other effects
    The update of all balances towards the disposal date will trigger additional effects that need to be recorded. The main effect is the accounting of deferred tax assets or liabilities. This requires that tax bases of all involved assets and liabilities are known and up to date. If necessary, the tax bases as of the disposal date have to be calculated. In addition to the accounting for deferred tax assets and liabilities, other effects may arise. One of these is the treatment of goodwill that is assigned to the associate at group level if the associate is part of a cash-generating unit.

Journal entries to be recorded as part of the preparation process are standard journal entries as executed for regular subsequent closing activities. While the profit and dividend recording of the equity method is already performed at parent level, a repetition at group level is not necessary. This limits the execution of standard journal entries around the disposal to a small set only.

Journal entries		Comment
dr.	Depreciation expenses	Applies to hidden reserves and burdens and non-accounted assets.
cr.	Investments in associates	
dr.	Deferred tax asset	Applies to unrealized profits (upstream).
dr.	Share of profit of the associate	
cr.	Inventory	

Journal entries considering further effects have to be applied as well. Journal entries can be complicated if the associate is a foreign investment, which will trigger translation effects.

If the associate and all dependencies of group relationships with the associate are updated, the accounting for the **disposal** at the disposal date will start. Executing the disposal will result in two profit elements recorded in the period:

• A profit or loss due to the regular operation of the associate up to the disposal date, and
• A gain or loss realized upon disposal of the associate.

The gains and losses realized on the disposal of the associate can be calculated by applying a direct or an indirect method. The **calculation of gains and losses** considers, not only the effects of the one-line consolidation but also any issues that exist at group level and the way the associate was integrated into the group. Therefore, the gain or loss at group level realized by the sale of the associate is always different from the gain or loss realized by the parent.

• Direct method
    The realized gains or losses of the disposal of the associate are calculated at group level only. Proceeds of the sale of the associate are deducted by the current equity value and those items that have a direct relationship with the carrying equity value of the associate. Those are particularly adjustments due to the recording of unrealized profits and the write-down and recording of assets and liabilities in the consolidated statement of financial position resulting from loss situations. In addition to these

specific associate-related items, further adjustments are necessary that are similar to those adjustments necessary if subsidiaries are disposed.[25]

The following scheme can be used in calculating the realized gain / loss:

	Net proceeds from the sale of interests in the associate
−	Equity value
+	Write-up of assets from upstream transactions
+	Write-up of devaluations due to loss situations
+	Elimination of acceptance of liability in loss situations
+/−	Effects of pro-rata capital adjustments
+/−	Differences due to foreign currency translations
+/−	Items of a revaluation surplus
+/−	Deferred taxes
+(/−)	Goodwill, if necessary also goodwill allocations due to cash generating units
=	Realized gain / loss

Tab. G-9   Gain / loss from the sale of an associate, the group's view

- Indirect method

This calculation starts with the investment in the associate, as recorded by the parent or any holding company. Proceeds from the sale of the associate are deducted by the carrying amount of the investment in associates disposed. The realized gain or loss in the parent's account is adjusted by a set of components that were accounted for at group level over the life in the group of the associate. These adjustments refer to changes of the initial purchase price allocation, particularly fair-value adjustments and depreciation and amortization of assets, alignments to group accounting policies, and again associate-specific items like the adjustment due to unrealized profits and the accounting of losses. Goodwill considered in calculating the realized gain / loss includes the goodwill directly attributable to the associate disposed which remains at group level. It can be adjusted by goodwill that belongs to the cash generating unit the associate was assigned to.

The following scheme can be used in calculating the realized gain / loss:

	Proceeds from the sale of interests in the associate
−	Carrying amount in separate financial statements (of the parent)
+/−	Pro-rata profits / losses of the current period
+	Dividends received
+/−	Fair-value adjustments
+/−	Differences due to accounting policies
+/−	Write-up of valuation adjustments and extraordinary depreciation
+	Depreciation of hidden reserves and non-accounted for assets
−	Release of hidden burdens
+/−	Equity changes due to unrealized profits
+	Write-up of devaluations due to loss situations
+	Elimination of acceptance of liability in loss situations
+/−	Deferred taxes
+(/−)	Goodwill, if necessary also goodwill allocations due to cash generating units
=	Realized gain / loss

Tab. G-10   Gain / loss from the sale of an associate, the parent's view

---

[25] See chapter J -3.2.1 on page 579 regarding these adjustments.

Both methods, direct and indirect, always produce the same result, and both have their advantages and disadvantages. The advantage of the direct method is its simplicity as all items are easily identifiable. By contrast, the advantage of the indirect method is the reconciliation between the realized gain / loss at parent level and the gain / loss at group level.

The expected (calculated) and realized gain or loss of the disposal of the associate can be measured in the consolidated financial statements as a result of the **accounting of the disposal**. The disposal itself will trigger the execution of a set of tasks necessary to remove all items that have a direct relationship with the associate from the consolidated statements of financial position. They are widely spread across the whole balance sheet.

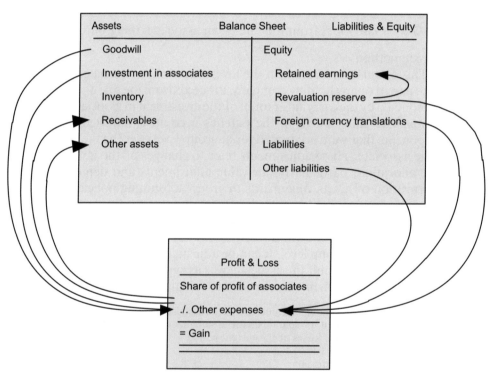

Fig. G-6 Accounting for full disposals

While the consolidated statement of financial position not only maintains the equity value of the investment in associated but also other items that have a close relationship with the associate, a full or partial disposal is required for those items. The amount attributable to be disposed has to be calculated individually for each asset and liability. The calculation is part of a set of dedicated tasks to be executed. Most of these tasks are part of deconsolidation activities.

Task	Explanation
Recording of the proceeds from the sale of the investment in associates	Those proceeds have to be recorded that are contractually agreed and that are due for payment. Any unearned proceeds have to be recorded in the balance sheet. The proceeds recorded at group level are usually identical to the proceeds recorded by the parent.
Removal of the carrying amount of the equity value of the associate	While the equity value of the investment in associates differs from the carrying amount of investments in subsidiaries recorded by the parent, the equity value has to be eliminated.
Recycling of items of other comprehensive income	As far as valuation adjustments to assets and liabilities are recorded through other comprehensive income that relate to the accounting of hidden reserves and burdens, non-accounted assets or contingent liabilities being part of the equity value, a recycling to profit & loss is required. The reason for recording in other comprehensive income is usually based on fair value adjustments or foreign currency translation differences.
	If an impairment test according to IAS 36 has unveiled an overstated carrying amount of goodwill of any other item which is part of the equity value of the investment in associates, the recorded write-down, as part of other comprehensive income, has to be reversed in line with IAS 28.23. Depending on the recording, reversals may relate to the depreciation and amortization on hidden reserves and identified non-accounted items for assets and the release of hidden burdens. Equity-changing unrealized profits and offset differences have to be considered as well.
Reclassification of items of other comprehensive income	Items recorded in other comprehensive income that are not eligible for recycling have to be reclassified to retained earnings.
Write-up of unrealized profits of assets of upstream-transactions	As far as assets are recorded in the consolidated statement of financial position that relate to upstream transactions with associates, the eliminated unrealized profits have to be added back as the associate now is treated as a third party. A recording at the lower base without unrealized profits is inappropriate. The write-up of unrealized profits applies to inventory as well as to non-current assets: fixed assets and intangible assets.
	The write-up amount is limited to the actual carrying amount in relation to the initial carrying amount.
Release of deferred tax assets or liabilities	As a consequence of adjusting items in the consolidated statement of financial position, any deferred tax assets or liabilities that are recorded in conjunction with these items have to be eliminated. This will always apply to assets where unrealized profits are eliminated. The adjustment has to be recorded either through profit & loss or through other comprehensive income depending on the initial recording. Therefore, the release of deferred tax assets or liabilities has to occur before any other comprehensive income is recycled or reclassified.
Write-up of other assets	If the investment in an associate (which is a financial asset) and any (long-term) assets that relate to the investment are written down or liabilities or provisions have been established due to the accounting of losses, the changes of these assets and liabilities have to be considered as well. Depending on the contractual situation of the sale and purchase agreement of the associate, any assets that are written down have to be reversed to reflect the situation as of and after the disposal date considering a deconsolidation took place. This applies particularly to loans the parent has granted to the associate as these loans will present assets against a third party (the associate's status after the disposal).
	The write-up is limited to the pro-rata profit of the associate.

Task	Explanation
Adjustments of liabilities and provisions	Guarantees given or underwritings assumed by the parent combined with the recording of corresponding items (either provisions or liabilities) due to a potential use liability have to be adjusted. If the parent remains liable for business transactions of the then former associate and a use is probable, an appropriate adjustment is necessary. The new carrying amount should reflect the expected exposure, adjusted by a discounting in case of long-term liabilities.
	If the risk is assumed to be not probable, a disclosure as a contingent liability combined with an elimination of the recognized amounts is required.
	The initial reason why such an item was established – either due to a loss situation or an expected failure of the associate – is not important.
Goodwill-adjustments	If the associate is part of a cash-generating unit, a fraction of the goodwill recorded at group level has to be disposed. The amount attributable to the associate is determined by the allocated goodwill to the cash-generating unit and the relative values of the associate compared to the value of the cash-generating unit (so all values of the entities belonging to the cash-generating unit) according to IAS 36.86.

Tab. G-11   Deconsolidation tasks upon the disposal of associates

The **date of the accounting** of the disposal of the associate from the group will be as flexible as a similar accounting for subsidiaries in case of the initial consolidation and the final deconsolidation. Both, the recording at the disposal date, or at the end of period, are possible.

- Recording at the disposal date demands that all accounts are up to date and reconciled, both at group and associate levels. Furthermore, the accounts of the associate might be subject to auditing activities. While valuation issues come along with the accounting of the deconsolidation, a delayed disposal accounting often takes place in practice. The advantage of this date is that the group centre is not so busy compared to regular accounting activities at the end of the period.
- Recording at the end at the period combines regular accounting activities as part of subsequent consolidations with the disposal of the group. The advantage is that all information of a deconsolidation and the subsequent disposal are available together with details of other assets and liabilities involved at group level. Nevertheless, a lack of details of the associate might get lost as the associate is not any longer in the influencing sphere of the parent.

Regardless of which approach is in favour to be applied, both have to ensure a clear cut-off at the disposal date. Even if the execution of the deconsolidation and disposal are realized later, the measurement base is always as of the disposal date. This measurement applies to all items involved, to assets and liabilities at group level and not only the equity value of the investment in associates.

While the elimination of the carrying amount of the investment in associates already took place in the parent's accounts, **journal entries** to be executed at group level consider only the difference between the carrying amount at parent level and at group level. Furthermore, the journal entries have to cover adjustments of all other accounts at group level. While some of the adjustments necessary to arrive at the realized gain or loss are recorded on the investment in associates account, the remaining balance covers these elements. A separate recording of a set of journal entries is therefore not necessary. The journal entries deal with the elimination and adjustment of assets and liabilities only. The recording of the sale of the associate is managed by the parent in its accounts. Consequently, an accounting of the sales transaction at group level is not necessary.

All adjustments can be combined into one standard journal entry which deconsolidates the associate from the consolidated statement of financial position and removes all related assets and liabilities in one step.

Journal entries		Comment
dr.	Liabilities	Relates to the adjustment of liabilities in loss situations or in case of a probable use of a guarantee granted by the parent and assumes that the guarantee will lapse upon the sale.
dr.	Inventory / non-current assets	Write-up due to the elimination of unrealized profits.
dr.	Other assets	Relates to the write-down of financial assets in loss situations.
dr.	Foreign exchange differences	Can also be a credit.
dr.	Revaluation reserves	Recycling of valuation adjustments.
cr.	Investment in associates	The remaining balance; includes elimination of unrealized profits, alignment to group accounting policies and other items.
cr.	Goodwill	If part of a cash-generating unit.
cr.	Gain on sale of associate	Can also be a loss (debit account instead).
dr.	Revaluation reserve	This journal entry is necessary if one or more components
cr.	Retained earnings	of the revaluation reserve are not subject to recycling.

If more transparency is demanded, this journal entry can be divided into several smaller journal entries. Several steps are necessary where each step records a defined asset, liability or equity component.

The presented solution assumes a division of work between the parent and the group. The recording of the equity method and the disposal of the carrying amount of investments in associates at parent level will result in an adjusted balance of the equity value at group level. The remaining balance carries only those items that relate to subsequent consolidation effects which are recorded during the lifetime of the associate in the group. Therefore, only the difference between the equity value and the carrying amount of investments in associates have to be removed (which is included in the above presented journal entry). The disadvantage of this method is the missing reconciliation of the disposed items at group level.

An alternate treatment is a reversal of the parent's journal entries at group level combined with the subsequent removal of the equity value at group level. The advantage of this method is that the components of the equity value can be reconciled upon disposal. In terms of journal entries the mentioned reversal can be realized using the following journal entry.

Journal entry			Comment
dr.		Investment in associates	Reversal of the journal entry at parent level.
	cr.	Gain on sale of associate	Can also be a loss.

The journal entry then to be executed is the same as before with different amounts.

Journal entries			Comment
dr.		Liabilities	Relates to the adjustment of liabilities in loss situations or in case of a probable use of a guarantee granted by the parent and assumes that the guarantee will lapse upon the sale.
dr.		Inventory / non-current assets	Write-up due to the elimination of unrealized profits.
dr.		Other assets	Relates to the write-down of financial assets in loss situations.
dr.		Foreign exchange differences	Can also be a credit.
dr.		Revaluation reserves	Recycling of valuation adjustments.
	cr.	Investment in associates	The remaining balance; includes elimination of unrealized profits, alignment to group accounting policies and other items.
	cr.	Goodwill	If part of a cash-generating unit.
	cr.	Gain on sale of associate	Can also be a loss (debit account instead).
dr.		Revaluation reserve	This journal entry is necessary if one or more components of the revaluation reserve are not subject to recycling.
cr.		Retained earnings	

The **presentation** of the disposal of the associate will take place in two separate items of the profit & loss statement. As far as the ordinary business activities are concerned, the profit of the period up to the disposal date and attributable to the parent is presents as "share of profit or loss of the associate" as part of the financial results. The gain or loss of the disposal of the associate can be presented in different positions of the profit & loss statement. IAS 28 is silent about any presentation requirements in this case. One option is the presentation in other earnings / other expenses similar to the disposal of non-current assets. As the investment in associates is also a financial asset, the disposal of the associate can be presented separately as part of the financial results. Even if both presentations are valid, the latter should be the preferred application as this presentation better reflects the nature of the associate and its regular accounting.

2.3.3. *IFRS 5 and disposals of associated companies*

The disposal of an associated company can be realized not only as an ordinary sale, as previously outlined, but it can also be classiffied as a discontinued operation or a disposal group, in line with IFRS 5. This opens up several options regarding the treatment of the sale for management. As there are many options available, various scenarios can be defined that can be applied to the disposal of associates. Regardless of which scenario is applied, conditions and requirements of IFRS 5 have to be satisfied upfront before an IFRS 5 accounting is applicable.[26]

---

[26] See chapter J -4 on page 601 for the application of IFRS 5 accounting. This chapter includes a detailed discussion on all steps necessary to disburse a company from the group.

Like all other companies subject to IFRS 5 accounting, an associated company has to run through all steps required to prepare the associate for an accounting that classifies the investment in associates as held for sale. This includes:

- Fulfilment of IFRS 5 criteria;
- Determination of the disposal date;
- Measurement applying IFRS 5 requirements;
- Accounting during the disposal period as a disposal group or discontinued operation;
- Sale of the disposal group or discontinued operation.

Upon the successful sale, a deconsolidation of the associated company is required applying deconsolidation procedures of associated companies as discussed before. Until this moment, the investment in the associate to be disposed is always presented as a non-current asset.

Accounting for disposals of associated companies depends on whether or not a full disposal is intended and decided by management:

- Full disposal
  If management intends a full disposal of an associated company that should be classified as held for sale, the associate will go through the same remeasurement procedure as an ordinary subsidiary.[27]

- Partial disposal
  Alternatively, the parent company might wish to retain an interest in the associated company. There are several reasons for this partial disposal. For example, the partial disposal is a standard procedure if the associate is itself a group and a subsidiary of that group will be sold, thus impacting the equity of the parent of that group.
  IAS 28.20 defines the allocation and accounting treatment of the portions to be disposed and retained. Based on this model, the initial task is a split-up between the two portions. The portion to be disposed is subject to the application of IFRS 5 while the retained portion is accounted for using the equity method.[28] The rationale behind the continuing use of the equity method until the disposal date is that the parent company still has significant influence in the associated company even if a portion is for sale. An accounting change for this portion may occur at the disposal date. Depending on the conditions of the remaining portion, this portion will either be subject to the accounting as a financial investment according to IFRS 9 or to the accounting as an associated company. The conditions have to be evaluated in accordance with IAS 28.5 to 28.15.

---

[27] See chapter J-4 on page 601 regarding the accounting in such a case.
[28] See chapter J-4 on page 601 regarding the accounting for the disposal portion.

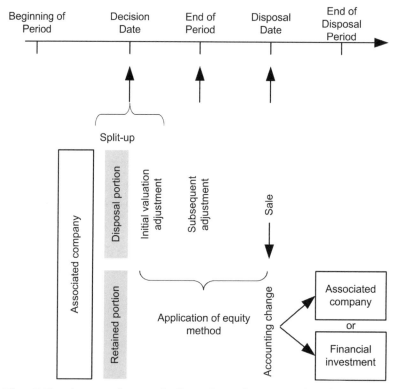

Fig. G-7 Accounting and allocation of an associated company due to IFRS 5 for partial disposals

The partial disposal will be complicated if the associate is fully integrated into a group: full integration often assigns an associate to a cash-generating unit. Such an assignment is often attended by an allocation of the cash-generating unit's goodwill to the associate. Therefore, similar to a full disposal, a partial disposal has to consider the allocation of a fraction of the cash-generating unit's goodwill to the disposed portion. In the absence of dedicated accounting rules, goodwill should be allocated to the disposal portion of the associate based on a determination of the relative values of the disposed assets (and liabilities) in relation to the cash-generating unit's value in accordance with IAS 38.86.

The presentation as held for sale according to IFRS 5 is limited to the disposal portion only.

The split-up of the associated company and separate accounting for the portion to be sold were introduced with the revised version of IAS 28, applicable from 1.1.2013. Applying the old accounting rule of IAS 28, the entire associated company would be reclassified as a disposal group available for sale (which in fact equals a full disposal).

Furthermore, this new accounting policy has to be applied to associated companies as well as to joint ventures.

3. TREATMENT OF LOSSES

The application of the equity method is mandatory in all situations, also when the associate has generated a loss. Losses may occur and they are not an exemption. Even if the equity method has to be applied, some specialities have to be considered, particularly if the associate produces on-going losses. On-going losses will not only reduce the carrying amount of the associate in the parent's accounts, they will also reduce the equity value at group level. In both financial statements, two activities will be triggered at the end of a period: the recording of a loss and the execution of an impairment test.

The general procedure is a reduction of the **carrying amount** of the investment in the associate. This reduction will continue in all subsequent loss periods until the carrying amount of the investment in associates will be zero. If additional losses still exist, the further handling depends on the financial commitment in the associate. If a loan was granted to the associate, the carrying balance of the financial asset has to be reduced. If guarantees or similar commitments are given, a liability has to be recorded provided that a payment is probable. If no further financial commitments are given, the accounting has to stop and any excess losses will not be recorded. Instead, losses should be recorded in the auxiliary calculation. The auxiliary calculation therefore has to trace the loss development until that moment the associate generates profits that will compensate the losses. To account for losses in structured ways, the following order has to be considered:

Step	Task
1	Reduction of the carrying amount of the investment in associated companies until the balance is zero.
2	If further losses exist, a reduction of the financial commitment of the parent company is mandatory. E.g. write-down of granted loans.
3	If an acceptance of liability or similar guarantees or commitments are given by the parent that result in an additional payment liability, a corresponding item can be recorded by the parent. This item is limited to the volume of the additional payment liability. A recognition of other liabilities or provisions is prohibited.
4	If losses still exist, accounting by applying the equity method has to be interrupted. The development of losses has to be recorded offsite.

Tab. G-12 Order of tasks regarding the treatment of losses

IAS 28.29 closed a regulatory gap for the treatment if the associate again generates profits: the standard now demands an application of the above-mentioned order in the reverse direction. All losses recorded in the auxiliary calculation have to be compensated for by profits first until this balance is zero. The next step is the elimination of liabilities followed by a write-up of the financial commitments given by the parent. If the balances of all balance sheet items are restored, the original balances are presented in the balance sheet, and the associate is still generating profits, then the investments in associates can be used to record profits. At that point, an auxiliary calculation is needed to trace all effects on the investment in associates accounts.

Independent from the above handling of assets and liabilities is the execution of an impairment test. On-going losses are always an indicator that the carrying amount of the investment in associates or its equity value is impaired: an impairment test is mandatory in such situations. If profits are generated in subsequent periods, the reason for an impairment might not be given any longer, in which case, a reversal of the recording of impairment losses is required.

> Treat the associated company as if it would be a subsidiary and execute the impairment test at the same time.

4. IMPAIRMENTS

IAS 28.40 requires an impairment test as part of the initial and subsequent consolidation. While investments in associates qualify as financial assets and goodwill is an implied item in the carrying amount of the investment in associates, a modified impairment test is also required by IAS 28.42. In fact, the test is similar to the requirements of IAS 36.80 that focus on business combinations. The difference from an ordinary impairment test is the item subject to testing. In regular impairment tests, goodwill is included, but while the goodwill of an associate is implied in the equity value, the whole equity value must be tested. Furthermore, the determination of the value in use differs from a regular determination as it combines the present values of the regular business and the (theoretical) ultimate disposal of the associate. The test itself is based on the requirements of *IAS 36 – Impairment of Assets.*[29]

The application of the equity method and the execution of impairment tests is not precise enough to derive a common scheme on the handling of impairment tests. In general, impairment tests are demanded by IAS 28.40 as outlined before. Nevertheless, IAS 28.32 also allows an application of an impairment test due to the wording in this paragraph: "… appropriate adjustments to the entity's share of the associate's or joint venture's profit or loss after acquisition are made for impairment losses such as for goodwill or property, plant and equipment …". By applying a strict interpretation of this wording, all assets, including goodwill, should be tested for impairment, similar to assets of consolidated financial statements.

Therefore, the execution order in testing associates for impairments has to be performed in the following way:

Step	Task	Where	Reference
1)	Recognition of any profit & loss the associate generates. This may include impairment losses already recognized by the associates.	Parent level	
2)	Recognition of any dividends received by the associate.	Parent level	
3)	Regular consolidations: • Elimination of unrealized gains and losses • Depreciation and amortization of any other assets • Adjustments of (contingent) liabilities and provisions	Group level	

---

[29] See chapter F -8.2 on page 348 regarding the application of impairment tests.

Step	Task	Where	Reference
4)	Impairment test of goodwill and any other assets subject to impairment testing. Two cases are possible:	Group level	IAS 28.32 (optional)
	a) The impairment test assumes that the associate has implied cash-generating units. Such a case is given if the associate is also a group that records goodwill. The measurement of goodwill by the associate can differ from the measurement by the parent due to different accounting policies which triggers additional impairment adjustments. This may lead to adjustments of impairment losses recognized by the associate.		
	b) Furthermore, impairment requirements many also arise by the recognition of items of the purchase price allocation, so by items not recognized by the associate.		
5)	Impairment test of the equity value of the associate.	Group level	IAS 28.40 (mandatory)
6)	Impairment test at group level of assigned goodwill if the associate is part of a cash-generating unit.	Group level	IFRS 3 / IFRS 10 / IAS 36

Tab. G-13 Execution order of impairments of associates

Depending on the treatment by the parent, the execution of step 4 is up to the discretion of management. Furthermore, an impairment test at parent level, regarding the carrying amount of the investment in associates, might be required if the associate does not perform and generates losses. This is a mandatory task in preparing separate financial statements of the parent.

Any impairment losses that arise on application of the equity value will not be allocated to any individual asset of the equity value. Instead, it should be recorded as a separate item. A treatment of any reversals of impairment losses will follow the same pattern.

Journal entry

dr.	Write-down of financial assets	
	cr.	Investment in associates

5. SPECIAL CASES

Accounting for investments in associates can become complex depending on the legal form, structure of the associate and the integration in a group. This is because specialities need to be considered: an associate with a legal shell based on a partnership requires special attention to properly handle the capital accounts of all partners, for example. An associate does not necessarily have a single entity. It can also be a group where its consolidated financial statements act as the basis for the ultimate parent. Furthermore, the treatment of the associate and the integration of the associate into the group require special attention. An associate can be treated as non-material, which does not trigger any accounting tasks. An associate can be closely integrated into the group as part of a cash-generating unit. An associate can also be involved in equity transactions with other group companies, e.g. through acquiring or selling of interests in group subsidiaries in the group, reciprocal interests in and with group companies and similar transactions.

So, a closer look into the accounting of such transactions is necessary.

5.1. Associates and cash-generating units

Even if associates do not have the status of a subsidiary, they can be embedded in dedicated **organizational units** of a group. These units often represent operating segments or business units or parts of business units. They often also form cash-generating units. As demanded by IAS 36.80, the goodwill of a group has to be allocated to cash-generating units. Therefore, an allocation of goodwill to a cash-generating unit will always cover all entities of that cash-generating unit. If an entity is to be disposed of, IAS 38.86 requires a disposal of a fraction of the allocated goodwill by using the relative values of the cash-generating unit. While the standard only mentions "entities" and not subsidiaries, an allocation of a fraction of goodwill to associates and joint ventures is required upon disposal. Therefore, associates may carry additional goodwill that is not part of the equity value of an associate at group level. This goodwill is more or less recorded in the goodwill position of the consolidated statement of financial position.

A second way for associates to become part of a cash-generating unit is through acquisition. In addition to a direct acquisition of interests in associates, interests in an associate can be acquired indirectly through the **acquisition of a group** where the parent of that group records investments in associates. The acquired group becomes a subgroup. The acquired group then will go through a purchase price allocation as demanded by IFRS 3. Procedures are the same except that the extent is broadened and all subsidiaries, associates and joint ventures have to be re-measured. Such a practice will result in two portions of goodwill for the associate: intrinsic goodwill deriving from the equity value alongside the group's goodwill.

Intrinsic goodwill arises if all assets and liabilities of the associate are remeasured to reflect their fair values as of the acquisition date.[30] There are three possible scenarios:

- Assumed goodwill
  The associate was acquired by the subgroup. Therefore, it has already gone through purchase price allocation; the determined goodwill is based on that purchase price allocation. Regular impairment tests were made; write-downs are not necessary.

  The acquisition of the subgroup and the then necessary purchase price allocation did not detect any changes in the associate's assets and liabilities. Therefore, the initial goodwill can also be assumed to be the associate's goodwill for group purposes.

---

[30] See chapter G -2.1.1 on page 432 regarding the purchase price allocation and the determination of goodwill.

- Adjusted goodwill

    The associate was acquired by the subgroup. Therefore, it has already gone through purchase price allocation; the determined goodwill is based on that purchase price allocation. Regular impairment tests were made.

    The acquisition of the subgroup and the necessary purchase price allocation unveiled new fair values of the associate's assets and liabilities and a different goodwill. Appropriate adjustments were made and the equity value now reflects the conditions as of the acquisition date by using adjusted goodwill.

- Initial goodwill

    The associate was either founded or acquired (without performing a purchase price allocation) by the parent of the subgroup. The purchase price allocation performed as part of the subgroup acquisition determined new fair values of assets and liabilities. Therefore, goodwill was initially established.

Other than the intrinsic goodwill that focuses on the fair values of the associate's assets and liabilities, **group goodwill** focuses on the role of the associate in the group. If the associate is embedded in a cash-generating unit structure and does not qualify as a separate cash-generating unit, a portion of the determined goodwill of the group is allocated towards the associate. The determination of that goodwill follows the ordinary accounting rules and practices for goodwill and cash-generating units as demanded by IAS 36.66. As a result, a portion of the goodwill at subgroup level is allocated to the associate but at a different level to the intrinsic goodwill.

5.2. Partnership as associate

Legal forms of associates may vary depending on the jurisdiction the associate resides, the legal environments the associate operates in and the risks associated with the business. In some cases, even partnerships qualify as associates. While partnerships follow different accounting rules in dealing with the partner's capital, a direct application of the equity of a legal entity on the capital of a partnership is not possible. Subsequently, an application of the equity method on partnerships requires a slight modification. The treatment of partner capitals and the application of the equity method will impact all levels in the group. Therefore, each level has to be reviewed individually.

- The partnership

    The net profit a partnership generates is not automatically allocable and distributable to partners. This is because the partnership may record expenses or earnings that are allocable directly to partners or that are not considered to be expenses. Traditionally, two transactions always require **adjustment**: services performed by partners and interest on partner capital accounts.

    While the partnership belongs to partners, these partners cannot be employed by themselves. Therefore, any salaries recorded by the partnerships for the services rendered by the partners are in fact drawings.

They need to be adjusted and reversed by the parent and by the executing group as a level I adjustment. A typical adjustment could look like this journal entry:

Journal entry
dr.   Drawing account partner
    cr.   Personnel expenses

The second traditional area deals with interest assigned to the partner's capital accounts. Often, partnership contracts state that the capital of the partner capital accounts have to be subject to interest. This would stipulate that the partner is treated like a creditor who lends money to the partnership. While a partner can't be a creditor to its own business, interest charged on the capital accounts has to be reversed, as with salaries. Other transactions may have similar impacts on the net profit of the partnership. They need to be reversed or adjusted as well.

Pro-rata net profits of the partnership and adjustments are only two components that build up the **capital account** of a partner. The capital balance has to consider also drawings by the partner that are recorded via the drawings account, as well as any investments.

Considering all the above-mentioned aspects, the profit of a partnership allocable to the parent can be calculated using the following scheme. The **calculation** considers both, the profit allocation and the changes in the partner's capital.

	Net profit / loss of the partnership
+	Expenses recorded due to the service of partners
+	Interest recorded on capital accounts of partners
+/−	Other adjustments
=	Adjusted net profit / loss of the partnership
−	Net profits allocable to other partners
−	Withdrawals by the parent
=	Carrying amount of the drawings account
+	Investments by the parent
+	Capital @ beginning of the period
=	Capital @ end of period

Tab. G-14   Calculation scheme for profits and capital of partnerships

The profit allocation of the partnership's profit to the parent is based on a pre-tax calculation. This is because **income tax** has to be paid by partners and subsequently by the parent recording the interests in associates. Due to this treatment a recording of income taxes at partnership level is not required.

The **presentation** of the partner's capital account in the financial statement of the partnership depends on the underlying partnership contract. While the capital accounts vary based on the business of the partnership and the drawings of the partners, capital accounts can be either classified as equity or liabilities. The classification depends on the requirements of *IAS 32 – Financial Instruments: Presentation* and the conditions as outlined in IAS 32.16A. If these conditions are fulfilled cumulatively, a presentation as equity is given, otherwise a presentation as liabilities is required:

- The partner is entitled to receive a pro-rata share of the partnership's net asset in case of liquidation.
- The partner's capital is subordinate to other classes of financial instruments (i.e. to payables to suppliers to fulfil their demands) and has not priorities or conversion rights included.
- All partners have the same arrangements; no partner should have any deviation or preferred agreements in his partner contract.
- The contractual obligation of the partnership is limited to the contractual compensation only. There are no further rights by the retiring partner for any additional payments or assets, neither to him or any third party.
- The partner's capital relates to the economic success of the partnership. It includes his portion of the profit & loss, any changes in net assets and any changes in the fair value or recognized and unrecognized assets (e.g. the increase of the market or fair value of land or the creation of intangible assets like a customer base by the partnership).

- The parent

   Applying the equity accounting by the parent to its share in the partnership, the parent has to record the profit & loss attributable to the parent as a partner, as well as any drawings the parent has taken during the period. Drawings represent dividends. The presentation of the investment in the partnership is the same as any other investments in associates.

   Due to the identical accounting at parent and partnership levels, the carrying amount of the investment in the partnership mirrors the partner's capital account of the partnership.

- The group

   Application of the equity method to partnerships at group level follows the same procedures as for any other associate. Due to the legal form of the partnership, slight adjustments are necessary that impact the equity consolidation and the determination of the equity value.

   Assuming that appropriate adjustments are made by the partnership to reflect the profit attributable to the parent, the determination of the equity value has to consider drawings that represent dividends as well as investments made by the parent in the partnership. All other items – such as adjustments to comply with group accounting policies, non-accounted assets, hidden reserves and burdens and other items that build up equity value – have to accounted for as usual. Considering all these effects, the determination of the equity value in the auxiliary calculation can be realized by applying a modified calculation.

Description	Goodwill	Hidden reserves & burdens	Non-accounted assets	Deferred taxation	Book value Investment	Equity value
Balance @ beginning of period	yyy	yyy	yyy	yyy	yyy	yyy
Other comprehensive income					yyy	yyy
Impairments	yyy					yyy
Depreciation & Amortization			yyy	yyy		yyy
Up- & downstream transactions					yyy	yyy
Unrealized profits					yyy	yyy
Adjusted profits					yyy	yyy
Investments					yyy	yyy
Drawings					yyy	yyy
Balance @ end of period	zzz	zzz	zzz	zzz	zzz	zzz

Fig. G-8 Auxiliary calculation for the investments in partnerships

Partnership contracts can be equipped with special agreements if partners retire or new partners will be accepted. These agreements usually provide detailed regulations about the handling of the partner capital accounts and the allocation of any fair values of assets attributable to partners. A typical agreement is a **compensation obligation** of the partnership on retirement of partners. Such an obligation is treated as a puttable instrument, and requires the partnership to present compensation obligations as liabilities, according to *IAS 32 – Financial Instruments: Presentation*, if the conditions as outlined in IAS 32.16A and discussed before are not fulfilled in total. The conditions are more or less the same as the ones used for a presentation of capital accounts as equity. Even if the conditions stay the same, the view of the conditions has changed while they have to be determined from a compensation obligation's point of view. In many cases, compensation obligations do not fulfil at least one of the listed conditions. This requires a presentation of the partner capital as a liability. To determine whether or not compensation obligations fulfil all these conditions, an individual check of the underlying partnership contract is necessary.

Presenting compensation obligations as liabilities will result in a misleading presentation of the performance and financial position of the partnership. This has to be reversed by the parent before the equity method can be applied.

5.3. Non-material associate becomes material

Similar to subsidiaries, an associate can be classified as non-material if its contribution to the group's performance and its omission does not have any material impact on the group's overall position. This classification is possible due to the **materiality concept** defined in the *framework*: as defined in F.30, an item is classified as non-material if the omission or misstatement is not relevant to the economic decision of users of financial statements. Therefore, the materiality concept is not only mandatory for business transactions, balance sheet and profit & loss items, it also covers consolidated financial statements and investments in associates treated as financial assets. Applying the materiality concept to a group, an associate may not be subject to consolidation, if the profit and total net assets of that subsidiary are not material to the group.

If an associate qualifies as a non-material company and is therefore not consolidated, the investment in that associate recorded by the parent company is also presented in consolidated financial statements. The presentation and the recording of the carrying amount of the investment in associates depends on the accounting by the parent. Some cases show how the parent has recorded the investment in a non-material associate:

- Parent records dividends only

  If dividends the associate distributes are recorded only, the carrying amount of the investment in the non-material associate equals the initial purchase price. The investment in that associate is recorded at cost. Typically, dividends are recorded by applying the following journal entry:

  Journal entry
  dr.   Cash
      cr.   Share of profits of associates

  According to IAS 28, recording dividends only is a violation of the accounting for investments in associates and can only be justified if the associate is also treated as non-material at parent level and the parent has elected to omit the application of the equity accounting for that associate. Such an accounting will demand a recording of deferred tax assets or liabilities as the tax base for investments in associates often considers both profits (and losses) and dividends distributed by the associate.

  A presentation as simple investments is also appropriate.

- Parent applies fair value accounting

  By applying the fair value accounting, the change in the investment in the non-material associate is recorded in other comprehensive income according to the accounting requirements of IFRS 9.

- Parent applies equity method

  Whether the associate is treated as material or non-material at parent level, an application of the equity method at parent level ensures a proper recording of profits and dividends.

If an **associate becomes material**, an application of the equity method is mandatory. Such a change in the status of the associate is often based on significant changes in the associate's business. The associate might enter into business transactions that significantly increase the net assets or the profit of the associate. The associate might also be engaged in acquisition of other companies. Regardless of the reasons why an associate becomes material, the application of the equity method will force accounting changes at parent and group level.

While IAS 28 is silent about the accounting, two solutions have been developed to cope with changes in the materiality status of an associate:

- Retrospective initial application

    IAS 8 – Accounting Policies, Changes in Accounting Estimates and Errors requires the full history of investments in associates to be rolled up back to the date of first acquisition. This roll-up should be performed as an off-site calculation to determine all carrying amounts of or in conjunction with the associate. An initial consolidation has to be performed using historical figures as of the acquisition date to determine the equity value, including all components as of that date. The equity value has to be advanced in all subsequent periods to arrive at the equity value as of the date the associate becomes material. Depending on the carrying amount and any subsequent changes in the carrying amount of the investment in the non-material associate, the determined equity value has to be used to adjust the carrying amount in the associate. Due to the retrospective application, the adjustment to arrive at the equity value at group level has to be recorded against retained earnings.

    <u>Journal entry</u>
    dr.   Investments in associates
        cr.   Retained earnings

    The calculation in determining the equity value of the non-material associate can be used as an auxiliary calculation for subsequent periods.

- Prospective application

    Again, in accordance with *IAS 8 – Accounting Policies, Changes in Accounting Estimates and Errors*, on the date when the associate becomes material, an initial consolidation has to be performed, using fair values for the investment in the associate and its net assets.

Regardless of which application is chosen to initially determine the equity value of the associate and to subsequently account for the associate, the new status of the associate will trigger additional tasks to be performed. These tasks belong to the ordinary accounting of associates during the preparation of consolidated financial statement as discussed for the subsequent consolidation.

H JOINT ARRANGEMENTS

About this chapter:

Joint arrangements are organizational forms of collaboration of two or more independent market participants. These market participants can be competitors or partners in the same or similar markets – even from different markets. The collaboration is often limited to a defined subject where the participants expect to achieve advantages. Due to the nature of the collaboration, there are dedicated agreements between the participants that need to be accounted for.

This chapter discusses all aspects of joint arrangements and their treatment for group purposes. This includes not only general characteristics but also accounting and consolidations aspects, the treatment of losses and other specific items attributable to joint ventures. The focus is on the company type and its integration in the group as consolidation requirements are more or less similar to associates.

1. BASICS

IFRS 11 generally defines the collaboration between two or more parties on a dedicated subject as a joint arrangement, which is accounted for according to IFRS 11 and IAS 28, depending on the classification of the arrangement. To be subject to the scope of IFRS 11, certain criteria have to be met. This requires an appropriate upfront check. The following workflow should be kept in mind when assessing whether or not a collaboration (so a joint business activity) between two or more parties qualifies as a joint arrangement.

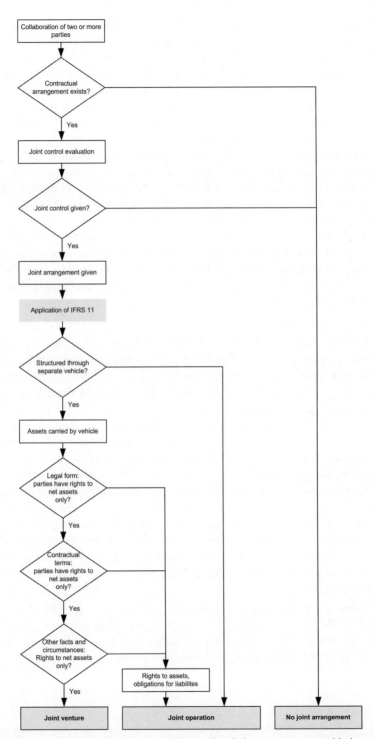

Fig. H-1   Scope check of IFRS 11 to determine joint ventures and joint operations

The workflow determines two items: Is the collaboration in the scope of an IFRS 11 accounting?; and, if yes, Is the accounting based on a venture or an operation? Accordingly, a set of checks has to be executed upfront to properly identify and allocate the collaboration. These checks usually have to be executed only at the inception of a joint business activity between two or more parties as conditions usually will not change afterwards. However, if conditions do change, the checks have to be repeated to determine if the joint activity is still within the scope of IFRS 11 or not. So, collaborations can subsequently qualify as joint arrangements. In addition to the scope-check, a determination regarding classification is necessary. A scope check, brought about by changes in conditions, might come to the conclusion that the collaboration still qualifies as a joint agreement; however, contractual terms or other issues may require reclassification from joint operation to joint venture, or vice versa.

IFRS 11.5 defines two conditions that have to be met to qualify a collaboration as a **joint arrangement**: a contractual arrangement and joint control. A separate determination of both elements is required. While joint control is often defined in or part of the contractual agreement, it is recommended to evaluate contractual agreements first.

- Contractual arrangement

    Contractual arrangement means that all collaborating parties are bound to an agreement. The type and content of the contractual agreement is not defined, it can therefore be any type of arrangement, either in writing (preferred!), oral or any other form. It does not necessarily to be certified by an independent person or authority like a notary. The only important element of the contractual agreement is its enforceability. IFRS 11.5 does not explicitly mention this requirement. It is more or less an implicit requirement due to the wording of IFRS 11.5 as parties are bound to the agreement.

    Contractual arrangements may be available at different levels. An agreement can consist of a contract between all parties ruling the collaboration, the duties of each party involved and other important items. An agreement can also exist at a lower level. This is when a carrying vehicle like a legal entity is used to host the collaboration. In such a case the articles or bylaws of that vehicle represent the contractual agreement binding all parties together.

    Even if the defined contents of a contractual agreement are missing, IFRS 11.B4 provides some hints about items that are typical for contractual agreements. The following checklist will help in determining typical elements of contractual agreements.

Item
Purpose, activity and duration of the joint agreement
Rights and duties of the parties, their voting rights and obligations
Appointment of the members of the board or an equivalent governing body of the joint arrangement
List of matters subject to decisions from parties as well as the required support from the parties
Party contribution duties, either by capital or other contributions
Sharing of assets and liabilities, revenues and expenses (or profit & loss) between parties

Tab. H-1 Checklist of typical content of contractual agreements[1]

- Joint control

   In addition to the contractual agreement, joint control is required. All parties control the joint arrangement equally. This requires a careful check of the existence of joint control as outlined in chapter C -2.[2] If the check confirms the existence of joint control, a joint arrangement is given. Contractual agreements may include regulations where joint control cannot be immediately detected or where joint control is not obvious. The following example represents a typical case where a threshold in the articles of incorporation will decide about whether or not joint control is given.

---

[1] Taken from IFRS 11.B4 and adjusted by other aspects.
[2] See page 55.

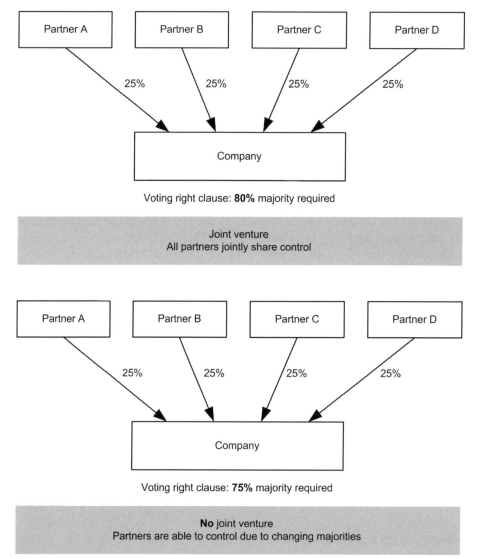

Fig. H-2 Examples of contractual agreements on voting rights and the impact on joint control

It is necessary to reassess joint control upon any changes to the joint arrangement. This should always include a verification of voting rights if joint arrangements are organized in separate vehicles.

> Ensure that no partner will gain control due to changes in voting rights by appropriate contractual agreements.

If the steps executed so far confirmed the existence of a joint arrangement, a classification of the joint agreement is required which is based on rights and obligations of the parties. IFRS 11.14 differentiates between joint operations and joint ventures. According to IFRS 11.15, a joint operation is given, if all parties have rights to the assets and obligations for the liabilities relating to the agreement. By contrast, according to IFRS 11.16, a joint venture is given, if all parties have rights to the net assets of the agreement. The difference between both definitions is the treatment of obligations, so is it a separate item or is it part of net assets. To determine the differences, a four-step approach needs to be executed. Depending on the underlying contractual agreement, the classification check as **joint operation or joint venture** can be stopped after each step.

1. Separate vehicle

    IFRS 11.A defines a separate vehicle as "a separately identifiable financial structure, including separate legal entities or entities recognized by statue, regardless of whether those entities have a legal personality". This broad definition covers all kinds of legal forms: incorporated legal entities as well as limited liability companies, unlimited companies, partnerships and trusts.

    The non-existence of a separate vehicle, hosting the activities, always suggests a joint operation as the risks and duties are with the parties. Consequently, all parties are obliged to account for their share of rights in assets and obligations for liabilities. If a separate vehicle is used further investigations are necessary requiring the execution of the next step.

2. Legal form

    Assuming a separate vehicle is used to host joint activities, the legal form has to be determined in respect of the assets and liabilities and the access of the parties to these assets and liabilities. As a general rule, if assets and liabilities carried by the vehicle are the property of the vehicle (so the vehicle has its own rights) the access of the parties is limited to net assets. By contrast, if the vehicle acts as a placeholder only and has no rights to the assets and liabilities or to their economic benefits, the rights in assets and obligations for liabilities are with the parties qualifying the joint agreement, again as a joint operation. Typical examples of such kind of legal forms are trusts and in some circumstances also partnerships (depending on the contractual agreement between the partners).

3. Contractual terms

    Contractual terms of legal forms can be modified in a way that specific treatments of rights and obligations may result. Thus, parties may benefit from rights to assets without being liable to any debts. This requires an assessment of contractual terms to ensure that both rights and obligations are carried by all parties: assignment of only one element to the parties is not sufficient in classifying the joint agreement as a joint operation. The following list, taken from IFRS 11.B27, provides guidance on classifying a joint venture or a joint operation.

	Joint operation	Joint venture
Terms or the contractual agreement	The contractual agreement provides the parties to the joint arrangement with its rights to the assets, and obligations for the liabilities, relating to the arrangement.	The contractual arrangement provides the parties to the joint arrangement with rights to the net assets of the arrangement (i.e. it is the separate vehicle, not the parties, that has rights to the assets, and obligations for the liabilities, relating to the arrangement).
Rights to assets	The contractual arrangement establishes that the parties to the joint arrangement share all interests (e.g. rights, title, in the assets relating to the arrangement in a specified proportion (e.g. in proportion to the parties' ownership interests in the arrangement or in proportion to the activity carried out through the arrangement that is directly attributed to them).	The contractual arrangement establishes that the assets brought into the arrangement or subsequently acquired by the joint arrangement are the arrangement's assets. The parties have no interests (i.e. no rights, title or ownership) in the assets of the arrangement.
Obligations for liabilities	The contractual arrangement establishes that the parties to the joint arrangement share all liabilities, obligations, costs and expenses in a specified proportion (e.g. in proportion to the parties' ownership interests in the arrangement or in proportion to the activity carries out through the arrangement that is directly attributed to them).	The contractual arrangement establishes that the joint arrangement is liable for the debts and obligations of the arrangement.
	The contractual arrangement establishes that the parties to the joint arrangement are liable for claims raised by third parties.	The contractual arrangement establishes that the parties to the joint arrangement are liable to the arrangement only to the extent of their respective investments in the arrangement or to the respective obligations to contribute any unpaid or additional capital to the arrangement, or both.
		The contractual arrangement states that creditors of the joint arrangement do not have rights of recourse against any party with respect to debts or obligations of the arrangement.
Revenue, expenses, profit or loss	The contractual arrangement establishes the allocation of revenues and expenses on the basis of the relative performance of each party to the joint arrangement. For example, the contractual arrangement might establish that revenues and expenses are allocated on the basis of the capacity that each party uses in a plant operated jointly, which could differ from their ownership interests in the joint arrangement. In other instances, the parties might have agreed to share their profits or loss relating to the arrangement on the basis of a specified proportion such as the parties' ownership interests in the arrangement. This would not prevent the arrangement from being a joint operation if the parties have rights to the assets, and obligations for the liabilities, relating to the arrangement.	The contractual arrangement establishes each party's share in the profit or loss relating to the activities of the arrangement.

Tab. H-2 Criteria on contractual terms

A special case is given if the parties provide guarantees to third parties to enable the joint arrangement to incur debt. IFRS 11.B27 clarifies that such guarantees are separate contracts and the joint arrangement is still the primary obligor.

4. Other facts and circumstances

In the rare event that the first three steps do not provide sufficient evidence to classify a joint arrangement as a joint operation or joint venture, other facts and circumstances have to be considered.

One such is an output related arrangement. If the joint arrangement is established to provide its output exclusively to the parties (where a sale to a third party is excluded) an output related approach can be applied for the measurement of the interest in the joint arrangement. Furthermore, in the absence of any other party benefiting from the joint arrangement it can be assumed that the liabilities of the joint arrangement can be allocated to the parties. If appropriate agreements regarding the rights in the asset of the joint arrangement exist, it can be assumed that such an output related joint arrangement qualifies as a joint operation.

To determine the impact of other facts and circumstances, the following check should be performed. If the answer to that check is a yes, then the joint arrangement classifies as a joint operation; otherwise it will be a joint venture:

"Have the parties designed the arrangement so that its activities primarily aim to provide the parties with an output (i.e. parties have rights to substantially all of the economic benefits of the assets held in the separate vehicle) **and** it depends on the parties on a continuous basis for settling the liabilities relating to the activity conducted through the arrangement?"

Once all these steps have been carefully taken, we have a joint operation, a joint venture – or even no joint arrangement.

Example

Yao Tung Ltd is a company that was founded in 2002 by Shenzhen Enterprises. The company manufactures and sells cables to the Asian market. Five years ago, Flexing Cables SE acquired a stake in the company from Shenzhen Enterprises. Since then, each of the partners has held a 50% stake in Yao Tung. Upon the acquisition of Yao Tung, the articles of incorporation and the by-laws were adjusted to reflect the involvement of Flexing Cables. The most important changes are summarized here:

- Each share of the company constitutes one voting right.
- All decisions regarding changes in the corporate structure, increase and decrease of share capital, the appointment and dismissal of company executives require an unanimous consent by the shareholders.
- Flexing Cables has the right to appoint a co-executive to run the company.

- The legal structure of the company is kept untouched. Shareholders have the right to participate in net assets only.
- Profit distributions are based on the participation quota.

To determine whether or not Yao Tung qualified as a joint venture, the workflow of the scope check would be applied:

- Yao Tung has two shareholders that act as two parties.
- The contractual arrangement both parties are bound to are the (changed) articles of incorporation.
- The articles of association require an unanimous consent on decisions, so no party can act on its own. Joint control is given.
- Yao Tung Ltd is a legal entity. According to IFRS 11.A, a separate vehicle is given.
- Due to the legal form as a limited company, no shareholder has access to selected assets or liabilities as they are the property of Yao Tung.
- As the underlying contractual arrangement is the articles of incorporation only, there are no further contractual terms that may give one party an advantage over the assets of Yao Tung.
- Other facts and circumstances are not identified.

As a result of this evaluation, Yao Tung had to be classified as a joint venture.

All the above-mentioned criteria to determine a joint operation or a joint venture assume straightforward behaviour of all parties. In practice, several different implementations can be found that require special attention.

A common practice between parties is arranging multiple activities by using one **collaboration framework** only. IFRS 11.18 has picked up this issue and demands a classification based on the activities. This requires following the workflow to determine rights in assets and obligations for liabilities separately for each activity. As there is no definition or guidance for an activity, extensive analysis is required to understand and identify the underlying activities that constitute an arrangement. This may include a determination of several vehicles if complex structures exist.

Another common practice is the hosting of several activities by **one vehicle** only. Again, rights and obligations have to be assessed at activity level. Hosting several activities require a strict separation of assets, liabilities (and other obligations), revenue and expenses (or profit & loss) for each activity. Furthermore, an assessment of the articles of incorporation or the by-laws is necessary to determine the treatment by the parties and whether or not a mixed treatment of activities as joint operations and joint ventures is possible.

As a general rule, a separate vehicle should carry one joint arrangement only as assets and obligations have to be allocated to that arrangement.

2. ACCOUNTING AND CONSOLIDATION

The accounting of the interest in joint arrangements depends on the classification of the arrangement as a joint operation or a joint venture. This will require a recognition of assets, liabilities, revenue and expenses in the accounts of the party with interests in the joint arrangement or an application of the equity method. IFRS 11.20 to 11.27 provides appropriate guidance on the accounting of joint arrangements.

> IFRS 11 is the successor of IAS 31. Several changes are implemented compared to the old standard:
>
> - Changed categories;
> - Modified choice of accounting methods.
>
> Allowed accounting methods are a recording of assets, liabilities, revenue and expenses (or profit & loss) or the application of the equity method. An application of a proportionate consolidation is not possible any longer.

A personal word on accounting methods:

IAS 31 allowed opting between the equity method and a proportionate consolidation to account for joint ventures in consolidated financial statements. However, IFRS 11 and IAS 28, as their successors, only accept the equity method and in very rare cases a recording of assets and liabilities by the parent. This has forced groups to transfer to the equity method. Large groups with significant joint ventures have been forced to present large drops in revenue and costs, combined with a related increase in the financial result of the group. This presentation requirement is more than questionable: it dilutes the group's real performance by overstating financial results and understating the business activities of the group. The overstating of financial results is not realized by financing activities of the group, but is based on the business of the group, which in fact mingles the financial results as this is not a financial but an operating issue.

2.1 Joint operations

IFRS 11.20 demands a recording of assets, liabilities, revenues and expenses directly in the accounts of a joint operator (which is in fact the party holding a share in the joint arrangement or in other words a parent or holding company of the group). The carrying amount of all recorded items has to be determined based on the contractual agreement and not on the share held in the joint arrangement. This demands a dedicated analysis of the **allocation** to the parties:

- Assets and liabilities provided by the parties
  Assets provided and liabilities assumed by the parent in respect of the joint operation have to be identified as used in the joint operation. This is required for an allocation of assets and liabilities. The accounting for these items is left unchanged and follows the ordinary accounting policy of the parent.

- Jointly held assets and liabilities – contractual agreement equals share in a joint arrangement

  Assets and liabilities that are established in the ordinary course of the business of the joint operation have to be recorded by all parties according to the agreement. While the contractual agreement equals the share in the joint arrangement, a proportionate allocation is possible. This allocation equals more or less a proportionate consolidation as applicable under the old standard (IAS 31).

- Jointly held assets and liabilities – contractual agreement does not equal to the share in a joint arrangement

  A different behaviour applies to assets and liabilities that are established in the ordinary course of the business if the share in the joint agreement does not reflect contractual agreements. The allocation of assets and liabilities jointly held is based on a prioritized order. If there is a contractual agreement on how to allocate assets and liabilities (either all, some or selected ones), an allocation based on the agreement has to be executed first. IFRS 11.B18 confirms this application. In the absence of any detailed handling in the agreement, a different accounting approach might be possible. This requires an evaluation of the contractual agreement. If there are any regulations on how to deal with gaps or not-covered items in the agreement, an evaluation is necessary. This evaluation has to determine if a treatment of assets and liabilities jointly held but not subject to any detailed regulations is required according to the agreement. If this is not the case, jointly held assets and liabilities might also be recorded based on the share in the joint arrangement. While a consistent application of all parties is required in such cases a consensus should be reached upfront (this is to ensure no double recording or any non-recording of assets and liabilities or part of them may result).

- Jointly incurred revenues and expenses

  Similar to the practice of recording assets and liabilities, revenues and expenses have to be recorded by all parties. Again, the extent of revenues and expenses to be recorded depends on the contractual agreements. A prioritized application of recording revenues and expenses similar to the recording of jointly held assets and liabilities is strongly recommended.

In most cases, contractual agreements and the share in a joint arrangement will result in an identical recognition. Nevertheless there might be situations where the contractual agreement and the share in the joint arrangement differ. One typical example is when two parties provide different types of asset (e.g. one is providing a production facility while the other one is providing the use of a patent) but both parties holding an equal share in the joint arrangement. In addition, additional assets and liabilities jointly held have to be allocated to the parties based on the contractual agreement. The allocation of revenues and expenses might be treated differently.

Another issue is **transactions with joint operations**. While the parent collaborates with the joint operation from a commercial perspective, regular business transactions exist. Nevertheless, from an accounting perspective, the parent would be engaged in commercial transactions with itself (for the share of the investment in the joint arrangement) and the other parties. This requires accounting adjustments due to the "dealing with itself". Similar to the accounting of business transactions with associates, downstream and upstream transactions require individual handlings.

- Upstream

  In an upstream transaction, goods are delivered or sold by the joint operation as the sending company to the parent that acts as the receiving company. In fact, such transaction can include all four basic intercompany transaction types.[3]

  Transactions **for immediate sale** and transactions **for own consumption** share similar handling. A recording of revenues of the joint operation and expenses of the parent that belong to the transactions are subject to non-recording to avoid an over- or under-statement of revenues and expenses.[4]

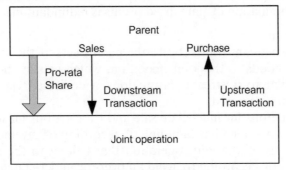

Fig. H-3   Business transactions with joint operations

Transactions **for later sale** require an elimination of unrealized profit. While the asset is recorded in the parent's accounts considering both, its own production costs as well as the production cost and profit mark-ups of the other parties, only the unrealized profit belonging to the parent has to be removed. Therefore, the unrealized profit subject to elimination can be calculated in the following way:

	Unrealized profit allocated in inventory
−	Unrealized profit attributable to other party: (1 − investment rate) × Unrealized profit
=	Unrealized profit attributable to parent (subject to elimination)
−	Deferred tax asset (Unrealized profit attributable to group × tax rate)
=	Adjustment of share of profit

Tab. H-3   Calculation of unrealized profit in upstream transactions

---

[3] See chapter F -5.1 on page 287 regarding details.
[4] Remember: A company cannot deal with itself!

The elimination together with the tax adjustment can be recorded in one combined journal entry.

<u>Journal entry</u>

dr.		Deferred tax assets
dr.		Profit & loss
	cr.	Inventory

The elimination requires certain knowledge about the profit mark-up that is included in inventory. Due to the nature of the joint operation, profit mark-up information should be available to the parent.

The accounting of transactions for own use is similar to the accounting of transactions for later sale. While both transaction types demand an elimination of unrealized profits, the calculation and procedure to be followed are identical. Deferred tax assets have to be considered as well. The recording will differ while non-current assets are involved that demands a use of appropriate accounts. Another issue may arise on the accounting for intangible assets. If accounting rules prohibit the capitalization of intangible assets, the capitalization is limited to the portion that belongs to the other parties. Elimination of unrealized profits is redundant in such a case.

- Downstream

    In downstream transactions, the parent acts as the sending company, delivering goods to the joint operation, which acts as the receiving company. Similar to upstream transactions, a dedicated view for each basic transaction is required.

    Transactions **for immediate sale** and transactions **for own consumption** share – again – a similar handling. A recording of revenues of the parent and expenses of the joint operation that belong to the transactions are subject to non-recording to avoid an over- or under-statement of revenues and expenses.

    Transactions **for later sale** require an elimination of unrealized profit. The asset is recorded in the parent's accounts considering both its own production costs, as well as the production costs and profit mark-ups of the other parties. Only unrealized profit belonging to the parent has to be removed. Therefore, the calculation of unrealized profits and its accounting is identical to the upstream case.

    Due to the allocation of the joint operation's assets to the parent, the accounting for transactions **for own use** is again identical to the upstream transaction.

The moment inventory is sold, the reversal has to be recorded. The reversal of the initial journal entry depends on the original journal entry.

<u>Journal entry</u>

dr.		Inventory
	cr.	Deferred tax assets
	cr.	Profit & loss

The need to eliminate unrealized profits can also result from transactions for own use. If goods are sold from or to the joint operation that are capitalized as fixed or intangible **assets**, the handling of the elimination of unrealized profits is similar to the one of inventory. The type of transaction (upstream or down) is not important as the reversal for both transaction types will result in the same journal entries.

Journal entry for the elimination of unrealized profits:

Journal entry
| dr. | Profit & loss | |
| | cr. | Fixed assets / intangible assets |

Journal entry for the subsequent adjustment of unrealized profits:

Journal entry
| dr. | Fixed assets / intangible assets | |
| | cr. | Depreciation expenses |

The **presentation** of joint operations in financial statements depends on the type of financial statement.

- Separate financial statements

   The requirement to account for assets, liabilities, revenue and expenses of joint operations in the accounts of a joint operator as demanded by IFRS 11.26a will result in including the joint operation directly in the separate financial statements of the parent. This may interfere with local accounting rules and regulations where companies are obliged to report separate financial statements based on local accounting standards. To achieve a consistent presentation, it is recommended not to record joint operations in separate financial statements using local accounting standards.

- Consolidated financial statements

   From a pure IFRS view, when recording transactions in separate financial statements, transactions will be also part of consolidated financial statements without any adjustments of otherwise modifications.[5] Therefore, carrying amounts of assets and liabilities in both statements should be the same. In practice, a dedicated view of the group and the transactions with joint operations is necessary that may result in a revised view.

   Every time a parent with interests in a joint operation has to prepare separate financial statements using local accounting standards, appropriate adjustments are necessary to comply with IFRS 11. It is recommended to record the joint operation at level II applying group and IFRS accounting policies.

---

[5] See also the frequently asked questions of the IASB staff regarding the presentation in separate and consolidated financial statements. Be aware that this paper is a non-official IASB guidance only!

The parent might be subject to consolidations if transactions between the joint operation and other group companies occur. Depending on the underlying business transactions, consolidation activities can include debt consolidations, consolidations of income and expenses and the elimination of unrealized profit. To ensure a proper identification of intercompany transactions, the joint operation should either be a separate reporting subject or the parent should fully incorporate the joint operation in its reporting duties.

2.2 Joint ventures

Other than the detailed accounting requirements for joint operations as defined in IFRS 11.20, **accounting** requirements for joint ventures are less detailed at first sight. IFRS 11.24 demands an application of the equity method for joint ventures only referencing to *IAS 28 – Investments in Associates and Joint Ventures* as the standard to be used regarding the accounting for joint ventures. The application of the equity method will finally result in a treatment of the joint venture as an associate. While IAS 28 does not differentiate between an associate and a joint venture, all accounting requirements have to be applied for the accounting of joints ventures as well. This includes such items as profit recording by the parent, transactions with joint ventures, accounting for losses of the joint venture and similar items.

IFRS 11.24 includes a regulation regarding **exemptions** of the application of the equity method for interests in joint ventures. It refers to the exemption provisions of IAS 28 as defined in IAS 28.17. IAS 28.17 refers to IFRS 10.4a regarding exemptions for preparing consolidated financial statements and has regulations similar to the exemption of IFRS 10.4a for the application of the equity method. General exemption rules can be applied.[6]

The **presentation** of joint ventures in financial statements depends on the type of financial statement.

- Separate financial statements
  According to IFRS 11.26b, the presentation of interests in joint ventures has to comply with IAS 27.10. Therefore, the interest in a joint venture has to be recorded either at cost or in accordance with IFRS 9. This is identical to the recording of investments in associates.

- Consolidated financial statements
  The presentation of interests in joint ventures in consolidated financial statements is not explicitly defined or mentioned in IFRS 11. Due to the referencing to IAS 28 as the relevant accounting standard for interest in joint ventures, the application of the equity method at group level including all consolidations tasks is also mandatory for joint ventures. Consolidation tasks for joint ventures are identical to consolidation tasks for associates.[7]

---

[6] See chapter B -2 on page 35 regarding any exemptions.

[7] See chapter G - on page 425 regarding the accounting and presentation in consolidated financial statements.

2.3 Interests in joint arrangements without joint control

There may be situations where parties have interests in joint arrangements without joint control. Even if no joint control is given, these parties have to fulfil some accounting requirements as their interests constitute assets that require recognition in their financial statements.

If the joint arrangement qualifies as a **joint operation** a dedicated treatment based on rights in assets and obligations of liabilities as set out in IFRS 11.23 is demanded. Therefore, two cases can occur:

* Rights and obligation exist

    If a party has rights and obligations but does not have joint control, that party has to account for its interest in the joint arrangement as if it *does* have joint control. Therefore, the accounting treatment is still the same as for parties with joint control.

* No rights and obligations

    If no rights in asset and no obligations for liabilities exist, IFRS 11.23 demand an accounting of the interest in a joint operation "in accordance with the IFRS applicable to that interest". The standard is silent about any accounting applications, any applicable IFRS and its consequences. In practice, the application would be limited to two standards: IAS 28 and IFR 11. If the party has a significant influence over the joint arrangement but no joint control, it has to account the interest in the joint arrangement according to the accounting standards of IAS 28. Thus, the joint arrangement will be accounted as an associate. If the party owns only "some" interests, an application of IFRS 9 is appropriate as the interest in the joint arrangement qualifies as a financial asset.

If the joint arrangement qualifies as a **joint venture**, an accounting as defined by IFRS 11.25 is necessary. Interests in joint arrangements that constitute significant influence have to be accounted for by applying IFRS 28. In other words, the joint arrangement has to be treated as an associate including the application of the equity method. This application is more or less identical to the accounting of interests in joint arrangements with joint control. If significant influence is not given, interests in the joint arrangement have to be treated as financial assets demanding an application of IFRS 9.

Both the accounting for interests in joint operations and joint ventures without joint control will result in a similar treatment as an associate or financial asset, demanding the application of IAS 28 or IFRS 9.

3. DISPOSALS / DECONSOLIDATION

Similar to other companies of the group, joint arrangements are subject to changes. These changes may result in a continuous application of already applied accounting methods, in a constitution of a new status in the group or an elimination while the joint arrangement may not any longer be part of a group. Other than the first case, the status of the joint arrangement ceases triggering additional accounting activities. Depending on the type and extent of these changes, a disposal or a deconsolidation or both activities have to be executed. Reasons why the status of a joint arrangement changes are manifold:

- Adjustments to contracts between all parties;
- Changes in facts and circumstances;
- Contractual termination due to fulfilment of the purpose of the joint arrangement;
- Termination by statue;
- Loss of joint control;
- Establishment of control;
- Sale of interest in joint arrangement.

All reasons can be subsumed into three accounting cases:

- Acquisitions of further interests in joint arrangements resulting in a change of control;[8]
- Partial sale of interest in joint arrangement;[9]
- Full disposal.

Other than the partial sale, the full disposal does not leave any interests in the joint arrangement. Such a disposal involves various levels where adjustments are necessary. Accordingly, the disposal has to be viewed from the parent's and the group's perspectives. These views also reflect the development of the carrying amount of the investment in joint arrangements as the account will have different balances at parent and at group level.

There are two types of joint arrangement that demand different accountings by the parent, but disposals also have to be treated differently. IFRS 11 is silent about the treatment of the disposal of interests in joint arrangements and their accounting treatment. The only place where some guidance is given about the disposal of interests in joint arrangements can be found indirectly in IFRS 5.5 (so as a treatment of assets held for sale or as discontinued operations). Due to the absence of any accounting guidelines, a careful determination of all facts and circumstances of the disposal is required before applying standard accounting procedures on disposals.

3.1 Joint operations

3.1.1 The parent's view

The parent needs to investigate the future of its assets and liabilities. This is a more sophisticated task when it involves joint assets and liabilities. An evaluation of the contractual terms regarding the treatment of joint assets and liabilities in

---

[8] See chapter I -3.6 on page 525 regarding the accounting in such situations.
[9] See chapters I -4.2 and I -4.3 on page 533 et. seq. regarding the accounting in such situations.

case the joint arrangement ceases is mandatory. Depending on the type of asset and liability, the following tasks are necessary:

- Own assets

    Own non-current assets (intangible, tangible and financial) that are used in joint operations are usually not subject to any special treatments due to the disposal of the joint arrangement. Nevertheless, an investigation regarding the nature of the assets and the intended further use or obsolescence is required. If the assets can be used as before but in a different environment, any adjustments to the carrying amounts of the assets are not necessary. By contrast, if further use as before is not necessary (e.g. due to the uniqueness of the assets), a determination of the future economic benefit is necessary. This requires the execution of an impairment test. Impairment tests are demanded by IAS 16.63 for property, plant & equipment, IAS 38.111 for intangible assets and IFRS 9.5.2.2 for financial assets.

    Own current assets used in the joint operation may exist as well. In principle, the treatment is the same as for non-current assets: future use depends on a potential sale to customers or own use. If the assets cannot be used as before, a revaluation is necessary to determine the lower of cost or net realizable value according to IAS 2.9.

    As far as the parent is accounting for assets in its balance sheet that are purchased from or sold to the joint operation, potential adjustments of unrealized profits have to be determined and – if present – accounted for.

- Share of joint assets

    Joint assets always require an investigation regarding the owner of the asset and any transfer in ownership. The moment the joint operation ceases, a decision is necessary regarding what to do with joint assets, which can either be sold or taken over by another party. This demands a recording of either a disposal or an acquisition. It is irrelevant if the assets are current or non-current, the treatment is always the same.

- Own liabilities

    As each party is responsible for its own liabilities, a settlement of these liabilities does not interfere with disposal of the joint operation and is based on the underlying settlement conditions.

    Additional liabilities can arise, based on contractual agreements due to the disposal and the duties of each party in closing the business. Appropriate consideration of any contingent liabilities arising is recommended.

- Share of joint liabilities

    The final category, the recording of the share of joint liabilities by each party, also demands a contractual assessment. These liabilities may be satisfied by the proceeds of the sale of joint assets or by a defined contribution or compensation by all or defined parties.

The gain or loss realized and recorded by a party can be estimated by applying the following calculation:

	Gains / losses due to the revaluation of own assets
+/–	Gains / losses of impairment tests on own assets
+	Proceeds from the sale of own assets
–	Carrying amount of own assets
+	Allocable proceeds from the sale of joint assets
+	Reimbursements due to the transfer of joint assets to another party
–	Carrying amount of share in joint assets
–	Obligations to settle own liabilities
–	Obligations to settle the share in joint liabilities
–	Additional obligations arising due to the disposal of the joint operation
+/–	Differences due to foreign currency translations
+/–	Changes in the carrying amount of deferred tax assets and tax liabilities
=	Realized gain / loss

Tab. H-4   Gain / loss of the disposal of a joint operation, the parent's view

Depending on the disposal and the agreement with the other parties, journal entries vary.

- Gain

  A gain due to the sale of non-current asset is usually presented as other income or other earnings in the profit & loss statement.

Journal entry			Comment
dr.		Other expenses	Recognition of any settlement obligations
	cr.	Trade payables (or other payables)	Recognition of additional liabilities
dr.		Impairment losses	Recognition of any impairment losses and revaluation adjustments
	cr.	Carrying amount of assets	
dr.		Trade receivables (or other receivables)	Recognition of the sale for own and joint assets
	cr.	Carrying amount of assets	Derecognition of own and joint assets
	cr.	Gain on sale of assets	

Differences due to foreign currency translations and changes in the carrying amount of deferred tax assets and tax liabilities follow the ordinary accounting rules for such items.

- Loss

  A loss due to the sale of a non-current asset is usually presented as other expenses in the profit & loss statement.

Journal entry		Comment
dr.	Other expenses	Recognition of any settlement obligations
	cr. Trade payables (or other payables)	Recognition of additional liabilities
dr.	Impairment losses	Recognition of any impairment losses and revaluation adjustments
	cr. Carrying amount of assets	
dr.	Trade receivables (or other receivables)	Recognition of the sale for own and joint assets
dr.	Loss on sale of assets	
	cr. Carrying amount of assets	Derecognition of own and joint assets

Again, differences due to foreign currency translations and changes in the carrying amount of deferred tax assets and tax liabilities follow the ordinary accounting rules for such items.

3.1.2 The group's view

The group's view of the disposal of a joint operation is primarily based on the parent's view. This is because all transactions recorded in the parent's account are also part of consolidated financial statements. The disposal on parent level will therefore automatically result in a disposal at group level without any further adjustments. An exception is given to consolidation tasks only. If assets of the joint operation were subject to consolidations tasks due to the engagement of the joint operation in business transactions with other group companies, a consolidation adjustment might be required if the carrying amounts of assets and liabilities subject to the joint operation were intentionally modified by consolidation entries. This applies particularly to any unrealized profits of inventories or non-current assets. These adjustments have to be reversed.

3.2 Joint ventures

3.2.1 The parent's view

The sale of all interests in a joint venture is the same as the sale of all interests in an associate. This is because for both types of investment, the same accounting methods have to be applied. The accounting methods require a development of the carrying amount of investments in joint ventures towards the disposal date. The following journal entries have to be applied:

Journal entries		Comment
dr.	Investments in joint ventures	Recording of the profit.
	cr. Share of profit of the associate	Can also be a debit in case of a loss situation.
dr.	Bank	Recording of the dividend.
	cr. Investments in joint ventures	

At the disposal date, the gain or loss realized by the disposal can be estimated using the following calculation:

	Proceeds from the sale of interests in joint ventures
−	Carrying amount of the interests in joint ventures
=	Realized gain / loss

Tab. H-5   Gain / loss of the sale of a joint venture, the parent's view

Journal entries are the same as for associates:

- Gain

Journal entry		Comment
dr.	Gain on sale of joint venture	Derecognition of investment which is a part of financial assets
	cr. Investments in joint venture	
dr.	Trade receivables (or other receivables)	Recognition of the sales transaction
	cr. Gain on sale of joint venture	

- Loss

Journal entry		Comment
dr.	Loss on sale of joint venture	Derecognition of investment which is a part of financial assets
	cr. Investments in joint venture	
dr.	Accounts receivables (or other receivables)	Recognition of the sales transaction
	cr. Loss on sale of joint venture	

Furthermore, deviations of cash flows due to variable elements have to be recorded if appropriate.

3.2.2 *The group's view*

The disposal of a joint venture at group level is a more sophisticated task as several accounting requirements have to be considered due to the application of the equity method. While the disposal of joint ventures at group level is identical to the disposal of associates at group level, all deconsolidation and disposal aspects discussed for associates can be applied to joint ventures as well (see chapter G -2.3.2 for the accounting of disposals).[10]

3.3 IFRS 5 and disposals of joint arrangements

Joint arrangements in general can also be subject to IFRS 5 and classify as held for sale: as assets or businesses, or discontinued operations prior to its subsequent sales. Due to the absence of any specific accounting guidelines for joint arrangements, standard steps and procedures have to be applied for full and partial disposals as defined by *IFRS 5 – Non-current Assets Held for Sale and Discontinued Operations*.[11]

---

[10] See page 458.

[11] See chapter J -4 on page 601 regarding the treatment for joint operations (so for assets held for sale) and chapters G -2.3.3 on page 466 and J -4 on page 601 regarding the treatment for joint ventures.

I CHANGES IN CONTROL

About this chapter:

Every time a share in a company is purchased or sold, the investment in that company changes. This also changes the control in the company. Depending on the type and status of the company in a group, the changed investment in the company has an impact not only on the accounting in the investment but also on the group's position. This chapter explains the accounting treatment of changes in control, both by the parent as well as the group.

Changes in control occur also upon the acquisition or sale of a company within a group. These transactions are slightly different to other changes in control as they have no interest in the company either before or after the transactions are executed. Therefore, both transactions (acquisition and sale of companies) are discussed in detail in other chapters.[1] This chapter focuses on changes in control which involve existing investments.

---

[1] See chapter E-2 on page 128 for the detailed discussion on initial purchase of investment in subsidiaries and chapter J - Disposals and deconsolidation on page 569 of the full disposal of all investments in a subsidiary.

1. BASICS

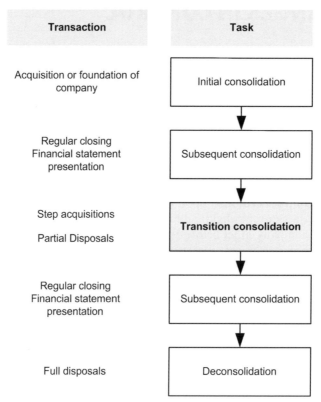

Fig. I-1   Lifecycle of a corporation: Transitional consolidation

All transactions that increase or decrease the interest in another company are subject to changes in control.[2] The reasons for these changes are manifold and often depend on the:

- overall strategy of management on how to develop the group,
- portfolio of companies in the group,
- options to be executed or that become due,
- cash demand of the group, and
- opportunity to increase voting rights.

Further reasons exist. All these reasons are based on the assumption that a consideration has to be received or paid which is usually cash or shares in the parent. In addition to these examples, changes in control can occur without any consideration involved. Such situations are often based on contracts

---

[2] See chapter C -1 on page 43 regarding the definition and application of control.

between shareholders. Examples of transactions that change control without any consideration transferred are:

- Changes in the article of a corporation or its bylaws,
- Contractual agreements regarding control between shareholders, or
- Dissenting voting rights.

Again, further scenarios may exist that trigger changes in control without any considerations.

The general accounting treatment of changes in control differs between the parent and the group. While the parent has to adjust its interest in subsidiaries only, a transitional consolidation by the group is required. The transitional consolidation can be triggered by step acquisitions, partial disposals or changes due to contractual agreements. It has to be executed anytime the investment will change.

While equity is a key element, transitional consolidations may include other consolidations as well. Depending on the status of the subsidiary, transitional consolidations may include debt consolidations, consolidations of earnings and expenses and adjustments of inventory, intangible and fixed assets. Transitional consolidations can have various characteristics. Sales as well as purchasing transactions may force to change the status of a company if the classification criteria for each specific category are met. Due to the various categories a company can be assigned to, various transitional consolidation scenarios are possible. Furthermore, if the company is not assigned to a new category, specific accounting guidelines may have to be followed. The following matrix provides support on transitional consolidations that may be appropriate based on the type of changes of control.

From			To	
	Financial Investment	**Associate**	**Joint Venture**	**Subsidiary**
Financial Investment	Status	Upwards	Upward	Upwards
Associated Company	Downwards	Status	Upwards or Status	Upwards
Joint Venture	Downwards	Downwards or Status	Status	Upwards
Subsidiary	Downwards	Downwards	Downwards	Status

Tab. I-1 Matrix of changes in control

In accordance with the status of a company in the group, the wording of the influence of the parent in its investment will change:

- Control is given every time a parent can direct its subsidiary without involving any other party.
- Joint control is given if the parent requires at least one other party to direct the joint venture in common.

- If the parent has a reasonable share in a company it also has significant influence. However, other parties may also have control on their own, or in joint arrangements, or as the result of a collaboration, or for many other reasons.

We will treat all these different wordings as subheadings of changes in control.

2. THE PARENT'S VIEW

Changes in control impact – like many other transactions – the parent as well as the group. From a parent's point of view, a purchase or a sale of interests in a subsidiary is a simple transaction to be executed in the accounts of the parent company. The accounting is similar to any purchase or sale of fixed assets where an increase or decrease in the carrying amount of a non-current asset is recorded. Even if these transactions are simple to execute, they can initiate changes in the group structure.

At the purchase date, all components of the purchase price have to be recorded as an increase in the carrying amount of the investment in subsidiaries. Even if an increase of an investment already made occurs, it follows the same principles as an initial acquisition.[3] If the contractual obligation includes variable elements, they are recorded based on the expected and discounted future cash flows using an appropriate discount rate that reflects the current market condition.

The new carrying amount of an investment in a subsidiary can be estimated by applying one the following calculations:

- Increase of interest in subsidiary

	Carrying amount of the interests in the subsidiary
+	Investments in the subsidiary purchased
=	New carrying amount of the interests in the subsidiary

Tab. I-2 Calculation of the carrying amount in subsidiaries for a sales activity, Increase of investment

- Decrease of interest in subsidiary

	Carrying amount of the interests in the subsidiary
–	Investments in the subsidiary sold
=	New carrying amount of the interests in the subsidiary

Tab. I-3 Calculation of the carrying amount in subsidiaries for a sales activity, decrease of investment

The journal entry of recording a **purchase** transaction is similar to all other transactions:

---

[3] See chapter E-3.3 on page 143 for elements that have to be considered as part of the purchase price.

Journal entry

dr.		Investment in subsidiaries
	cr.	Trade payables (or other payables)

The journal entry of recording a **partial disposal** will result either in a gain or loss. Therefore, journal entries may vary depending on the sale.

- Gain

    A gain due to the sale of a non-current asset is usually presented as other income or other earnings in the profit & loss statement.

Journal entries			Comment
dr.		Gain on sale of subsidiary	Derecognition of investment which is a part of financial assets
	cr.	Investments in subsidiaries	
dr.		Trade receivables (or other receivables)	Recognition of the sales transaction
	cr.	Gain on sale of subsidiary	

- Loss

    A loss due to the sale of a non-current asset is usually presented as other expenses in the profit & loss statement.

Journal entries			Comment
dr.		Loss on sale of subsidiary	Derecognition of investment which is a part of financial assets
	cr.	Investments in subsidiaries	
dr.		Accounts receivables (or other receivables)	Recognition of the sales transaction
	cr.	Loss on sale of subsidiary	

The group's view of the transaction of the parent is more complex. Increases and decreases of investments in subsidiaries, joint ventures, associates and other investments have an impact on the status of the investment in the group. Depending on the investment before the increase or decrease and the transaction of the parent, different tasks are necessary at group level. These tasks may include purchase price allocations, equity consolidations, equity transactions and disclosures in the notes. In some cases, the parent's transactions also impact the profit of the group as adjustments of selected assets and liabilities may be necessary that are recorded through profit & loss.

3. INCREASE IN INVESTMENTS

Increase in investments occur if the parent company is able to expand its investment in another company. Such transactions are usual if the other company is stock-listed and there are only limited opportunities in bulk transactions. As a consequence, small investments are acquired. It is assumed that there is an initial interest. An increase in investments may result in an increase in control. Increases in control are also discussed as "step acquisitions" or "acquisitions achieved in stages" in literature. It is not important how many steps are executed, the accounting for incremental increases in an investment always follows the same model. Common to all increases is a change of the status of the company in the group and the questions: "What is purchased?" and "What are the corresponding acquisition costs?". Changes can span over all company categories – from financial investments to subsidiaries.

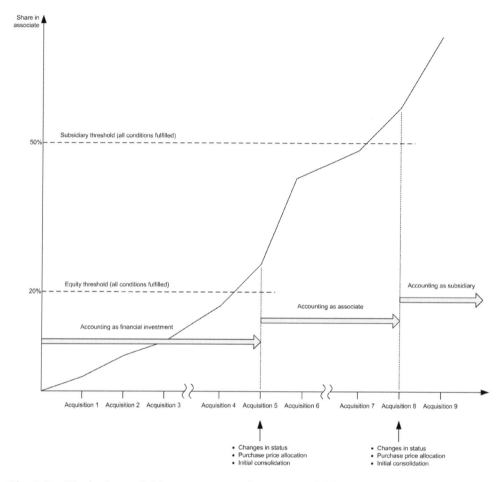

Fig. I-2   Typical acquisition structure of step acquisitions

3.1. Financial investment to associate

A transition of a financial investment towards an associate occurs if the purchasing of additional investments in that company constitutes significant influence. This will be assumed if the investment in associates results in more than 20% of the voting power. Reasons why a change occurred are not important. As an initial investment is present, the whole transaction is treated as a step acquisition according to IAS 28.32. Depending on the accounting of the financial investment, the accounting that is based either on *IAS 39 – Financial*

Instruments: Recognition and Measurement or *IFRS 9 – Financial Instruments* will change towards the accounting according to *IAS 28 – Investment in Associates and Joint Ventures.* The relevant date is that date when all conditions to account for as an associate are fulfilled. Accordingly, up to this date, the interests in that company are treated as financial investments with an appropriate measurement.

As the change in status from financial investment to associate requires a minimum of two purchase transactions, a step acquisition is always given. Steps acquisitions can be realized by the parent or any other subsidiary of the group already carrying an initial interest that is presented as a financial investment. They can also be made by any other parent, holding company or subsidiary of the group. It is not important which group company executes the acquisition as long as significant influence can be established, either directly or indirectly.

From an accounting perspective, the (new) associate will be initially accounted for applying the provisions of IAS 28.32. IAS 28.32 demands separate recognition of differences between the cost of the investment and share of the net fair value (identifiable assets and liabilities) of the associate at the date the financial investment becomes an associate. This will trigger an initial consolidation including a purchase price allocation and an initial equity consolidation.[4] The steps of the initial consolidation of associates have to be expanded by an additional task. Therefore, it is recommended to execute all activities in the following order:

Step	Task	Comment
1)	Recording of the (last) acquisition of interest in associates by the parent	
2)	Estimation of the cost of the investment	This is the additional task to be executed in step acquisitions!
3)	Execution of a purchase price allocation	
4)	Consolidation	
5)	Search and accounting for any pre-existing relationships	
6)	Execution of impairment tests	

Tab. I-4 Execution order of step acquisitions by the parent for financial investments to associates

The **first step** – estimation of acquisition costs – relates only to the last acquisition of interests in the associate that establish significant influence. The estimation of the purchase price follows the same rules than any other acquisition costs. It consists of the purchase price and any acquisition-related costs.[5]

---

[4] See chapter G -2.1 on page 430 regarding details of the initial consolidation.

[5] See acquisition costs on page 464 and acquisition-related costs on page 428 regarding considerable elements.

An identification and determination of these acquisition costs should be manageable without any problems including those items that deal with variable elements such as future compensation.

More attention has to be given to the **second step**, the calculation of the costs of financial investments currently held. This calculation is necessary as this is one element of the purchase price as of that date where significant influence is established. IAS 28.10 and 28.32 demand only recognition of the investment in an associate at cost (which should reflect the purchase price). The standard is silent about the definition and composition of this cost. It is also silent about the application of an appropriate accounting method and the recording of any gains and losses arising on the initial investment. Therefore, a set of accounting options is available to determine the (deemed) costs.

- Analogy to IFRS 3

    As with IFRS 3, the original investments will be sold for fair value and an acquisition of the same investment will be simulated at the date the financial investment became an associate. This will result in a recognition of a gain or loss in the profit & loss statement.

    Treatment in analogy to IFRS 3 can run into the same problem as for subsidiaries: How to measure the original investment? Is a simple extrapolation of the consideration sufficient or is a full revaluation required? A simple extrapolation does not consider the relationship in the market between the existing and new interests as well as any implied premium due to bulk acquisitions. For a proper fair value measurement, the correct method would be a complete revaluation as significant influence is achieved, which would have to consider an elimination of any premiums to arrive at the fair value. Therefore, it is recommended to apply the following guideline in determining the fair value of financial investment. If all acquisitions are time dependent, a simple extrapolation is suitable. If this timely dependency is not given, a complete valuation of existing interests is required. Such a valuation depends on the status of the acquiree. If the acquiree is a publicly listed corporation, market values can be used to determine the fair value. If the acquiree is a privately held corporation, an application of discounted cash flow methods is appropriate in determining an entity value. The expected cash flows are subject to discounting in subsequent periods, based on the planned business activities.[6]

    The consolidation profit for the adjustment of the carrying amount of the financial investment can be calculated using the following scheme assuming that all adjustments are recorded through profit & loss.

---

[6] See Appendix I: Fair value measurement on page 751 regarding more details on applicable valuation measurement methods.

	Gains from the addition of financial investments @ fair value
−	Losses from the disposal of financial investments @ carrying amount
+/−	Fair value changes recorded in other comprehensive income
=	Consolidation gain / loss

Tab. I-5 Calculation scheme for determining consolidation gain/losses financial investments to associates

The following journal entry can be used.

Journal entry			Comment
dr.		Investments in associates	Deemed costs
dr.		Profit & loss	Recording of valuation adjustment
	cr.	Financial investment	Carrying amount of financial investment

- Retrospective revaluation

Retrospective revaluation of the original investments through other comprehensive income is also appropriate for arriving at deemed costs. This requires knowledge about the situation of the financial investment at previous acquisition dates. In particular, any implied unrecorded assets and liabilities, hidden reserves and burdens have to be known that have to be advanced to the date the financial investment becomes an associate. This requires retrospective application of a purchase price allocation or a similar method to determine carrying amounts of these additional items. Keeping this in mind, deemed costs for each acquisition of interests in financial investments can be calculated.

	Acquisition costs of original financial investment
+	Retained earnings not distributed to investors
+/−	Adjustments and depreciations on non-accounted items, hidden reserves and burdens
+/−	Valuation adjustments due to measurement of financial investment @ fair value
+/−	Effects of foreign currency translations
=	Deemed costs

Tab. I-6 Calculation scheme of deemed costs

In this case, gains or losses arising from the comparison of deemed costs with the carrying amount of financial investments will be recorded directly in equity. If the original investments are treated as available for sale and any fair value adjustments are recorded through other comprehensive income, a recycling of these items in profit & loss is not appropriate. Adjustments will result in the following journal entry.

Journal entry		Comment
dr.	Investments in associates	Deemed costs
dr.	Other comprehensive income	Recording of valuation adjustment
cr.	Financial investment	Carrying amount of financial investment

• Prospective application

Some argue that an adjustment of the original investments is not necessary and that the carrying amount of these investments can be used as it is. This will result in a pure reclassification using a single journal entry.

Journal entry	
dr.	Investments in associates
cr.	Financial investments

Special attention is – again – required if financial investments are treated as available for sale. In such cases a recycling is necessary.

Journal entry		Comment
dr.	Other comprehensive income	Can also be a credit.
cr.	Profit & loss	

Due to the regulatory gap of IAS 28 on the **application of an appropriate method** to account for step acquisitions and the cost of investment, a discussion can be found in literature about the proper method to be applied; there are divergent opinions. Some argue that, in the absence of any accounting requirements, it is for the preparers to apply the method of their choice, while others prefer consistent application of accounting options and methods. The latter propose retrospective application, as this is consistent with IFRS 1, and particularly IFRS 1.40A. The downside of this argument is the preparation of a third statement.

Even if these accounting options are available, a selection of one option is an accounting policy choice. Therefore, all subsequent acquisitions – and particularly step acquisitions – of associates have to follow the selected accounting treatment to ensure a consistent application.

All other steps to be executed are identical to the initial consolidation of associates. The revaluation of assets and liabilities purchased, the execution of a purchase price allocation, the initial equity consolidation, the consideration of pre-existing relationships and an impairment test are standard tasks.

3.2. Financial investment to joint venture

By acquiring additional shares, either due to purchase from another shareholder or an increase in share capital, a financial investment may become a joint venture if appropriate agreements are made between shareholders, and joint control will be established. A determination of contractual conditions is mandatory to prove a proper status as a joint venture.

IAS 28 no longer differentiates between associates and joint ventures and instead requires uniform application of the equity method for both types of investment. However, the accounting of a step acquisition of a joint venture is identical to the accounting of a step acquisition of an associate (which was explained in detail in the previous chapter).

3.3. Financial investment to subsidiary

By acquiring additional shares or similar equity instruments of a company that is currently recorded as a financial investment, control may be constituted. Such an acquisition assumes that the voting rights will be increased from less than 20% to more than 50% to establish control. As investments are already present, this transaction is a step acquisition according to IFRS 3. The acquisition date is determined as date where conditions are met that constitutes control.

To account for step acquisitions, IFRS 3.42 demands that investments in the acquiree held have to be remeasured to reflect fair value as of the acquisition date before applying the acquisition method. From an abstract view of IFRS 3, establishment of control has two basic elements: the acquisition of new shares – paid for in cash, or assets or liabilities, or equity instruments – and an exchange transaction that converts the carrying amount of the current investment into a fair value. This exchange transaction is treated as a disposal of the financial investment with its current value combined with a fictitious acquisition of these investments at fair value. As a consequence, the increase in investment has to be accounted for in two blocks: The first block focuses on the measurement of interests currently acquired and existing interests, while the second block applies the acquisition method by executing a purchase price allocation.

Consequently, the first block is subject to an accounting in the separate financial statements of the parent. In addition to the measurement of the interest acquired and the interest remeasured, a reclassification from financial investment to investments in subsidiaries is required. It is recommended to execute all activities in the following order:

Step	Task
1)	Estimation of consideration transferred that relate to the acquired items
2)	Calculation of the fair values of financial investment currently held
3)	Accounting of a disposal of the currently held financial investments @ carrying amount
4)	Accounting of an acquisition of the currently held financial investment @ fair value (this transaction automatically implies the reclassification)

Tab. I-7 Execution order of step acquisitions by the parent for financial investments to subsidiaries

The **first step**, the accounting for the consideration transferred in step acquisitions, is identical to the determination of the purchase price or the consideration transferred in every other acquisition. Consequently, the standard procedures of purchase price allocation can be applied that relate to the determination of considerations transferred.[7]

The **second step**, the calculation of the fair value measurement of existing financial investments at the acquisition date, is demanded by IFRS 3.42. While this standard is silent about the measurement of existing financial investments, there is a regulatory gap when determining the appropriate fair value of these investments. An observed practice is that the value of the existing interests is calculated by a simple extrapolation of the consideration transferred of the current acquisition in relation to the existing portion. This practice does not consider the relationship in the market between existing and new interests, or any implied control premium. For a proper fair value measurement, the correct method would be a complete revaluation as control is achieved. Such a revaluation has to consider an elimination of a control premium to arrive at the fair value. In practice, control premiums cannot be estimated reliably which may result in a non-consideration. Therefore, it is recommended to apply the following guideline in determining the fair value of the existing interests.

If all acquisitions are time dependent, a simple extrapolation is suitable. If this timely dependency is not given, a complete valuation of existing interests is required. Such a valuation depends on the status of the acquiree. If the acquiree is a publicly listed corporation, market values can be used in determining the fair value. Instead, if the acquiree is privately held, an application of discounted cash flow methods is appropriate in determining value. Subject to discounting are the expected cash flows in subsequent periods based on the planned business activities. The entity value then can be used for the calculation of the fair value of the existing investment.[8]

A side-effect is accounting for deferred taxes. Deferred taxes on existing investments may have been recorded upon any fair value adjustments of financial investments compared to the tax position of financial investments. The disposal will release these deferred tax assets or liabilities while the fictitious acquisition will establish another deferred tax asset or liability. In consequence, a deferred tax item will be recognized due to the adjustment to fair values because from a tax perspective no changes occurred.

The consolidation profit for the fair value adjustment can be calculated using the following scheme assuming that all adjustments are recorded through profit & loss. This scheme can be used for all acquisitions of interests that trigger transitional consolidations according to IFRS 3.

---

[7] See chapter E-3.3 on page 143 regarding the accounting for considerations transferred.

[8] See Appendix I: Fair value measurement on page 751 regarding more details on applicable valuation measurement methods.

	Gains from the addition of existing investments @ fair value
−	Losses from the disposal of existing investments @ carrying amount
+/−	Fair value changes recorded in other comprehensive income
+/−	Deferred taxes[9]
=	Consolidation gain / loss

Tab. I-8　Calculation scheme for determining consolidation gain/ losses financial investments to subsidiary.

The **third step**, accounting for the disposal of the existing financial investment, removes the carrying amount and depends on the initial recording. If the investment was recorded through other comprehensive income, the removal has to be accounted also through other comprehensive income. If the investment was classified as trading, the removal is recorded through profit & loss. This requires knowledge about the initial accounting of the financial investments as these investments are subject to the classification and measurement according to either IAS 39 or IFRS 9.

> IFRS 3.42 was modified with the introduction of IFRS 9. Under the old standard, any fair value adjustment needed to be recorded through profit & loss. The revised standard now differentiates between an adjustment through profit & loss and other comprehensive income. Which adjustment is applicable depends on the initial recording of financial investments (held to maturity or trading).

Journal entries vary depending on the initial recording of financial investments.

- Through profit & loss

Journal entry
dr.　　　　Other expenses
　　cr.　　　　Interests in financial investments　　Carrying amount

- Through other comprehensive income

Journal entry
dr.　　　　Other comprehensive income
　　cr.　　　　Interests in financial investments　　Carrying amount

---

[9] Deferred taxes are often not considered in determining the consolidation gain or loss in other literature. This is due to the focus on the calculation of fair value adjustments only. As the accounted financial investments are subject to deferred taxes in separate financial statements of the parent upon the subsequent measurement according to IFRS, taxation effects may exist that trigger the accounting of deferred taxes. Consequently, to have a complete picture of the impact on profit & loss, deferred taxes are considered.

The **fourth step**, the recording of a fictitious acquisition of the existing financial investments, adds existing financial investments to investment in subsidiaries considering fair value. Similar to the disposal, the acquisition follows the initial recognition of the underlying financial investment. The accounting change in IFRS 3.42 is also applicable to the acquisition. In parallel, the journal entry not only considers the change in value but also the reclassification by using a different account.

Journal entries vary depending on the initial recording of financial investments.

- Through profit & loss

Journal entry		Comment
dr.	Investment in subsidiaries	Fair value to be used
cr.	Other expenses / Other earnings	Depends if separate presentation or netting is applied

- Through other comprehensive income

Journal entry		
dr.	Investment in subsidiaries	Fair value to be used
cr.	Other comprehensive income	

Even if the separate accounting of disposal and acquisition of the existing financial investment offers a transparent approach, an **alternate treatment** of the third and fourth step can be observed in practice. Journal entries are combined and executed in one step to document the dependencies between the accounts. This requires the determination of the difference between the fair value and the carrying amount of the financial investment. Again, journal entries have to distinguish the recording between profit & loss and other comprehensive income.

- Through profit & loss

Journal entry		Comment
dr.	Investment in subsidiaries	
cr.	Other earnings	Can also be a debit.
cr.	Interests in financial investments	

- Through other comprehensive income

Journal entry		Comment
dr.	Investment in subsidiaries	
cr.	Other comprehensive income	Can also be a debit.
cr.	Interests in financial investments	

Having successfully adjusted the carrying amount of the investment in subsidiaries, the second block executes the application of the acquisition method. Up to this point, only the consideration transferred has been recognized by the parent (or any holding company or subsidiary of the group). What is left is the application of a purchase price allocation. From a group's perspective, the transaction of increasing the interest in financial investments is identical to a full initial consolidation. A purchase price allocation as discussed in chapter E -3 has to be applied. The calculation of goodwill is identical to the calculations presented before:

	Consideration transferred to obtain control
+	Fair value of any previously held interest in acquire
+	Amount of non-controlling interests
–	Fair value of identifiable net assets of the acquire
=	Goodwill / badwill attributable to the acquirer

Tab. I-9   Calculation of goodwill / badwill

All further activities, particularly the consolidation techniques for the initial recording as a subsidiary, follow the steps discussed in detail in chapter E -5.

3.4. Associate to joint venture

The formation of a joint venture using an existing company is a task that is realized at shareholder level. The shareholders have to enter into a contractual agreement to share the control of a joint venture in a way that requires an unanimous consent. This sharing does not necessarily mean that the investment in the company that acts as the joint venture will change or has to be adjusted. Nevertheless, adjustments are often made to align control with the investment in the joint venture.

From a commercial perspective, the investment in an associate can be used by the parent in a way that the investment in an associate will act as the contribution of the parent if forming the joint venture. Therefore, the status of the associate changes to a joint venture. Also, a change from significant influence to join control occurs.

From an accounting perspective, both types of investment – the associate as well as the joint venture – are accounted for by application of the equity method if there are no special considerations that require a recording of assets and liabilities in the parent's accounts. The accounting method therefore does not change. The carrying amount of the investment in the associate at parent level and the equity value at group level have to be advanced as if there was no change in the status of the associate. IAS 28.24 explicitly demands a continuation of the equity method without any adjustments or remeasurements of the carrying amount at parent and group level due to the change in the status. Consequently, no accounting tasks are necessary.

3.5. Associate to subsidiary

When additional shares, or similar equity instruments, of a company that is currently recorded as an associate are acquired and control is constituted, a change in the accounting method is mandatory. The status of the associate will change towards a subsidiary. This acquisition assumes that the voting rights will establish control by increasing from more than 20% but less than 50%, to more than 50%. As investments in a company are already present, this transaction is a step acquisition according to IFRS 3. The acquisition date is determined as that date where conditions constituted control.

The accounting is the same as for financial investments, IFRS 3.42 is also applicable. The difference between a step acquisition that starts with financial investments and a step acquisition that starts with an associate is the carrying amount of the investment in associates, which includes adjustments due to the application of the equity method. The carrying amount has to be adjusted towards the acquisition date.

Having an abstract view of the accounting requirements as defined in IFRS 3, the transaction that establishes control consist of two basic elements: an acquisition of new shares that are paid in cash or assets or liabilities or equity instruments and an exchange transaction that converts the carrying amount of the investment in associates into a fair value. This exchange transaction is treated as a disposal of the investment in associates with its current value combined with a fictitious acquisition of these investments at fair value. As a consequence, the accounting for an increase in the investment has to be realized in two blocks: The first block measures interests acquired and existing, while the second block applies the acquisition method by executing a purchase price allocation. Again, the procedure is identical to a financial investment becoming a subsidiary.

Consequently, the first block is subject to an accounting in the separate financial statements of the parent. In addition to the measurement of the interest acquired and the interest remeasured, a reclassification from investment in associates to investments in subsidiaries is required. It is recommended to execute all activities in the following order:

Step	Task
1)	Application of the equity method during the period until the acquisition date
2)	Estimation of consideration transferred that relate to the acquired items
3)	Calculation of the fair values of investments in associates currently held
4)	Accounting for a disposal of the currently held investments in associates @ carrying amount
5)	Accounting for an acquisition of the currently held investment in associates @ fair value (this transaction automatically implies the reclassification)

Tab. I-10 Execution order of step acquisitions by the parent for investments in associates

The **first step**, the adjustment of the carrying amount of the investment in associates, is a pure application of the equity method described in chapter G. All transactions that influence the carrying amount have to be advanced to the acquisition date. If necessary, the auxiliary calculation has to be updated to reconcile with the carrying amount at the acquisition date. Tasks to be executed are in particular:

- Recognition of any profits realized between the beginning of the period and the acquisition date.

- Recording of any dividends received before the acquisition date.
- Amortization of intangible assets until the acquisition date.
- If necessary, adjustment of contingent liabilities assumed and provisions.
- Adjustments of deferred taxes based on asset / liability adjustments.
- Execution of an impairment test for goodwill and recording of any impairment losses in applicable.

The impairment test is usually a mandatory annual task that should be executed at least at the acquisition date to ensure that the implied goodwill is not overstated. Any impairment test should be agreed with the auditors for each individual case.

The **second step** – accounting for the consideration transferred during step acquisitions – is identical to determining a purchase price or the consideration during any acquisition. Consequently, standard procedures for purchase price allocation can be applied.[10]

Calculation of fair value in associate investments as of the acquisition date – the **third step** – is required by IFRS 3.42. While the standard is the same for financial investments and associates, the valuation issue discussed in detail for financial investments is also valid for associates. Therefore, the regulatory gap that exists when determining appropriate fair value also applies to investments in associates. Again, a simple extrapolation of the consideration transferred from the current acquisition in relation to the existing associate investment is applied also to associates. This practice does not consider the relationship in the market between the existing and new interests as well as any implied control premium. For a proper fair value measurement, the correct method would be a complete revaluation as control is achieved. Such a revaluation has to consider an elimination of a control premium to arrive at the fair value. In practice, control premiums cannot be estimated reliably, which may result in a non-consideration. Therefore, it is recommended to apply the following guideline in determining the fair value of the existing interests.[11]

If all acquisitions are time dependent, a simple extrapolation would be suitable. If there is no such dependency, a complete valuation of existing interests is required, which depends on the status of the acquiree. If the acquiree is a publicly listed corporation, market values can be used in determining the fair value. Instead, if the acquiree is a privately held corporation, an application of discounted cash flow methods is appropriate in determining an entity value. Cash flows expected in subsequent periods are subject to discounting. The entity value then can be used for the calculation of the fair value of the existing investment.[12]

A side effect is the accounting for deferred taxes. Deferred taxes on existing investments in associates may have been recorded upon any additional task required

---

[10] See chapter E -3.3 on page 143 regarding the accounting for considerations transferred.

[11] The following passage is a repetition of the passage in chapter I -3.3.

[12] See Appendix I: Fair value measurement on page 751 regarding more details on applicable valuation measurement methods.

by the application of the equity method compared to the tax position of the investment in associates. There are three levels where deferred taxes are recorded:

- Company level: Deferred tax assets and liabilities (due to inside basis differences I) are not subject to any adjustment as these items are recorded by the associate.
- Level III: Deferred tax assets and liabilities (due to inside basis differences II) as a consequence of the purchase price allocation. Reasons for a deviation of the carrying amounts are caused by identified hidden reserves and burdens, non-accounted assets, contingent liabilities and goodwill subject to depreciation or impairment tests. These items are part of the carrying amount of investments in associates.
- Parent level: Deferred tax assets or liabilities (due to outside basis differences) accounted for separately from the investment in associates.

The disposal will release deferred tax assets or liabilities due to outside basis differences while the fictitious acquisition will establish another deferred tax asset or liability. In consequence, a deferred tax item will be recognized due to the adjustment to fair values because from a tax perspective no changes occurred.

The consolidation profit for the fair value adjustment can be calculated using the following schemes assuming that all adjustments are recorded through profit & loss. This scheme can be used for all acquisitions of interests that trigger transitional consolidations according to IFRS 3. Two options exist to calculate a consolidation profit:

- Option 1

	Proceeds from the addition of old shares @ new value
−	Expenses from the disposal of old shares @ carrying amount
+/−	Fair value changes recorded in other comprehensive income
+/−	Differences due to foreign currency translations
+/−	Deferred taxes
=	Consolidation gain / loss

Tab. I-11 Calculation scheme for determining consolidation gain/ losses associated company to subsidiary, option 1

- Option 2

	Addition of valuation differences between new and old value of investments in associates
−	Disposal of recorded profits
+	Addition of dividends paid
+/−	Fair value changes recorded in other comprehensive income
+/−	Differences due to foreign currency translations
−	Deferred taxes
=	Consolidation gain / loss

Tab. I-12 Calculation scheme for determining consolidation gain/ losses associated company to subsidiary, option 2

Both options will deliver the same results.

The **fourth step**, the accounting of the disposal of the investment in associates, will remove the carrying amount of the investment in associates. The removal is recorded through profit & loss or other comprehensive income depending on the original journal entries. This requires a history of all movements of the balances of investments in associates including knowledge on the contra-account used. In most cases, the removal is recorded through profit & loss. A recording through other comprehensive income may occur due to valuation adjustments.

> IFRS 3.42 was modified with the introduction of IFRS 9. Under the old standard, any fair value adjustment needed to be recorded through profit & loss. The revised standard now differentiates between an adjustment through profit & loss and other comprehensive income. Which adjustment is applicable depends on the original recording of transactions that modify the carrying amount of investment in associates.

Journal entries vary depending on the initial recording of financial investments.

- Through profit & loss

Journal entry		Comment
dr.	Other expenses	
cr.	Investments in associates	Carrying amount

- Through other comprehensive income

Journal entry		Comment
dr.	Other comprehensive income	
cr.	Investments in associates	Carrying amount

A combination of both journal entries might also be appropriate.

The journal entries have to be executed at that level where the differences between the equity value (at group level) and the carrying amount of the investment in associates of the parent is recorded.

The **fifth step**, the recording of a fictitious acquisition of the investment in associates, will add the investment in associates to the investment in subsidiaries considering the fair value. Similar to the disposal, the acquisition follows the initial recognition of the underlying financial investment. The accounting change in IFRS 3.42 is also applicable to the acquisition. In parallel, the journal entry not only considers the change in value but also the reclassification by using a different account.

Journal entries vary depending on the original recording of investment in associates.

- Through profit & loss

Journal entry		Comment
dr.	Investment in subsidiaries	Fair value to be used
cr.	Other expenses / Other earnings	Depends if separate presentation or netting is applied

- Through other comprehensive income

Journal entry		Comment
dr.	Investment in subsidiaries	Fair value to be used
cr.	Other comprehensive income	

Even if the separate accounting of disposal and acquisition of the investment in associates offers a transparent approach, an **alternate treatment** of the fourth and fifth step can be observed in practice. Journal entries are combined and executed in one step to document the dependencies between the accounts. This requires the determination of the difference between the fair value and the carrying amount of the investment in subsidiaries. Again, journal entries have to distinguish the recording between profit & loss and other comprehensive income.

- Through profit & loss

Journal entry		Comment
dr.	Investment in subsidiaries	
cr.	Other earnings	Can also be a debit.
cr.	Investment is associates	

- Through other comprehensive income

Journal entry		Comment
dr.	Investment in subsidiaries	
cr.	Other comprehensive income	Can also be a debit.
cr.	Investment in associates	

Another item that needs attention is the treatment of **foreign currency** translations. Differences in respect to foreign currency translations recorded in equity also influence the fair value accounting. IFRS 3.42 and IAS 21.48 require that changes in the value of the equity interest have to be accounted for "on the same basis as would be required if the acquirer had disposed directly of the previously held equity interest".[13] In other words, cumulative exchanges differences have to be reclassified from equity to profit & loss.

Journal entry		Company
dr.	Other expenses	Can also be a credit.
cr.	Differences of foreign currency translations	

The separation between effects recorded in profit & loss and other comprehensive income due to the accounting change will last until the subsidiary will

> Record the fair value adjustment at level III. You will be in line with all fair value adjustments of assets acquired and liabilities assumed due to the purchase price allocation. Furthermore, the initial (and also the subsequent) consolidation at group level can be executed without any modifications or special considerations.

---

[13] This requirement is also consistent to IAS 28.23.

be finally disposed. At that moment, a recycling of amounts recognized in other comprehensive income to profit & loss occurs.

Having successfully adjusted the carrying amount of the investment in subsidiaries, the second block executes the application of the acquisition method. Up to this point, only the consideration transferred has been recognized by the parent (or any holding company or subsidiary of the group). What is left is the application of a purchase price allocation. From a group's perspective, the transaction of increasing the interest in financial investments is identical to a full initial consolidation. A purchase price allocation as discussed in chapter E -3 has to be applied. The calculation of goodwill is identical to the calculations presented before:

	Consideration transferred to obtain control
+	Fair value of any previously held interest in acquire
+	Amount of non-controlling interests
–	Fair value of identifiable net assets of the acquire
=	Goodwill / badwill attributable to the acquirer

Tab. I-13 Calculation of goodwill / badwill

All further activities, particularly the initial consolidation techniques, are discussed in detail in chapter E -5. Nevertheless, the status of the associate may force additional activities. It can be assumed that there is some kind of business activity between the parent or other companies of the group and the associate; this should be considered as a pre-existing relationship and dissolved. This may require the execution of a consolidation that has to be expanded on debt and unrealized profits of inventory. Finally, deferred tax assets and liabilities due to outside basis differences have to be determined and accounted for.

Example

As part of its strategy to control the sales channels, Flexing Cables's management usually tries to control sales subsidiaries through the majority of voting rights. Wherever possible, management tries to acquire additional shares in companies they have some kind of interest in to control them. As part of this strategy, management has taken the opportunity to acquire the remaining 70% of the interests in Chorunta Cables. There had been several unsuccessful attempts to acquire the remaining shares in the past. But now Chorunta Cables would be a wholly-owned subsidiary of Flexing Cables Holding as the acquisition was realized by the holding company. The amount Flexing Cables Holding has to transfer for these additional interests is 4,200 k EUR. The transaction took place at the end of March transferring control to Flexing Cables as of 1 April.

At **parent level** (Flexing Cables Holding), the acquisition will be recorded like any other ordinary purchase transaction. Furthermore, a reclassification from investments in associates to investments in subsidiaries might be required.

Journal entry

dr.	Investment in subsidiaries	4,200	
cr.	Liabilities		4,200

The carrying amount of the investment in Chorunta Cables, Flexing Cables Holding is recording, is 325 k EUR at the acquisition date. This amount represents the initial investment in Chorunta Cables of 170 k EUR, profits recorded amounting to 278 k EUR and dividends received amounting to 123 k EUR. Profits of the current period as well as dividends received are not considered. Flexing Cables has to record the following journal entries that reflect the non-considered subjects:

Journal entries				Comment
dr.	Investments in associates	9		Share of profit period 1.1. to 31.3.
	cr.	Share of profits of associates	9	
dr.	Bank	16		Dividends distributed relating to fiscal year 2012
	cr.	Investments in associates	16	

The carrying amount of investments in associates will now be 318 k EUR.

At **group level**, a dedicated view is necessary as several tasks have to be performed. These tasks follow the execution order for step acquisitions.

- Step 1 – Application of equity method

    While the acquisition of the remaining shares in Chorunta Cables was realized end of March, the application of the equity method has to be continued until this moment. This is necessary to ensure that the profits realized by Chorunta Cables are included pro-rata in the financial results of the consolidated profit & loss statement. Furthermore, the equity value of the investment in Chorunta Cables is required as this amount has to be considered in determining the consolidation gain or loss.

    At the end of the previous period, the auxiliary calculation unveiled the following composition of the equity value recorded in the consolidated statement of financial position:

Item	Goodwill	Non-accounted assets	Deferred taxation	Book value investment	Equity value
Balance @ initial recognition	48	35	(9)	96	170
Depreciation & amortization		(14)	4		(10)
Unrealized profits				(12)	(12)
Profits					
• Cumulative				246	246
• Current period				32	32
Dividends				(123)	(123)
Balance @ end of period	48	21	(5)	239	303

The auxiliary calculation has to be advanced to the acquisition date by considering the following issues:

- In February, 50% of the previous period profits are distributed as dividends.
- At the acquisition date, Chorunta Cables carrying amount relating to inventory purchased from companies of the Flexing Cables group is 506 k EUR.

- The profit realized by Chorunta Cables for the period from 1.1. to 31.3. is 31 k EUR.
- The annual depreciation on non-accounted assets (which consists of a customer base only) is 4 k EUR.
- Chorunta Cable's tax rate is 25.5%.
- No items were recorded in other comprehensive income.

Having executed all transactions, the auxiliary calculation at the acquisition date will be:

Item	Goodwill	Non-accounted assets	Deferred taxation	Book value investment	Equity value
Balance @ initial recognition	48	35	(9)	96	170
Depreciation & amortization		(15)	4		(11)
Unrealized profits				(12)	(12)
Profits					
• Cumulative				278	278
• Current period				9	9
Dividends				(139)	(139)
Balance @ end of period	48	20	(5)	232	295

The following journal entries have to be recorded at level II to reflect the above-mentioned transactions:

Journal entries				Comment
dr.	Revenues	0.5		Elimination of unrealized profits; calculation is based on transfer pricing rules.
	cr.	Investments in associates	0.5	
dr.	Share of profits of associates	1		Regular depreciation on non-accounted assets.
	cr.	Investments in associates	1	
dr.	Investments in associates	0.2		Adjustment to deferred taxation due to depreciation.
	cr.	Share of profits of associates	0.2	

- Step 2 – Estimation of considerations transferred

A scanning of any of any unusual items in the sales and purchase agreement that may impact group accounting was not detected. Accordingly, the consideration transferred equals the amount Flexing Cables Holding has recognized in its investment in subsidiaries amounting to 4,200 k EUR.

- Step 3 – Calculation of fair values

While Chorunta Cables is a privately held company, the determination of the fair values of the old investments in the company is based on the company's mid-term plans to develop the business. The determination unveils an entity value for the whole company of 5,600 k EUR. Accordingly, the portion that relates to the old investment is 1,680 k EUR (5,600 k EUR *30%).

- Step 4 – Accounting for disposal of currently held investments

    While Flexing Cables Holding is recording its investments in associates at cost, modified by pro-rata profits and dividends, adjustments necessary to arrive at the equity value are historically recorded at level II. To align the equity value to the carrying amount of investment in associates, the difference between these two figures has to be disposed at level II:

Carrying amount investment in associates as of 31.3.	318
− Equity value as of 31.3.	295
= Consolidation gain I	23

Journal entry

dr.	Investments in associates	23	
	cr.	Gain on sale of associate	23

    Executing the journal entry will eliminate all adjustments at level II.

- Step 5 – Acquisition of currently held investments

    The step-up of the investment in associates to arrive at the fair value is recorded at level III. The following consolidation gain will result from this transaction:

Fair value of old investment in associates as of 31.3.	1,680
− Carrying amount investment in associates as of 31.3.	318
= Consolidation gain II	1,362

Journal entry

dr.	Investments in subsidiaries	1,362	
	cr.	Gain on sale of associate	1,362

- Step 6 – Purchase price allocation and initial consolidation

    Having executed all adjustments of the consideration transferred (old and current investments), a regular purchase price allocation as demanded by IFRS 3 has to be executed.[14] The purchase price allocation unveiled the following facts:

- There are no hidden reserves or burdens.
- The value of short-term orders to be processed by the end of the period is 450 k EUR.
- The value of long-term orders to be processed within the next fiscal years is 370 k EUR.
- A customer base valued at 2,300 k EUR.
- Deferred tax liabilities relating to non-accounted assets have a value of 701 k EUR.

    The following journal entry is recorded at level III:

Journal entry

dr.	Intangible assets	3,120	
	cr.	Deferred tax liabilities		701
	cr.	Retained earnings		2,419

---

[14] See chapter E-3 on page 136 regarding details. These tasks will not be presented in this example.

The goodwill to be established at group level can be calculated as follows:

	Consideration transferred		5,880
	IFRS net assets of the company as of 1.4.2013	814	
+	Customer orders, s.t.	450	
+	Customer orders, l.t.	370	
+	Customer base	2,300	
–	Deferred tax liabilities	(701)	
=	Total assets Chorunta Cables	3,233	
–	Assets allocable to the Flexing Cables Holding	100%	3,233
=	Goodwill attributable to Flexing Cables Holding		2,647

Based on this calculation and all recorded carrying amounts, the initial consolidation for the group of Chorunta Cables is reflected by the following journal entry:

Journal entry				Company
dr.		Share capital	50	Chorunta Cables
dr.		Retained earnings	3,183	Chorunta Cables
dr.		Goodwill	2,647	Group
	cr.	Investments in subsidiaries	5,880	Flexing Cables Holding

• Subsequent accounting

As from 1.4.2013, Chorunta Cables is a wholly-owned subsidiary of Flexing Cables. Accordingly, it will be treated like any other subsidiary for preparing consolidated financial statements. The only item to consider is a revenue cut-off for the period from 1.1. to 31.3. as this has associate status. The cut-off can be realized on any level by executing the following journal entry (one line item per account required):

Journal entry			
dr.		Revenues	1,401
	cr.	Expenses	1,370
	cr.	Retained earnings	31

3.6. Joint venture to subsidiary

There are situations where a joint venture becomes a subsidiary. According to the definition in IFRS 11.16, a joint venture is a joint arrangement, whereby the parties that have joint control of the arrangement have rights to the net assets of the arrangement. Consequently, a status transition from a joint venture to a subsidiary can only occur, if one or more partners have forwarded their rights in the joint venture to another party presuming that contractual conditions are met. Reasons for and the handling of the forwarding of rights are usually based on the underlying contractual agreement that binds all partners together. There are many:

- Omission of partners (individuals, corporations) due to death, insolvency, decisions by court or similar reasons;
- Lapsing of a defined period that binds partners together;
- Lapsing of a defined period combined with a forced retirement;
- Termination or lapsing of the underlying contractual agreement;
- Contractual agreement of transfer of rights upon the occurrence of defined events or circumstances;
- Other reasons as appropriate.

Regardless of how a transfer of rights occurs, a check of contractual conditions is mandatory in such cases. The check has to focus on the transfer of rights, the share owned in the joint venture and any limitations that exist due to contractual agreements. Various scenarios may result in control.

Rights	Contractual condition	Evaluation
Transfer of voting rights in joint venture combined with retirement, control given	Two partners only.	Joint venture ceases. Status of the joint venture changes towards subsidiary.
Transfer of voting rights in joint venture combined with retirement of one or more partners, control given	More than two partners. No changes in joint control possible. No changes of contractual agreement possible (e.g. due to limitations or thresholds to be passed).	Joint venture remains. Even if control could be established through voting rights, they are limited due to contractual conditions.
Transfer of voting rights in joint venture combined with retirement of one or more partners, control given	More than two partners. No changes in joint control possible. Changes of contractual agreement possible.	Joint venture ceases in the moment the underlying contractual agreement is changed. This change is only possible if the party that owns the majority of voting rights also has the power to change the contractual agreement. Status of the joint venture changes towards subsidiary.
Transfer of voting rights in joint venture combined with retirement of one or more partners, **no** control given	More than two partners. No changes in joint control possible.	Joint venture remains, no changes.

Tab. I-14 Scenarios of changes in joint ventures

While these scenarios assume that control is established through voting rights, there may also be contractual agreements that can establish control through other rights.[15] It is important to check the contractual agreement.

The transition of a joint venture towards a subsidiary follows the same accounting pattern as a transition of an associate towards a subsidiary. The rationale for the same handling is based on the application of the equity method

---

[15] See chapter C -1 on page 44 regarding rights that are capable to establish control.

that is mandatory for both associates, and joint ventures.[16] Therefore, the accounting methods and procedures described for associates have to be applied to joint ventures.[17]

> With a change from IAS 31 to IFRS 11 for the accounting of joint ventures, a change of the accounting methods occurred. The mandatory accounting method for joint ventures is now the equity method; proportionate consolidation is no longer possible.

4. DECREASE IN INVESTMENTS

In contrast to the increase in control, a loss of control occurs anytime an interest in a company is reduced without full disposal. Such reductions are named partial or step disposals. Usually they occur if a portion of the interest in a company is sold that will result in a consideration received by the parent or any holding in the group. Nevertheless, there are cases where a loss of control takes place without any consideration received. Such situations are deemed disposals that require a special treatment. Common to all decreases in control is a change of the status of the company in the group. Again, changes can span over all company categories – from subsidiaries to financial investments.

4.1. Associate to financial investment

The partial disposal of an interest in an associate is a transaction that not only requires the execution of specific accounting procedures according to IAS 28; it requires also a fair value recording of the remaining interests in the then financial investment.

> The revision of IAS 28 as part of the new consolidation suite has introduced a new handling of partial disposals of associates. While the old version requested an application of the carrying amount of the old shares as the basis for the remaining interests, the new version now requires a fair value measurement considering a recycling of other comprehensive income.

The partial disposal will result in an execution of three separate transactions that interact:

- Discontinuing the use of the equity method combined with an appropriate deconsolidation.

---

[16] If IAS 31 is still applied for the accounting in joint ventures, a transition to IFRS 11 is recommended before the accounting of the transition from a joint venture to a subsidiary can start. This is important in cases, where a pro-rata consolidation is applied to joint ventures.

[17] See previous chapter for a detailed explanation.

- Recording of a sales transaction.
- Remeasuring the remaining interest.

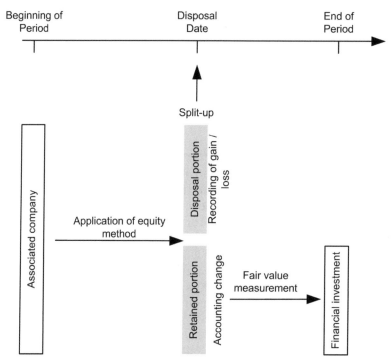

Fig. I-3 Timing of partial disposals of associates

Based on the required activities, a set of tasks can be derived.

Step	Task	Where to execute
1)	Advancement of all accounting tasks towards the disposal date	Parent and group level
2)	Fair value measurement of retained portion	Parent level
3)	Suspending of the application of the equity method	Group level
4)	Recording of sales transaction and recognition of gain / loss	Parent and group level
5)	Clean-up activities	Parent and group level

Tab. I-15 Execution order of partial disposal of an associate

The **first step** in determining the equity split is the advancement of all items towards the disposal date. This requires that the associate's accounting is up to date, including a set of financial statements as of the acquisition date. It also requires that the equity value are at group level is up to date and adjustments of the equity value are accounted for, including an update of the auxiliary calculation. This is to ensure that profits of the associate are properly recorded as part of the group's performance up to the disposal date.

The **second step**, remeasurement of retained interests in the associate, has to be based on a fair value approach according to the provisions of IFRS 9. The standard is silent about the measurement methods and any underlying rationales. A set of techniques is available to determine the fair values of the remaining interests in the former associate depending on its status. If the associate is a publicly listed company, fair values of the remaining interests can be obtained from market values. If the associate is a privately held company a calculation of an entity value based on a discounted business plan can be used, which acts as the basis in determining fair values of the remaining interest.[18] It is not appropriate to simply extrapolate the price obtained. This is because the sale price includes not only the fair value of the related interests, but also a sales premium (if the associate is profitable) or other compensations (e.g. if the associate is making a loss). Having determined the fair value of the remaining interests, these fair values act as the starting point for subsequent measures of the then financial investment.

Suspension of the equity method as the **third step** includes a set of activities and dependencies, similar to the full disposal of an associate. Furthermore, tasks depend on the accounting activities performed by the parent due to the sale on an interest portion in the associate. Therefore, it is important to advance the fair value measurement of the second step regarding the place of recognition.

IFRS 28.22b demands measurement of the remaining interests at fair value only. In addition to the missing guidance on the accounting methods, the standard does suggest where to account for the remaining interests. A **fair value allocation** is required. The following scenarios might be possible.

Scenario	Carrying amount on		Comment
	Parent level	**Group level**	
1)	Fair value	None	
2)	Book value	Adjustments to fair value	
3)	None	Fair value	Not appropriate as financial investments are assets to be recorded by the parent.

Tab. I-16   Accounting scenarios of remaining interests in associate

Which scenario has to be selected depends on the accounting by the parent regarding the presentation in its separate financial statements. If the parent applies IFRS, it will be forced to measure the financial investments as financial assets, according to IFRS 9.5.2.1 in combination with IFRS 9.4.1.4 at fair value, unless measurement at cost is required. In this case, the first scenario might be applicable. If the parent is applying any other accounting system or IFRS that requires measurement of the carrying amount of financial investments at cost or

---

[18] See Appendix I: Fair value measurement on page 751 regarding more details on applicable valuation measurement methods.

book value, the second scenario has to be applied. The book value can be estimated by a simple calculation.

$$\text{Book value} = \text{Remaining interest} * \frac{\text{Carrying amount of investment in associates}}{\text{Interest in associate}}$$

Fig. I-4   Calculation of remaining book value

The remaining interest can be calculated by a subtraction of the interest in
the associate sold from the interest in the associate. Any adjustments to arrive at
fair value have to be recorded at group level (preferably as a level II adjustment)
to comply with IAS 28.22b's requirement of a fair value measurement in consolidated financial statements. If it is known how much needs to be recorded at group
level, deconsolidation can be executed.

The **calculation of gains and losses** is similar to the calculation of a full disposal. Both, the direct as well as the indirect method of determining the realized
or loss can be applied.

- Direct method

    The realized gains or losses of the partial disposal of the associate
    are calculated at group level only. Proceeds of the sale of investments in
    associates are deducted by the current equity value and those items that
    have a direct relationship with the carrying equity value of the associate,
    adjusted by the fair value of the remaining interests.

    The following scheme can be used in calculating the realized gain / loss:

	Net proceeds from the sale of interests in the associate
−	Equity value
+	**Portion of equity value attributable to remaining interests (fair value)**
+	Write-up of assets from upstream transactions
+	Write-up of devaluations due to loss situations
+	Elimination of acceptance of liability in loss situations
+/−	Effects of pro-rata capital adjustments
+/−	Differences due to foreign currency translations
+/−	Items of a revaluation surplus
+/−	Deferred taxes
+(/−)	Goodwill, if necessary also goodwill allocations due to cash generating units
=	Realized gain / loss

Tab. I-17   Gain / loss from a partial sale of an associate, the group's view

- Indirect method

    The calculation of gains and losses via the indirect method considers
    any accounting activities of the parent. Proceeds from the partial sale of
    investment in associates are deducted by the disposed carrying amount.
    The realized gain or loss in the parent's account is adjusted by a set of
    components that were accounted for at group level over the life in the
    group of the associate. Additional adjustments of the realized gain or loss
    arise due to the fair value measurement of the remaining interests.

The following scheme can be used in calculating the realized gain / loss:

	Proceeds from the partial sale of interests in the associate
+	**Fair value of remaining interests**
−	Carrying amount in separate financial statements (of the parent)
+/−	Pro-rata profits / losses of the current period
+	Dividends received
+/−	Fair-value adjustments
+/−	Differences due to accounting policies
+/−	Write-up of valuation adjustments and extraordinary depreciation
+	Depreciation of hidden reserves and non-accounted for assets
−	Release of hidden burdens
+/−	Equity-changes due to unrealized profits
+	Write-up of devaluations due to loss situations
+	Elimination of acceptance of liability in loss situations
+/−	Deferred taxes
+(/−)	Goodwill, if necessary also goodwill allocations due to cash generating units
=	Realized gain / loss

Tab. I-18   Gain / loss from a partial sale of an associate, the parent's view

Regardless of which method is applied, both direct and indirect methods will always produce the same result. Both have their advantages and disadvantages. The advantage of the direct method is its simplicity: all items are easily identifiable. By contrast, the advantage of the indirect method is the reconciliation between the realized gain / loss at parent level and the gain / loss at group level.

The discontinued use of the equity method demands a **deconsolidation** to adjust carrying amounts of items in the statement of financial position. Activities due to the deconsolidation are identical to the accounting of full disposals of associates. The following activities are typical elements of a deconsolidation that require a check whether or not they are necessary.[19]

Activity
Recording of the proceeds from the sale of the investment in associates
Removal of the carrying amount of the equity value of the associate
Recycling of items of other comprehensive income
Reclassification of items of other comprehensive income
Write-up of unrealized profits of assets of upstream-transactions
Release of deferred tax assets or liabilities
Write-up of other assets
Adjustments of liabilities and provisions
Goodwill-adjustments

Tab. I-19   Deconsolidation tasks upon the partial disposal of associates

---

[19] See accounting of the disposal on page 462 regarding detailed explanations.

When the fair value of the remaining interests is known, the sales price and all deconsolidation tasks have been achieved, the **fourth step** can be executed. This task records the sales transaction of the investment in associates and any revaluations that finally result in recognition of the resulting gain or loss. Any transactions that are recorded at parent level have to be considered in determining the required **journal entries**. It is not necessary to account for the sales transaction at group level as such transactions are limited to the difference between the equity value and the carrying amounts at parent level. All adjustments can be combined in one journal entry which deconsolidates the associate from the consolidated statement of financial position and removes all related assets and liabilities in one step.

Journal entry			Comment
dr.		Financial investments	Either fair value or adjustments to fair value.
dr.		Liabilities	Relates to the adjustment of liabilities in loss situations or in case of a probable use of a guarantee granted by the parent and assumes that the guarantee will lapse upon the sale.
dr.		Inventory / non-current assets	Write-up due to the elimination of unrealized profits.
dr.		Other assets	Relates to the write-down of financial assets in loss situations.
dr.		Foreign exchange differences	
dr.		Revaluation reserves	Recycling of valuation adjustments.
	cr.	Investment in associates	The remaining balance; includes elimination of unrealized profits, alignment to group accounting policies and other items.
	cr.	Goodwill	If part of a cash-generating unit.
	cr.	Gain on sale of associate	Can also be a loss (debit account instead).

This solution assumes a division of work between the parent and the group. Even if all items are combined into only one journal entry, this method faces a disadvantage: the missing reconciliation of the disposed items at group level. If more transparency is demanded, this journal entry can be divided into several smaller journal entries. Several steps are necessary where each step records a defined asset, liability or equity component.

An alternate treatment is a reversal of the parent's journal entries at group level combined with the subsequent removal of the equity value at group level. The advantage of this method is that the components of the equity value can be reconciled upon the disposal. This application is identical to a full disposal.

Journal entry		Comment
dr.	Investment in associates	Reversal of the journal entry at parent level.
cr.	Gain on sale of associate	Can also be a loss.

The journal entry then to be executed is the same as before with different amounts.

Journal entry			Comment
dr.		Financial investments	Fair value.
dr.		Liabilities	Relates to the adjustment of liabilities in loss situations or in case of a probable use of a guarantee granted by the parent and assumes that the guarantee will lapse upon the sale.
dr.		Inventory / non-current assets	Write-up due to the elimination of unrealized profits.
dr.		Other assets	Relates to the write-down of financial assets in loss situations.
dr.		Foreign exchange differences	
dr.		Revaluation reserves	Recycling of valuation adjustments.
	cr.	Investment in associates	The remaining balance; includes elimination of unrealized profits, alignment to group accounting policies and other items.
	cr.	Goodwill	If part of a cash-generating unit.
	cr.	Gain on sale of associate	Can also be a loss (debit account instead).

The journal entries executed so far focus on recording the sales transaction and a revaluation of the remaining interests. While this is just one part of recording the **fifth step** acts as a **clean-up task** considering additional requirements. IAS 28.22c and IAS 28.23 particularly demand an adjustment of other comprehensive income (e.g. due to fair value adjustments or foreign currency translations). Items recorded in other comprehensive income that belong to the disposed associate have to be recycled to profit & loss as far as they would have been recorded on a direct disposal.

Journal entry		Comment
dr.	Revaluation reserve	
	cr. Gain on sale of associate	Can also be a loss (debit account instead).

Those items that are not recycled either have to be reclassified to retained earnings or kept as they are. The criterion whether or not a reclassification is necessary depends on the fair values of retained interests and on the dependency between the fair value of the retained interests and its measurement type.

Journal entry		Comment
dr.	Revaluation reserve	This journal entry is necessary if one or more components of the revaluation reserve are not subject to recycling.
	cr. Retained earnings	

4.2. Joint venture to financial investment

The need of changing the status of a joint venture to a financial investment may have various reasons:

- The contractual purpose of the joint venture is fulfilled.
- Contractual agreements demand a forced sale.
- Contractual agreements demand a residual interest in the former joint venture.

- Rights or obligation due to the former joint venture still exist.
- Other reasons.

Whatever the underlying reason is, the change in status is accompanied by two major items: loss of joint control and sale of an interest in the joint venture. Accordingly the application of the equity method has to be discontinued (IAS 28.22) and a sale has to be recorded. While these tasks are identical to the accounting of a partial disposal of an associate, the accounting treatment of associates can be applied (explained in detail in the previous chapter).

4.3. Joint venture to associate

Joint ventures are established for specific purposes. Once the purpose has been fulfilled, there is no longer any need for shareholders to maintain a joint venture. Shareholder contracts are usually terminated in such situations, resulting in a loss of joint control. However, the investment in the company remains, and should be accounted for as an investment in an associate. Therefore, the status of the joint venture will change to an associate, along with a change from joint control to significant influence.

From an accounting perspective, both types of investment – associate, as well as joint venture – are accounted for by an application of the equity method, as long as there are no special conditions that require a recording of assets and liabilities in the parent's accounts (for joint operations). The method, therefore, does not change. The carrying amount of the investment in the joint venture at parent level and the equity value at group level have to be advanced as if there was no change in the status of the joint venture. IAS 28.24 explicitly demands a continuation of the equity method without any adjustments or remeasurements of the carrying amount at parent and group level due to the change in the status. Consequently, no accounting tasks are necessary. This is exactly the same issue as with an increase in investments, so when an associate becomes a joint venture.

4.4. Subsidiary to financial investment

The sale by a larger investment in subsidiaries can result in a situation where the subsidiary changes its status towards a financial investment. This is much the same as when an associated company becomes a financial investment. The underlying approach is again an application of fair value principles on the remaining interest. IFRS 10.25 always treats a status change as a loss of control and demands an execution of three steps to account for it:

- A derecognition of all assets and liabilities of the former subsidiary from consolidated financial statements.
- A recognition of a financial investment at its fair value for the interest retained.
- A recognition of a gain or loss due to the transaction.

The **derecognition of all assets and liabilities** is identical to a disposal in conjunction with a full deconsolidation of a subsidiary. A gain or loss will be recorded by the parent in its separate and consolidated financial statements.

The actions required are described in detail in chapter J -3 - Deconsolidation techniques.[20]

The **recognition of a financial investment** requires a determination of the fair value of the retained interest using fair value methods: market values are usually not available for subsidiaries (unless there are rare circumstances where subsidiaries are publicly listed and non-controlling interests are traded in the market).[21] Similar to other transitional consolidations a determination of the fair value of the remaining interests based on any purchase or sales prices is not appropriate as they include premiums that are not appropriate in determining fair values. Instead, the fair value of the financial investment has to be determined based on an entity value of the former subsidiary and the relative portion of remaining interest.

There is a minor accounting issue of where to record the fair value of the financial investment. IFRS 10.25 does not provide any guidance due to the focus on consolidated financial statements. Therefore, an investigation regarding the accounting of the disposal at parent level is necessary. The following scenarios might be possible.

Scenario	Carrying amount on		Comment
	Parent level	**Group level**	
1)	Fair value	None	
2)	Book value	Adjustments to fair value	
3)	None	Fair value	Not appropriate as financial investments are assets to be recorded by the parent.

Tab. I-20 Accounting scenarios of remaining interests in subsidiaries: financial investments

If the parent applies IFRS, it might be forced to measure the financial investments as financial assets according to IFRS 9.5.2.1 in combination with IFRS 9.4.1.4 at fair value unless a measurement at cost is required. In this case, the first scenario might be applicable. If the parent is applying any other accounting system or an IFRS that forces to measure the carrying amount of financial investments at cost or book value the second scenario has to be applied. The book value can be estimated by a simple calculation.

$$\text{Book value} = \text{Remaining interest} * \frac{\text{Carrying amount of investment in subsidiaries}}{\text{Interest in subsidiary}}$$

Fig. I-5 Calculation of remaining book value

---

[20] See page 575.

[21] See Appendix I: Fair value measurement on page 751 regarding more details on applicable valuation measurement methods.

The remaining interest equals a substraction of the interest in the subsidiary sold from the interest in the subsidiary. Any adjustments to arrive at fair value have to be recorded at group level (preferably as a level II adjustment) to comply with the requirement of IFRS 10.25b for a fair value measurement in consolidated financial statements.

The **recognition of gains and losses**, demanded by IFRS 10.25c, is a purely technical task. Gains and losses have to be recorded in the statement of income by executing the journal entries of the first two tasks. Several options are suitable: the journal entries presented here is just one of them. It assumes that the parent has recorded a partial disposal combined with a reclassification of the remaining interests to financial investments.

Journal entry			Comment
dr.		**Financial investments**	Allocation of retained interest in subsidiary.
dr.		Receivables	
	cr.	Investment in subsidiaries	Release of carrying amount.
	cr.	Gain on sale of subsidiary	

Based on the parent's journal entry, the following journal entry will be executed at group level. If appropriate, parts of this journal entry have to be recorded at the appropriate valuation levels (I to III) due to any adjustments to comply with group accounting policies or valuation step-ups due to the initial purchase price allocation.

Journal entry			Comment
dr.		**Financial investments**	Fair value step-up.
dr.		Liabilities	Liabilities of subsidiary.
dr.		Investment in subsidiaries	Reversal of parent journal entry to enable reversal of initial equity consolidation.
dr.		Revaluation surplus	Initial equity consolidation due to step-up of carrying amounts of assets and liabilities.
dr.		Non-controlling interests	
	cr.	Share capital	Initial equity consolidation.
	cr.	Capital reserve	Initial equity consolidation.
	cr.	Retained earnings	Initial equity consolidation and items recorded as other comprehensive income.
	cr.	Assets	
	cr.	Goodwill	Initial equity consolidation but balance can vary due to goodwill allocation of cash-generating units.
	cr.	Gain on sale of subsidiary	Can also be a loss (debit account instead).
	cr.	Gain non-controlling interests	Can also be a loss (debit account instead).

Even if IFRS 10.25 assumes two independent transactions, the change from a subsidiary towards a financial investment can be calculated as one transaction. The **calculated gain or loss** has to be equal to the gain or loss recorded for each separate transaction. In determining the realized gain or loss, the calculation of the full disposal can be used, modified by the fair value measurement of the remaining interest.

- Direct method

	Proceeds from the sale of interests in the subsidiary
+	**Fair value of remaining interest**
−	Level II assets of the sold company
+	Level II provisions and liabilities of the sold company
+/−	Differences due to foreign currency translations
+/−	Items of the revaluation surplus
+/−	Deferred taxes
+(/−)	Goodwill, if necessary also goodwill adjustments due to cash-generating units
+	Non-controlling interests
=	Realized gain / loss

Tab. I-21 Gain / loss due to transition from subsidiary to financial investment applying the direct method, the group's view

- Indirect method

	Proceeds from the sale of interests in the subsidiary
+	**Fair value of remaining interest**
−	Carrying amount of the interests in the subsidiary in the parent's accounts
=	Realized gain / loss in the parent's accounts
+/−	Fair value adjustments recorded through profit & loss according to IFRS 9
−	Accumulated exceptional depreciation
+	Impairments of goodwill included in net book value
+/−	Hidden reserves and burdens of purchase price allocations released through profit & loss
+/−	Net profit of the period of the sold company
+/−	Revaluation surplus, neutrally reclassified
+/−	Foreign currency translations, neutrally reclassified
+/−	Deferred taxes
+/−	Goodwill adjustments due to cash-generating units
+	Non-controlling interests
=	Realized gain / loss

Tab. I-22 Gain / loss due to transition from subsidiary to financial investment applying the indirect method, the group's view

Similar to disposals, a partial sale can also be subject to **accounting tricks and misuse**. IFRS 10.25 and 10.B97 focus on the loss of control as the underlying rationale. However, a decrease in investment follows the same practices as a disposal demanding a commercial view of the sales transaction.[22]

4.5. Subsidiary to associate

The sale of a controlling interest in a subsidiary may result in the retention of significant influence. Accordingly, the status of the subsidiary changes towards associate with loss of control. All kinds of losses are accounted for, regardless of the company's status after the disposal of the subsidiary's shares. In fact, the sales

---

[22] See chapter J -3.3.4 on page 600 regarding the requirements on multiple sales arrangements.

transaction forces an accounting according to the provisions of IFRS 10.25. It again demands an execution of three steps to account for the loss of control:

- A derecognition of all assets and liabilities of the former subsidiary from consolidated financial statements.
- A recognition of an interest in associates at its fair value for the interest retained.
- A recognition of a gain or loss due to the transaction.

These accounting requirements are the same as for retained interests that qualify as financial investments even if some modifications are necessary.

The **derecognition of all assets and liabilities** of the former subsidiary from consolidated financial statements is identical to disposal in conjunction with full deconsolidation of a subsidiary. A gain or loss will be recorded by the parent in its separate and consolidated financial statements.

Activities to be performed are described in detail in chapter J -3 - Deconsolidation techniques.[23]

The **recognition of an interest in associates** is based on a three-step approach.

- Step 1

   IFRS 10.B98b(iii) demands recognition of the retained interest at fair value – the necessary first step. The determination of the fair value is similar to that in financial investments. Again, fair value measurement methods have to be applied because market values are rarely available for subsidiaries (except when subsidiaries are publicly listed and non-controlling interests are traded in the market).[24] The method of choice is a discounted cash-flow method to derive fair values from planned future profits.

- Step 2

   Having determined fair values of the retained interests, an allocation to parent and / or group level is necessary depending on the accounting performed by the parent in the same manner than for financial investments. The following scenarios are possible.

Scenario	Carrying amount on		Comment
	Parent level	**Group level**	
1	Fair value	None	
2	Book value	Adjustments to fair value	
3	None	Fair value	Not appropriate as financial investments are assets to be recorded by the parent.

Tab. I-23 Accounting scenarios of remaining interests in subsidiaries: associates

---

[23] See page 575.

[24] See Appendix I: Fair value measurement on page 751 regarding more details on applicable valuation measurement methods.

If the parent applies IFRS, it might be forced to measure the financial investments as financial assets according to IFRS 9.5.2.1 in combination with IFRS 9.4.1.4 at fair value unless a measurement at cost is required. In this case, the first scenario might be applicable. If the parent is applying any other accounting system or IFRS that forces it to measure the carrying amount of financial investments at cost or book value the second scenario has to be applied. The book value can be estimated by a simple calculation.

$$\text{Book value} = \text{Remaining interest} * \frac{\text{Carrying amount of investment in subsidiaries}}{\text{Interest in subsidiary}}$$

Fig. I-6 Calculation of remaining book value

The remaining interest equal a substraction of the interest in the subsidiary sold from the interest in the subsidiary. Any adjustments to arrive at fair value have to be recorded at group level (preferably as a level II adjustment) to comply with the requirement of IFRS 10.25b for a fair value measurement in consolidated financial statements.

- Step 3

    The final step is a transfer of the fair value of the remaining interest into the equity value of the then associate at the date of loss of control; the fair value acts as the starting point for the equity accounting. This transfer demands a purchase price allocation, an initial consolidation and the preparation of the necessary auxiliary calculation (described in detail in chapter G -2.1 Initial consolidation[25]).

    If the sales transaction occurred during the period, the carrying amount of the investment in associates has to be advanced towards the end of the period applying regular accounting activities as appropriate for associates.

The **recognition of gains and losses**, demanded by IFRS 10.25c, is a purely technical task, identical to that when a subsidiary becomes a financial investment, except for the accounts to be used for the remaining interest. Journal entries presented here assume that the parent has recorded a partial disposal combined with a reclassification of the remaining interests to investments in associates.

Journal entry		Comment
dr.	**Investment in associates**	Allocation of retained interest in subsidiary
dr.	Receivables	
cr.	Investment in subsidiaries	Release of carrying amount
cr.	Gain on sale of subsidiary	

Based on the parent's journal entry, the following journal entry will be executed at group level. If appropriate, parts of this journal entry have to be recorded at the appropriate valuation level (I to III) due to any adjustments to

---

[25] See page 430.

comply with group accounting policies or valuation step-ups due to the initial purchase price allocation.

Journal entry		Comment
dr.	**Investment in associates**	Fair value step-up.
dr.	Liabilities	Liabilities of subsidiary.
dr.	Investment in subsidiaries	Reversal of parent journal entry to enable reversal of initial equity consolidation.
dr.	Revaluation surplus	Initial equity consolidation due to step-up of carrying amounts of assets and liabilities.
dr.	Non-controlling interests	
	cr. Share capital	Initial equity consolidation.
	cr. Capital reserve	Initial equity consolidation.
	cr. Retained earnings	Initial equity consolidation and items recorded as other comprehensive income.
	cr. Assets	
	cr. Goodwill	Initial equity consolidation. Balance may vary due to goodwill allocation of cash-generating units.
	cr. Gain on sale of subsidiary	Can also be a loss (debit account instead).
	cr. Gain non-controlling interests	Can also be a loss (debit account instead).

Even if IFRS 10.25 assumes two independent transactions, the change from a subsidiary towards an associate can be calculated as one transaction. The **calculated gain or loss** has to be equal to the gain or loss recorded for each separate transaction. In determining the realized gain or loss, the calculation of the full disposal can be used modified by the fair value measurement of the remaining interest.

- Direct method

	Proceeds from the sale of interests in the subsidiary
+	**Fair value of remaining interest (equity value of associate)**
−	Level II assets of the sold company
+	Level II provisions and liabilities of the sold company
+/−	Differences due to foreign currency translations
+/−	Items of the revaluation surplus
+/−	Deferred taxes
+(/−)	Goodwill, if necessary also goodwill adjustments due to cash-generating units
+	Non-controlling interests
=	Realized gain / loss

Tab. I-24   Gain / loss due to transition from subsidiary to associate applying the direct method, the group's view

- Indirect method

	Proceeds from the sale of interests in the subsidiary
+	**Fair value of remaining interest (interest in associate)**
−	Carrying amount of the interests in the subsidiary in the parent's accounts
=	Realized gain / loss in the parent's accounts
+/−	Fair value adjustments recorded through profit & loss according to IFRS 9
−	Accumulated exceptional depreciation
+	Impairments of goodwill included in net book value
+/−	Hidden reserves and burdens of purchase price allocations released through profit & loss
+/−	Net profit of the period of the sold company
+/−	Revaluation surplus, neutrally reclassified
+/−	Foreign currency translations, neutrally reclassified
+/−	Deferred taxes
+/−	Goodwill adjustments due to cash-generating units
+	Non-controlling interests
=	Realized gain / loss

Tab. I-25   Gain / loss due to transition from subsidiary to associate applying the indirect method, the group's view

In addition to all described tasks, the associate might be part of a cash-generating unit requiring a goodwill allocation.

Similar to disposals, a partial sale can also be subject to **accounting tricks and misuse**. While IFRS 10.25 and 10.B97 focus on the loss of control as the underlying rationale, a decrease in an investment so that significant influence is established follows the same practices as a disposal demanding a commercial view of the sales transaction.[26]

4.6. Subsidiary to joint venture

In some cases, a subsidiary will be changed to a joint venture. This occurs if the parent actively contributes its subsidiary to a joint venture. To identify any accounting activities, a determination on how the subsidiary became a joint venture is important. There are generally two ways of establishing a joint venture:

- Through a sales transaction where shares in the subsidiary are sold to the other parties of the joint venture.
- Through a contribution where the other partners contribute other assets to the joint venture.

Both ways of establishing a joint venture require individual accounting treatments.

In a **sales transaction**, the parent is selling interests in the subsidiary to one or more parties that are involved in the joint venture. In addition to these sales transactions, either a binding contract between the parties or a change in the articles and by laws of the subsidiary in respect of the joint venture will be established. The purpose of these legal tasks is to define and clarify all matters of the joint venture, the purpose, the role of the parties and similar items. From an accounting perspective, the sales transaction has to be treated in the same manner as a

---

[26] See chapter J -3.3.4 on page 600 regarding the requirements on multiple sales arrangements.

transitional consolidation from a subsidiary to an associate, as discussed in the previous chapter.[27]

In addition to the sales transaction, a **contribution transaction** requires a dedicated view as a loss of control occurs without any accounting requirements by the parent. From a parent's perspective there is a loss of control and a reduction of the relative interest rate, but the carrying amount is left untouched. The parent is only forced to reclassify the interests held.

<u>Journal entry</u>

dr.		Investment in joint ventures
	cr.	Investment in subsidiaries

A more sophisticated accounting is required at group level. The loss of control again requires an accounting according to the provisions of IFRS 10.25 and 10.B98. The same steps are applied but in a modified way as there is no consideration received involved:

- A derecognition of all assets and liabilities of the former subsidiary from consolidated financial statements.
- A recognition of an interest in associates at its fair value for the interest retained.
- A recognition of a gain or loss due to the transaction.

The **derecognition of all assets and liabilities** of the former subsidiary from consolidated financial statements is identical to a disposal in conjunction with a full deconsolidation of a subsidiary. A gain or loss will be recorded by the parent in its consolidated financial statements only.

Activities to be performed are described in detail in chapter J -3 - Deconsolidation techniques.[28]

The **recognition of an investment in joint ventures** at fair value requires a company valuation to determine the entity value of the former subsidiary. There are in principle two ways of determining the fair value:

- Entity value of the joint venture
  Determining this considers the contributions of all parties of the joint venture. The entity value is derived from the planned performance of the joint venture based on the planned operations and business activities and an application of discounted cash-flow methods.[29] The entity value of the joint venture allocable to the parent is based on the (new) share of the parent in the joint venture.

- Entity value of the subsidiary
  An alternative is to determine the entity value of the subsidiary as of the date it becomes part of the joint venture. In most cases, the value is needed anyway to determine the contribution of the parent and the other partners

---

[27] See chapter I -4.5 on page 537.

[28] See page 575.

[29] An application of other methods might be appropriate as well as long as they are appropriate to the intended measurement objective.

to the joint venture as comensations or adjustments to the contribution are necessary to ensure an equal contribution of all partners. The determined entity value has to be adjusted by synergies that arise from the contribution of the other partners: the joint venture may have a different scope to the subsidiary, resulting in different performances and values. The problem in practice is the measurement of synergies as they represent hopes and estimations of management that often cannot be measured or realized.

Any changes between the determined fair value and the carrying amount in the parent's accounts have to be recorded as a valuation step-up at level II.

While associates and joint ventures are accounted for according to the provisions of IAS 28, an initial consolidation is again required to determine the equity value and to set-up the auxiliary calculation as described in detail in chapter G -2.1 Initial consolidation.[30]

The third step, the **recognition of gains and losses** as demanded by IFRS 10.25c is a purely technical task identical to the other transitional consolidations. The journal entry presented here assumed only the reclassification performed by the parent and will be executed at group level. Any differences between the fair value determined and the (unchanged) carrying amount in the parent's account is recorded as a valuation step-up at level II. If appropriate, parts of this journal entry have to be recorded on the appropriate valuation levels (I to III) due to any adjustments to comply with group accounting policies or valuation step-ups due to the initial purchase price allocation.

Journal entry			Comment
dr.		**Investment in joint ventures**	Fair value step-up.
dr.		Liabilities	Liabilities of subsidiary.
dr.		Investment in subsidiaries	Reversal of parent journal entry to enable reversal of initial equity consolidation.
dr.		Revaluation surplus	Initial equity consolidation due to step-up of carrying amounts of assets and liabilities.
dr.		Non-controlling interests	
	cr.	Share capital	Initial equity consolidation.
	cr.	Capital reserve	Initial equity consolidation.
	cr.	Retained earnings	Initial equity consolidation and items recorded as other comprehensive income.
	cr.	Assets	
	cr.	Goodwill	Initial equity consolidation. Balance may vary due to goodwill allocation of cash-generating units.
	cr.	Gain on sale of subsidiary	Can also be a loss (debit account instead).
	cr.	Gain non-controlling interests	Can also be a loss (debit account instead).

Even if IFRS 10.25 assumes two independent transactions, the change from a subsidiary towards a joint venture can be calculated as one transaction. The **calculated gain or loss** has to be equal to the gain or loss recorded for each separate transaction.

---

[30] See page 430.

- Direct method

	Equity value of joint venture
−	Level II assets of the sold company
+	Level II provisions and liabilities of the sold company
+/−	Differences due to foreign currency translations
+/−	Items of the revaluation surplus
+/−	Deferred taxes
+(/−)	Goodwill, if necessary also goodwill adjustments due to cash-generating units
+	Non-controlling interests
=	Realized gain / loss

Tab. I-26 Gain / loss due to transition from subsidiary to joint venture applying the direct method, the group's view

- Indirect method

	Fair value step-up
+/−	Fair value adjustments recorded through profit & loss according to IFRS 9
−	Accumulated exceptional depreciation
+	Impairments of goodwill included in net book value
+/−	Hidden reserves and burdens of purchase price allocations released through profit & loss
+/−	Net profit of the period of the sold company
+/−	Revaluation surplus, neutrally reclassified
+/−	Foreign currency translations, neutrally reclassified
+/−	Deferred taxes
+/−	Goodwill adjustments due to cash-generating units
+	Non-controlling interests
=	Realized gain / loss

Tab. I-27 Gain / loss due to transition from subsidiary to joint venture applying the indirect method, the group's view

In addition to all the tasks described, the associate might be part of a cash-generating unit requiring a goodwill allocation.

Similar to disposals, a partial sale can also be subject to **accounting tricks and misuse**. While IFRS 10.25 and 10.B97 focus on the loss of control as the underlying rationale, a change in the status from a subsidiary to a joint venture follows the same practices as a disposal demanding a commercial view of the sales transaction.[31] Even a change from control to joint control is a loss of control.

5. ACQUISITIONS AND DISPOSALS WITHOUT CHANGES IN CONTROL

Some transactions increase or decrease the interest in a company without a change in the status of the company within the group. While there is no change

---

[31] See chapter J -3.3.4 on page 600 regarding the requirements on multiple sales arrangements.

in status, and control may only change slightly, these transactions need special attention. Again the transactions behind the changes of interest in a company can be acquisitions and disposals achieved in stages. For each company category, an individual accounting treatment is necessary.

5.1. Financial investment

A financial investment is a financial asset that is a contractual right to receive cash or another financial asset. In other words, a financial investment is an investment in another company that entitles to receive a dividend. These investments represent equity instruments of the other company which are typically shares, convertible bonds and similar instruments that are equipped with voting rights. The investment in that company is less than 20%: investments of more than 20% presume significant influence and therefore require accounting for such an investment as investment in associates. As long as such investments are not used as a parking position for excess cash (and therefore presented as current assets), the purpose of financial investments is based on a long-term view as a strategic investments. Financial investments are presented in the statement of financial position as non-current financial assets usually measured by their fair values or amortized costs.

There are three measurement options available to account for financial investments in subsequent periods:

- At fair value through other comprehensive income (which is the default measurement method) according to IFRS 9.4.1.4.
- At amortized costs if the business model of the company holding financial investments is based on asset holding in order to collect cash flows at specified dates that include solely payments of principals and interests only according to IFRS 9.4.1.2.
- At fair value through profit and loss according to IFRS 9.4.1.5 to avoid accounting mismatches.

In most cases, the first option will be chosen where financial investments are recorded at fair value through other comprehensive income. Financial investments usually pay dividends based on their performance and therefore do not have specified dates where payments are made that consist of principals and interests. Keeping the general accounting options in mind, step acquisitions and disposals that do not constitute a status change are accounted for by applying these measurement principles.

Financial assets are accounted for using either the trade date or settlement date accounting for sales and purchases. Trade date accounting recognizes the asset when purchased and any changes in value until the financial investment is delivered at the settlement date. By contrast, the settlement date accounting recognizes all changes in value between the trade date and settlement date and the asset when it is delivered. Both accounting methods will finally generate the same result.

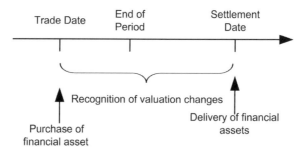

Fig. I-7   Timing of purchases of financial investments

5.1.1. Step acquisitions

The purchases of financial investments at different dates are step acquisitions without a change in the status. Each purchase is measured by its fair value in accordance with IFRS 9.5.1.1. In addition to the fair values, any transaction costs have to be considered. This will usually increase the carrying amount of the financial investment. The carrying amount at the acquisition date that consists of the fair value and the transaction costs is subject to a fair value adjustment in subsequent periods.

Transaction costs are incurred on purchase of financial investments that otherwise would not arise. Typical transaction costs according to IAS 39.AG13 are fees, commissions, levies by regulatory agencies, transfer taxes and duties. These costs can be paid to agents, brokers, and similar institutions. As transaction costs relate to external transactions and services, these costs do not cover debt premiums, discounts and financing costs as well as any internal costs due to administration or similar purposes.

The **journal entries** reflect ordinary transactions for purchasing and valuation adjustments. [32]

- Purchasing, initial recognition

Journal entry			Comment
dr.		Financial investments	The investment itself
	cr.	Bank	
dr.		Financial investment	Any fees and commissions that relate to the purchase.
	cr.	Bank	Alternate account: trade payables

- Subsequent recognition

    The subsequent recognition considers any fair value changes and adjusts of the carrying amount of financial investments to reflect the fair value through other comprehensive income. Even if the change in fair

---

[32] These journal entries assume that the financial instruments are delivered immediately, so there is no difference between the trade date and settlement date.

value of the financial instrument is recorded through other comprehensive income, any dividends received have to be recorded through profit and loss according to IFRS 9.5.7.6.

Journal entry		Comment
dr.	Financial investments	Can also be a credit.
	cr. Other comprehensive income	

5.1.2. *Partial disposals*

If parts of financial investment are sold, the accounting of that sales transaction is treated as a partial disposal of a financial investment. The sales transaction, like the purchase, has to be accounted for in accordance with IFRS 9. To qualify for a disposal, IFRS 9.3.2.3 demands that the contractual right to cash flows from financial assets expires, or the right to receive cash flows and substantial risks and rewards is transferred. A disposal (including partial disposal: so a sale of all or part of a financial investment) usually fulfils these requirements.

The measurement of the partial disposal is based on the provisions of IFRS 9.3.2.13, which demands an allocation of the carrying amount between the parts that are sold and the ones that are retained. The allocation of the carrying amount is based on the relative fair values of the disposed and retained assets. Fair values have to be determined at the date of transfer. Any gains or losses due to the transfer have to be recognized in profit & loss. Additionally, if the financial asset is qualified as available for sale and any valuation adjustments to the carrying amount subsequent to the initial recognition are recorded in other comprehensive income, a recycling to profit & loss is required. Based on these accounting requirements, the realized gain or loss of the disposal can be calculated.

	Consideration received
−	Carrying amount attributable to the disposal
+/−	Revaluation surplus, neutrally reclassified
+/−	Foreign currency translations, neutrally reclassified
=	Realized gain / loss

Tab. I-28   Gain / loss on partial disposal of financial investment

The measurement of financial investments is based on a fair value approach as already mentioned. Determining a fair value of a financial investment depends on the type of investment.

- Publicly listed
    A financial investment in a publicly listed company is an investment in an equity instrument issued by that company. As market data is available, a fair value measurement can be based on quoted price in the market.

- Privately held
    A financial investment of an interest in a privately held company is also an investment in an equity instrument. As the company is privately held, market data to determine the fair value is not available. In such a case,

appropriate valuation techniques have to be applied to determine the fair value.[33] A typical application is the use of a discounted cash flow method on the planned operations and business. Nevertheless, it is questionable if an access to such data is given. IFRS 9.5.2.1 in combination with IFRS 9.B5.4.14 to 9.B5.4.17 have picked up that issue and allow a measurement at costs if fair values cannot be reliably measured.

The **accounting** of the disposal depends not only on the fair value measurement at the date of transfer but also on the accounting by the parent. If the financial investment in the parent's accounts is recorded at historical costs, any fair value adjustments due to subsequent measurements are recorded as level II adjustments. If the financial investment is established due to step acquisitions, the question arises to which acquisition the disposed financial investments have to be allocated. An application of valuation methods like weighted average or FIFO might be suitable as long as a direct allocation to any tranche fails. Another proven practice is to apply movements of bank deposits or bank statements if financial investments relate to publicly listed companies. The accounting of the disposal is treated like any other disposal of any current or non-current assets. Depending on the accounting of the parent, appropriate adjustments can be determined and accounted for at group level. Any costs due to the disposal have to be recorded as an expense.

Having calculated the carrying amount to be disposed at parent level, a simple journal entry is sufficient to record the disposal.

Journal entry		Comment
dr.	Receivables	
cr.	Financial investment	
cr.	Gain on sale of financial investment	Can also be a loss (debit account instead).

Any valuation adjustments to arrive at fair value at group level and the related disposal should be preferably recorded at level II.

Journal entry		Comment
dr.	Revaluation surplus	Can also be a credit.
dr.	Other comprehensive income	Foreign currency translations and revaluations. Can also be a credit.
cr.	Financial investment	Difference between carrying amount at parent level and fair value.
cr.	Gain on sale of financial investment	Can also be a loss (debit account instead).

5.2. Associate

Equity transactions with a parent can change the equity of an associate without impacting on its status. Changes in an associate's equity require the execution

---

[33] See Appendix I: Fair value measurement on page 751 regarding more details on applicable valuation measurement methods.

of an initial consolidation or a disposal accounting (IAS 28.25 gives some guidance on such situations).

5.2.1. *Acquisitions and increases in capital*

Increases in the carrying amount of an investment in an associate are treated as **step acquisitions**. They will increase the influence in the associate but without any changes in the status of the associate; significant influence is retained. Reasons for such step acquisitions are manifold. In most cases the acquirer intends to increase its investment in a company until control is constituted because the associate has a strategic meaning to the parent or the group and sufficient shares in the associate to constitute control cannot be acquired in one step. Step acquisitions can be arranged in various ways, with or without consideration. The standard case of step acquisitions is the ordinary purchase of shares by the parent in exchange for cash or an equity instrument of the parent. This purchase transaction will initiate a new initial consolidation at the purchasing date of the new shares. The accounting is similar to step acquisitions that demand a change in the status of the company. The accounting for step acquisitions is discussed in detail in chapter 3.1.[34]

In addition to step acquisitions, **changes in an associate's equity** may also trigger an increase in investment without changing the associate's status. Changes in equity are equity transactions executed on the associate level. They do not necessarily demand an involvement of the associate's shareholder by providing more capital to the associate. Changes can also be realized by allocation transaction in the equity structure of the associate. Increases in equity of the associate can be allocated to the following categories:

- Proportionate increase in capital

    A proportionate increase in capital and therefore a change in equity or the equity structure can be realized through equity allocations and capital contributions by the associate's shareholders. All shareholders contribute based on their individual portions in the associate.

    Equity allocations assign retained earnings to share capital or capital reserves, increasing the share capital but leaving the absolute equity unchanged. The allocation requires the prior approval of shareholders as it impacts their rights.

Journal entry		Comment
dr.	Retained earnings	
cr.	Capital reserves	Can also be share capital.

Capital contributions are common practice if shareholders plan to strengthen the capital base of a company. The capital contribution does not necessarily require cash; other assets contributed to the associate may fulfil the same purpose. Each shareholder's contribution depends on his

---

[34] See page 576.

individual investment in the associate. It has to be calculated based on the agreed total increase in equity of the associate. Furthermore it assumes that – again – all shareholders contribute to the equity increase. The increase in equity can be realized either through the issuing of new shares or through an increase in capital reserves. Issuing new shares follows the ordinary accounting rules for issuing equity instruments which has to consider the par value per share and the related market value. This value depends on the shareholder resolution how to increase the associate's equity in return for a defined number of shares. The following journal entries are required by the **associate**:

Journal entry			Comment
dr.	Cash		For each shareholder in relation to its share in the associate.
	cr.	Share capital	Issuing of new shares, par value of shares only.
	cr.	Capital reserves	Difference between par and market value of the shares.

Much easier than issuing shares is the recording of capital contributions if no new shares are issued:

Journal entry			Comment
dr.	Cash		For each shareholder in relation to its share in the associate.
	cr.	Capital reserves	Just an increase in capital reserves, no new shares.

Common to both scenarios is an increase in equity without any changes in the relative portion of each shareholder in the associate.

The recording of capital contributions by the **parent** is treated like all other acquisitions. The capital contribution will increase the carrying amount of investments in associates.

Journal entry		
dr.	Investment in associates	
	cr.	Cash

While the capital contribution is executed by all shareholders, the pro-rata share of the investment in the associate does not change. Consequently, the parent is still entitled to participate in the associate's profit & loss, its changes in net assets and any changes in fair values of non-accounted assets and liabilities. Therefore, an application of an initial consolidation to determine a new equity value at group level is not necessary. The application of the equity method is left unchanged.

• Disproportionate increase in capital

A more sophisticated approach is for the parent to make a contribution which provides more capital than the other shareholders to the associate, resulting in an increased pro-rata share for the parent.

The accounting at associate and parent levels does not change; both companies record the contribution as if a proportionate increase in capital had occurred. Due to the increased pro-rata share in the associate, accounting tasks at group level will be initiated. The changed pro-rata share is treated like a new share acquisition which – again – demands the execution of a purchase price allocation like a step acquisition. The equity value of the associate has to be adjusted based on the determination of hidden reserves and burdens, non-accounted assets, goodwill and similar items and an update of the auxiliary calculation.[35]

The disproportionate increase in capital unfolds subsequent effects. The parent is entitled to a larger portion of the profit & loss realized by the associate as well as increased dividends. Furthermore, the effects of the new purchase price allocation (e.g. depreciation and amortization) will impact the contribution of the associate to the group's performance.

- Disproportionate less decrease in capital

  A (real) decrease in capital will force a company to distribute share capital to its shareholders where all shareholders will receive either cash or other types of asset according to their shares in the company. Such a distribution does not impact the relative share in the company and is therefore not a disposal.

  A special case is the decrease in capital where a shareholder will contribute disproportionately less to the capital decrease. This shareholder will therefore benefit from the capital decrease by expanding its relative share in the company. IFRS are silent about the treatment of such transactions. Even if the capital decreases, the reduced decrease, compared to other shareholders, qualifies as an acquisition of additional shares in the company and is therefore a step acquisition.

  The disproportionately smaller decrease in capital will trigger accounting activities at all levels. The **associate** has to record the distribution of capital:

Journal entry
dr.   Share capital
dr.   Capital reserves
   cr.   Cash

The **parent** has to reduce its carrying amount of investments in associates:

Journal entry		Comment
dr.	Cash	For each shareholder in relation to its share in the associate.
cr.	Investment in associates	

---

[35] See chapter G -2.1 on page 430 regarding the purchase price allocation and the initial consolidation of new shares in the associate.

At group level, the lesser decrease in capital has to be determined. The amount can be calculated by comparing the effective decrease in capital with a proportionate decrease in capital. The difference between these two amounts represents the acquisition costs of the additional shares in the associate. This equals a step acquisition. Based on the additional shares and the acquisition costs, a purchase price allocation is required to determine the new equity value at group level including an update of the auxiliary calculation.[36]

Subsequent effects are the same as for the disproportionate more increase in capital.

Common to all categories of capital increases are missing dedicated accounting guidelines. Therefore, there are several solutions to accounting for increases in capital. Which solution is the appropriate one to be applied has to be determined in each individual case.

5.2.2. *Partial disposals and decreases in capital*

A **partial disposal** of an investment in associates can reduce the investment in the associate without losing the significant influence in the associate. In such cases, the application of the equity method is still required. Usually, a partial disposal is a sales transaction of shares with consideration (i.e. by receiving cash). Even if reasons for such transactions are manifold, the accounting of partial disposals still follows the same pattern.

A reduction of the pro-rata share in an associate might also be realized by a **decrease in capital** which is finally a change in equity and which depends on the involvement of shareholders. Such decreases are also called deemed disposals.[37] Changes in equity are equity transactions executed on the associate level. They do not necessarily demand an involvement of the associate's shareholder. Changes in equity can also be realized by allocation transaction in the equity structure of the associate. Changes in equity that will result in a decrease in equity of the associate can be allocated to the following categories:

- Proportionate decrease in capital
  In general, a decrease in capital is not identical to a disposal. A disposal always reduces the pro-rata share in the associate while a decrease in capital only reduces share capital (or equity) without touching the interests of shareholders in the associate as long as a proportionate decrease occurs. Decreases in capital can be realized with and without the involvement of shareholders.

  Decreasing capital without involving shareholders is realized through an **allocation within equity**. These allocations are usual to cover losses

---

[36] See chapter G-2.1 on page 430 regarding the purchase price allocation and the initial consolidation of new shares in the associate.
[37] See chapter I-6.2 on page 567 for further information on deemed disposals.

generated by the associate. The absolute equity remains unchanged. It requires the prior approval of shareholders as this impacts the rights of the shareholders.

Journal entry		Comment
dr.	Capital reserves	Can also be share capital.
cr.	Retained earnings	

Capital decreases involving shareholders are always capital disposals. Disposals do not necessarily require cash, other assets distributed by the associate may fulfil the same purpose. The capital distribution to each shareholder depends on his individual investment in the associate. It has to be calculated based on the agreed total decrease in equity of the associate. Furthermore, it assumes that all shareholders benefit from the equity decrease. The decrease in equity can be realized either by retiring the number of shares outstanding or by a decrease in capital reserves. Retiring shares outstanding follows the ordinary accounting rules for equity instruments which has to consider the par value per share and the related market value. This value depends on the shareholder resolution how to decrease the associate's equity in return for a defined number of shares. The following journal entries are required by the **associate**:

Journal entry		Comment
dr.	Share capital	Par value of shares only.
dr.	Capital reserves	Difference between par and market value of the shares.
cr.	Cash	For each shareholder in relation to its share in the associate.

Much easier than retiring shares is the recording of capital distribution if the number of shares is left unchanged:

Journal entry		Comment
dr.	Capital reserves	Just a decrease in capital reserves, no retiring of shares.
cr.	Cash	For each shareholder in relation to its share in the associate.

Common to both scenarios is a decrease in equity without any changes in the relative portion of each shareholder in the associate.

The recording of capital contributions by the **parent** is treated like all other acquisitions. The capital contribution will decrease the carrying amount of investments in associates.

Journal entry	
dr.	Cash
cr.	Investment in associates

While capital distribution is executed by all shareholders, the pro-rata share of the investment in the associate does not change. Consequently, the parent is still entitled to participate in the associate's profit & loss, its changes in net assets and any changes in fair values of non-accounted assets and liabilities. Therefore, the application of the equity method at group level is left unchanged. It has to be applied to the changed equity.

- Disproportionate more decrease in capital

A disproportionate more decrease in capital is a more challenging accounting approach than an ordinary capital distribution. Due to the higher decrease in capital of the parent, less capital is held by the parent than the other shareholders hold in the associate. Such a capital distribution will result in a decreased pro-rata share of the parent in the associate.

The accounting on associate and parent level will not change. Both companies will record the capital distribution as if a proportionate decrease in capital would occur. Due to the decreased pro-rata share in the associate, accounting tasks at group level will be initiated. The change in the pro-rata share in the associate is treated like a partial disposal which – again – demands a disposal accounting. The equity value of the associate has to be adjusted based on a calculation of new carrying amounts of hidden reserves and burdens, non-accounted assets, goodwill and similar items and an update of the auxiliary calculation.[38]

The disproportionate decrease in capital unfolds also subsequent effects. The parent is entitled only to a smaller portion of the profit & loss realized by the associate as well as decreased dividends. Nevertheless, the effects of the adjusted equity value (e.g. due to changed depreciation and amortization) will positively impact the contribution of the associate to the group's performance.

- Disproportionate less increase in capital

A disproportionately less increase in capital occurs every time a company plans to increase its share capital but some shareholders refuse to attend at this capital increase or they attend only with a smaller percentage. As a consequence, the relative share in the associate will be reduced depending on the equity structure of the associate in relation to the shareholders engagement. Again, IFRS are silent about the treatment of such transactions. Even if the capital increases, the extent of the lesser increase compared to other shareholders qualifies as a disposal of shares in the company and is therefore a partial disposal.

The increase will trigger accounting activities at all levels. The **associate** has to record the capital contribution:

---

[38] See chapter G -2.3 on page 456 regarding the accounting for disposals and deconsolidations of the associate.

Journal entry
dr.   Cash
    cr.   Share capital
    cr.   Capital reserves

Depending on the involvement of the **parent** in the capital contribution, either no activity is required or an increase in the carrying amount of investments in associates has to be recorded:

Journal entry		Comment
dr.	Investment in associates	
cr.	Cash	For each shareholder in relation to its share in the associate.

At **group** level, several accounting options are available to deal with the non- or reduced involvement of the parent in the capital contribution. Even if a disproportionate less increase in capital occurs and the share of the parent in the associate decreases, a step-up in the investment in associates and / or the equity value might be given that needs to be accounted for.

Journal entry		Comment
dr.	Investment in associates	Can also be a credit.
cr.	Share of profit of associates	

Further adjustments to the equity value may be required depending on the share of the parent in hidden reserves and burdens, non-accounted assets, goodwill and other items. This also requires an update of the auxiliary calculation.

Subsequent effects are the same as for the disproportionate more increase in capital.

Both a partial disposal and a decrease in capital demand the execution of a set of **accounting tasks**. Even if only a portion of the investment in associates is disposed, the tasks are similar to a full disposal. Tasks include a proportionate expensing of investments in associates, recording of the sales transaction and a deconsolidation at group level and any other adjustments, particularly follow-up effects of the one-line consolidation.[39] All effects are recorded as gains or losses in the profit & loss statement unless a reclassification of other comprehensive income to retained earnings is demanded.

An issue will arise if the investment in associates is acquired in **step acquisitions**. The carrying amount of the investment in associates comprises of interests in associates with different amounts per share. This will force a decision on the sale of shares: Which shares have to be sold and how to measure them at parent and at group level?

---

[39] See chapter G -2.3 on page 456 regarding details of all disposal tasks.

- Parent level

  At parent level, the carrying amount of the investment in associates has to be determined that has to be expensed due to the sales transaction.

- Group level

  At group level, the equity value consists of hidden reserves and burdens, non-accounted assets and goodwill. As these items are built up by different amounts due to the various acquisitions, appropriate adjustments are required based on the sales transactions.

Solving this issue requires an evaluation of the sales contract in combination with the shares sold. If shares sold are **registered shares**, a direct allocation of the shares to their acquisition is recommended and possible in determining the carrying amount to be expensed and the adjustment necessary of identified and accounted components of the equity value. If shares sold are **bearer shares** that are maintained in a collective deposit of a bank, a direct allocation of the appropriate action is not possible. This requires the application of valuation techniques. As a general rule, the valuation technique that best characterized the behaviour of the interests in associates should be chosen in determining the carrying amount to be expensed and the equity value amount to be adjusted. In most cases, the applications of weighted average method, FIFO or LIFO qualify for an application. While FIFO and LIFO often fail for an application, the use of the weighted average method is often observed in practice. It is the preferred method because of its simplicity.

If shares are maintained in a collective deposit of a bank, the use of the bank's valuation is preferred before an application of any valuation techniques will be applied.

5.3. Joint venture

Acquisitions and disposals without changes in control of a joint venture is a special case due to the nature of the joint venture. They can only occur due to the retirement of an old party or an acceptance of a new party presuming that the contractual conditions of the joint venture still will be met and joint control is still given. Changes in the structure of the parties engaged in a joint venture require consent by all parties. Not part of changes in the structure of parties is the replacement by one party through another party presuming that the party will step into the conditions as valid for the old party.

The accounting of such changes depends on whether new parties are accepted, old parties retire and the way they will contribute to the joint venture. The following figure provides a comprehensive overview of changes in joint ventures and their accounting.

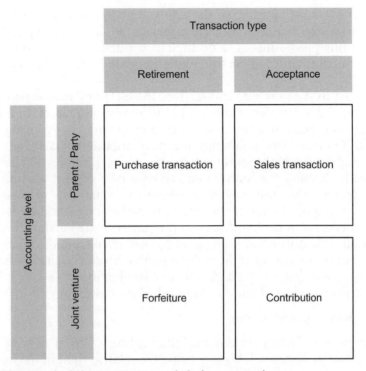

Fig. I-8 Changes in joint ventures and their accounting

5.3.1. *Retirement of parties*

The retirement of one or more parties in a joint venture is – from an accounting perspective – a step acquisition. This is because fewer parties are involved and have joint control. Regardless of how many parties retire, at least two parties have to remain to ensure that a joint venture can exist. This may increase the relative share of all parties left that are still engaged in the joint venture. The retirement of a party can be realized in two ways:

- Through a purchase transaction;
- Through a forfeiture of shares.

Both ways of rearranging the joint venture require individual accounting treatments.

In a **purchase transaction**, the remaining parties purchase the interest in the joint venture of the retiring party in a way that joint control continues. If necessary, terms and conditions of the binding contract between all parties involved or the articles and by laws of the joint venture have to be adjusted to reflect the new composition of the remaining parties in the joint venture. From a parent's (as one party) perspective, the purchase of additional interests in the joint venture from the retiring party is a step acquisition that increases the interest in the joint venture whereby the application of the equity method continues unchanged. This is identical to a step acquisition of an associate requiring the application of the same accounting procedures. As a result, a new initial consolidation in combination with a purchase price allocation and an update of the auxiliary calculation is required.[40]

In contrast to the purchase transaction, the **forfeiture transaction** pushes the accounting of the retirement of a party to the joint venture level. In this case, the joint venture is obliged to compensate the retiring party by reducing the equity through a forfeiture of shares in return for the distribution of cash or other assets. The remaining parties in the joint venture enhance their interests in the joint venture indirectly through the reduced equity base of the joint venture. From an accounting perspective, this way of handling the retirement of a party equals an increase in capital for the remaining parties that is realized by a disproportionate less decrease in capital.[41] As a consequence, a step acquisition has to be applied based on hypothetical acquisition costs derived from the relative changes of proportionate changes in equity of the joint venture. Similar to the purchase transaction, a new initial consolidation in combination with a purchase price allocation and an update of the auxiliary calculation is required.

5.3.2. *Acceptance of new parties*

An acceptance of new parties in the joint venture is – from an accounting perspective – a partial disposal. This is because the relative right in the joint venture will be reduced for each existing party and allocated to the new party to ensure joint control. In principle, the acceptance of parties can be realized in two different ways:

* Through a sales transactions where shares in the joint venture are sold to the new party by all current parties.
* Through a contribution where the new party contributes assets to the joint venture.

Both ways of establishing a joint venture require individual accounting treatments.

In a **sales transaction**, the parent (and all other parties) is selling a part of his interest in the joint venture to the new party. In addition to the sales transaction, either an update of the binding contract between the parties or a change in the articles and by laws of the joint venture in respect of the new party needs to be established. The purpose of these legal tasks is to ensure that joint control is still obtained and the rights and duties of the current parties are also assigned to the new party. From an accounting perspective, the sales transaction has to be treated in the same manner as a partial disposal of an interest in an associate without changing the status as an associate as discussed in the previous chapter.[42] This is

---

[40] See chapter I -5.2.1 on page 549 and chapter G -2.1 on page 430 regarding the accounting procedures to be applied.

[41] See Disproportionate less decrease in capital on page 551 regarding accounting details with the specialty that no accounting tasks are necessary by the parent.

[42] See chapter I -5.2.2 on page 552.

because the joint venture is already accounted for by applying the equity method and it will be accounted for after the acceptance of the new party by still applying the equity method. The interest in the joint venture will be reduced together with the percentage held in it. As this is a transaction between the parties of the joint venture (and therefore the shareholders of the joint venture), the joint venture itself is not involved and affected.

Other than the sales transaction, a **contribution transaction** requires a dedicated view as a reduction in the relative share in the joint venture occurs without any accounting requirements by the parent and without a loss of joint control. Due to the missing accounting requirements by all parties, the accounting is pushed down to joint venture level. Even if the accounting takes place at joint venture level, legal tasks may be processed by the parties of the joint venture similar to the sales transaction to ensure that joint control is maintained. As the accounting takes place at joint venture level, changes in capital occur due to the issuing of new shares to the new party in return for the agreed contribution of the party (which can be cash, current or non-current assets, rights and any other type of assets). From a parent's perspective, this way of accepting a new party equals a disproportionate less increase in capital (or a deemed disposal). The accounting by the parent is – again – similar to a partial disposal of an associate.[43]

All the discussed topics so far belong to the parent and are recorded either on parent or associate level. Even if there are similarities for both ways, the accounting for an acceptance of a new party at group level is subject to the provisions of IAS 28.25. While the equity method is still applied, any changes reducing the ownership interest in the joint venture demands a reclassification of elements other comprehensive income to profit & loss.

5.4. Subsidiary

An increase or decrease of the investment in a subsidiary by a parent that already has control is treated again as a step acquisition or partial disposal. The acquisition of additional shares in the subsidiary can increase the absolute voting level from its current level to a maximum 100%. The same applies to partial disposals. Investment in a subsidiary can be reduced from 100% to any voting level at which control is retained ($\geq 50\% + 1$ share) unless other facts and circumstances ensure control. The accounting treatment of such transactions was not defined in the past. IAS 27 (rev. 2008) and IFRS 10 now have defined the general accounting treatment of increases and decreases of interests in subsidiaries without any change of control as equity transactions between shareholders (defined in IFRS 10.23). Accordingly, any assets and liabilities, including goodwill of the subsidiary, that are part of consolidated financial statements will not change as the sphere of the subsidiary is not involved.

Due to the accounting as an equity transaction between shareholders, these transactions impact only the equity of consolidated financial statements. Transactions are accounted for as reclassifications in equity between non-controlling interests and reserves. IFRS 10.B96 requires a reclassification of the difference

---

[43] See decrease in capital on page 552.

between the fair value of consideration paid or received (so the purchase price) and an "adjustment amount" of non-controlling interests. The standard is silent about any measurement methods and any presentation in equity which is particularly an issue if any non-controlling interests are retained or established the first time.[44] In accounting for equity transactions the following items have to be considered:

- Fair value of non-controlling interests

     The fair value of non-controlling interests is not necessarily identical to the carrying amount as recorded in consolidated financial statements. Differences to the carrying amount can arise from the application of the full-goodwill or partial-goodwill methods during the initial recognition of a subsidiary. Furthermore, the fair value of non-controlling interests is affected by the business of the subsidiary in subsequent periods and the creation of any hidden reserves and burdens as well as any non-accounted assets in the ordinary course of the business. These items are material if the subsidiary was acquired a long time ago and had a profitable history. Therefore, a determination of the entity value of the subsidiary might be appropriate or necessary to calculate the fair value of non-controlling interests.

- Purchase price

     The negotiation of and agreement on a purchase price is a process that is influenced by facts and emotions. Therefore, a purchase price will vary depending on the parties involved in the negotiation process and the course of the negotiation process. A wise party selling a stake in a company will always consider the fair value of the stake plus a sales premium. Once the price is fixed, the form and the elements how to pay the price has to be agreed.

     The negotiated purchase price or consideration transferred to acquire or dispose of an additional tranche in the subsidiary might include various elements in addition to cash.[45] The measurement of these items should be performed similar to the measurement according to IFRS 3. Equity instruments have to be considered by their market values, variable elements have to be considered by their present values and non-monetary items by their fair values. Measuring non-monetary items by their fair values might require a valuation adjustment of the carrying amount of these items through profit & loss. This is the only exception to equity transaction where profit & loss is involved.

> Applying the same procedures to the determination of the purchase price than used in business combinations will ensure a proper treatment of all components.

---

[44] The IFRS assume that non-controlling interests are usually established through a business combination and not through an equity transaction between shareholders.

[45] See chapter E -3.3 on page 143 regarding typical purchase price elements.

While the standard is silent about any measurement and accounting methods, accounting options are available which are linked to the initial recognition of non-controlling interests. The measurement basis in such cases can be based on

- Proportionate shares

    The use of proportionate shares is recommended when the partial goodwill method is applied. In such cases, the adjustment of non-controlling interests will generally result in a higher "swing" of equity as the fair values of the stake in the subsidiary sold or purchased is part of the purchase price.

    The amount attributable to the equity transaction can be determined applying the following calculation:

$$\text{Attributable amount} = \text{Carrying amount non-controlling interests} * \frac{\text{Percentage of non-controlling interests transferred}}{\text{Percentage of non-controlling interests before transaction}}$$

Fig. I-9 Calculation of attributable non-controlling interests based on percentages

- Fair values

    The use of fair values is recommended when the full goodwill method is applied. While the "swing" of equity is reduced to fair value adjustments only, the swing is less than if the method is based on proportionate shares.

    The amount attributable to the equity transaction can be determined applying the following calculation:

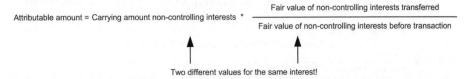

$$\text{Attributable amount} = \text{Carrying amount non-controlling interests} * \frac{\text{Fair value of non-controlling interests transferred}}{\text{Fair value of non-controlling interests before transaction}}$$

Two different values for the same interest!

Fig. I-10 Calculation of attributable non-controlling interests based on fair values

For both alternatives, the carrying amount of non-controlling interests after the transaction is:

	Carrying amount of non-controlling interests before transactions
−	Attributable amount (of non-controlling interests to parent)
=	Carrying amount of non-controlling interests after transaction

Tab. I-29 Calculation of new non-controlling interests

IFRS 10 is also silent about the accounting for any **acquisition-related costs incurred** due to the equity transaction. Costs incurred are all acquisition-related costs that arise in each acquisition of interests in a company.[46] Common sense is that costs incurred due to these equity transactions have to be accounted for

---

[46] See chapter E -3.3 on page 143 regarding examples of acquisition and acquisition-related costs.

similar to other equity transactions of the parent like the issuing or acquisition of own equity instruments. Therefore, IAS 32.37 should be applied regarding the accounting of costs incurred. IAS 32.37 demands that costs directly attributable to a transaction have to follow the underlying transaction. In other words, costs incurred that relate directly to the equity transaction have to be recorded in equity as well. Transaction related costs recorded in equity are limited to incremental costs only. Those costs would not have been incurred if the transaction had not taken place (so direct costs).

IFRS 10 does not provide any guidance regarding the **presentation in equity** and therefore where to record the transaction in equity. The only requirement is to record the transaction in equity and to present the effects in a separate schedule, according to IFRS 12.18. A single line item in the consolidated statement of changes in equity might satisfy this disclosure requirement. As a consequence, an inconsistent accounting of these transactions is observed in practice. Some record the equity transaction in retained earnings, others record them in capital reserves. While sales and purchases of non-controlling interests are equity transactions similar to issuing and acquisition of own equity instruments that does not impact profits, a recording in capital reserves is the preferred recording.

5.4.1. Step acquisition

An acquisition of a further interest in a subsidiary is a step acquisition where the parent usually is obliged to transfer a consideration. Assuming that the consideration includes the fair value of non-controlling interests and a sales premium, the equity transaction can be calculated.

	Consideration paid
−	Carrying amount of non-controlling interests attributable to the transaction
=	Equity movement of parent

Tab. I-30 Calculation of equity movement in a purchase transaction of non-controlling interests

The carrying amount of non-controlling interests is taken from the accounts as it is. It is a cumulative figure based on historical movements due to the performance of the subsidiary. It can be calculated considering all historical allocations to non-controlling interests.

	Non-controlling interest of initial consolidation
+/−	Profit & loss allocable to non-controlling interests in subsequent periods
−	Payments to non-controlling shareholders
+/−	Changes in fair values
+/−	Revaluation surplus
+/−	Foreign currency translations
+/−	Deferred taxes
+/(−)	Goodwill, if necessary also goodwill allocations due to cash generating units
=	Carrying amount of non-controlling interests at acquisition

Tab. I-31 Calculation on non-controlling interests based on historical movements

The accounting of a step acquisition is identical to all other acquisitions of financial assets. The **parent** has to recognize its acquisition costs that consist of considerations transferred and acquisition-related costs by applying the following journal entry. The journal entry assumes that all elements of the consideration transferred are properly measured.

Journal entry		Comment
dr.	Investment in subsidiaries	
cr.	Cash	
cr.	Liabilities	Future payments like earn-out options.

While the recording of an acquisition of a non-current asset in the parent's account has to be treated as an equity transaction at group level, movements in investments in subsidiaries have to be allocated to non-controlling interests. The final journal entry allocates that amount from non-controlling interests to equity that reflects the equity transaction. The remaining balance on the non-controlling interest account reflects the remaining share of non-controlling shareholders in the subsidiary. It will be zero if all non-controlling interests are acquired.

Journal entries		Comment
dr.	Non-controlling interests	
cr.	Investment in subsidiaries	
dr.	Capital reserves	Recognition of equity movement.
cr.	Non-controlling interests	

The journal entries at group level have to be repeated in all subsequent periods to reflect the changes due to the step acquisition. As an alternative, the journal entry of the initial consolidation has to be adjusted by the effects of the step acquisition.

Example

After several years, Flexing Cables was able to acquire the remaining 25% interest in Wilmington Ltd from the old founder family. The price, Flexing Cables had to pay was a fixed amount of 2,500 k EUR, which had to be transferred upon the signature of the sales and purchase agreement. The sales transaction was closed on October 1st. Flexing Cables has realized the acquisition through its subsidiary, Flexing Cables Holding. Additional costs arising from the sales transaction amounted to 35 k EUR, which were expensed.

Flexing Cables Holding had recorded the acquisition of interests in Wilmington like any other acquisition of assets.

Journal entry			
dr.	Interests in subsidiaries	2,500	
cr.	Cash		2,500

At group level, the increase in the carrying amount of interests in subsidiaries has to be reversed. Furthermore, non-controlling interests have to be eliminated. Non-controlling interest include the amount carried forward, any distribution of dividends, foreign exchange effects and the profit of the period from the beginning of the period to the acquisition date. The remaining amount to be recorded in equity is determined by the following calculation:

	Consideration paid	2,500
–	Carrying amount of non-controlling interests	946
–	Pro-rata profit of the period attributable to non-controlling interests	1,309
=	Equity movement of parent	245

Accordingly, the following journal entry has to be executed at group level:

Journal entry				Company
dr.	Non-controlling interests	2,255		Group
dr.	Capital reserves	245		Group
cr.	Interests in subsidiaries		2,500	Flexing Cables Holding

5.4.2. Partial disposals

A sale of interest in a subsidiary is a partial disposal where the parent is obliged to deliver the interest sold. Having determined the fair value of non-controlling interests sold, the equity transaction can be calculated. The determination of the fair value is based on fair value measurement techniques of the entity value of the subsidiary and the percentage of interests in the subsidiary sold.

	Consideration received
–	Fair value of the interest in subsidiaries sold
=	Equity movement of parent

Tab. I-32 Calculation of equity movement in a sales transaction of non-controlling interests

The accounting of a partial disposal is identical to the sale of any other non-current assets. The **parent** is performing a standard journal entry of a non-current sale applied to the investment in subsidiaries account.

Journal entry		Comment
dr.	Receivables	
cr.	Investment in subsidiaries	
cr.	Gain on sale on investment	Can also be a loss (debit account instead).

While the recording of an acquisition of a non-current asset in the parent's account has to be treated as an equity transaction at group level, movements in investments in subsidiaries have to be allocated again to non-controlling interests. This procedure is identical to a step-acquisition (except that credits and debits are exchanged). The final journal entry performs the equity transaction. It allocates that amount from equity to non-controlling interests to reflect the fair value on non-controlling interests in the consolidated statement of financial position. If the subsidiary was a wholly-owned company, non-controlling interests are established the first time and not created by a business combination.

Journal entries		Comment
dr.	Investment in subsidiaries	
cr.	Non-controlling interests	
dr.	Non-controlling interests	Recognition of equity movement.
cr.	Capital reserves	

Similar to step acquisitions, these journal entries at group level have to be repeated in all subsequent periods to reflect the changes due to the partial disposal. As an alternative, the journal entry of the initial consolidation has to be adjusted by the effects of the partial disposal.

6. SPECIAL CASES

Subsidiaries and associates including their control and significant influence are subject to further details. If changes in the ownership structure of subsidiaries and associates occur, a reassessment is required to determine any changes in control and the impact on separate and consolidated financial statements of the (ultimate) parent. In addition to ordinary changes in control that arise from acquisitions and disposals of interests in companies, from time to time special cases may also affect control. Some of these areas where changes in control can occur are listed in this chapter. They often cover the following topics:

- Changes in control when the affiliate is part of discontinued operations;
- Deemed disposals;
- Changes in control without any external involvement;
- Other issues that constitute changes in control.

These cases are discussed in the following chapters.

6.1. Discontinued operations

Changes in control can also be applied to affiliated companies (e.g. a subsidiary) that belong to discontinued operations according to IFRS 5. As IFRS 5 focuses on the classification of companies as held for sale, changes in control can only refer to a loss of control where the parent company retains some kind of control or influence in the disposed company.[47] The most common cases where a loss of control takes place are those ones of subsidiaries and associated companies. Joint ventures classified as held for sale is one of the rare cases.

---

[47] For a full disposal and the associated loss of control refer to chapter J -4 on page 601 for subsidiaries, chapter H -3 on page 494 for joint ventures and chapter G -2.3 on page 456 for associated companies.

The following table will help in determining if the interest in a company can be classified as held for sale according to IFRS 5 if a change in control takes place:[48]

Type of change in control	IFRS 5 application	Reason
Subsidiary to subsidiary	No	Control retained
Subsidiary to joint venture	Yes	Control lost
Subsidiary to associate	Yes	Control lost
Subsidiary to financial investment	Yes	Control lost
Joint venture to joint venture	No	Joint control retained
Joint venture to associate	Yes	Joint control lost
Joint venture to financial investment	Yes	Joint control lost
Associate to associate	No	Significant influence retained
Associate to financial investment	Yes	Significant influence lost

Tab. I-33 Application matrix of IFRS 5 on changes in control

Changes in control considering IFRS 5 can also be one part of a disposal achieved in stages. To avoid any misuse, the disposal should be analyzed and measured in its entirety as far as there are any timing dependencies.

Like a full disposal, an affiliated company has to be allocated as a disposal group at group level if recognition criteria of IFRS 5 are met. IFRS 5.8A confirms that it is not important whether a full disposal occurs or a non-controlling interest is kept in the company. Due to this practice, a combination of accounting tasks has to be followed in accounting of a partial disposal of an affiliated company (at group level):

- IFRS 5 classification

   The assets and liabilities or the investment in associates of the affiliated company have to be accounted for as a discontinued operations or a disposal group according to IFRS 5. All steps of the IFRS 5 procedure have to be executed; particularly the criteria to establish an IFRS 5 case have to be fulfilled.[49]

- Transitional consolidation

   Once assets and liabilities or the investment in associated companies of the affiliated company are classified as a discontinued operations (or disposal group) held for sale and a binding commitment of the purchase of a portion of the interests held in that affiliated company is available, a

---

[48] Table taken from Deloitte, iGAAP 2013 and adjusted for own purposes.

[49] See chapter J-4 on page 601. Steps 1 to 4 have to be processed. Depending on the sale, step 5 might be applied as well.

transitional consolidation is required. This consolidation depends on the current (before the partial disposal) and the new (after the partial disposal) status of the company. An appropriate consolidation technique has to be chosen and executed.[50]

At parent level, the accounting of investment in the affiliated company will be split up into two elements following the further sales or retention intention as required by IAS 28.20.[51]

Both the transactions at parent and group level demand an accounting of deferred taxes.

6.2. Deemed disposals

Changes in control can occur through transactions that are initiated by subsidiaries and associates. These transactions are either out of the control of the parent or based on toleration or omission by the parent due to a missing activity. Regardless how the change in control occurs, the parent has always a passive part. Reasons for deemed disposals are manifold:

- A full entitlement in rights issues is not taken;
- Payment of scrip dividends are not taken;
- Shares are issued to other shareholders;
- Options or warrants granted to other parties are exercised by these parties.

Other reasons are possible. As a result, the parent's stake in the subsidiary or associate dilutes. This dilution demands an adjustment in consolidated financial statements either through additional consolidations, reclassifications or simple adjustments of carrying amounts of balance sheet items. Which method is the appropriate one depends on the status of the company affected, the volume of changes in control and transitional effects that require a change in the status.[52] Regardless of which method is applied, the accounting of changes in control has to be recorded through profit & loss resulting in gains or losses.

6.3. Other constitutions of control

Changes in control may apply even if no acquisitions, disposals (either deemed or part or full) or internal transactions take place that finally focus on a change in voting rights. The origin of such changes is based on other facts apart from any voting rights. Typical examples are interests by and transactions on interests between investors and other parties.

---

[50] Depending on the sale, one of the cases discussed in chapter I -4 applies. The consolidation tasks described in the appropriate chapter has to be adopted.

[51] See chapter G -2.3.3 on page 466 for a detailed explanation.

[52] The accounting of deemed disposals depends on resulting effects. It is treated either as a change in the status of the company or a disposal without changes in control. See chapters I -4 on page 527 and I -5 on page 544 regarding the required accounting.

J DISPOSALS AND DECONSOLIDATION

About this chapter:

A deconsolidation is that task required if a subsidiary of a group is sold by the parent. Like an acquisition, the composition of the group will change due to the disposal. The sale of a subsidiary triggers a follow-up activity for the group as all those assets and liabilities that are sold have to be removed from consolidated financial statements as well. Preceding sale, management decisions are often made regarding the sale and the structure of the group.

This chapter discusses all aspects that relate to the sale of a subsidiary, from a parent's point of view as well as the group's point of view.[1] Profits achieved during the life of the subsidiary in the group are discussed in detail as well as consolidation methods down to journal entries. Special attention is given to the accounting as a discontinued unit according IFRS 5 before the final sale is executed.

---

[1] Disposals of associated companies and joint ventures are discussed in chapters G -Associated companies and H -Joint.

1. BASICS

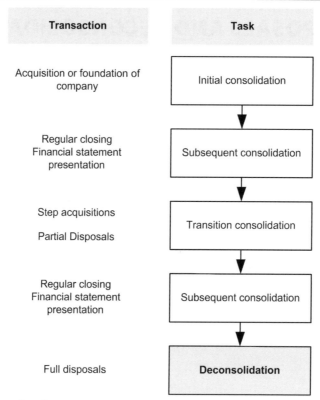

Fig. J-1   Lifecycle of a corporation: Deconsolidation

A sale (disposal) of a subsidiary by its parent company is often based on management decisions based on various intentions. Typical examples of a disposal are:

- Strategic changes in the scope of the group's business;
- The subsidiary does not any longer fit to the group and its core business;
- Attractive conditions on the sale like the sales price;
- Cash demands of the group for further or new investments;
- On-going losses of a subsidiary;
- Group restructuring.

Regardless of the intention of management to dispose of the subsidiary, the sale (or disposal) of all interests in an affiliated company (e.g. a wholly owned subsidiary) triggers the final stage of the lifecycle of a company in a group. With this sale, the investment of the parent in its subsidiary will be eliminated from the parent's statement of financial position. Total loss of control is given. Furthermore, the subsidiary also leaves the group, which requires the elimination of all assets and liabilities from the group's consolidated statement of financial position.

Depending on how the decision is made to dispose of the subsidiary and how the subsidiary is treated since then opens several accounting options to record the disposal. In general, a regular disposal is subject to IFRS 10. *IFRS 10 – Consolidated Financial Statements* provides the framework for these activities, IFRS 10.25 and IFRS 10.B97 to B99 define the tasks to be executed upon the loss of control. If a subsidiary is handled in a special way that it is available for sale, an application of *IFRS 5 – Non-current Assets Held for Sale and Discontinued Operations* may be applicable.

Accounting for the sale of a subsidiary involves not only the investment in a subsidiary at parent level and its assets and liabilities at group level, it will result in a set of transactions that ensure a full release of both statements of financial positions. In addition to the recording of the sale, a major transaction is the removal of the subsidiary from the group. This will be realized by executing a deconsolidation that has to ensure that all assets and liabilities are removed. As part of the deconsolidation, the following items have to be considered:

- Determination of the date of loss of control. The determination of the disposal date is directly linked to contractual agreements regarding the transfer of control to the acquirer. It also acts as the cut-off point for all kinds of allocations of carrying amounts of balance sheet items and profits / losses attributable to the group.
- The carrying amounts of assets and liabilities at group level at the disposal date. They consist of the balances at local level and all adjustments on other levels. The preparation of an interim closure of the subsidiary at the disposal date is strongly recommended.
- Existing hidden reserves and burdens as well as assets not accounted for that are accounted for at group level.
- Goodwill. Goodwill has to be considered in the context of cash generating units and impairment tests.
- Revaluation surplus as far as they relate to balance sheet items of the subsidiary.
- Reserves for foreign exchange differences.
- Non-controlling interests.

Each item requires special attention regarding their accounting and their consideration during the deconsolidation.

The deconsolidation will trigger additional requirements in preparing consolidated financial statements. While a disposal – like an acquisition – is always an extraordinary transaction, follow-up activities are necessary for presentation purposes. The disposal will affect not only the balance sheet due to investments, assets and liabilities assigned to the subsidiary but also the statement of income and the statement of cash flows as there is always an impact of the consolidated profit of the group and the cash flows achieved upon the disposal. Furthermore, analysis and detailed information provided in the notes are impacted as well. A typical example is the fixed asset schedule that may have to be expanded by additional columns for analysis. Last but not least, details on the disposal have to be provided in the notes explaining also the rationale behind the disposal.

1.1 Transitional consolidation without external involvement

All the above-mentioned transactions assume an external purchase or sales transaction on the equity of a subsidiary, joint venture or associate that induces a change in control. But changes in control can occur even without the involvement of any external transactions executed by the parent. These changes are based on other transactions that always trigger equity consolidation tasks to reflect the new conditions of the subsidiary, joint venture or associate. They are sometimes out of scope or control of the parent. Depending on the type of transaction, transitional consolidations or even deconsolidations apply. An approval of the parent as the shareholder is required in most cases.

Reasons for changes in control are manifold. The following list provides examples of transactions that impact control even without any sales or purchases of the parent:

- Changes in the article of a corporation or its bylaws;
- Control contracts, particularly establishment and termination of control contracts with the parent company or establishment or termination of control contracts with other parties (shareholders);
- Changes in voting rights to establish control;
- Dissenting voting rights;
- Acceptance of new shareholder through issuing of new shares by the subsidiary;
- Compensation of old shareholders through share repurchases by the subsidiary;
- Insolvency of a subsidiary;
- Changes in risks and rewards of special purpose entities.

Some of the examples listed qualify also as deemed disposals.

Accounting for changes in control according to the above-mentioned examples requires either a deconsolidation or a transitional consolidation. This is independent from the carrying amount of the investment in the subsidiary, joint venture or associate, the equity of the company or the percentage of interests in the company held. The only trigger is the change in control. Which consolidation finally has to be applied depends on the situation after the change. Due care has to be used to evaluate the reasons, to determine the accounting implications and to apply the appropriate transitional consolidation (including a deconsolidation). Knowing the impact on the consolidation, one of the presented transitional consolidation methods has to be applied.

> Checking for reasons for changes in control should be a standard task in preparing consolidated financial statements. This task should be one of the initial tasks to be executed before any accounting activities start.

2. CONTROL

As control is an integral element of defining groups and the composition of groups, a closer look on control is required also in the context of disposals and deconsolidation. As long as control is given, the subsidiary over which control is executed has to be considered as a part of the group. Nevertheless, there are situations where control is not given any longer, even if a disposal of the subsidiary did not take place. Such situations can arise from changes in the shareholder structure in which the parent did not participate (so called deemed disposals), or contractual conditions, or due to legal or court orders. Typical reasons for loss of control for the latter ones are:

- The subsidiary is controlled by government, court, administrator or regulator based on court orders.
- Insolvency where the subsidiary is controlled by a liquidator (to be checked if control is really lost).
- Seizure by government which is particularly valid for overseas investments in selected countries.

Like a sales transaction, the loss of control due to these reasons will also initiate a deconsolidation. The difference from a sales transaction is the presentation of these transactions in the separate and consolidated statements of financial position. While a sales transaction fully eliminates the investment in a subsidiary in the separate statement of financial position, and the assets and liabilities attributable to the subsidiary in the consolidated statement of financial position, an investment in a subsidiary is presented in separate and consolidated statements of financial position by applying a pure deconsolidation. This presentation assumes that the investment in the subsidiary is still given. In case of an insolvency a write-down or write-off of the investment in the subsidiary is required. Such a transaction is a variation of a sales transaction. Therefore, we will focus on a sales transaction that removes a subsidiary from its group, requiring a deconsolidation.

Nevertheless, the general treatment of loss of control can be summarized as follows:

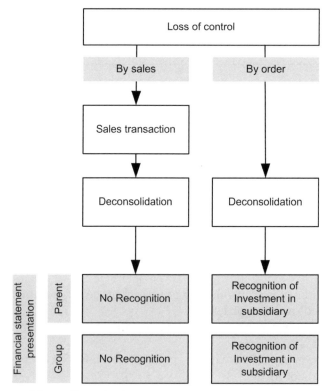

Fig. J-2   Types of loss of control

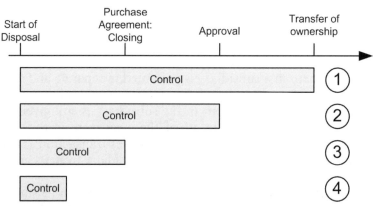

Fig. J-3   Transfer of control

From an accounting perspective, the sale of all interests in an affiliated company will result in a loss of control or in other words: control is transferred to an
external party. The loss of control depends on the conditions defined in the sale &
purchase agreement. Therefore, the sale & purchase agreement has to be scanned
regarding all arrangements that relate to the sale. In determining the effective date

a company departs from the group (the disposal date), the same techniques can be used as when determining the date of control of an acquisition.[2] The transfer of risks and rewards and other forms of transferring control should be kept in mind.

In some cases, the sale of all investments in a subsidiary is linked to **several transactions**. These transactions may occur simultaneously or step by step or depend on each other. The loss on control and its effective date is therefore not easy to determine. In such cases, IFRS 10.B97 provides guidance that all transactions have to be treated as one due to the commercial effect behind the transaction.

The sale of a subsidiary might also be subject to **approval** by antitrust or competition authorities. These situations occur if the acquirer and the subsidiary sold will dominate a business or market. The loss of control might be given in the first instance as the ownership transfers to the acquirer. But control may be established at a later stage upon the rejection of the approval by antitrust or competition authorities.

A common practice is the **backdating** of a purchase agreement towards the beginning of the period. The intention of a backdating is often based on a simplified agreement on the purchase price and on the allocation of profits of the current period. From an accounting point of view, a backdating is just an allocation issue of the purchase price that does not impact the effective date.

> Use the same techniques to identify the effective date for acquisitions and disposals.

The implications of loss of control and the stage and date where control is lost trigger the disposal accounting. As the presentation and recording of a subsidiary in separate and consolidated financial statements vary the implications for the parent company and the group will also vary. They will be solved by the application of dedicated consolidation techniques.

3. DECONSOLIDATION TECHNIQUES

Removing a subsidiary from the consolidated financial statement requires special deconsolidation techniques. These techniques have to consider a set of issues that arise in the ordinary course of the business of a group and as a result of the initial consolidation of a subsidiary. The issues always deal with equity effects and include the following items:

- Options used as part of IFRS 1 First time adoption;
- Goodwill depending on the initial consolidation (full vs. purchased goodwill);
- Cash generating units;
- Non-controlling interests;
- Discontinued operations;
- Cut-off issues of profit if the subsidiary is disposed during the period.

---

[2] See chapter C -1 on page 44 in determining control.

The deconsolidation itself can be realized either in one step or in multiple steps. Both methods will always produce the same results.

- Multi-step deconsolidation

  A multi-step deconsolidation removes all assets and liabilities from consolidated financial statements by executing two journal entries. The first journal entry removes assets and liabilities in relation to the own stake in the subsidiary; the second removes the stake of non-controlling interests in assets and liabilities. This journal entry depends on the initial recognition on non-controlling interests. If non-controlling interests are recorded by applying the full-goodwill method, a portion of the group's goodwill has to be eliminated as well. If the partial-goodwill method is applied, no further adjustments are necessary.

- One-step deconsolidation

  The one-step deconsolidation does not differentiate between own stakes and non-controlling stakes. All assets and liabilities are removed from the consolidated balance sheet in one journal entry by eliminating investments in subsidiaries and non-controlling interests. An identification of all assets and liabilities is required. This applies particularly to any goodwill attributable to the disposed subsidiary.

In addition to the described effects, dependencies and follow-ups need to be considered. It is recommended to consider them by posting additional journal entries. Typical examples are goodwill adjustments due to cash generating units and adjustments due to the accounting of the subsidiary as a discontinued unit.

3.1 The parent's view

The sale of all interests in a subsidiary is a simple transaction to be executed in the accounts of the parent. The accounting is similar to any sale of fixed assets where a gain or loss due to the sales transaction is recorded. At the purchase date, the interest in a subsidiary has to be expensed. In parallel, the parent records earnings based on the agreed sales price. Earnings have to include any other contractual contribution to be received, measured by their fair values at the purchase date. Usually, a receivable will be recorded in the balance sheet until payment. If the contractual obligation includes variable elements, they are recorded based on the expected and discounted future cash flows using an appropriate discount rate that reflects the current market condition.

The gain or loss realized can be estimated by applying the following calculation:

	Proceeds from the sale of interests in the subsidiary
–	Carrying amount of the interests in the subsidiary
=	Realized gain / loss

Tab. J-1 Gain / loss from the sale of subsidiaries, the parent's view

Recording earnings and expenses due to the sale will result either in a gain or loss. Therefore, journal entries may vary depending on the sale. These journal entries do not differ from a partial sale.

- Gain

    A gain due to the sale of a non-current asset is usually presented as other income or other earnings in the profit & loss statement.

Journal entries			Comment
dr.		Gain on sale of subsidiary	Derecognition of investment which is a part of financial assets
	cr.	Investments in subsidiaries	
dr.		Trade receivables (or other receivables)	Recognition of the sales transaction
	cr.	Gain on sale of subsidiary	

- Loss

    A loss due to the sale of a non-current asset is usually presented as other expenses in the profit & loss statement.

Journal entries			Comment
dr.		Loss on sale of subsidiary	Derecognition of investment which is a part of financial assets
	cr.	Investments in subsidiaries	
dr.		Accounts receivables (or other receivables)	Recognition of the sales transaction
	cr.	Loss on sale of subsidiary	

If expected cash flows that are based on variable elements deviate from the initial expected cash flows, an adjustment is required in that year the variable element becomes due for payment. In such a situation, an additional gain or loss has to be recorded. The journal entry to be executed is again subject to gains or losses.

- Gain

Journal entry			Comment
dr.		Cash	Payments exceed the initial expectation.
	cr.	Trade receivables (or other receivables)	
	cr.	Gain on sale of subsidiary	

- Loss

Journal entry			Comment
dr.		Cash	Payments fall below the initial expectation.
dr.		Loss on sale of subsidiary	
	cr.	Trade receivables (or other receivables)	

> **Example**
>
> Based on the sale and purchase agreement signed on 28 February, the interests in Cuivre Manufacture had to be eliminated from the accounts of Flexing Cables SE. In addition to the already mentioned conditions, the sale and purchase agreement included the following topics:[3]
>
> - The sales price for the shares held in Cuivre Manufacture was 18,000 k EUR.
> - The sales price included the profit of the company realized between the beginning of the period and the date of the transfer of the ownership.
>
> Flexing Cables had acquired the interests in Cuivre Manufacture 25 years before for a purchase price of 1,090 k EUR. The company had been almost profitable since then, so adjustment to the carrying amount of the investment in Cuivre Manufacture, due to impairment, was not necessary. Accordingly, the following profit was realized on the disposal:
>
> | | | |
> |---|---|---|
> | | Sales price | 18,000 |
> | – | Carrying amount of interests in subsidiaries | 1,090 |
> | = | Realized gain | 16,910 |
>
> Flexing Cables SE recorded the following journal entries for the disposal:
>
> Journal entries
> | | | | |
> |---|---|---|---|
> | dr. | Receivables | 18,000 | |
> | cr. | Gain on sale of subsidiary | | 18,000 |
> | dr. | Gain on sale of subsidiary | 1,090 | |
> | cr. | Investment in subsidiaries | | 1,090 |

3.2 The group's view

A more sophisticated view of the sale of the interest in a subsidiary is the group's view. Due to the one-entity theory, assets and liabilities are disposed at group level. This requires that all assets and liabilities that belong to the subsidiary sold can be identified. The identification includes all levels in the group. In other words, not only those assets carried in the accounts of the subsidiary subject to disposal have to be identified, but also any further adjustments:

- at level I due to the alignment of the subsidiary's accounting standard to the parent's accounting standard,
- at level II due to different accounting policies,
- at level III for assets and liabilities recognized as part of a business combination (e.g. the original acquisition), and
- at group level due to additional valuation and measurement tasks.

As long as the sale relates to a subsidiary, the identification of assets should not be an issue to address. The same applies if a set of subsidiaries will be sold that represents a business unit, an operation, a major line of operation, a segment or a similar organizational unit of the group. The identification may become an

---

[3] See the example in chapter C -3 on page 62 regarding further details of the disposal.

issue, if a part of a subsidiary or a dedicated business in a subsidiary will be sold. In such cases an allocation of the subsidiary's asset to the business is required. In some cases, an asset of the subsidiary may serve different business units. Here, it has to be checked if the asset is allocable to several business units and if not how to treat the asset upon the sale.

An item at group level that requires special attention is goodwill. If goodwill is directly allocated to the subsidiary, it can be treated like any other asset. If the subsidiary is part of a cash-generating unit where goodwill is allocated to, a pro-rata consideration is required.

The thoughts of dealing with assets and liabilities in the group have to be reflected by the tasks required to deconsolidate the subsidiary:

- Calculation of gains and losses;
- Asset and liability elimination;
- Goodwill;
- Other comprehensive income;
- Consolidation tasks to be executed.

Some of the tasks can be performed in one step as part of the one-step or multiple-step deconsolidation. The tasks can also be affected by additional activities that arise from the IFRS, e.g. by IFRS 5 if the subsidiary to be deconsolidated has the status of a discontinued operation classified as held for sale. Regardless of those specialities, IFRS 10.B98 defines the activities in broad terms that have to be executed.

3.2.1 Calculation of gains and losses

The gain or loss realized at group level due to the disposal of the subsidiary can be calculated by applying either the direct or indirect method. Both methods assume that any non-controlling interests are already eliminated. The elimination of non-controlling interests will result in **adjusted assets and liabilities** that are used in determining the realized gain or loss on the sale of the subsidiary:

- Direct method

    The calculation of gains or losses starts directly at group level. Proceeds from the sale of the subsidiary are deducted by all assets at local level as well as all level II adjustments. Provisions and liabilities at local level and level II are added to the proceeds. Further adjustments relate to items recorded in other comprehensive income (e.g. valuation reserves, foreign currency translations), to deferred taxes and goodwill (if there is any goodwill left).[4] The goodwill considered in calculating the realized gain / loss includes the goodwill directly attributable to the subsidiary disposed. It can be adjusted by goodwill that belongs to the cash generating unit the subsidiary was assigned to.

---

[4] Deferred taxes as part of the realized gain / loss are often ignored in literature. Deferred taxes that are directly attributable to the subsidiary disposed and that have to be eliminated are considered in calculating the realized gain/ loss to provide a full picture on the effective gain / loss. This applies also to the indirect method.

The following scheme can be used in calculating the realized gain / loss:

	Proceeds from the sale of interests in the subsidiary
−	**Adjusted** level II assets of the disposed company
+	**Adjusted** level II provisions and liabilities of the disposed company
+/−	Differences due to foreign currency translations
+/−	Items of a revaluation surplus
+/−	Deferred taxes
+(/−)	Goodwill, if necessary also goodwill adjustments due to cash-generating units
=	Realized gain / loss

Tab. J-2   Gain / loss from the sale of subsidiaries using the adjusted direct method, the group's view

• Indirect method

The calculation of gains or losses by applying the indirect method starts with the investment in subsidiaries as recorded by the parent or any holding company. Proceeds from the sale of the subsidiary are deducted by the carrying amount of the interest in the subsidiary disposed. The realized gain / loss in the parent's accounts is adjusted by group specific components accounted for during the life in the group. These components relate to items of the initial purchase price allocation (e.g. all level II adjustments due to hidden reserves and burdens), to items recorded in other comprehensive income (e.g. valuation reserves, foreign currency translations), any fair value adjustments according to IAS 39, accumulated depreciation, impairment losses recorded, deferred taxes and goodwill. Again, the goodwill considered in calculating the realized gain / loss includes the goodwill directly attributable to the subsidiary disposed which remains at group level. It can be adjusted by goodwill that belongs to the cash generating unit the subsidiary was assigned to.

The following scheme can be used in calculating the realized gain / loss:

	Proceeds from the sale of interests in the subsidiary
−	**Adjusted** carrying amount of the interests in the subsidiary in the parent's accounts
=	Realized gain / loss in the parent's accounts
+/−	**Adjusted** fair value adjustments recorded through profit & loss according to IAS 39
−	Accumulated exceptional depreciation
+	Impairments of goodwill included in net book value
+/−	**Adjusted** hidden reserves and burdens of purchase price allocations released through profit & loss
+/−	**Adjusted** net profit of the period of the sold company
+/−	Revaluation surplus, neutrally reclassified
+/−	Foreign currency translations, neutrally reclassified
+/−	Deferred taxes
+/−	Goodwill adjustments due to cash-generating units
=	Realized gain / loss

Tab. J-3   Gain / loss from the sale of subsidiaries using the adjusted indirect method, the group's view

Regardless of which method is applied, the direct and indirect methods always produce the same result. Both methods have their advantages and disadvantages. The advantage of the direct method is its simplicity as all items are easily identifiable. By contrast, the advantage of the indirect method is the reconciliation between the realized gain / loss at parent level and the gain / loss at group level.

The calculations presented consider only the effects of the group. To estimate the effects on non-controlling interests – and particularly the realized gain / loss attributable to non-controlling interests – an expansion by another column may help. This expansion has the advantage that it supports a reconciliation of all necessary adjustments for assets and liabilities. A calculation scheme could look like this:

		Group	Non-controlling interests
	Proceeds from the sale of interests in the subsidiary		
–	Level II assets of the sold company		
+	Level II provisions and liabilities of the sold company		
+/–	Differences due to foreign currency translations		
+/–	Items of the revaluation surplus		
+/–	Deferred taxes		
+(/–)	Goodwill, if necessary also goodwill adjustments due to cash-generating units		
=	Realized gain / loss		

Tab. J-4 Example of calculation scheme considering non-controlling interests

To avoid an adjustment for **non-controlling interests**, both methods can include non-controlling interests to arrive at the realized gain or loss. Again, these calculations will produce the same results as before.

- Direct method

	Proceeds from the sale of interests in the subsidiary
–	Level II assets of the sold company
+	Level II provisions and liabilities of the sold company
+/–	Differences due to foreign currency translations
+/–	Items of the revaluation surplus
+/–	Deferred taxes
+(/–)	Goodwill, if necessary also goodwill adjustments due to cash-generating units
+	**Non-controlling interests**
=	Realized gain / loss

Tab. J-5 Gain / loss from the sale of subsidiaries using the non-controlling interests direct method, the group's view

- Indirect method

	Proceeds from the sale of interests in the subsidiary
−	Carrying amount of the interests in the subsidiary in the parent's accounts
=	Realized gain / loss in the parent's accounts
+/−	Fair value adjustments recorded through profit & loss according to IAS 39
−	Accumulated exceptional depreciation
+	Impairments of goodwill included in net book value
+/−	Hidden reserves and burdens of purchase price allocations released through profit & loss
+/−	Net profit of the period of the sold company
+/−	Revaluation surplus, neutrally reclassified
+/−	Foreign currency translations, neutrally reclassified
+/−	Deferred taxes
+/−	Goodwill adjustments due to cash-generating units
+	**Non-controlling interests**
=	Realized gain / loss

Tab. J-6 Gain / loss from the sale of subsidiaries using the non-controlling interests indirect method, the group's view

You may feel that the direct method considering non-controlling interests is easier to manage as there is a direct relationship with the journal entries of the deconsolidation without managing complex adjustments.

Example

This example continues the example of the previous chapter!
To determine the gain or loss to be achieved at group level due to the disposal of Cuivre Manufacture from the group, group level details were necessary.

- Assets and liabilities of the disposed subsidiary
  While Cuivre manufacture applied group accounting policies in its local accounts, any level I and level II adjustments are not necessary. The carrying amounts of all assets and liabilities as of the separate statement of financial position as of the disposal date can be used directly in determining the realized gain on the sale:

IFRS Statement of financial position Cuivre Manufacture as of 28.2.2014 (in k EUR)

Assets		Liabilities & Equity	
Cash at hand & bank	781	Trade payables	2,483
Trade receivables	1,623	Tax liabilities	105
Inventory	2,586	Accruals	1,637
Other assets	943	Loans	100
Current assets	**5,933**	Other payables	635
		Current liabilities	**4,960**
Property, plant & equipment	16,294		
Intangible assets	78	Loans	1,100
Non-current assets	**16,372**	Pensions	182

Deferred taxes	137
Non-current liabilities	**1,419**
Share capital	150
Capital reserve	1,500
Retained earnings	14,276
Equity	**15,926**

Total assets	**22,305**	**Total liabilities & equity**	**22,305**

IFRS Statement of income Cuivre Manufacture as of 28.2.2014 (k EUR)		**IFRS Statement of income Cuivre Manufacture as of 28.2.2014 (k EUR)**	
Revenues	7,321	Revenues	7,321
Changes in inventory	(163)	Cost of goods sold	(5,495)
Work performed and capitalized			
Other income	286	**Gross margin**	**1,826**
Total performance	**7,444**		
		Sales & distribution expenses	(388)
Raw materials and consumables	(2,871)	Administration expenses	(329)
Employee expenses	(1,857)	Research & development expenses	(81)
Depreciation and amortization expenses	(268)	Other income	286
Other expenses	(1,425)	Other expenses	(291)
Operating profit	**1,023**	**Operating profit**	**1,023**
Finance expenses	(74)	Finance expenses	(74)
Profit before tax	**949**	**Profit before tax**	**949**
Income tax expenses	(316)	Income tax expenses	(316)
Net profit for the period	**633**	**Net profit for the period**	**633**
Thereof:		Thereof:	
• Profit allocable to non-controlling interests	253	• Profit allocable to non-controlling interests	253
• Profit allocable to the group	380	• Profit allocable to the group	380

• Group history

At the original acquisition date of Cuivre manufacture, the following items were recognized at level III:

Asset / liability	Amount
Fair value adjustments land	240
Customer orders	120
Customer base	330
Deferred taxes	(230)
	460

All items were recorded in retained earnings in accordance with IFRS 1.11. Group policies prefer the application of the cost model and do not allow an application of the revaluation model. Accordingly, a revaluation surplus does not exist. As of the disposal date, only the fair value adjustment and a corresponding deferred tax liability amounting to 80k EUR existed at level III.

- Other comprehensive income[5]

  Appraisal gains on pension provisions require consideration.

- Goodwill[6]

  Two items would be considered: The goodwill of Cuivre manufacture as of the initial consolidation and an additional goodwill portion of the copper solutions business unit (which represents a cash-generating unit).

- Non-controlling interests

  The carrying amount of non-controlling interests represented the situation as of the disposal date including allocation of profits, distribution of dividends and other compensations. The carrying amount at the beginning of the period was 6.235 k EUR. This balance did not include the profit of the period attributable to non-controlling interests.

Having considered all above discussed issues, the realized gain on the disposal could be calculated:

		Group	Non-controlling interests	Total
	Proceeds from the sale of interests in the subsidiary	18,000		
−	Level II assets of the sold company	(13,383)	(8,922)	(22,305)
+	Level II current liabilities of the sold company	2,976	1,984	4,960
+	Level II provisions and non-current liabilities of the sold company	851	568	1,419
−	Level III assets	(144)	(96)	(240)
+	Level III deferred taxes	48	32	80
−	Recycling of other comprehensive income	(81)	(55)	(136)
−	Goodwill	(490)		
−	Goodwill adjustments due to the cash-generating unit	(976)		
+	Non-controlling interests (carrying amount at the beginning of the period)		6,235	
=	Realized gain / loss	6,800	(253)	

3.2.2 *Asset and liability elimination*

The core of the deconsolidation is the removal of assets and liabilities belonging to the disposed subsidiary from the consolidated financial statements. The appropriate standard, IFRS 10.25 to 10.26 is extremely lean in providing detailed instructions on the accounting for loss of control. According to the standard

[5] See the example in chapter J -3.2.4 on page 588 for details.
[6] See the example in chapter J -3.2.3 on page 585 for details.

- Assets and liabilities have to be derecognized, and
- A gain or loss is recognized associated with the loss of control.

Even if these are only a very few requirements, the elimination itself depends on the deconsolidation method applied. Common to both methods is that the balances of all assets and liabilities at the date of loss of control have to be available, preferably by using the interim closure of the subsidiary.

- Multi-step deconsolidation

    Applying multi-step consolidation requires an adjustment of assets and liabilities. This adjustment restates the carrying balances of all assets and liabilities by that amount that belongs to the non-controlling interest. The remaining carrying amounts of assets and liabilities are subject to the deconsolidation.

- One-step deconsolidation

    This removes non-controlling interests, together with the parent's, from the balance sheet; a specific consideration or treatment of assets and liabilities is not required. They can be taken as they are for deconsolidation purposes.

Often, the sale of a subsidiary is bound to **specific conditions**. One of the most common conditions is that subsidiaries are sold cash and debt free leaving defined financial assets and liabilities with the parent. This has to be considered within the deconsolidation. The easiest way to account for these (and also for other) conditions is to transfer those assets and liabilities that are excluded from the sale of the subsidiary to that entity of the group that has to carry the obligation. This is either the parent or a holding of the group. Once the transfer is done, the regular deconsolidation will be initiated.

> **Example**
>
> This example continues the example of the previous chapter!
> The corporate centre has decided to apply the one-step deconsolidation. Accordingly, assets and liabilities attributable to Cuivre Manufacture are removed in one step by charging the carrying amount to two accounts in the profit & loss statement: gains on sale of investment in subsidiaries and gains on eliminating non-controlling interests. These accounts are charged in relation to the participation quota.

3.2.3 *Goodwill*

Like all other assets, goodwill is an asset that has to be eliminated from the consolidated financial statement if there is a relationship with the disposed subsidiary. To understand how goodwill has to be removed, an analysis of the business of the subsidiary and the group is required. Usually, an acquired subsidiary becomes part of a business unit or form a new business unit. This depends on the nature of the group's business, the business of the subsidiary and the intention why the subsidiary was acquired (e.g. expansion of market share, expansion into other geographical regions, gathering new sales channels or new product lines). If the initial intention was to expand the group's activities into other business areas, the subsidiary may act as an own business unit and also as a cash-generating unit. By contrast, the subsidiary may become part of a business unit and a cash-generating unit, if the initial intention was to strengthen the current business of the group.

Usually, goodwill will arise from the acquisition if the purchase price exceeds all assets acquired. This goodwill has to be allocated to the cash-generating units that benefit from the synergies of the acquisition of the subsidiary as stated in IAS 36.80. This allocation has to be executed even if the allocation of goodwill is independent to the allocation of assets and liabilities. In most cases, the allocation occurs to that cash-generating unit the subsidiary belongs to. The intention of this rule is an allocation based on an economic view rather than on a subsidiary's view. An individual allocation is not given any longer.

At disposal, a calculation is necessary to determine that amount that has to be considered in the deconsolidation. It is not sufficient to take the initial goodwill as this goodwill is allocated to cash-generating units and the goodwill could be subject to an impairment test in the past. IAS 36.86 demands that a pro-rata portion of the goodwill has to be disposed. This portion should reflect the proportion of values within the cash-generating unit. A calculation of the goodwill to be disposed can be based on the following formula:

$$\text{Goodwill disposed subsidiary} = \text{Goodwill of CGU} * \frac{\text{Carrying amount disposed subsidiary}}{\text{Carrying amount of CGU}}$$

Fig. J-4   Goodwill calculation on disposal

A simplification to this method is given, if the subsidiary still resides as an own business unit and as an own cash-generating unit. Only in this case, the goodwill may equal the initial goodwill where a determination of the goodwill to be disposed is not required. A calculation is not required as the full amount of goodwill has to be considered.

Deviation from the goodwill allocation is acceptable only in such cases where the goodwill allocation will result in a mismatch. Other methods may be applicable to allocate goodwill that will not let into a mismatch, if the other method can demonstrate that it better reflects the relationship of operations of the cash-generating unit. An appropriate documentation is recommended to deliver the evidence required for auditors.

An exemption is given if goodwill (based on previous GAAP) is recognized during the first-time adoption of IFRS as a deduction from equity. Recognition of this goodwill in the opening IFRS statement of financial position is prohibited. Consequently, this goodwill is also prohibited from reclassification issues. An allocation from equity towards profit & loss at the date the subsidiary will be disposed is not appropriate according to IFRS 1.C4i)(i).

The allocation of goodwill depends also on the shareholder structure of the subsidiary. All above discussed issues can be taken if the subsidiary is a wholly-owned subsidiary. If the parent company does not hold the full stake in the subsidiary and non-controlling interests exist, the accounting of the disposal of goodwill depends also on the initial goodwill allocation method. We therefore have to differentiate between these two methods:

- Partial goodwill method

  The partial goodwill method reflects only the shareholder's stake in goodwill. It can be taken as discussed before.

- Full goodwill method

  The full goodwill method unveils the whole goodwill of the subsidiary including the portion attributable to the non-controlling interests. In absence of specific accounting guidelines, the goodwill attributable to non-controlling interests has to be treated in the same way as the other goodwill.

Example

This example continues the example of the previous chapter!

Cuivre Manufacture is – together with Germain de Paris – part of copper solutions business unit. This business unit is also a cash generating unit due to its specific products. A mutual interference with other parts of the group is not given. A goodwill amount of 4,624 k EUR is assigned to that business unit. The goodwill assigned is built up by the individual goodwill of the companies belonging to the business unit:

- Cuivre Manufacture 490 k EUR;
- Germain de Paris 4,134 k EUR.

These goodwills belong to the initial consolidations of the companies and were never subject to any impairment adjustments.

As a pro-rata portion of the business unit's goodwill has to be allocated to the disposal of Cuivre Manufacture, the carrying amounts of the business unit and Cuivre Manufacture have to be determined by applying the provisions as outlined in IAS 36.74 et seq. Taken from regular impairment tests, the following information is available:

- The fair value of the business unit is assumed to be 61,004 k EUR, the fair value of Cuivre Manufacture is 19,494 k EUR.
- Based on the planning of the business unit, the value in use is assumed to be 58,525 k EUR.
- Corporate assets allocable to the business unit have a value of 1,500 k EUR.
- Disposal costs of the business unit are assumed to be 1,000 k EUR. These costs are external costs only.

Based on the available information, the fair value less cost of disposal of the business unit is 61,504 k EUR (which includes corporate assets allocated to the business unit as well as the assumed disposal costs). While this amount is higher than the value in use, the recoverable amount of the business unit used for goodwill allocation is 61,504 k EUR. By applying the above mentioned formula, the goodwill attributable to Cuivre Manufacture is 1,466 k EUR (4,624 k EUR * 19,494 k EUR / 61,504 k EUR). Considering the goodwill of Cuivre Manufacture's initial consolidation, an amount of 976 k EUR has to be allocated from the business unit's goodwill to Cuivre Manufacture.

3.2.4 Other comprehensive income

During life in a group, a subsidiary may have had transactions that are not recorded in profit & loss. These include usually valuation issues with corresponding unrealized gains and losses. These transactions are usually recorded in **other comprehensive income** and are therefore part of the group's equity. Upon disposal, other comprehensive income has to be "cleaned" by removing these items to its appropriate positions. The removal is based on the initial assets and liabilities and has to follow them. As assets are expensed due to the disposal, any gains or losses associated with the assets have to be recycled (so moving them from other comprehensive income to comprehensive income). The same applies to liabilities.

Other than the application to gains and losses is the treatment of a **revaluation surplus**. The general rule is that the revaluation surplus follows the underlying assets so that it has to be forwarded to profit & loss. Nevertheless, there is an exception to this rule. If a revaluation surplus that relates to an asset that would be transferred directly to retained earnings upon the disposal of the asset, the valuation surplus then has to be allocated to retained earnings according to IFRS 10.B99.

In addition to valuation adjustments recorded in other comprehensive income, **foreign currency effects** arising due to the translation of foreign operations have to be considered. IAS 21.48 provides appropriate guidelines. The rule requires that the cumulative effect of foreign currency translations, recorded through other comprehensive income and presented separately in equity for that particular subsidiary has to allocate to profit & loss.

Example

This example continues the example of the previous chapter!

A review of changes in equity of Cuivre Manufacture's capital accounts and a reconciliation with profits recorded unveiled that unrealized gains and losses had been recorded by the company that related to pensions. The total amount was 135 k EUR. While the revaluation method was not a group requirement, no revaluation surplus existed. Furthermore, the local currency of Cuivre manufacture was identical to the group currency. Accordingly, no foreign currency effects were recorded in retained earnings or other equity categories.

3.2.5 Consolidation tasks

In addition to the removal of assets and liabilities from the consolidated financial statement, several consolidation tasks have to be executed to ensure that the transition to the new owner of the subsidiary and the deconsolidation will be smooth. These tasks have to ensure that the preparation of consolidated financial statements at later stage will not be infected by the disposal of the subsidiary.

As the disposal of a subsidiary often takes place during the period, **profit cut-off issues** have to be considered. Depending on the date of the loss of control, profits realized up to this date belong to the group. They have to be presented in the consolidated statement of income as profits from continuing operations. Profits realized after the loss of control belong to the new owner of the subsidiary. Therefore, the deconsolidation has to consider the profit achieved which remains with the group until the disposal. To ensure a proper profit allocation, a deconsolidation at the date of loss of control is the preferred solution. This requires an interim closure of the diposed subsidiary as of that date. While there are situations where this is either not possible or not practical or not necessary to prepare consolidated financial statements at that date, the deconsolidation will often be postponed to the next regular group closure date (either interim date or balance sheet date) where consolidated financial statement are required. The interim closure of the disposed subsidiary will be used for deconsolidation issues. The profit of the subsidiary as well as all other elements of profit & loss will be kept as they are because they reflect the business during the period belonging to the group. Due to the use of the interim closure, profits after the date of loss of control are not added and therefore not considered ensuring a proper cut-off. Assets, liabilities and selected items of equity have to be deconsolidated. The remaining equity rested in retained earnings will stay as it is.[7]

There are situations where **interim closures** are not made or are not available. Such situations occur for example if a purchasing agreement is made between the parent and the buyer where the profit of the period of the subsidiary is not important for determining the purchase price. Other reasons for not preparing an interim closure may also exist. In such situations, the last available financial statements or the last available reporting packages of the subsidiary have to be used for deconsolidation. The numbers available have to be developed – if doable – towards the date of loss of control. This may reduce the level of errors and differences that arise due to incomplete figures of the subsidiary. Nevertheless, the missing interim closure will always result in an erroneous presentation of the group's profit. If such an error is non-material to the group's profit the auditor will usually accept such mistakes. Otherwise, further investigations are necessary to retrieve more detailed information from the former subsidiary – again, if doable.

The practice of **backdating** the purchase agreements towards the beginning of the year is irrelevant to the accounting, as control is still given until the date of loss of control. The profit of the subsidiary up to this date has to be considered as part of the group's profit. Therefore, the backdating practice has only an influence on the purchase price.[8]

The disposal of the subsidiary and the deconsolidation trigger some **administrative tasks** in accounting, particularly if the then former subsidiary is still doing

---

[7] It will be increased or decreased in the following year by the profit realized during the period up to the loss of control and the gain or loss realized due to the sale of the subsidiary.

[8] See chapter E -3.2 and particularly the remarks on backdating on page 140.

business with companies of the group. As of the date of loss of control, the subsidiary has to be reclassified from an internal company to an external one. All new balances companies of the group are recording have to be recorded on the external accounts. Revenues, expenses, receivables, payables and all other items have to be recorded on external accounts and not on intercompany accounts. This is important, because otherwise differences may arise on debt and earnings-/expense consolidations if the "former" subsidiary is still marked for intercompany transactions. The same applies to the treatment of inventory. The elimination of unrealized profits has to be abandoned.

> A formal process should be initiated by the corporate centre to rule the new accounting treatment of transactions with the then former subsidiary. This has to be rolled-out to all companies of the group.

> **Example**
>
> This example continues the example of the previous chapter!
> Due to the disposal date 28.2.2014, Cuivre Manufacture's profits allocable to the group that amount to 380 k EUR have to stay in Flexing Cables SE's consolidated statement of income. A recording or presentation of profits amounting to 253 k EUR allocable to non-controlling interests is not appropriate because of the disposal of the subsidiary during the period.

3.2.6 Journal entries

All disposal tasks, as well as the deconsolidation of the subsidiary, result in a limited set of journal entries only.[9] This set depends upon the deconsolidation type elected (either multi-step or one-step). While both types include the deconsolidation of equity and equity journal entries are identical, they can be executed first.

Equity journal entries have to consider the situation and the transactions recorded by the parent company. This is because the journal entries initiated by the parent company upon the disposal of its investment in the subsidiary will arrive at group level via the aggregated trial balance.[10] Due to these journal entries, the balance on the "investments in subsidiaries" account is missing at group level. On the other hand, the journal entry of the initial equity consolidation is still present at group level. This situation will trigger a set of issues that need to be solved:

- A balance on the "investment is subsidiaries" account is required for the initial equity consolidation.
- Goodwill established by the initial equity consolidation may be allocated to cash generating units so that goodwill is still required at group level.

---

[9] Not to inflate the presentation of journal entries, we will assume that the disposal of the subsidiary will result in a gain. Journal entries for recording the disposal with a loss will be very similar (some accounts need to be debited instead of credited and vice versa).

[10] See page 576 for the parent's journal entries.

- Applying the full goodwill method upon initial consolidation, non-controlling interests have a stake in goodwill.
- The journal entry of the initial equity consolidation has to be removed as part of equity deconsolidation.
- Some goodwill of the cash-generating unit has to be allocated to the disposed subsidiary.

There are many solutions to cope with these issues. If the subsidiary is a **stand-alone** cash-generating unit that has no non-controlling interests, a simple reversal of the initial equity consolidation is sufficient.

Journal entry		Comment
dr.	Investment in subsidiaries	Reversal journal entry using the balances of the initial consolidation.
cr.	Goodwill	
cr.	Share capital	
cr.	Capital reserve	
cr.	Retained earnings	

If there are many additional effects involved, other solutions may be appropriate. One solution that solves the discussed issues is the application of the **modified equity deconsolidation** method. This method considers all effect that may arise on equity. The modified equity deconsolidation method works in a way that it splits up the initial consolidation and records both parts through profit & loss. The first part eliminates those items that deal with the investment in subsidiaries and the equity accounts of the subsidiary.

Journal entry		Comment
dr.	Investment in subsidiaries	Reversal journal entry using the balances of the initial consolidation.
cr.	Share capital	
cr.	Capital reserve	
cr.	Retained earnings	
cr.	Gain on sale of subsidiary	

This will leave goodwill as it is but produces an additional gain. Depending on the deconsolidation type and the conditions of the disposed subsidiary, this gain will be adjusted in the next step by the allocation of goodwill to the disposed subsidiary. At the end, the remaining gain reflects effect of changes in goodwill due to cash-generating units and non-controlling interests attributable to the disposed subsidiary.

Subsequent to the cleaning of equity accounts, all other assets and liabilities of the subsidiary have to be removed. The removal depends on the deconsolidation type (one-step or multiple step deconsolidation) that initiates different journal entries. All journal entries have to consider assets and liabilities recorded on several levels: from local level to level III.[11]

---

[11] The aggregated trial balance includes all levels, so we don't need to care about assets and liabilities we have to consider.

• Multi-step deconsolidation

This separates deconsolidation of the parent's investment in the sub-sidiary and investment in the non-controlling interest in the subsidiary. Separate journal entries are required. To determine the gain / loss on the sale of the subsidiary, a cleaning of **non-controlling interests** have to be initiated in the first step by executing journal entries that eliminate the non-controlling interests. The journal entries depend on the initial recognition. If the full goodwill method was applied, journal entries have to consider goodwill. If the purchased goodwill method was applied, a pro-rata elimin-ation of goodwill is not necessary.

1) Pro-rata elimination of assets and liabilities

Journal entry			Comment
dr.	Liabilities		Pro-rata liabilities of the subsidiary
dr.	Non-controlling interests		
	cr.	Assets	Pro-rata assets of the subsidiary

2) Pro-rata elimination of goodwill attributable to the subsidiary (full goodwill method only!)

Journal entry		
dr.	Non-controlling interests	
	cr.	Goodwill

3) Pro-rata elimination of foreign currency translations

Journal entry		
dr.	Non-controlling interests	
	cr.	Retained earnings	Can also be a subaccount or a separate account

Depending on foreign currency effects, this journal entry can also be the other way around (dr / cr exchange).

4) Pro-rata elimination of the revaluation surplus

Journal entry		
dr.	Revaluation surplus	
	cr.	Gain on sale of subsidiary

5) Pro-rata elimination of the net profit of the period allocable to the non-controlling interests

Journal entry		
dr.	Gain on sale of subsidiary	
	cr.	Non-controlling interests

This journal entry eliminates the net profit of the period allocable to non-controlling interests. Therefore, the consolidated statement of income will only present the profit of the period without the non-con-trolling portion which is appropriate as the profit of the period cannot have a non-controlling portion due to the sale of the subsidiary (and the disposal of the accompanying non-controlling interests).

Having adjusted assets and liabilities by removing the non-controlling interest's portion, a regular deconsolidation of the subsidiary for the **parent**'s interest will be executed.

6) Elimination of assets and liabilities

Journal entry			Comment
dr.		Liabilities	Pro-rata liabilities of the subsidiary
dr.		Gain on sale of subsidiary	
	cr.	Assets	Pro-rata assets of the subsidiary

7) Elimination of goodwill attributable to the subsidiary considering effects of cash-generating units

Journal entry		
dr.		Gain on sale of subsidiary
	cr.	Goodwill

8) Elimination of foreign currency translations

Journal entry			Comment
dr.		Gain on sale of subsidiary	
	cr.	Retained earnings	Can also be a subaccount or a separate account

Depending on foreign currency effects, this journal entry can also be the other way around (dr / cr exchange).

9) Elimination of the revaluation surplus

Journal entry		
dr.		Revaluation surplus
	cr.	Gain on sale of subsidiary

- One-step deconsolidation

  The one step deconsolidation combines a set of transactions with one or more journal entries. A dedicated view of the parent company and non-controlling interests will not be taken.

  1) Elimination of all assets and liabilities

Journal entry			Comment
dr.		Liabilities	All liabilities of the subsidiary
dr.		Gain on sale of subsidiary	
	cr.	Assets	All assets of the subsidiary

  2) Elimination of goodwill attributable to the subsidiary. This may involve goodwill of a cash-generating unit.

Journal entry		
dr.		Gain on sale of subsidiary
	cr.	Goodwill

3) Elimination of foreign currency translations

Journal entry		Comment
dr.	Gain on sale of subsidiary	
cr.	Retained earnings	Can also be a subaccount or a separate account

Depending on foreign currency effects, this journal entry can also be the other way around (dr / cr exchange).

4) Elimination of the revaluation surplus

Journal entry	
dr.	Revaluation surplus
cr.	Gain on sale of subsidiary

5) Elimination of non-controlling interests

Journal entry		Comment
dr.	Non-controlling interests	
cr.	Gain non-controlling interests	This is a P&L account!

6) Allocation of pro-rata gain to non-controlling interest

Journal entry	
dr.	Gain on sale of subsidiary
cr.	Gain non-controlling interest

The balance on the "gain non-controlling interest" account should match the profit of the period to be allocated to non-controlling interests. As this is a profit & loss account, no further journal entry is required in adjusting the net profit of the period by the portion allocable to non-controlling interest.

Both deconsolidation types eliminate the subsidiary in full. The only item left are retained earnings the subsidiary has contributed during its life as part of the group. Follow-up activities to be considered are the administrative tasks as discussed before.

Journal entries have to be executed on the level where the consolidation is performed. If it is on account level, a journal entry for each account of the disposed subsidiary may be required!

Use a separate interim account for removing non-controlling interests to verify that non-controlling interests in the profit & loss statement balance with the profit of the period attributable to non-controlling interests.

Example

This example continues the example of the previous chapter!

To deconsolidate Cuivre Manufacture from the group by applying the one-step deconsolidation, the following journal entries were necessary. These journal entries take into account that Flexing Cables SE, as the parent, had already removed its investment in Cuivre Manufacture from its local accounts.

- Reversal of parent's journal entry

  To properly eliminate all items at group level, the initial equity consolidation had to be repeated ultimately. This is necessary as goodwill and non-controlling interests needed to be established for adjustment and elimination. Flexing Cables SE had already removed the interest in Cuivre Manufacture from its balance sheet and it was necessary to reverse that journal entry, as follows:

Journal entry				Comment
dr.	Investment in subsidiaries	1,090		Level II
cr.	Gain on sale of subsidiary		1,090	

  Subsequent to this journal entry, the initial equity consolidation can be repeated.

Journal entry				Company
dr.	Share capital	150		Cuivre Manufacture
dr.	Retained earnings	850		Cuivre Manufacture
dr.	Goodwill	490		Group
cr.	Investment in subsidiaries		1,090	Flexing Cables SE
cr.	Cash at hand & bank		400	Non-controlling interests

- Removal of assets and liabilities at level II

Journal entries				Comment
dr.	Gain on sale of subsidiary	469		Pro-rata
dr.	Gain non-controlling interests	312		Pro-rata
cr.	Cash at hand & bank		781	
dr.	Gain on sale of subsidiary	974		Pro-rata
dr.	Gain non-controlling interests	649		Pro-rata
cr.	Trade receivables		1,623	
dr.	Gain on sale of subsidiary	1,552		Pro-rata
dr.	Gain non-controlling interests	1,034		Pro-rata
cr.	Inventory		2,586	
dr.	Gain on sale of subsidiary	566		Pro-rata

dr.		Gain non-controlling interests	377		Pro-rata
	cr.	Other assets		943	
dr.		Gain on sale of subsidiary	9,776		Pro-rata
dr.		Gain non-controlling interests	6,518		Pro-rata
	cr.	Property, plant & equipment		16,294	
dr.		Gain on sale of subsidiary	47		Pro-rata
dr.		Gain non-controlling interests	31		Pro-rata
	cr.	Intangible assets		78	
dr.		Trade payables	2,483		
	cr.	Gain on sale of subsidiary		1,490	Pro-rata
	cr.	Gain non-controlling interests		993	Pro-rata
dr.		Tax liabilities	105		
	cr.	Gain on sale of subsidiary		63	Pro-rata
	cr.	Gain non-controlling interests		42	Pro-rata
dr.		Accruals	1,637		
	cr.	Gain on sale of subsidiary		982	Pro-rata
	cr.	Gain non-controlling interests		655	Pro-rata
dr.		Loans, s.t.	100		
	cr.	Gain on sale of subsidiary		60	Pro-rata
	cr.	Gain non-controlling interests		40	Pro-rata
dr.		Other payables	635		
	cr.	Gain on sale of subsidiary		381	Pro-rata
	cr.	Gain non-controlling interests		254	Pro-rata
dr.		Loans, l.t.	1,100		
	cr.	Gain on sale of subsidiary		660	Pro-rata
	cr.	Gain non-controlling interests		440	Pro-rata
dr.		Pensions	182		
	cr.	Gain on sale of subsidiary		109	Pro-rata
	cr.	Gain non-controlling interests		73	Pro-rata
dr.		Deferred tax liabilities	137		
	cr.	Gain on sale of subsidiary		82	Pro-rata
	cr.	Gain non-controlling interests		55	Pro-rata

- Removal of assets and liabilities at level III

Journal entries					Comment
dr.	Gain on sale of subsidiary	144			Pro-rata
dr.	Gain non-controlling interests	96			Pro-rata
cr.	Property, plant & equipment		240		
dr.	Deferred tax liabilities	80			
cr.	Gain on sale of subsidiary		48		Pro-rata
cr.	Gain non-controlling interests		32		Pro-rata

- Recycling of other comprehensive income

Journal entry				Comment
dr.	Gain on sale of subsidiary	81		Pro-rata
dr.	Gain non-controlling interests	55		Pro-rata
cr.	Other comprehensive income		136	

- Goodwill elimination

Journal entry				Comment
dr.	Gain on sale of subsidiary	490		Cuivre Manufacture's own goodwill
cr.	Goodwill		490	
dr.	Gain on sale of subsidiary	976		Business unit's goodwill
cr.	Goodwill		976	

- Removal of non-controlling interests

Journal entry			
dr.	Non-controlling interests	6,235	
cr.	Gain non-controlling interests		6,235

Just to verify that the recorded journal entries reconcile with the calculation of the calculated gain on the disposal of Cuivre Manufacture, the following accounts will be reviewed in detail (across all levels).

dr.		Gain on sale of subsidiary		cr.
Removal of carrying amount in subsidiary, recorded by Flexing Cables SE	1,090	Sales price of disposal, recorded by Flexing Cables SE	18,000	
Cash at hand & bank	469	Reversal of removal	1,090	
Trade receivables	974	Trade payables	1,490	
Inventory	1,552	Tax liabilities	63	
Other assets	566	Accruals	982	
Property, plant & equipment	9,776	Loans, s.t.	60	
Intangible assets	47	Other payables	381	
Property, plant & equipment, level III	144	Loans, l.t.	660	
Other comprehensive income	81	Pensions	109	
Goodwill	490	Deferred tax liabilities	82	
Goodwill	976	Deferred tax liabilities, level III	48	
	16,165		22,965	
		Balance	**6,800**	

dr.		Gain non-controlling interests		cr.
Cash at hand & bank	312	Trade payables		993
Trade receivable	649	Tax liabilities		42
Inventory	1,034	Accruals		655
Other assets	377	Loans, s.t.		40
Property, plant & equipment	6,518	Other payables	254	
Intangible assets	31	Loans, l.t.	440	
Property, plant & equipment, **level III**	96	Pensions	73	
Other comprehensive income	55	Deferred tax liabilities	55	
		Deferred tax liabilities, level III	32	
		Non-controlling interests	6,235	
	9,072			8,819
Balance	253			

The calculated realized gains and losses are confirmed. Furthermore, the balance of the "gain non-controlling interests" account is equal to that amount allocable to non-controlling interests in the consolidated statement of income. As a debit it will reduce the profit contribution of Cuivre Manufacture to that amount attributable to the group without requiring a separate disclosure (while the subsidiary is already disposed).

3.3. Special cases

The deconsolidation of a subsidiary is not limited to the consolidated statement of financial position and the statement of income. Other items of financial statements are affected as well. The most important ones are the statement of cash flows and the fixed asset schedule being part of the notes. Furthermore, special transaction may cause a deconsolidation even if there is no change in the investment in the subsidiary.

3.3.1. Statement of cash-flow

Disposals of subsidiaries impact the statement cash-flow as the sale of a subsidiary is often combined with cash payments by the acquirer that has to be presented in the statement of cash flows. IAS 7.16 d) requires disclosing the sale of a subsidiary and its related cash flows as "cash receipts from sales of equity or debt instruments of other entities and interests in joint ventures" within in the investing activities category.

While the disposal of a subsidiary equals a disposal of assets and liabilities at group level, the consolidated statement of cash flows also will present changes in assets and liabilities in the first instance. Changes in assets and liabilities that relate to the disposal have to be identified and isolated from other changes of assets and liabilities. If changes relate to current assets, they have to be reallocated from the operating activities category towards the investing activities category. If changes relate to non-current assets, a reallocation within the investing activities section may be appropriate. In some cases, the financing activities section may be involved as well (if loans that relate to the subsidiary are disposed of as well). Finally, these changes have to be adjusted by non-cash items.

If the disposal applies to a foreign investment, foreign currency effects mingle with cash and non-cash related changes of assets and liabilities. These foreign currency effects have to be isolated and presented in a separate line item of the statement of cash flows.

The following list includes all steps necessary to properly present a disposal in the statement of cash flows:

Step	Task
1)	Identify all changes in assets and liabilities that relate to the disposal of the subsidiary in each category of statement of the cash flows.
2)	Isolate these changes from other changes in assets.
3)	Reclassify these changes to a separate line item in the investing activities category (line item called "cash receipts from sales of investments in subsidiaries").
4)	Remove all non-cash related changes.
5)	Remove and reclassify foreign currency effects from the line item towards a line item below net changes in cash.
6)	If the sale of the subsidiary involves the transfer of cash at the subsidiary: Adjust cash funds by a reclassification of the cash transferred (line item often called "changes in cash funds due to changes in the group's composition" or a similar description).
7)	Reconcile the line item with cash actually received due to the sale of the subsidiary.

Tab. J-7   Steps to adjust the statement of cash flows for disposals

3.3.2 *Fixed asset schedule*

Like the statement of cash flows, the fixed asset schedule is involved anytime a disposal occurs. This is because a disposal of a subsidiary always includes a disposal of non-current assets associated with the subsidiary. While the presentation of a pure disposal in the fixed asset schedule is not appropriate, a separate presentation is required to distinguish between disposals of assets due to the end of their useful life or the lack of future economic benefits and the disposal (of useful non-current assets) as part of the sale of a subsidiary. IAS 16.73 e) is picking up this topic. The reconciliation of non-current assets has to consider:

- Assets allocated to a disposal group according to IFRS 5;
- Acquisition through business combinations.

In practice, changes in the fixed asset schedule that relate to acquisitions and disposals of subsidiaries in the group are often presented within on reconciliation item. This is often labelled as "change in consolidation status" or has a similar description.

The balance to be presented in that section can be derived from the deconsolidation journal entries, particularly from items that deconsolidate non-current assets.

3.3.3 Group-internal transactions

Disposals can be subject to group-internal transactions. A parent of a subgroup or a holding company is disposing a subsidiary that is bought by another company of the group. From an ultimate parent's perspective, such transactions are group restructurings that have no impact on the ultimate group at all: there is a division of work. The parent of the sub-group of the holding company is accounting a disposal as an ordinary transaction to comply with local accounting standards and regulations for their separate financial statements. The same does the purchasing company of the group. At group level preferably at level II or level III, the disposal as well as all subsequent effects arising from the disposal is reversed.

3.3.4 Multiple arrangements and misuse

As IFRS 10 demands a recognition of any gains and losses in profit & loss, **accounting tricks and misuse** might be applied to minimize losses and maximize gains due to these transactions. Typical applications are step disposals where interests in a subsidiary are recorded in a number of separate transactions.

One or more initial transactions are treated as equity transactions where control is still obtained. The interest in the subsidiary will be reduced to a level slightly above the control threshold (50%). Subsequent transactions will then finalize the disposal by recording a gain or loss in profit & loss for the remaining interest in subsidiaries sold. This transaction structure offers two areas which management can play with: A shift of profits & losses from the consolidated statement of income to equity, and vice versa; and an allocation of the consideration received to the transactions to generate profits or losses in each transaction.

To avoid misuse by using such structures, IFRS 10.B97 provides additional guidance. The underlying rationale of the accounting of structured transactions is a check from a commercial perspective. If a sale is structured in a way that the overall commercial (or economic) impression indicates one economic transaction, all separate transactions have to be accounted for as one transaction only.

IFRS 10.B97 lists four cases that indicate multiple transactions to be treated as one single transaction only:

- Transactions take place at or entered into the same time or in contemplation of each other.
- Transactions are designed to achieve an overall commercial effect as a single transaction.
- The occurrence of one transaction depends on the occurrence of another transaction.
- Transactions on their own are not economically justified. They will be economically justified only in combination with other transactions.

IFRS 10.B97 provides an example for the last case where one transaction is priced below market price while another transaction is priced above market price.

> A check regarding multiple arrangements and their commercial or economic effects should be a standard activity in the accounting of disposals.

4. DISCONTINUED OPERATIONS

There are many reasons why the operations of a subsidiary, a set of subsidiaries or even a business unit are discontinued. At the end of the day, all reasons can be allocated to one of the following areas:

- Strategic changes in the scope of the business of a group

    The subsidiary does not fit any longer in the portfolio of the group due to products manufactured / sold, services rendered, business shifts inside the group towards other areas or other reasons.

- On-going losses of a subsidiary

    The subsidiary produces on-going losses the parent company is not willing any longer to carry or a continuing recapitalization does not deliver the required results.

- Group restructuring

    A group restructuring is expected to improve the position of the group in the market either due to changes in products, services, market penetration or similar reasons. This can also result from a loss situation in the group that is not necessarily caused by one subsidiary. In any case, the subsidiary does not fit any longer in the group structure.

A common feature in all areas is that a management decision is required. This management decision usually covers also the decision how to treat the future life of the subsidiary in the group and if or not to dispose of the subsidiary. If such a decision is made, an alternate accounting for the subsidiary as a disposal group or a discontinued operation is possible as defined in *IFRS 5 – Non-current Assets Held for Sale and Discontinued Operations.*[12] This alternate accounting assumes that the carrying amount of the interest in a subsidiary will be substantially recovered through a sale rather than through its continuing use.

IFRS 5 covers the treatment of a set of assets and a combination of assets. There are different means for each type of asset. To avoid any misunderstandings, the following list explains the various types of asset, their content and the application to a subsidiary:

---

[12] This chapter only discusses the treatment of financial assets, particularly subsidiaries, joint ventures, associated companies and investments in securities (companies) to be measured in accordance with IAS 39. It does not discuss any aspects on other non-current assets.

Asset type	IFRS 5 definition[13]	Application to a subsidiary
Current asset	An entity shall classify an asset as current, if • It expects to realize the asset, intends to sell or consume it in its normal operating cycle; • It holds the asset primarily for the purpose of trading; • It expects to realize the asset within 12 months after the reporting period; or • The asset is cash or cash equivalent […].	Current assets are just an element of a subsidiary's total assets. They are scoped-out for valuation issues.
Non-current asset	An asset that does not meet the definition of a current asset.	Non-current assets are another element of a subsidiary's total assets. Depending on the type of non-current asset, these assets are either scoped-in or scoped-out.
Disposal group	A group of assets to be disposed of, by sale or otherwise, together as a group in a single transaction, and liabilities directly associated with those assets that will be transferred in the transaction. The group includes goodwill acquired in a business combination if the group is a cash-generating unit to which goodwill has been allocated in accordance with […][14] or if it is an operation within such a cash-generating unit.	Due to the definition of a disposal group, a subsidiary can be identical to a disposal group. This is the smallest group of assets a subsidiary can be allocated to unless the subsidiary equals a cash generating unit.
Cash generating unit	The smallest identifiable group of assets that generate cash inflows that are largely independent of the cash inflows from other assets or group of assets.	Depending on the structure of a group, a subsidiary can be • identical to a cash generating unit. In this case, the cash generating unit is also equal to a disposal group. • only a part of a cash generating unit. In this case, a subsidiary may qualify as a disposal group or a part of it. Cash generating units may also be part of a larger disposal group.
Discontinued operation	A component of an entity that either has been disposed of or is classified as held for sale and: • Represents a separate major line of business or geographical area of operations, • Is part of a single co-ordinated plan to dispose of a separate major line of business or geographical area of operations or • Is a subsidiary acquired exclusively with a view to resale.	Again, depending on the group's structure a subsidiary may qualify as a discontinued operation if the definition requirements are fulfilled. As discontinued operations may cover several business units, several cash generating units and several subsidiaries, a detailed check regarding contents and dependencies and the position of a subsidiary in this context is required to be aware of all accounting effects.

Tab. J-8 Asset types as defined in IFRS 5

---

[13] Definitions taken from IFRS 5 Appendix A.
[14] Specific reference to IAS 36.

The allocation of a subsidiary to one of the asset types is appropriate, if the subsidiary is the only one to be disposed. But there are often situations in which the subsidiary is just an element of a larger disposal. The subsidiary can be combined or grouped with other assets or subsidiaries.[15] In this case, it can be part of a cash-generating unit, a business unit or a major line of business or geographical area of operations. In all cases the accounting according to IFRS 5 will not change; the only subject that changes is the volume of assets to be disposed and therefore the workload associated with the disposal in measuring each asset for disposal.

The interaction between a disposal group or a discontinued operation according to IFRS 5, and group accounting according to IFRS 10, requires that the sale of a subsidiary and its deconsolidation from the group has to be executed in a special way. This is because disposal groups and discontinued operations have to be separated from the on-going business of the group, requiring also a separate presentation. To do so, all balance sheet items have to be developed towards the decision day where a subsidiary qualifies as a disposal group or a discontinued operation including appropriate valuation adjustments of all balance sheet items. The subsidiary then has to be removed from the consolidated balance sheet and presented separately until its sale. The following list includes all steps necessary to execute the deconsolidation and sale of a subsidiary by treating it as a disposal group or a discontinued operation.

Step	Task
1)	Check, if requirement of IFRS 5 apply
2)	Develop all balance sheet items towards the "decision date"
3)	Measurement (Revaluation of assets and execution of impairment tests)
4)	Recording as disposal group or discontinued operation
5)	Sale of subsidiary
6)	Deconsolidation

Tab. J-9   Deconsolidation tasks by considering IFRS 5

By carefully executing each step, the spin-off of a subsidiary will be easily realized.

4.1 Step 1 – IFRS 5 Check

The first step that has to be executed is an "IFRS 5 check". To benefit from the alternate accounting, a set of requirements has to be fulfilled, before accounting according to IFRS 5 is possible. Each requirement has to be checked carefully as a cumulative fulfilment is required. It is also recommended to prepare a

---

[15] In this chapter, the words "subsidiary" and "disposal unit" cover a subsidiary, an associated company, a joint venture, a set of them, a business unit and a segment according to IFRS 8. It can either be a cash-generating unit or part of a cash-generating unit. Both words used will have the same meaning and should reflect the disposal object.

documentation for audit purposes that all requirements are fulfilled. The application of checklists may help in this situation. All requirements are summarized in IFRS 5.7 and 5.8. While some requirements have only a vague description and are often not that clear at the first instance, some hints are given for support. The following requirements have to be fulfilled:

- Non-current assets

    IFRS 5 accounting is limited to non-current assets. As subsidiaries, joint ventures, associated companies and business units belong to financial assets; this requirement is always fulfilled at parent level. At group level, additional requirements have to be fulfilled as outlined in IFRS 5.31 and 5.32. These requirements demand that the subsidiary's business or area of operations qualifies as a cash generating unit. Three options are available where the subsidiary:

    - represents a major line of business or geographical area of operations;
    - is part of a single co-ordinated plan to dispose of a major line of business or geographical area of operations;
    - is acquired exclusively with a view to resale.

    Assuming that these requirements are fulfilled the subsidiary is treated as a discontinued operation, otherwise it will classify as a disposal group.

    Even if this list defines some business areas, they do not interact with segments according to IFRS 8 because a major line of business can be just one part of a segment. The easiest way to define a business or area of operation is to identify the cash flows associated with that business as recommended by IFRS 5.BC 70. This is also in line with the requirement of a cash generating unit.

- Available for immediate sale

    The subsidiary has to be in a sufficient condition that it can be sold. The criterion as outlined in IFRS 5.7 is diffuse. While an investment in a subsidiary is more than an ordinary asset, a preparation of the subsidiary may be necessary depending on what part of a subsidiary will be sold. This may require that certain business transactions have to be executed before the sale. Therefore, the present condition of a subsidiary has to align to the management's plan on what to sell. Conditions have to be checked individually for each sale.

- Sale is highly probable

    IFRS 2.Appendix A defines the phrase "highly probable" as "significantly more likely than probable" where probable means "more likely than not". In other words, highly probable means in this context that a sale is expected to occur. To qualify as an expected sale, a set of requirements has to be fulfilled cumulatively. It is not sufficient if only some requirements are fulfilled. These requirements act as indicators to prove the expected sale.

- Sales plan

"A **plan** is typically any diagram or list of steps with timing and resources, used to achieve an objective."[16] In the context of IFRS 5, the objective is to sell a subsidiary and the plan reflects the activities, the company will undertake to spin off the subsidiary. There is no distinct definition about the type and the contents of a plan. For documentation purposes, a formal description of the plan should be available to prove that a sales plan is in place. This description should include a specification about what to sell from the subsidiary (assets / business) and which steps are required to bring the subsidiary with its assets into a sellable condition. The description should also include the intended activities to actively market and sell the subsidiary.

The plan has to be supported and **committed by management**. IFRS 5.8 explicitly mentions that this commitment has to be given by an appropriate level of management with the power and authority to decide on the sale of the subsidiary and a willingness to execute the plan. The management definition can span from a holding's management on a lower level in the group to the board of the group. The level of management depends on the structure of the group, the authorizations in the group and the type of subsidiary to be sold. In rare situations, approvals by the board or shareholders may be required. For accounting purposes (also for auditor demands) a formal documentation on the management's commitment should complement the plan's documentation.

> Documentation can be derived from management meeting notes or meeting papers.

- Active programme and actively marketed

The sales plan initiated or supported by management has to include activities that search for a buyer and actively market the subsidiary. One activity of the sales plan is an "**active programme** to locate a buyer". It is not sufficient to just declare a subsidiary as a discontinued operation; it has to be ensured that the subsidiary finally will be sold. Therefore, it is necessary to prove that systematically search for a potential buyer is initiated, either by the parent or by an external service provider (e.g. an investment bank). Even if the search for a buyer is not defined by IFRS, a structured approach in locating a potential buyer is favourable as it provides evidence that the programme is actively running.

The sales plan also has to ensure that the subsidiary is "**actively marketed**". This phrase should be interpreted as an active offer of the subsidiary in the market. The active offer precludes that information to the

---

[16] Definition taken from Wikipedia.

general public is available that the subsidiary can be purchased (passive marketing). The offer also assumes that the subsidiary is presented to potential buyers once they are identified (active marketing).

The degree and intensity of both items, the active programme and the active marketing, depend on the business and attractiveness of the subsidiary, its market and their practices, the competition and similar reasons. Therefore, activities have to be adopted as appropriate.

- Reasonable price

The sales price the subsidiary is marketed for should be reasonable to the fair value of the subsidiary. The standard only emphasizes the price that is used to market the subsidiary. This precludes that the fair value of the subsidiary is known. A fair value calculation has to be available before an expected sales price is fixed.

Even if the sales price should be reasonable to the fair value of the subsidiary, there is no distinct definition about this condition. Therefore, it is up to management's discretion to define what is reasonable. A sales price that is slightly above the fair value of the subsidiary is doubtless reasonable. In some cases, a sales price equal to or slightly less than the fair value may be reasonable. This depends on the economic conditions and the environment when and where the subsidiary is offered. An extraordinary deviation from the relation between the expected sales price and the fair value of the subsidiary is definitely not reasonable. If there is such a condition, the auditors may require an additional explanation. In some cases similar subsidiaries may be available for sale by other parties in the market. If their sales prices deviate from the own sales price – particularly if the companies offered are more or less identical – an adjustment of the expected sales price towards market conditions may be necessary. Such an adjustment always qualifies as an extraordinary deviation. To document a deviation in this case, a comparison of offered prices for the other companies is recommended.

As the final sales price results from a negotiation process with the buyer, a deviation from the initial sales price usually occurs. This deviation is subject to the accounting for the sale of the subsidiary that may result in a gain or loss. It does not interfere with the criteria when to account for a subsidiary as a discontinued operation.

- Completion within 12 months

An important indicator that the sales activity is highly probable is the completion of the sale within one year from the date of classification. Management has to ensure that all activities necessary are arranged in such a way that the sale is completed at the end of that period. If the sale failed within that period (the **12 month period** is **not met**), the sale is not regarded as highly probable. As a consequence, the requirements of IFRS 5 are not met and the subsidiary has to be integrated into consolidated financial statements as an ordinary subsidiary.

The date of classification is not defined in IFRS 5. It is up to management to decide on that date. In practice, the date of classification will be that day, when a formal decision by management is made to remove the subsidiary from the group and the sales plan is approved by management.

The one-year criterion is not always a fixed one. The period can be extended according to IFRS 5.9 if events or circumstances delay the sale that cannot be influenced by the parent company and the management or is outside their control. The **extension of the total disposal period** together with its reasons should be documented. Nevertheless the commitment to sell the subsidiary still has to be in place and the sales plan will be executed as planned considering a new timing. IFRS 5. Appendix B set out the requirements when an expansion of the 12 month period is appropriate. According to these requirements, an extension is only possible in three cases:

1. **Third parties** have to be involved setting conditions to the sale of the subsidiary provided that a firm purchase commitment or agreement with a buyer is made in the meantime or is highly probable. Typical examples of third parties are antitrust or competition authorities. While their decisions usually depend on the whole sales transaction and the implications to the market, the approval of this third party will take some time which cannot be influenced. The period will then be expanded until the third party has approved the sale (with or without any conditions on the sale).

2. The buyer imposes **unexpected conditions** on the transfer of a subsidiary that are not discussed or otherwise known before a firm purchase commitment is obtained from the buyer. These conditions may not necessarily be set by the buyer; unexpected conditions may also be set by others. To obtain a prolongation of the period, timely actions are required to solve the conditions and a favourable solution is reached. Unexpected conditions can have manifold reason. A typical example is an environmental pollution not earlier detected.

3. **Changes in circumstances** occur that were initially assumed to be unlikely and will result in a non-sale of the subsidiary. Provided that appropriate reactions on the changes in circumstances occur within the 12 month period and the subsidiary will be actively marketed considering the changes in circumstances, an extension is given. Other criteria as outlined before still have to be met. Typical examples are changes in market prices due to economic reasons.

- No significant changes

  Another requirement is that "it is unlikely that **significant changes** to the plan will be made or that the plan will be withdrawn". This assumes that a plan, once decided, should be executed as agreed. In practice, this criterion always provides problems as companies often operate in volatile environments where changes in market conditions are often the case. Changes in the market may force management to think of alternative solutions to sell, restructure or retain the subsidiary. If such cases apply, the subsidiary either may have to be re-integrated into the group or will be subject to a different plan, maybe as one part of a changed disposal unit.

  As the wording in the standard refers to significant changes only and there is no **definition of** what is "**significant**", it is up to management's discretion to decide on what significant changes are. Usually, significant changes are those ones where market conditions, the composition of the subsidiary or other factors will change, that have a direct impact on the fair value of the subsidiary, on the ability to market the subsidiary or the sales price to be achieved. An individual view is required for each disposal. On the other hand, as long as changes are not significant, the plan can be executed as intended.

  A variation of changes in a plan is a **withdrawal**. This always requires a further decision by management not to sell the subsidiary but to retain it for whatever reason. If such a decision is made, the subsidiary has to be re-integrated into the group and in its consolidated financial statements.

Like the availability for immediate sale, the criteria listed as part of a highly probable sale are also diffuse. Therefore, the whole context of an expected sale and all activities planned or realized should be considered in deciding if a sale will take place and if the conditions of a highly probable sale are met. A commercial view is recommended provided that accounting information needs are fulfilled.

A good documentation is the key to success an auditor will accept. The documentation of the plan should contain at least the following items:

- A description of what exactly should be sold;
- Activities necessary to bring the subsidiary into the condition that all items subject to a sale are available for immediate sale;
- The management decision and the date of the decision;
- Intended tasks to locate a buyer;
- Intended tasks to market the subsidiary;
- A calculation of the fair value of the subsidiary to estimate the expected sales price;
- A timing of all activities and tasks.

Provided that all criteria are met the subsidiary can be accounted for as a discontinued operation held-for-sale. For accounting purposes, the subsidiary with its assets and liabilities will be treated as a disposal group.

4.2. Step 2 – The decision date

If the check of fulfilling IFRS 5 requirements passed successfully, the accounting of the subsidiary as a discontinued operation can start. The exact starting point is that date where all requirements are met and a formal management decision was made. In most cases, the starting point will be the management's **decision date** unless the subsidiary is not yet in the condition for an immediate sale. If this is the case, the decision date has to be postponed to that date where the subsidiary will be available for immediate sale as intended (to account for the subsidiary according to IFRS 5).

A balance sheet and a profit & loss statement of the subsidiary have to be available at the decision date. This is necessary because all **balance sheet items** (assets and liabilities) may be subject to a revaluation at that date and the balances of the revaluated assets and liabilities are needed for the deconsolidation. Assets and liabilities will be available by preparing a provisional close at the decision date. The decision date will act also as a cut-off point for the allocation and measurement of assets and liabilities belonging to a disposal group. All profits and changes in assets and liabilities belonging to the disposal group have to be allocated to the consolidated financial profit & loss statement and presented separately. Therefore, all balance sheet items have to be developed towards the decision date.

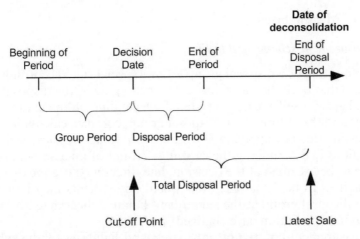

Fig. J-5   IFRS 5 disposal timing and the decision date

A special issue at the decision date is the allocation of assets. All assets that belong to the discontinued operation have to be identified. This is a simple task as long as assets and liabilities are easy to identify. In some cases a separation of assets is difficult as these assets may serve more than just the discontinued operation. Depending on the nature of this asset it has to be either split up or allocated to the group or the discontinued operation combined with a service level agreement or replaced by another appropriate asset. Which solution is the appropriate one has to be decided for each case individually. The allocation of liabilities has to occur in a similar way.

While the decision date is different from the balance sheet date, **presentation** requirements arise only at the balance sheet date. Nevertheless, some preparation activities at the decision date are necessary as they are needed at the balance sheet date. They are usually based on the deconsolidation and deal with the identification of assets belonging to the discontinued operation.

A special case applies if the subsidiary becomes a discontinued operation **after the end of the period** but before consolidated financial statements are authorized and published. Due to the matching principle, an adjustment of consolidated financial statements of the prior period is prohibited. All activities are subject to the period the decision date belongs to. Nevertheless, the classification as a discontinued operation will be an important event after the balance sheet date that has to be disclosed in the management discussion (if required by local accounting standards) and in the notes (according to IFRS 5.12).

Another special case is the treatment of **abandoned operations**. Subsidiaries belonging to this type of operation have to be accounted for as before. This is because they may be used for future purposes. An abandoned operation can be classified as a discontinued operation anytime the criteria of step 1 are met. Again, the starting point will be the decision date, as explained before.

4.3. Step 3 – Measurement

4.3.1. Measurement scheme and timing

The accounting of a disposal group follows special rules according to IFRS 5, which ensure that both the individual assets belonging to the disposal group and the disposal group itself are not overstated. Depending on the nature of the individual asset and the nature of the disposal group, complex calculations involving fair value estimations by applying *IFRS 13 – Fair Value Measurement* may occur. All calculations in determining the carrying amount of an asset and the disposal group have to be executed at the decision date directly before the disposal group will be classified as held for sale. Subsequent adjustments may be necessary to present the disposal group at the subsequent balance sheet date if conditions of the discontinued operation have changed.

The measurement covers not only assets and liabilities of the subsidiary. If the subsidiary was acquired and accounted for as a business combination, level II and level III adjustments may be present. They need to be considered in measuring the carrying amount of a disposal group.

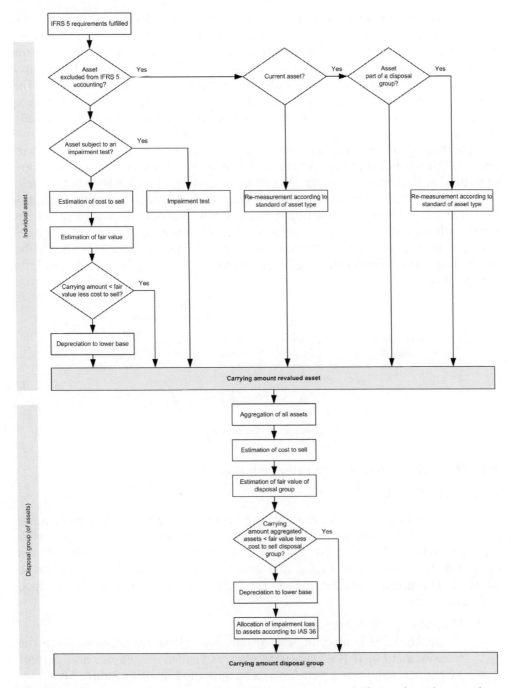

Fig. J-6   Measurement scheme for disposal groups and discontinued operations

The underlying principle in measuring assets at the decision date is a valuation of an asset at the lower of its carrying amount and the fair value less costs to sell. This is the standard requirement that applies to assets and disposal groups equally. An exception to this measurement principle is the disposal to shareholders. Only in that case the subsidiary will be measured at the lower of the carrying amount and the fair value less cost to distribute. Both cases will execute the same calculation, the same measurement and a similar recording. The only differences are cost items that relate to a sale or distribution.

The timing of the discontinued operation interacts with the carrying balances of the disposal group. At the decision date, all assets and liabilities are measured at the lower of the carrying amount and its fair value less costs to sell. These remeasured assets and liabilities keep their adjusted carrying amounts until the sale occurs. An additional write-down of assets or a reversal of an initial adjustment may be necessary at the balance sheet date if conditions have changed that require a new measurement. No further adjustments should be made, not even a depreciation of non-current assets as IFRS 5.25 prohibits depreciation.

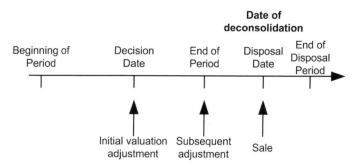

Fig. J-7   IFRS 5 Timing of valuation adjustments

4.3.2. Individual assets

As already mentioned, the estimation of the carrying balance of the disposal group is executed at the decision date. At this point the disposal group's **assets** carrying balance will be adjusted as appropriate. The adjustment itself is based on a two-step calculation. In the first instance, the individual asset has to be adjusted. This adjustment depends on the type of the asset that can be grouped three categories:

- Non-adjustable assets

  IFRS 5.5 lists a set of **non-current** assets that are excluded from the measurement of IFRS 5. These assets are so called scoped-out non-current assets. Instead, these assets have to be measured by other standards:

Asset	Measurement base
Deferred tax assets	IAS 12 – Income Taxes
Assets arising from employee benefits	IAS 19 – Employee Benefits
Financial assets within the scope of IFRS 9	IFRS 9 – Financial Instruments
Non-current assets that are accounted for in accordance with the fair value model in IAS 40	IAS 40 – Investment Property
Non-current assets that are measured at fair value less costs to sell in accordance with IAS 41	IAS 41 – Agriculture
Contractual rights under insurance contracts	IFRS 4 – Insurance Contracts

Tab. J-10 List of non-current assets requiring a different measurement base than IFRS 5

As the scope of IFRS 5 is the disposal of non-current assets, disposal groups and discontinued operations, the standards require remeasuring non-current assets only. Therefore, the measurement of all **current** assets is not covered and an adjustment of current assets is not required. Nevertheless, a remeasurement for current assets will come through the "back door". IFRS 5.15 requires measuring the disposal group as a whole at its fair value. This requires also current assets to be measured at their fair values. Again, the measurement occurs according to the asset's relevant standards.

> Check the existence of a disposal group upfront! Only if a disposal group is given, a remeasurement of current assets should be initiated!

- Assets subject to an impairment test

    IFRS 5.20 requires that an impairment test has to be executed for those assets that are subject to an impairment test as defined in IAS 36.[17] The impairment test is an event-driven impairment test based on the conditions at the decision date. All assets that require a fair value measurement or adjustment by any standard have to be considered. Items to be covered by impairment test are in particular:

Asset	Standard
Inventories measured at their fair values	IAS 2 – Inventories or IFRS 9 – Financial Instruments
Financial instruments	IAS 39 – Financial Instruments or IFRS 9 – Financial Instruments
Property	IAS 16 –Property, Plant and Equipment
Intangible assets with an indefinite useful life	IAS 38 – Intangible Assets
Goodwill	IFRS 3 – Business Combinations

Tab. J-11 Assets subject to an impairment test

---

[17] See chapter F -8.2 on page 348 for a detailed application of the impairment test.

Even if the impairment test is mandatory at the decision date, it may be conducted twice. A repetition of the test may be required at the balance sheet date if the carrying amount of the disposal group may be interfered by significant changes in their conditions.

An adjustment for selected current assets might be necessary as a consequence of an impairment test if current assets are excluded from remeasurements required by IFRS 5. A typical example is the write-down of accounts receivable due to their non-collectability. As accounts receivable – even if they are current – are financial assets according to IAS 39, they are subject to an impairment test.

> Be careful! Current assets can also be subject to impairment tests.

- All other assets

    All other assets that are not subject to the above-mentioned categories have to go through a regular remeasurement check. These are so called scoped-in assets. The check will – similar to an impairment test – compare the carrying amount of an asset with its fair value less costs to sell. An adjustment is required if the carrying amount exceed its fair value less costs to sell. Only in such a case, a write-down to the lower fair value is necessary. The write-down has to be expensed reducing the profit for the period. The carrying amount of an asset can be determined directly from the accounts (as long as the asset can be identified in the accounts). The determination of the fair value less costs to sell is more difficult to realize as two items have to be assumed.

    IFRS 5. Appendix A defines **costs to sell** as "the incremental costs directly attributable to the disposal of an asset (or disposal group), excluding finance costs and income tax expense". Therefore, costs to sell should cover at least:

    - Fees for lawyers, advisors, auditors and similar parties involved,
    - Legal costs,
    - Insurance,
    - Stamp duties,
    - Costs of removing the asset,
    - Transportation costs, and
    - Similar costs.

Excluded from recognition as costs to sell are all those costs that relate to facility-holding costs (e.g. insurance, utilities and similar costs) and to other internal costs. Such costs relate to the operation of a subsidiary and have no relationship with the disposal because they would be incurred whether the asset would be sold or not.

In some situations, subsequent costs will arise from the sale of a subsidiary. These costs have their origins in the (planned) sale and are triggered and initiated by them only. Typical examples are staff compensation, redundancy payments and payments due to legal obligations.

As there is no guidance about such items, it is up to management discretion to consider these items as costs to sell as long as they are judged to be incremental and are directly assignable to the disposal.

Cost to sell may be subject to discounting if the total disposal period exceeds the defined period of 12 months according to IFRS 5.17. If an extended period is assumed and an appropriate discount rate is chosen, all effects relate to discounted costs to sell have to be recorded as financing costs.

IFRS 5.A requires that costs to sell do not include taxes and financing costs. These costs always belong to continuing operations.

> It might be more appropriate to account for subsequent costs to sell rather than considering them as part of costs to sell only.

In addition to the costs to sell, the **fair value** of the asset has to be estimated. The fair value equals that price that would be received if the asset was sold in a market (so in fact it is a transfer between market participants). While some assets do not have active markets, the use of fair value measurement methods as outlined in IAS 13 is required.[18] In general, two types of asset valuations can be identified:

- Assets that can be traded in an active market

    Selected assets are traded in active markets. The fair value of these assets can be directly determined by choosing their market values at a defined date. This does apply particularly to all kinds of financial assets and financial instruments. It can also apply to assets of property, plant and equipment as long as these assets are traded in specific markets. Typical examples are cars and used machines that have separate and active markets. In these cases, the fair value can be derived from transactions of similar assets in the market.

- Assets that have no active market

    Several assets are not traded in active markets as the nature of such assets is too specific to a company that a market could exist. In such cases, the use of valuation techniques is appropriate. These techniques derive a fair value from market, cost or income approaches. The latter makes use of future cash flows that will be achieved by using the specific asset. Choosing the appropriate approach depends on the underlying asset, its behaviour and the valuation intention.

Similar to the remeasurement of assets to its fair value, liabilities have to be adjusted as appropriate. The adjustment of liabilities is not directly mentioned in IFRS 5 but it can be derived from IFRS 5.4 and 5.18 that refer to the remeasurement of liabilities part of a disposal group. IFRS applicable to liabilities have to be used for remeasurement.

---

[18] See Appendix I: Fair value measurement on page 751 for details regarding fair value measurement.

4.3.3. Disposal groups

Having taken the first instance, assets and liabilities remeasured will be used in determining whether or not the **disposal group**'s carrying amount does not exceed its fair value less costs to sell. This task is more or less a repetition of all tasks executed for the individual assets, even if the scope is slightly different.

- Carrying amount

  The carrying amount of a disposal group consists of all individual assets and liabilities that belong to the disposal group as outlined in IFRS 5.4. It is sufficient to aggregate all assets and liabilities to arrive at a net-asset position of the disposal group.

- Fair value less costs to sell

  The determination of the fair value less costs to sell is in principle similar to the determination of an individual asset's fair value less costs to sell. Differences arise in the fair value estimation while now a whole set of assets has to be considered. This will change the scope of the fair value determination. The composition of costs to sell will also change.

  The **Cost to sell** a disposal group can cover all those elements that apply also to an individual asset. While the scope of the asset changes, some costs that are important for the sale of an individual asset may be irrelevant for a disposal group. For example, if a large machine will be sold, costs of removing the machine and transportation costs may be a major element in determining costs to sell as a relocation of the machine takes place. If that machine is part of a production unit that includes buildings and other facilities and if that production unit represents the disposal group, costs to sell for the individual asset have to be ignored for the disposal group as the machine will not change its location. Therefore, the costs to sell an individual asset cannot automatically be transferred to the disposal group. Instead, an individual assessment of costs to sell for the disposal group is required.

  A similar idea is behind the assessment of the **fair value** of a disposal group. While the disposal group includes various assets and liabilities that may have the capability to generate cash, a dedicated view of the contents of a disposal group is required to decide on the fair value measurement of the disposal group. The definition of fair value in IFRS 5. Appendix A directly refers to the application *of IFRS 13 – Fair Value Measurement*. According to IFRS 13.9 the fair value of an asset (or a group of assets) is that value that would be achieved in an orderly transaction between market participants.

  The application of IFRS 13 to a disposal group has to be treated depending on the composition of assets and liabilities of the disposal group. If the disposal group includes just a bunch of assets, the assets have to be measured in the same way as the measurement for individual assets occur. Dependencies between assets should be considered. Instead, if the disposal group equals a cash-generating unit, valuation techniques can be used to measure cash flows of the disposal group in determining the fair value. In such a situation discounted cash flow methods are the preferred methods to be applied. Such methods demand that future cash flows are known. Cash flows can be directly derived from budgets of the cash-generating unit adjusted by non-cash items. An appropriate discount rate has to be used that reflect market conditions.

While the disposal group includes goodwill from the initial acquisition of a subsidiary or from a goodwill-carrying cash generating unit, an impairment test is required to ensure that the goodwill reflects the current condition of the disposal group. Therefore, the established standards of IAS 36 have to be applied.[19]

4.3.4. Impairment losses

Due to the measurement scheme, impairment losses arise on two levels. The first level carries all impairment losses that are allocated to **individual assets**. If the carrying amount of an individual asset exceeds its fair value less costs to sell, an impairment loss has to be recorded. In fact, the carrying amount of an asset will be reduced by recording the impairment loss.

The second level carries the impairment losses of a **disposal group**. If the carrying amount of revaluated assets exceeds the fair value less costs to sell, an additional impairment loss has to be recognized. As this impairment loss involves all assets and liabilities, an allocation of the impairment loss is required. IFRS 5.23 requires applying the allocation rules of IAS 36.104 a) and b). Therefore, an impairment loss has to be allocated to non-current assets by reducing their carrying amount in the following order:

- Goodwill
  This is that goodwill that belongs to the disposal group. It can be either goodwill due to the initial consolidation of a subsidiary or the goodwill belonging to a cash-generating unit or only a portion of it.

- Scoped-in non-current assets
  If any impairment loss is left that is not absorbed by goodwill (so in fact goodwill allocated to the disposal group has to be zero), an allocation to non-current assets is required. The allocation has to consider all scoped-in non-current assets, whether their carrying amounts reflect their fair values or not. It will be executed pro-rata on the basis of the carrying amounts of the involved assets.
  Scoped-out non-current assets and current assets are not subject to an adjustment of their carrying amounts.

Even if the allocation order and requirement is based on IAS 36 (due to the referencing of IFRS 5 to IAS 36 – IFRS 5.23 in conjunction with IAS 36.104 a and b), the scope is narrowed. In this case, the allocation of impairment losses is

---

[19] See chapter F -8.2 on page 348 for the detailed application of the impairment test.

limited to goodwill and those non-current assets that are subject to remeasurement according to IFRS 5. The extent, to which an asset's carrying amount will be reduced, is determined by IFRS 5 only. Therefore, the write-down of an asset according to IFRS 5 will differ from that according to IAS 36.

In some cases, the **impairment loss** of a disposal group **exceeds** the cumulative **carrying amounts** of scoped-in non-current assets. Such a situation may occur if the carrying amounts of scoped-in non-current assets are small and fair value adjustments are triggered by either scoped-out non-current assets or current assets. IFRS 5 is silent about such situations. Therefore, it is up to the preparer to decide on an adequate accounting treatment that reflects the initial intention. It is recommended to adopt the accounting treatment as an accounting policy of the group. The following options may be appropriate:

- Allocation of the remaining impairment loss to scoped-out non-current and current assets;
- Recognition of an additional liability;
- No recognition but tracking of impairment losses in an off-balance sheet calculation that might be important in case of subsequent valuation adjustments.

There are different opinions and interpretation regarding the proper accounting treatment in such situations.[20] A strict interpretation according to IFRS 5.23 would discard the first two options leaving only the last option as the valid one because IFRS 5.23 require to allocate impairment losses to scoped-in non-current assets only. Therefore, if such a situation occurs, a discussion with the group's auditors should always take place to agree on an appropriate accounting treatment as there might be circumstances where a different accounting of such effects is more appropriate.

There is a set of **exemptions** regarding the measurement and the accompanying calculation of assets and liabilities at the decision date.

- Foreign operations

  These usually require a currency translation at the end of each period where translation differences are recorded in other comprehensive income. According to IAS 21.48, a reclassification of all translation differences from equity to profit & loss is required upon the date of disposal. For IFRS 5 accounting purposes, a recycling has to occur at the date, the disposal group is sold. A recycling at the decision date is not appropriate as this only changes the status of the subsidiary to be sold from an on-going to a discontinued operation. IFRS 5.BC37 and BC38 confirm this practice.

- Issues with sales price

  The adjusted carrying amount of a disposal group does not necessarily reflect the sales price. This is because the sales price may include other

---

[20] E.g. Lüdenbach, §29, Rz. 33 in IFRS Kommentar.

items that are not considered at the decision date. Furthermore, items recorded in other comprehensive income have to be recycled. This includes for example the "PUF"-elements: pensions, unrealized gains and losses and foreign exchange differences.

- Liabilities exceed assets

    Having adjusted non-current assets due to impairment losses may result in a mismatch between assets and liabilities. Liabilities now exceed assets so that negative sales proceeds are expected. Such a situation often occurs in practice when loss-making operations are to be disposed. Due to a different presentation of assets and liabilities, an accounting for such a situation is not necessary at the decision date but it will be subject to the recording of the final sale.

Regardless of which level is involved in carrying an impairment loss, the underlying journal entry is always the same.

Journal entry

dr.	"Disposal expenses"	
	cr.	Goodwill / impaired asset

All measurement activities are finally cumulated into two figures: the carrying amount of all assets classified as held for sale and the carrying amount of all liabilities belonging to assets classified as held for sale. While these two figures may include more than one non-current asset, a disposal group or a discontinued operation, it is recommended to document the composition of these two figures in an auxiliary calculation. This calculation should contain a breakdown by the disposal groups and the carrying balances of their assets / liabilities. It should also contain, on an item-by-item basis, impairment losses allocated to assets and non-taken depreciation.

> The auxiliary calculation helps you in subsequent measures at later stages.

4.4. Step 4 – Life as a discontinued operation

Once the subsidiary has been removed from the group and its consolidated financial statements, life as a discontinued operation starts. Even if this "new" life offers a certain freedom for the subsidiary, it is still linked to the group. Therefore, it has to be included in all statements of the group following the presentation requirement of IFRS 5.

4.4.1. *Presentations*

The presentation of the discontinued operation in the **consolidated statement of financial position** has to occur separately from assets and liabilities of the continuing operation. Therefore, all assets of the discontinued operation have to be aggregated into one balance sheet item only. This balance sheet item is named "Non-current assets classified as held for sale" and presented in the consolidated statement of financial position below all assets of the group. It has to be developed forward to the balance sheet date for presentation purposes. The same presentation applies to all liabilities of the discontinued operation. The description is slightly different ("Liabilities directly associated with non-current assets classified as held for sale"), the remainder stays the same. A netting of assets and liabilities of the discontinued operations to present assets on a net basis is prohibited according to IFRS 5.38. Like assets and liabilities, any profits recognized during the period and belonging to equity have to be presented separately. IFRS 5 recommends labelling that equity item as "Amounts recognized in other comprehensive income and accumulated in equity relating to non-current assets held for sale".

Assets		Liabilities & Equity	
Non-current assets	X	Equity	X
Current assets	X	Amounts recognized in other comprehensive income and accumulated in equity relating not non-current assets held for sale	X
Non-current assets classified as held for sale	X	**Sub-Total**	**XX**
		Non-current liabilities	X
		Current liabilities	X
		Liabilities directly associated with non-current assets classified as held for sale	X
Total	**XX**	**Total**	**XX**

Fig. J-8 Sample balance sheet including the presentation of discontinued operations

The presentation of non-current assets classified as held for sale and liabilities directly associated with non-current assets classified as held for sale is based on consolidated figures. Therefore, an allocation of all assets and liabilities in their defined positions is required triggering the execution of the following journal entries for reclassification.

Journal entries			Comment
dr.		Assets classified held for sale	
	cr.	Assets	Level II assets of the subsidiary
dr.		Liabilities	Level II liabilities of the subsidiary
	cr.	Liabilities classified held for sale	

IFRS 5 does not demand retrospective application, not even for comparative figures of the prior period. Therefore, non-current assets classified as held for sale may be presented in the current period only without the restatement of the prior period. Subsequently, if a discontinued operation is sold, it may be presented in the prior period but not in the current one.

As with the consolidated statement of financial position, the **consolidated statement of income** has to present the effects of the discontinued operation separately to the continuing operations. Again, the presentation of discontinued operations in the profit & loss statement is also reduced to one line item only that has to be presented net of tax. Therefore, it is recommended to place the presentation below the continued operation as suggested by the examples of IAS 1.IG6.

	Current period	Prior period
Revenue	X	X
Cost of sales	X	X
Gross profit	**XX**	**XX**
Distribution costs	X	X
Adminstrative expenses	X	X
Other expenses	X	X
Finance costs	X	X
Profit before tax	**XX**	**XX**
Income taxes	X	X
Profit / loss from continued operations	XX	XX
Profit / loss from discontinued operations	X	X
Net profit for the period	**XX**	**XX**

Fig. J-9 Sample profit & loss statement including the presentation of discontinued operations

Due to the requirement of IFRS 5.33 to disclose " … the total of the post-tax profit or loss of discontinued operations …", the profit / loss disclosure of the disposal group covers the total period, not only the portion after the decision date. Other than the presentation in the consolidated statement of financial position, the presentations demand comparable figures for the prior period according to IFRS 5.34. This is an inconsistent treatment as there is no similar retrospective application required for the balance sheet. It also requires that a separate calculation of prior period results has to be executed for presentation.

Even if the presentation is limited to one line item only, an analysis of the results of the discontinued operations is required. This analysis has to contain the following items:

- Revenue;
- Expenses;
- Pre-tax profits (or losses);
- Income tax expenses;
- Gains and losses recognized due to the fair value measurement of noncurrent assets or a disposal group.

It is up to the discretion of management to present this analysis in the profit & loss statement or in the notes.

> To boost the readability of financial statements, place the analysis in the notes as practiced by most companies. There you have the space to dedicate an own chapter to discontinued operations. You should also include all other mandatory disclosure requirements in this chapter.

Even if a reclassification of balance sheet and profit & loss items is a simple task it may produce misleading presentation as there are general **presentation conflicts** arising from IFRS 5 and IFRS 10. IFRS 5.4 demands an allocation of all assets and liabilities that belong to a disposal group to be presented separately from other assets and liabilities of the group in consolidated financial statements. By contrast, IFRS 10.B86 demands that all intercompany balances on assets and liabilities should be eliminated in full. IFRS 5.BC53 confirms the IASB's view of the consolidation and separate presentation of disposal groups. These requirements will generate a conflict if assets and liabilities of a disposal group refer to intercompany transactions. Either assets and liabilities will be consolidated, resulting in an insufficient presentation of the disposal group's assets and liabilities, or assets and liabilities will not be consolidated, resulting in a proper presentation of the disposal group but generating a violation of the consolidation requirements of IFRS 10. Regardless of which solution will be chosen, an error will always arise. Which error is more material has to be checked and discussed with the auditor. A fall-back to the principles of the framework might be appropriate to find a suitable solution for this dilemma.

As with assets and liabilities, the presentation of continuing and discontinuing operations in the statement of profit & loss may end in misleading results. This is particularly the case if a sales subsidiary is subject to a disposal group that significantly contributes to the group's revenue and profits. Applying the consolidated view demanded by IFRS 10, external revenue of that subsidiary will be classified as part of discontinued operations which are falsifying the performance of the group (In this case, the revenue of the group is understated because, even if the subsidiary is sold, revenue may still accrue to the group from the previous relationship – so sales from the group to the then former subsidiary will stay.). A consistent application with the accounting solution for balance sheet presentation is mandatory to solve the presentation issue in the consolidated statement of profit & loss.[21]

> If you detect such kinds of conflicts, involve your auditor upfront to find a suitable agreement. A decision has to be made regarding the leading standard, IFRS 5 for a presentation that reflects the true conditions of the disposal group or IFRS 10 that formally complies with the standard. Consider the implication on all statements as they are all involved!

There is an option for the presentation of cash-flows. Required disclosures can either be taken in the **statement of cash flows** or in the notes. IFRS 5.33c requires a separate disclosure of cash flows of the discontinued operation for all

---

[21] See also IDW RS HFA 2, Tz. 112 ff. for a detailed example of these conflicts.

three categories; operating, financing and investing activities. This includes the current as well as the prior period.

Items of discontinued operations have to present also in the **fixed asset schedule**. IAS 16.73(e) (ii) requires that a reclassification of all non-current assets to discontinued operations have to be disclosed separately.

4.4.2. Subsequent measurement

Subsequent to the measurement at the decision date, disposal groups are subject to specific accounting treatment. The idea behind this treatment is to "freeze" or conserve the assets of the disposal as they are due to the expected sale. Therefore, a continuous recognition of interests and other expenses should occur, but a further depreciation to adjust the carrying amount of non-current assets is prohibited according to IFRS 5.25.

An integral accounting requirement is a subsequent measurement of the disposal group and its assets and liabilities as requested by IFRS 5.19. This measurement shall ensure that assets of the disposal group are not overstated and the criteria of a discontinued operation are still given. Therefore, a subsequent remeasurement of the disposal group is required if a regular fiscal period ends during the total disposal period. As the standard is silent about any other subsequent measurement dates, remeasurement may also be appropriate if there is the possibility of non-current asset impairment.

The first step of the subsequent measurement is the measurement of scoped-out assets and liabilities. These have to be measured according to their individual IFRS. Gains and losses that have to be recorded due to the remeasurement of non-current assets of the disposal group that do not meet the definition have to be recorded in continuing operations; IFRS 5.37 provides guidance.

Subsequent to the first step, the measurement of all scoped-in assets and the disposal group will follow. This measurement is identical to the initial estimation of the fair values of non-current assets and the disposal group. The procedure of the initial measurement can be used that will result in a new calculation of fair value less costs to sell combined with the recording of either an additional impairment loss or gain. If a recognition of assumed impairment losses at the decision date did not take place, this recognition should be caught up at the date of the subsequent measurement. The origin of the change in fair value is irrelevant. A decrease of the fair value of a disposal unit can be caused by non-current assets, current assets and even by liabilities. In all cases, impairment losses are allocated to those non-current assets that are subject to IFRS 5 accounting.

There might be situations where the fair value of a disposal group has been increased compared to the situation at the decision date. The reason for an increase may be subject to the accounting of selected assets that have to be measured with their fair values and that drive the fair value of the whole disposal group. Typical examples are financial instruments classified as trading. A gain due to the increase of the fair value of the disposal group can only be recognized if two criteria are fulfilled:

- The gain is limited to the cumulative impairment loss of scoped-in non-current assets. This includes the write-down to the lower base at the decision date and any subsequent measurements as well as previously recognized impairment losses in accordance with IAS 36.
- The gain was not already recognized for scoped-out non-current assets. It should only be recognized once.

4.5. Step 5 – Sale of discontinued operations

The disposal period always stops at that date where the disposal group is sold. This assumes that the location of a potential buyer was successful and a binding agreement between both parties is signed (which is usually a sale & purchase agreement). The determination of the exact date (the disposal date) follows the same procedures as for ordinary disposals and acquisitions of subsidiaries.[22] At the disposal date, a set of accounting activities are triggered:

- Recording of the disposal by the parent;
- Recording of the disposal by the group;
- Recycling of items recognized in other comprehensive income.

The **recording of the disposal by the parent** of a subsidiary subject to IFRS 5 accounting is exactly the same as for an ordinary subsidiary. The parent records a gain or loss due to the disposal in the statement of profit & loss by eliminating the carrying amount of the investment in the subsidiary and the recognition of the conditions defined in the purchase agreement. Journal entries will not change.

The **recording of the disposal by the group** is slightly different. As assets and liabilities are presented in separate and defined balance sheet positions (non-current assets classified as held for sale and liabilities directly associated with non-current assets classified as held for sale), an elimination of the carrying amount of these items is required. Also, assets and liabilities are still consolidated, requiring an unwinding of intercompany transactions. The procedure is the same as for the disposal on an interest in a subsidiary.

As far as assets of the subsidiary are adjusted to fair value through other comprehensive income, the gains and losses recorded in other comprehensive income have to be recycled to profit & loss. If other comprehensive income includes foreign currency translations of the subsidiary, these translation differences have to be recycled as well. The **recycling** will impact the gain or loss realized at group level due to the disposal.

The gain / loss due to the disposal of the subsidiary at the disposal date can be calculated in the same way as the **calculation** of ordinary disposals occurs by applying either the direct or indirect method. The difference from those

---

[22] See chapter J -1.1 on page 572 for ordinary disposals of subsidiaries and chapter E -3.2 on page 140 for acquisitions of subsidiaries.

calculations is that the remeasured and reclassified assets and liabilities have to be used for disposal groups as outlined in the following example:[23]

	Proceeds from the sale of interests in the subsidiary
−	Level II **assets classified as held for sale**
+	Level II **liabilities directly associated with assets classified as held for sale**
+/−	Differences due to foreign currency translations
+/−	Items of the revaluation surplus
+/−	Deferred taxes
+/−	Further adjustments due to subsequent measurements (not realized so far)
+	Non-controlling interests
=	Realized gain / loss

Tab. J-12 Example of determining gains / losses from the sale of disposal group using the direct method

Special attention has to be given to disposals resulting in **negative sales proceeds**. In such cases, the buyer of a disposal group will receive additional cash or equity or any other form of payment to accept the disposal group as it is. Reasons for negative sales proceeds may be that:

- disposal groups produce continuous losses, or
- liabilities exceed assets of the disposal group after remeasurement.

IFRS 5 is silent about such cases. An accounting as a disposal group may be appropriate as long as formal IFRS 5 requirements are fulfilled. Nevertheless, it is recommended to assess the substance of such a disposal group, whether it is worth disposing of the group rather than liquidating it.

4.6. Step 6 – Deconsolidation

Having remeasured all assets of the disposal group, the subsidiary is now prepared for deconsolidation. A deconsolidation in the context of IFRS 5 accounting is slightly different from that of an ordinary disposal as additional tasks are necessary due to the presentation as assets / liabilities classified as held for sale and their different measurement base. All deconsolidation activities should take place at the disposal date. If a deconsolidation will take place at the next ordinary balance sheet date, the balances of the subsidiary at the disposal date have to be used for deconsolidation.

The extent of the deconsolidation required covers all areas:

- Equity elimination
  Full elimination of equity in the parent's accounts. Furthermore, a removal of the initial equity consolidation is necessary. Goodwill effects due to cash-generating units and effects of non-controlling interests have to be considered. Transactions at group level have to be considered.

---

[23] Determining gains and losses using an indirect method is also appropriate. See chapter J -3.2.1 on page 579 for the application of the indirect method.

- Asset and liability removal

    Removal of the carrying amounts of assets and liabilities at the disposal date. These carrying amounts will differ from the ones at the decision date and the balance sheet date.

- Earnings / expense consolidation

    An elimination of intercompany transactions up to the disposal date is required not to overstate revenues and profit in the consolidated statement of income. This consolidation interacts with presentation issues for the disposal group as discussed before!

- Adjustment of unrealized profits

    Adjustments of unrealized profits will apply, if the classification and the disposal will result in changes of unrealized profit. An adjustment is not required for those assets that relate to transactions after the disposal date.

- Further administrative tasks

    Administrative tasks are similar to the ones of an ordinary disposal.[24]

Before the deconsolidation can take place, effects due to the presentation of discontinued operations have to be reversed. Even if a disposal group's non-current assets are "freezed" and do not change their balances, the disposal group will have a running business that has an impact on current assets and liabilities as the ordinary bookkeeping of the subsidiary will not stop. Therefore, carrying amounts of assets and liabilities of the subsidiary differ between the decision (or the subsequent balance sheet date) and the disposal date. To solve the differences, a reversal of journal entries at the decision date (or the subsequent balance sheet date) is appropriate at group level for presentation purposes.

Journal entries			Comment
dr.		Assets	
	cr.	Assets classified held for sale	Level II assets of the subsidiary
dr.		Liabilities classified held for sale	Level II liabilities of the subsidiary
	cr.	Liabilities	

Any consolidations and transactions at group level due to interim financial reporting as required by *IAS 34 – Interim Financial Reporting* that relate to discontinued operations have to be reversed or adjusted if they have an impact on the deconsolidation.

Having prepared the disposal group, the sale of the subsidiary and its deconsolidation is now ready to be executed. The deconsolidation follows exactly the same procedure as an "ordinary" deconsolidation.[25]

---

[24] See page 589.

[25] See chapter J -3.2.6 on page 590 for a description of all journal entries to be executed.

4.7. Special cases

4.7.1. Distributions to owners

Discontinued operations may also arise if a distribution to owners is planned. A typical reason for this kind of distribution is a company split. The distribution type just differs (asset distribution instead of cash); all other conditions regarding a distribution stay the same. In some jurisdictions, shareholder approval may be required for such a distribution.

The procedure of classifying a subsidiary as a discontinued operation held for distribution to owners is the same as an ordinary discontinued operation. It has to follow the same rationale including measurement, deconsolidation and subsequent measures but it has to consider specific distribution rules. They should be incorporated into the sales plan.

The measurement of assets distributed to owners also does not change. The accounting follows the same procedures as for other disposals. Nevertheless, special attention is given to costs to distribute. These costs may differ from costs to sell. Even if the definition of "incremental costs directly attributable to ..." does not change, the scope and composition is different as different types of cost may be involved. An analysis of tasks to be executed upon the distribution to owners might be useful in assuming costs to distribute.

4.7.2. Changes to sales plan, criteria not any longer met

Situations to account for a subsidiary to be presented as a discontinued operation and accounted as a disposal group may change. Reasons for such changes may be:

- Management's intention to dispose of the subsidiary has changed;
- External (market) effects make the disposal uncomely;
- There is no buyer;
- An agreement on the sales price could not be reached;
- Other reasons.

These reasons may mean that requirements as summarized in IFRS 5.7 and 5.8 to recognize a subsidiary according to IFRS 5 are not any longer met.[26] Instead, changes to a plan of sale apply. Regardless of the underlying reasons, a management decision is again necessary not to sell the subsidiary. Therefore, as of the decision date not to sell the subsidiary, the subsidiary has to be removed from the disposal group and accounted for as an ordinary part of the business as it was accounted before. It will be classified as held for use.

IFRS 5.26 to 5.29 set out the accounting requirement in such a case. In fact, assets have to be restated as if they would never have been part of a disposal group considering that a potential impairment may have occurred. This requires a reversal of all adjustments due to impairment losses and the execution of all

---

[26] See chapter J -4.1 on page 603 for a summary of all criteria that have to be met.

non-taken depreciation. The then calculated asset's value has to be compared to a recoverable amount as of the decision date not to sell the subsidiary where the recoverable amount reflects its fair value. It is – again – an impairment exercise that has to be taken here. The final carrying amount of the asset will be the lower of the calculated asset's value and the recoverable amount. Any adjustment to the asset to arrive at its intended carrying amount has to be recorded through profit & loss, preferably in those categories, where the initial recording on gains or losses took place. If both, the allocation of the subsidiary to a disposal group and its later reallocation to its initial position took place within a period, profit & loss effects compensate.

In conjunction with adjustments required by IFRS 5, a consolidation is required at group level restoring the group as if the subsidiary had never left the group.

A variation of the non-disposal of a subsidiary is the removal of only one asset or liability from a disposal group. In this case it has to be checked if the remaining assets and liabilities of the disposal group meet the requirements of IFRS 5.7 and 5.8:

- If this is the case, the remaining assets and liabilities still qualify as held for sale. Any adjustments to these assets and liabilities are not necessary. An adjustment applies to the removed asset only. The asset removed has to go through the same valuation process to restore the carrying amount as if the asset had never been treated as held for sale.
- By contrast, if the remaining assets and liabilities fail to qualify as held for sale, all assets and liabilities that not any longer qualify as held for sale have to be reclassified to held of use requiring an appropriate valuation adjustment.

4.7.3. *Purchase of subsidiary for immediate sale*

There are situations where subsidiaries were purchased that are subject to an immediate sale. Typical reasons may differ for such purchase / sales transactions:

- The subsidiary can be purchased at a favourable price expecting an appropriate profit on sale;
- Customers are already available that demand such subsidiaries;
- The subsidiary was part of a larger purchase but does not fit in the group's strategy.

Regardless of the reason why a subsidiary will be immediately sold, the accounting for an immediate sale follows specific rules. IFRS 5.11 requires that the subsidiary will be directly classified as held for sale at the acquisition date. This classification is tied to two conditions:

- The 12 month period criterion has to be met at the acquisition date;
- It is highly probable that the other criteria as outlined in IFRS 5.7 and 5.8 are met in a short period after the acquisition date. This period should not exceed three months.

The classification as held for sale at the acquisition date results in a mixture of requirements according to IFRS 5 and requirements according to IFRS 3. Therefore, elements of IFRS 5 have to be considered directly as part of the business combination:

- Estimated costs to sell are not recognized as expenses. Instead, they are considered in goodwill as part of the business combination. This will increase goodwill.

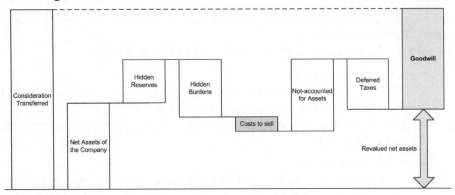

Fig. J-10   Costs to sell as part of business combinations

- The subsidiary is subject to consolidation according to IFRS 10.[27] IFRS 5.BC53 confirms that there is no exception that may lead to a non-consolidation. Thus, a consolidation is mandatory even if the company resides only for a limited period with the group.

  The initial consolidation may be executed at the same time the deconsolidation will take place. This depends on the availability of a potential buyer and a closure of the disposal deal. As a consequence, a simplified consolidation may be appropriate with the focus on equity consolidation. Other consolidation tasks, particularly equity consolidation, depend on the subsidiary. There might be transactions already before the acquisition that have to be eliminated. As IFRS 5 requires only limited disclosures, simplified consolidations may be appropriate.

4.7.4. Disposal groups without any non-current assets

There may be situations in which a business is treated as a discontinued operation but the disposal group representing this operation does not include any non-current assets subject to IFRS 5 remeasurement at all. IFRS 5 is silent about such a situation. In fact, the standard also has conflicting definitions that may lead to various accounting assumptions. IFRS 5.2 states, that the application of

---

[27] The accounting rules have changed. Under IAS 27 (old version), an exemption from consolidating these disposal groups was given. This rule was removed by the introduction of IFRS 10.

IFRS applies to "… all recognized non-current assets and disposal groups […], except for those assets listed in paragraph 5 which shall continue to be measured in accordance with the Standard noted …". Using this definition only, a disposal group is always subject to IFRS 5 accounting, even if there is no non-current asset that meets the IFRS 5 definition. Furthermore, IFRS 5.4 states, that if "… a non-current asset within the scope of the measurement requirements of this IFRS is part of a disposal group, the measurement requirements of this IFRS apply to the group as a whole, …". This can be interpreted as there always has to be a non-current asset that meets the definition of IFRS 5 to qualify as a disposal group for measurement.

Two interpretations may be derived from this wording:

- No remeasurement
  Due to missing non-current assets that meet the definition of IFRS 5, the whole measurement principle of IFRS 5 does not apply. Therefore, any gain or loss due to the sale of the disposal group will be realized at the date of the final sale.

- Full remeasurement
  Due to the missing guidance, the missing requirement explicitly with a non-current asset "on board" that qualifies for IFRS 5 accounting and the wording of IFRS 5.2, a full remeasurement may be appropriate. This is even supported by the idea, that disposal groups should be measured at the expected amount to be realized as derived from the underlying principle of IFRS 5.15 (the measurement at the lower of its carrying amount and fair value less costs to sell). Therefore, all assets and liabilities have to be remeasured at the decision date according to their individual standards. The gain or loss will be realized earlier, at the decision date.

Regardless of which position is taken for the accounting of such cases, a consistent application is required.

K SPECIAL AREAS

About this chapter:

All aspects of the lifecycle of a subsidiary as part of a group and the processes belonging to each stage of the lifecycle have already been discussed. Nevertheless, groups are confronted with additional items arising in the ordinary course of the business that have to be considered. Such items occur frequently and are usually not avoidable.

This chapter is picking up all areas where additional accounting tasks due to the business or the structure of a group are necessary. These areas are:

- Treatment of foreign currencies and their translation;
- Taxation, particularly the accounting for deferred taxes in groups;
- Cash-Flow statements;
- Partnerships;
- Restructuring of a group.

For each area, a detailed explanation is given regarding the effects that can occur in a group and the accounting for these effects. It will distinguish between effects that arise at local level in the accounts of a subsidiary and at group level.

1. CURRENCY TRANSLATION OF FOREIGN OPERATIONS

1.1. Basics

Foreign currency translations are regular tasks as part of the preparation process of consolidated financial statements. They occur if:

- foreign operations using a different currency than the parent have to be considered in consolidated financial statements,
- transactions are executed in a foreign currency, or
- a presentation currency other than the group currency is used.

The accounting of foreign currency translations is ruled in "*IAS 21 – The effects of Changes in the Foreign Exchange Rate*". This standard not only considers the handling of currency translations, it also covers accounting for hyperinflation in accordance with IAS 29.[1] Even if the standard defines the treatment of foreign currencies, selected transactions and items are excluded. These are covered by other standards: derivative transactions of financial instruments by IFRS 9, hedge accounting for foreign currency items by IAS 39, presentations of cash flows in a foreign currency by IAS 7.

A foreign operation is defined as "… an entity that is a subsidiary, associate, joint arrangement or branches of a reporting entity […] conducted in a country or currency other than those of the reporting entity". So in fact, if a parent has some kind of business outside its domestic market in a currency other than its base currency, currency translations apply.[2] While this definition also includes branches, there may be several currencies allocable to a legal entity's various operations. As branches also have consequences for taxation, companies tend to avoid such configurations by using legal entities for its foreign operations.

Currency translations follow a defined process. Depending on the currencies to be considered, several translations may be necessary. They are embedded in the preparation process of consolidated financial statements. To capture all transactions that are based on foreign currencies, all levels have to be considered. Therefore, a foreign currency translation should take place at level II after any adjustments but before the consolidation. If level II adjustments are necessary using the currency of the group, the currency translation occurs upfront. The translation covers all elements of financial statements:

- Statement of financial position;
- Statement of income;
- Statement of cash flows;
- Statement of changes in shareholder equity;
- Notes, particularly all charts and tables in the notes.

---

[1] Accounting for hyperinflation is not discussed in this book.

[2] The focus in this chapter will not be on transactions in a foreign currency but on the translation of foreign operations.

A dedicated view regarding the translation has to be executed for each element of financial statements.

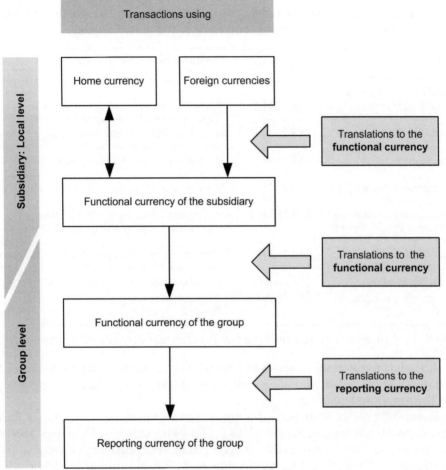

Fig. K-1 System of currency translations

The core of currency translations is the **concept of the functional currency**. IAS 21.11 defines the functional currency as that currency that primarily generates and expends cash. To determine that currency, criteria used are the currency applied for sales prices of goods and services and the currency applied for labour, material and other costs. In most cases, the functional currency will be the domestic currency of an affiliate company. Therefore, the functional currency can only change if the economic environment in which the company operates also changes. Nevertheless, there are cases where the company has to apply a different currency than the domestic currency as its functional currency. In such cases, subsidiaries operate in an international environment, generating revenues due to exports or imports that are invoiced in a foreign currency or using a key currency for their businesses. While a mixture of criteria can occur, it is up to management discretion to decide about the appropriate functional currency based on the overall nature of the business integral to the group. The following table may help in determining the functional currency of an affiliate company in a group. If indicators prove that independence from the group is given, the affiliate company has an own functional currency. Otherwise, the functional currency of the group applies.

Item	Reference	Indicator for own functional currency
Competitive forces and regulations	IAS 21.9a (ii)	Determination of prices in domestic currency
Debt management	IAS 21.11d	Cash flow of operating activities sufficient to repay debt / no funds support by group
Financing of operations	IAS 21.10a	Financing independent from group, domestic currency (but not necessarily)
Expense impact	IAS 21.9b	Expenses (e.g. salaries) are paid in its domestic currency
Intercompany transaction	IAS 21.11b	Low volume of intercompany transactions compared to external business
Impact on group cash flows /remittance of cash flows to group	IAS 21.11c	No impact of the group on cash flows given / autonomous management of cash flows[3]
Local or autonomous management	IAS 21.11a	Degree of which the operation is linked to the group / independence of business
Operating cash flows	IAS 21.10b	Cash flows are based on domestic currency
Sales price for goods and services	IAS 21.9a (i)	Denomination and settlement in domestic currency

Tab. K-1 Indicators in determining the functional currency of a subsidiary

A similar requirement applies to selected transactions using a currency other than its domestic or functional currency. Those transactions have to be translated into the functional currency.

Depending on the structure of a group and its business, a group may have to apply several functional currencies. This is always the case if subsidiaries operate in foreign markets with foreign currencies compared to the currency of the group. The identification of functional currencies has to follow additional guidelines. If the subsidiary qualifies as a foreign operation and has a certain degree of autonomy, the functional currency is the currency the subsidiary applies. If the subsidiary is closely linked to the parent and acts as an extension to the parent, the functional currency of the subsidiary is the functional currency of the parent. Regardless of which functional currency is applied by subsidiaries, from a group's perspective the currencies are always foreign currencies that have to be translated.

In addition to the functional currency, IAS 21 defines a **presentation currency** that can be used to present consolidated financial statements. Usually, the presentation currency is identical to the functional currency of the group. Nevertheless, there are situations where consolidated financial statements have to be presented

---

[3] Subsidiaries are often linked to cash pools. In such a case it has to be checked how the cash pool is managed in financing the group.

in a different currency than the functional currency of the group. The translation into a presentation currency is used for these purposes. This translation is also used in groups and not only at group level. Subsidiaries with their own functional currencies can apply this translation to have their separate financial statements translated into the group's currency.

Currency translations in groups can combine both the functional and reporting currency. The application depends on the structures in a group. Fig. K-2 lists typical translation scenarios that may be used in translating foreign investments into the group's currency.

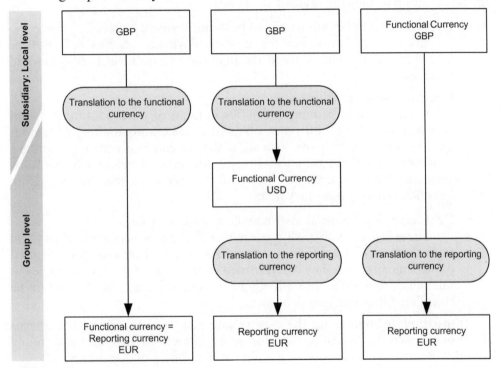

Fig. K-2   Translation scenarios

> Ensure that each subsidiary has a functional currency whenever possible! This simplifies the currency translation.

1.2. Translation to the functional currency

The translation of financial statements into the functional currency is realized by a method that presents the translated financial statements as if they were already prepared using the functional currency. Therefore, an analysis of the nature of each item is required in determining the translation. An item can either have a monetary or non-monetary character.

1.2.1. Monetary items

Monetary items are defined as a "... units of currency held and assets and liabilities to be received or paid in a fixed or determinable number of units of currency". So, monetary items are all those items that will generate fixed cash receipts and payments. A list of all monetary items is provided in Tab. K-5. Monetary items are always translated using the closing rate. Any exchange differences have to be recorded through profit & loss.

Even if the definition is simple, some types of asset and liabilities require special attention as they are difficult to classify:

- Defined benefit obligations due to post-employment benefits

    Even if the provision for post-employment benefits will not be determinable, the payments to the plan have to occur at fixed dates and fixed amounts.

- Decommissioning obligations

    If the decommissioning obligation consists of a contract for payment that a third party fulfils the obligation, decommissioning obligations qualify as monetary items. Instead, if the obligation is accounted for as a provision, cash flows are uncertain and difficult to estimate. Furthermore, subsequent adjustments may apply to provisions so that the obligation qualifies as a non-monetary item.

- Debt securities (financial instruments, available for sale)

    These instruments qualify as monetary items. Nevertheless, changes in fair values may have different reasons. As long as these changes are based on an amortization they are recorded in profit & loss. Other changes in fair value are recoded through other comprehensive income. This has to be considered in classifying debt securities.

Translating an item using the closing rate may lead to divergent balances in the other currency. An obligation for an adjustment of this item due to any accounting regulations (e.g. due to a higher-value principle) does not exist.

Monetary items can also be a part of the **net investment in a foreign operation**. Typical examples of such monetary items are loans, receivables or payables that have a long-term character. If there are no defined conditions on repayment or settlement in a foreseeable future, special accounting rules apply in preparing consolidated financial statements. In the absence of a definition for a "foreseeable future", the application has to be derived from historical patterns on settling intercompany relationships. Short-term items that are rolled forward and / or renewed on a regular basis do not fulfil the requirement of a long-term character. Also due to the definition of IAS 21.15, items like trade receivables, trade payables or any type of guarantees given are excluded and do not belong to net investments.

The net investment in a foreign operation can be made either directly or indirectly via a subsidiary. It is not important which company of the group grants the loan to the foreign operation as long as control is established over the company of the group that made the investment.

As with other monetary items, gains and losses on exchange differences are recorded through profit & loss, either by the company granting the loan or receivables of the foreign operation. Which company records the exchange differences depends on the currency used:

- Currency used equals the functional currency of the company granting the loan: foreign operation records exchange differences.
- Currency used equals the currency of the foreign operation: company granting the loan records exchange differences.

At group level in consolidated financial statements, the initial exchange differences have to be recorded through other comprehensive income. This requires reclassification from profit & loss to other comprehensive income as part of the consolidation process; reclassification from other comprehensive income to profit & loss is only applicable on the disposal of the foreign operation.

1.2.2. Non-monetary items

While there is no distinct definition, non-monetary items are, as the name suggests, all those items that are not monetary. IAS 21.16 highlight this interpretation by the missing right to receive fixed or determinable amount of cash. This definition should always be followed if there is any doubt whether or not a balance sheet item classifies as a monetary or non-monetary item. A list of monetary items relating to this definition is provided in Tab. K-5.

The translation of non-monetary items and the application of the appropriate **exchange rate** differ depending on their measurement at historical cost or fair value:

- A measurement at historical cost requires the use of a historical exchange rate which is the rate at the date of the transaction.
- A measurement at fair value requires the use of an exchange rate which is the rate at the date the fair value was measured.

Most non-monetary items will use historical exchange rates as they are measured at cost. By contrast, items measured at its fair value are limited in nature. Usually, financial assets and liabilities, investments in subsidiaries, associates and joint ventures, investment properties and biological assets are those items measured at their fair values.

1.2.3. Translation tasks and techniques

A translation of financial statements into the functional currency has to occur on an item by item base. This is necessary due to the classification of balance sheet items as monetary or non-monetary and the application of the appropriate exchange rate.

While some balance sheet items are based on transactions denominated in a foreign currency, the **initial recording** of the transaction and its translation into the functional currency has to be based on the exchange rate at the date of the transaction. This is the historical exchange rate that has to be applied or considered in all subsequent translations for the specific transaction.

Translations into the functional currency in **subsequent periods** are subject to the dedicated translation rules on monetary and non-monetary items. The translation has to follow these rules:

- Monetary balance sheet items are translated using the closing rate.
- Non-monetary balance sheet items measured at historical costs are translated using the exchange rate at the date of the transaction.
- Non-monetary balance sheet items measured at fair value are translated using the exchange rate at the date of the fair value determination.
- Items of the profit & loss statement are translated using the exchange rate at the date of the transaction.

If the accounting is maintained in a currency other than the functional currency, all amounts have to be translated at the end of the period into the functional currency by applying the above rules. This requirement, as defined in IAS 21.34, should ensure that the foreign operation presents its figures in the functional currency as if it had applied the functional currency right from the beginning. Even if this requirement sounds feasible, it will raise concerns regarding the handling. In such a situation, an accounting system is required that supports multi-currency handling or translation methods. A manual translation is not recommended as translations might go down on a transaction base which makes a manual translation difficult to realize.

If all transactions are translated at their adequate rates, a translated **statement of income** will automatically result. If a manual translation of the statement on income at the end of the period is necessary, average exchange rates should be applied. Even if average exchange rates do not meet real conditions, they are close to it which ensures a minimum deviation. This can even be refined by applying historical rate for selected transaction. Typical examples are depreciations and amortizations of non-current assets.

Exchange differences resulting from settlements, remeasurements or translations are recorded in profit & loss either as a gain or loss according to IAS 21.20. Financial instruments measured in accordance with IFRS 9 are excluded from these translations as they have their own rules. Differences can only arise on monetary items as they have to use the closing rate for translations. While the application of historical rates is demanded for non-monetary items, exchange differences will not arise. The only reasons why exchange differences on non-monetary items may arise are remeasurement requirements or a disposal of the item in a currency other than the functional currency. If exchange differences on non-monetary items are identified that are not caused by either a change in the carrying amount of the underlying asset / liability or a disposal, further investigation is required. In most cases, the application of an improper exchange rate at the end of the period is the reason for these unexpected differences.

As a general rule, gains and losses due to exchange differences always follow the underlying transaction. Therefore, if transactions are recorded in profit

& loss, gains and losses due to exchange differences are recorded in profit & loss as well. If transactions are recorded in other comprehensive income, gains and losses due to exchange differences have to be recorded in other comprehensive income as well. This applies particularly for non-current assets as changes in fair value are (often but not always) recorded in other comprehensive income.

> Maintain a dedicated account for foreign currency effects in equity to document translation effects and, if necessary, add attributes to allocate them on an entity by entity base at group level. This ensures that a recycling at a later stage is given.

The translation technique follows the rationale of monetary and non-monetary items. Due to the application of different exchange rates, differences will arise across the trial balance. These differences represent the cumulative exchange differences that need to be recorded in profit & loss. As historical rates have to be used for non-monetary items, a detailed analysis of selected accounts is required and items of these accounts have to be translated on an item by item base. This applies particularly to non-current assets like property, plant & equipment, to all types of intangible asset and to equity. Special attention has to be given to retained earnings and profit & losses carried forward. Their translation is based on the annualized results of previous periods that require an additional documentation. To ensure a proper translation the following steps should be applied:

Step	Task
1)	Estimation of exchange rates to be used.
2)	Translation of all monetary items.
3)	Translation of all non-monetary items except equity. This translation depends on the composition of balance sheet items in respect of their historical rates.
4)	Translation of equity. The translation of retained earnings and profit & loss carried forward depends on the annualized results and dividends.
5)	Translation of the statement of income by applying an average rate and individual rates for selected items.
6)	Accumulation of the carrying amounts of all translated accounts, sorted by debits and credits.[4]
7)	Calculation of the total difference between debits and credits.
8)	Allocation of gains or losses due to differences that demand recognition in other comprehensive income into that category.
9)	Additionally at group level: Allocation of monetary items that belong to net investments in foreign operations to other comprehensive income.
10)	Consideration of the remaining difference as a gain or loss in the statement of income

Tab. K-2 Translation steps of the conversion into a functional currency

---

[4] Steps 6 and 7 can be combined into one step by considering the sign-convention of the trial balance.

1.2.4. *Changes in the functional currency*

As outlined before, the functional currency is closely linked to the business and the environment of an operation. Therefore, a change in the functional currency occurs only in rare cases. Typical reasons for changes in a functional currency are:

- Scope of the business has changed.
- Relocation of business took place.
- "Release from the group" so that the subsidiary has attained more independence.

If the underlying business justifies a change in the functional currency, the new currency chosen has to reflect the business of the subsidiary in the same way the old functional currency did.

When the change in the functional currency should be applied is based on the change of the underlying business. In most cases, a specific **date** cannot be determined while changes in business occur creeping over a period of time unless there are no hard facts like the invoicing in a new currency determinable. While a change in the business can occur during the period, any date could be specified for changing the functional currency. Evidence is required for auditors that the date selected reflects the change in business.

> Select a date at the beginning or end of a most recent period, interim period or any other period applicable.

The change in the functional currency demands a **perspective application** of the new functional currency on all monetary and particularly on all non-monetary items. As monetary items always have to be measured by the closing rate, the focus is on non-monetary items. Due to the requirement of IAS 21.37, non-monetary items will be translated using the rate of the change date. This rate will act as the new historical rate. Any gains and losses arising on this conversion have to be recorded as if a translation of a foreign currency towards the functional currency took place. So a recording in profit & loss or other comprehensive income is mandatory. The previous recorded gains and losses on exchange differences recognized in other comprehensive income stay as they are because a recycling is not necessary as the underlying assets are not disposed.

1.2.5. *Special cases*

Translations into the functional currency affect also items that are subject to remeasurement at the end of the period. This applies to several items: inventory and deferred taxation.

Inventory consists of raw materials, unfinished goods, finished goods and often also prepayments on raw materials. Materials are bought in the past; goods are assembled or under construction where the unfinished part is also subject to past activities. Therefore, cash flows cannot be expected and consequently, inventory is always classified as non-monetary requiring the application of historical rates. Nevertheless, inventory is also subject to remeasurement at the end of the period by applying the lower of cost or market method. The lower market will result in a fair value view that demands a closing rate. As this will result in a mixture of translations on non-current assets, IAS 21.25 has clarified that both exchange rates apply even if a rededication of the closing rates occurs. In practice, inventories are often translated by using the closing rate assuming an application of the net realizable value.

Impairments of non-current assets are usually based on the same method. Therefore, *IAS 36 – Impairment of Assets* and any other standards that measures assets at the lower of cost or market method have to apply the same technique of using different rates for measuring balances of assets.

1.3. Translation to the presentation currency

The translation of financial statements into the presentation currency is – compared to the translation into the functional currency – a method that can be realized at group level. In such a case, the functional currency is with the subsidiary. The advantage of applying a translation into a presentation currency is its simplicity compared to the translation into a functional currency. A differentiation between monetary and non-monetary assets does not take place; all items are treated the same way.

A translation into the presentation currency will apply only at the end of a period. An initial translation like for the functional currency is not required. The translation has to follow these rules:

- All balance sheet items except equity are translated using the closing rate.[5]
- Equity is translated using historical rates.
- Items of the profit & loss statement are translated using the exchange rate at the date of the transaction.

IAS 21.39 clarifies that the exchange rate at the date of the statement of financial position has to be applied; this is usually the end of the period.

Special attention is required for the translation of **equity** as historical rates are demanded. Due to the application of historical rates equity may be subject to additional exchange differences that arise on movements on equity. IAS 21 is silent about the treatment of such movements. Therefore, these rates should be applied individually on all components of equity:

- Common stock
    The rates at each date of an increase or decrease in common stock have to be applied.

- Capital reserves
    The rates at each date of a capital injection or reduction have to be applied.

---

[5] In fact, IAS 21.39 defines only the translation of assets, liabilities and profits of the period. This automatically will result in an application of historical rates for equity as equity is a residual item in this case.

- Revaluation surplus

  The rates at the date of each revaluation of non-current assets have to be applied.

- Retained earnings and profits / losses carried forward

  For each transaction in retained earnings, the appropriate rate has to be applied. Increases in retained earnings due to the profit of a period are based on the average exchange rate of that year. Decreases of retained earnings due to dividend payment require special attention. Dividend payments that relate to a distinct period are based on the rate of the transaction date. The rate of this date differs from the average rate of the period the dividend belongs to which triggers an additional exchange difference. Dividends that relate to previous periods (so more than one period) usually cannot be allocated to dedicated periods unless there is some kind of evidence that enables an allocation to a dedicated period. Such evidence can be a shareholder resolution that defines the allocation of dividends. Exchange differences that arise on dividend payment of several periods can be estimated by applying valuation methods such as weighted average or first in-first out. The method that best reflects the underlying dividend payment should be chosen.

- Profit of the period

  The profit of the period is based on the average exchange rate of the period.

Apply a separate history for each category of equity in your documentation. Based on the individual movements and their associated rates, an average exchange rate can be determined for each category. An auxiliary calculation will help due to its content on information: average exchange rates, movements of equity, documentation for auditors. This simplifies the translation as historical details need not to be retrieved for each close. Make use of it!

Example

Flexing Cables Canada is a sales company that supplies the Canadian market with products of the Flexing Cables group. Accordingly, its functional currency is the Canadian Dollar. To consolidate the company, its financial statements reporting to the parent have to be converted into the reporting currency of the group, the Euro. The following balance sheet and profit & loss statements are subject to the currency conversion.

IFRS Statement of financial position Flexing Cables Canada as of 31.12.2013 (in k CAD)

Assets		Liabilities & Equity	
Cash at hand & bank	2,161	Trade payables	3,437
Trade receivables	3,194	Tax liabilities	200
Inventory	4,275	Prepayments	320
Other assets	1,515	Accruals	497
Current assets	**11.145**	Loans	500
		Other payables	1,204
Property, plant & equipment	214	**Current liabilities**	**6,158**
Intangible assets	35		
Non-current assets	**249**	Deferred taxes	28
		Non-current liabilities	**28**
		Share capital	50
		Retained earnings	5,158
		Equity	**5,208**
Total assets	**11,394**	**Total liabilities & equity**	**11,394**

IFRS Statement of income Flexing Cables Canada as of 31.12.2013 (k CAD)		IFRS Statement of income Flexing Cables Canada as of 31.12.2013 (k CAD)	
Revenues	41,705	Revenues	41,705
Changes in inventory		Cost of goods sold	(36,224)
Work performed and capitalized			
Other income	210	**Gross margin**	**5,481**
Total performance	**41,915**		
		Sales & distribution expenses	(2,096)
Raw materials and consumables	(23,670)	Administration expenses	(1,798)
Employee expenses	(7,388)	Research & development expenses	
Depreciation and amortization expenses	(38)	Other income	210
Other expenses	(9,127)	Other expenses	(105)
Operating profit	**1,692**	**Operating profit**	**1,692**
Finance expenses	(40)	Finance expenses	(40)
Profit before tax	**1,652**	**Profit before tax**	**1,652**
Income tax expenses	(438)	Income tax expenses	(438)
Net profit for the period	**1,214**	**Net profit for the period**	**1,214**

To convert the financial statements, the following exchange rates are applied:

Subject	Exchange rate	Comment
Share capital	1.4423	Exchange rate as of the day of incorporation
Retained earnings	1.4028	Weighted average exchange rate as of all previous periods
Net assets	1.4724	Closing rate
Profit & loss statement	1.3681	Weighted average exchange rate of the period

All differences that arise during the translation are recorded in other reserves. Based on the above applied exchange rate, the translated balance sheet and profit & loss statement will be:

IFRS Statement of financial position Flexing Cables Canada as of 31.12.2013 (in k EUR)

Assets		Liabilities & Equity	
Cash at hand & bank	1,468	Trade payables	2,334
Trade receivables	2,169	Tax liabilities	136
Inventory	2,903	Prepayments	217
Other assets	1,029	Accruals	338
Current assets	**7,569**	Loans	340
		Other payables	818
		Current liabilities	**4,183**
Property, plant & equipment	145		
Intangible assets	24	**Current liabilities**	
Non-current assets	**169**	Deferred taxes	19
		Non-current liabilities	**19**
		Share capital	35
		Retained earnings	3,699
		Other reserves	198
		Equity	**3,932**
Total assets	**7,738**	**Total liabilities & equity**	**7,738**

IFRS Statement of income Flexing Cables Canada as of 31.12.2013 (k EUR)		**IFRS Statement of income Flexing Cables Canada as of 31.12.2013 (k EUR)**	
Revenues	30,484	Revenues	30,484
Changes in inventory		Cost of goods sold	(26,478)
Work performed and capitalized			
Other income	154	**Gross margin**	**4,006**
Total performance	**30,634**		
		Sales & distribution expenses	(1,532)
Raw materials and consumables	(17,301)	Administration expenses	(1,314)
Employee expenses	(5,400)	Research & development expenses	
Depreciation and amortization expenses	(28)	Other income	154
Other expenses	(6,671)	Other expenses	(77)
Operating profit	**1,237**	**Operating profit**	**1,237**
Finance expenses	(29)	Finance expenses	(29)
Profit before tax	**1,208**	**Profit before tax**	**1,208**
Income tax expenses	(320)	Income tax expenses	(320)
Net profit for the period	**888**	**Net profit for the period**	**888**

The **statement of income** has to be translated using the exchange rate at the date of the transaction. This might be appropriate if a company has only a few transactions; it is definitely not practical for companies with thousands of transactions. Therefore, average rates can be used for translation. The average rate used should approximate the exchange rates at the dates of transactions as outlined by IAS 21.40.[6] Constraints in applying an average exchange rate for the period are similar to those of the functional currency translation.

Due to the closing and average rates required, **exchange differences** are unavoidable. That applies particularly for depreciation and amortization, for discounting of provisions, changes in inventory and similar transactions. All these transactions affect the statement of financial position and the statement of income equally but are translated using different rates. Exchange differences arise also due to movements of exchange rates between the periods. Even if an asset was not touched during the period, it will have a different translated carrying amount at the end of the period than it has before. Due to the simplicity of the translation, exchange differences can be calculated by applying two calculations for those items, whose rates differ from the closing rate according to IAS 21.41:

- Statement of income: profit of the period * (average rate – closing rate);
- Statement of financial position: carrying amount net assets @ the beginning of the period * (closing rate prior period – closing rate current period).[7]

> Translations can be simplified in spreadsheets, even if a translation at account level is required. Convert each account of the trial balance by using its appropriate exchange rate (closing, average or historical). Do not convert the account that carries the accumulated balance of exchange differences. The sum of all accounts of the trial balance represents your exchange differences for the current period you simply need to add to the exchange differences account.

As a general rule, gains and losses due to exchange differences are not recorded in profit & loss. Instead, exchange differences are always recorded in other comprehensive income. The rationale behind this rule is the theory that the translation is just for presentation issues and that no impact on current or future cash flows is given. While exchange differences due to translations exist, a separate presentation in equity is mandatory.

Even if the translation is simplified and differences are presented at a dedicated place, the translation task for presentation purposes is very similar to the translation task to the functional currency:

---

[6] Please refer to chapter K -1.4 on page 646 regarding the discussion about the selection of an appropriate exchange rate.
[7] Some interpret the requirement of using net assets for calculating exchange differences as using equity. In fact, both, net assets and equity, will deliver the same result.

Step	Task
1)	Estimation of exchange rates to be used.
2)	Translation of all balance sheet items using the closing rate.
3)	Translation of the statement of income by applying an average rate.
4)	Translation of equity using historical rates. The translation of retained earnings and profit & loss carried forward depends on the annualized results and dividend.
6)	Accumulation of the carrying amounts of all translated accounts, sorted by debits and credits.[8]
7)	Calculation of the total difference between debits and credits.
8)	Allocation of gains or losses due to differences in other comprehensive income.

Tab. K-3   Translation steps of the conversion into a presentation currency

There is no accounting guidance on **changes in the presentation currency**. A group can present their financial statement in any currency that is appropriate for their purposes and, if necessary, also in different currencies at the same time. IAS 21.BC13 confirms this view.

1.4. The exchange rate

The determination of exchange rates applied is defined by IAS 21.21. The standard only requires using the spot rate as the exchange rate, which is that rate used at the date of the transaction to convert a foreign currency into the functional currency, or as of the end of the period (the so called closing rate). As spot rates are available at different times and closings, either an appropriate rate is offered or available or an average of ask and bid spot rates can be used to calculate the rate applied. The standard is silent about all other applications of exchange rates. This includes topics like the type of spot rate to be used, sources of exchange rate, calculations of average exchange rates and determination of historical rates.

Despite the volatility of exchange rates, the rate of a specific date has to be used. This is particularly important on the closure of periods. Even if there are significant movements of the exchange rate before and after the balance sheet date the exchange rate as of the balance sheet date has to be applied. Nevertheless, significant movements may be important for disclosure in conjunction with *IAS 10 – Events after the Reporting Period*.

Available **sources** in selecting the appropriate exchange rates can be internet sites offering exchange rates for free or institutions like federal reserve's providing data on official exchange rates. Regardless of which source is selected, the source should be applied in a consistent manner and be free of peaks or similar issues. Furthermore, the source selected should provide exchange rates for all currencies used in the group. If there are several sources it's possible that two sources for the same currency may yield different exchange rates.

While sources provide official and **unofficial exchange** rates, the application of official exchange rates is preferred. The standard itself is silent about the use of official exchange rates. If unofficial exchange rates are used for currency conversions and translations, an error according to IAS 8.41 may arise, but their use is not prohibited and is widely and legally applied. If transactions will be settled by applying the unofficial rate an application might be appropriate. Nevertheless, the auditor will ask for evidence of such a material error. Good documentation may help.

---

[8] Steps 6 and 7 can be combined into one step by considering the sign-convention of the trial balance.

Occasionally, an exchange rate may **be unavailable**. In such situations, the first available subsequent rate should be used.

On the other hand, there are situations and circumstances where more than one exchange rate is available. In case of **several exchange rates**, an exchange rate has to be chosen that best reflects future cash flows upon settlement.

While exchange rates are sometimes not available for a specific date, difficult to obtain or not practical in application the use of a rate that approximates the rate of that date is appropriate. IAS 21.22 and 21.40 suggest applying an **average rate** for the week or month as an appropriate rate assuming that this rate will be applied to all transactions for the period covered by the rate. If the volatility and fluctuation of an exchange rate is in an appropriate bandwidth, the application of an exchange rate for the period might also be appropriate. Nevertheless, IAS 21.22 and 21.40 prohibit the application of such an average exchange rate in case of significant fluctuations of that rate.

Average exchange rates should always be calculated as a **weighted average**, preferably on a daily basis. Such an average rate is close to the application of rates on a daily basis that ensures a minimal deviation. Good currency websites offer the selection and download of appropriate rates as a time series that enables a simple calculation of a weighted average rate. Estimating the average as an **arithmetic average** based on the closing rates or prior and current period is not prohibited due to the absence of dedicated rules. The application of such an average rate only makes sense, if rates do not fluctuate significantly or have a constant increasing or decreasing tendency. In most cases, these average rates will be more imprecise than a weighted average rate as markets have different behaviours. Therefore, the application of an arithmetic average exchange rate should be avoided.

Some countries fix exchange rates on a periodical basis (in most cases on a monthly base) through their federal reserves combined with a mandatory application of that **fixed exchange rate** for companies residing in that country with international business. Therefore, the group has to consider that specific rate for translation and conversions tasks.

Example

To convert foreign currencies into the group's currency, Flexing Cables SE uses a single source for all currencies applied in the group. The source provides official exchange rates. To calculate the weighted average exchange rates, the company is calculating the rate based on daily published exchange rates. The determination is based on the following calculation model (here calculated for CAD to convert the financial statements of Flexing Cables Canada):

Date	Exchange rate	1/365
1.1.13	1.3139	0.003599
2.1.13	1.3130	0.003597
3.1.13	1.3073	0.003582
...	...	...
...	...	...
30.12.13	1.4721	0.004033
31.12.13	1.4724	0.004034
Sum		**1.3681**

1.5. Currency translations in practice

The methods described to translate a foreign currency into a functional or reporting currency can initiate complex transactions. The complexity depends on the applied method, the history and the available information of a subsidiary. To avoid this, companies tend to assure that subsidiaries qualifying as foreign investments operate in a business environment where their local currencies act as the functional currency. This eliminates the burden for complex conversions where historical information is required. A reduction in complexity can also be achieved by picking up proper translation strategies. The translation strategy should always focus on simple and direct translations into the reporting currency of the group: hierarchical stacked functional currencies, multi-level currency translations, interim currencies and similar items should always be avoided.

If a translation into a **functional currency** cannot be avoided, this translation should always be executed by the subsidiary. The reasons for this translation place are details required for translation. A corporate centre usually does not have the details required for this kind of translation. Reporting all details to the corporate centre also does not add value due to the volume of information required and the workload that results to such a solution. Recommendation in summary: foreign investments should always use a functional currency that is directly translated in the reporting currency. Translation into a functional currency is the responsibility of the foreign investment.

Several tendencies are observed regarding the application of the translation into the **reporting currency** of a group. Some groups require the reporting of financial information by using the reporting currency as defined by the corporate centre. The translation has to be executed by the foreign investment. Other groups simplify the reporting of financial information by using the local or functional currency of the foreign investment. Translation into the reporting currency is done by the corporate centre. Both concepts have their advantages and disadvantages; whichever is applied depends on the ability and knowledge of the foreign investment in translations of foreign currencies. If there are any uncertainties regarding the correct treatment at the foreign investment, it is recommended that translations into the reporting currency are done by the corporate centre.

> Let the subsidiary only be involved in the currency translation in the functional currency! This currency should be used for reporting purposes. Any other currency translation should be managed by the corporate centre.

If accounting systems do not support currency translations, manual translation is required. A manual translation can be realized by using spreadsheets. The closing balance at the end of the period of each account of the trial balance has to be converted by using the closing rate for balance sheet items, the historical rate for equity or the average rate for profit & loss items. Due to the different exchange rates, the converted trial balance will not balance. The difference between debits and credits represents the cumulated exchange differences of the currency translations. They have to be added to the exchange differences account.

More challenging is the preparation of the statement of cash flows and the fixed asset schedule. Both include analyses that are based on figures from the previous period. As a restatement of previous period figures using the exchange rates of the current period is not applicable due to the presentation rules of financial statements, the additional presentation effects are also subject to translation. To identify the translation effects of the current period in relation to the previous period, a double translation is required. The first translation will be executed by using the exchange rates of the previous period while the second translation uses the exchange rate of the current period. Differences between account balances of these two translations are exchange differences of the current period. As an alternative, differences between exchange rates can be used by directly calculating exchange differences. The translation practice using two translations to identify translation differences is a proven method.

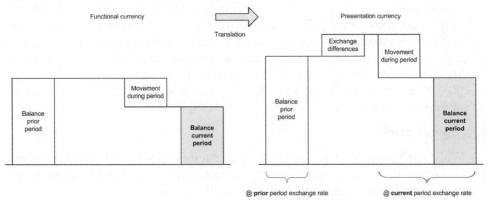

Fig. K-3 Exchanges differences due to different exchange rates

While the **statement of cash flows** reconciles the carrying amount of cash between the current and prior period an exchange difference is required to adjust cash funds of the prior period. This difference is presented separately from other items according to IAS 7.28 below net changes in cash flows but before prior period cash funds. There are also exchange differences for all other assets and liabilities that require adjustment in order to reconcile movements between the periods. While these differences are also based on exchange rate movements and no cash flows are associated with them, elimination is required. Again, the same procedures in estimating these differences apply.

Like the statement of changes in cash flows, the **fixed asset schedule** reconciles movements in the carrying amounts of non-current assets. The behaviour of non-current assets is still the same as for cash items. An exchange difference has to be determined for each non-current asset. Due to the separate presentation of acquisition or manufacturing costs and depreciation, a separate row or column (depending on the presentation style) for each item of the fixed asset schedule is required to present exchange differences due to currency translation. This requires a split-up and allocation of exchange differences between acquisition or manufacturing costs and depreciation. In most cases, the asset modules of accounting systems are capable in handling these requirements.

A detailed view is required for the **statement of changes in equity**. As this statement is a reconciliation of equity movements exchange differences cannot arise on all equity components due to their measurement at historical rates. Nevertheless, this statement includes a reconciliation of all movements of foreign currency translations.

While several elements of the balance sheet and cash flow statement have to be explained in the **notes**, items subject to translations have to be disclosed as well. Foreign currency disclosures are often divided between: general principles of currency translation – as part of accounting policies – and detailed effects on selected items in the statements of financial position and income (and other statements as appropriate).

1.6. Taxation

Translations into the functional currency and the presentation currency will not only result in exchange differences that are recorded in profit & loss or in other comprehensive income, but also in changes in the carrying amount of balance sheet items. Due to the impact on the carrying amount, tax effects may arise that qualify as outside basis differences. They have to be accounted for as deferred tax assets or deferred tax liabilities. IAS 21.50 is picking up this issue and demands an accounting according to *IAS 12 – Income Taxes* for these items.[9]

1.7. Special cases

While the rationale of a group is focused on its business and does not necessarily follows any currency thoughts, special cases arise in groups that require special attention. Typical cases are discussed briefly below.

1.7.1. Goodwill and non-controlling interests

Special attention is required for goodwill and non-controlling interests as these two items relate to equity of the foreign operations (directly and as subgroups) and are considered during the equity consolidation.

Goodwill as defined in IFRS 3 is always a residual value that reflects the surplus of the investment of the parent in its subsidiary. Goodwill may be recorded as full goodwill, representing the parent's and the non-controlling interest's portion, or partial goodwill representing the parent's portion only. Both types of goodwill belong to the subsidiary and are subject to foreign currency translation. IAS 21.47 and 21.BC28 define goodwill as an asset of the subsidiary. Due to the treatment as an asset of the subsidiary, goodwill is subject to any exchange differences arising on subsequent translations compared to the initial recognition due to different exchange rates. These differences have to be recorded in other comprehensive income. It is not important, if goodwill is part of a cash-generating unit or not.

If goodwill is allocated to a **cash-generating unit**, any movement due to impairment tests or disposals will affect associated exchange differences. Upon the date

---

[9] See chapter K -2.3.3 on page 669 regarding the accounting of deferred taxes on foreign currency translations.

of allocating goodwill to the cash-generating unit, the exchange rate as of that date has to be used. It is recommended to allocate goodwill to a cash-generating unit at the acquisition date. IAS 21.BC32 confirms that there are different levels for goodwill, the one where goodwill is tested (usually the foreign currency level) and the one where goodwill is allocated to (the functional currency). Due to different levels, exchange differences will impact the recording of any impairment losses.

Exchange differences, whether they refer to an initial goodwill or goodwill belonging to a cash-generating unit and recorded in other comprehensive income have to be reclassified to profit & loss. IAS 21.48 and 21.48C clearly state that exchange differences relating to foreign operations have to be reclassified. Strict interpretation of these accounting rules suggests that there is no dependency between goodwill and exchange differences upon disposal. Another interpretation may conclude that a breakup of exchange differences into separate components that are allocable to the underlying assets and liabilities is not required by the standard. Nevertheless, there may be different interpretations about the allocation of exchange differences to various items. Furthermore, exchanges differences relating to goodwill can be reclassified in full or on a proportionate share basis.

> If such situations occur, involve your auditors upfront on the accounting solution you prefer.

Goodwill can also have an impact on **non-controlling interests**, if the full goodwill method is applied for goodwill accounting. Any exchange differences that arise from the translation of goodwill in subsequent periods have to be allocated to other comprehensive income and to non-controlling interests. Instead, if the partial goodwill method is applied, exchange differences are allocated to other comprehensive income only. An allocation to non-controlling interests is gratuitous. Exchange differences on the translation of all other assets and liabilities are allocated to non-controlling interests based on the share of non-controlling interests in the subsidiary. The remaining portion is allocated to other comprehensive income.

Due to the different treatment of goodwill, exchange differences cannot be allocated to non-controlling interests based on their investment. Instead a calculation is required to estimate the final amount of exchange differences attributable to non-controlling interests.

Upon the disposal of a subsidiary, the non-controlling interests are subject to any exchange differences. Exchange differences due to translations have to be derecognized as demanded by IAS 21.48. This means that exchange differences that are allocable to non-controlling interests have to be recorded against them. Reclassification to profit & loss is prohibited.

1.7.2. *Currency effects of intercompany relationships*

Like any other business transaction with third parties, **trade** business transactions with other companies of the group are also subject to foreign currency translations. On the other hand, currency effects will arise due the **translation** of financial statements from one currency to another currency. So, there are two currency effects requiring separate treatment.

Principles of Group Accounting under IFRS

Intercompany transactions, either trading or similar ones, are subject to IAS 21.20 and 21.23. They qualify in most cases as monetary items. Any exchange differences according to a settlement of those transactions or a revaluation of corresponding assets and liabilities are recorded in profit & loss, either at the date of the settlement or at the balance sheet date. All those accounting activities are recorded in the separate financial statements of the sending or receiving company. Who is in charge of recording these differences has to be determined by the agreed transaction currency and its relationship to the functional currency.

Translating intercompany balances of monetary items from a functional currency into a reporting currency will create additional exchange transactions. These are now recorded in other comprehensive income. As a consequence, two differences are recorded on one business transaction due to accounting requirements. One is recorded at local level (so in separate financial statements) while the other one is recorded at group level in consolidated financial statements. A compensation of both effects is not allowed.

Recording exchange differences due to foreign exchange translations in profit & loss is something nobody likes as these differences have the potential to reduce or even disturb the profit of the period. The number of differences recorded depends on the volatility of exchange rate movements and the volume of the business executed in foreign currencies. From a single company's point of view, exchange differences can be avoided by always using the functional currency as the agreed transaction currency. This may work in some situations and in some markets. Nevertheless, some markets have agreed on defined currencies where an invoicing in a different currency is almost uncommon. A typical example is the oil industry that used the USD. Exchange differences in groups are also unavoidable if functional currencies of the group's companies differ. Nevertheless, differences can be minimized by applying clever netting systems.[10]

The only chance to avoid a dilution of profit due to exchange differences is an allocation of assets and liabilities to net investments. Other than business transactions focusing on trading in the group are **net investments** as they focus on the investment in foreign operations. As outlined before, only selected monetary items qualify as net investments. Exchange differences on the translation of net investments are always recorded in other comprehensive income according to IAS 21.32 at group level. They are reclassified to profit & loss only in the case of a full or partial disposal of the investment. If receivables are classified belonging to net investments and these receivables are settled, there is a partial disposal, which requires the reclassification of a portion of the foreign exchange translation account to profit & loss.

Investments in foreign investments may be subject to **hedging**. Hedging net investments is an appropriate method according to IAS 39.86c used to secure currency effects. Hedging effects are recorded in other comprehensive income as required by IAS 39.102a unless there is an ineffective portion. The ineffective portion has to be recognized in profit & loss. Like exchange differences, the portion of the hedged item recognized in other comprehensive income has to be allocated

---

[10] See chapter F -4.4.3 on page 284 regarding the application of netting systems.

to profit & loss upon the disposal of the net investment of the foreign operation. Further requirements on hedging are outlined in IFRIC 16:

- Hedging have to be applied to all net investments of foreign operations.
- Hedging is only applicable to currency effects between the functional currency of the foreign operations and the functional currency of the parent.
- Hedging is limited to the net assets. The hedged item is always equal or less than the carrying amount of the net assets.
- The hedging relationship can occur between any parent in the group and the foreign operation but only one hedge on the net assets is permitted in consolidated financial statements.

1.7.3. Disposal of foreign operations

Upon the disposal of a foreign operation, translation differences that are cumulated in equity have to be adjusted. The disposal can have different forms: sale of interests, liquidation and repayment of share capital are just some examples that classify as a disposal. IAS 21.48 requires a reclassification of exchange differences that relate to the foreign operation from other comprehensive income to profit & loss in these cases. In other words, equity is cleaned by effects that belong to that operation. The amount that has to be reclassified depends on the disposal and on the percentage of the interests in the foreign operations. Therefore, the recycling of foreign currency translations to profit & loss follows pro-rata to the disposal (relationship between the portion disposed to the total engagement).

There are two **exceptions** where a partial disposal always triggers a full reclassification of translation differences. These exceptions are based on the assumption that the companies will get a new status in the group:

- Loss of control of a subsidiary;
- A joint arrangement or an associate becomes a financial investment.

Due to the introduction of *IFRS 11 – Joint Arrangements*, a differentiation between a full and a partial disposal is made in IAS 21. The loss of control depends on the type of investment and the nature of the disposal. Even if a partial disposal (in terms of the percentage disposed) occurs, a full disposal of translation differences might be the case. IAS 21.48A – 48D and IAS 21.BC36 – BC40 provide details.

All requirements of IAS 21.48A – 48D regarding a reclassification of exchange differences from other comprehensive income to profit & loss will be reflected by the following matrix:

From	To			
	Financial Investment	Associate	Joint Venture	Subsidiary
Financial Investment	Partial			
Associate	Full	Partial		
Joint Arrangement	Full	Partial	Partial	
Subsidiary	Full	Full	Full	Partial

Tab. K-4 Matrix of reclassifications of exchange differences from other comprehensive income to profit & loss

A full or a partial disposal will always result in a decrease of the ownership in an interest in the foreign operation (so either a subsidiary, a joint arrangement or an associate) and in its carrying amount in that company. Therefore, if the parent writes down the carrying balance due to other reasons, a disposal is not given, as the percentage of ownership has not changed. Consequently, recycling exchange differences is prohibited. Examples of these write-downs are:

- Continuous losses;
- Impairment write-downs;
- Abandonment of business.

Dividends are not treated as disposals. IAS 21.BC35 clarifies that dividends distributed that relate to the "pre-group" era and exceed the distributable profit generated since the acquisition is always a dividend payment and not a disposal.

A **discussion** of the terms "partial disposal" and "proportionate share" as used in IAS 21.48C and IAS 21.BC40 can be found in literature. Some interpret these terms that a percentage of the portion disposed in relation to the total interest has to be applied to the reclassification of exchange differences. Others have the opinion that a qualitative interpretation and analysis is required of the items disposed to estimate the proportionate share. Such an issue may arise if a partial disposal occurs that has to consider goodwill belonging to a cash-generating unit. The disposal of goodwill related to the cash-generating unit will shift the proportionate share from a pure percentage disposal towards a different level.

The accounting of goodwill and non-controlling interests was discussed in section 1.7.1.

1.7.4. Currency translation in multi-level groups

A more complex issue is the translation into functional or presentation currencies in multi-level groups. Currency translations and the recording of exchange differences always follow the method of the consolidation. Therefore, a differentiation depending on the consolidation type is required.

- Chain or intermediate consolidation

   The chain consolidation consolidates the group step by step at each subgroup level, so a foreign currency translation has to occur at each level. All subsidiaries of a subgroup have to be converted to the functional currency of the parent of the subgroup. Exchange differences arising due to the conversion have to be recorded in other comprehensive income of that subgroup. The then consolidated financial statement of that subgroup is subject to a further currency conversion at the next level up. Again, exchange differences are recorded in other comprehensive income of that higher (sub-)group. These currency translations have to be executed until the ultimate parent consolidates its group. As a result, exchange differences arise at all levels of the group.

   Currency translations in chain consolidations will result in a different composition of exchange differences if different functional currencies of subgroups exist. To avoid these exchange differences, subgroups should have the same functional currencies the ultimate parent has. A special case is the situation in which exchange differences occur when a subsidiary uses the same functional currency as the ultimate parent but translations to functional currencies of several subgroups have to be executed. These exchange differences are system intrinsic and not avoidable.

- Simultaneous consolidation

    Applying simultaneous consolidation is much easier than a chain consolidation. All subsidiaries with its functional currencies are translated directly into the functional currency of the group and their exchange differences are recorded in other comprehensive income. The advantage of this translation is not only a simple handling but also less exchange differences because of one translation only.

The composition of exchange differences recorded in other comprehensive income due to the different consolidation systems has an impact on a disposal of a subsidiary or subgroup.

1.8. Classifications of balance sheet items for translations

The following list provides support for translation of balance sheet items into a functional currency.

Item	Category	Rate
Trade payables	Monetary	Closing
Trade receivables	Monetary	Closing
Accruals (expenses and income)	Monetary	Closing
Advances paid	Non-monetary	Historical
Advances received	Non-monetary	Historical
Allowances		
• for doubtful debts	Monetary	Closing
• for inventory obsolescence	Non-monetary	Historical
Bank balances	Monetary	Closing
Capital reserves	Non-monetary	Historical
Cash & cash equivalents	Monetary	Closing
Debts securities	Monetary	Closing
Deferred income	Non-monetary	Historical
Deferred taxes	Monetary	Historical
Deposits	Monetary	Closing
Employee benefit liabilities	Monetary	Closing
Depreciation	Non-monetary	Historical
Equity	Non-monetary	Historical
Finance leases (payables)	Monetary	Closing
Financial assets		
• Trading	Monetary	Closing
• Available for sale	Monetary / non-monetary	Closing
• Held to maturity	Monetary / non-monetary	Historical
Goodwill	Non-monetary	Historical

(continued)

Item	Category	Rate
Intangible assets	Non-monetary	Historical
Inventory	Non-monetary	Closing
Investment in associates	Non-monetary	Historical
Loans	Monetary	Closing
Non-controlling interests	Non-monetary	Historical
Other assets	Monetary / non-monetary	Closing / Historical
Other liabilities	Monetary / non-monetary	Closing / Historical
Prepayments		
• Refundable	Monetary	Closing
• Non-refundable	Non-monetary	Historical
Property, plant & equipment	Non-monetary	Historical
Provisions	Monetary	Closing
Retained earnings	Non-monetary	Historical
Revaluation surplus	Non-monetary	Historical
Taxes		
• Payable	Monetary	Closing
• Refundable	Monetary	Closing
Unfinished goods	Non-monetary	Closing

Tab. K-5   Classification of balance sheet items for foreign currency translations

2. DEFERRED TAXES IN GROUPS

2.1. Basics

2.1.1. The temporary concept

Deferred taxes are in integral element in the accounting of taxable transactions and items in financial statements. The relevant standard for accounting of deferred taxes is *IAS 12 – Income taxes*. The standard does not only apply to deferred taxes, it covers also the accounting for income taxes.

Accounting for deferred taxes is based on the **temporary concept** that uses differences of balance sheet items between their carrying amounts and tax bases. The differences are subject to calculating deferred taxes. While differences in groups have manifold reasons, a systematic view of the preparation of consolidated financial statements is necessary to cover all aspects. Due to the nature of financial statements, required adjustments and consolidations for group needs, differences may arise in different forms at each level. Differences at all levels can be divided into three types of difference:

- • Temporary differences
    These are time limited. Differences revert at a foreseeable time when the date and difference lapse can be determined. These differences have their origin in different accounting regulations of IFRS and tax laws. Both accounting regulation will lead to the same carrying amounts of balance sheet items after a defined period, as illustrated in the following example.

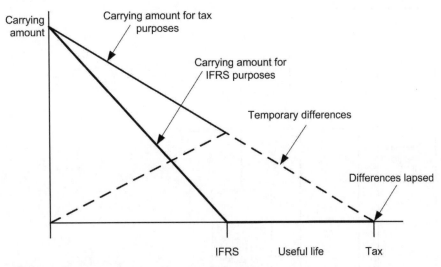

Fig. K-4   Example of temporary differences

Temporary differences are the core of the temporary concept.

- Quasi-permanent differences

  As a special type, these differences differ from temporary differences regarding the time of reversion. Quasi-permanent differences have usually an indefinite time. These differences have their origins in the recognition and measurement of balance sheet items that are not subject to regular depreciations and use impairment tests instead. Quasi-permanent differences are also subject to the temporary concept.

- Permanent differences

  Unlike temporary differences, these have no future reversion date and are not accounted for.

The **system** of accounting for deferred taxes uses temporary differences as a starting point. Based on these differences, deferred taxes are calculated and recorded either as deferred tax assets or deferred tax liabilities. These assets and liabilities are adjusted in subsequent Periods in proportion to the changes of temporary differences: no temporary differences, no deferred taxes.

The system described above applies to separate as well as consolidated financial statements. Therefore, it is not sufficient to focus on separate financial statements of subsidiaries and add them together. Instead, temporary differences at all **levels** in the group have to be considered when arriving at deferred taxes in consolidated financial statements:

- At local level based on the original transactions;
- At level I due to adjusted transactions for IFRS purposes;
- At level II due to the alignment to group accounting policies;
- At level III due to the recognition of additional assets and liabilities;
- At group level due to consolidation tasks.

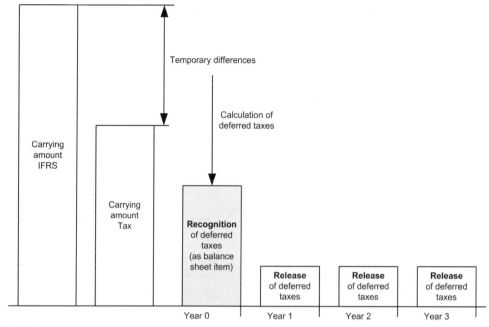

Fig. K-5   System of deferred taxes

To ensure that all differences are identified and considered, it is recommended to check temporary differences in the order they are formed level by level.

2.1.2. Accounting for deferred taxes – Recognition

Depending on the type of differences, deferred taxes are recognized either as assets or liabilities. The recognition follows the ordinary rules of the framework in recognizing assets and liabilities.

Deferred tax assets are recognized if:

- The carrying amount of assets under IFRS accounting is lower than its tax base.
- The carrying amount of debt and liabilities under IFRS accounting is higher than its tax base.
- An asset is not accounted for under IFRS rules.
- Debt and liabilities are not accounted for under tax regulations.
- There are tax losses that have to be accounted for.

Deferred tax liabilities are recognized if:

- The carrying amount of assets under IFRS accounting is higher than its tax base.
- The carrying amount of debt and liabilities under IFRS accounting is lower than its tax base.
- An asset is not accounted for under tax regulations.
- Debt and liabilities are not accounted for under IFRS rules.

The following figure summarizes the recognition of deferred tax items.

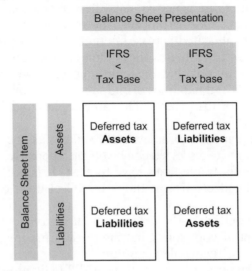

Fig. K-6 Deferred tax matrix

The general rule is a **recognition** of deferred tax assets and deferred tax liabilities through profit & loss. This rule applies to the initial and the subsequent recognition. A deviation of this principle is permitted for selected transactions only. In such cases, changes of the carrying balances are recorded either in other comprehensive income or directly in retained earnings. Transactions that require a profit neutral recording are

- The first time adoption of IFRS. All changes in deferred tax assets and liabilities are recorded as retained earnings.
- Financial instruments that are classified as held to maturity.
- Fixed and intangible assets that are accounted for using the revaluation method.
- Changes in pension plans.
- Foreign currency translations.

In addition to these general principles, dedicated rules prohibit the recognition of deferred tax items. IAS 12.15 (a) and 12.21 prohibit the recognition of temporary differences on goodwill. IAS 12.15 (b) prohibit the recognition of transactions that are not part of business combinations and that neither accounting nor taxable profit are affected.

Netting of deferred tax assets and liabilities require a special treatment. The default rule, as stated in IAS 7.74, is a separate presentation of deferred assets and liabilities. An exception to this rule is given, if current tax assets and liabilities belong to the same tax authority and there is an enforceable right of the company as the taxable entity to offset them. In such cases, deferred tax assets and liabilities can be netted. A netting is also possible for a set of entities that settle their tax obligation on a net basis or simultaneously. If conditions are met, deferred tax assets and liabilities can be netted, regardless of the timing of reversals of the underlying transactions. This netting rule allows only limited netting in groups if group companies are allocated across different tax legislations. Netting at local level and level I is easy to realize as they belong to the subsidiary. Netting on all other levels is usually not possible due to different tax authorities. This is because the valuation of assets and liabilities of the subsidiary is based on a different taxation base (so the one of the parent). The same applies to differences that arise at group level.

The offsetting of current tax assets and liabilities as one requirement for netting implies that income taxes levied can be offset. Therefore, either the same type of income taxes or offsettable taxes have to exist. It is not sufficient that a tax authority levies and collect taxes as they can collect taxes on behalf of various authorities.

An exception to netting is the taxation via tax groups. As one entity acts as the taxpayer for a set of companies, netting of deferred tax assets and liabilities can cover companies of the whole tax group.

Temporary differences may arise from a different presentation of balance sheet items compared to their presentation for tax purposes. The presentation can take place at different reporting positions, can be combined or netted with other balance sheet items. Regardless of the presentation, the carrying amount of balance sheet items and their tax bases have the same balances. As a consequence unreal temporary differences appear that have no economic background. Therefore, reclassifications are necessary to compensate and eliminate those false temporary differences.

2.1.3. Accounting for deferred taxes – Measurement

The measurement of temporary differences is based on the **tax rate** of that period when deferred tax assets are realized or settled according to IAS 12.47. Therefore, a future tax rate has to be applied. As such a tax rate is not foreseeable, the tax rate at the end of the period has to be applied that is enacted or substantially enacted by tax authorities or the government or parliament, or similar institutions.

Even if deferred taxes have a non-current character, IAS 12.53 prohibits the **discounting** of deferred tax assets and liabilities. The reason for this relief has its origin in the transactions that trigger temporary differences. To discount deferred tax assets and liabilities would require a discounting of each temporary difference by considering their individual timing. The IASB's opinion is that such a requirement would be impracticable or highly complex that led to the discounting relief.

The measurement of temporary differences in groups requires – depending on the level and types of difference – a company specific view. The reason for this dedicated view is the use of company individual tax rates for all temporary differences of adjusted separate financial statements. In addition temporary differences at group level will require the application of the parent's tax rate.

2.2. Differences

As mentioned several times, temporary differences follow the underlying transactions. The adjustment of these transactions in groups at different levels will also trigger differences and deferred taxes at each level. These differences are called "inside basis differences" as they compare the carrying amounts of balance sheet items with their tax bases. Depending on the level and type of difference, specific tasks have to be performed.

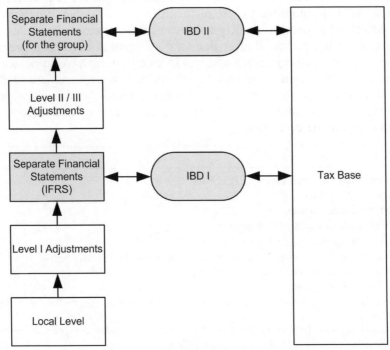

Fig. K-7   Inside basis differences – scheme

In addition to differences of subsidiaries, differences at parent level that relate to the investment in subsidiaries arise. These differences are called "outside basis differences" and are a mandatory accounting item of deferred taxes.

Well-managed companies are able to track temporary differences asset by asset at all levels.

2.2.1. *Inside basis differences I*

Deferred taxes of separate financial statements are recorded and based on temporary differences at local level and – if necessary – adjusted at level I to comply with IFRS rules. They are also called "inside basis differences I" for group purposes. Differences are based on and driven by the operating activities of the company and can cover the parent and its subsidiaries. As these differences are recorded at local level, the tax rules applicable for the company have to be used in determining temporary differences. Due to the operating activities, differences can occur in almost all balance sheet items. Chapter K2.4 provides a table with the most important reasons for differences of these balance sheet items.[11]

While deferred taxes have to be recorded in local financial statements, they have an impact on the process of preparing local accounts. The preparation process requires with a preliminary close of the accounts available. Furthermore, the tax base has to be known to identify temporary differences. In some legislations, tax returns are often prepared after financial statements have been prepared. In such cases, a process change is necessary: tax calculations have to be available in parallel to the preparation of financial statements. If tax returns are prepared by an external advisor, the advisor has to be integrated into the process of preparing financial statements. Therefore, the following steps are recommended in preparing and accounting deferred taxes.

Step	Task
1)	Preparation of a preliminary IFRS close
2)	Update of tax bases
3)	Differences calculation
4)	Elimination of permanent differences
5)	Reclassifications
6)	Determination of temporary differences, if required by transactions
7)	Determination of the appropriate tax rate
8)	Calculation of deferred taxes
9)	Calculation of deferred taxes due to tax losses of the period and tax losses carried forward
10)	Classification of deferred taxes: through profit & loss or other comprehensive income
11)	Adjustment of deferred tax assets and liabilities
12)	Preparation of the final IFRS financial statements

Tab. K-6 Steps in preparing deferred taxes

The calculation of temporary differences and deferred taxes subject to inside basis differences is based on the tax legislation the company resides. A detailed calculation of differences by balance sheet item is necessary because the allocation of deterred taxes, either assets or liabilities, to balance sheet items is a required disclosure of IAS 12.81 and 12.82. The accounting is based on a calculation where all effects can be combined into a maximum of four journal entries. The journal entries depend on the recognition.

---

[11] See page 677 for the table.

Journal entries		Classification
dr.	Deferred tax assets	Profit & Loss
cr.	Deferred tax earnings	
dr.	Deferred tax expenses	Profit & Loss
cr.	Deferred tax liabilities	
dr.	Deferred tax asset	Other comprehensive income
cr.	Equity[12]	
dr.	Equity	Other comprehensive income
cr.	Deferred tax liabilities	

Example

In its opening IFRS balance sheet, Solenta has recorded several items with a deviating tax base. As the opening balance sheet is part of Solenta's separate financial statements, the differences in the bases have to be considered as deferred tax assets or deferred tax liabilities. Subject to the accounting are those items that have been remeasured according to fulfil IFRS requirements and those items that require a recording of deferred tax assets or liabilities due to local GAAP. The following table lists those balance sheet items that have been remeasured to comply with IFRS.[13]

Item	IFRS carrying amount	Tax base	Differences	Deferred tax impact	
				Assets	Liabilities
Intangible assets	4,061	3,448	613		(183)
Property, plant & equipment	59,432	52,660	6,775		(2,019)
Trade receivables	21,701	21,275	426		(127)
Deferred items	0	5	(5)	2	
Pension provisions	(7,200)	(6,330)	(870)	259	
Other provisions	(2,592)	(2,928)	336		(100)
Total			(5,107)	261	(2,429)

The differences for assets and liabilities are calculated by subtracting the tax base from the carrying amount. Positive differences constitute deferred tax liabilities while negative ones deferred tax assets. The differences are multiplied by the tax rate to arrive at the amounts to be recorded. The tax rate to be applied is the local tax rate of Solenta, 29.8%.

2.2.2 Inside basis differences II

The adjustment of separate financial statements by group accounting policies will initiate additional differences. Due to the accounting at level II temporary differences that relate to these adjustments are also called "inside basis differences II" for group purposes. In addition to adjustments for group accounting purposes, inside basis differences II often also cover the effects of level III. By including items that belong to the subsidiary and measured from the group's point of view,

---

[12] "Equity" acts as a placeholder for the accounts to be used. Such accounts can be revaluation surplus, retained earnings or similar accounts.

[13] See example on page 122 regarding the underlying items.

all temporary differences that belong to a subsidiary are bundled into these inside basis differences. The general principles in determining and measuring temporary differences have to be applied to this level as well. Measuring temporary differences means that the tax base of the subsidiary has to be applied. The calculation of deferred tax assets and liabilities has to follow the same procedure like inside basis differences I. They are needed for disclosures and the recording. The journal entries are equal to entries of inside basis differences I.

Journal entries		Classification
dr.	Deferred tax assets	Profit & Loss
cr.	Deferred tax earnings	
dr.	Deferred tax expenses	Profit & Loss
cr.	Deferred tax liabilities	
dr.	Deferred tax asset	Other comprehensive income
cr.	Equity[14]	
dr.	Equity	Other comprehensive income
cr.	Deferred tax liabilities	

Example

Those items, that are uncovered during the purchase price allocation of the Solenta acquisition, are subject to the recording of deferred tax assets and liabilities. They have to be recorded on the same level the underlying assets and liabilities are recorded on. The following table lists those balance sheet items and their balances that are identified and measured during the purchase price allocation.[15]

Item	IFRS carrying amount	Tax base	Differences	Deferred tax impact	
				Assets	Liabilities
Patents	17,800	0	17,800		(5,304)
Customer base	3,000	0	3,000		(6,705)
Pending orders	22,500	0	22,500		(1,162)
Property (land)	900	0	900		(268)
Financial assets	9	0	9		(3)
Bad debt allowances	220	0	220		(65)
Environmental pollution	(3,000)	0	(3,000)	894	
Patent infringement	(8,000)	0	(8,000)	2,384	
Total				3,278	(13,507)

While the listed items are unknown for taxation, the tax base is always zero. Accordingly, deferred tax assets and liabilities are measured based on the carrying amount of the underlying assets and liabilities. Positive carrying amounts constitute deferred tax liabilities while negative ones deferred tax assets. Their carrying amounts are multiplied by the tax rate to arrive at the amounts to be recorded. The tax rate to be applied is the local tax rate of Solenta, 29.8%

---

[14] "Equity" acts as a placeholder for the accounts to be used. Such accounts can be revaluation surplus, retained earnings or similar accounts.

[15] See the various examples in chapter E -3.4 regarding the underlying items and their measurement starting on page 152.

2.2.3. *Outside basis differences*

Outside basis differences reflect the parent's view on its subsidiaries, branches, associates and joint ventures through its investments in them. They are the third element of deferred taxes in groups and are established at parent and group level. Due to the nature of these investments, two comparisons ensure to detect temporary differences:

- Investments in subsidiaries, branches and associates or investments in joint ventures of the parent and its tax base;
- Group's investments in subsidiaries, branches and associates or investments in joint ventures and the parent's tax base.

Accounting for these temporary differences is defined in IAS 12.38, as long as certain conditions are not met which prohibit this type of accounting. These conditions focus on the control of the parent to influence the timing of difference reversals and the probability that the differences will not reverse in the foreseeable future. These conditions are always met in the case of subsidiaries, because the parent can control temporary differences by deciding on dividend distributions. Therefore, non-recording of deferred taxes for subsidiaries is mandatory. If a subsidiary is scheduled for sale and there is an intention from management to do so, deferred taxes relating to outside basis differences have to be recorded. The same applies to associated companies. Even if significant influence is given the parent does not have control over the associate and can therefore not control the timing of difference reversals.

If conditions are not met, deferred taxes due to differences with the outside have to be recognized. Depending on the legal form of the parent and its subsidiaries, temporary differences may vary in separate as well as consolidated financial statements.

In separate financial statements, legal forms of the subsidiary are the subject of estimating outside basis differences. While partnerships have to use the taxable partner contribution accounts of each partner, corporations use the tax bases of assets and liabilities. Typical examples of outside basis differences are:

- Extraordinary depreciations that are non-tax-deductible;
- Allocation of a subsidiary as discontinued unit according to IFRS 5.15 (and therefore measurement at the lower of its carrying amount and fair value);
- Classification of a subsidiary as available for sale;
- Write downs for tax purposes that are not accounted for under IFRS;
- Dividend distributions that are non-tax-deductible in partial or in full.

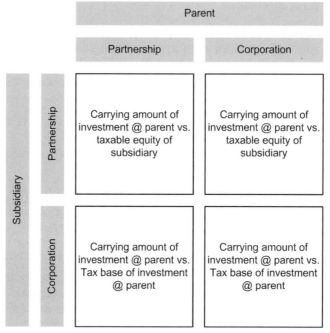

Fig. K-8 Outside basis differences of the parent

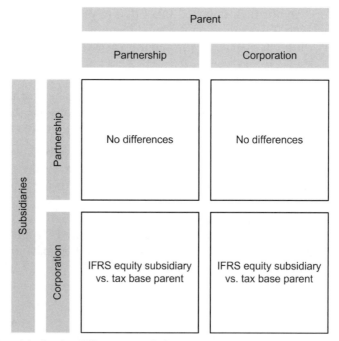

Fig. K-9 Outside basis differences of the group

In groups, only corporations are subject to outside basis differences. Due to the tax treatment of partnerships, which is identical to IFRS, differences cannot arise. According to the one-entity theory – the breakup of investments in subsidiaries into assets and liabilities – net assets of the subsidiary have to be compared to their tax bases at group level. This is particularly important in the case of a disposal.

2.3. Special cases

Some transactions, at local and group levels require dedicated analysis as they may trigger temporary differences that are not so obvious at first sight. Transaction types vary as they can be initiated for commercial or tax reasons, or by the measurement of assets and liabilities. The following items represent typical transactions initiating temporary differences.

2.3.1. *Intangible assets and goodwill*

Intangible assets with an indefinite life, according to IAS 38.88, are subject to an annual impairment test as they are not depreciated on a regular base. The test according to IAS 36 has "to ensure that the assets should be carried at no more than their recoverable amount". The tax base of intangible assets with an indefinite life is usually measured at cost. Typical examples of such kinds of assets are internet domain names and non-expireable concessions. Due to the nature and the accounting of these intangible assets, quasi-permanent differences exist, which will change every time adjustments are made to the carrying amount based on the results of the impairment test. Their tax base will not change.

Those intangible assets with an indefinite life that are acquired as part of a business combination require a dedicated view. If these assets are already accounted for by the acquired company, a tax base may exist so that differences can be calculated based on the carrying amounts. If assets require a step-up in their carrying amounts, differences are calculated on the carrying amounts plus their step-up. If assets are recognized as part of the application of the acquisition method, no tax base exists. These assets, as well as any step-up of assets, are recorded as level III items calculating deferred taxes on the full carrying amount. In addition to the general recognition principles, intangible assets that are measured by applying the income approach have to consider a tax amortization benefit. This tax amortization benefit considers future tax advantages due to depreciation. Such an approach may not work for the assets discussed due to infinite life. Therefore, an adequate useful life has to be assumed.

Goodwill is treated similarly to intangible assets. Like intangible assets with an indefinite life, goodwill is also subject to regular impairment test. Nevertheless, as goodwill represents the residual amount in a business combination it is not subject to deferred taxes according to IAS 12.21 (b).

2.3.2. *Unused tax credits and tax losses*

Unused tax credits and tax losses are assets that have to be accounted for. They reflect tax reliefs that are deductible in future periods. As credits and losses can only be utilized against future profits, the company has to prove that a use is probable. The reason for this proof is justified in the history of those tax losses. Losses arise from non-performance of corporations. The corporation therefore has to show a way to turn the business from a loss into a profit situation – by planning for the future. As uncertainty increases with increasing time, the planning should cover a period of three to five years only. This is a period where a reliable assumption can be made with a manageable risk exposure. The planning has to consider the situation of the company, its product portfolio, the market and market position. Auditors will usually check if the planning is consistent to internal and external facts and give a true and fair view of the planned future using realistic assumptions.

> The tax planning has to be consistent with the company's business planning!

The planning is used to capitalize deferred assets that relate to tax credits and tax losses and, therefore, needs to cover the next few foreseeable periods. It should consider all tax aspects. IAS 12.34 requires recognizing deferred taxes only to the extent that they will be utilized (so that future tax profits will be available).

To calculate deferred taxes due to tax credits and tax losses the application of a two-step calculation is recommended. In the first step, expected tax burdens of the planning period are calculated without the consideration of any tax credits and tax losses. In the second step, the same calculation will be executed, considering tax credits and tax losses this time. The difference between both calculations reflects the maximum recoverable taxes that can be capitalized. If tax credits and tax losses are less than the maximum recoverable taxes, the whole amount can be capitalized. Otherwise the capitalization is limited to the calculated maximum recoverable amount. The result is an unrecognized deferred tax asset that is subject to an annual reassessment. The reassessment has to consider any changes in parameters, assumptions and the underlying data. Once a revised planning is available, the above described calculation has to be executed to verify that any additional unused deferred tax assets may be recorded or not.

The accounting for deferred tax assets for tax credits and tax losses is treated in a similar way as deferred tax assets for temporary differences. While these items do not depend on other balance sheet items, simple journal entries fulfil the need to account for tax credits and tax losses.

Journal entries		Comment
dr.	Deferred tax assets	Consideration of tax credits / tax losses
cr.	Deferred tax earnings	
dr.	Deferred tax expenses	Use of tax credits / tax losses
cr.	Deferred tax assets	

Special attention is required for business combinations. IAS 12.68 requires a dedicated accounting of deferred tax assets due to tax losses carried forward:

Time / Date	Subject	Task
Acquisition date	Recording of deferred tax asset	Recording by reduction of goodwill's carrying balance
Measurement period (12 months)	a) New information available about facts and circumstances existed at the balance sheet date	Adjustment of deferred tax asset by adjustment of goodwill's carrying balance
	b) New information but goodwill is zero	Adjustment of deferred tax asset through profit & loss
After measurement period	New information available about facts and circumstances existed at the balance sheet date	Adjustment of deferred tax asset through profit & loss

Tab. K-7 Steps in recording deferred tax assets as part of business combinations

2.3.3. *Foreign currency translation*

If a subsidiary – or in general a foreign operation – has a functional currency that differs from the reporting currency of the parent, a foreign currency translation is required. IAS 21.39 defines the application of the procedures that record translation differences as part of equity with an impact on other comprehensive income. Due to this recording differences qualify as outside basis differences. A deferred tax asset or liability has to be recognized, assuming recognition criteria are met.

The accounting of deferred taxes on foreign currency differences is limited by IAS 12.39 and 12.40. If, in the foreseeable future, dividend payments and the subsidiary's sale are not expected, recognition of deferred taxes is prohibited – even if the parent can control the reversal of timing differences.

A challenge is the identification of foreign currency translation differences; they belong to balance sheet items that already vary due to increases and decreases, acquisitions and disposals and timing issues. To identify exchange rate fluctuations, an appropriate accounting structure is necessary considering the group structure and systems used in the accounting department. If the accounting systems do not support a foreign currency translation, a manual conversion is necessary to identify their effects.[16]

While foreign currency translation differences are recorded in equity, deferred tax assets and liabilities have to follow them. Therefore, the recording is compared to other temporary differences slightly different.

a) Temporary differences trigger deferred tax assets

Journal entries		Classification
dr.	Deferred tax assets	Recording of deferred tax asset
cr.	Other comprehensive income[17]	
dr.	Other comprehensive income	Release of deferred tax asset
cr.	Deferred tax assets	

---

[16] See chapter K -1 on page 632 regarding the procedure of manual foreign currency translations.

[17] This acts as a placeholder for the dedicated deferred tax account in equity (usually somewhere in retained earnings).

b) Temporary differences trigger deferred tax liabilities

Journal entries		Classification
dr.	Other comprehensive income	Recording of deferred tax liability
cr.	Deferred tax liability	
dr.	Deferred tax liability	Release of deferred tax liability
cr.	Other comprehensive income	

2.3.4. *Tax groups*

A tax group or fiscal unity is an instrument to optimize the tax position of a set of companies. Tax groups are linked very closely to national tax rules and have to fulfil a set of requirements before they will be accepted by tax authorities. Some tax legislations require a profit & loss transfer agreement that requires the companies of a tax group to transfer any profits and losses to a defined company – usually the parent or controlling company.[18] Within a tax group, this company acts as the taxpayer. It is in charge of filing tax returns and submitting tax payments for all companies of the tax group. The calculation of taxable profits and losses, as well as the calculation of related taxes, rests with each company of the tax group. The advantage of such a system is the compensation of taxable profits of companies with taxable losses of other companies within the tax group to reduce the tax burden. Additional tax benefits may arise depending on tax regulations.

Tax groups can be initiated to cover different tax types, the best known being income and value added tax (VAT). Tax groups subject to other types of tax may exist as well; they are not that important for groups.[19] In the context of groups, both mentioned tax types are important. Income tax is the only relevant tax type that triggers temporary differences. VAT groups instead have an impact on intercompany transactions only. Therefore, tax groups dealing with VAT have to be considered as one part of the elimination of intercompany transactions and balances.[20]

The reasons for temporary differences due to tax groups vary. Usually, they are based on profit and loss allocations within the tax group and on dividend distributions. Even if profits (or losses) are distributed fully in the tax group, some profits may rest with a company in the tax group due to local accounting requirements by IFRS or local GAAP. A similar case might be dividend distributions to owners that classify as non-controlling interests. Such payments are often based on contractual agreements between shareholders or on legal requirements. Therefore, appropriate adjustments may be necessary in addition to account for any differences. Payments to non-controlling interests qualify as permanent differences while profit allocations within the group are treated as temporary differences. As temporary and permanent differences are mingled, appropriate procedures have to be in place to isolate the permanent ones.

---

[18] The parent company of a group is not necessarily the controlling company of a tax group. Larger groups may have several tax groups on various levels.

[19] And therefore not discussed yet.

[20] Eliminations of intercompany balances due to income taxes exist as well!

Tax groups do not necessarily equal groups. As tax groups are totally independent tax vehicles, a detailed view of the interactions between a tax group and a group is required. Two **allocation types** need to be considered:

- Full integration into the group

    This is a simple case. All companies of the tax group are also part of the group and the consolidated companies. The controlling company can record all tax effects of the tax group that will be considered in preparing consolidated financial statements.

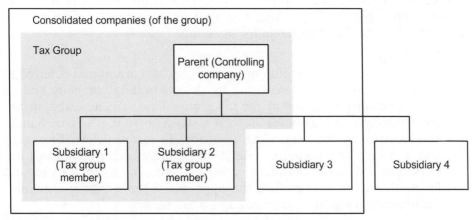

Fig. K-10   Tax group fully integrated into a group

- Partial integration into the group

    This is more complex. Such scenarios may occur if companies are not considered as consolidated companies due to materiality or other reasons, even if they belong to the group. A partial integration requires a cut-off of income and deferred taxes of the tax group between the part that belongs to the group and the consolidated companies and the companies that are not consolidated.

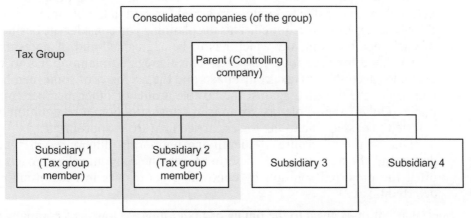

Fig. K-11   Tax group partially integrated into a group

In larger groups, tax groups may be arranged in **tax chains** where a controlling company of a tax group may be a member of another tax group. This kind of structure is often used to realize different tax effects at different levels in a group. This requires a group with several levels, which is often realized by holding companies that act as intermediaries. Chains of tax groups are linked to several requirements by tax authorities. If one or more requirements are not fulfilled, either there is no tax group or all tax groups are treated as one. Both cases would result in a failed tax structure that may lead to tax disadvantages.

IFRS does not cover **accounting** for tax groups or the treatment of deferred tax assets and liabilities. In practice, two approaches account for deferred tax assets and liabilities of companies in the tax group.

- Formal approach

  In line with the definition of a tax group, all current and deferred tax assets and liabilities are recorded by the controlling company and not by any member company of the tax group. This is because the member companies have no tax bases for their assets as any tax issues are handled and recorded by the controlling company. To record deferred tax assets and liabilities all temporary differences of the member companies have to be assigned to the controlling company and considered in its separate financial statement. Therefore, this approach requires extensive auxiliary calculations to ensure consistency and transparency.

- Economical approach

  This approach (also called the stand-alone method) treats each member company of the tax group individually. It assumes that there is no tax group and that each member company has its own temporary differences. Calculated deferred tax assets and liabilities of each member company are assigned to the controlling company in the next step which accounts for them. The calculation is based on the tax rate of the controlling company.

  If some member companies are in a loss situation, deferred tax assets that relate to tax losses carried forward have to be considered in preparing the tax position of the tax group. To decide on any capitalization of deferred tax assets due to tax losses carried forward, a tax planning across the whole tax group is required. This tax planning will consider the business of each member company which has to be aggregated and, if necessary, consolidated for tax group purposes. The aggregated planning has to be expanded according to tax group effects and the tax losses of some member companies are offsetted against the taxable profits of other member companies. Only if the whole tax group is in a loss situation, a recognition of deferred tax assets due to tax losses carried forward is appropriate.

  Due to the procedure of identifying temporary differences in a tax group and the accounting of deferred taxes, the economical approach is often the preferred solution by controlling companies in accounting of deferred taxes.

Special attention is given to the **timing** of tax groups. As long as a company is a member of a tax group, it has to follow the rules of that group. Therefore, tax issues that relate to transactions prior to the formation of tax-groups may have to be re-evaluated depending on the approach applied. In applying the formal approach, deferred tax assets and liabilities that related to temporary differences before the formation of the group, have to be released. These differences have to be recorded by the controlling company using the tax rate of this company. In applying the economical approach, deferred tax assets and liabilities that relate to temporary differences before the formation of the tax group stay as they are. Most fiscal legislations require a specific treatment of tax losses carried forward. If they exist before the formation of the tax group tax losses carried forward are usually frozen during the membership to a tax group. They revive after the termination of the tax group. Therefore, deferred tax assets that relate to these pre-tax groups have to be released.

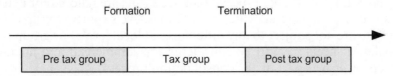

Fig. K-12 Timing of tax groups

> Have documentation regarding pre-tax losses available if it is foreseeable that the subsidiary might leave the group at a later stage.

Tax groups also impact the **netting** of deferred assets and liabilities. As the controlling company is in charge as the tax debtor, all deferred tax items of the tax group are subject to netting. The netting considers not only all member companies of the tax group it also considers all levels and is not limited to one level only.

2.3.5. Partnerships

Partnerships have – in contrast to corporations – a set of special tax issues that have to be considered in determining temporary differences. As partnerships are taxed on the owner level for income taxes instead of on the partnership level, tax authorities often consider additional items that impact the profit attributable to the partners. Usually, these items have their origins in uncovered and accounted former hidden reserves, assets and liabilities that are owned by the partner but are used as necessary assets and similar issues. Adjusting these items may result in an increase or decrease of taxable profit. Such practices are unknown by IFRS accounting.

Balance sheet enhancements carry valuation adjustments of the partnership's assets that are directly allocated to partners; there is one balance sheet enhancement per partner. Valuation adjustments are established every time a change in the partnership structure occurs, either due to the retirement of a partner or the acceptance of a new partner. In such cases any hidden reserves or burdens of assets have to be uncovered because of the fair value assignment to all partners. The valuation adjustments have to be developed in subsequent periods and considered as one part of the taxable profits of each partner. For IFRS accounting, balance sheet items are already accounted for by using fair value principles. Therefore, these balance sheet enhancements are not required for IFRS accounting. In determining temporary differences, a comparison of the balance sheet with the balance sheet for tax purposes and its balance sheet enhancements is required. Deferred tax assets and liabilities based on these temporary differences are recognized only for those taxes where the partnership (and therefore not the partners) acts as the taxpayer. Typical examples of such taxes are commercial taxes.

Partnerships as subsidiaries in groups require an enhanced tax calculation. Profits of the partnership are taxable by the parent company. Therefore, balance sheet enhancements that belong to the parent company have to be considered for determining temporary differences for income taxes.

Special balance sheets carry assets and liabilities that are owned by dedicated partners. They are considered as required items of the partnership for tax purposes by tax authorities. These special balance sheets are ignored for deferred tax purposes because they are allocated to different levels (partner vs. partnership), and therefore are not subject to any differences at local level. For group purposes, special balance sheets have to be considered for commercial and income taxes. Both effects reverse as part of the consolidation process.

Temporary differences and deferred taxes of partnerships can be summarized:

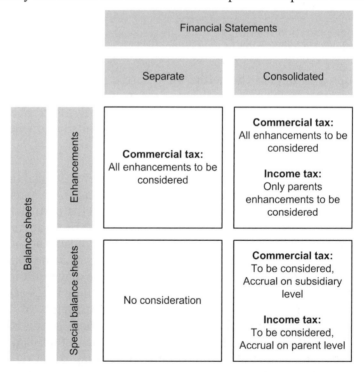

Fig. K-13 Combinations of temporary differences of partnerships

2.3.6. Associates

The accounting of investments in associates, their business transactions and the integration in the group will trigger differences between the carrying amounts of investments in associates (both, on parent and at group level) and other items in consolidated financial statements and their corresponding tax bases. Therefore, the accounting of deferred tax assets and liabilities is influenced by several issues at several levels. In fact, three levels need to be considered:

- The associate itself

    While the measurement of assets and liabilities follow IFRS accounting rules, the associate itself has to determine differences between the carrying amounts of assets and liabilities and their corresponding tax bases. Based upon these differences, a deferred taxation takes place. The accounting for deferred tax assets and liabilities therefore follows the standard procedures every company has to apply.

- The parent

    Investments in associates held by a parent qualify for an accounting for deferred tax assets or liabilities as the differences between the carrying amount of an investment in associates and their tax bases are treated as outside basis differences. Therefore, the standard accounting for outside basis differences has to be applied as discussed in chapter 2.2.3.[21] Nevertheless, some specialities exist for associates that require special attention.

    According to IAS 12.42, the status of an associate establishes only significant influence but not control. Therefore, the parent is not able to control the dividend policy of the associate. This requires the recording of a deferred tax liability. Nevertheless, a recording of a deferred tax liability is not possible if there are arrangements to include a non-distribution agreement in the foreseeable future.

- The group

    Due to the accounting of investment and business transactions in associates two types of deferred tax require dedicated attention. These items exist at group level and are often established due to consolidation tasks.

    - Intrinsic

        Deferred tax assets and liabilities are **part of the equity value** of an investment in an associate at group level. They are established as part of the initial purchase price allocation and the one-line consolidation. Deferred tax assets and liabilities are remeasured in subsequent consolidations due to changes of the carrying amount of the underlying assets and liabilities that are also part of the equity value. The underlying assets and liabilities are created due to the application of a purchase price allocation. These items are usually hidden reserves and burden and non-accounted assets that are accounted for on a pro-rata basis.

---

[21] See page 665 for details.

- Extrinsic

Deferred tax assets and liabilities can be established due to transactions between group companies and associates. These items are recorded **separately from the equity value** of the investment in associates and are accounted for at group level only. A typical example of deferred tax assets and liabilities is the adjustment of inventory by unrealized profits that result from upstream transactions.

2.3.7. Restructuring

A restructuring is often initiated by management to adjust the structure of a group to market demands, to optimize tax positions in the group or to realize hidden reserves due to dividend distributions. From an accounting point of view, a restructuring does not have an impact on consolidated financial statements because an internal relocation of assets and liabilities does not impact its external presentation. Nevertheless, restructuring may have an impact on the tax positions of all companies involved in a restructuring. The reason for this impact is initiated by tax regulations. Restructurings can be realized by using various options for taxation, e.g. a revaluation of assets and liabilities. The temporary differences arising from restructurings are almost inside basis differences.

As restructurings may have long-term effects, a simulation of all impacts in the current and subsequent periods is recommended to understand all tax implications. Depending on the intention of the restructuring, its volume and the involvement of (several) fiscal legislations tax effects may have various consequences. In such cases, detailed further analyses are necessary.

2.4. Tax reconciliation

A tax reconciliation is a disclosure requirement defined in IAS 12.81 (c). The reconciliation is used to explain any differences between actual and expected tax expenses. The expected tax expense is based on the net profit of the period by applying the current tax rate. All effects that have a tax impact have to be considered in reconciling tax expenses to the net profit of the period. As this tax reconciliation is required for the consolidated statement of income, all tax effects of all group companies have to be considered. To capture all tax effects, a tax reporting is required that requires subsidiaries to disclose details on local taxes and their fiscal legislation.

The preparation of a tax reconciliation in a group can be achieved in several ways. It is recommended that each company of the group prepares a tax reconciliation. This should be part of the tax reporting package. The tax reconciliations of all subsidiaries are aggregated and – if necessary – consolidated.

It is recommended to structure the tax reconciliation into logical sections. In practice, the following sections are applied by most companies:

- Deviations from the taxable base;
- Tax rate deviations;
- Deferred tax assets;
- Aperiodic effects;
- Other effects.

All tax effects that may have an impact on tax expenses have to be allocated to one of these categories. Depending on the fiscal legislation, additional tax effects have to be considered.

Item	Section
Changes due to foreign tax rates	Tax rate deviations
Depreciations on non-tax deductible items	Taxable base
Effects of changes in commercial and similar tax rates	Tax rate deviations
Effects of changes in income tax rates	Tax rate deviations
Effects of tax audits	Aperiodic effects
Impairment effects of equity consolidation	Taxable base
Impairment of tax losses carried forward	Deferred tax assets
Local taxes	Tax rate deviations
Non-recording	Deferred tax assets
Non tax deductible expenses	Taxable base
Prepayments for future years recognized in P&L	Aperiodic effects
Tax credits	Taxable base
Taxes of previous years	Aperiodic effects
Tax reimbursement due to tax losses carried back	Aperiodic effects
Tax-free dividends	Taxable base
Tax-free earnings	Taxable base
Write-downs, write-ups of remeasured assets	Taxable base
Write-ups	Deferred tax assets

Tab. K-8   ABC of elements of tax reconciliations

In groups that do not maintain a track record of tax effects per subsidiary, some deviation between actual and expected tax expenses may not be explainable. Such unexplained differences are often combined as compound items belonging to other effects and should not exceed 5% of expected tax expenses.

2.5. Classification of deferred tax elements

The classification of elements subject to deferred taxes depends on the tax treatment. Most fiscal legislations have dedicated rules and regulation regarding the accounting and acceptance of financial statements. Therefore, each transaction and balance sheet item has to be considered individually by both, the application of IFRS and tax regulations. The following classifications may help in identifying potential differences between IFRS and tax bases of assets and liabilities.

Item	Type	Additional explanation
Accruals	Temporary	Reasons for temporary differences: Recognition and timing of accruals.
Development costs, capitalization	Temporary	Only development expenses are capitalizable, no research expenses. Most fiscal legislations prohibit the capitalization of development expenses, therefore temporary differences.
Foreign currency translations	Temporary	Only if foreign operations with a different functional currency than the parent are integrated into consolidated financial statements.

(continued)

Item	Type	Additional explanation
Goodwill	Usually temporary	Established through business combinations. Subject to impairment test.
Grants relating to assets	Temporary	IAS 20.24: Either a deduction of the carrying amount of the assets or recognition of deferred income. Temporary differences if recorded as other income for tax purposes, subject to tax regulations.
Intangible assets acquired, non-depreciable	Quasi-permanent	Subject to impairment tests. Reasons for temporary differences: Measurement, residual value, impairments.
Intangible assets acquired, depreciable	Temporary	Reasons for temporary differences: Measurement, useful life, residual value.
Inventory	Temporary	Reasons for temporary differences: Measurement (cost elements, particularly for work in progress and finished goods), haircuts, lower of cost or net realizable value principle as defined in IAS 2.9.
Liabilities	Temporary	Reasons for temporary differences: Recognition and discounting using different discount rates.
Non-controlling interests	Permanent	Dividend payments to non-controlling interests are out of scope as such differences do not revert.
Pension provisions	Temporary	Reasons for temporary differences: Underlying assumptions and parameters, pension plans and other facts. Tax regulations often have dedicated rules for accepting pension plans as tax deductible.
Property, plant and equipment	Temporary	Reasons for temporary differences: Measurement (cost elements), depreciation methods, useful life, residual value.
		IFRS specifics: Component approach, revaluation model.
		Additional tax specifics need to be considered.
PPE: Grants	No recognition or temporary	Deduction of the carrying amount of the asset. Temporary differences if treated differently for tax purposes.
PPE: Leasing	No recognition or temporary	Applicable to finance leases only.[22] Financial legislations usually have own regulations on leasing.
Receivables	Temporary	Reasons for temporary differences: Impairment of receivables, lump-sum allowances.
Securities	Temporary	Reasons for temporary differences: Application of fair value measurement according to IAS 39.46 vs. carrying amounts according to tax regulations.
Special items	Temporary	Relate to tax regulations. No recording under IFRS.
Subsidiaries	Temporary or permanent	Driven by tax regulations: Tax exemptions, special tax treatments. Additional effects may arise by applying the equity method and dividend recognition or distributions.
Tax groups	Temporary	Applies to profit allocation and dividend distribution in the tax group.
Tax liabilities, current	No deferred item	In case of different presentation form: reclassification only.
Provisions	Temporary, permanent or no deferred item	Reasons for temporary differences: Discount rates, recognition criteria.

Tab. K-9 ABC of deferred tax elements

---

[22] The current standard will be replaced. At the published date of this book the IASB has published ED/2013/6 as a draft version of the final standard.

3. CASH FLOW STATEMENTS

3.1. Basics

IAS 1.10 defines a set of four statements and the notes as the mandatory elements that have to be presented in financial statements:

- Statement of financial position;
- Statement of comprehensive income;
- Statement of changes in equity;
- Statement of cash flows.

All statements are presented equally next to each other. As the IFRS do not differentiate between separate and consolidated financial statements, a cash flow statement is required at group level as part of consolidated financial statements where the same accounting rules have to be applied as for separate financial statements. These rules, particularly the presentation of cash flow statements, its structure and content are defined in *IAS 7 – Cash Flow Statements*.

The purpose of the cash flow statement is to provide information about the changes in cash in a structured way. The statement is therefore a reconciliation of changes in cash on bank accounts between the end of the last and current period. IAS 7.10 defines three major **categories** that have to be presented within the cash flow statement:

- Operating activities

    The main focus of this category is to inform about cash flows that arise from the ongoing business. It is an indicator about the current performance of a company in generating cash. Operating activities include all transactions that are derived from revenue producing activities of an entity. These revenue producing activities may either result in a profit and loss or changes in current balance sheet items. IAS 7.14 lists a set of examples that belong to operating activities.

- Investing activities

    Cash flows from investing activities inform about the intensity in investments during the period. These investments are an indicator about the investment in the future and the potential ability of the company to generate future cash flows. Investing activities include all transactions that change non-current balance sheet items, particularly intangible assets, property, plant & equipment and financial assets of all kind. Changes include the acquisition as well as disposals of assets. IAS 7.16 lists a set of examples that belong to investing activities.

- Financing activities

    Cash flows from financing activities inform about the ability of the company to repay its debt in future periods. It also provides information about the financing of the company through debt and equity as well as any debt settlements. Therefore, financing activities include all capital transactions of the company. IAS 7.16 lists a set of examples that belong to investing activities.

The presentation of the contents of each category (line items) is not covered by IAS 7. This gap enables preparers to define the items to be presented in each category as it is appropriate for their business. An analysis of published consolidated financial statements unveils that companies often use this freedom to summarize transaction details into a few line items per category only. Even if formal requirements are fulfilled, such cash flow statements lack transparency about cash flows details that might be important for investors.

IAS 7.18 dictates the format for cash flows from operating activities. There are two **methods**:

- Direct method

  This method presents gross receipts and payments, grouped by classes of similar transactions. IAS 7 encourages this method. As IAS 7.18 (a) requires a gross presentation of receipts and payment, an offset is not appropriate.

  To prepare a cash flow statement using this method, receipts and payment information have to be extracted directly out of the accounting system. As most systems are not able to generate such information, most companies prefer to use the indirect method.

- Indirect method

  The indirect method derives cash flows from the balance sheet using the profit of the period as a starting point. This profit will be adjusted by all non-cash transactions.

Non-cash items to be adjusted
Depreciation
Increase or release (non-use) of provisions
Increase or release (non-use) of accruals
Deferrals
Deferred taxes
Unrealized foreign currency gains and losses
Undistributed profit of associates

Tab. K-10 List of adjustments in cash flow statements applying the indirect method

Furthermore, the profit has to be adjusted by items that belong to investing and financing activities. Some items like interest paid and received, taxes paid, have to be disclosed separately (IAS 7.31 and IAS 7.35). As these items are also part of the profit a reclassification is required. Reclassifications are often presented in cash flow statements as other adjustments. To complete cash flow of operating activities, changes in items of the balance sheet have to be added. This applies to all balance sheet items except for non-current assets as they belong to investing activities, to equity and current and non-current debt (e.g. loans and borrowings) as they belong to financing activities.

Even if there is no requirement, it is good practice to add a subtotal that covers the profit for the period and all non-cash adjustments. This subtotal, called "cash earnings" represents the cash performance that is generated by ordinary sales activities.

As the standard only requires using "profit" as a starting point and a definition about "profit" is missing, the starting point may differ. Some use net profit of the period, others opt for profit before taxation or even EBIT and EBITDA. IAS 7. Appendix A mentions profit before taxation as a starting point. Applying a strict interpretation, the net profit of the period should be used as the starting point for cash flow statements applying the indirect method. The advantage of this starting point is the consistency between the cash flow statement, the statement of comprehensive income and the statement of financial position where the net profit of the period in presented in equity.

As cash in- and out-flows should be presented separately, **netting** is prohibited. Due to this requirement, cash flows arising from receivables cannot be netted with cash flows from payables for example. Nevertheless, an aggregation of similar cash flows is permitted. An example is the summary of cash flows from receivables and cash flows from other assets. Even if netting is prohibited, IAS 7.22 lists some exceptions from this rule. A netting is allowed under the following circumstances:

- Receipts and payment on behalf of a customer can be netted, if they reflect the activities of that customer;
- Receipts and payments that relate to items with quick turnovers, large amounts and short maturities.

Selected transactions require the allocation to its proper category. These transactions are included in another category due to the procedure in preparing cash flow statements. Such **reclassifications** are necessary for all items that have a profit impact: typically, capitalized assets or purchase price allocations that are often part of operating activities but belong to investing activities.

3.2. Group effects

Cash flow statements of consolidated financial statements have – compared to cash flow statements of separate financial statements – special requirements regarding the preparation and presentation. As the cash flow statement reconciles cash and cash equivalents balances from the previous period with the current period, financial statements of the subsidiaries – as well as all group effects of the period – have to be considered in addition to previous period balances:

- Changes in the group composition;
- Consolidation and elimination of intercompany transactions and balances;
- Foreign currency translations and valuations;
- Affiliated companies.

Automation of cash flow statements is limited to group level. Even if integrated accounting software is able to prepare cash flow statements (and also at group level), details of group specific events cannot be covered by these systems.

Therefore, automatically prepared consolidated cash flow statements can provide a solid cash flow base only. The base has to be adjusted by additional effects and items to arrive at the final cash flow statement. Usually, manual adjustments have their roots in the divergent evaluation and measurement of transactions at group level. This also includes reclassifications and nettings, if appropriate. To be aware of transactions that impact the cash flow statement, reporting systems used in the group have to consider cash flow requirements.

3.2.1. Changes in the group composition

There may be different reasons for changes in the group composition, the most common being changes that impact the cash flow statement, such as acquisitions and disposals of subsidiaries. In some cases changes in the group may occur without a change in control by the parent company. All changes are accompanied by additional disclosures in the notes.

- Acquisition of subsidiary

   Both the acquisition of a subsidiary and the purchase price allocation have a direct impact on the consolidated cash flow statement. Due to the single asset acquisition theory and the consolidation process, assets and liabilities are presented as changes in cash flows of operating activities. The consolidation process sums-up all line items of the balance sheet of all subsidiaries including the acquiree. The aggregated carrying amount of each balance sheet item at the end of the reporting period is then compared with the carrying amount at the end of the previous period. The movements therefore also include the changes due to the acquisition of the subsidiary. Due to the presentation layout of the cash flow statement, balance sheet items of the acquiree are spread across the whole cash flow statement: in operating activities for current assets and liabilities, in investing activities for non-current assets, in financing activities for all kinds of debt and changes in equity and in the cash funds for cash and cash equivalents of the acquiree. While IAS 7.39 requires a separate disclosure of acquisitions of subsidiaries as part of investing activities, adjustments are necessary. These adjustments consist of reclassifications of movements due to the carrying amount of balance sheet items of the acquiree in each reporting position of the cash flow statement to a line item in investing activities dealing with cash outflows due to investments in subsidiaries. IAS 7.40 requires additional items to be disclosed that will result in further adjustments of the cash flow statement:

   - Only the consideration paid has to be presented. Therefore, any deferred payments, any future payments subject to earn-out options, warranties for share based payments and similar items that have no cash effects have to be eliminated. Accordingly, deferred payments have to be reported in those future periods, when such a payment will take place.

- If considerations received include an exchange of assets, such transactions have to be eliminated as well because they do not include cash transfers.
- As acquisitions of subsidiaries may include cash balances in the financial statements of the subsidiaries, these balances have to be presented separately. Cash balances at the subsidiary represent cash inflows that will reduce the cash outflow due to the acquisition.

- Disposal of subsidiary

    Disposals of subsidiaries follow the same rules and guidelines as acquisitions. They have to be presented separately from acquisitions according to IAS 7.39.

- Changes in control

    Changes in the group may occur through changes in ownership and other reasons than acquisitions and disposals. As changes in ownership do not result in a loss or establishment of control, all cash flows have to be reported as financing activities according to IAS 7.42A and 7.42B.

    Changes that are not based on acquisitions or disposals can be treated differently in cash flow statements. The reason therefore is a missing regulation in IAS 7. To handle such changes, two opinions can be found in literature. One opinion is a neutral treatment of such changes. Another opinion is to include these changes in the cash flow statement as a separate line item.

3.2.2. Consolidation

The principle to eliminate all intercompany relationships in consolidated financial statements is also valid for the cash flow statement. Therefore, all group internal cash-flows have to be eliminated as well to present consolidated financial statements. The consolidation is linked to the preparation of cash flow statements. If the cash flow statement is derived from the consolidated profit & loss statement and the consolidated statement of financial position, a consolidation of the cash flow statement is unnecessary. If the cash flow statement is derived from local statements, a distinct consolidation is required.[23]

3.2.3. Foreign currency translations

Similarly to the statement of financial position and the statement of income, cash flow statements have to cope with the same problems of foreign currency translation. The reasons for these problems are the same: the volume of transactions together with their translation at different times with different exchange rates. To solve these problems, translations average exchange rates are applied as an approximation.

---

[23] See page 689 for detailed explanations on both methods.

Foreign currency translations as part of cash flow statements initiate a set of problems. They are induced via adjusted financial statements of all companies in the group combined with the consolidation at group level. The underlying reason for these issues is the focus on cash flows. Therefore, a differentiated view of transactions is necessary:

- Ordinary transactions
  All cash flows from ordinary transactions have to be adjusted by changes in exchange rates. An identification of these exchange rate effects is sometimes not easy to realize because transactions often include changes of balance sheet items. Therefore, a separation combined with individual treatments is required.

- Changes in exchange rates
  Non-realized gains and losses that belong to exchange rate translations or changes in exchange rates have to be "eliminated non-cash".

- Recognition in profit & loss
  Effects of foreign currency translations recorded in profit & loss have to be eliminated in full.

- Cash and cash equivalents
  Cash and cash equivalents of foreign currencies have an implied currency effect. They have to be adjusted and presented in a separate line item. Most cash flow statements present such a line item as "Effect on exchange rates on cash and cash equivalents" close to changes in cash and cash equivalents.

- Translation of foreign operations
  A translation of balance sheet items of foreign operations may result in changes of those items even if there is no change in the original balance sheet. Such kinds of changes have to be eliminated in full.

Regardless of which transaction applies the identification of foreign currency effects is always a critical issue. The identification can be realized by a multiple translation: The opening and the closing balance sheet of the period should be converted by using the exchange rates of the last fiscal year. The balance sheets should also be converted by using the exchange rate of the current fiscal year. The differences are exchange rates effects that need to be considered and adjusted. This procedure has to be applied for each company of the group that prepares financial statements using a different currency than the parent company. The procedure is costly but safe and the preferred method, if accounting systems do not support a foreign currency handling.

Multiple currency translations should always be applied in case of a manual preparation of a cash flow statement.

3.2.4. *Associates and joint ventures*

Associates differ from affiliated companies due to the reduced investment in those companies and the lack of control. Even if control is not given, associated companies and their performances are considered as part of consolidated financial statements. Therefore, dedicated accounting rules apply also for cash flow purposes.

The recording of profits from **associates** is based on the application of the equity method. The recognition of the share of the associate's profit is always a non-cash transaction and has to be eliminated. An elimination is not required, if the profit recognition and the distribution occurs in the same period. If the distribution happens in a different (e.g. subsequent) period, the distribution has to be considered in that period as a cash receipt. The same applies to any advance payments on dividends on the associate.

Any capital step-ups and step-downs that are based on a shift from or to retained earnings are non-cash transactions that need to be eliminated. The same applied to any write down's of the carrying balance of the investment in the associate.

Adjustments of cash flows of **joint ventures** follow the way as joint ventures are included in consolidated financial statements. If they are included in the consolidated financial statements on a proportional base, cash flows have to be considered also proportional. If joint ventures are included by applying the equity method, all cash flows that relate to distributions, payments and receipts between the joint venture and the group are considered on a proportional basis applying the share in the joint venture as required by IAS 7.38.

3.3. Other effects

In addition to group effects, other effects have to be considered in preparing cash flow statements. These effects are independent from any group specialties and occur in almost every cash flow statement.

Taxes require a differentiated view as they combine several elements that need to be adjusted. As a general rule, all non-cash transactions have to be eliminated and reclassifications are required to disclose taxes paid as a separate line item according to IAS 7.35. While taxes consist of deferred and current income taxes, different tasks are necessary.

- Deferred taxes

    These are recorded in the balance sheet and profit & loss statement; as they present future tax effects based on current or past events, they are classified as non-cash items that need to be eliminated in full. They are recorded as deferred tax assets or deferred tax liabilities in the balance sheet. Any changes in the carrying amount are either recoded through profit & loss of other comprehensive income (which is part of equity). Therefore, the elimination has to include all accounts or balance sheet items that carry any tax balances.

In some cases, deferred tax items may be part of assets or liabilities acquired and adjusted in business combinations. These tax items have to be eliminated in full as well.

- Current income taxes

  These record all tax obligations as part of the ongoing business: prepayments made during the period or accrued obligations for outstanding payments. Therefore, tax payments made and recorded as an expense in the profit & loss statement have to be reclassified within operating activities while all accrued tax obligations have to be eliminated in full.

Taxes in the group are the aggregate of all subsidiaries' tax expenses. To eliminate non-cash transactions of the subsidiary the parent has the choice to implement an appropriate reporting toolbox. This can be realized by either with separate reporting positions of tax details or additional forms that cover tax details.

Like tax, **interest** follows a similar pattern. The net profit of the period has to be adjusted by recorded interest earnings and expenses followed by an elimination of non-cash elements. IAS 7.31 requires disclosure of interest received and paid as separate line items. In addition, IAS 7.33 assumes that interest has to be disclosed as an operating activity because the underlying borrowings are linked to the generation of profit or loss. Interest may be allocated to investing and financing activities if it can be proven that the interest arose from those activities. If interests aros due to for different reasons, the interest must be split up and allocated to the proper categories. To automate such allocations it is recommended to have separate interest accounts per category available, which avoids any manual adjustments and relocations.

Any **excess cash** that is not required in the ordinary course of the business is often used for investments in securities, funds or similar financial assets. As these investments are used as a "parking position" for the excess cash, they have a short-term character and do not represent long-term strategic investments. Therefore, interest earnings generated from these kinds of investments are always classified as operating activities.

3.4. Preparation techniques

The procedure in preparing cash flow statements **automatically** depends on the accounting system used. Most accounting systems are able to prepare a cash flow statement based on balance sheet movements during the period. As these automatically generated cash flow statements not always cover all cash flow details, manual adjustments are necessary. Typical adjustments are additional eliminations of non-cash transactions, reclassifications of selected cash flow items and allocations of transactions.

If accounting systems do not support the preparation of cash flow statements, a **manual** preparation is necessary. All steps an accounting system usually performed have to be executed by hand. The advantage in preparing manual cash flow statements is the incorporation of those manual adjustments of automatically prepared cash flow statements.

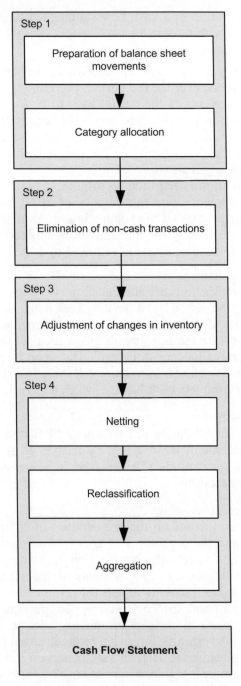

Fig. K-14 Preparation scheme of cash flow statements

The manual preparation of a cash flow statement using the indirect method can be realized usually within four steps:

1. Balance sheet movements

    The first step is to prepare movements of all balance sheet items. The movements have to cover the full period; therefore the balance sheets at the beginning and the end of the period have to be used. It is recommended to prepare the movements at account level because the accounts have to be assigned to an appropriate category of the cash flow statement. If all accounts are assigned, the sum of all movements should equal the changes in cash and cash equivalents.

    Special attention is required to intangible assets as well as property, plant and equipment. The movements of those items include capital expenditures, disposals as well as depreciation. As all three movements have to be disclosed separately, the reconciliations of fixed assets as required by IAS 16.73 and intangible assets as required by IAS 38.118 are needed.

2. Non-cash transactions

    Non-cash transactions are eliminated in two steps. The first step adjusts the net profit of the period by eliminating such items like depreciation, effects of exchange rates, discounting, adjustments of provisions and similar items. The counterparts of these adjustments follow the underlying transactions and adjust movements of balance sheet items. The second step eliminates all other non-cash transactions. These transactions can arise from valuation adjustments that affect other comprehensive income, which is recorded in equity.

3. Valuation adjustments

    The net profit of the period is subject to further adjustments if the profit & loss statement is presented by nature. In such cases changes in inventory as well as capitalized assets have to be considered if they belong to non-cash transactions.

4. Netting and Reclassifications

    The final step focuses on the presentation of the cash flow statement. If appropriate and the conditions of IAS 7.22 are met, cash flows have to be netted. The netting usually occurs within one category. Reclassifications cover all three categories and adjustments of the net profit of the period. The first set of reclassifications adjusts the profit of the period by allocating items to the appropriate category. This applies particularly to interests and taxes. The second set of reclassifications allocates cash flows between the categories. A typical example for such a reclassification is the presentation of acquisitions of subsidiaries. The third set focuses on reclassifications within a category. An example is the disclosure of cash outflows due on the purchase of fixed assets and the proceeds resulting from disposals of fixed assets.

    To present the cash flow statement in its final form, line items are aggregated to reporting positions. The aggregation follows the presentation policy of the (parent) company.

> The steps will guide you safely through the preparation process!

The above steps are valid for the preparation of all kinds of cash flow statements. Preparing consolidated cash flow statements for **groups**, additional tasks are necessary. All effects that may arise in groups have to be considered and to be either eliminated, consolidated or allocated. Consolidated financial statements can be prepared by applying either a top-level or bottom-up approach.

- Top level

    The top level approach is identical to the traditional way of preparing cash flow statements. The cash flow statement is derived directly at group level from the consolidated statements of financial positions and of income. This requires detailed knowledge about all transactions in all subsidiaries. Such a requirement is manageable only in small groups because the volumes of details subsidiaries have to deliver to corporate centre contradict an efficient preparation of consolidated financial statements. An advantage of the top level approach is the omission of any consolidation tasks.

- Bottom up

    This method of preparing consolidated cash flow statements allocates the preparation to all companies in the group. In the first instance, each company has to prepare a cash flow statement based on their local financial statements of the period. These local cash flows statements are subject to consolidation procedures similar to the preparation of consolidated profit & loss statement and the statement of financial position. They have to be translated to the reporting currency of the group and adjusted by all level II items if cash relevant. All adjusted cash flow statements are aggregated and consolidated. Corporate centre has to deal with the challenge of consolidating all the intercompany cash flows. These cash flows have to be derived from the debtors and creditors subledgers. Even if this approach is more time consuming and an involvement of subsidiaries is required, it offers a simplified preparation process at group level because the corporate centre does not need to know all cash flow details in all group companies.

Reporting requirements differ according to the approach chosen. Applying the top level approach, dedicated information has to be reported by subsidiaries while the reporting requirement of the bottom up approach only requires a cash flow statement. The reasons for the simplified reporting requirement can be found in the reporting packages itself as all other information are already included for debt and income & expense consolidations.

3.5. Classification of cash flow elements

The following table provides a comprehensive summary of the position of profit & loss and balance sheet items in cash flow statements. This table assumes that the indirect method is applied.

Item	Category	Additional explanation
Trade payables	Operating	
Trade receivables	Operating	
Accruals	Operating	
Acquisition of subsidiaries	Investing	Elimination of assets and liabilities in operating activities and presentation as a separate line item in investing activities.
Acquisitions, variable components	None	Full elimination in the period the acquisition takes place. Instead, presentation in the period where payments of variable components occur.
Acquisitions, cash and cash equivalents received	Investing	To be netted with payment related acquisitions.
Capital reserves	Financing	
Current taxes	Adjustment / Operating	Reclassification from profit of the period to operating activities as separate line item and elimination of the non-cash portion.
Deferred taxes	None	Full elimination.
Depreciation	Adjustments	Full elimination.
Differences arising from foreign currency translations	Various	See chapter 1.3 for a detailed explanation.
Discounting	Adjustments	Full elimination.
Dividends, paid	Financing	Date of payment is relevant, not the date of the dividend resolution.
Dividends, received	Operating	Only if dividends declared and accounted for are received. Otherwise full elimination.
Financial assets	Investing	Only non-current financial assets. If financial assets classify as current a presentation in operating activities is appropriate.
Intangible assets	Investing	Either capital expenditures or disposal of assets. Separate presentation for both transactions required.
Interests	Adjustment	Elimination of interest earnings and expenses.
Interests paid	Operating	Always operating unless it can be proven that the underlying transaction belongs to investing or financing activities. In such cases a reclassification is required.
Interests received	Operating	Always operating unless it can be proven that the underlying transaction belongs to investing or financing activities. In such cases a reclassification is required.
Internally generated intangible assets	Investing	
Internally produced and capitalized assets	Investing	Reclassification from operating activities.
Inventory	Operating	
Investments	Investing	
Loans	Financing	Always financing, whether loans are presented as current or non-current.
Other assets	Operating	
Other liabilities	Operating	
Property, plant & equipment	Investing	Either capital expenditures or disposal of assets. Separate presentation for both transactions required.
Provisions	Operating	
Share capital	Financing	
Shareholder Transactions	Financing	

Tab. K-11   ABC of cash flow statement elements

4. PARTNERSHIPS

A partnership as a proven model has a variety of forms: limited, unlimited or with protected partners. In general, partners run the business and are therefore liable for their business activities. A common feature is taxation at partner level. Depending on the underlying business, a partnership can be established for a dedicated purpose, for a limited period or even for a longer period. The binding element is the partner contract that rules the duties, risks and rewards for each partner and therefore also the control a partner has in the partnership. Another feature is the liquidation of a partnership that is easily managed than for a stock company. Due to these advantages, partnerships are popular also for groups to arrange a part of a business in a partnership. A traditional example is the use of partnerships for joint ventures.

Partnerships in groups can be found at every level. Traditionally, partnerships are subsidiaries, joint ventures or associates established for business reasons. Partnerships can also act as parents if shareholders have agreed to bundle or concentrate investments in other companies through a partnership. In such a case, the partnership is obliged to prepare consolidated financial statements.

Partnerships as subsidiaries have to follow the same accounting and consolidation principles as every other subsidiary of the group.[24] To qualify as a subsidiary, control has to be given demanding the application of the control concept on partnerships. This requires a preparation for consolidations as well as an execution of equity-, debt- and other consolidations.

- Preparation

  Preparing a partnership for consolidation requires adjustments for all kinds of services performed, recorded expenses that are not expenses from a group's perspective as well as interests on partner capital accounts. These adjustments are usually subject to the partner's drawing accounts which could be realized as level I adjustments. A typical adjustment could look like this journal entry:

  Journal entry
  dr.   Drawing account partner
       cr.   Other expenses

  All other items like adjustments to comply with group accounting policies, non-accounted assets, hidden reserves and burdens and other items that build up the equity value have to accounted for as usual.

- Equity consolidation

  Partnerships usually do not have the equity structure of a stock company. Instead partnerships maintain capital and withdrawal accounts for each partner. Depending on the articles of the partnership, these accounts

---

[24] See chapter G -5.2 on page 473 regarding partnerships as associates.

may qualify for a presentation as liabilities which have to be considered when applying the equity consolidation. The equity consolidation of a partnership always follows the same logic as for every other company. The equity accounts of the subsidiary have to be replaced by the partnership account instead. Therefore, a standard journal entry for an equity consolidation of a partnership would be:

Journal entry		Company	Comment
dr.	Goodwill	Group	
dr.	Capital account partner	Subsidiary	
dr.	Withdrawal account partner	Subsidiary	
dr.	Profit / losses carried forward	Subsidiary	Only if appropriate.
dr.	Revaluation reserve	Subsidiary	Only if appropriate. Can also be a credit.
dr.	IFRS opening balance	Subsidiary	Only if appropriate. Can also be a credit.
	cr. Investment in subsidiaries	Parent	
	cr. Receivables	Parent	Relates to withdrawal account. Only if appropriate.
	cr. Deferred taxes revaluation reserve	Subsidiary	Only if appropriate. Can also be a debit.
	cr. Foreign exchange differences	Group	Can also be a debit.

The other partners are treated as minority interests.

Journal entry		Company	Comment
dr.	Capital account partner	Subsidiary	
dr.	Withdrawal account partner	Subsidiary	
dr.	Profit / losses carried forward	Subsidiary	Only if appropriate.
	cr. Non-controlling interests	Group	

- Debt and other consolidations

    Presuming that adjustments are properly executed, the consolidation of debt, earnings and expenses and unrealized profits follows the standard procedures applied in every subsequent consolidation.

In addition to specialities of the equity consolidation, effects to be recorded by the parent have to be considered. These effects are independent from any preparation activities but influence the preparation process of consolidated financial statements.

- Taxation

    Due to the legal form of a partnership, the taxation of the partner's profits occurs on partner level. Therefore, the parent has to ensure that taxes are recorded (and paid) by the parent. A record of income taxes at partnership level is not required. Nevertheless, local or commercial taxes might qualify for a recording at partnership level.

- Drawings account

    The accounting practice of a partnership will record all profit & loss attributable to the parent as well as any drawings the parent has taken during the period on the drawings account. Therefore, drawings represent dividends that are subject to elimination.

Due to the identical accounting on parent and partnership level, the carrying amount of the investment in the partnership mirrors the partner's capital account of the partnership.

5. RESTRUCTURING OF GROUPS

5.1. Basics

Restructuring as a common task is often used to improve the composition, structure and management of a group and to optimize the performance or the tax position of a group. Having a closer look to the underlying intentions for restructurings, typical **reasons** are:

- Alignment of the group to the new corporate strategy, to market and customer requirements;
- Financial restructuring to improve profits or to eliminate losses;
- Tax optimization to reduce the tax burden or to make use of tax losses and credits;
- Realization and lifting of hidden reserves in subsidiaries for equity step-ups or dividend distributions;
- Limitations of risks due to guarantees, liabilities or contingent liabilities;
- Sale of subsidiaries or sub-groups;
- Changes in the shareholder structure on various group levels, even at parent level. This also affects non-controlling interests and investments in associates and joint ventures.

This is not an exhaustive list.

Restructuring a group means that the composition and structure of the group will change. Changes can relate to subsidiaries (on a legal level), to business units (on a management level), to products and service offered and other organizational units of the group. The restructuring of products and services are typical topics of management accounting whilst a restructuring of subsidiaries is a typical financial accounting topic. The restructuring of business units often involves both accounting disciplines. This is because a business unit is built up by several legal entities or parts of entities, which involves financial accounting. Management accounting is involved due to performance measurements, plans and budgets and their management. While a group restructuring is based on dedicated intentions and group structures vary, several options of restructurings are available:

- Sale of subsidiaries or sub-groups, e.g. due to non-performance or changed business scope;
- Allocation of subsidiaries to new or different business units, either in total or in part;
- Separation or combination of businesses and / or subsidiaries.

While restructuring of groups always affect the individual subsidiary and its relationship with other group companies, a view is required on restructurings in its entirety. There are always **three players** involved:

- The group that is based on IFRS accounting;
- Local laws and regulations that can have dedicated requirements on restructurings;
- Tax jurisdictions that may have dedicated tax rules on restructurings.

Depending on the realization of restructurings, rules and regulations of these players may contradict each other. To find appropriate solutions, complex restructurings may be the case. Therefore, a "cookbook accounting" is not possible – each restructuring requires an individual solution.

Another issue that is closely linked to all three players is their dependency on each other and the **impact on the group**. Restructurings usually impact the individual company: either as the one subject to the restructuring or the one with the interest in the subsidiary to be restructured, or the one who will hold the interest in the subsidiary. As all restructuring activities have to be accounted for in local accounts by applying local GAAP and the related tax rules, modified separate financial statements will result. Due to the consolidation process, all changes at local level that are induced by the restructuring will be passed through to consolidated financial statements of the group. While IFRS 10.B86 requires an elimination of group internal transactions, the restructuring has to be checked to what extent group-internal effects are included. This check should include two items, a pure restructuring and an acquisition. Dedicated tasks have to be executed depending on these items.

- Pure restructurings

    A pure restructuring is a group-internal transaction that does not include any external elements. Therefore, nothing has changed from an external perspective; no impact on the position of the entire group is given. As a consequence, the whole restructuring has to be reversed to present the group as it was before. The reversal is a dedicated part of the preparation process of consolidated financial statements.

    Even if the group has to present itself without any changes, there is one impact that cannot be changed. Restructurings always impact also the tax position of the restructured subsidiary. The tax position can be identical to local GAAP; the tax position also can deviate. This may trigger the accounting of deferred tax assets or liabilities at local level. Even if the restructuring is reversed to present the group as it was before, the tax position cannot be reversed. As a consequence, deferred tax assets and liabilities that relate to the restructuring are presented in consolidated financial statements.

- Acquisitions

    If the restructuring of a group includes acquisitions an external element is given. In such a case, it has to be checked, how the acquisition occurred and which IFRS has to be applied for the accounting of the transaction. This is because the acquisition either is a collection of assets and liabilities where their appropriate IFRS have to be applied or a business is given that demands a purchase price allocation. Such restructuring tasks will definitely change the presentation of consolidated financial statements.

The impact on a group does not only impact the current and the intended structure but also the **long-term orientation**. Restructurings will develop long-term effects that have to be understood and considered.

> Restructurings are often performed at short notice, under time pressure and even sometimes without the necessary vision. Subsequent effects are therefore not sufficiently considered. Therefore, take your time and simulate a restructuring over a longer period of time. Consider tax, local GAAP and IFRS. If you think that such a restructuring is reasonable and realizable, the risks are manageable and acceptable, you should execute the restructuring.

5.2. Types of restructuring

Restructurings can be realized in different ways. There is no golden way available as restructurings depend on group structures and the intention for the restructuring. Nevertheless, all group restructurings are based on four basic cases. These cases can be combined, simultaneously or step by step executed or otherwise arranged so that they apply to the intended restructuring of the group.

1. New parent

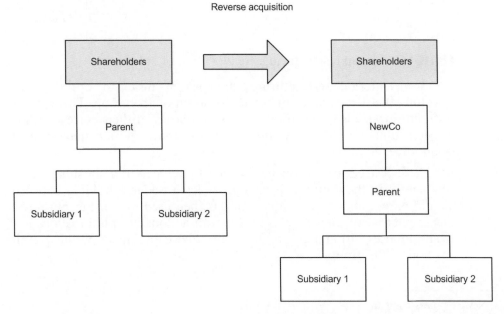

Fig. K-15 Group restructuring: New parent

The intention of installing a new parent is often driven by changes in the shareholder structure. Typical applications are venture capital companies that acquire larger shares of investment in the group by using a "NewCo" as the financing vehicle.[25] By using these solutions, the debt financing of the acquisition is pushed-down to the old parent. Such transactions are often combined with a merger of the new ultimate parent with the old parent.

If a new parent should be established as the ultimate parent, the issue arises how the new parent should be established. Such restructurings may also qualify as reverse acquisitions.[26]

2. Group-internal restructuring

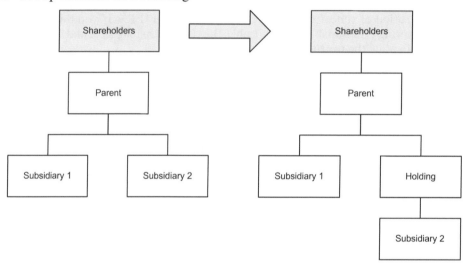

Fig. K-16   Group restructuring: Reallocation of subsidiary

Group-internal restructurings are proven tasks to optimize the structure, the performance or the tax position of the group. This type of restructuring is also used to allocate subsidiaries to their corresponding business units so that they are easier to handle from a management perspective.

These restructurings can be realized by allocating a subsidiary to a new parent in the group, it is also possible to wedge a holding between the old parent and the subsidiary that is then used for further purposes. The impact is still the same. As these transactions are pure reallocation of subsidiaries within a group, they do not have an impact on the overall position of the group.

---

[25] NewCo = New company.

[26] See chapter E -6.1 on page 217 regarding reverse acquisitions.

The allocation of a subsidiary in a group is usually based on sales transactions. This will open several accounting options and duties on the level of the selling and buying companies:

- The investments in the subsidiary can be sold with a profit
- The selling company can utilize tax losses and tax credits
- The buying company can remeasure the investment in the subsidiary
- Hidden reserves of the subsidiary can be raised through a purchase price allocation

As an indirect effect, sub-groups can be established if the sales transaction involve companies that do not yet have subsidiaries. It has to be checked if a group accounting due to local laws and regulations becomes necessary.

While there are no changes at group level, all transactions have to be caught and reversed during the consolidation process. This involves not only equity consolidations and transactions at group level but also the elimination of unrealized profits and debt and income & expense consolidations.

3. Mergers and splits of companies

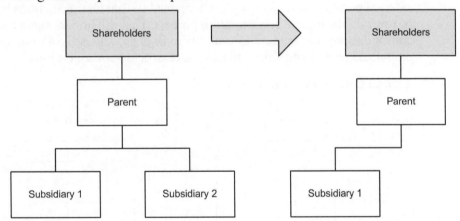

Fig. K-17 Group restructuring: Mergers

Mergers of companies are popular in two cases: To clean-up the group structure by reducing the number of subsidiaries and to combine subsidiaries with similar structures or business activities so that the business activities of the merged companies complement each other.

Similar to mergers, company splits are used mainly in two cases: to separate businesses that are hosted by a legal entity into two or more separate subsidiaries and for the distribution on non-cash assets to owners.

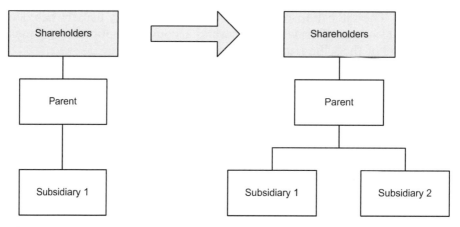

Fig. K-18   Group restructuring: Splits

Both methods, mergers and splits, are often combined with other basic cases to realize complex group internal restructurings.

This type of restructuring follows the same rationale as a group-internal restructuring as long as both subsidiaries stay within the group. From an external point of view, nothing has happened so that all transactions have to be reversed during the consolidation process. This will impact against equity consolidations and transactions at group level as well as the elimination of unrealized profits and debt and income & expense consolidations.

4. Transactions under common control

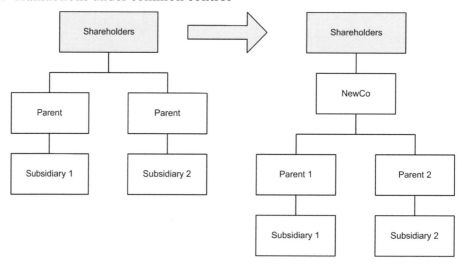

Fig. K-19   Group restructuring: Transactions under common control

Special applications are transactions under common control. If shareholders dominate two groups that are combined into one group by using a new ultimate parent, several accounting options are possible. The transaction can be accounted for as a business combination by applying IFRS 3 as well as a combination by two groups based on their carrying amounts.[27]

The intention to combine two groups into one is solely a "shareholder issue". Shareholders benefit from less administrative tasks like attending one annual general meeting only. The groups benefit from reduced administration costs like preparing one set of consolidated financial statements or maintaining one annual general meeting only.

5.3. Restructuring methods

A careful analysis of the four basic restructuring types will unveil a limited set of commercial transactions that are used to realize restructurings. These transactions are either used standalone or in combination of each other. In fact, restructurings are realize by a combination of three methods:

- sales transactions,
- mergers, and
- splits.

In addition to these three commercial transactions, the use of **shell companies** is an important restructuring element. Shell companies are used as placeholders to realize restructurings. They can be used in different ways, particularly for:

- holding purposes,
- the carrying of investments in or financing of subsidiaries for a defined period before they are merged with the subsidiary,
- the establishment of new companies, or
- the transfer of businesses.

Other uses are thinkable as well depending on the intention of the restructuring and the need for legal vehicles that support the restructuring.

Restructuring methods are directly influenced by **taxation**. While any changes of the legal entity, whether they apply to the business of the entity, to their assets and liabilities or to the legal shell have a direct impact on the taxation of the entity, jurisdictions have often developed tax rules and regulations that have to be applied upon any changes in the structure of an entity. In some cases these tax rules interact with the corresponding commercial rules. The intention of these tax rules is to ensure that the taxation after the restructuring is similar to the taxation before the restructuring and that the restructuring does not result in a reduced taxation or with items that are not any longer subject to taxation. Even

---

[27] Please note: If different shareholders are involved, the formation of a new group by using an ultimate parent has to be accounted for as a business combination in accordance with IFRS 3 only!

if taxation is ensured, subsequent tax effects may arise. Typical examples are the retirement of unused tax credits or losses, changes in exemptions, tax penalties upon improper restructuring ways and similar effects.

> Restructurings may generate tax impacts that are not directly obvious. Therefore, involve your tax advisor upfront when starting the planning of the restructuring to avoid unexpected tax effects.

Due to the application of *IAS 12 – Income Taxes*, the tax effects of restructuring will be recorded in consolidated financial statements. To understand the impacts in consolidated financial statements, the overall restructuring process and the tax impact on each company involved in the restructuring have to be reviewed from a tax perspective. If cross-border restructurings occur, the review has to consider the taxation systems of each jurisdiction. Based on these activities, the tax position of each company has to be developed. The tax position has to consider the tax base of each asset and liability of the balance sheet to determine the resulting deferred tax assets or liabilities. The preparation of deferred tax assets and liabilities in consolidated financial statements due to the restructuring follows the normal preparation process of tax positions.[28]

The combination of local taxation rules and regulations in combination with the accounting for the resulting tax effects according to IAS 12, a presentation of tax effects due to the restructuring in consolidated financial statements occurs, even if all intended effects have to be adjusted while there are no changes from an external view in the group composition at all.

5.3.1. Sales

Sales transactions as part of restructuring activities are standard procedures to move a company from one to another parent in the group. Due to the nature of the sale, a change in the shareholder structure of the sold company occurs that requires appropriate contracts, often by involving a notary as such activities have to be filed with commercial registers.

As the sales price is subject to negotiation, the **sending parent** can negotiate any price ranging from book values to fair values. An appropriate gain has to be recorded in profit & loss upon the sale of the investments in subsidiaries.

Journal entry
dr.		Receivables
	cr.	Investment in subsidiaries
	cr.	Other earnings

On the other hand, the **receiving parent** is not only recording the investment in subsidiaries in their separate financial statements. A purchase price allocation, as required by IFRS 3 (and may result in additional intangible assets, contingent liabilities and goodwill), is not necessary as long as the transaction is a

---

[28] See chapter K -2 on page 656 regarding the accounting of deferred tax assets and liabilities in groups.

pure group-internal transaction or the receiving parent is exempt from preparing consolidated financial statements – as long as they are prepared by the ultimate parent in the case of external involvement.

Journal entry

dr.	Investment in subsidiaries	
	cr.	Payables

Sales transactions are often combined with mergers.

5.3.2. Mergers

Mergers transactions are standard procedures for restructuring a group. The intention of a merger is to combine the businesses of two legal entities into one. There are several **types** of merger: horizontal, vertical, conglomerate, market extension and product extension. Such mergers are common in markets, between competitors or across the supply chain. Mergers in groups are slightly different as there are no independent companies involved that can cause changes in competition in markets. They can be upstream, downstream or sidestream:

- Upstream

    Here a subsidiary merges with its parent (also called a vertical merger). Such mergers are in favour if a dedicated business of the subsidiary has to be moved to the parent. Upstream mergers are often combined with an antecedent acquisition of the subsidiary.

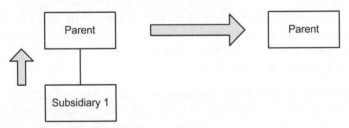

Fig. K-20   Upstream merger

- Downstream

    Also a vertical merger, in this case the parent moves towards the subsidiary.

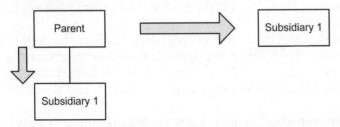

Fig. K-21   Downstream merger

- Sidestream

    Here the two companies have the same parent, either directly or indirectly (also called a horizontal merger). This type of merger is often used if identical businesses have to be combined or business effects across the supply chain are expected.

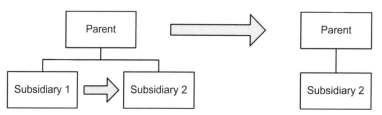

Fig. K-22   Sidestream merger

All types of merger can be arranged in two ways:

- By absorption

    The entities have defined tasks: one is to be merged, the other one will absorb the former. The legal entity that is merged will lose its legal existence. The absorbing entity will keep its legal form. The investment of the parent in the absorbing subsidiary will be expanded by the former investment in the merged subsidiary.

- By new formation

    Mergers can also be arranged in a way where both entities will be merged into a new entity. Both entities will lose their legal existence. The parent's investment in the former subsidiaries will be replaced by the investment in the new subsidiary.

Mergers are embedded in a **legal environment** that requires defined tasks before a merger can be legally accepted. These tasks may change from legislation to legislation, but some are common to all legislations even if the contents may vary. A common task is the execution of formal requirements. This includes merger contacts, filings with commercial registers, audits of mergers, accounting requirements and financial settlements in case of dissenting shareholders. While the initial intention of mergers is focused on markets and not on group-internal restructurings, competitive issues in markets and antitrust regulations are often linked to mergers. Appropriate documentation regarding market effects is therefore another common task.

Even if companies subject to mergers in groups have to fulfil the same requirements as everybody else, topics that relate to market conditions, antitrust regulations or similar issues are easy to fulfil as there will be no market impacts. This is because relationships to each and between the companies and the markets do not change.

The **accounting** of mergers is an area that is not fully captured by IFRS: dedicated rules do not exist and can only be found indirectly in some standards. In general, a merger of two companies in a group is not treated as a business combination. IFRS 3 is not applicable according to IFRS 3.2c and IFRS 3.B1. The reason for this non-application of IFRS 3 is that the ultimate parent that has control before the merger and still has control after the merger. In such cases, there is a business combination under common control, which is excluded from IFRS 3 accounting. Due to the non-application of a business combination, the merger can be accounted for as an ordinary acquisition of assets and liabilities in exchange for shares in the absorbed or newly formed company. This offers accounting options for mergers, particularly for the measurement of assets and liabilities. The measurement of assets and liabilities of the merged company can be assumed by the absorbing company based on book values, partial step-ups of the carrying amounts and on fair values.

- Book values

  The absorbing company will assume the carrying amounts of the merged company's assets and liabilities as they are, without any fair value adjustments.

- Partial step-ups

  A partial step-up may be appropriate in situations where a step-up in the value of selected items is appropriate without recognizing full fair value.

- Fair values

  The measurement of all assets and liabilities at their fair values is an option that will be used to create additional distributable equity.

Similar to all other business transactions, different views are required on mergers regarding their **accounting impacts**, the view of the entities involved and group views.

- Group

  From a group's perspective, the merger is just a reallocation of the subsidiary in the group. Therefore, no changes in consolidated financial statements should occur due to the merger. Any adjustments (step-ups in the carrying amounts up to the fair value) to the carrying amount of assets and liabilities of the merged companies have to be reversed.

- Subgroup

  The principle that no changes occur applies to subgroups if subgroups are controlled by the ultimate parent. This also requires a reversal of any adjustments to the carrying amount of the merged companies if the absorbed company does not assume the book values for assets and liabilities of the merged companies. A different accounting treatment might be required if the parent of the subgroup is publicly listed. While the subgroup has dedicated reporting requirements to fulfil, a full elimination might provide misleading information to shareholders and investors.[29]

---

[29] Consolidated financial statements of such subgroups are often treated by the separate entity approach.

Therefore, a presentation of merger effects might be appropriate. A check regarding a potential reverse acquisition has to be considered.

- Company
    The absorbing company accounts for the merger based on the assumed values for assets and liabilities. These can be book values, partial step-ups and fair values.

A special case is the handling of **non-controlling interests** that relate to a merged company, which are transferred to the absorbing company like any other assets and liabilities. In the absence of any detailed accounting requirements, a partial step-up of the carrying amounts of assets and liabilities to reflect the non-controlling interests's pro rata portion of the fair values of all assets and liabilities is one option. This option does not care about any step-ups in values that are allocable to the parent's equity portion. The other option is accounting based on book values.

5.3.3. Splits

The third important commercial transaction is a company split. The company is divided into several parts depending on how the split is to be realized. This can affect one or more businesses of the company as well as a collection of assets and liabilities. A typical example is the transfer of financial assets, particularly interest in other companies into separate legal entities. The newly formed entities then can act as holdings or can be used for further restructuring activities like mergers with other companies or to be sold to other companies of the group. Even if such transactions could be realized more efficiently, local commercial, accounting and taxation rules and regulation that have to be followed may force more complex realizations of the intended restructuring.

Typical **types** of split are dispersions, spin-offs and split-offs. These splits have a direct interconnection with the ownership structure. Depending on the type of the company split, the new asset carrying unit may have the same shareholders, shareholders hold interests in different entities or the new asset carrying unit will be a subsidiary of the old one. While groups may have complex structures, splits can be used to allocate parts of the split company throughout the group, even if a direct interest is not given.

- Dispersion
    A dispersion divides the business and the assets of the company into two or more businesses or asset carrying units, which then become legal entities: the old legal entity no longer exists. The shareholders of the former company receive shares in the new legal entities. Allocation options are available. Shareholders may get a proportionate share in all new legal entities but an allocation of the new entities to defined shareholders is also possible. The latter option is often used when companies have to be divided due to inheritance.

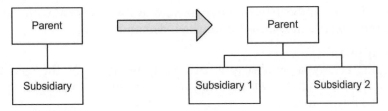

Fig. K-23 Company dispersion

- Split-off

Similar to dispersions are split-offs. The intention is still the same – assets or the business are split into two or more parts – but the big difference is the handling of the old company. While a dispersion will result in an expiration of the old company, the old company still exists after the split. The split will result in a capital decrease in the old company by the portion that is transferred. The allocation of shares to shareholders for both entities is similar to the dispersion, either on proportionate basis or by assigning dedicated entities to dedicated shareholders.

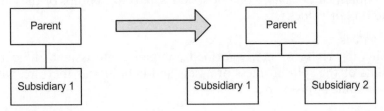

Fig. K-24 Company split-off

- Spin-off

A spin-off (or spin-out) is slightly different to the first two methods: assets are split and the old company remains. The difference from the other methods is the handling of the ownership structure. The asset carrying unit becomes a subsidiary of the old company; thus, the company will record an interest in subsidiaries instead of the transfered assets and liabilities. The ownership structure of the old company does not change.

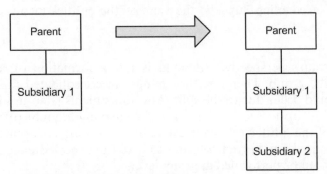

Fig. K-25 Company spin-off

All types of split can be arranged in two ways. Both ways deal with the asset carrying unit that has been spun-off and which demands a legal shell.

- By absorption

    Splits arranged by absorption transfer the assets of the split to an existing entity. This entity is granting additional shares to the shareholders in return for the assets.

- By new formation

    Splits based on a new formation will establish a new legal entity that will carry assets of the split. Shareholders will receive shares in the entity in return for the assets transferred.

The **accounting** of splits is identical to the accounting of mergers. As splits within groups are transactions under common control, they are also exempt from the application of IFRS 3 as a business combination due to the requirements of IFRS 3.2c and IFRS 3.B1. This offers accounting options for splits as ordinary acquisitions of assets and liabilities in exchange for shares, particularly for their measurement. The measurement of assets and liabilities of the newly formed or absorbing company can be based on book values, partial step-ups of the carrying amounts and on fair values.

- Book values

    The absorbing or newly formed company will assume the carrying amounts of the split business or assets and liabilities as they are, without any fair value adjustments.

- Partial step-ups

    A partial step-up may be appropriate in situations where a step-up in the value of selected items is appropriate without recognizing full fair value.

- Fair values

    The measurement of all assets and liabilities at their fair values is an option that will be used to create additional distributable equity.

Similar to all other business transactions, different views are required on splits regarding their **accounting impacts**, the view of the entities involved and group views.

- Group

    From a group's perspective, the split is just a formation of a new subsidiary in the group. Therefore, no changes in consolidated financial statements should occur due to the split. Any adjustments (step-ups in the carrying amounts up to the fair value) to the carrying amount of assets and liabilities of the splitted companies have to be reversed. An application of book values is the preferred solution to avoid unexpected effects and additional tasks to be performed at group level.

- Subgroup

    The principle that no changes occur, applies to subgroups if subgroups are controlled by the ultimate parent. This also requires a reversal of any adjustments to the carrying amount of the absorbed or newly formed companies if the companies do not assume book values for assets and liabilities. A different accounting treatment might be required if the parent of the subgroup is publicly listed. While splits and subsequently the shareholder assignment can be arranged across the whole group, the subgroup might be involved only with a fraction of the split. As dedicated reporting requirements are demanded by the parent of the subgroup and consolidated financial statements do not cover the whole split transactions, a full elimination is not possible. Therefore, a presentation of the effects of the split is appropriate which have to be reversed by the ultimate parent.

- Company

    The absorbing or the newly formed companies are accounting the assets and liabilities based on the assumed values for assets and liabilities. These can be book values, partial step-ups and fair values.

5.4. Special case: Shareholder initiated restructurings

In addition to all the reasons discussed, restructurings can be caused or initiated by shareholder decisions or due to shareholder demands. Even if a big spread is given to shareholder decisions and demands, two cases are of particular interest that will trigger a restructuring of a group:

- Distribution of non-cash assets

    Shareholders may demand a distribution of non-cash assets instead of cash dividends. Non-cash assets can include all kinds of assets, starting with individual fixed assets and ending with a whole business. Such distributions may force the parent to apply dedicated accounting tasks to fulfil shareholder demands. The accounting for a distribution of a non-cash assets requires a consideration of all facts and circumstances of the distribution. One fact is related to recipients of non-cash distributions as the accounting will differentiate between internal and external shareholders.

    - Distributions to external shareholders

        The accounting of distributions of non-cash assets to external shareholders is defined and clarified in *IAS 17 – Distribution of Non-cash Assets to Owners*. A set of **requirements** has to be fulfilled to account for distributions. All owners of a class of equity instruments have to be treated equally. Classes of equity instruments can be common shares and preferred shares for example. The owners shall gain control over the distributed non-cash assets the first time (so no control before the distribution). Furthermore, a formal decision has to be made to declare and pay a dividend which needs the authorization of shareholders. Distributions to external owners usually fulfil these requirements.

The **accounting** of the distribution is straightforward: Non-cash assets have to be measured by their fair value and distributed to shareholders. As the carrying amount of assets differs from their fair value, a fair value step-up or -down is required. While the fair value of assets is usually higher than the carrying amount, a gain can be expected. Measurement base is the balance sheet date. The step-up amount has to be recorded in profit & loss according to IFRIC 17.14.

The **timing** of all journal entries is based on the standard procedure of dividends. At the date of approval by the shareholders, the parent has to record the dividend liabilities.

Journal entry		Comment
dr.	Retained earnings	Amount reflects the fair value as of the balance sheet date
cr.	Liabilities to shareholders	

At the date of the distribution of the non-cash assets, the step-up has to be recorded. This journal entry assumes that there are no significant changes in the fair value of the assets to be distributed.

Journal entry		Comment
dr.	Liabilities to shareholders	
cr.	Assets	
cr.	Other earnings	Step-up amount

If changes in the fair value occur between the balance sheet date and the date of distribution, a further fair-value adjustment is necessary. This assumes a review of the assets to be distributed. The fair value swing has to be recorded in equity.

Journal entry		Comment
dr.	Liabilities to shareholders	
cr.	Assets	
cr.	Other comprehensive income	Can also be a debit.
cr.	Other earnings	

- Distributions within the group

A distribution within a group will lead to a situation where the ultimate parent has control over the distributed non-cash assets before and after the distribution. Therefore, an application of IFRS 17 is not given for distributions within groups according to IFRIC 17.5.

From a group's perspective, the distribution of non-cash assets is just a transfer of assets between two companies in the group. The distribution is qualifying as a simple intercompany transaction. Therefore, the elimination rules for intercompany dividends (that assume cash dividends) apply also to the distribution of non-cash assets.[30]

---

[30] See chapter F -9.1.2 on page 378 regarding the accounting for the elimination of intercompany dividends.

- Mixed models

    The distribution of non-cash assets can also apply to group-internal and external shareholders. A common case is the existence of minority shareholders if the distributing subsidiary is not wholly owned by the parent. Due to the requirements of IFRIC 17.4 (the equal treatment of all shareholders) and IFRIC 17.5 (parent has control before and after the distribution), an application of IFRIC 17 is not given for mixed models.

    As IFRS 17 focuses on accounting for distributions by the dividend paying entity, the accounting at the receiving (external) shareholders is not covered. The accounting of dividends received by internal shareholders is defined in IFRS 10.B86c (so the elimination of group internal transactions).

- Retirement of shareholders

    A retirement of shareholders may also cause restructuring activities if the compensation is taken from the parent's assets instead of a compensation transferred by other shareholders. Such retirements can be found often at privately held companies. They are linked to the legal form of the parent and the articles of incorporation. Typical examples of such legal forms are partnerships and limited liability companies (LLC). Not all legal forms allow such a retirement agreement. Furthermore, the compensation will have an impact on equity so that additional commercial rules have to be considered that relate to the legal form of the parent.

    The compensation due to the retirement of shareholders is in the first instance a purely local issue that requires the application of local accounting and taxation rules and regulations. The compensation usually is based on the value of the group (so the parent and all of its subsidiaries and other investments) and the stake the shareholder has in the parent. The estimation of that value is subject to appraisals and should be assumed to be a given. In most cases, the value exceeds the corresponding equity portion so that a gain will be created the parent and the retiring shareholders have to account for.[31]

    From a commercial point of view, the retirement is a simple exchange transaction. The parent distributes assets (either cash or non-cash assets) measured at their fair values to its retiring shareholder in exchange for the shares the retiring shareholder has in the parent. The sum of the fair values of the distributed assets reflects the value determined by the underlying appraisal. Such an exchange transaction is a typical repurchase of treasury shares according to IAS 32.33 that reduces the carrying amount of equity. Therefore, the standard journal entry in case of a cash transaction is:

Journal entry		Comment
dr.	Treasury shares	Reduction of equity equals the fair value
cr.	Cash	

---

[31] Taxation effects that arise for the shareholder will not discussed here.

As far as non-cash assets or even a business are involved, a step-up (revaluation) of the carrying amount of the distributed assets is necessary before the distribution occurs. Depending on the items subject to the distribution, the following activities are necessary:

Item	Step-up handling	Reference
Current assets	Current assets rarely include hidden reserves. Therefore, their carrying amounts have to be remeasured to reflect market conditions.	Various IFRS, e.g. • IAS 2 for inventories • IFRS 9 for trade receivables
Non-current assets	Non-current assets like fixed and intangible assets or financial assets are remeasured by their corresponding standards using either revaluation models or derecognitions. Full recognition of hidden reserves.	Various IFRS, e.g. • IAS 16 for property, plant & equipment • IAS 38 for intangible assets • IFRS 9 for financial assets
Current liabilities	Handling similar to current assets.	IFRS 9
Non-current liabilities	Are usually treated as financial liabilities, therefore consideration at fair value.	IFRS 9

Tab. K-12 Step-up tasks of assets and liabilities to be distributed to shareholders

The journal entry has to consider the step-up of all assets and liabilities distributed. The recording through profit & loss is derived from the derecognition criteria of the appropriate standards (e.g. IAS 16.68 or IAS 38.113) and is in line with distribution on non-cash assets as dividends as outlined in IFRIC 17.

Journal entry		Comment
dr.	Treasury shares	Reduction of equity equals fair value
dr.	Liabilities	Carrying amount of liabilities
cr.	Assets	Carrying amount of assets
cr.	Other earnings	Gain from step-up of assets and liabilities

The handling of treasury shares – either a retirement of shares or a placement in the stock market – is a separate transaction that does not belong to the retirement of shareholders.

As the compensation impacts the equity of the parent, it also has an impact on consolidated financial statements. All the effects the parent has to account for, are moved one by one into consolidated financial statements. Therefore, the retirement of shareholder does not only impact the consolidated statement of financial position, other statements are involved as well (consolidated statement of cash flows: cash flows from financing activities, payment to owners to redeem shares; consolidated statement of changes in shareholder equity: Transactions with shareholders).

L MANAGEMENT CONSOLIDATION

About this chapter:

Consolidation as part of the preparation of consolidated financial statements is that activity that has the highest priority for group accounting, and is therefore the most discussed. But there are also situations where a consolidation of the whole group is not applicable due to the loss of information necessary to run the group, its business units and subsidiaries. Another situation is the preparation of detailed reports that need to be incorporated into consolidated financial statements. Typical examples are segments, business units, profit centres and similar units of a group. In such cases, management consolidations are required that deliver this information, a group consolidation is not able for. This chapter tries to give an outlook on management consolidation based on underlying business requirements and the dependency between management consolidation and the preparation of consolidated financial statements.

1. BASICS

All topics discussed so far focus on the consolidation of a whole group. Subsidiaries are considered if they belong to the companies subject to consolidation. In preparing consolidated financial statements, subsidiaries are included as a whole without any consideration of their internal structures. This is sufficient as consolidated financial statements have to present the position of the group as a whole. Even if the basic statements contain total numbers of the group, more detailed information and analysis are required in some cases. The reasons for detailed information can be classified in two major areas: Disclosures required as part of the notes, and management information to run the group or parts of the group. Depending on the type of information and its use, the sources of information can arise from unconsolidated items, consolidated items and pre- or partially consolidated items.

- Unconsolidated items are often balance sheet or profit & loss components of companies that are subject to transactions that are unusual, extraordinary or material to the group and that require separate disclosure.
- Consolidated items are prepared for general disclosures and analysis of selected components of the basic statements.
- Pre- or partially consolidated items are consolidated figures of parts of the group.

Pre- or partially consolidated figures of the group are more detailed summaries of financial data. They are used for disclosure, e.g. for business unit information or segment information as required by IFRS 8 due to the management approach. They are also used in running the business of the group as partially consolidated figures provide useful information to managers responsible for parts of the group. Such figures are also used for a set of tasks like performance measurement, valuations and calculation of bonuses and commissions. Depending on the type of information required, these partial consolidations can include several parts of a group. All types of consolidation that are required due to which reason ever and do not focus on the whole group are treated as management consolidations. By contrast, the consolidation of the group is treated as a financial consolidation.

While there are different addressees of consolidated data and information, several levels of consolidation exist. Levels may vary depending on the size and composition of the group, its product and service portfolios and the geographical presence. The definition, extent and application of consolidation levels interact with the structure of the group. A typical group has at least three levels that represent the activities of a group. Further levels may exist in large groups. In addition to these levels, projects and cost units are subject to consolidation.

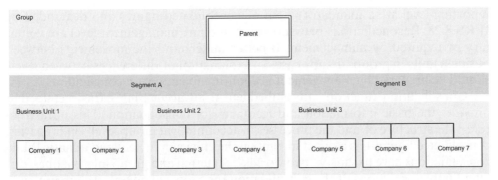

Fig. L-1   Typical structure of a group

- Group
    The group level carries the financial consolidation of the group as a whole.
- Segment
    The segment reporting required by IFRS 8 requires the consolidation of units belonging to the segments. Such information is part of consolidated financial statements and disclosed in the notes.

- Business unit
    Business units are defined based on activities, products and similar reasons. It may include subsidiaries or parts of subsidiaries that have to be consolidated.

- Project and cost unit
    Projects and cost units might be subject to consolidation if they are spread across the group.

Management consolidation to run the business and particularly the **use** for performance measurement of business units is widely discussed among groups. The question from management accounting is whether or not consolidation tasks should be executed to measure the performance of a business unit. There are pros and cons in applying management consolidations. Arguments for management consolidation are the enhanced accuracy of data particularly in groups that have complex intercompany relationships and simplified calculation of bonuses and commission that depend on the performance of business units. Arguments against management consolidation are the enhanced workload in preparing consolidated figures and the small advantage of consolidated figures compared to unconsolidated figures. Such arguments are often used by groups that have an easy-to-manage business without any complex dependencies between and in business units. Therefore, both situations can be found in practice. Application, as well as non-application, of management consolidation is appropriate depending on management discretion.

Consolidation on several levels will often lead to irritation as figures do not match across these levels. Therefore, the dependencies and interactions of consolidated figures between group, segment, business unit and other levels have to be explained by reconciliations. **Reconciliations** between group and segment reporting level are a mandatory item of consolidated figures and demanded by IFRS 8.28. Reconciliations between group and any management level are voluntary or required by management to better understand the movements between business units in groups. In any case, an explanation of differences between levels should be prepared by management accounting to support reconciliations.

Consolidation functions are embedded in an **accounting infrastructure** that provides the basic information and resources for consolidation. This infrastructure – the structure of and the processes in accounting at group level – in preparing consolidated figures has a direct impact on the efficiency, extent and quality. While consolidations have to satisfy "two worlds" – external and group internal ones, different implementations of the consolidation function can be observed in practice.

- Separate structures

    Separate structures consist of separate consolidations. While financial or statutory consolidations that prepare consolidated financial statements are located in the finance accounting department, management consolidations are handled in the management accounting department. Synergies in preparing consolidated figures are not used, consolidation skills are found in both departments. Separate structures are expensive and often not efficient.

- Integrated services

    Integrated services follow a different approach. Consolidations – regardless which ones – are prepared by a separate department that serves as a provider to management and financial accounting. The focus is on an efficient consolidation with lean structures. Nevertheless, such services require changes in accounting processes and defined interfaces between all accounting and related departments.

Both structures have their advantages and disadvantages. As a general rule, the larger the group and the more complex intercompany transactions are the more favourable is an accounting infrastructure based on integrated services.

2. BUSINESS UNITS

Management consolidations that prepare consolidated figures (profit & loss statements, balance sheets, cash flow statements) for business units depend on the structure of the group and the allocation of subsidiaries to business units. Business units are defined as logical parts or organizational units of a group that represent defined business functions or activities that are independent from other parts of the group. A business unit is part of the overall organizational structure of a group that is managed separately. It has its own performance measurement a business unit manager signs responsible for.

Due to the functional view of the group, a mapping of the legal structure to business structure is required. This mapping has to allocate all affiliates and associates into the business structure. A direct mapping of a company to a business unit is not always given. Often, companies act only as a legal shell. The activities of several business units are united in one company. Such setups are common if a group operates in developing countries or tries to explore new markets or want to introduce a new business in a region where other businesses of the group are well established. There are several advantages to using an existing company as a legal shell:

- Own administration expenses can be minimized;
- No external registration or filing fees and service costs for a new company;
- No delay in introducing a new business;
- No processing time due to the formation of a new company;
- Quick market presence;
- Other commercial advantages.

By making use of companies that act as a legal shell, companies of the group may be spread across business units or even segments as illustrated by the following figures.

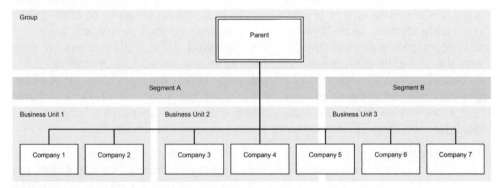

Fig. L-2 Group structure example 1

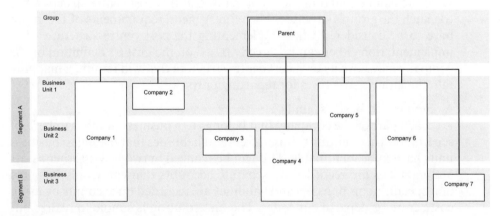

Fig. L-3 Group structure example 2

Even if the advantages are obvious, from the group's point of view such structures are difficult to handle regarding the management of business units, the legal entity and the preparation of consolidated figures:

- Several reporting lines from one company into several business units require data separation at local level.

- At least one manager has to sign responsible for the legal unit. This may result in conflicts if that manager is also in charge of a business unit while several other business units are hosted by the company. Decisions to be made and targets assigned to the company might be interpreted in favour for that business unit the manager also signs responsible for due to the dependencies of bonuses and other incentives.
- Allocation of parts of the company, particularly profits, assets and liabilities to business units are mandatory for management and allocation purposes.

As a general guideline in defining group structures, an allocation of companies to more than one business unit or across reportable segments should be avoided. Whenever possible, a company should be directly allocated to one business unit only. If such an allocation is not possible and an allocation across business units is needed, the company that is spread across business units has to be allocated to a reportable segment. An allocation of a company to several business units and across reportable segments should always be avoided. Such allocations are only acceptable if legal requirements exist that negatively impact the operation.

Assuming that an allocation of a company across business units takes place, **organizational and accounting aspects** dominate the structure of the company. These aspects have to be followed to enable the corporate centre to allocate and consolidate the financial position and performance of business units.

- Cost centres

    As a minimum requirement, the company which hosts various businesses have to have an organization structure that can be used for allocation purposes. Therefore, an underlying cost centre structure is necessary. Usually, such a structure can be found in every company. But this cost centre structure has to match the group's structure. Therefore, general requirements of the group have to be considered when implementing the cost centre structure.[1] The implementation either can be directly based on the group's definition or the company may have its own cost centre structure that will require a mapping into the group's structures for reporting purposes.

- Assignment to business units

    Each part of the company that belongs to a business unit has to be kept separately in accounting terms. Assets and liabilities that belong to business units have to be identifiable. This can be realized in two ways: Either assets and liabilities are recorded on separate accounts that carry only business unit specific items or assets and liabilities are recorded on accounts by using cost centre or department codes. The first solution is simple to realize but it inflates the account structure by with several accounts for similar assets and liabilities. The second solution is more sophisticated as account–cost centre combinations have to be used to allocate assets and liabilities to their corresponding business units. In practice, an account–cost centre combination is used for consolidation.

---

[1] See organization of the group on page 91 regarding further explanations.

In addition to assets and liabilities, all revenues and expenses of the period (and also the profit of the period) have to be assigned to business units as well. The assignment can be realized in the same way as the allocation of assets and liabilities by using account–cost centre combinations. There is a direct relationship between the profit and equity allocations. Retained earnings have to be allocated to business units in the same way the allocation of profit was handled.

- Handling of non-allocated assets

  Having allocated all mentioned items to business units, some assets, liabilities and equity may remain that are not allocable to any business unit. Non-allocable items often refer to corporate assets that serve all business units. Such assets have to be treated similar to corporate assets as defined by *IAS 36 – Impairment of Assets*.

- Intercompany

  An important organizational aspect is the identification and allocation of intercompany items (so assets, liabilities, revenue and expenses) to their corresponding business units. The allocation is necessary for management consolidation. The recording of intercompany items is based on ordinary accounting tasks. In addition to the correct intercompany account and the company code of the corresponding entity, a cost centre or department code is needed. The recording is not limited to intercompany transactions with other companies of the group. Even intercompany transactions between different business units inside the company have to be recorded. While such a recording would result in an overstatement of revenues and expenses as well as assets and liabilities, a reversal is required when preparing separate financial statements of the company.

- Use of resources and cost allocation

  Even if the company is treated as a legal shell and host the various businesses, these businesses also consume resources of the company. That is particularly office and other space in combination with utilities or administration services like accounting, payroll, human resources and IT. Furthermore, some businesses may consume and provide services at the same time. Regardless of the configurations, resources are shared across business units. Such a sharing requires also an allocation of their underlying costs. Underlying costs will always include direct costs; they may include overhead costs as well. This allocation can be based on traditional cost allocation techniques like cost allocation sheets used in management accounting. An alternate treatment is the use of transfer prices if rendered services shall include a profit mark-up. As long as transfer prices are used within the company only, the calculation of transfer prices can be based on commercial aspects only by neglecting any tax impact.

  The accounting for cost allocation has to ensure that the integrity of the business unit allocation is not injured. A pure cost allocation is not

sufficient as this will create a trial balance checksum error even if the
overall allocation side the company does not create any issues. Instead,
a double allocation similar to journal entries has to be performed. This
requires special attention as outlined below:

Journal entry		Cost Centre	Comment
dr.	Office expenses	100	Allocation of office expenses from one cost centre to another
cr.	Office expenses	200	one. Both cost centres belong to different business units.

Fig. L-4   Example of an improper cost allocation

The journal entry allocates costs from one cost centre to another
without impacting on the performance of the company. Nevertheless, from
a business unit's view the trial balances of both business units do not add
to zero raising a checksum error.

Journal entries		Cost Centre	Comment
dr.	Office expenses	100	
cr.	Transfer account	200	Interim balance sheet account
dr.	Transfer account	100	
cr.	Office expenses	200	

Fig. L-5   Example of a correct cost allocation

These journal entries allocate cost in a proper way. The balance of the
interim account is always zero from the company's point of view. Dividing
the trial balance into business units will not raise a checksum error, as a
double entry ensures data integrity.

• Reporting

Reporting for management consolidation purposes is advanced
compared to the reporting for statutory purposes. This is because more
details are needed. A reporting using dedicated forms or reports is
not appropriate in this case while data-quadruples are needed. These
quadruples always consist of accounts, cost centres, the contra company
and the resulting balance per reporting company.

Company ID	Account	Cost Centre	Contra company ID	Balance
xxx	xxxx.yyy	zzz	xxx	123,45

Fig. L-6   Data quadruple required for consolidation

Data quadruples may be enhanced if business is done with companies
that also host various businesses. In such cases, a contra company ID is not
sufficient. A combination of contra company ID and a contra cost centre
is needed which will inflate the reporting volume.

Company ID	Account	Cost Centre	Contra company ID	Contra Cost Centre	Balance
xxx	xxxx.yyy	zzz	xxx	zzz	123,45

Fig. L-7   Data multiple required for consolidation

Due to the reportable content, a reporting of a trial balance that includes quadruples or multiples is preferred. Such a reporting has to be managed in an electronic form due to the volume of possible combinations of accounts, cost centres and group companies involved.

In addition to organizational aspects of companies, **consolidations aspects** at group level require special attention. This attention is necessary as the consolidation has to consider business-internal transactions that are subject to consolidation only. These transactions can be understood as virtual intercompany transactions. Business transactions with other business units are treated in the same manner as with group-external parties like customers or suppliers. As a consequence, consolidation tasks & techniques have to be aligned to the business unit level.

- Data separation

  While a consolidation is performed on business unit level, only those data have to be considered that belongs to the business unit. Therefore, a data separation is necessary. This separation has to extract all data from the reported trial balance where the cost centre belongs to the business unit. This can be one or more cost centres depending on the group structure and the implementation by the hosting company. The checksum of the extracted trial balance has to add to zero!

- Data aggregation

  Data aggregation is an interim step to ensure that the data required for consolidation is aggregated on an appropriate level. By default, the data separation is serving the lowest level with the most details due to the account–cost centre combination. If such a detailed level of information is not necessary, a data aggregation has to condense all details up to the level that is required for consolidation. The desired level can be any level from single cost centres to the business unit itself as long as the aggregations sticks to the cost centre hierarchy. An aggregation is achieved by a summary of all account–cost centre combinations where the cost centres belong to a cost centre of a higher level up to the business unit.

Company ID	Account	Cost Centre	Balance	
xxx	1234.567	101	100,00	
xxx	1234.567	102	100,00	Cost centres on detail level
xxx	1234.567	110	50,00	
xxx	1234.567	100	250,00	Aggregated data at cost centre on higher level

Fig. L-8 Cost centre aggregation

The data aggregation has its limitations where contra companies and / or contra cost centres exist. An aggregation without the consideration of such details would result in a loss of details that is required for consolidation. Every time details are presented, the aggregation on a higher cost centre level will result in additional data quadruples or multiples.

Company ID	Account	Cost Centre	Contra company ID	Balance	
xxx	1234.567	101		100,00	⎤
xxx	1234.567	102	500	100,00	⎬ Cost centres on detail level
xxx	1234.567	110		50,00	⎦
xxx	1234.567	100		150,00	⎤ Aggregated data at cost centre
xxx	1234.567	100	500	100,00	⎦ on higher level

Fig. L-9 Cost centre aggregation using more details

- Trial balance preparation

    The preparation of an aggregated trial balance follows the same procedures as every other preparation for financial or statutory consolidations. All subsidiaries of the group that belong in full or in part to the business unit have to be considered in preparing the aggregated trial balance. The mixture of companies is not important. Therefore, a data separation and aggregation has to be performed of each company of the business unit that hosts more than one business. This is to ensure that only that part of a company will be considered that really belongs to the business unit.

    The aggregation, so the summation of all account balance across all companies have to consider again data quadruple: the account, the contra company, the contra cost centre and the balance. A pure aggregation by considering accounts only is not sufficient due to the loss of mandatory detail information.

    All companies that belong to the business unit have to perform the same adjustments that are necessary for statutory purposes. Therefore, a conversion towards IFRS and the application of group accounting principles are mandatory. This will result in level I to level III adjustments. Again adjustments necessary for hosting companies have to consider only that portion that belongs to the business unit. A data separation is required as well for the adjustments.

- Consolidation

    Once an aggregated trial balance is available that reflects the business unit financial position and performance, the intended management consolidation can start. The consolidation is similar to any other consolidation and consists of an elimination of all business-internal transactions. The following items have to be executed:[2]

---

[2] See chapters F-4 to F -6 regarding detailed descriptions of all consolidation tasks and activities.

- Debt consolidation;
- Income–expense consolidation;
- Elimination of unrealized profits.

An equity consolidation depends on the group structure. If a holding company or a parent is part of the business unit that record investments in subsidiaries that belong to the business unit, an equity consolidation eventually combined with an accounting of non-controlling interests is necessary. In all other cases, equity consolidation can be ignored.

Due to the focus on business-unit internal transactions, the **consolidation** journal entries required to eliminate transactions vary. If there are intercompany transactions that belong in full to a business unit, standard journal entries can be applied for elimination.

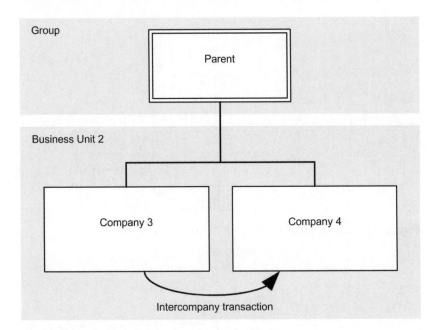

Fig. L-10 Elimination between two companies

Journal entry		Company	Comment
dr.	Liabilities	Sending company	Debt consolidation
cr.	Assets	Receiving company	
Journal entry		Company	Comment
dr.	Revenues	Sending company	Income–expense consolidation
cr.	Expenses	Receiving company	

A more sophisticated elimination is required if one of the two companies belong only in part to the business unit. It is not any longer sufficient to consider the companies in total. The contra cost centre has to be part of the journal entry. This is the cost centre as defined in the data aggregation. In can be the original cost centre or a cost centre at a higher level.

Journal entry		Company	Cost Centre	Comment
dr.	Liabilities	Sending company	Receiving cost	No cost centre
cr.	Assets	Receiving company	centre	information required

Journal entry		Company	Cost Centre	Comment
dr.	Revenues	Sending company	Receiving cost	No cost centre
cr.	Expenses	Receiving company	centre	information required

A similar elimination of intercompany transactions is required if two companies are involved that belong in part to the business unit. In such a case, the contra cost centre and the cost centre of the reporting company have to be used. The cost centre of the company is that cost centre used for data separation.

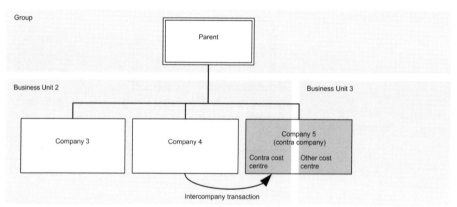

Fig. L-11   Elimination with one hosting company

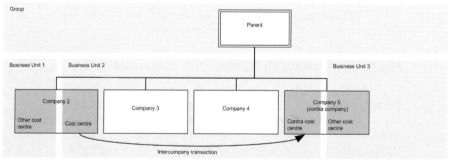

Fig. L-12   Elimination with two hosting companies

Journal entry		Company	Cost Centre
dr.	Liabilities	Sending company	Sending cost centre
cr.	Assets	Receiving company	Receiving cost centre
Journal entry		Company	Cost Centre
dr.	Revenues	Sending company	Sending cost centre
cr.	Expenses	Receiving company	Receiving cost centre

As with a standard consolidation, a consolidation matrix can be established for management consolidations as well. The difference from a standard consolidation matrix is again the enhanced content as it is not sufficient to consider only company IDs as references. Instead, a combination of company IDs and cost centres is required for the sending as well as the receiving company. The consolidation matrix can be used for double checks of reconciling intercompany balances and any differences due to improper accounting on cost centre level.

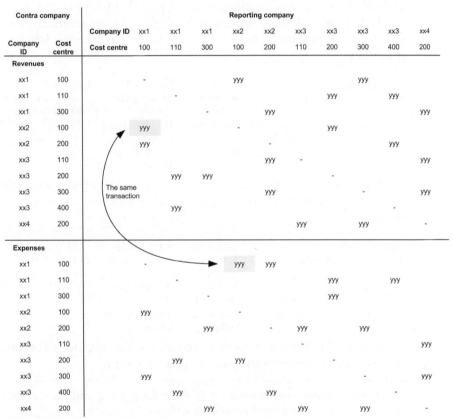

Fig. L-13 Intercompany consolidation matrix

Due to the involvement of various cost centres for one company, the consolidation of intercompany transactions of one company can require more than one journal entry. The number of journal entries depends on the number of cost centres involved. The use of cost centres in consolidations enables intercompany eliminations even within a company. The company ID will be indeed the same but cost centre IDs differ. The price for such a comfortable intercompany elimination is performing extended journal entries combined with eliminations of the extended journal entries when preparing separate financial statements.

Another important topic is the elimination of **unrealized profit**, which arises in transactions for later sale and own use. The elimination procedure and the calculation of the embedded unrealized profit do not differ between management and statutory consolidations.[3] The only difference is the journal entry to be executed as this journal entry has to consider again cost centres. Due to the reason for unrealized profits and the presentation style of the statement on income, four journal entries may apply.

If the profit & loss statement is based on a structure by nature, the following journal entry has to be used to eliminate unrealized profits in inventory:

Journal entry			Company	Cost Centre	Comment
dr.		Revenues	Sending company	Sending cost centre	Cost centres depend on which company is the one hosting the business.
	cr.	Changes in inventory	Receiving company	Receiving cost centre	
	cr.	Inventory	Receiving company	Receiving cost centre	

If the profit & loss statement is based on a structure by function, this journal entry has to be applied for the elimination of unrealized profits in inventory:

Journal entry			Company	Cost Centre	Comment
dr.		Revenues	Sending company	Sending cost centre	Cost centres depend on which company is the one hosting the business.
	cr.	Cost of goods sold	Sending company	Sending cost centre	
	cr.	Inventory	Receiving company	Receiving cost centre	

If unrealized profit resides in fixed assets, the inventory account has to be replaced by the appropriate fixed asset account.

> Keep in mind: An elimination of unrealized profit will raise deferred tax issues even for management consolidation!

A successful execution of the consolidation step will result in a consolidated trial balance for the business unit.

---

[3] See chapter F -6 on page 310 regarding the handling of unrealized profits.

- Other tasks

    Preparing consolidated financial statements usually requires the execution of a set of other tasks:

    - Group transactions;
    - Netting;
    - Reclassification.

    As far as management consolidations are concerned, the question will arise whether or not these tasks are necessary for the management of the business unit and the extent of information these tasks are able to contribute. As there are not legal requirements for a complete close of business units, a soft close might be sufficient. By contrast, if the remaining tasks have a material impact on the management of the business unit, these tasks have to be performed and a hard close is demanded in that case. To decide whether or not a full close is necessary, cost-benefit aspects, required preciseness and quality of consolidated business unit figures and other criteria should be considered.

    Nettings and reclassification, in the context of management consolidation, occur exactly in the same way as for statutory consolidations. Special attention is required for group transactions. Group transactions refer to valuation issues at group level like bad debt allowances, provisions or adjustments of goodwill. Some of these valuation adjustments may belong to business units so that a consideration on business unit level is appropriate.

    The final activity to complete business unit consolidations is the deriving of the balance sheet and profit & loss statement of the business unit which is more or less an automated task that requires no manual involvement.

Consolidation tasks & techniques focus on management consolidation for business units and can be applied to all kinds of levels that demand consolidation. Potential candidates for such management consolidations are **segments** as segments are also subject to an external reporting as demanded by *IFRS 8 – Operating Segments*. While segments reside on business units and are therefore the next higher level, consolidation techniques do not significantly change, even if there is a change in the scope of consolidation. A limited set of adjustments has to be considered:

- The cost centre hierarchy has to ensure consistency. Cost centres have to roll-up into business units and business units have to roll-up into segments. A distinct allocation is necessary identical to the allocation of cost centres (so no allocation of business units to more than one segment).
- The data separation and aggregation have to consider all companies of the segment. While a company may host several businesses, some of these businesses may belong to the same segment. This requires a modified data separation. The same applies to data aggregation.

- The consolidation and elimination of segment-internal transactions have to be executed across all companies of the group.
- Other tasks have to be executed when segment consolidations are part of consolidated financial statements published in annual reports. A soft close is not appropriate in such situations.

Management consolidations are – compared to statutory consolidations – more challenging as a further dimension, the cost centre, has to be considered in the consolidation process. A valid question therefore is on the automation of management consolidations. To avoid any manual activities, as many steps should be automated as possible. This is subject to the consolidation software used.

Consolidated business unit figures (so balance sheet and profit & loss statements and other derived financial information) will help the manager in charge to run the business unit. If these figures are not comparable and reconcilable with other figures in the group, a **reconciliation** is necessary to explain the effects and changes between different views of the performance of the group, the business unit and other organizational units. Typical reconciliations used in groups are:

- The group's consolidated profit & loss statement with the aggregated consolidated profit & loss statements of all segments. This is also a mandatory disclosure in consolidated financial statements according to *IFRS 8 – Operating Segments*. The disclosure has to include several segment information and particularly total assets and total liabilities, group internal and external revenues, profits, depreciation, interests and income tax expenses.
- The segment's consolidated profit & loss statement with the aggregated consolidated profit & loss statements of all business units. Such a reconciliation is necessary if the segments are actively managed.
- The business unit's consolidated profit & loss statement with the aggregated consolidated profit & loss statements of all companies of the business unit.

To prepare such reconciliations, management consolidations have to be performed several times. The reconciliation between the group's performance and segments, a statutory consolidation of the whole group and management consolidations for all segments are required. Similar, a reconciliation between a segment and its business units require a management consolidation of the segment and all business units. As such tasks may result in time-consuming consolidation activities, approximations are often used in practice. These approximations prepare aggregated figures. Intercompany eliminations are based on a rough estimation accepting errors. These errors are acceptable up to a certain extent and depends on the discretion of management.

3. PROJECTS AND COST UNITS

Projects and cost units can be subject to management consolidation, like business units, and are required if projects and cost units are spread across the group involving intercompany transactions. The ownership of management consolidations on projects and cost units is with management accounting. The intention of management consolidations on projects and cost units is to gain a better understanding of the financial position of a project or cost unit in a group which usually consists of assets involved, costs, financial resources and any revenues. A pure aggregation of costs, financial resources and revenues would not result in a fair presentation of the financial position as over- and under-statements will exist due to intercompany transactions involved.

Management consolidations on projects and cost units are used for different purposes. Typical applications of such consolidations are the calculation of products at group level, the performance monitoring of large projects or the calculation of inventory at group level. A common feature is the intention for the use of management consolidations as explained before. Therefore, management consolidations are often separate tasks, they can stand on their own and be not necessarily part of group accounting tasks in preparing consolidated financial statements. Nevertheless, they will be used for the assessment of the absolute position of a project or cost unit when this has to be capitalized.

In general, two views can be taken on projects and cost units – calculation and performance. Both views have their existence rights and are needed at different stages.

- The calculation view is a preview of a project or cost unit (e.g. like the development of a new product). It will be taken upfront to gain an understanding about the expected profits and costs incurred, in total and / or per unit involved. If necessary calculations will be expanded to lifecycle views of projects and cost units, either on a stand-alone basis by considering only costs and expenses or on a profit base by considering also expected and assumed revenues.
- The performance view is an on-going or final view depending on the stage of the project's or cost centre's activities, and considers revenues in addition to costs so that a profit measurement becomes possible. Furthermore, cost comparisons are possible when comparing the actual cost position with calculated or planned costs. Such views are popular to get an understanding on the profit that was achieved with the project or product.

3.1 Projects

Projects are defined as activities with a limited duration. The duration of a project depends on the business of the group, the volume and its complexity: from a few months to several years. At the end of the project's duration, a measurable result can be observed, whether this result consists of a constructed asset, services provided or knowledge gained.

Projects subject to management consolidation are usually larger projects in which several subsidiaries, business or other organizational units are involved. The **structure and organization** of these types of project is arranged in a way that one instance (a department, a business unit or any other organizational unit) is responsible for the project while all departments, business units, or other organizational units involved allocate some of their resources to the project.

These resources are usually managed and maintained by a local person in charge who is serving the project.

A central aspect in running these projects is a dedicated **workflow**. Each party involved has to be aware of his tasks and activities, his deadlines and the resource to be used. The workflow is usually managed and monitored by the responsible party to track progress, appropriate reporting structures and project meetings.

Projects can be arranged internally and externally. Group internal projects often focus on the improvement of defined subjects in groups. By contrast, group external projects are those to be sold to customers. These projects generate revenue and therefore profits that contribute to the group's performance while internal projects usually generate costs only. Whether a project is arranged internally or externally, they have more or less the same cost structures including similar **cost components**. The standard cost components of projects consist of materials, personnel costs, charges and other overhead costs. It is irrelevant where these costs are generated as long as these costs can be assigned to projects.

From an **accounting perspective**, accounting for projects is a mixture of financial and management accounting tasks. Projects have to be treated as unfinished goods at the end of a period and require a capitalization based on the progress of the project unless there is no revenue recognition based on the application of the percentage of completion method. Capitalization as unfinished goods follows the ordinary accounting rules that have to be applied for any other unfinished goods. The extent of capitalizing costs that belong to the project has to consider all organizational units involved with their local costs. This requires an extended project reporting to track all intercompany transactions together with their costs involved. This reporting has to be embedded in a consolidation environment that is capable to separate project costs from other costs and to consolidate only these costs.

3.2 Cost units

Cost units are management accounting items used to collect all kinds of costs. A cost unit is often used for a product or a similar item that carries a set of costs. The intention if using cost units is to track the costs and the performance of a product. Common applications are the initial calculation of a product, the continuing measurement of the performance and profits of a product and the determination of a product's contribution to the company's or group's performance. Compared to projects, cost units have a different focus, they are not limited like projects. They collect costs as long as this is appropriate, and if the cost units are used for products, these units will exist as long as the product does.

To manage cost units, the units are embedded in a **structure** that is able to identify and allocate costs to these units. A common practice is to build hierarchies of cost units to aggregate and allocate costs along the value chain or the manufacturing process of products and within product groups. This not only applies to production within a single corporation, but also to groups where several parties are involved in manufacturing and selling products.

Typical **cost components** are direct materials, direct labour and work overheads. An extended view will consider other cost components that arise either directly or indirectly from the product or its application. Typical cost components allocable to cost units are: development costs, packaging and handling costs, tools used in production and any other directly allocable costs. Such an extended view often extends the accounting towards a lifecycle costing system for products (and services).

From an **accounting perspective**, the application of cost units requires special attention regarding the determination and application of costs in a hierarchical system. Costs have to be accounted for only once and not at several stages along the manufacturing process. Costs also have to be free from any unrealized profit and cost items that do not belong to production costs is a narrow view.

3.3 Consolidation tasks and techniques

The consolidation of projects and cost units is different from a consolidation of an entity or business unit. This is because management consolidations dealing with projects and cost units do not have to ensure that all financial figures and the related journal entries have to balance. Instead, only defined or dedicated items have to be considered in the consolidation procedure. This requires detailed knowledge of cost structures, profit calculation, group structures and the workflow and value creation chain in a group.

As the complexity of management consolidations increases with that of the processes and structures of products and groups, an application of methods and processes that can cope with these requirements is required. Current implementations often make use of the application of a standard costing system in combination with transfer pricing systems. Such applications enable a consolidation without requiring a too detailed knowledge on structures and processes. The corporate centre is provided with standardized information that simplifies the consolidation procedure. Even if methods and processes are applied that simplify management consolidations, the consolidation of projects and cost units require intimate knowledge about the structure and behaviour of projects and products.

Consolidation tasks focus on the elimination of unrealized profits along the value chain and the determination of the current position of a project or product (its costs and performances) from a group's perspective. This is a typical activity of cost or management accounting to monitor the performance of projects and products, which can be performed at any point during the period. In addition to these voluntary activities, a management consolidation is required at the end of the period if projects and products have to be capitalized as finished or unfinished goods or services.

Consolidation techniques of management consolidations do not differ significantly from techniques for statutory consolidations. The difference between both consolidations is their focus and precision. Due to the purpose of projects and cost units, a reconciled handling like in financial accounting is not necessary. While the focus is on the collection and allocation of costs and their refinancing through sales at a later stage, typical accounting elements such as financial trial balances are not necessary. Therefore, the consolidation is treated in a slightly changed way. The techniques applied to management consolidation are not new and mostly use tools that are derived from proven cost accounting practices.

The elimination of **intercompany transactions** that are assigned to projects and cost units follows the same pattern as the consolidation of business units. A consolidation using a combination of accounts and cost units and – if appropriate cost centres – is necessary to eliminate these intercompany transactions.[4]

Another consolidation technique in determining project and product costs is the use of **consolidation sheets**, which summarize the cost structure of each company, business unit, subproject or sub-cost unit involved. Relationships between these areas are eliminated by applying ordinary consolidation procedures. To comply with accounting requirements, contractions and extensions can be used for adjustments to arrive at consolidated figures for group purposes.

	Reporting company				Sum	Adjustments			Group
	xx1	xx2	xx3	xx4		Consolidations	Extensions	Contractions	
Production costs:									
Direct material	yyy	yyy	yyy	yyy	xxx	yyy	yy1		zzz
Direct labour	yyy	yyy	yyy	yyy	xxx	yyy			zzz
Works overhead	yyy	yyy	yyy	yyy	xxx	yyy			zzz
Costs of goods manufactured	xxx	xxx	xxx	xxx	xxx	xxx	xxx	xxx	zzz
Allocated costs:									
Sales costs	yyy	yyy	yyy	yyy					
Packaging, freight and related costs	yy1		yy1			Costs of group internal transactions			
Administration costs	yyy	yyy	yyy	yyy					
Profit mark up	yyy	yyy	yyy	yyy					
Sales price	xxx	xxx	xxx	xxx					

Fig. L-14 Consolidation sheet for the determination of cost units for group purposes

Consolidation sheets require detailed knowledge of the cost structures in each company, business unit, subproject or sub-cost unit involved. Furthermore, the relationships between these areas have to be known. If consolidations sheets are applied for products, relationships reflect the bill of materials and assembly instructions.

4. DEPENDENCY BETWEEN MANAGEMENT CONSOLIDATIONS AND CONSOLIDATED FINANCIAL STATEMENTS

Consolidated financial statements that are prepared by applying statutory consolidations and management consolidations have a strong dependence. This is because management consolidation is often used to calculate selected balance sheet items and profit & loss items and for the preparation of accompanying

---

[4] See chapter L -2 on page 714 for further details.

financial figures that are required for disclosure purposes. Furthermore, both consolidations make use of the same underlying financial data and information, even if their views of the underlying data are different.

To enable statutory and management consolidations using the same underlying data requires a data preparation that is able to serve both consolidations. Data for management consolidation require more details than data for statutory consolidations, so management consolidation requirements take priority. This includes:

- An allocation of data that are aggregated on an account to one or more accounts or to one or more cost centres, and
- Data extensions by additional information (e.g. cost centre, cost units) that are not needed for statutory purposes.

Statutory consolidations usually do not require this richness of detail. Data at account level per subsidiary is often more than sufficient. To ensure a coexistence of data use for various purposes, preparation needs of underlying data have to be evaluated in each individual case before implementing them in accounting systems. Data structures that are able to carry all information for consolidation needs are often realized by using data warehouses in combination with OLAP tools for data retrievals.

The dependency between both consolidations is also driven by organizational aspects. If statutory and management consolidations are handled in different departments, a workflow between both departments is necessary for year-end closings including all typical workflow elements like responsibilities of tasks and activities, timing, interfaces and data formats, information and other issues. If in contrast the consolidations are handled in one department, both consolidations can be combined into one central instance.

M CONSOLIDATED FINANCIAL STATEMENTS

About this chapter:

The consolidation is done. Now, consolidated financial statements have to be prepared which is much more than just to compile all data into one set of accounts and derive the required statements. Additional explanations are required due to the disclosure requirements of IFRS. Furthermore, some legislation requires the preparation of management discussions that need to be integrated into consolidated financial statements. This chapter highlights all topics that are required in preparing the full set of consolidated financial statements.

1. THE BASICS

The preparation of the required statements and accompanying documents of consolidated financial statements is the final task before audit. All consolidated data have to be brought in a reportable and readable format that complies with the reporting requirements of IAS 1 – the purpose of the audit. Parents use this opportunity by preparing annual reports that include not only consolidated financial statements together with their accompanying documents but also information about the group, their products, services and business activities and governing letters from the chairmen of the board and the management and other important information. These annual reports are usually available as a glossy.

The financial section of annual reports includes mandatory as well as **voluntary items**. Voluntary elements are often included as consolidated financial statements under IFRS are accepted by some legislations as a substitute to consolidated financial statements based on local accounting standards if mandatory items of these accounting standards are part of consolidated financial statements under IFRS. As IFRS do not reject such an attempt through restrictions but encourage disclosing additional information as appropriate, consolidated financial statements often act as multi-purpose statements.

Part of voluntary items is also the management discussion about the current financial position and current and planned performance. As this is not an IFRS at this stage but a practice statement it is not a mandatory item. Nevertheless, the IASB is planning to make such disclosures mandatory in the future.

Mandatory items of consolidated financial statements are defined in IAS 1.10. The standard requires the following items to be included in consolidated financial statements:

- Statements
  - [Consolidated] statement of financial position
  - [Consolidated] statement of comprehensive income
  - [Consolidated] statement of changes in equity
  - [Consolidated] statement of cash flows;
- Notes;
- Comparative information;
- Additional statement of financial position upon retrospective application of accounting policies or restatements.

The contents of each item are defined either by IAS 1 or by other standards. All statements have the same prominence.

Even if not explicitly mentioned, the auditor's opinion on the consolidated financial statements is also a mandatory item to be disclosed.

2. STATEMENTS

IAS 1.10 only defines items being part of consolidated financial statements, some of them are subject to further requirements. The standard itself lists layouts alternative and a set of minimum contents to be presented. Preparers have to include only these minimum contents but are free to add other content as appropriate. For example, IAS 1.85 encourage preparers to add additional items when such presentation is relevant for an understanding of the group's financial performance.

As IAS 1 does not differentiate between separate and consolidated financial statements all requirements have to be applied to consolidated statements.

*   [Consolidated] statement of profit or loss and other comprehensive income

    The statement comprises two sections that are often presented as separate statements – a section on the ongoing performance of the group (presented often as a consolidated statement of income) and a section about other changes of equity, often presented in a statement of comprehensive income or in the consolidated statement of changes in equity. IFRS 1.IG6 (Part I) provides examples about acceptable integrated and separate presentations of these sections in one or more statements. Observed practice is a separate presentation of the performance of the group: a [consolidated] statement of income and a [consolidated] statement of comprehensive income.

    The structure of the profit & loss section depends on the chosen alternative. IAS 1.99 accepts a presentation of profit & loss by nature and by function. The chosen form directly interacts with the consolidation tasks outlined in chapter F -5.2.

    > As the presentation by function is the preferred and internationally accepted form, investors will benefit from choosing this form.

    The structure of the other comprehensive section is based on a classification by nature. It comprises all changes in equity that are caused in the ordinary course of the business but outside profit & loss.

*   [Consolidated] statement of financial position

    The statement of financial position covers all assets and liabilities of the group. In addition to the items to be included in the statement, the main focus is on the presentation of these items. In general, all assets and liabilities have to be presented separately as current and non-current items. The classification depends on the definition of IAS 1.61. Items that are expected to be settled or recovered within 12 months have to be presented as current. A specific sorting order within the categories is not required, IAS 1.57 expressly confirms this. The freedom to prepare the statement of financial position as appropriate to preparer's needs has resulted in an application of presentations derived from local accounting standards. Anglo-Saxon companies, for example, often prepare the statement using an increasing order of liquidity. European companies as another example often prefer a presentation based on a decreasing sorting order of liquidity by considering the function of assets.

- [Consolidated] statement of cash flows

    The presentation of the statement of cash flows is based on *IAS 7 – Statement of Cash Flows*. According to the standard, cash flows can either be prepared by the direct method or indirect method as outline in chapter K -3.1.[1] Even if preparers have the choice between these two presentation methods, the preferred method from a preparer's perspective is the indirect method. This is because the ability to prepare cash flow statements using the direct method is difficult, as EDP systems often do not offer an extraction ability of data required.

    Due to the detailed requirements on the presentation of cash flows, alternative treatments and presentation options are not given. The only option a preparer has is to decide about the level of detail to be presented for each cash flow category.

- [Consolidated] statement of changes in shareholder equity

    The statement of changes in equity is more or less a reconciliation of changes in equity. For each category of equity the movements – sorted by profit & loss, other comprehensive income and transactions with owners – have to be presented. Categories of equity are not fully defined; IAS 1.106 and 1.108 list only some items. Usually, categories of equity are those ones presented also in the statement of financial position. They often consist of:

    - Share capital;
    - Capital reserves;
    - Retained earnings;
    - Other reserves;
    - Treasury shares;
    - Non-controlling interests.

    Due to the requirements of the standard, a presentation as a table is often chosen where columns reflect categories of equity and rows reflect their changes. As transactions during the periods may change, the rows of the statement will also change as needed.

---

[1] See page 679.

| Item | Share capital | Capital reserves | Retained earnings | Other reserves | | | | | Treasury shares | Equity attributable to owners | Non-controlling interests | Total equity |
				Pensions	Financial instruments	Hedges	Foreign currency translations	Revaluation Surplus				
Equity @ beginning of period	yyy	yyy	yyy	yyy	yyy	yyy	yyy	yyy	yyy	zzz	yyy	zzz
Changes in accounting policies			xxx		xxx		xxx	xxx		xxx	xxx	xxx
Corrections of errors			xxx	xxx	xxx	xxx	xxx			xxx	xxx	xxx
Restated equity @ beginning of period	yyy	yyy	yyy	yyy	yyy	yyy	yyy	yyy	yyy	zzz	yyy	zzz
Net profit & loss of the period			xxx							xxx	yyy	xxx
Other comprehensive income												
Unrealized gains / losses				xxx	xxx	xxx	xxx			xxx	xxx	xxx
Other changes								xxx		xxx	xxx	xxx
Deferred taxes				xxx	xxx	xxx		xxx		xxx	xxx	xxx
Transactions with shareholders												
Increase / Decrease of share capital	xxx	xxx								xxx	xxx	xxx
Dividends			xxx							xxx		xxx
Treasury shares		xxx	xxx						xxx	xxx	xxx	xxx
Other transactions		xxx	xxx							xxx	xxx	xxx
Reclassification		xxx	xxx							xxx	xxx	xxx
Equity @ end of period	yyy	yyy	yyy	yyy	yyy	yyy	yyy	yyy	yyy	zzz	yyy	zzz

Fig. M-1 Example of consolidated statement of changes in equity

The above-mentioned structure of the statement is expanded by a further row for reclassifications. Such a row is necessary if shareholder resolutions are made to allocate equity to specific purposes. A typical example is an allocation of capital from retained earnings to capital reserves.

Some IFRS demand a retrospective application of selected transactions, particularly if new IFRS are endorsed that have to be applied. A retrospective application may also occur due to corrections of errors according to *IAS 8 – Accounting Policies, Changes in accounting estimates and errors*. As such transactions have to be recorded at the beginning of the period; it is good practice to present restated equity due to these effects.

3. NOTES & GROUP DISCLOSURES

Notes are an integral element of consolidated financial statements as they include complementary information and analyses about items presented in the consolidated statement of financial position, the consolidated statement of income, the consolidated statement of cash flows and the consolidated statement of changes in equity. IAS 1.10e states that notes are the element of financial statements that contain a summary of significant accounting policies together with other explanatory information. The structure and basic contents to be disclosed in notes are defined in IAS 1.112 to 1.138. Other contents of the notes are defined as disclosure requirement in other standards.[2]

3.1. Structure of notes

The very rough structure of the notes is proposed in IAS 1.114. According to this definition, notes should be structured in the following order:

- Statement of compliance with IFRS;
- Summary of significant accounting polices applied;
- Supporting information for items presented in the statements;
- Other disclosures.

This structure is not obligatory. Alternative structures might be applied in some circumstances. Based on these prerequisites, notes as applied in practice are divided into three sections:

- General descriptions and information
    This section contains a summary of general information and the basis for the preparation of consolidated financial statements.
    - Introduction to the parent and the group. This includes at minimum the legal form of the parent, its residence, the nature of the entities operation and details on the ownership (privately held or publicly listed,

---

[2] Due to the extent of reporting requirements and the level of detail demanded for disclosure, this chapter includes only basic explanations of notes. This explanation covers the structure and general contents only. IFRS as published by the IASB should be used for any details that have to be disclosed.

often combined with the place of trading and it's ID) as demanded by IAS 1.138. In rare cases, other information such as markets and products and services offered is provided.

- Compliance statement with IFRS as demanded by IAS 1.16. This statement should provide assurance that the financial statements comply with all IFRS. As far as any changes to accounting standards occurred, a description of the changed standards, the impacts on the consolidated financial statements and any early application and their (expected) impacts have to be disclosed.
- Disclosures required for the first time application of IFRS.
- Applied accounting policies.
- Structure of the group and changes in the group.

- Explanation and supporting disclosures of statements.
     This section contains explanations and analysis of the items presented in the four basic statements.

- Other information and disclosures
     All other information and disclosures, either mandatory or voluntary that are required by IFRS and that are not allocable to any items of the statements are combined in this section. Typical examples that belong to this section are:
  - Risks;
  - Related parties;
  - Management remuneration.

As a courtesy to users of financial statements, stick to the structure applied in practice unless you have good reasons to apply a different structure.

3.2. Accounting policies and group disclosures

Compared to notes of separate financial statements, notes of consolidated financial statements include additional disclosures for group and consolidation purposes. These additional disclosures are either reported separately or integrated into general accounting policies. A tendency is not observable. Regardless of a separate or combined reporting, accounting policies of consolidated financial statements always consist of accounting principles applied in measuring and presenting financial items and group policies and methods applied in preparing consolidated financial statements.

Accounting principles applied consist of a detailed description of how to account for dedicated business transactions and balance sheet items. This description includes a brief explanation of the underlying business transactions as well as the measurement practice applied. The order, accounting policies are presented usually follows the presentation style of the statements and the set-up of the statements. Most companies start with a description of the policies belonging to the consolidated statement of income followed by a description of the items belonging to the consolidated statement of financial position. Accounting policies are complemented by other disclosures that have the same prominence even if these items are not subject to accounting. Typical examples of such items are the handling of contingent liabilities, product warranties and legal proceedings.

The description of accounting principles applied for consolidated financial statements is identical to the principles required for separate financial statements. There is no difference.

Group policies and methods are an expansion of the accounting principles towards the group. Items to be disclosed are consolidation methods and currency translations. The intention of these disclosures is to enable readers of consolidated financial statements to estimate the impact of the consolidation process on consolidated financial statements. The disclosures usually include a description of the extent of consolidations, of consolidation methods applied (equity, debt, income & expense and unrealized profits), any exceptions to consolidations (e.g. due to non-material reasons) and the application of underlying principles, particularly the handling of any deviations of subsidiary's financial statements from the reporting date of the group and the application of uniform recognition and measurement principles.

An integral part of group policies is the treatment of foreign currency translations. The treatment of foreign currencies has to include a description of the translation methods applied and how any differences are recorded. Furthermore, if the functional currency of foreign companies is different to the group's functional currency, the translation methods to convert these companies into the group's functional currency has to be described.

In addition to group policies, disclosures of the group are demanded by IFRS. These **group disclosures** are often organized in a separate chapter that belongs to general descriptions and information. Some companies even combine this information with group policies applied. The intention of group disclosures is to inform about the structure of the group, its subsidiaries as well as any changes of the group composition. Changes of the group composition include both, acquisitions and divestitures, particularly of those companies subject to consolidation.

- Acquisitions

    Disclosures relating to acquisitions target on business and financial information of the company acquired. In addition to a formal description of the subsidiary acquired, the nature of its business and the fit to the group, financial information has to be disclosed as demanded by IFRS 3.B64 to 3.B67. In addition to the carrying amount of assets acquired and liabilities assumed, disclosures have to consider fair value adjustments and any residual value to be recognized as goodwill or gains.[3] The standard also requires the disclosure of pro-forma performance information of the period where the company is acquired.[4]

    Due to the extent of information to be disclosed acquisitions are usually arranged in subchapters where a subchapter comprises all disclosures per acquisition.

---

[3] See chapter E -4.2 on page 193 for an example of a reconciliation schedule of a purchase price allocation and disclosures demanded by IFRS 3.

[4] See chapter E -1.2 on page 119 regarding the handling of pro-forma periods.

- Divestitures

    Similar to acquisitions, extended disclosures are required upon the sale of subsidiaries. These disclosures include a description of the sales transaction together with the gain or loss achieved by this disposal. A brief description together with a presentation of the net gain / loss is often sufficient.

	Sales proceeds	xxx
-	Net assets	xxx
+/-	Other gains or losses incurred	xxx
Net gain / loss		**xxx**

Fig. M-2   Schedule of gains / losses generated due to divestitures

Other disclosures in the context of divestitures are subsidiaries that are classified as discontinued operations according to the accounting requirements of IFRS 5. These disclosures include a description of the business or subsidiary that is classified as a discontinued operation together with explanations why this operation is for sale. IFRS 5.41 provides a list of detailed requirements that relate to the descriptions and explanations demanded. A common practice is to disclose the composition of the net assets that reflect the discontinued operation.

While divestitures directly impact the financial position and performance of the group, a summary of all disposals and the impact on the group and its performance is often provided in the notes.

3.3. Disclosures

Disclosures that relate to the statements are the core element of notes. These disclosures include various elements ranging from general descriptions to calculations, detailed analyses and impacts on the group. The items, facts and circumstances that will be integrated into the notes depend on the requirements of the individual standards. The **origin** of information to be added in notes is widely spread across all applied standards. Each standard defines its individual items that have to be included in the notes. There is no option on ignoring or omitting disclosures. Other than details in financial statements that can be ignored due to materiality reasons, disclosures have to be published in full. To ensure that all disclosure requirements are met, a scan of all standards regarding their disclosure requirements in a mandatory task if not other tools are used that ensure disclosure compliance with IFRS.

> Use publicly available checklists to determine which disclosures are required.

Disclosures are structured by following the individual statements and the structure of each statement. While there is no guidance on the order how items are disclosed, two tendencies on the **structure** can be observed in practice. Parents often structure the disclosures by starting with the consolidated statement of

Item	Carrying amount
Non-current assets	
Intangible assets	xxx
Goodwill	xxx
Property, plant & equipment	xxx
Financial assets	xxx
Other assets	xxx
Current assets	
Inventory	xxx
Receivables	xxx
Other assets	xxx
Cash & cash equivalents	xxx
Assets of discontinued operation	**xxx**
Non-current liabilities	
Pensions	xxx
Debt	xxx
Other provisions & liabilities	xxx
Current liabilities	
Prepayments	xxx
Debt	xxx
Payables	xxx
Accruals	xxx
Other liabilities	xxx
Liabilities of discontinued operation	**xxx**
Net assets	**xxx**

Fig. M-3   Schedule of net assets of a discontinued operation

income (often combined with information on other comprehensive income) followed by the consolidated statement of financial position and the remaining statements (consolidated statement of cash flows and consolidated statement of changes in shareholder equity). An observed alternative form is starting with the consolidated statement of financial position followed by the consolidated statement of income and again all other statements.

To allocate financial figures provided in the statements to disclosures in the notes, **references** are used. Each financial item in a statement that is explained by additional information, analysis or details carries a reference. This reference can be found in the section of the notes dealing with the accompanying disclosures. References are numbered in a logical order following the presentation order of the statements and the structure in the statements.

The **content** to be disclosed varies. As the content depends on the business of the group and the extent of items to be disclosed due to the requirements of the appropriate standards, there is no general guidance how to arrange the content. The arrangement of the content has to be defined by each group individually to reflect its business. The presentation of the content is usually based on a mixture that consists of a verbal description of facts and circumstances and tables that carries analyses and break-downs of financial figures into single components. If necessary, comparisons of current period figures with previous period figures are used to explain changes, trends or other developments.

3.4. Other disclosures

Disclosures of accounting policies, the group and dedicated analysis of financial items of all statements are complemented by other disclosures, which are either mandatory due to other IFRS rules and regulations, or voluntary due to information that is important for investors and other stakeholders. They can cover the group as a whole or focus on selected businesses of the group or even on some details where management believes that they need to be disclosed.

- Mandatory disclosures

    Mandatory disclosures summarize all disclosures required by IFRS that do not belong to accounting policies or any financial items of the basic statements. Typical examples of such disclosures deal with leases, related parties or first time adoption of IFRS.

    Mandatory disclosures can also relate to the laws and regulations of the country in which the parent resides; they are often not mandatory from an IFRS perspective, and therefore complementary. Typical examples of such disclosures are information about dedicated expense information or management remuneration.

    Other mandatory disclosures are often demanded by stock exchanges. These disclosures are required to be listed in stock exchanges and have to be disclosed on a regular base. Publicly listed companies often incorporate these items in their financial statements. Typical disclosures relate to trading information of stock, filings and financial calendars.

- Voluntary disclosures

    In contrast to mandatory disclosures, voluntary disclosures are not under any publishing constraints. The information disclosed is wholly based on the discretion of management to provide other useful information to investors and other stakeholders. Consequently, such information can include all kinds of items that either has a connection to financial figures or are independent from them.

The less important other disclosures are the closer they are placed towards the end of the notes.

3.5. Preparation process

The preparation of notes can become a time-consuming exercise, particularly when prepared for the first time. This is because the disclosures subject to integration in the notes are widely spread across all applied standards. Initial preparation therefore requires special attention as there is no choice in what should be included when mandatory. Once prepared though, these notes can act as a template for subsequent preparations of notes to consolidated financial statements. Updates due to changes in the group structure, changes in applied group accounting policies or the application of new IFRS can be easily made without completely rewriting.

To ensure safe preparation of notes, checklists should be used, comprising disclosures required by all standards, often grouped by categories as demanded by the structure of notes. Due to the changes in accounting standards, initialized by the introduction of new standards, the replacement of existing standards by new ones or by annual improvement projects, the most up to date checklists should be used.

> Checklists are offered by all large auditor companies. They are often available for free in the download areas of auditor's websites.

If the preparation process of notes to consolidated financial statements is based on checklists, several scans of the checklist used are required to ensure an appropriate disclosure of all facts and circumstances. It is recommended to apply the following preparation order:

Step	Activity	Tasks / Explanations
1)	Initial scan	The initial scan is used to identify those standards and disclosures that are applied for the preparation of consolidated financial statements and therefore have to be considered in the notes.
2)	Data gathering	Depending on the IFRS involved, data subject to the notes have to be gathered. Depending on the size and structure of the group, several departments and / or entities have to deliver dedicated information:[5] <ul><li>Accounting: Accounting policies, details on all financial items like balance sheet items, fixed asset schedules and similar information.</li><li>M&A: Details on companies acquired.</li><li>Legal: List of companies of the group, changes in the group and similar information.</li><li>Cost accounting: Details on the profit & loss statements, management and segment information, capitalized assets and similar information.</li><li>Treasury: Information and details on cash, liquidity, loans, financial instruments and similar information.</li></ul>

---

[5] This is a typical scenario of data gathering in midsize groups. Other types of sources and data allocation to sources may be possible depending on group structures.

Step	Activity	Tasks / Explanations
3)	Draft version and secondary scan	Based on the information and data gathered, a first draft can be prepared. This draft should be structured according to the recommendations given. The content of each section of the notes has to be established by using checklists the second time. This time, each entry of the checklist of the relevant standards have to be checked regarding the following criteria:

		• Applicable
		• Not applicable
		• Not material

If an applicable disclosure is identified, this information has to be incorporated in the notes at its appropriate place. If a disclosure applies but is marked as not material it is up to the preparer to omit this information if it is in line with the group policies on disclosures. A documentation should be available for auditor discussions on non-material items.

The extent of disclosures will result in a time consuming activity of preparing notes which requires an appropriate lead time.

| 4) | Other standards | While the mandatory content on disclosures as demanded by IFRS is prepared in step 3, disclosures demanded by other standards and rules have to be incorporated. The origins of these disclosures are either based on local accounting and / or taxation rules & regulations or disclosures demanded by stock exchanges where the parent is listed. Disclosures may vary depending on the jurisdiction the parent resides. |

| 5) | Voluntary information | Some groups add further voluntary information to notes to provide enhanced information to users of consolidated financial statements. The items disclosed, their extent and level of detail are subject to management discretion. Therefore, notes to financial statements vary if groups are compared, even within the same industry. |

Typical examples of voluntary information are:

• Remuneration details of the board and other governing bodies
• Services rendered by auditors
• Declarations according to local laws (e.g. governance codex)
• Additional details of segments and business units
• Separate financial statements of the parent

| 6) | Finalization | Due to the details some disclosures require, the data already gathered might not be sufficient. Therefore, an additional data gathering process will be necessary. This process should be initiated after the draft version of the notes is prepared and the extent of additional data and information necessary is known. The data gathering then can be limited to detailed requests only. |

Once notes are finalized, a further cross-check with the basic statements is recommended due to the interaction of all items. This applies particularly to the references in the statements to the position in the notes as well as the balances disclosed in the statements and explained in the notes. Another cross-check is required if management reports are prepared that include financial details of the period. It has to be ensured that the information in management reports not only ties to the statements but also to the accompanying notes. The cross-check should be done by a different person to minimize potential misstatements and misinformation.

Tab. M-1 Preparation order of notes to consolidated financial statements

An exception to the preparation process is the **first time application** of IFRS, which requires additional disclosures (IFRS 1). This is a one-off activity which has to be removed in subsequent periods.

As already mentioned, notes of previous periods can be used as a **template** to prepare notes for the current period. Using templates requires special attention due to changes that occur in the group and in accounting standards:

- Group changes

    Changes in the group require an update of group disclosures, particularly on the group structure and its affiliates and associates. While changes in the group structure can occur due to acquisitions, divestitures or restructurings, appropriate disclosures describing the changes in the group's composition are required. In particular the mandatory disclosures dealing with acquisitions and divestitures have to be added.

- Accounting standards

    IFRS are dynamic, even if this is not observable at first sight. Changes in accounting standards as issued by the IASB may relate to the IFRS themselves (so new, changed or omitted standards), annual improvement projects (changes in some details only) or IFRIC (new ones). Parents are obliged to report about the changes related to the IFRS and their application to the group. Depending on the application of these changes, disclosures may change compared to previous periods. This requires an update of the notes. To ensure that the notes reflect the actual IFRS, the most recent checklists should be used. The scanning of the checklists can be limited to those areas where changes occurred. Accordingly, the areas in the notes that relate to the changes have to be updated. This will be the case for all disclosures that relate to financial information of the statements as well as accompanying information.

The updated template can be used to prepare the final notes. Current financial figures of previous notes becomes previous financial figures of current notes. Current financial figures of current notes have to be added based on the data gathering process.

4. MANAGEMENT REPORT

In addition to consolidated and separate financial statements, a management reports is a typical element that complements financial statements. A management report is a summary by management that reflects the management's view of the economic environment, the economic situation of the group, the activities during the period and the outlook to the near future based on management's expectation and assumptions. It should be readable as a stand-alone report without referring to financial statements or other sources or references.

A management report is not a mandatory element of consolidated financial statements based on IFRS. The requirement of adding a management report to financial statements is more or less derived from local GAAP where such a report is often a mandatory element. Management reports prepared due to local requirements and consolidated financial statements according to IFRS are combined when local laws and regulations allow an application of IFRS instead of local GAAP.

Because of their significance, these reports have to be audited like consolidated financial statements. The auditor has to express an opinion about the true and faithful presentation of the activities during the period and the outlook of the expected business in subsequent periods.

The scope of and the items to be considered in a management report will change based on the company preparing the report and the underlying business. A management report that is prepared by a company of the group or by the parent will only consider the activities, events and other required information for that company. A management report that is prepared for the group has to consider all activities, events and other required information for all companies of the group. Therefore, the group management report is much broader in its content. When preparing such a report, the question arises to what level of detail the report should be prepared. Larger groups often include information down to business unit level. Even if the general information of the business of the group is available on business unit level, extraordinary, unusual or significant transactions of some companies of the group may require disclosure in the notes if they have a material impact on the group, on its performance, its financial position or on the risks position.

In addition to the scope of the management report, the contents of management reports vary based on local GAAP and other local requirements. Those countries that have a certain tradition of preparing management reports have dedicated requirements on management reports. Management reports can be embedded in a broader context. This broader context demands additional information: for example, disclosures of publicly listed companies of the environment the group operates in.

While several legislations demand management reports, the IASB has picked up these issues and has developed an **IFRS**-based reporting framework summarized in *IFRS Practice Statement – Management Commentary*. The practice statement is not a standard and therefore not mandatory for application. It is more or less a recommendation that can be followed when preparing management reports.[6]

The preparation of a management commentary is based on a set of principles:

- As the commentary is a discussion about the performance, position and progress of the company prepared by management, it should be prepared from a management's perspective.
- The information provided in the management commentary should complement the information presented in [consolidated] financial statements.

---

[6] We will align the management commentary to groups. The alignment is presented by square brackets.

- The management commentary should focus on forward looking information.
- The information given in the commentary should fulfil the qualitative characteristics as outlined in the framework. This includes particularly the characteristics of relevance and materiality, a faithful presentation, comparability, verifiability, timeliness and understandability.
- The presentation of the information given in the commentary should be clear and straightforward. It should be easily understandable by the intended audience.

While the IASB's intention of management commentary is to provide useful information that relates to [consolidated] financial statements, the content of the management commentary is limited to a set of complementary information:

- Nature of the business
  The nature of the business includes a description of the company and its business. Typical elements of this description are the branch the company operates in, the main markets including the competitive position of the company in the market, significant features of the legal, regulatory and macro-economic environment, the main products and services, business processes and distribution methods as well as the [group's] structure and how it creates value.

- Management objectives and its strategies to meet those objectives
  Management objectives are useful information to understand the rationale of management decisions in relation to the execution of a strategy. Any significant changes in management objectives and / or the strategy should be discussed in the commentary.

- Most significant resources, risks and relationships
  Resources, risks and relationships to be considered in management reports are those items that affect the performance and value of the [group]. Resources to be mentioned are those ones that are critical for the [group's] success. Relationships are those ones with various stakeholders that impact the business of the [group]. This is combined with a description of the principal risks by [groups], changes to these risks and its management and the effectiveness of the management.

- Results and prospects of operations
  Results and prospects are not limited to financial performance. Non-financial performance has to be considered as well: performance and progress during the period, its impact on the overall performance, together with significant changes to the financial position of the group. Based on the results of operation an outlook on the future, the targets set and strategies together with related risks to achieve those targets complements the results and prospects of the operations.

- Critical performance measures and indicators used by management to evaluate the performance

Performance measures and indicators that reflect the critical success factors used by management have to be quantified and disclosed together with an explanation of why and how the measures have changed. This disclosure should be supported by a brief explanation of the relevance of these performance measures and indicators.

The disclosures provided in the management commentary are just basics. They can be expanded by other voluntary facts as appropriate to present the group and its activities as a whole.

Compared to the IFRS' management commentary, management reports that are mandatory by **local GAAP** often demand either additional information about the structure, activities and position of a group or dedicated information relevant to publicly listed companies. The content of these reports therefore change depending on the reporting purpose. The following two examples will provide a brief overview of required structures and contents of management reports and how these reports deviate from each other.

- Example USA

  Management reports are only demanded and mandatory for companies applying US-GAAP that are publicly listed. These reports are called "management discussion & analysis" (MD&A) and have to be filed annually together with financial statements and other documents and information to the Securities & Exchange Commission (SEC) using the forms 10-K (item 7, for domestic filers) or 20-F (item 5, for foreign filers).[7] As the preparation of consolidated financial statements is mandatory for publicly listed companies, the MD&A have to be prepared at group level as well.

  The reportable content that is asked for in the forms is defined in the 1933 Securities Act (regulation S-K item 303). According to this act, companies have to disclose group information on:

  - Operating results;
  - Liquidity and capital resources;
  - Research & development, patents and licences, etc.;
  - Trend information;
  - Off-balance sheet arrangements;
  - Tabular disclosure of contractual obligations;
  - Safe harbour.

  Detailed explanations of each disclosure are demanded. These explanations may include dedicated items to be highlighted if they have a current or future effect and therefore an impact on the group.

  The MD&A only focuses on financial information that is important for investors. The filing requirements of the SEC also includes information on other items like the organizational structure, a business overview,

---

[7] Filings of these forms can be inspected in the EDGAR-database of the SEC which is publicly available.

directors, senior management, advisors and employees, compensation of directors and senior management and board practices. These details are kept separate for SEC purposes; other legislations demand such details as part of a management report. To fully understand the position of a public US-listed company, additional required information should be considered in analyzing US management reports.

- Example Germany

    Management reports based on German GAAP are a mandatory element of annual reports. These reports are called "Lagebericht" and have to be prepared by all companies whether they are publicly listed or privately held. Management reports have a long tradition in Germany; the first legal requirements to prepare reports can be traced back to the year 1884. The contents to be reported are defined in para. 289 for single entities and para. 315 for groups of the German Commercial Code including an interaction between these two definitions for groups. Disclosure exemptions depend on the size of the reporting company. Management reports have to be readable as separate documents without any references to the [consolidated] financial statements.

    The reportable content is divided in dedicated reports that cover selected areas to be reported:

  - General structure of the group;
  - Economic report;
  - Report on branches and offices;
  - Report on material effects after the balance sheet date;
  - Report on projections, chances and risks;
  - Risk report on the application of financial instruments;
  - Report on internal controls and risk management;
  - Report on acquisition-relevant information (for publicly listed companies only);
  - Remuneration report of officers and board members (for publicly listed companies only);
  - Management declaration.

    The management report is complemented by other reports, particularly by a sustainability report that should inform about environmental issues and a corporate governance report.

    The extent of each report depends on the reportable content as well as the structure, size and business of the group.

The IFRS management commentary and the two examples provided illustrate the broad approaches these reports follow. Even if the contents vary and a more or less exhaustive disclosure about the activities and business of the group is given, all reports have a common core that is based on the financial performance and position of a group, the risks associated with the business and activities of management to handle and mitigate these risks. They are combined with the future opportunities and risks of the group.

N APPENDIX I: FAIR VALUE MEASUREMENT

While the fair value concept is an integral element of IFRS, it cannot be ignored in preparing consolidated financial statements. There are several transactions in groups where fair value is an important element. Fair value issues arise always on the acquisition of subsidiaries and their disposals. Depending on the carrying assets of group companies, these issues may also arise in preparing regular consolidated financial statements. As fair value measurement affects the preparation of consolidated financial statements at various opportunities, this appendix will explain some relevant concepts, methods and tasks necessary to prepare the statements.[1]

1. HISTORY

The treatment of fair values and their measurement has been discussed for several years. This is because definitions and elements of fair value are spread across several IFRS, are sometimes not consistent or do not meet the desired objective. Often, additional guidance on how to apply fair value measurements is missing. As a consequence, the IASB and the FASB jointly have developed common requirements for measuring fair value and disclosing fair value information. The results of these activities are published in *IFRS 13 – Fair Value Measurement*.

IFRS 13.C1 requires the application of this standard for periods beginning on or after 1 January 2013, even if earlier application is permitted. As the application of this standard is relatively recent, two cases require attention as fair values may have different definitions:

- IFRS 13 adopted

    If IFRS 13 is adopted, all measurement issues of fair values follow the definition as outlined in IFRS 13.9: "This IFRS defines fair value as the price that would be received to sell an asset or paid to transfer a liability in an orderly transaction between market participants at the measurement date".

---

[1] This appendix explains only selected aspects of fair value measurement and valuation techniques important for groups. Valuation techniques and methods are described only in general. It is recommended to make use of other literature, particularly valuation literature, for a full scope of fair value measurement and the application and handling of appropriate valuation techniques including the details required by each method.

> • IFRS 13 not yet adopted
>
>   If not yet adopted, a transition to IFRS 13 is required. IFRS 13.C2 requires a prospective transition, so a retrospective adjustment is not necessary simplifying the transition. The transition also changes the definition of fair value. Older IFRS have different definitions, e.g. IFRS 5.A: "The amount for which an asset could be exchanged, or a liability settled, between knowledgeable, willing parties in an arm's length transaction".

2. DEFINITION

IFRS 13.9 defines fair value as the price that would be received to sell an asset or paid to transfer a liability in an orderly transaction between market participants at the measurement date. Due to this definition, the price determined is an exit price (assuming a sale). Even if this definition is very comprehensive, several facts and circumstances have to be determined in assuming the fair value:

- Assets that are subject to a fair value measurement

    Subject to fair value measurements are all assets and liabilities that require a recording at fair values. IFRS 13.5 addresses the application if any standard requires a fair value measurement. Accordingly, some items are exempt from an application.

Item	Covered by standard	Scope	Exemptions	Comment
Intangible assets	IAS 38	Yes		Only if revaluation model is applied
Property, plant & equipment	IAS 16	Yes		Only if revaluation model is applied
Asset measurement: value in use	IAS 36	No		Similarity to fair value given but not fair value
Asset measurement: fair value less cost of disposal	IAS 36	Yes	Yes	Disclosures not required
Financial assets	IFRS 9	Yes		
Investment property	IAS 40	Yes		
Agricultural assets	IAS 41	Yes		
Mineral resources	IFRS 6	Yes		Only if revaluation model is applied
Inventories	IAS 2	No		
Share-based payments	IFRS 2	No		Disclosures not required
Leasing	IAS 17	No		
Pensions: plan assets	IAS 19	Yes	Yes	Disclosures not required
Retirement benefit plan investments	IAS 26	Yes	Yes	Disclosures not required
Business combinations	IFRS 3	Yes		Applies to purchase price allocation
Financial liabilities	IFRS 9	Yes		
Provisions, liabilities	IAS 37	No		

Tab. N-1   List of assets subject to fair value measurement

Depending on the nature of assets and liabilities, a fair value measurement occurs on a recurring basis or if specified circumstances or events exist. This requires a consideration of the characteristics of the assets and liabilities, particularly any restrictions and uses.

The fair value measurement can be applied to individual assets and liabilities as well as to a group of them.

A determination of fair value is not limited to specific types of asset. An application is required for financial as well as non-financial assets. Non-financial assets are all those assets that are not measured in accordance with IAS 39 or IFRS 9. A common feature of those assets is often a missing active market.

- The principal market of that asset and its participants

  The principal **market** is the market where trading of assets frequently occurs with sufficient volume to determine pricing information on an ongoing basis. If there is no principal market, the most advantageous market has to be determined. If there are several markets with different prices, the principal market has to be applied. Both the principal and the most advantageous markets are active markets. Access to the market must exist.

  Market **participants** have to be unrelated parties dealing at arm's length principle for their own economic interest.

- The price

  The price is a fair value that has been achieved for the sale of an asset in an orderly transaction. The price considers the fair value of the asset only. Therefore, no transactions costs are included. An adjustment might be necessary to have the asset available for the market. IFRS 13.24 mentions transportation costs as one example for those adjustments.

- Appropriate valuation techniques

  In the absence of an active market, valuation techniques have to be applied to determine an active market. This assumes that an estimation of a fair value can be derived from the asset and its use.

3. MEASUREMENT

The measurement of assets and liabilities covers the whole lifecycle and therefore has to consider the initial as well as subsequent measurements. Therefore, fair value measurement requirements apply at different **stages**.

- Initial recognition

  Usually, it is assumed that the price paid to acquire an asset or a group of assets or assume liabilities is based on an arm's-length transaction so that the price reflects the fair value of the asset.[2] Nevertheless, there are situations where an asset is obtained at a price different than its fair value.

---

[2] The price paid is also called the entry price.

To adjust the initial price asset to its fair value, day one gains or losses arise. Reasons for those dissenting prices are:

- Transactions between related parties;
- Transaction executed under duress;
- Transaction covers a group of items;
- Transactions in different markets and not in the principal market.

- Subsequent measurement
    Measuring the fair value of an asset in subsequent periods assume an exit price, so a price that can be achieved on an active market. The full set of fair value tools can be applied.

Regardless of which method is applied to determine the fair value of an asset or liability, IFRS 13.72 defines a **fair value hierarchy** that has to be applied. This hierarchy is a "guideline" regarding which inputs are most suitable when valuation techniques are used. The intention of this hierarchy is to increase consistency and comparability.

Level	Rationale	Comment
1)	Quoted prices in active markets	Quoted prices are always unadjusted prices. An adjustment is only appropriate if • Large amounts of similar assets and liabilities are held but the quoted price is not readily accessible. • Quoted price does not equal fair value (e.g. due to timing issues, the fair value measurement date does not equal the acquisition date or significant events have changed the fair value). • Observed identical assets and liabilities are subject to adjustments. Active markets trade assets frequently and in a certain volume. This is primarily the principal market and only in the absence of this market the most advantageous market.
2)	Other observable inputs:	Only if level 1 inputs are not available, level 2 has to be applied. Similar assets and liabilities are not defined any further by IFRS 13. Identifying such items requires not only judgement but also an understanding of the terms and other factors that affect the fair value and an identification and assessment of any differences in the terms compared to the asset subject to measurement.
2a)	Quoted prices for similar assets and liabilities in active markets	
2b)	Quoted prices for identical or similar assets and liabilities in non-active markets	Similar to quoted prices, adjustments to quoted prices for identical or similar assets may be necessary to reflect the behaviour of the asset subject to measurement. Typical examples are risk alignments, conditions and locations.
2c)	Inputs other than quoted prices for assets and liabilities	
2d)	Market-corroborated inputs	
3)	Unobservable other inputs	Level 3 inputs are only appropriate if any market relationship is missing. Therefore, internal inputs based on the group's own data are used. If – again – evidence is given that other market participants use other data, appropriate adjustments are considered to reflect at least some market aspects.

Tab. N-2   Fair value hierarchy

The order of the fair value hierarchy ensures that observable inputs have to be preferably applied as they are market related (external) and therefore provide more assurance than internal ones.

If assets cannot be reliably measured by using similar assets in active markets, the application of **valuation techniques**, as outlined in IAS 13.61, is an appropriate method in deriving fair value. Valuation techniques vary depending on the nature of the underlying asset to be measured. IFRS 13.62 provides three valuation approaches that can be used:

- Market approach;
- Cost approach;
- Income approach.

Various valuation techniques are available for each approach.

3.1. Market approach

This approach uses market data to derive fair value for the asset under review. Market data can be derived from transactions with similar or comparable assets. Data can also be derived from current or similar markets. Due to the various market data and the application on the asset to be valued, several methods are available.

- Analogy methods

    Analogy methods observe transactions with similar assets in active markets and try to derive a value for the asset subject to valuation from these transactions. The challenge in applying analogy methods is to find active markets and similar assets. Active markets are markets where the group operates in. Similar assets mean that these assets have to have the same characteristic and service capacity as the original asset. If observed assets deviate from the original asset appropriate adjustments are necessary. Analogy methods apply to assets that are traded in markets. Typical examples of markets and assets are merger & acquisition transactions of companies or markets for new or used machines. Analogy methods regularly fail for self-constructed assets or assets with specific purposes. To get better confidence, peer groups (a set of similar transactions) are often used.

- Multiples

    Similarly to analogy, this method determines the value of an asset through observation. The value of the comparable asset is transferred to standardized values relative to key statistics to calculate valuation multiples. These multiples are applied to the asset subject to estimate it's value. Multiples must have a relationship with the market. They are often based on earnings, cash flows or other market measures like enterprise values or price-earnings ratios. Like analogy methods, multiples face the same challenges in identifying assets and markets.

- Matrix pricing

  This is a mathematical method where the value of an asset is derived against several benchmarks or quoted prices in the market. So a multiple reference is used to determine the fair value. Matrix pricing is a common method used for financial instruments (so assets and liabilities).

- Direct market prices

  The asset's value can be taken directly from the market. Direct prices interfere with the size of the market. Also, the volume of an asset's trade in the market, compared to the volume of the asset subject to valuation, has to be considered. This is important in the case of assumed bulk sales of the asset: such transactions have the ability to change the observed market price. Direct market prices are often applied to financial assets and liabilities, such as securities.

3.2. Cost approach

This approach focuses on the asset itself and reflects the amount required to replace the asset in its current condition. Replacing an asset can occur in two ways: either by replacing the asset through a substitute (a product that is available in the market) or by rebuilding the asset. Appropriate valuation methods are available for both ways.

- Replacement costs

  The replacement cost method assumes that the asset can be replaced by a substitute, so an asset with the same characteristics as the original one. The substitute has to have the same service capacity as the original asset. Replacement costs might be adjusted by obsolescence if necessary. Obsolescence comprises physical deterioration, technological and economic obsolescence.

- Reproduction costs

  The reproduction cost method assumes that the asset in its current condition is built up right from scratch. Any improvements to the product due to new standards, production processes and similar issues are not considered. The method uses historical costs that are indexed to adjust historical costs to current conditions. This adjustment has to consider all costs incurred: labour costs, materials as well as an appropriate overhead portion.

3.3. Income approach

This approach is based on the ability of an asset to generate future cash flows or profits. The amount determined reflects the market expectation of the fair value of these future cash flows. Applying the income approach demands an application of discounted cash flow models and consequently an estimation of discount rates (e.g. by using weighted average costs of capital based on capital asset pricing models), planning data of future cash flows the asset will generate, market parameters like inflation and market growth rates and tax effects. In particular, planning data is important as this data reflects the underlying business. Therefore, management accounting is involved in preparing the data by considering pricing and volume of products and services, cost structures related to the asset and the product portfolio, so the mix of products and services expected to be sold or delivered.

As future cash flows depend on the underlying assets and its character, a set of measurement methods is available:

- Option pricing models

  These models are mathematical methods which determine the fair value of an equity option by considering various market metrics. The most known models are the Black-Scholes model and the binominal model proposed by Cox, Ross and Rubinstein. Option pricing models are applicable for financial assets.

- Direct cash flows

  These methods apply only if an asset has the ability to generate measureable cash flows. These cash flows might be subject to adjustments as appropriate before discounting to determine the value of the asset.

- Incremental cash flows (ICF)

  The incremental cash flow method compares the cash flows of the company carrying the asset with a fictitious company with similar cash flows but without the asset. The difference between both cash flows represents the cash flow attributable to the asset.

  Incremental cash flows are popular not only for determining the value of an asset but also for determining the consequences of management decisions, the profitability of projects and investments. The method usually ignores any sunk cost and overhead costs but considers opportunity costs, side effects and changes in net-working capital.

- Comparative income differential method (CIDM)

  Similar to incremental cash flows, this method estimates the income differential of an asset between its utilization and its absence. Applying this method requires appropriate knowledge about the assets and its use and utilization. The more complex an asset is the more effects require attention. Typical effects are cost savings, interactions with other assets and revenue impacts.

- Multi-period excess earnings method (MEEM)

  This method estimates the fair value based on expected future economic earnings that is generated by a business unit or a group of assets. The method is the preferred choice if cash flows generated by an asset cannot be reliably directly measured. To determine the fair value of an asset, charges for all other assets involved are deducted from cash flows of the business unit or group of assets. The residual cash flow then represents the cash flow assigned to the asset which will be discounted to arrive at the value of the asset.

- Relief from royalty method (RFR)

   The relief from royalty method is a measurement method based on savings of license payments to third parties. RFR is usually applied to intangible assets that are legally protected. It assumes that these protected intangible assets (e.g. patents, trademarks or similar rights) could be licensed in an arm's-length transaction from an unrelated party at a royalty rate that represents market conditions. The fees to be paid to ensure access and use to these rights are the basis. The associated cash flows will be discounted to arrive at the fair value of the asset.

   The challenge of this method is the determination of the appropriate royalty rate to be paid. Therefore, actual licensing agreements of the same or similar assets are the best references to be used. Either single agreements or a pool of agreements act as a benchmark. This requires a database research for identifying actual licensing agreements that match the assets subject to valuation. Appropriate adjustments to the royalty rate are necessary to align the licensing agreement to the asset if a perfect fit is not given. Typical reasons for adjustments are industry specific application, technology, remaining useful lives, exclusivity of the asset and other aspects.

4. MEASUREMENT TECHNIQUES FOR SELECTED ASSETS AND LIABILITIES

The following table provides an overview of measurement techniques that are available for or can be applied to selected assets and liabilities.

Item	Primary category	Alternate category	Applicable measurement methods	Comments
Assembled workforce	Cost	Income	Multi-period-excess-earnings method	One charge of the model
Capitalized intangible assets	Cost			Discount due to ageing!
Copyrights	Income	Market		
Customer relationships, non-contractual	Income	Market	Multi-period-excess-earnings method	
Distribution networks	Cost	Income		
Franchise rights	Income	Market		
In process research & development	Cost			
Inventory	Income			
Management information software	Cost	Market		
Non-compete agreements	Income		CIDM	
Orders	Income			

Item	Primary category	Alternate category	Applicable measurement methods	Comments
Other rights	Income	Market		
Patents	Income	Market	Relief from royalty method	
Product software	Income	Market		
Self-constructed and used non-current assets (fixed assets)	Cost		Replacement costs, Indexing	
(Tax amortization benefits)	Income		Multi-period-excess-earnings method	One charge of the model
Trademarks, trade names and brands	Income	Market	Relief from royalty method, Incremental cash flow method	

Tab. N-3   Measurement methods for selected assets and liabilities

APPENDIX II: IFRS – US-GAAP COMPARISON

This comparison should provide a brief overview of the major differences for group accounting and for the preparation of consolidated financial statements between IFRS and US-GAAP.

Area	Subject	IFRS	Reference	US-GAAP	Reference
Consolidated financial statements					
	Preparation	Preparation considering all subsidiaries unless a subsidiary is marked as non-material to the group.	IFRS 10	• Preparation considering all subsidiaries. • Industry-specific guidance given that may preclude consolidation by certain organizations.	ASC 810
	Exemptions from preparing consolidated financial statements	• Parent who are itself wholly-owned subsidiaries. • Investment companies by default unless specific conditions exist that demand consolidation. Fair value measurement of subsidiary required.	IFRS 10.4	No exemptions.	
Control					
	Determination of control	Control concept. Determination is based on power, rights to return and the link between power and returns. Assessment of the entity, its purpose, operation and environment.	IFRS 10 IFRS 10.5	Two tier model: • Variable interest entity (VIE) Determination of primary beneficiary through controlling financial interest. If power to direct activities and right to receive benefit (or obligation to absorb losses) exists. Assessment of the entity, its purpose, operation and environment. • Voting interests model To be applied for all other entities. Only actual voting rights to be considered which will result in effective control. Contractual arrangements to be considered! Assessment of VIE first before determining control through voting rights.	ASC 810
	Voting rights	Control is established if there is more than 50% of voting rights. Consideration of direct and indirect voting rights.		No difference from IFRS.	
	Contractual arrangements	Alternate for establishing control to voting rights. May establish control even if there is no majority of voting rights.		Similar application than IFRS.	

(continued)

Area	Subject	IFRS	Reference	US-GAAP	Reference
	Potential voting rights	Substantive potential voting rights to be considered in assessing power. Not currently exercisable but have to be exercisable if decisions need to be made in future. Consideration in determining significant influence.		No guidance on potential voting rights. No consideration in determining significant influence.	
	De facto control	Control through other options than through voting rights. Careful evaluation demanded.		No de facto control due to the effective control concept.	
	Joint control / shared power	More than one controlling party. Parties jointly control the entity. No party can act on its own, collaboration is required.		Shared power of unrelated parties will lead to no consolidation. Applies to VIE.	
	Loss	Loss of control: Derecognition. Loss of joint control or significant influence: Remaining investment qualifies as financial asset. Measurement at fair value through profit and loss.		Loss of control: Derecognition. Loss of joint control or significant influence: Measurement at carrying amount.	
Accounting policies	General rule	Uniform accounting policies for all companies of the group. This does not only include subsidiaries but also associates and joint ventures. For "like transactions and events in similar circumstances".		Uniform accounting policies for all companies of the group. Nevertheless associates do not have to comply with this requirement if they apply an acceptable alternative US-GAAP treatment.	
	Exceptions	No exceptions.		Industry-specific policies applied by subsidiaries permitted.	
	Reporting date	Subsidiaries with a different reporting date may be consolidated, provided that • Deviation is less than three months. • Adjustment of significant transactions are made.		Subsidiaries with a different reporting date may be consolidated, provided that • Deviation is less than three months. • Disclosure or adjustment of material transactions are made.	
Business combinations			IFRS 3		ASC 805

Area	Subject	IFRS	Reference	US-GAAP	Reference
	Contingent consideration	Initial recognition at fair value. Subsequent measurement at fair value (through profit & loss or other comprehensive income) or IAS 37 or other IFRS as appropriate.		Initial recognition at fair value. Subsequent measurement at fair value through profit & loss until contingency is resolved.	ASC 805-30
	Acquired assets and assumed liabilities	No recognition of contingent assets. Contingent liabilities are recognized at fair value (assuming they can be measured reliably).		Contingent assets and liabilities are recorded at fair value provided they can be measured reliably during the measurement period. If no fair value measurement possible, accounting is based on existing guidance.	
	Goodwill	Either standalone or assigned to cash-generating unit (if business will be assigned to a cash-generating unit). Annual and event-driven testing for impairment. One-step approach: Adjustment to recoverable amount (the higher of value in use and fair value less cost of disposal) through profit & loss. The impairment loss may reduce the carrying amount of assets if it exceeds the carrying amount of goodwill.		Assigned to reporting unit. Annual and event-driven testing for impairment. Two-step approach: Step 1 compares the fair value with the carrying amount (including goodwill) of the reporting unit under test. Step 2 is performed only if the fair value is less than the carrying amount. This step determined the goodwill impairment amount by measuring the excess of the carrying amount over the implied value of goodwill. The recorded impairment loss is limited to the carrying amount of goodwill.	ASC 805-20
	Non-controlling interests	Two options to measure the carrying amount of non-controlling interests: Full fair value of non-controlling interests which results in the application of the full goodwill method. Proportionate fair value of net assets acquired which results in the application of the partial goodwill method.		Always measured at fair value.	
	Entities under common control	Topic not covered by current IFRS.		Business combinations of entities under common control are recorded at predecessor's costs.	

(continued)

Area	Subject	IFRS	Reference	US-GAAP	Reference
	Push-down accounting	Topic not covered by current IFRS. Issue is solved by applying adjustments at higher levels.		Substantially wholly-owned subsidiaries (> 95%) are required to apply the basis for accounting of the new parent in their separate financial statements. Application mandatory for publicly listed companies, voluntary for privately held companies.	ASC 323
Interests in joint ventures	Definition	Joint arrangement: An arrangement to which two or more parties have joint control.	IFRS 11 IFRS 11.A	Joint Venture: Corporation formed, owned and operated by two or more businesses (venturers) as a separate and discrete business or project (venture) for their mutual benefit.	
	Types	• Joint operation • Joint venture (usually separate entity)		Jointly controlled (separate) entities	
	Realization & Accounting	• Joint control • Joint operation: Joint control of the arrangement with direct access and rights to assets and obligations for liabilities. Each party accounts for its share in assets and liabilities, revenues and expenses. • Joint venture: Joint control of the arrangement with rights to net assets and outcome of the arrangement only. Each party accounts for interests in the joint venture by applying the equity methods. Recording of a (partial) gain in case of non-monetary asset contributions. Exceptions to this principle apply in selected cases.		• Shared control • Participating rights of each venturer • Content must be given to operating, investing and financing decisions. • Accounting depends on determination of joint venture: • If joint venture is VIE consolidation may apply. • If joint venture is not a VIE, application of equity method applies. • Proportionate consolidation applies in selected cases and certain industries. • Contributions to joint venture recorded at cost. Non-cash contributions may require recording a gain.	
Equity method	Exemption	Exemptions for selected investment companies given if investment is recorded at fair value through profit & loss.	IAS 28	Accounting option: Either application of equity method or recording at fair value through profit & loss.	ASC 323

Area	Subject	IFRS	Reference	US-GAAP	Reference
	Acquisition date excess fair value over costs	Recognition of day one gains if investment is measured at fair value.		Recognition and amortization. No day one gain recordable.	
	Impairments and losses	Regular impairment tests required. Losses in excess of the investment amount are recorded in steps: reduction of carrying amount in investment, recording or adjusting other items and finally no loss recording.		Concept of temporary decline. If the fair value of an investment is not temporarily below its carrying amount, impairment is required. Full loss recording in excess of investment account (either negative balance or liability) if return to profitability can be assured.	ASC 350, ASC 360
Fair value measurement			IFRS 13		ASC 820-10

APPENDIX III: IFRS

IFRS, IFRIC and SIC listed are effective as of 1.1.2013. As far as any effective dates are mentioned, these dates refer to the initial application of the standard or any amendment that becomes effective after the effective date of the current IFRS. Effective dates that relate to any annual improvements are not mentioned and therefore also not listed.

1. LIST OF IFRS

IFRS	Description of standard	Group core[3]	Group secondary[4]	Effective Date
IAS 1	Presentation of Financial Statements	X		2013 (Amendment: Presentation of items of other comprehensive income)
IAS 2	Inventories			
IAS 7	Statement of Cash Flow		X	
IAS 8	Accounting Policies, Changes in Accounting Estimates and Errors		X	
IAS 10	Events after the Reporting Period		X	
IAS 11	Construction Contracts			
IAS 12	Income Taxes		X	2013 (Amendment: Presentation of items of other comprehensive income) 2014 (Amendment: Investment entities)
IAS 16	Property, Plant and Equipment			
IAS 17	Leases			
IAS 18	Revenue			
IAS 19	Employee Benefits			2013 (Amendments)
IAS 20	Accounting for Government Grants and Disclosure of Government Assistance			
IAS 21	The Effects of Changes in Foreign Exchange Rates	X		
IAS 23	Borrowing Costs			
IAS 24	Related Party Disclosures		X	
IAS 26	Accounting and Reporting by Retirement Benefit Plans			
IAS 27	Separate Financial Statements	X		2013

[3] "Group core" means that this standard is a core standard of group accounting.
[4] "Group secondary" means that this standard is important to be considered.

IFRS	Description of standard	Group core[3]	Group secondary[4]	Effective Date
IAS 28	Investment in Associates and Joint Ventures	X		2013
IAS 29	Financial Reporting in Hyperinflationary Economies			
IAS 31	Interests in Joint Ventures	X		Dispensed due to the application of IFRS 11
IAS 32	Financial Instruments: Presentation		X	2013 (Amendment Disclosures – off-setting financial assets and financial liabilities)
				2014 (Amendment: Investment entities)
IAS 33	Earnings per Share		X	
IAS 34	Interim Financial Reporting		X	
IAS 36	Impairment of Assets	X		
IAS 37	Provisions, Contingent Liabilities and Contingent Assets			
IAS 38	Intangible Assets			
IAS 39	Financial Instruments: Recognition and Measurement	X		
IAS 40	Investment Property			
IAS 41	Agriculture			
IFRS 1	First-time Adoption of International Financial Reporting Standards		X	2013 (Amendment: Government loans)
				2014 (Amendment: Investment entities)
IFRS 2	Share-based Payment			
IFRS 3	Business Combinations	X		
IFRS 4	Insurance Contracts			
IFRS 5	Non-current Assets Held for Sale and Discontinued Operations		X	
IFRS 6	Exploration for and Evaluation of Mineral Resources			
IFRS 7	Financial Instruments: Disclosures			2013 (Amendment Disclosures – off-setting financial assets and financial liabilities)
				2014 (Amendment Investment entities)
IFRS 8	Operating Segments			
IFRS 9	Financial Instruments	X		2015
IFRS 10	Consolidated Financial Statements	X		2013
IFRS 11	Joint Arrangements	X		2013
IFRS 12	Disclosure of Interests in Other Entities	X		2013
IFRS 13	Fair Value Measurement	X		2013

2. IFRIC AND SIC INTERPRETATIONS

IFRIC / SIC	Description of standard	Group basic[5]	Group secondary[6]	Effective Date
SIC 7	Introduction of the EURO			
SIC 10	Government Assistance – No Specific Relation to Operating Activities			
SIC 12	Consolidation – Special Purpose Entities	X		Dispensed due to the application of IFRS 10
SIC 13	Jointly Controlled Entities – Non-Monetary Contribution by Venturers	X		Dispensed due to the application of IFRS 11
SIC 15	Operating Leases – Incentives			
SIC 21	Income Taxes – Recovery of Revalued Non-Depreciable Assets			Dispensed due to amendments of IAS 12
SIC 25	Income Taxes – Changes in the Tax Status of an Entity or its Shareholders		X	
SIC 27	Evaluating the Substance of Transactions Involving the Legal Form of a Lease			
SIC 29	Service Concession Agreements: Disclosures			
SIC 31	Revenue – Barter Transactions Involving Advertising Services			
SIC 32	Intangible Assets – Web Site Costs			
IFRIC 1	Changes in Existing Decommissioning, Restoration and Similar Liabilities			
IFRIC 2	Member's Shares in Cooperative Entities and Similar Instruments	X		
IFRIC 4	Determining whether an Arrangement contains a Lease			
IFRIC 5	Rights to Interest arising from Decommissioning, Restoration and Environmental Rehabilitation Funds			
IFRIC 6	Liabilities arising from Participating in a Specific Market – Waste Electrical and Electronic Equipment			
IFRIC 7	Applying the Restatement Approach under IAS 29 Financial Reporting in Hyperinflationary Economies		X	
IFRIC 8	Scope of IFRS 2			Dispensed due to amendments of IFRS 2
IFRIC 9	Reassessment of Embedded Derivatives			Dispensed due to amendments of IFRS 9

[5] "Group core" means that this standard is a core standard of group accounting.

[6] "Group secondary" means that this standard is important to be considered.

IFRIC / SIC	Description of standard	Group basic[5]	Group secondary[6]	Effective Date
IFRIC 10	Interim Financial Reporting and Impairment	X		
IFRIC 11	IFRS 2 – Group and Treasury Share Transactions	X		Dispensed due to amendments of IFRS 2
IFRIC 12	Service Concession Agreements			
IFRIC 13	Customer Loyalty Programmes			
IFRIC 14	IAS 19 – The Limit on a Defined Benefit Asset, Minimum Funding Requirements and their Interaction			
IFRIC 15	Agreements for the Construction of Real Estates			
IFRIC 16	Hedges of a Net Investment in a Foreign Operation	X		
IFRIC 17	Distributions of Non-cash Assets to Owners	X		
IFRIC 18	Transfer of Assets to Customers			
IFRIC 19	Extinguishing Financial Liabilities with Equity Instruments		X	
IFRIC 20	Stripping Costs in the Production Phase of a Surface Mine			2013

REFERENCE LIST

Baumann, Konsolidierung mehrstufiger Konzerne, Springer Fachmedien, Wiesbaden 2000

Bellandi, The handbook to IFRS transition and to IFRS U.S. GAAP dual reporting, Wiley, Chichester 2012

Berentzen, Die Bilanzierung von finanziellen Vermögenswerten im IFRS-Abschluss nach IAS 39 und IFRS 9, EUL-Verlag, Köln 2010

Bragg, Fast Close, A guide to closing the books quickly, Wiley & Sons, Hoboken 2009

Bragg, GAAP 2013, Interpretation and application of Generally Accepted Accounting Principles, Wiley & Sons, Hoboken 2012

Deloitte, iGAAP 2013, Lexis Nexis, London 2013

Ernst & Young, Verrechnungspreise, Stollfuß, Bonn 2003

Ernst & Young, Transition guidance amendments for IFRS 10, IFRS 11, and IFRS 12, London 2012

Fischer, Mehrkomponentenverträge, Wiley, Weinheim 2010

Frölich, Praxis der Konzernrechnungslegung, Linde, Wien 2007

Fuchs / Stibi, IFRS11, Joint Arrangements – lange erwartet und doch noch mit (kleinen) Überraschungen?, published in: BetriebsBerater 23.2011

Gräfer / Scheld, Grundzüge der Konzernrechnungslegung, 9. Edition, Erich Schmidt Verlag, Berlin 2005

Grant Thornton, Intangible Assets in a Business Combination, London 2008

Hoehne, Veräußerung von Anteilen an Tochterunternehmen im IFRS-Konzernabschluss, Gaber, Wiesbaden 2009

IASB, International Financial Reporting Standards 2013, IASB, London, 2013

KPMG, IFRS aktuell, 5. Edition, Schäffer-Poeschel Verlag, Stuttgart 2012

Lüdenbach / Hoffmann, IFRS Kommentar, Haufe, Freiburg 2012

Müller / Stute / Withus, Handbuch Lagebericht, Erich Schmidt Verlag, Berlin 2013

Niebecker / Kirchmann, Group Reporting und Konsolidierung, Schäffer Poeschel, Stuttgart 2011

OECD, OECD Transfer Pricing Guidelines for Multinational Enterprises and Tax Administrations, OECD Publishing, Paris 2010

PWC, IFRS and US-GAAP: Similarities and differences, Philadelphia 2013

Reinke, Impairment Test nach IAS 36, Erich Schmidt Verlag, Berlin 2010

Renz / Wilmanns, Internationale Verrechnungspreise, Wiley, Weinheim 2013

Säuerlich, Immaterielle Vermögenswerte im Rahmen einer PPA nach IFRS3, Deloitte, Berlin 2006

Scherrer, Konzernrechnungslegung nach HGB und IFRS; 2. Edition, Vahlen, München 2007

SEC, A comparison of U.S. GAAP and IFRS, Staff paper, SEC 2011

Shamrock, IFRS and US-GAAP, A comprehensive comparison, Wiley, Hoboken 2012

Sommer, Case Study Impairment Test, FAS, Berlin 2009

Wiley Text, International Financial Reporting Standards 2014, Wiley, Weinheim 2014

Wirth, Firmenwertbilanzierung nach IFRS, Schäffer-Poeschel, Stuttgart 2005

GLOSSARY

Item	Definition / meaning[1]
Acquiree	The business or businesses that the acquirer obtains control of in a business combination.
Acquirer	The entity that obtains control of the acquiree.
Acquisition date	The date on which the acquirer obtains control of the acquiree.
AICPA	American Institute of Certified Public Accountants.
Annual report	An aggregation of an entity's activities during a fiscal year. Financial statements form usually a part of annual reports.
Assembled workforce	An existing group of employees that permits an acquirer to continue operating the acquired business without hiring and training new employees to perform the same functions.
Asset	Probable future economic benefits obtained or controlled by an entity as a result of a past transaction or event.
Asset-backed securities	An asset-backed security is a security whose performance is derived from a set of underlying assets.
Associate	An associate in an entity over which an investor has significant influence.
Balance sheet date	The last day of a fiscal period.
Bulk transaction	A bulk transaction is a transaction (e.g. sales or purchase) where a larger number of items (e.g. shares) is transferred from one party to another one.
Business	An integrated set of activities and assets that is capable of being conducted and managed for the purpose of providing a return in the forms of dividends, lower costs or other economic benefits directly to investors or other owners, members or participants.
Business combination	A transaction or other event in which the acquirer obtains control of one or more businesses. Transactions sometimes referred to as "true mergers" or "mergers of equals" are also business combinations as that term is used in IFRS.
Chart of accounts	The chart of accounts is a structured list of accounts used by an entity.
CoA	Chart of Accounts.
Comparative information	Comparative information is information on financials and non-financials of the preceding period.
Consideration transferred	Considerations transferred are all those items that are given in exchange to a share in an acquiree in a business combination.
Consolidated financial statements	Consolidated financial statements are the statements of a group in which assets, liabilities, equity, income, expense and cash flows of the parent and its subsidiaries are presented as those of a single economic entity.
Consolidation	Consolidation is the process of merging or combining several items into one item.

(continued)

---

[1] Most of these definitions are taken from the official International Financial Reporting Standards.

Item	Definition / meaning[1]
Contingent consideration	Usually, an obligation of the acquirer to transfer additional assets or equity interests to the former owners of an acquiree as part of the exchange of control of the acquiree if specific future events occur or conditions are met.
Contingent liability	A contingent liability is a possible obligation that arises from past events and whose existence will be confirmed only by the occurrence or non-occurrence of one or more uncertain future events not wholly within the control of the entity.
Control	An investor controls an investee when it is exposed to, or has the rights, to variable returns from its investment with the investee and has the ability to affect those returns through power over the investee.
Creep acquisition	Creep acquisitions are increases in voting rights through dividend reinvestment plans instead of distributing dividends.
CUP	Comparable uncontrolled price method.
Debentures	A long-term debt not secured by any collateral.
Debt security	Any debt instrument with defined conditions that can be purchased and sold between two or more parties.
Deconsolidation	A deconsolidation is a task that removes the financial statement of an entity from consolidated financial statements.
Deemed disposal	A deemed disposal is a loss of control by an investor that is out of his control.
De facto control	De facto control is a situation where an investor can control the investee through his dominant position at an annual general meeting without having real control.
Deferred tax asset	Deferred tax assets are income taxes recoverable in future periods due to deductible temporary differences and the carryforward of any unused tax credits or tax losses.
Deferred tax liability	Deferred tax liabilities are income tax payables in future periods.
Defined benefit obligations	The defined benefit obligation is the expected future payment required to settle the obligation resulting from employee services in the current and prior periods.
Disclosure	Information and details on selected items, transactions or similar topics unveiled in financial statements.
Discount rate	The rate used to arrive at the present value of one or more future payments.
Dividend	A dividend is a payment by an entity to its shareholders.
Due diligence	Due diligence is a risk assessment (or an investigation) of a business prior to signing a purchase contract in acquiring this business.
EBIT	Earnings Before Interest and Taxes
EBITDA	Earnings Before Interest, Taxes, Depreciation and Amortization
Equity instrument	An equity instrument is a contract that evidences a residual interest in the assets of an entity after deducting all of its liabilities.
Equity method	The equity method is a method whereby the investment is initially recognized at cost and adjusted thereafter for the post-acquisition change in the investor's share in the investee's net assets.
Exchange rate	The exchange rate is the ratio of exchange for two currencies.
Fair value	Fair value is the price that would be received to sell an asset or paid to transfer a liability in an orderly transaction between market participants at the measurement date.
FASB	Financial Accounting Standards Board

Item	Definition / meaning[1]
Financial investment	A financial investment is an (long-term) investment in an entity with the expectation of capital appreciation, dividends of other forms of benefits.
Foreign operation	A foreign operation is an entity that is a subsidiary, associate, joint arrangement or branches of a reporting entity conducted in a country or currency other than those of the reporting entity.
Free float	The free float represents the portion of shares in an entity that are held by public investors and traded in the market.
Future economic benefit	The future economic benefit represents the potential to contribute, directly or indirectly, to the cash flows and cash equivalents of an entity.
Gain	Gains are increases in equity based on transactions other than revenue recognition and transactions with owners.
Goodwill	An asset representing the future economic benefits arising from other assets acquired in a business combination that are not individually identified and separately recognized.
Group manual	A manual that comprises rules, regulations and similar items of a group.
Group restructuring	Group restructuring is a reorganization or new composition of the legal, operational or other structure of a group for the purpose of an increased profitability.
IAS	International Accounting Standards.
IASB	International Accounting Standards Board.
IBD	Inside Bases Differences.
IFRS	International Financial Reporting Standards.
IFRIC	International Financial Reporting Interpretations Committee.
Impairment	Impairment is a situation where a decline in the value of an asset occurs resulting in a situation where the recoverable amount of an assets is continuously below its carrying amount.
Income tax	The amount of tax to be paid to tax authorities to the profits of an entity.
Indemnification	Indemnifications are payments of the vendor if outcomes of contingencies or uncertainties regarding selected assets or liabilities are outside given promises or contractually agreed conditions.
Inflation rate	The inflation rate reflects the rise in the general price level of an economy over a period of time.
Initial consolidation	A process that integrates a new subsidiary in consolidated financial statements.
Insolvency	Insolvency is the inability of an individual or organization (the debtor) to meet its financial obligations and accordingly pay its debt.
Intangible asset	An identifiable non-monetary asset without physical substance.
Investment entity	An investment entity is an entity that obtains funds from one or more investors for the purpose of providing to those investors with investment managing services and returns from capital appreciations and investment income on a fair value basis.
IPO	Initial Public Offer
Joint arrangement	A joint arrangement is an arrangement in which two or more parties have joint control.
Joint control	Joint control is a contractually agreed sharing of control in an arrangement, which exists only when decisions about the relevant activities require the unanimous consent of the parties sharing control.

(*continued*)

Item	Definition / meaning[1]
Joint venture	A joint venture is an arrangement whereby the parties that have joint control of the arrangement have the rights to the net assets of the arrangement.
Liability	Probable future outflow of economic resources arising from present obligations.
Lucky buy	A lucky buy represents a business combination where the consideration transferred is less than the fair value of assets acquired and liabilities assumed.
Measurement period	The measurement period is the period after the acquisition date during which the acquirer may adjust the provisional amounts recognized for a business combination.
Monetary item	A monetary item is a unit of currency held and assets and liabilities to be received or paid in a fixed or determinable number of a unit of currency.
Mutual entity	A mutual entity is an entity that provides dividends, lower costs or other economic benefits directly to its owners, members or participants.
Netting	Netting is an activity to offset the balance of one item with the balance of another item.
Non-controlling interests	The equity in a subsidiary not attributable, directly or indirectly, to a parent.
Non-financials	Non-financials are data and information that complement financial information.
Non-monetary item	A non-monetary item is an item other than a monetary item.
Nominal rate	Interest rate before adjustment to inflation or compounding effects.
OBD	Outside Bases Differences.
OECD	Organization for Economic Co-Operation and Development.
OLAP	Online Analytical Processing.
Onerous contract	An onerous contract is a contract in which the unavoidable costs of meeting the obligations to fulfil the contract exceed the expected economic benefit of the contract.
Opening balance sheet	The opening balance sheet is the balance sheet at the beginning of a (fiscal) period or at the beginning of an application of new accounting standards or at the formation of a new entity.
Other comprehensive income	Other comprehensive income comprises items of income and expense (including reclassification adjustments) that are not recognized in profit & loss as required of permitted by certain IFRS.
Overhead	Overhead are general (administrative) required costs to run a business that cannot be attributed to revenue-generating activities. Overhead in production are production costs that are neither direct material or direct labour costs.
Parent	An entity that controls one or more entities.
Pivot table	A pivot table is a simple version of an OLAP tools. It is a data summarization tool that aggregates, analyzes and sorts data by various aspects.
Potential voting rights	Potential voting rights are rights to obtain voting rights of an investee, such as those arising from convertible instruments or options, including forward contracts.
Pre-existing relationship	Pre-existing relationships are relationships between an acquirer and the acquiree that already existed before the acquisition date in a business combination.

Item	Definition / meaning[1]
Prepaid expenses	Prepaid expenses are amounts paid to secure the use of an asset or the receipt of services at a future date or continuously over one or more future periods.
Present value	The present value represents a future amount of money that has been discounted to the current date.
Pro-forma period	The period between the beginning of a period and the acquisition date.
Proportionate consolidation	A proportionate consolidation is a method of accounting whereby a venturer's share of each of the assets, liabilities, income and expenses of a jointly controlled entity is combined line by line with similar items in the venture's financial statements or reported as separate line items in the venturer's financial statements.
Profit distribution	The transfer of dividends (the profits generated by an entity) to its shareholders.
Protective rights	Rights designed to protect the interests of the party holding those rights without giving that party power over the entity to which those rights relate.
Purchase date	The date when interests in a subsidiary, a joint venture or an associate are acquired (view from the acquirer) or sold (view from the seller).
Purchase price	The amount of money or the (fair) value of an asset to be transferred to another party in exchange for another asset.
Reacquired right	A right that was previously granted to an acquiree to use the acquirer's intangible assets and that was reacquired as part of a business combination.
Reclassification	A reclassification is an activity that allocates an item or a portion of an item from one location to another one to properly reflect its presentation in financial statements.
Reciprocal interests	A reciprocal interest is an interest of two or more parties in each other.
Reimbursement	A reimbursement is a pay back of money or other form of compensation from one party to another one.
Revaluation surplus	The revaluation surplus is an element of equity that carries any increases in the fair value of an asset above the cost-based measurement when applying the revaluation model.
Reporting date	Usually the balance sheet date. The date on which financial statements are prepared and published.
Residual value	The residual value of an asset is the estimated amount that an entity would currently obtain from a disposal of the asset, after deducting the estimated cost of disposal, if the asset were already of the age and in the condition expected at the end of its useful life.
Restatement	Restatement is correcting the recognition, measurement and disclosure of amounts of elements of financial statements.
Retained earnings	Undistributed profits of an entity of current and prior periods.
Retrospective application	Retrospective application is applying a new accounting policy to transactions, other events and conditions as if that policy had always been applied.
Right to return	The contractually agreed right of a party to return the item acquired (either an asset or a business) to the vendor.
SEC	Securities & Exchange Commission.
Seizure	Seizure transfers the possession of assets or businesses to a government or a unit that act on the government's behalf.

(continued)

Item	Definition / meaning[1]
Separate financial statements	Separate financial statements are those presented by a parent or an investor or any other entity.
Shared services	Shared services in a group is the bundling of similar functions and tasks into one organizational unit that serves these functions and tasks to all clients in an efficient way.
Shell company	An empty company with no business.
Significant influence	Significant influence is the power to participate in the financial and operating policy decisions of the investee but is not control or joint control of those policies.
Significant transaction	A transaction that is material to an operation
Spot rate	The spot rate is the (current) price used to settle a security, currency or other financial asset.
Structured entity	A structured entity is an entity whose activities are restricted to the extent that those activities are, in essence, not directed by voting or similar rights. Definition as per ED10.
Subsidiary	A subsidiary is an entity, including an unincorporated entity such as a partnership that is controlled by another entity (known as the parent).
Substantive rights	Substantive rights are the rights of an investor relating to the investee that are exercisable when decisions need to be made.
TNMM	Transactional net margin method
Transfer pricing	Transfer pricing is a system of group-internal pricing of goods and services.
Treasury shares	Treasury shares are shares in an entity bought back from the market and held by this entity.
Trust	A trust is an entity that holds and manages assets for the benefit of another party.
Unrealized profit	Changes in the value of an asset that is not sold or otherwise realized or remeasured.
Variable returns	Variable returns are the returns of an investee that will vary depending on the performance of the investee.
VAT	Value added tax.
Withdrawal account	A withdrawal account is an equity account of a partner in a partnership that records the withdrawals of the partner during the financial period.
Withholding tax	A tax that has to be transferred to tax authorities by the dividend issuing entity in case of dividend payment or other distributions of profit. The withholding tax usually reduced the dividend payment.
Write-down	A reduction of the carrying amount of an asset or liability to a lower value due to a decline in value.
Write-up	An increase of the carrying amount of an asset or liability to a higher value. The higher value is limited to the fair value of an asset.

INDEX

779

Index compiled by Terry Halliday